£7.95
MC.

To Heather
from Marcus
Southampton 19-4-78

# MONETARY ECONOMICS: READINGS ON CURRENT ISSUES

# MONETARY ECONOMICS: Readings on Current Issues

**William E. Gibson**
*University of California, Los Angeles*

**George G. Kaufman**
*University of Oregon*

**TATA McGRAW-HILL PUBLISHING COMPANY LTD.**
**New Delhi**

MONETARY ECONOMICS : **Readings on Current Issues**



**T M H Edition 1975**

*Reprinted in India by arrangement with McGraw-Hill, Inc. New York.*

This edition can be exported from India only by the Publishers, Tata McGraw-Hill Publishing Company Ltd.

Published by Tata McGraw-Hill Publishing Company Limited and Printed by Mohan Makhijani at Rekha Printers Pvt. Ltd., New Delhi-110015.

# CONTENTS

# CONTENTS BY AUTHOR

# PREFACE

Interest in monetary economics and policy has intensified greatly in recent years for a number of reasons, including an increasing dissatisfaction with the performance of fiscal policy for economic stabilization and the generation of a substantial stream of evidence relating money importantly and in a predictable fashion to income, output, and prices. The increase in interest has been accompanied by a rapid growth both in the number of articles written on monetary economics and in the number of professional journals devoted in whole or in part to monetary economics, policy and institutions. Because of the proliferation of articles and the increasing inaccessibility of their sources, it has become difficult for both students and teachers to remain abreast of current developments. This volume brings together a collection of important recent contributions originally published in a wide variety of professional economic journals.

The articles have been selected both to guide the reader through the more important developments in the recent rekindling of interest in monetary economics and policy and to put these developments in perspective. The developments have not been without controversy, and this volume attempts to capture both the highlights and the spirit of the period. Recent advances in monetary economics have differed somewhat from past developments in that they have been primarily empirical. Alternative hypotheses of monetary behavior have been subjected to vigorous empirical analysis using scientific methods of testing hypotheses and new statistical techniques. Professor Milton Friedman has recently noted that "the basic differences among economists are empirical, not theoretical."[1] As a result, the emphasis of the readings in this collection is empirical. But numbers without theory or application have little meaning. Thus the articles have been selected to provide the reader with both the theoretical foundations of the analyses and the policy implications of the new evidence presented.

The volume is designed for use as a primary or supplementary readings text in upper-division and graduate courses in monetary economics and macroeconomics. This book may also be of value as supplementary reading in courses in money and banking and to practitioners in this area who wish to keep abreast of current developments. The articles assume some familiarity with the basic theories of that field and with the institutions of the financial sector.

The collection is divided into six major parts. Part I discusses the theory and evidence underlying the use of monetary policy for stabilization. The other five parts discuss important contemporary issues in monetary economics. The readings selected are by leading writers of the schools of thought involved. Because the issues are unresolved, we have attempted to present all sides of the debate as equitably as possible.

Many of the topics considered have not been included in textbooks or previous books of readings. Three of the six topics—Indicators of Monetary Policy; Money, Price Expectations, and Interest Rates; and The

[1] Milton Friedman, "A Theoretical Framework for Monetary Analyses," *Journal of Political Economy,* vol. 78 (March/April, 1970) p. 234.

Incidence of Monetary Policy—have only recently been thoroughly explored by contemporary monetary economists. The other three parts feature articles developing new evidence concerning Money, Monetary Policy, and Economic Activity; The Definition of Money; and Federal Reserve Control of the Money Stock. With the exception of readings in section A of part I, almost all the articles selected have been published since 1967.

Although the selections are ultimately our own, we acknowledge the assistance of many of our colleagues and friends, in particular, Professors Michael DePrano, Edward Kane, Larry Mote, Allan Meltzer, Frank Steindl, and Richard Zecher, in evaluating the literature and supporting the project. The authors are also grateful to Mrs. Marian Lang, Sharon Sowden, Mrs. Sally Mobley, and the Federal Deposit Insurance Corporation for their valuable assistance in the initial production process. Portions of the work on the volume were completed while Professor Gibson was at the Brookings Institution and the Federal Deposit Insurance Corporation on leave from the University of California, Los Angeles, and while Professor Kaufman was at the University of Southern California on leave of absence from the Federal Reserve Bank of Chicago.

*William E. Gibson*
*George G. Kaufman*

**MONETARY ECONOMICS:**
**READINGS ON**
**CURRENT ISSUES**

# I MONEY, MONETARY POLICY, and ECONOMIC ACTIVITY

Economists have long recognized that variations in the stock of money influence the economy. There has been less universal agreement on precisely what in the economy money affects, how the effects are transmitted, the strength of the effects, the length of time before the effects are observed, and the stability of the relationships. Nineteenth-century economists tended to assume full employment to be a normal situation and tended to emphasize the influence of changes in the supply of money on only the price level. Monetary authorities at the time also tended to accept this assumption and focus on stabilizing foreign exchange rates and national gold stocks. In this process, changes in prices, money, and interest rates often occurred as a means of attaining the objective of external balance, rather than for internal balance. Rules of the gold standard limited the use of discretionary policy to times of war and financial crisis. As industrialization accelerated, however, fluctuations in aggregate employment and production increased in both frequency and amplitude. Before 1930, economists had substantial faith both in the underlying stability of the economy and in the ability of the economy to regain equilibrium quickly once disturbed, and they continued to consider monetary policy as appropriate primarily for achieving stability in prices and exchange rates. This view prevailed despite the fact that beginning at least with Henry Thornton in 1797 some writers had recognized that money had an influence on real income, although the nature of this relationship was not always rigorously articulated.

The sharp and prolonged widespread depression of the early 1930s weakened faith both in the ability of monetary policy to attain full employment and in the automatic tendency of the economy to achieve full employment equilibrium at stable prices. There was a widespread view that the inherited strategy of monetary policy was tried and found wanting. Alternative nonmonetary proposals for stabilization, particularly those derived from Keynes' General Theory, were accepted as a replacement for monetary policy.[1] These policies were tried not because they had been proven successful but because monetary policy was considered to have been tried to its fullest extent without success. The large volume of excess bank reserves concomitant with a decline in the supply of money and low interest rates accompanied by a low level of investment were considered evidence of the impotency of monetary policy.

[1] While some early interpreters of the General Theory downgraded the influence of money and monetary policy, this seems not to have been Keynes' intentions. See Axel Leijonhufvud, *On Keynesian Economics and the Economics of Keynes,* New York, Oxford University Press, 1968.

This was further documented by surveys that found that business firms tended to give scant attention to financial variables in their investment decisions. Money seemed to matter little if at all. Monetary policy was further relegated to a secondary position of maintaining interest rates at minimum levels by the decision to finance World War II expenditures largely through monetary expansion, rather than higher taxes, and by the subsequent postwar fear of precipitating a decline in bond prices. Not until the Treasury–Federal Reserve Accord in 1951 was monetary policy once again freed for general stabilization use.

This is not to say that all economists in this era considered money and monetary policy impotent. Clark Warburton, for one, published frequent articles during the 1940s emphasizing the linkage between money and business activity.[2] A decade later Milton Friedman and his associates began to generate an almost continuous stream of evidence supporting the close and regular relationship between money, income, and prices throughout the world.

Immediate post-Accord experience with monetary policy during the 1950s was not entirely satisfactory. Changes in policy were frequent and abrupt and were accompanied by equally frequent and abrupt changes in economic activity. The inauguration of President John Kennedy in 1961 marked the beginning of an era of active fiscal experimentation under the leadership of Walter Heller. After an initial period of apparent major achievements, the failure to contain inflation with much-heralded fiscal measures and the continued development of additional evidence of a close relationship between money and economic activity by Friedman and a small but growing and vocal group of monetarists dampened enthusiasm for fiscal policy while increasing enthusiasm for monetary policy.

The articles reprinted in part I conduct the reader through the more recent developments in this scenario.[3] The first selection by Friedman summarizes the considerable amount of evidence he and others have collected relating money, prices, and income in a number of countries over long periods of time. In large measure, the article reviews the findings of his monumental book *A Monetary History of the United States 1867-1960*, written in collaboration with Anna Schwartz.[4] The article suggests that all major economic fluctuations in United States' history are attributable to marked and preceding movements in the nominal money stock. Money is considered the primary cause of changes in the price level and, at times of great monetary instability, also of changes in output and employment. However, the lengths of time between changes in money and the resulting changes in economic activity are found to be both long and variable, suggesting to Friedman that monetary policy can make its major contribution to economic stabilization by providing for a steady growth of the money stock.

Although written specifically as critical reviews of the Friedman-Schwartz book, the next two selections are relevant also to Friedman's analysis in general. Clower discusses primarily Friedman's method of evaluating hypotheses empirically by their ability to explain general historical experience rather than by the consistency of their internal logic fortified by selected illustrations. He concludes that, when qualified by the accompanying caveats, Friedman's findings are on the whole supported by the evidence presented. Tobin examines the economics of the argument. He questions the usefulness of the definition of money used, takes issue with the independent causal role Friedman assigns to money, and emphasizes the instability of the money-income relationship caused by velocity changes. In addition, he argues that the Federal Reserve could not control the supply of money closely even if it wished to do so.

---

[2] A collection of Warburton's articles appears in Clark Warburton, *Depression, Inflation and Monetary Policy*, Baltimore, Johns Hopkins Press, 1966.

[3] References to earlier developments may be found in Harry G. Johnson, "Monetary Theory and Policy," *American Economic Review*, vol. 52 (June 1962) pp. 335–384, and George G. Kaufman, "Current Issues in Monetary Economics and Policy: A Review," *The Bulletin*, no. 57, New York University, Institute of Finance, May 1969.

[4] Milton Friedman and Anna Jacobson Schwartz, *A Monetary History of the United States 1867-1960*, National Bureau of Economic Research, Studies in Business Cycles, no. 12, Princeton, Princeton University Press, 1963.

The result of these and similar exchanges was that both sides reevaluated their positions and respecified their hypotheses more carefully.[5] Two streams of alternative hypotheses developed. Advocates of heavy reliance on fiscal policy conceded a greater influence to money, while the monetarists devoted more attention to illuminating the processes by which money influenced economic activity, the so-called "black box." The next series of selections presents examples of this reevaluation. Samuelson and Smith describe hypotheses representative of modern neo-Keynesian thought in which money possesses an important but not primary policy role in affecting economic activity, and Fand delineates the differences between hypotheses assigning weak and strong roles to money.[6]

The testing of these alternative hypotheses has been conducted in a new intellectual context. The introduction of the electronic computer revolutionized empirical investigation in economics. Not only could more complex hypotheses be empirically examined for longer periods of observation, but the tests could be conducted in greater accord with scientific method. Davis and Brunner present fragmentary evidence in support of the neo-Keynesian and monetarist hypotheses, respectively. Shortly after publication of their findings, Andersen and Jordan startled the economics profession by developing a three-variable single equation that predicted both nominal income as well as many larger models and suggested that monetary policy has a stronger, quicker, and more reliable impact than fiscal policy.[7] If their equation is accepted, the efficacy of fiscal policy rather than of monetary policy is in question. Davis subjects the Andersen-Jordan analysis to careful scrutiny. He concludes that while the evidence in favor of a strong role for money in affecting economic activity cannot be dismissed lightly, the failure to describe the process by which money affects national income weakens the plausibility of the findings.[8]

The exchange between the monetarists and their critics served to clarify considerably the usefulness of single or limited equation reduced form system in economic analysis. The primary value of these equations appears to be in predicting, their lowest value in hypotheses testing. For example, many forces other than economic policy affect the economy. If executed with perfection, policy would reinforce some of these forces and off-

[5] Another exchange that contributed greatly to the development of more refined hypotheses involved the following articles: Milton Friedman and David Meiselman, "The Relative Stability of Monetary Velocity and the Investment Multiplier in the United States, 1897-1958," in Commission on Money and Credit, *Stabilization Policies,* Englewood Cliffs, N.J., Prentice-Hall, 1963, pp. 165–269; Donald Hester, "Keynes and the Quantity Theory: A Comment on the Friedman-Meiselman CMC Paper," *Review of Economics and Statistics,* vol. 46 (November, 1964) pp. 364–368; Albert Ando and Franco Modigliani, "The Relative Stability of Velocity and the Investment Multiplier," *American Economic Review,* vol. 55 (September, 1965) pp. 693–728; Michael DePrano and Thomas Mayer, "Test of the Relative Importance of Autonomous Expenditures and Money," *Ibid.*, pp. 729–752; Friedman and Meiselman, "Reply," *Ibid.*, pp. 753–775; Ando and Modigliani, "Rejoinder," *Ibid.*, pp. 786–790; DePrano and Mayer, "Rejoinder," *Ibid.*, pp. 791–792.

[6] The differences between the quantity theory and "Keynesian" models are also examined in a recent article by Milton Friedman, "A Theoretical Framework for Monetary Analysis," *Journal of Political Economy,* vol. 78 (March/April 1970) pp. 193–238. Similarly, the differing implications of the alternative theories for the process by which monetary shocks are transmitted to the real sector are clarified by William L. Silber, "Monetary Channels and the Importance of Money Supply and Bank Portfolios," *Journal of Finance,* vol. 24 (March, 1969) pp. 81–87.

[7] This equation also serves as the primary equation in the more complete monetarist model of the United States economy subsequently developed by economists at the St. Louis Federal Reserve Bank. Leonall C. Andersen and Keith M. Carlson, "A Monetarist Model for Economic Stabilization," *Review,* Federal Reserve Bank of St. Louis, April 1970, pp. 7–25.

[8] The Andersen-Jordan analysis was also subjected to critical examination by deLeeuw and Kalchbrenner, who raised a number of important questions on the exogenous nature and completeness of specification of the two policy variables. In a subsequent reply, Andersen and Jordan defended their analysis. Frank deLeeuw and John Kalchbrenner, "Monetary and Fiscal Actions: A Test of Their Relative Importance in Economic Stabilization—Comment," *Review,* Federal Reserve Bank of St. Louis, April, 1969, pp. 6–11, and Leonall C. Andersen and Jerry L. Jordan, "Reply," *Review,* Federal Reserve Bank of St. Louis, April, 1969, pp. 12–16.

set others so that the economy would operate at optimum levels at all times. In simple models, this would be reflected by high correlations between the policy variables and the goal variables when policy reinforces the other influences on the economy and low correlations between the two when policy offsets such influences. Hence, evaluating the effectiveness of policy only by the strength of the correlation may yield a misleading image of the effectiveness of a particular policy.

The introduction of the computer also accelerated the effort to construct large-scale structural econometric models of the economy. DeLeeuw and Gramlich describe a number of policy simulations on the FRB-MIT model, one of a small number of operative large models of the U.S. economy. This model is of particular interest for monetary analysis because it includes a reasonably fully developed financial sector and specifies three linkages between the financial and real sectors. Besides the traditional interest rates as a cost of capital linkage, the FRB-MIT model contains a short-run credit rationing link and a wealth effect generated through adjustments of portfolios. The model suggests that both monetary and fiscal policies influence activity significantly, although monetary policy does so with a reasonably long lag.

The final selection is a warning by Friedman not to expect too much from monetary policy. While Friedman concedes that changes in money can affect real variables in the short run, he argues that in the long run they affect primarily prices and that real variables such as employment and output are affected primarily by nonmonetary forces such as technology, population, resource endowment, and education. Friedman concludes by arguing that the Federal Reserve can make its most important contribution to economic stability by preventing instability in money rather than by introducing instability into money in an effort to offset other sources of instability in the economy. In his view attempts to fine tune would be self-defeating and lead to greater instability.

# A. Secular Evidence

## 1 | THE MONETARY STUDIES OF THE NATIONAL BUREAU*

MILTON FRIEDMAN
*University of Chicago*

To the theologian, money is the "root of all evil." To the economist, money had hardly less importance up to the early 1930's. It was then widely accepted that long-period changes in the quantity of money were the primary source of trends in the level of prices and that short-period fluctuations in the quantity of money played an important rôle in business cycles and might be the major explanation of them. For example, in his monumental book on business cycles published in 1913, Wesley C. Mitchell, while by no means promulgating or accepting an exclusively monetary theory of the cycle, gave much attention to monetary factors, constructing new estimates of various monetary components which are still part of the statistical underpinning of our present series on the stock of money.

The Keynesian revolution in economic thought in the mid-1930's produced a radical change in the attention paid by economists to money. The fact that the Federal Reserve System did not stem the Great Depression was interpreted as meaning that money was of secondary importance, at most a reflection of changes occurring elsewhere. Though this conclusion was a *non sequitur*, it was nonetheless potent. And it was all the more readily accepted because Keynes provided an intellectually appealing alternative explanation of the Great Depression. For nearly two decades thereafter, money became a minor matter in most academic economic writing and research, to be mentioned almost as an afterthought. And economic research on money was notable by its absence.

Recently there has been a revival of interest in money and a great increase in the amount of economic research on money. Several causes combined to produce this revival of interest. One was dissatisfaction with the predictions yielded by the Keynesian analysis—the most dramatic being the failure of the much-predicted postwar depression to occur. A second was the emergence of inflation as a major problem in all countries that adopted the easy-money policy, widely regarded as called for by the Keynesian analysis. No country succeeded in stemming inflation until it replaced the easy-money policy by more "orthodox" monetary measures. A third was scholarly criticism and analysis of Keynes' theoretical structure, and the resulting attribution of an important theoretical role to the so-called "real-balance" effect. A fourth was the accumulation of empirical evidence bearing on the behavior of money and its relation to other economic magnitudes. The combined effect has been striking. Ten years ago, we at the National Bureau and an associated group at the University of Chicago were almost the only academic economists working intensively on money. Today, I am glad to say, we have a host of competitors.

* Reprinted from *The National Bureau Enters Its 45th Year, 44th Annual Report,* © 1964 by the National Bureau of Economic Research, pp. 7–25, by permission of the author and the National Bureau of Economic Research.

## 1. The Studies Covered by This Report

The National Bureau's monetary research has throughout been closely connected with its studies of business cycles. Wesley Mitchell's preliminary manuscript on business cycles contained a long chapter on the role of money and credit in the cycle. For that chapter, he had collected many series bearing on money and credit, which remain the backbone of the Bureau's collection of series in this area. The chapter was the starting point of the studies covered by this report, as other chapters were of so many of the major National Bureau studies.

This report covers only those monetary studies of the Bureau for which Anna J. Schwartz, Phillip Cagan, and I have had responsibility. The group of studies, begun well over a decade ago, is now, I am glad to report, nearly completed. Hence, this report deals mostly with work already done or nearly done. Needless to say, just as our studies built on the earlier work of the Bureau and other investigators, so, I trust, they will in their turn open up new avenues of future research for the Bureau and for others. The test of success in any scientific research is dual: the questions it answers and, even more, the new questions it raises. Though I shall refer incidentally to some of the questions our work raises and on which further research is needed, I shall not attempt a comprehensive survey. Research must lead its own life. I am all too aware how much our own work departed from the lines we initially expected it to follow to want to peer too deeply into that clouded (and crowded) crystal ball.

As our work proceeded, we came to plan three monographs. One, *A Monetary History of the United States, 1867-1960,* by Anna J. Schwartz and myself, was published in 1963. A second, "Determinants and Effects of Changes in the Money Stock, 1875-1955," by Phillip Cagan, will soon go to press. The third, "Trends and Cycles in the Stock of Money in the United States," by Anna Schwartz and myself, is in first draft form. The major unfinished work is the substantial revision and expansion of the present draft, which was completed years ago and then put aside while we finished the *Monetary History*. We hope that by the next annual meeting we can report that this monograph too is ready or nearly ready for review by the Board of Directors.

In addition, four other Bureau publications have come from our studies. "Money and Business Cycles," by Friedman and Schwartz (Conference on the State of Monetary Economics, *Review of Economics and Statistics*, Feb. 1963 suppl.), is something of a preview and advance summary of one part of our projected volume, "Trends and Cycles." Friedman, *The Demand for Money* (O.P. 68, 1959), is a preliminary version of another chapter of that work, and Friedman, *The Interpolation of Time Series by Related Series* (T.P. 16, 1962), is a byproduct of our monetary estimates. Phillip Cagan's *The Demand for Currency Relative to Total Money Supply* (O.P. 62, 1958) is a preliminary version of part of his monograph.

## 2. The Meaning of "Money" and Our Estimates of the Quantity of Money

It will help put our work in proper perspective to distinguish at the outset between different senses in which the word "money" is used. In popular parlance, there are three main senses—as in pocket money, money market, and making money. In the first sense money refers to a class of assets of wealthholders; in the second, to credit; in the third, to income. Our work has been concerned with money in the first sense. We have of course had to consider both credit conditions and income: credit conditions as affecting the quantity of money, as being in turn affected by changes in the quantity of money, and as one of the channels through which changes in the quantity of money may affect income; similarly, income as perhaps the central total whose fluctuations constitute business cycles, as a source of changes in the quantity of money, and as itself affected by changes in the quantity of money. We have repeatedly been impressed in the course of our work with the importance of clearly distinguishing between money as an asset—as a stock at a point in time—and these other phenomena for which the word money is frequently used. Indeed, a key finding in our *Monetary History* is that the confusion of money and credit has been a primary source of difficulty in monetary policy. And recent experience indicates this is still so.

Credit conditions are affected by a much broader range of factors than those linked to the quantity of money and they require study in their own right. This is being done in the National Bureau studies of consumer credit, interest rates, and the quality of credit.

Our emphasis on money as an asset led us to take as our first major project the construction of a consistent and continuous set of estimates on the quantity of money for as long a period as possible. This turned out to be a more arduous task than anticipated, involving as it did piecing together numerous bits of data from a wide variety of sources. The final series starts in 1867, is for semi-annual or annual dates to 1907, and monthly thereafter. Though the series is now available (in an appendix to *A Monetary History*), a full description of sources and methods, and supplementary tables giving various components of the series and related series, are yet to be published. They will be included in our planned volume, "Trends and Cycles."

These estimates, as well as our subsequent work, brought to the fore the more specific question of precisely how to define money. Should it include only literal pocket money —that is, paper currency and coin? Or also demand deposits subject to transfer by check? Commercial bank time deposits? Mutual savings bank deposits? Savings and loan shares? Cash surrender values of life insurance policies? Series E bonds? And so on toward the outer bound defined by some of the broad concepts of liquidity; or, in a different and more appealing direction, toward weighted aggregates of the several elements.

Our statistical estimates, so far as feasible, give the components separately, so that each user can make his own choice within the limits of what we could estimate. In our work, we have generally found that the most useful single total is an intermediate one—currency held by the public, plus demand deposits adjusted of commercial banks, plus time deposits of commercial banks. Hence, we have termed this total "money" for our purposes and have used other expressions for other totals. The forthcoming volume on trends and cycles will discuss the question of definition in some detail and present the empirical evidence which led us to adopt this particular definition. So far as I can see, no issue of principle is involved in the choice of definition, but only a question of the empirical usefulness of one or another admittedly imperfect approximation to a theoretical construct. So far as I can see, no important substantive issues are involved either. Judged by the criteria we used, alternative definitions are not much inferior to the one we adopted, so that a strong case against them cannot be made. Whenever possible, we have tried systematically to see whether any substantive conclusion is affected by substituting an alternative concept. Typically, none is, though some of the numerical relations may be different for one concept than for another. The occasional impression in the scientific literature that important substantive issues are involved generally turns out to be a result of the use of the word money to refer to different things.

All of our studies have been heavily dependent on the new estimates of the quantity of money we constructed. Our *Monetary History* "traces the changes in the stock of money . . . examines the factors that accounted for the changes, and analyzes the reflex influence that the stock of money exerted on the course of events."[1] In his monograph Cagan examines intensively the sources of changes in the stock of money and gives a detailed statistical analysis of the cyclical and secular behavior of each of the proximate determinants of the quantity of money, as we term them: high-powered money, the ratio of deposits at banks to their reserves, and the ratio of the public's holdings of deposits to its holdings of currency. The "Trends and Cycles" volume will, besides giving the basis for our new estimates, present a full statistical analysis of the secular and cyclical behavior of the stock of money and of monetary velocity in relation to other economic magnitudes. We shall rely heavily on the standard Bureau techniques to determine characteristic cyclical amplitude and timing. We plan also to supplement these techniques with both correlation techniques and—hopefully

[1] *A Monetary History*, p. 3.

—spectral analysis, to see whether different techniques give consistent results.

The major scientific contribution of the studies probably will prove to be their quantitative findings about a host of specific magnitudes and relations. Most of our findings to date are summarized in the final chapter of *A Monetary History*, in the final chapter of Cagan's monograph, and in "Money and Business Cycles." They constitute building blocks to be incorporated in that general theory of the cycle which is the ultimate aim of scholars in the field.

Rather than try to summarize those findings here again, I should like instead to give something of the flavor of our work by considering an important specific issue, outlining the kind of evidence that is available from our published work on it, and giving some additional evidence from our unpublished work. I shall then summarize the general qualitative conclusions we have reached, with special stress on their limitations, and, finally, illustrate the applicability of some of our results to the interpretation of recent economic changes.

### 3. The Direction of Influence between Money and Business

The specific issue I propose to consider is in some ways the central issue in dispute about the role of money in business cycles, namely, whether the cyclical behavior of money is to be regarded as a major factor explaining business fluctuations or as simply a reflection of business fluctuations produced by other forces. In Irving Fisher's words, the issue is whether the cycle is largely a "dance of the dollar" or, conversely, the dollar is largely a dance of the cycle. Stated still differently, the issue is whether the major direction of influence is from money to business or from business to money.

In each of these statements of the issue, I have used an adjective like "major" or "largely." One reason is that the alternatives contrasted are not mutually exclusive. Undoubtedly there can be and are influences running both ways. Indeed, insofar as the cycle is in any measure self-generating and not simply a response to external shocks, and insofar as money plays any systematic role in producing the cycle, the influences must run both ways, the changes in the stock of money producing changes in business that produce changes in the stock of money that continue the cycle.

A second reason for the qualifying words is that there can be and almost certainly are factors other than money that contribute to the cycle, whatever may be the role of money. The question at issue is, therefore, whether money exerts an important independent influence, not whether it is the only source of business fluctuations and itself wholly independent of them.

What kind of evidence can be cited on this issue?

#### (1) *Qualitative Historical Circumstances*

Perhaps the most directly relevant kind of evidence emerges from an examination of the historical circumstances surrounding changes in the quantity of money. They often have decisive bearing on whether the changes could have been an immediate or necessary consequence of contemporary changes in business conditions. This is particularly true about policy changes deliberately instituted by monetary authorities, which is why, as we say in *A Monetary History*, "the establishment of the Federal Reserve System provides the student of money a closer substitute for the controlled experiment to determine the direction of influence than the social scientist can generally obtain."[2]

From such evidence, it is possible to identify a number of occasions on which monetary changes have clearly been independent of contemporaneous changes in business conditions. On those occasions, the monetary changes have been accompanied by economic changes in the same direction, monetary contractions (or more precisely, reductions in the rate of change in the stock of money) being accompanied by contractions in money income, prices, and output; and monetary expansions, by the opposite. The relation between monetary and economic change at those times also has been very much the same as on other occasions when historical circumstances were less decisive about the source of the monetary change. We ended our summary of this evidence in the final chapter of *A Monetary History* as follows: "Mutual interaction, but with money rather clearly the senior partner in longer-run movements and in major cyclical

[2] *A Monetary History*, p. 687.

movements, and more nearly an equal partner with money income and prices in shorter-run and milder movements—this is the generalization suggested by our evidence."

### (2) *The Behavior of the Determinants of the Money Stock*

In his monograph, Cagan provides a rather different kind of evidence. Any change in the money stock can be attributed to changes in the three proximate determinants, mentioned earlier: high-powered money, the deposit-reserve ratio, and the deposit-currency ratio. Any influence of business conditions on money must operate through one or more of these determinants. If this is the major direction of influence, the determinants separately should be more closely related to business conditions than the money stock as a whole is; moreover, the observed relation should be consistent with what we know about the character of the monetary institutions regarded as producing it. Hence, examination of the relation of money and each determinant separately to business conditions provides evidence on the direction of influence.

For secular movements, Cagan finds that high-powered money is the major source of changes in the stock of money. During most of the period studied, increases in prices would be expected to have reduced the quantity of high-powered money by discouraging gold output and encouraging gold exports. Conversely, decreases in prices would have encouraged gold output and stimulated gold inflows. Yet the actual relation is the other way: price increases are associated with a higher than average rate of rise in high-powered money; price decreases, with a lower than average rate of rise. Moreover, there is a closer relation between income and changes in the total money stock than between income and the separate determinants. Cagan concludes that, for secular movements, the predominant direction of influence must run from money to income. "To explain secular movements in prices," he writes, "we should look primarily to the supply of money and then secondarily to nonmonetary factors that may also have been important."

For cyclical fluctuations, Cagan finds the evidence more mixed. It is clearest for the severe business contractions. For these, he does not find it possible to attribute the changes in the stock of money to the effect of business on the determinants of the stock of money. Hence, the uniform coincidence of severe monetary contraction and severe economic contraction seems persuasive evidence for an influence running from money to business. As Cagan writes, "a monetary explanation of why some business contractions become severe, whatever may have started them, is hardly novel, but the supporting evidence is much stronger than is generally recognized." Incidentally, this explanation of severe business contractions is not necessarily inconsistent with an alternative explanation suggested by Moses Abramovitz in his work on long cycles. The relation between the two explanations will be examined in our "Trends and Cycles" volume.

For business cycles not containing severe contractions, Cagan finds clear evidence of the influence of business on money operating through the determinants. The deposit-currency ratio was the most important single source of cyclical fluctuations in the rate of change in the money stock. Cagan attributes most of the fluctuations in the deposit-currency ratio to the effect of the contemporaneous cyclical movements in economic activity. Similarly, he regards the fluctuations in the reserve ratio as reflecting cyclical movements in credit demands. For mild cycles, there is therefore clear evidence of a feedback effect of business on money. But Cagan also finds evidence of the same kind of effect of money on business which is so clearly present in secular movements and severe contractions. That evidence is the fact that the relation between money and business during mild cycles remains the same over a long period despite substantial changes in the institutional structure connecting business and the separate determinants.

### (3) *Consistency of Timing on Positive and Inverted Basis*

A third type of evidence is provided by the cyclical timing of monetary changes. However, to explain the relevance of this evidence, I shall have to digress briefly to describe our measures of the cyclical timing of money.

In studying the cyclical timing of money, we have found it more useful to examine the rate of change in the money stock than its absolute level. The reason is that the upward secular trend in the quantity of money has been so strong that the quantity of money has frequently tended to rise during both cyclical expansions and cyclical contractions. Cyclical forces show up much more clearly in the rate at which the stock of money rises than in whether it rises; or, alternatively, cyclical forces show up more clearly in the deviations of the stock of money from a secular trend.

We have used two alternative methods to describe the timing of the cyclical fluctuations in the rate of change in money. One is the standard Bureau specific cycle analysis: we date the months in which the series reaches peaks and troughs, and designate the resulting dates, the peaks and troughs in the rate of change. However, we have been hesitant to rely on this method alone. The major reason is purely statistical. Rate-of-change series are very erratic and jagged, having a characteristic saw-tooth appearance. This often makes it difficult to choose a particular month as the peak or trough. Several months, sometimes separated by a long interval, often seem about equally plausible. A subsidiary reason we have been hesitant to rely on the rate-of-change peak and trough dates alone is analytical. What feature of the money series is most relevant to the cycle is by no means clear, whether the rate of change alone, or some cumulative total such as the deviation from a trend.[3]

Accordingly, we have used a second method of dating suggested by the empirical observation that the rate-of-change series often seemed to move around the same level for a time and then shift abruptly to a new level. This suggested approximating the rate-of-change series by a set of horizontal steps, which turn out typically to alternate between high and low steps. We designate as a "step peak" the month in which a high

[3] For a fuller discussion of this point and also some of the other points considered in this subsection see Friedman, "The Lag in Effect of Monetary Policy," *Journal of Political Economy*, Oct. 1961, pp. 447–466.

**TABLE 1. COMPARISON OF TIMING MEASUREMENTS OF RATE OF CHANGE IN MONEY STOCK ON POSITIVE AND INVERTED BASIS, 1870–1961**

| | Kind of Specific Cycle Turn in Rate of Change in Money Stock | | | |
|---|---|---|---|---|
| | *Last month of step at:* | | *Trough or peak in rate of change at:* | |
| | Reference troughs | Reference peaks | Reference troughs | Reference peaks |
| Mean lead (−) or lag (+), in months | | | | |
| Positive basis | −4.0 | −6.1 | −13.2 | −16.9 |
| Inverted basis | 19.5 | 15.6 | 12.8 | 6.4 |
| Standard deviation of lead or lag, in months | | | | |
| Positive basis | 5.6 | 7.1 | 6.0 | 7.6 |
| Inverted basis | 11.7 | 15.8 | 15.1 | 12.3 |
| Number of observations | 21 | 21 | 21 | 21 |

NOTE: Matching with reference turns follows Arthur F. Burns and Wesley C. Mitchell, *Measuring Business Cycles*, New York, NBER, 1946, pp. 115–128, with a few exceptions. Strict adherence to the Burns and Mitchell procedure would not reverse the finding that the standard deviations are larger on the inverted basis than on the positive basis.

SOURCE: Money stock: 1870–1946, from *A Monetary History*, Table A-1, col. 8; 1947–61, *Supplement to Banking and Monetary Statistics*, Sect. 1, Board of Governors of the Federal Reserve System, Oct. 1962, pp. 20–22.

step ends and is succeeded by a low step, and as a "step trough" the month in which a low step ends and is succeeded by a high step. It turns out that these dates approximate the dates at which the deviation from a trend would reach a peak or trough. Their use obviates the necessity of actually fitting a trend.

We had hoped that one of these methods would yield dates bearing a more consistent relation to the timing of reference cycles than the other, giving us a basis for choosing between the two methods. So far, this hope has not been realized (see Table 1); the two yield about equally consistent timing measures. Hence, we have continued to use both, regarding this as a way both to average out errors and to take account of different characteristics of the money series.

Both the rate-of-change peak and the step peak in the money series tend regularly to come earlier than the peak in general business (the reference peak) to which we match them, and both the rate-of-change trough and the step trough to come earlier than the matched reference trough. The interval is somewhat longer at peaks than at troughs, and decidedly longer for the rate-of-change turning points than for the step turning points. On the average of twenty-one matched cycles (from 1870 to 1961) the rate-of-change peak comes 17 months earlier than the reference peak, and the step peak, 6 months earlier; the rate-of-change trough comes 13 months earlier than the reference trough, the step trough, 4 months earlier. As to consistency, the rate-of-change turning point comes earlier than the reference turning point at every one of the 42 turning points included in the above averages; the step turning point does so in 29 out of the 42.

These regular and sizable leads of the money series are themselves suggestive of an influence running from money to business but they are by no means decisive. One reason is that both the monetary changes and the business changes might be the common consequence of some other influences which have their effect on money more promptly than on business. A second is that the characteristics of business change affecting money may not be those that are dated by the Bureau reference dates.

The most important reason, however, why the consistent leads of the money series are not decisive is that, given a recurrent cyclical process, these leads may be simply the reflection of an earlier influence of business on money; they may be a statistical artifact resulting from our matching the turning points in money with the wrong turning points in business. Instead of matching a peak in the money series with the subsequent reference peak, we could match it with the prior reference trough; similarly, we could match the rate of change trough with the prior reference peak. This procedure yields shorter average timing differences for the rate-of-change dates—an average lag of 6 months at reference peaks and 13 months at reference troughs—and longer average timing differences for the step dates—an average lag of 16 months at reference peaks and 19 months at reference troughs.[4]

The question whether it is preferable to interpret the money series as mainly conforming positively to the cycle with a lead or invertedly with a lag is therefore relevant to the more general question whether the predominant direction of influence is from money to business. All theoretical analysis I know of which would explain how money can play an independent role in the cyclical process also implies that the connection is positive, that is, that unusually high rates of rise in money promote business expansion, unusually low rates, business contraction. Hence, inverted conformity, whether with a lag or a lead, would sharply contradict the existence of a strong influence from money to business, and positive conformity, especially with a lead, would be consistent with such an influence. On the other hand, many of the links between business and money, as Cagan has shown, may be expected to produce an inverted response; the clearest example is the tendency of business expansion to produce gold outflows and hence downward pressure on high-powered money. Inverted conformity with a lag

[4] Of course, given a recurrent cycle, a money peak could be matched with a prior reference peak as well, and similarly for the trough, implying a long-delayed positive effect of business on money; or a money peak and trough, with a succeeding reference trough and peak, implying a long-delayed inverted effect of money on business, and so on. We have restricted the discussion to the simplest alternative interpretations.

would therefore be entirely consistent with an influence running from business to money. Positive conformity could be, too, since some of the effects of business on money are in a positive direction, for example, the effect of business expansion on bank reserve ratios. However, it is not easy to rationalize positive conformity with a lead as reflecting supply response.

The nub of these considerations is that

**TABLE 2. RANK DIFFERENCE CORRELATION BETWEEN CHANGE IN ONE CYCLE PHASE AND CHANGE IN NEXT SUCCEEDING CYCLE PHASE, RATE OF CHANGE IN MONEY AND TWO INDICATORS OF GENERAL BUSINESS, 1879 – 1961, EXCLUDING WAR CYCLES AND 1945 – 1949**

| Series correlated with itself | Annual and semiannual data 1879–1908 | Monthly data 1908–1961 | Whole period 1879–1961 |
|---|---|---|---|
| Expansion in indicated series and succeeding contraction in same series | | | |
| 1. Rate of change in money stock, per cent per month in specific cycles | –.02 | .33 | .24 |
| 2. Moore index, in specific cycle relatives (indicator of physical change in general business) | –.07 | .10 | .10 |
| 3. Clearings-debits, in reference cycle relatives (indicator of dollar-value change in general business) | –.05 | –.39 | .15 |
| Number of pairs | 8 | 10 | 18 |
| Contraction in indicated series and succeeding expansion in same series | | | |
| 4. Rate of change in money stock, per cent per month in specific cycles | .83 | .68 | .74 |
| 5. Moore index, in specific cycle relatives | .71 | .85 | .86 |
| 6. Clearings-debits, in reference cycle relatives | –.17 | .46 | .26 |
| Number of pairs | 8 | 7 | 15 |

NOTE: War cycles 1914–19 and 1938–45 are omitted because of their special characteristics. The 1945–49 cycle is omitted because the expansion is skipped by the rate-of-change in money series. Specific cycles are those matched with reference cycles in the column headings. There was a one-to-one correspondence between specific and reference cycles.

SOURCE: Money stock: see Table II-1. Specific cycle analysis follows Burns and Mitchell, *Measuring Business Cycles*, pp. 115–141.

Moore index: Unpublished memorandum by Geoffrey H. Moore, extending table in *Measuring Business Cycles*, p. 403, and revising and updating table in *Business Cycle Indicators*, Vol. I, p. 104. An average of three trend-adjusted indexes of business activity—A.T.&T., Persons-Barrons, and Ayres—each of which was analyzed for specific cycles, suppressing specific cycle turns not corresponding to reference cycle turns.

Clearings-debits: Bank clearings outside New York City, monthly,

1879–1919: bank debits outside New York City, monthly, 1919–1961.

1879–1942: Seasonally adjusted from *Historical Statistics of the United States, 1789–1945*, Bureau of the Census, 1949, pp. 324–325, 337–338.

1943–61: Board of Governors of the Federal Reserve System, Division of Bank Operations, mimeographed table, "Bank Debits and Rates of Turnover" (C.5, Revised Series, 1943–52), Dec. 23, 1953; thereafter *Federal Reserve Bulletin*, adjusted for seasonal variation by NBER. Reference cycle analysis follows Burns and Mitchell *Measuring*, pp. 160–170.

Values of the rank-difference correlation coefficient that would be exceeded in absolute value by chance in the indicated proportion *P* of independent samples are:

| Value of *P* | 7 | 8 | 10 | 15 | 18 |
|---|---|---|---|---|---|
| .10 | .71 | .64 | .56 | .44 | .40 |
| .05 | .79 | .74 | .65 | .52 | .48 |
| .01 | .93 | .88 | .79 | .69 | .63 |

inverted conformity would clearly contradict a predominant influence of money on business; positive conformity would be consistent with such an influence and, especially with a lead, would constitute evidence in favor of it but would not rule out an influence of business on money. And, of course, as with the more general question, positive and inverted conformity are not mutually exclusive; both exist, and both are plausible. The question is, which is dominant.

How can our timing measures help us choose between positive and inverted conformity? One obvious answer is by seeing which interpretation yields more consistent timing measures. Are the leads or lags more nearly the same from cycle to cycle on one interpretation than on the other?

Table 1, which comes from our unfinished manuscript, "Trends and Cycles," contains the relevant evidence. It gives, for all cycles from 1870 to 1961, the dispersion (as measured by the standard deviation) of the leads and lags as computed under the two interpretations and as determined both from rate-of-change and step dates. The dispersion is uniformly lower when the money series is treated as conforming positively, and the difference is substantial.[5] So far as this evidence goes, it clearly supports positive conformity.

### (4) *Serial Correlation of Amplitudes of Cycle Phases*

A very different kind of evidence on positive versus inverted conformity is provided by the size of cyclical movements in money. In order to explain what this evidence is, I shall again have to digress, this time to describe a most interesting feature of business cycle behavior which has implications for many problems besides the one under discussion.

The feature in question is the relation between successive phases of business cycles. Is the magnitude of an expansion related systematically to the magnitude of the succeeding contraction? Does a boom tend on the average to be followed by a large contraction? A mild expansion, by a mild contraction? To find out, we have used two different measures of the amplitude of cyclical phases: one, the Moore index,[6] as an indicator of the change in the physical volume of activity; the other, the volume of bank clearings or debits, as an indicator of the change in money values. Lines 2 and 3 of Table 2 (which, like Table 1, is taken from the present draft of "Trends and Cycles") show that, when the amplitude of an expansion is correlated with the amplitude of the succeeding contraction, the resulting correlation is negligible for both measures. Surprisingly, perhaps, there appears to be no systematic connection between the size of an expansion and of the succeeding contraction, whether size is measured by physical volume or by dollar value.

Let us now ask the same question, except that we start with a contraction and ask how its amplitude is related to that of the succeeding expansion. As lines 5 and 6 of Table 2 show, the results are very different for the physical-volume measure though much the same for the dollar-value measure. A large contraction in output tends to be followed on the average by a large business expansion; a mild contraction, by a mild expansion.

This phenomenon, if it should be confirmed by a fuller analysis of data for the United States and other countries, would have important implications for the analysis of business cycles in general, not solely for our monetary studies. For one thing, it would cast grave doubt on those theories that see as the source of a deep depression

[5] If the standard deviations on the two interpretations could be regarded as statistically independent of one another and each based on independent observations, the ratio of the larger to the smaller that would be exceeded by chance less than one time in twenty would be 1.46, and less than one time in 100, 1.73. For three of the four comparisons in Table 1, the ratio considerably exceeds the latter level, and for the fourth, the former. The specified conditions are not satisfied by these data but it is not clear in which direction the comparison is biased.

[6] The Moore index is our designation of an average of three trend-adjusted indexes of general business used by Burns and Mitchell (*Measuring Business Cycles*, p. 403) as a broad indicator of the amplitude of cycles, and revised and extended by Geoffrey H. Moore (*Business Cycle Indicators*, G. H. Moore, ed., Princeton for NBER, 1961, Vol. I, p. 104; and an unpublished memorandum).

the excesses of the prior expansion.[7] For another, it would raise serious questions about both the analytical models, in terms of which most of us have come to approach the analysis of cycles, and the statistical methods we use to analyze them.

Our analytical models generally involve a conception of a self-generating cycle, in which each phase gives rise to the next, and which may be kept going by a sequence of random shocks each giving rise to a series of damped perturbations. The corresponding physical analogy is of an electrical network in which responses are described by sine waves. The asymmetric serial correlation pattern suggests that this analogy may be misleading, that a better one is what can be termed a plucking model. Consider an elastic string stretched taut between two points on the underside of a rigid horizontal board and glued lightly to the board. Let the string be plucked at a number of points chosen more or less at random with a force that varies at random, and then held down at the lowest point reached. The result will be to produce a succession of apparent cycles in the string whose amplitudes depend on the force used in plucking the string. The cycles are symmetrical about their troughs; each contraction is of the same amplitude as the succeeding expansion. But there is no necessary connection between the amplitude of an expansion and the amplitude of the succeeding contraction. Correlations between the amplitudes of successive phases would be asymmetric in the same way the correlations in lines 2 and 5 of Table 2 are. Expansions would be uncorrelated with succeeding contractions, but contractions would be correlated with succeeding expansions. Up to this point, the peaks in the series would all be at the same level. To complete the analogy, we can suppose the board to be tilted to allow for trend and the underside of the board to be irregular to generate variability in the peaks, which would also introduce something less than perfect correlation between the size of contractions and subsequent expansions.

In this analogy, the irregular underside of the rigid board corresponds to the upper limit to output set by the available resources and methods of organizing them. Output is viewed as bumping along the ceiling of maximum feasible output except that every now and then it is plucked down by a cyclical contraction. Given institutional rigidities in prices, the contraction takes in considerable measure the form of a decline in output. Since there is no physical limit to the decline short of zero output, the size of the decline in output can vary widely. When subsequent recovery sets in, it tends to return output to the ceiling; it cannot go beyond, so there is an upper limit to output and the amplitude of the expansion tends to be correlated with the amplitude of the contraction.

For series on prices and money values, the situation is different. The very rigidity in prices invoked to explain the decline in output may mean that the declines in prices vary less in size than the declines in output. More important, there is no physical ceiling, so that there is nothing on this level of analysis to prevent the string from being plucked up as well as down. These differences make it plausible that the asymmetric correlation would be much less marked in money-value series than in output and perhaps entirely absent in price series. This is so for the correlations in Table 2, which are small for clearings-debits. The same conclusion is suggested also by graphic inspection of a wide variety of physical volume and price series. A symmetric pattern of downward pluckings can be clearly seen in many of the physical volume series; such a pattern is much less clear in the price series; and, in some price series, symmetric upward pluckings seem about as numerous.

The contrast between the physical-volume and dollar-value or price series can be put somewhat differently. The indicated pattern in physical-volume series is readily understandable regardless of the reason for the cyclical fluctuations in the series—of the source of the pluckings, as it were. A similar pattern in value or price series would have to be explained by some similar pattern or asymmetry in the source of the cyclical fluctuations, some factor that prevents up-

[7] The major qualification that must be attached to our result for this purpose is the definitions of the cycle and of expansion and contraction phases on which it rests. Proponents of the view cited might well argue that what matters is the cumulative effect of several expansions, as we define them, and that the relevant concept of expansion is of a "major" expansion or a phase of a long cycle.

ward plucking from being as important as downward plucking.

Let us now return to our major theme and see how we can use this feature of business cycles to get additional evidence on the appropriate interpretation of the money series. If positive conformity is dominant, and if the monetary changes are linked with physical-volume changes, then the serial correlations for money should be the same as for the Moore index. On the other hand, if inverted conformity is dominant, and changes in business produce later changes in the opposite direction in money, then the correlations for money should be the opposite of those for the Moore index, that is, the amplitude of an expansion should be correlated with that of the succeeding contraction; and the amplitude of a contraction should be uncorrelated with that of the succeeding expansion.

The relevant correlations for the specific cycle amplitudes of the rate of change in money are given in lines 1 and 4 of Table 2. We have as yet no parallel analysis for step amplitudes, though we plan one. The correlations we have for money are roughly the same as for the Moore index. The simplest interpretation of this result is that the pattern for business is a reflection of the pattern for money. In terms of our analogy, every now and then the money string is plucked downward. That produces, after some lag, a downward movement in economic activity related in magnitude to the downward movement in money. The money string then rebounds, and that in turn produces, after some lag, an upward movement in economic activity, again related in magnitude to the upward movement in money. Since the downward and subsequent upward movements in money are correlated in amplitude with one another, so are downward and subsequent upward movements in economic activity. Since the upward and subsequent downward movements in money are not correlated in amplitude, neither are the upward and subsequent downward movements in economic activity.

Personally, I find this bit of evidence in favor of dominant positive conformity particularly persuasive for two reasons. The first is that I have been unable to construct an explanation of how the observed asymmetric correlation pattern for money could be produced by an inverted response of money to business cycles. The second is that our historical studies have uncovered a number of episodes that correspond precisely to the notion of downward pluckings of the money string.

### (5) *Evidence from Foreign Countries*

All the evidence so far cited is for the United States. In addition, there is much evidence of a similar kind for other countries.[8] Cagan's earlier work on hyperinflations provides some striking results of a positive relationship for rather extreme monetary episodes.[9] Several studies on Chile, done by students or faculty members of the University of Chicago, provide persuasive evidence of a more moderate though still substantial inflation.[10] Some unpublished work on Canada by George Macesich demonstrates that the timing relations between monetary and economic change there are very similar to the relations in the United States.

In order to expand the range of evidence on this and related issues, I went on something of a fishing expedition last year (on leave from both the University of Chicago and the National Bureau) to explore the

---

[8] I exclude the well-known studies which deal chiefly with long-period secular rather than short-period cyclical relations, such as Earl J. Hamilton's classic work on the price revolution in the sixteenth century as a result of the inflow of specie from the New World, or J. E. Cairnes' "Essays Toward A Solution of the Gold Question" (*Essays in Political Economy*, London, Macmillan, 1873, pp. 1–165), in which he analyzed in advance the effects to be expected from the gold discoveries in Australia and California and then after the event added postscripts checking his predictions with the actual outcome—one of the earliest and still one of the best applications of the scientific method in economics.

[9] Phillip Cagan, "The Monetary Dynamics of Hyperinflation," in *Studies in the Quantity Theory of Money*, Milton Friedman, ed., University of Chicago Press, 1956.

[10] John Deaver, "The Chilean Inflation and the Demand for Money," unpublished Ph.D. dissertation, University of Chicago, 1960; Arnold C. Harberger, "The Dynamics of Inflation in Chile," in Carl Christ *et al.*, *Measurement in Economics*, Stanford University Press, 1963, pp. 219–250.

data available for foreign countries differing as widely as possible from the United States, and to learn something about their monetary arrangements. The countries I studied in some detail were Yugoslavia, Greece, Israel, India, and Japan. For each, I collected data on the quantity of money, income, prices, indexes of industrial production, interest rates, and the like. There is no doubt that sufficient data are available to make comparative studies feasible.

So far, I have been able to do little analysis of the data I gathered. But even that superficial analysis has uncovered some interesting bits of additional evidence on the direction of influence. For Yugoslavia, for example, there happens to be an episode for which the direction of relation is hardly doubtful: the stock of currency (which seems the appropriate measure of "money" for such a country) and income in current prices both have been rising rather rapidly in the past decade, with one marked exception in both. There is one year in each series in which the upward trend is replaced by a horizontal movement. That year comes one year earlier in the currency series than in the money income series! For Israel, the data, which are carefully compiled, show roughly the same relation between rates of change as for the United States, with rates of change in currency leading rates of change in income by about a year. For Japan, cyclical fluctuations of the past ten years or so seem readily interpreted as a strictly self-generating monetary cycle in response to changes in the rate of change in the money stock. The contractionary monetary changes are produced by the reactions of the monetary authorities to recurrent balance of payments difficulties, which are a response to prior expansionary monetary changes that occur when the balance of payments eases. The Japanese data show about a three- to six-months' lead of the rate of change in the money supply over the rate of change in production and prices. We have as yet no conceptually similar timing comparisons for the United States, though we are in the process of making them. Perhaps the closest are the timing comparisons between the step dates and reference turns. Those show a roughly similar lead.

### (6) *The Combined Weight of the Evidence*

In a scientific problem, the final verdict is never in. Any conclusion must always be subject to revision in the light of new evidence. Yet I believe that the available evidence of the five kinds listed justifies considerable confidence in the conclusion that the money series is dominated by positive conformity, which reflects in some measure an independent influence of money on business. The feedback effect of business on money, which undoubtedly also exists, may contribute to the positive conformity and may also introduce a measure of inverted conformity.

In the "Trends and Cycles" volume, we hope to carry farther our analysis of the evidence based on the timing and amplitude of fluctuations in the money series (subsections 3 and 4). We have no present plans for doing any further work on the qualitative historical evidence or on that provided by the determinants of the money stock (subsections 1 and 2). Data for foreign countries (subsection 5) merit much fuller analysis, and I have interested a number of students in research for doctoral dissertations which will make a start in that direction. However, this is not part of the Bureau's program, though it is obviously relevant to our common intellectual interests.

## 4. Our Central Qualitative Conclusions and Their Limitations

The central conclusion we have reached in our studies is of a piece with that reached on the specific issue considered in the preceding section, and like that, though still tentative, in our opinion justifies much confidence. Stated simply, it is that money does matter and matters very much. Changes in the quantity of money have important, and broadly predictable, economic effects. Long-period changes in the quantity of money relative to output determine the secular behavior of prices. Substantial expansions in the quantity of money over short periods have been a major proximate source of the accompanying inflation in prices. Substantial contractions in the quantity of money over short periods have been a major factor in producing severe economic contractions. And cyclical variations in the quantity of money may well be an important element in the ordinary mild business cycle.

These qualitative conclusions, and even more specific quantitative findings, are important. But they are also limited. Because they go sharply counter to what has been so widely believed for nearly two decades, there has been some tendency to interpret our claims as being far more than they are. For example, one newspaper story referring to similar views interpreted them as asserting that "the growth of the money supply is the single most important factor affecting the nation's economy"—which is very far indeed from what we are saying. To avoid misunderstanding, let me state explicitly some of the limitations of our conclusions.

One limitation is linked to the distinction between "real" magnitudes—relative prices, quantities of output, levels of employment, efficiency of production, accumulation of capital, and the like—and "nominal" magnitudes—absolute prices, quantity of money, nominal money income, and so on. The quantity of money in general appears not to be an important factor affecting secular changes in the real magnitudes. They are determined primarily by such basic phenomena as the kind of economic system, the qualities of the people, the state of technology, the availability of natural resources, and so on. These, not monetary institutions or policy, are the critical factors that ultimately determine the "wealth of nations" and of their citizens. In general, the major long-run impact of the quantity of money is on nominal magnitudes, and especially on the absolute level of prices. Our conclusions are in no way inconsistent with that celebrated—and much misunderstood—statement of John Stuart Mill, "There cannot, in short, be intrinsically a more insignificant thing, in the economy of society, than money; except in the character of a contrivance for sparing time and labor. It is a machine for doing quickly and commodiously, what could be done, though less quickly and commodiously, without it; and like many other kinds of machinery, it only exerts a distinct and independent influence of its own when it gets out of order."[11]

[11] *Principles of Political Economy* (1848), Ashley, ed., Longmans, Green, 1929, p. 488.

What we can now add to this is a much more explicit specification of what it means for the machinery of money to "get out of order." It gets out of order, we have tentatively concluded, when the quantity of money behaves erratically, when either its rate of increase is sharply stepped up—which will mean price inflation—or sharply contracted—which will mean economic depression—and especially when such erratic movements succeed one another. One of our major findings is that, over periods spanning several cycles, the average rate of growth of the stock of money—so long as it is relatively stable and within moderate limits—has no discernible effect on the rate of growth of real output. Differences in monetary growth are reflected instead in prices. Our findings give no support to the view, now widely popular, that long-run inflation is favorable to economic growth. Deviations from the average rate of growth of the stock of money, if sharp, account for the inflations or severe contractions already referred to. If mild, the deviations are linked to the usual business cycle, and appear to be reflected partly in prices and partly in quantity, though we know little as yet about what determines how much of the effect is on prices and how much on quantity. The general subject of the division of changes in money income between prices and quantity badly needs more investigation. None of our leading economic theories has much to say about it. Yet knowledge about it is needed for better understanding of the impact not only of monetary changes but also of other factors significant in the business cycle.

A second limitation is linked to the distinction between average behavior and behavior in a particular episode. The fact that we can predict within fairly narrow limits the number of heads that will come up in a thousand tosses of a fair coin does not enable us to predict what will come up the next time. As students of business cycles, we are concerned largely with average behavior. The data for any particular episode are bound to be subject to considerable errors of measurement and to be affected by casual events peculiar to that episode. We can largely compensate for both bad data and erratic behavior by constructing averages for a number of episodes. The results may be well established, on the average, yet not reliable for predicting an individual case. Our earlier discussion of cyclical timing is an excellent example. As noted above, data on the month-to-month changes in the quantity of money are highly erratic and irregular, and there is often much uncertainty for an individual cycle about which month shows the highest rate of change (rate-of-change peak), or which month is followed by a shift in the rate of change to a lower level (step peak). Hence there is also much uncertainty about the difference in time between the rate-of-change peak and the reference peak or between the step peak and the reference peak—a date which is itself subject to error. But such errors may be expected to cancel out, so the average timing may be well determined. For example, in the course of 21 matched cycles from 1870 to 1961, the estimated difference in timing between the step peak and the reference peak varied from a lag of 4 months to a lead of 17 months with a standard deviation of 7 months. These estimated differences average out to a lead of 6 months, and this average is rather accurately determined. The standard error of the *average* is only 1.6 months, which means that the odds are 2 to 1 that the error in the average time is less than 1.6 months and 20 to 1 that it is less than 3.2 months.

Looked at another way, the fact that, on the average, the step peak comes 6 months before the estimated reference peak does not enable us to say very much about any particular occasion. Even if we could know that an observed shift to a lower rate of growth of the money stock is one that we would later regard as a step peak—much easier to know by hindsight than at the time—about the most we could say would be that there was roughly a 50-50 chance that a turn in business that we could later regard as a reference peak would occur between 1 and 11 months later. Our inability to be more precise may reflect our inability to measure the various magnitudes very accurately, or it may reflect inherent variability in the economic response to monetary stimuli. At the present stage of our knowledge, we do not know which.

Our assertion that money matters is therefore very far indeed from an assertion that we know enough about the role it plays and can measure sufficiently accurately the relevant magnitudes to predict precisely what effect an observed change in the quantity of money will have in a particular case. Needless to say, the aim of further research is to improve the precision of such predictions.

A third limitation, and the last one I shall mention, is that we are still a long way from having a detailed and tested theory of the mechanism that links money with other economic magnitudes. For long-period secular changes, for short-period rapid inflations, and for severe contractions, there exist reasonably well-formulated theories and a good deal of empirical evidence on transmission mechanisms. But for the ordinary business cycle, we are in a much less satisfactory position. In "Money and Business Cycles," we sketched very broadly some of the possible lines of connection between monetary changes and economic changes "in order," as we wrote, "to provide a plausible rationalization of our empirical findings . . . to show that a monetary theory of cyclical fluctuations can accommodate a wide variety of other empirical findings about cyclical regularities, and . . . to stimulate others to elaborate the theory and render it more specific."[12] We shall try to improve and elaborate this sketch in our "Trends and Cycles" volume, but I am not sure just how far we can get within the limits we have imposed for ourselves. Identification of the channels through which short-run monetary changes work their effects, and specification in quantitative terms of the characteristics of the channels and of the effects exerted through them, remain major tasks for future research.

## 5. The Stock of Money and Recent Economic Changes

A look at recent history will enable us to illustrate many of the points made in the preceding sections and to show the relevance of some of our findings to current problems.

The upper panel of Chart 1 shows for the past seven years three series: (1) the money stock, as we define it, which is to say currency plus all commercial bank deposits adjusted; (2) currency plus demand depos-

[12] Friedman and Schwartz, "Money and Business Cycles," p. 59.

its adjusted only, an alternative concept which is often referred to as the money supply; (3) the Federal Reserve index of industrial production, as a single index of the physical volume of general economic activity. The vertical scale is logarithmic, to show relative not absolute changes.

The two money series illustrate why the total stock of money is not of itself a very useful magnitude for studying cyclical movements. The series are smooth and dominated by their trends. Cyclical fluctuations show up in the form of waves about the trend and only occasionally in the form of

**CHART 1** Comparison of changes in money and production, 1957–1963.
*The horizontal broken lines represent high and low steps in the rate of change.* T *and* P *show reference cycle turning points.*

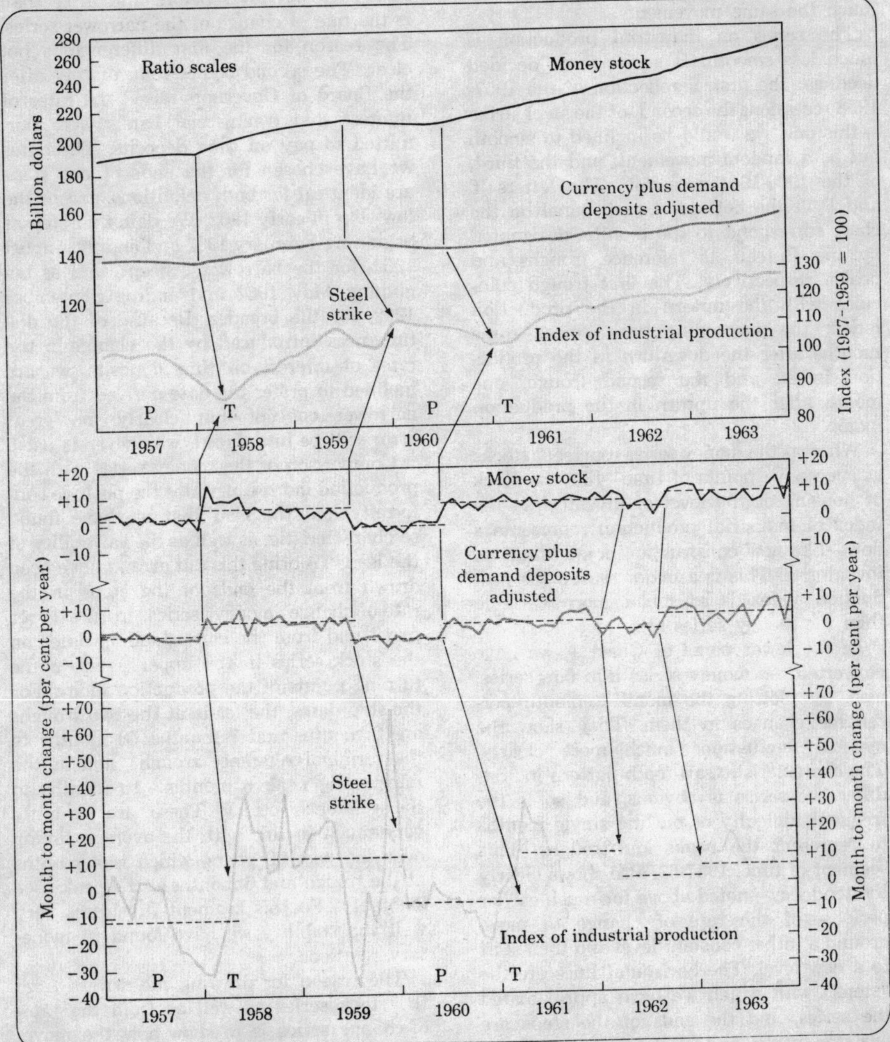

absolute ups and downs. For this period, there is only one absolute decline in the money stock series (from 1959 to 1960). The trends of the two series differ much more for that period than for most, reflecting the recent rapid rise in the time deposits of commercial banks, apparently largely in response to the successive rises in the rates of interest banks have been permitted, and have been willing, to pay on them. But aside from the trend, it is perhaps obvious even from these series that the two show very much the same movements.

The series on industrial production is much less smooth. It shows three decided declines: the first, a reflection of the 1957-1958 recession; the second, of the steel strike —this one, we would be inclined to smooth out as a random movement; and the third, of the 1960-1961 recession. The letters T and P at the bottom of each panel on the chart correspond to the months designated by the Bureau as reference troughs and peaks, respectively. The first trough coincides with the upturn in the production index; the succeeding peak comes three months after the downturn in the production index; and the second trough, one month after the upturn in the production index.

Whereas the money series represent stocks at successive points of time—like the stock of housing or the level of inventories—the index of industrial production represents a flow—like new construction or additions to inventories. This is a major reason the production index is so much more variable than the money series are.

In the lower panel of Chart 1, we have converted the money series into flow series, also, by plotting the month-to-month percentage changes in them. They show the cyclical fluctuations much more clearly. The characteristic saw-tooth pattern in first-difference series is obvious, and so is the frequent difficulty of picking single months to represent the peaks and troughs. This segment of time, 1957-63, also shows clearly the tendency—noted above for much earlier periods—of the rate of change to move around a rather constant level and then shift to a new level. The horizontal lines are the "steps" with which we have approximated the series, and the ends of the steps are our step peaks and step troughs. For this segment, the step dates seem less ambiguous than the specific cycle dates, but for other segments the opposite is true.

Comparison of the two money series in the lower panel illustrates our general finding that the substantive results do not depend on which particular definition is used. The two series are obviously closely parallel. The only appreciable differences are in early 1958 and in early 1962, when the rate of change of the broader series is higher relative to its level before and after than is the rate of change of the narrower series. The reason for the first difference is not clear. The second comes immediately after the Board of Governors raised the rates of interest that commercial banks were permitted to pay on time deposits. The dates we have chosen for the ends of our steps are identical for both definitions, except the low step in early 1962. We date that step as beginning February 1962 and ending August 1962, for the narrower concept, and as beginning May 1962 and ending September 1962, for the broader. Because of the disturbances introduced by the change in the rates of interest on time deposits, we are inclined to prefer the date derived from the narrower concept—but clearly, no great error will be introduced, whichever is used.

Comparison of the money series with the production index illustrates the positive conformity and the lead that we have found so characteristic, as well as the variability of the lead. To bring this out arrows have been drawn from the ends of the steps in the rate-of-change money series in the lower panel and from the corresponding dates on the stock series in the upper panel to the turning points of the production index. For the step dates, the leads at the two troughs are 3 months and 7 months (8 months to the terminal reference trough) and at the intervening peak 6 months (10 months to the reference peak). These are certainly very much in line with the average timing over the past 90 years, which is 4 months at the trough and 6 months at the peak (see Table 1). So this segment illustrates very well the stability we have found in monetary relations.

The reason for drawing the arrows from the stock series as well as from the rate-of-change series is to show how the movements which show up so clearly in the rate-of-change series can be seen also in the stock series, once one looks for them.

The money series show a low step in 1962 that we have so far not matched with any corresponding movement in the upper panel for the production index. However, though the production index has risen since early 1961 except for an occasional month, it is clear that there was a distinct retardation in late 1962. The retardation was the source of much concern at the time and was associated with the lower level of national income attained than had been forecast early in the year. To bring that movement into sharper relief, we have used the same technique for the production index as for the money series, namely, plotted month-to-month percentage changes. This series is even more erratic than the money series, but there is clearly a low step in 1962 to correspond with the low step in the money series. Its onset, as we have dated it, comes 2 months after the beginning of the low step in currency and demand deposits, and 1 month before that in the broader money total. The shift to a new higher level comes 5 months after the shift to a higher level in the rate of change in money.

This minor perturbation in industrial production will not and should not be classified by the National Bureau as a reference cycle; hence, neither its occurrence, its correspondence to the shift in money, nor the timing of the two movements would be revealed in a standard Bureau cyclical analysis. This is one of that species of subcycles that Ruth Mack has brought to our attention. The existence of such episodes is one of the reasons we plan to supplement the standard cycle analysis in our "Trends and Cycles" volume with correlation analysis of at least quarterly series.

The chart shows very much wider fluctuations in industrial production than in the rate of change in money series. If instead of industrial production a measure of aggregate output had been used, the contrast would have been narrower but still present. The contrast is even greater for aggregate money income than for output. We reported in "Money and Business Cycles" that, on the average, the percentage fluctuations in income were twice as large as those in the rate of change in money and offered a hypothesis to explain why this should be so.

So far, I have used the recent period to illustrate some of our technical problems and some of our descriptive findings. But it can also serve to illustrate the problems of interpretation. I have described Chart 1 entirely in terms of a positive conformity of the money series; trying to describe it in terms of inverted conformity will perhaps suggest some of the difficulties we have found with such an interpretation and some of the reasons we have rejected it. The still more important question is whether we should interpret the positive conformity as reflecting the influence of money on business, or of business on money. If these were the only alternatives, I would find the former much more appealing for this segment of time in particular. There have been in this period five rather clear-cut shifts in monetary action—as judged by the rate of change in the stock of money. Each has been followed after some months (with one possible exception, early 1962, if the link is made with the broader money series) by a shift in the same direction in the rate of growth of economic activity, as judged by the production index. Perhaps this pattern reflects the common effect of some third force; it is hard to explain it by any direct influence of business on money.

# 2 MONETARY HISTORY AND POSITIVE ECONOMICS*

ROBERT W. CLOWER
*Northwestern University*

We economists are essentially only dilettanti in the field of historical research, with the usual faults of all dilettantism: over-hasty conclusions, insufficient criticism of sources, tendentious colouring of facts, and even, on occasion, unconscious fabrication of them.

Knut Wicksell

## I

If successful prediction were the sole criterion of the merit of a science, economics should long since have ceased to exist as a serious intellectual pursuit. Accurate prognosis is not its forte. The real strength of the discipline lies in another direction —namely, in its apparently limitless capacity to rationalize events after they happen. This helps explain the indifference of most economic theorists to "the lessons of history"; men to whom all things are possible have little to learn from experiments conducted in the laboratory of time. It also helps explain the indifference of most economic historians to abstract theory; what have they to learn from a subject that "yields no predictions, summarizes no empirical generalizations, provides no useful framework of analysis"?[1]

Recent years have, of course, witnessed some changes in the attitude of theorists toward economic history and in the attitude of economic historians toward theory. Rummaging in attics and excavating ancient files have not yet become popular sports, but the production of historical statistics is very nearly one already. The problem is to put the data now becoming available to good use. This is hardly a novel problem; men have been debating the merits of alternative epistemologies since the dawn of time. But economic history is currently in a state of flux, forced by external pressures to become less humane, torn by internal discord as to how this should be done.[2] Thus the future direction of the subject may well depend as much on the methodological views of economists playing at history as on the attitudes of economic historians. Whether this bodes well or ill for economic history, I cannot pretend to say. Much depends on just who the "dilettanti" are, for economics

* Reprinted from *Journal of Economic History,* vol. 24 (September, 1964), pp. 364–379, by permission of the author and the Economic History Association.

[1] Milton Friedman, "The Marshallian Demand Curve," in *Essays in Positive Economics* (Chicago: University of Chicago Press, 1953), p. 92.

[2] See papers by Rostow, Meyer and Conrad, and Kuznets on "The Integration of Economic Theory and Economic History," *Journal of Economic History,* XVII (Dec. 1957), 509–553 (Kuznets' "Summary of Discussion and Postscript" is especially relevant); also Lance E. Davis, Jonathan R. T. Hughes, and Stanley Reiter, "Aspects of Quantitative Research in Economic History," *Journal of Economic History,* XX (Dec. 1960), 539–547; Douglass C. North, "Quantitative Research in American Economic History," *American Economic Review,* LIII (Mar. 1963), 128–130; and Robert W. Fogel, "Reappraisals in American Economic History—Discussion," *American Economic Review,* LIV (May 1964), 377–389.

proper is not devoid of methodological factions either.[3]

These considerations lend peculiar interest and significance to the volume under review. To be sure, Friedman and Schwartz's *History* merits close attention in its own right; it is not every day, or even every decade, that an outstanding economic theorist joins forces with another able scholar to produce a major work in economic history. But Milton Friedman is not just an outstanding theorist. He is the leading exponent of a radical research methodology which views much of formal economic analysis as "disguised mathematics"; which regards theories as useful only if they "fit as full and complete a set of related facts about the real world as it is possible to get"; which is contemptuous of any test of the validity of a hypothesis other than "comparison of its predictions with experience."[4] And he is also the author or coauthor of some highly impressive testimonials to the virtue of these views.[5] Surely this lends additional allure for both economic historians and their "dilettante" brothers to Friedman and Schwartz's venture into Clio's realm.

## II

No brief summary can convey an accurate impression of the range and depth of Friedman and Schwartz's *History*. To be sure, the discussion is highly selective; as the authors state (p. 3): "Throughout, we trace one thread, the stock of money, and our concern with that thread explains alike which episodes and events are examined in detail and which are slighted." Nevertheless, the books reads more like a general economic history than even its authors seem to suppose. And this is as it should be; to distinguish sharply between "monetary" and "other" aspects of the history of a money economy would be artificial as well as misleading.

The book was originally conceived as a single chapter in a statistical study of monetary factors in the business cycle (Preface, p. xxi). It now covers 860 pages, comprises thirteen chapters and two appendices,[6] and appears in print in advance of the study which gave it birth.

Economic historians will probably find most to arouse their interest in the first few chapters, which cover the relatively tranquil years between 1867 and 1914. Here the authors' central theme is the untrammeled development of the economy in response to the working of natural economic forces, "avarice explaining all, always."[7] The argument is detailed, penetrating, and for the most part convincing. For sheer ingenuity in marshaling evidence, few historical narratives can match Friedman and Schwartz's discussion of "Special Problems Connected with the Greenback Period" (ch. ii, sec. 5), their analysis of the "Great Deflation" (ch. iii, sec. 1), or their account of the Panic of 1907 (ch. iv, sec. 3).

The theme of the middle portion of the *History* (chs. v through xi) is the response of the economy to the vicissitudes of international affairs and domestic politics, with special emphasis on the growing power of the Federal Reserve System as an agent of economic control. Specialists in monetary economics will find these chapters a valuable source of factual and theoretical insight into the working of financial mechanisms. Economic historians are less likely to enjoy

[3] See H. Laurence Miller, Jr., "On the 'Chicago School of Economics,'" *Journal of Political Economy*, LXX (Feb. 1962), 64–69, and comments by M. Bronfenbrenner and George J. Stigler in the same issue; also G. C. Archibald, "Chamberlin *versus* Chicago," *Review of Economic Studies*, XXVIII (Oct. 1961), 2–28, and later responses by Stigler and Friedman, *ibid.* XXX (Feb. 1963), 63–67.

[4] Friedman, *Essays in Positive Economics*. The quoted phrases are torn out of context from pp. 12, 300, and 9, respectively. Friedman himself would never express views so extreme as these [compare his reply to Archibald (*Rev. Ec. St.*, XXX), pp. 65 ff.].

[5] I refer especially to Friedman, *A Theory of the Consumption Function* (Chicago: University of Chicago Press, 1957); to Friedman and Kuznets, *Income from Independent. Professional Practice* (New York: NBER, 1945); and to Friedman and Schwartz, "Money and Business Cycles," *Review of Economics and Statistics*, XLV (Feb. 1963 suppl.), 32–64. But these are just a few choice items in a long and distinguished list.

[6] Reference should also be made to the thoughtful and interesting "Director's Comment" by Albert J. Hettinger, Jr., which appears at the very end of the book (pp. 809–814).

[7] I owe this phrase to my erstwhile colleague, Meyer Burstein.

or profit from the discussion; too much of it is concerned with technical monetary details and with lengthy accounts of the policy deliberations of the monetary authorities. Like other readers, however, they will be intrigued by Friedman and Schwartz's unconventional views on the "Great Contraction" and other episodes of the interwar period.

The penultimate chapter, on the post-World War II rise in the income velocity of money, seems to be more in the nature of a journal article than a contribution to monetary history, but it is of considerable interest all the same. The final chapter provides a concise but remarkably complete account of the authors' main conclusions.[8]

## III

The preceding summary emphasizes the narrative rather than the analytical aspects of the *History*. Appearances to the contrary notwithstanding, the emphasis of the book is the other way around. The authors themselves do not appear to recognize the distinction; indeed, they blend analysis so effectively with narrative that one can hardly tell which of their historical judgments rest on fact and which on theoretical fancy. The difficulty lies, however, not in the authors' exposition, which is generally lucid, but rather in their failure to provide an explicit account of their methodology. My purpose in the pages that follow is to fill this gap.

The essentials of Friedman and Schwartz's analytical procedure are adumbrated in the opening paragraph of their final chapter (p. 676):

> The varied character of U.S. monetary history [from 1867 to 1960] renders this century of experience particularly valuable to the student of economic change. He cannot control the experiment, but he can observe monetary experience under sufficiently disparate conditions to sort out what is common from what is adventitious and to acquire considerable confidence that what is common can be counted on to hold under still other circumstances.

I interpret this observation to say something as follows. We may view historical time-series observations as rough measures of the values assumed in various intervals of time by the variables of a general dynamic system.[9] If the values of certain variables are observed to follow some regular pattern in relation to one another, we may abstract this pattern from the data and use it as a tentative benchmark to distinguish between "equilibrium" and "disequilibrium" states of the system. The very existence of such a pattern may be taken to mean that the economic system is basically stable.[10] Accordingly, we may assert with some confidence that departures from "equilibrium," as indicated by breaks in the pattern, will tend to be self-restoring, and we may use this stability principle as a basis for predicting the probable behavior of the economy starting from any given initial situation. Moreover, we may attribute obvious deviations from "normal" behavior to various "shocks," some of which can be identified with specific historical events. In this manner, we may assign "causal" significance to particular classes of events—"monetary," "political," "technological," etc.—and perhaps even go so far as to assess the relative importance of each as a source of economic change.

I hope this interpretation does not do serious injustice to the views actually held by Friedman and Schwartz. It portrays with reasonable accuracy a research strategy which seems to me to make some sense and with which I have considerable sympathy. And it is consistent with what I know about the methodological views of the patron saint of "positive economics," Alfred Marshall.[11]

[8] I omit comment on the two appendices, except to say: (1) the statistical work underlying the basic tables in Appendix A and the charts and tables appearing elsewhere in the book is clearly of the highest quality (a full explanation of the estimates prepared by Friedman and Schwartz is to appear in their forthcoming study of "Trends and Cycles in the Stock of Money," another National Bureau project) and (2) the discussion of "the proximate determinants of money" in Appendix B does not add much of value to the argument in the text (most of the relevant information is already given in sec. 4 of ch. ii).

[9] Compare Friedman and Schwartz, "Money and Business Cycles," pp. 29–63.

[10] At least, for all practical purposes. On this, compare R. L. Basmann, "The Causal Interpretation of Non-Triangular Systems of Economic Relations," *Econometrica*, XXXI (July 1963), 442–443, 453.

[11] See Marshall, "The Present Position of Economics," in *Memorials of Alfred Marshall*, A. C. Pigou, ed. (London: Macmillan, 1925), pp. 166–169; also Friedman, "Marshallian Demand Curve," pp. 89-92.

The difficulty is to put the strategy to practical use, for it is by no means clear how one is supposed to distinguish between what is "common" and what is "adventitious," between patterns that are "regular" and patterns that are not.

But here we may draw on "the methodology of positive economics." Clearly, if we are required to judge a theory not by precept but by practice, then we should judge a research strategy in the same way: that is, not by what its exponents say it can do but rather by what it enables them to accomplish. If this is our procedure, then the difficulty mentioned above may be passed over for the time being; a look at the facts may suffice to allay any doubts we have about our ability to "sort out what is common from what is adventitious."

## IV

It is common knowledge that changes in money income and employment are more or less closely associated with changes in prices, financial flows, holdings of physical assets, bank deposits, etc. What is not known is the precise character of these associations, their magnitude, reliability, and causal significance. Friedman and Schwartz begin their attack on these problems by studying outwardly relevant time-series data in the hope that these will reveal patterns of association of sufficient clarity to provide a tentative foundation for further analysis.

Referring to the 93-year period from 1867 to 1960, they find that the "stock of money" (defined as currency plus commercial bank deposits) grew from less than $2 billion to more than $200 billion, while income (as measured by Kuznets' unpublished annual estimates of net national product in current prices)[12] grew from less than $6 billion to more than $200 billion (pp. 3-5 and charts 1 and 62). The income velocity of money changed substantially during the period as a whole, falling fairly steadily between 1869 and 1915 (from a value of 4.6 to a value of 2.1), oscillating around an uncertain trend from 1916 to 1946, rising to a level somewhat above that for 1915 during the years 1947-1960. Population more than quadrupled during the same period, per capita holdings of money increased more than thirtyfold, per capita income more than tenfold.

The clearest secular patterns which seem to emerge from the data involve the stock of money, on the one hand, and income and the stock of "high-powered money,"[13] on the other. All three of these magnitudes are found to display strong upward trends, money generally rising faster than high-powered money, high-powered money generally rising faster than income. The suggestion is that rates of growth of the three series have been roughly proportional to one another; but the relationship is far from exact.

Friedman and Schwartz's analysis of cyclical variations in the stock of money and in money income produces sharper results. Although the numerical value of income velocity is discovered to vary considerably from one cycle to another, velocity is found to display "a systematic and stable movement about its trend, rising during expansion and falling during contraction" (p. 682). Moreover, observed year-to-year changes in the value of velocity are "less than 10 per cent in 78 out of the 91 year-to-year changes from 1869 . . . to 1960. Of the 13 larger changes, more than half came during either the Great Contraction or the two world wars, and the largest change was 17 per cent" (p. 682).

These results imply a strikingly good correlation between changes in the stock of money and changes in income, comparable in important respects to the familiar time-series correlation between income and consumption.[14] Whatever view one takes of the probable causal significance of this re-

[12] These estimates are available on request from the National Bureau of Economic Research, but are not presented in the *History*, except in charts.

[13] Defined as "the total amount of hand-to-hand currency held by the public plus vault cash plus, after 1914, deposit liabilities of the Federal Reserve System to banks" (p. 50).

[14] See Friedman and David Meiselman, "The Relative Stability of Monetary Velocity and the Investment Multiplier in the United States, 1897-1958," *Stabilization Policies*, research study prepared for the Commission on Money and Credit (Englewood Cliffs, N. J.: Prentice-Hall, 1963), pp. 165–268, especially Charts II-4 and II-6, pp. 194 and 196. Also, Ando, Brown, Solow, and Kareken, "Lags in Fiscal and Monetary Policy," in the same volume, pp. 14–24.

lation, its practical importance cannot be denied. No theory of a money economy which is incapable of generating the kind of behavior required by the correlation can be taken very seriously. Conversely, any theory which is capable of generating such behavior deserves consideration, at least tentatively, as a descriptive and explanatory device. Considered from either point of view, the correlation constitutes a promising point of departure for further research.

## V

Friedman and Schwartz's procedure at this stage is to ask, as it were, What is the simplest relation between the stock of money and money income that is capable of rationalizing the behavior patterns suggested by the statistical evidence? It should be emphasized that they do not concern themselves at this point with "causality" or related philosophical issues. Their question relates simply to the behavior of empirical data, not to the behavior of people or markets. How the economic system *really* works is irrelevant; what Friedman and Schwartz want to know is whether the system works *as if* its object were to ensure the maintenance of some "normal" relation between the stock of money and money income.

To cut a long story short, the answer which I interpret Friedman and Schwartz to give to their question is that, to a first approximation, the *normal* stock of money ($M_n$) and *normal* income ($Y_n$) are related by an equation of the form $M_n = KY_n^a$, where $K$ is a constant representing the reciprocal of the "normal" income velocity of money, and $a$ is a constant ($a > 1$) representing the "normal" income elasticity of demand for money balances. Of course, the "normal" magnitudes $M_n$ and $Y_n$ are not directly observable. To connect them with corresponding *measured* magnitudes (M and Y), it is necessary to introduce certain "transitory" variables $u_m$ and $u_y$, defined by the equations

$$M \equiv M_n + u_m$$

and

$$Y \equiv Y_n + u_y$$

These identities, together with the initial assumption

$$M_n = KY_n^a$$

imply that the measured stock of money and measured money income are connected by the relation

$$M = K[Y - u_y]^a + u_m$$

Friedman and Schwartz's inquiry into monetary history is thus directed, in effect, at characterizing the general properties of the transitory magnitudes $u_m$ and $u_y$, studying their interrelations, and identifying independent variations in each with specific historical events—wars, crises, international gold flows, actions by the Federal Reserve authorities, etc.

They do not couch their argument in these terms; the language and symbols that I am using are mine, not theirs, and so is the interpretation.[15] The purpose of my free translation is to suggest to the reader something that I did not begin to realize until after I started to write this review: that the conceptual framework of Friedman and Schwartz's *History* is virtually indistinguishable from that of Friedman's earlier *A Theory of the Consumption Function*. Once this analogy is grasped, the whole of Friedman and Schwartz's analytical narrative is seen to follow a purposeful pattern; what at first sight seems a slightly untidy argument is instead discovered to be a masterly mosaic of logic and facts.

But is it "history"? Most historians would probably want to reserve judgment about the non-narrative portions of the argument, on the ground that the establishment as distinct from the verification of "laws" of social development is not an essential aspect of history *qua* history. On the other hand, most economists would probably say that the entire argument is strictly history, on the ground that evidence about past human endeavor, however important it may be for testing economic hypotheses, is not a necessary, sufficient, or reliable basis for formulating them.

This conflict of viewpoint raises some

[15] For a very similar symbolic presentation, however, see Friedman and Schwartz, "Money and Business Cycles," pp. 56–58.

delicate and controversial issues. To what extent is Friedman and Schwartz's argument directed toward the establishment of causal rather than merely descriptive relations among economic phenomena? Is there any meaningful way to distinguish between the two; that is, what objective criteria, if any, might be used to distinguish between relations that do and relations that do not have causal significance? It seems to me that these issues go to the heart of the problem with which this review is primarily concerned, which is to assess the "importance" of Friedman and Schwartz's book as a "contribution to knowledge." Accordingly, it is on these issues that I shall mainly focus in the pages that follow.

## VI

As I emphasized earlier, Friedman and Schwartz do not initially concern themselves with questions of causality. However, the tenor of their argument gradually runs in that direction until it becomes the dominant note of the book. How do they accomplish this transmogrification? I shall not try to recapitulate the details of their argument, but I shall try to reproduce the main outlines.

The first step in the process is to show that the basic theoretical model is useful for summarizing the salient facts of U. S. monetary history since 1867. To be sure, the procedure used to derive the model in the first place guarantees that its fit to the original money and income series will be reasonably satisfactory; but the model works better than this remark might seem to suggest. Indeed, if one were simply confronted with the model and told to fit it to the data (using moving averages of measured money and measured income as estimates of the corresponding "normal" variables), I daresay he would be amazed at the results.[16]

The second step is to show that where the model does not perform almost perfectly (as during the two depression decades, 1870-1880 and 1930-1940, and during the post-World War II period of rising income velocity), this is attributable not to any basic inadequacy of the model but rather to exceptional variations in the transitory components of money or income, the "causes" of which can be at least tentatively identified. Thus, the imperfections of the model for describing monetary experience during the period 1870-1880 are explained in part by errors in Kuznets' estimates of net national product for this period (pp. 36–41). Similarly, the partial breakdown of the model during the period 1930-1940 is traced to the ineptitude of the Federal Reserve authorities in failing to take adequate measures to stem the tide of the Great Contraction (pp. 693–694). And the failure of the model to account for the rise in income velocity after 1946 is attributed (after lengthy evaluation of other possible explanations, such as rising interest rates, the growth of financial intermediaries, etc.) to "changing patterns of expectations about economic stability" (p. 673).

The third and final step is to conduct some "crucial" thought experiments with historical data, the argument being that "the examination of a wide range of qualitative evidence . . . provides a basis for discriminating between [alternative] possible explanations of observed statistical covariation [so that one can] go beyond the numbers alone and, at least on some occasions, discern the antecedent circumstances whence arose the particular movements that become so anonymous when we feed the statistics into the computer" (p. 686). This technique is applied to a number of cases (including the Gold Inflation of 1897-1914, the monetary expansions accompanying World Wars I and II, the resumption and silver episodes, and the recessions of 1920, 1931, and 1937). In every instance, it is concluded that "the major channel of influence is from money to business" (p. 694), although "there have clearly also been influences running the other way" (p. 695).

Whether or not one considers the evidence and arguments introduced at each of these steps to be completely persuasive (and I do not), he can hardly fail to be jolted by their cumulative impact (as I was). True, the entire demonstration rests in the final anal-

[16] But perhaps not. On this, see Ames and Reiter's fascinating sampling experiment involving time series drawn at random from *Historical Statistics of the U. S.*, "Distributions of Correlation Coefficients in Economic Time Series," *Journal of the American Statistical Association*, LVI (Sept. 1961), 637–656.

ysis on the assumption that the original theoretical model is basically valid, which is the point at issue. True, it is one thing to use a model to summarize facts, another to use it as a basis for positive judgments about "what might have been" or "what is to be." True, Friedman and Schwartz nowhere provide an explicit statement of the manner in which changes in the stock of money are linked with changes in income.[17] Hence, Friedman and Schwartz cannot be said to have explained the nature of the causal mechanism whose existence seems to be implied by their historical judgments. Nevertheless, they make a case that is not easy to answer, and one which strongly supports the view to which they effectually commit themselves in their final chapter; that is, that *income and prices will typically be found "dancing to the tune called by independently originating monetary changes"* (p. 686, my italics).[18]

Such a conclusion—particularly when it is backed up by over six hundred pages of detailed evidence—is bound to be a bit upsetting to those whose vision of the working of the economic system is informed by neo-Walrasian theoretical conceptions, which is to say, to all but a small handful of contemporary economists.[19] For it is an essential feature both of post-Keynesian income analysis and of contemporary monetary theory that *money does not matter much except in the long run.* More specifically, neo-Walrasians typically argue[20] that, in a closed economy, the absolute levels of money prices and aggregate money income depend *ultimately* on the quantity of *legal tender means of payment* as determined by the fiscal and monetary operations of government; but that the *impact* effects of autonomous changes in the stock of legal-tender money cannot be disentangled from other and equally important sources of economic disturbance—technological, psychological, etc.—not, at least, by visual inspection of historical time-series data and casual study of related events.[21] More pointedly, legal-tender money—which does not include either demand or time deposits—is merely one of many generally acceptable means of payment. The great bulk of objects which people regard as "money" at any given point in time[22] consists of debt instruments, the amounts of which are determined in the short run not by government authorities but by the general public. Facts and arguments to the contrary notwithstanding, therefore, it is absurd to assign a prominent role in cyclical movements to variations in the stock of legal-tender money, and it is even more absurd to treat the total "stock of money," however one might define it, as an independent variable. So the issue is joined.

---

17 An account of sorts is given in Friedman and Schwartz, "Money and Business Cycles," and criticized in the same issue by Hyman P. Minsky and Arthur Okun (pp. 68–72, 74).

18 See also Friedman and Schwartz, "Money and Business Cycles"; Milton Friedman, "The Quantity Theory of Money: A Restatement," *Studies in the Quantity Theory of Money* (ed. Milton Friedman; Chicago: University of Chicago Press, 1956), pp. 3–21; Friedman and Meiselman, "Relative Stability," pp. 166–170.

19 The term "neo-Walrasian" refers to the general point of view underlying such modern classics as Hicks' *Value and Capital* and Samuelson's *Foundations of Economic Analysis.* The distinctive characteristic of this point of view as contrasted with that of Marshall, the neo-Classics, and Friedman and Schwartz, is that market demand and supply relations are explicitly defined in terms of underlying microeconomic decision processes. This aspect of the neo-Walrasian literature stands out with particular clarity in recent contributions to the general equilibrium theory of money. See, for example, Don Patinkin, *Money, Interest and Prices* (Evanston: Row Peterson, 1956); G. C. Archibald and R. G. Lipsey, "Monetary and Value Theory: A Critique of Lange and Patinkin," *Review of Economic Studies,* XXVI (Oct. 1958), 1–22.

20 See M. L. Burstein, *Money* (Cambridge: Schenkman Publishing Co., 1963), pp. 749 ff.; P. A. Samuelson, "Reflections on Central Banking," *National Banking Review,* I (Sept. 1963), 15–28.

21 For a clear statement of representative views, see H. G. Johnson, "Monetary Theory and Policy," *American Economic Review,* LII (June 1962), 335–384; also, R. G. Lipsey and F. P. R. Brechling, "Trade Credit and Monetary Policy," *Economic Journal,* LXXIII (Dec. 1963), 618–641.

22 The time qualification is important; for example, in times of prosperity practically any asset may be regarded as "money," whereas in times of "panic" even demand deposits may sell at a discount (compare *History,* p. 161). What constitutes "legal tender" is also a problem: greenbacks were " 'lawful money' and legal tender for all debts, public and private, except customs duties and interest on the public debt, both of which were to be payable in coin," to quote Alonzo Barton Hepburn, *A History of Currency in the United States* (New York: Macmillan Co., 1915), p. 185.

The difference between Friedman and Schwartz and those whom I have called neo-Walrasians may at first sight appear to turn on questions of fact. If the neo-Walrasians are right (it may be said), they should be able to produce a better explanation of historical experience than that offered by Friedman and Schwartz. If they cannot do this, they should give up the game. But who is to decide if one model is "better" than another? And what does "better" mean if the purposes of alternative models are significantly different—for example, if one model is intended roughly to summarize experience covering nearly a century, and the other is intended to predict with a high degree of accuracy what will happen during a period of a few weeks or months if a certain policy action is taken now? I think there can be no doubt about the answer: *there are no objective standards for evaluating the descriptive validity of theoretical hypotheses; standards that serve for one purpose or period may not do at all for others.* This is quite sufficient to show that the real point at issue cannot be settled by appealing to "facts."

The question whether there exist objective criteria for distinguishing between relations that are "causal" and relations that are "merely descriptive" remains to be decided. This is obviously a matter for philosophers of science rather than for economists. However, since philosophers have now been debating the issue for more than two millenia, we may sensibly infer that "facts" will never resolve it. To date, the only thing on which all philosophers seem agreed is that most scientists have a strong psychological propensity to regard all correlations that are not known to be spurious as manifestations of some underlying causal process. Whether or not this propensity has a solid foundation in fact is beside the point; what is important is that the propensity itself drives scientists to think and act in certain interesting ways.[23]

## VII

Thus we come at last to methodological differences as the ultimate basis for the revulsion of neo-Walrasians from the "monetomania" of Friedman and Schwartz. These differences are, I think, greater in practice than they appear to be in principle. No judicious writer on methodology ever takes a completely unqualified stand on any basic issue, knowing full well that some arcanum of science will be dredged up by opponents and used to show him wrong. Real methodological differences are aired in private, usually by groups of people who have fault to find with approaches used by other groups. I propose to be injudicious: to say bluntly and without qualification some things about the methodology of Friedman and Schwartz and that of the neo-Walrasians that I would normally not commit to print.

Friedman and Schwartz, like all other economists, start with certain vague notions about the working of a money economy: banks and businesses act "as if" they want to make money; households act "as if" they want to eat and work; markets act "as if" their object is to arrive at prices that equate demands with supplies. They then proceed *immediately* to give these notions definite form by shaping them in the light of empirical knowledge. There is no sharp distinction in their world between "theory" and "fact"; theory is simply an organized description of consilient inductions drawn from related sets of empirical observations. Nor is there any question of using facts to "illustrate" rather than "test" hypotheses, for this would be to illustrate facts with more facts. Whether or not Friedman and Schwartz regard personal intuitions as "facts" is uncertain; but my hunch is that they do not. If they did, they would have to pay at least some attention to the intuitive plausibility (that is, "realism") of their assumptions, and this would violate a fundamental tenet of the "methodology of positive economics."[24]

The neo-Walrasians (like Friedman and Schwartz) start with certain vague notions about the working of the economic system.

[23] For an elaborate discussion of "causality" and its various behavior manifestations, see Ernest Nagel, *The Structure of Science* (New York: Harcourt, Brace and World, 1961), ch. x.

[24] See Friedman, "The Methodology of Positive Economics," *Essays*, pp. 16–23; and more significantly, *Consumption Function*, p. 231. I should remark explicitly that my interpretation of Friedman and Schwartz's methodological position is based not so much on what they say, here or elsewhere, jointly or singly, as on what they do—and similarly for the neo-Walrasians.

However, these notions are shaped initially not in the light of concrete experience but rather with reference to *stylized facts* (that is, intuition and common sense). There is no pretense of "descriptive realism" in this procedure, but there is a very real concern with the intuitive plausibility of basic assumptions. Personal reflections about one's own objective responses to external stimuli are, after all, as real and reliable as are any observations of external events.[25]

The *crucial* test of the empirical validity of a model, for the neo-Walrasians just as for Friedman and Schwartz, is the conformity of its predictions with experience.[26] But one of the major objectives of theorizing is to avoid having to perform needless experiments. Why put to factual test a model that is logically inconsistent or trivial, analytically unmanageable, intuitively absurd, or devoid of empirical implications even under ideal conditions? Abstractness, elegance, and generality are *not* irrelevant criteria for evaluating the potential empirical fruitfulness of a theoretical model; all have an immediate bearing on one or more of the preliminary tests listed above.

As for the familiar indictment that facts are typically used not to test but merely to illustrate preconceived hypotheses, the neo-Walrasians must certainly plead "guilty" —but only to the specification of being cautious, not to the specification of producing barren abstractions. No doubt most neo-Walrasian models are excessively general (whatever that may mean). The proper way to specialize models is gradually to modify them by reference to results obtained by refined statistical analysis of empirical data *and by reference to other relevant critical procedures.*[27] Economics is an unsettled research science, not a systemized body of established truths. It is still relatively youthful, its subject matter is complex, and its procedure is largely nonexperimental. Progress in shaping economic hypotheses to bring them to bear on concrete problems is bound to be uncertain and slow. Accordingly, neo-Walrasians may be justly charged with being excessively patient —"like highly trained athletes who never run a race,"[28] but men who are passionately "anxious to do good," who have a "burning interest in pressing issues of public policy, . . . who desire to learn how the economic system really works in order that that knowledge may be used,"[29] are perhaps better employed in politics than in basic scientific research.

These remarks are not intended to settle anything; only to clarify some issues and clear some air. I have so far stressed points of apparent disagreement between the neo-Walrasians and Friedman and Schwartz. I should now like to emphasize two points of fundamental importance on which there is clearly complete accord: first, *the essential art of the empirical scientist is that of inventing conjectures;* second, *this art is bound by no fixed rules.* There are countless "patterns of plausible inference," all potentially fruitful, none capable of *proving* anything.[30] Methodological disputes are generally idle because they are concerned with means rather than ends; the scientific worth of a conjecture does not depend on its methodological pedigree. Methodological differences are nevertheless worthwhile, be-

[25] This is an important reason for attaching significance to so-called scientific paradoxes; see my "Permanent Income and Transitory Balances," *Oxford Economic Papers*, XV (July 1963), 177 ff.

[26] I should emphasize once more the inherent ambiguity of the "prediction" criterion (see last paragraph of preceding section). For a concise but exceptionally lucid discussion of the problems involved, see H. Theil, *Economic Forecasts and Policy* (Amsterdam: North-Holland Publishing Company, 1958), pp. 204–207.

[27] On this, see Karl R. Popper, *Conjectures and Refutations* (London: Routledge and Kegan Paul, 1963), ch. i; also K. Klappholz and J. Agassi, "Methodological Prescriptions in Economics," *Economica*, N. S. XXVI (Feb. 1959), pp. 60–74.

[28] Samuelson, *Foundations of Economic Analysis* (Cambridge: Harvard University Press, 1947), p. 4.

[29] Friedman, "Lange on Price Flexibility and Employment: A Methodological Criticism," *Essays*, p. 300.

[30] For details, see G. Polya, *Patterns of Plausible Inference* (Princeton: Princeton University Press, 1954).

cause diversities of intellectual perspective are a mainstay of vigorous scientific criticism. Whether Friedman and Schwartz are right or wrong, their views, as expressed in the *History* and elsewhere, will invite attention and promote much worthwhile research. Failing the will or the ability to produce equally provocative works, neo-Walrasians will have to take such comfort as they can from the maxim that "the path to useful knowledge is paved with false conjectures."

## VIII

As a general rule, every historical narrative may be expected to display one or more instances of each of Wicksell's "faults of dilettantism"; and the longer and more elaborate the narrative, the easier it is likely to be for a critic to spot them. Friedman and Schwartz's *History* is no exception to the rule, but neither is it any easy mark; the range is too great and the target too small for even a diligent critic to accumulate anything but a pitiful score. Nuances aside, I have no fundamental quarrel with any of Friedman and Schwartz's substantive conclusions. My only doubts concern the evidential force and practical significance of some of their historical judgments. The comments that follow are therefore confined to certain general aspects of Friedman and Schwartz's argument that have influenced my assessment of their work.

Research strategies may be considered effective in roughly the same measure as they help us formulate and solve worthwhile problems. The strategy implicit in "the methodology of positive economics" strikes me as being especially effective for uncovering important empirical regularities, directing attention to useful and intellectually challenging areas of research, and posing problems in a clear and forceful manner. It is not irrelevant in this connection to mention that the consumption function, the accelerator relation, and the "Phillips Curve," were all products of research procedures similar to that espoused by Friedman and Schwartz. By contrast, I cannot recall offhand a single instance in which neo-Walrasian research procedures have yielded *empirical* results of fundamental novelty or importance. Considered from this point of view, the neo-Walrasian approach must probably be adjudged relatively barren.

Of course, procedures that are efficient for formulating problems may or may not be efficient for solving them. As concerns the latter criterion, however, I do not myself see any objective grounds for preferring the strategy of the neo-Walrasians to that of Friedman and Schwartz. It is perhaps more natural to associate modern techniques of econometric research with neo-Walrasian economics; and there can be no doubt about the value of these techniques for evaluating the quantitative significance of regularities discovered by other means. But econometric analysis is hardly a monopoly of the neo-Walrasians.[31]

In the final analysis, the real strengths and weaknesses of the *History* depend not on its authors' research strategy but rather on their inferential tactics. Since my outlook on economics is basically that of a neo-Walrasian (though not, I think, to the point of fanaticism), I should be the last to claim that my appraisal of this aspect of Friedman and Schwartz's book is devoid of bias. Readers may therefore place more than usual credence in my acknowledgment that Friedman and Schwartz's tactical performance is superbly ingenious and effective. This theme merits further elaboration.

Those who view the economic system through neo-Walrasian spectacles will be quick to find fault with such assertions in the *History* as:

> The stock of money shows larger fluctuations after 1914 than before 1914 and this is true even if the large wartime increases in the stock of money are excluded. The blind, undesigned, and quasi-automatic working of the gold standard turned out to produce a greater measure of predictability and regularity—perhaps because its discipline was impersonal and inescapable—than did deliberate and conscious control exer-

[31] However, see Friedman, "Methodology," n. 11, pp. 12–13. For some interesting observations on a related topic, see Polya, *Plausible Inference*, pp. 40–41.

cised within institutional arrangements intended to promote monetary stability [pp. 9–10];

or,

The monetary collapse [following 1929] was not the inescapable consequence of other forces, but rather a largely independent factor which exerted a powerful influence on the course of events. . . . Prevention or moderation of the decline in the stock of money, let alone the substitution of monetary expansion, would have reduced the contraction's severity and almost as certainly its duration. The contraction might still have been relatively severe. But it is hardly conceivable that money income could have declined by over one-half and prices by over one-third in the course of four years if there had been no decline in the stock of money [pp. 300–301];

or, more generally,

While the influence running from money to economic activity has been predominant, there have clearly also been influences running the other way, particularly during the shorter-run movements associated with the business cycle. . . . Changes in the money stock are therefore a consequence as well as an independent source of change in money income and prices, though, once they occur, they produce in their turn still further effects on income and prices. Mutual interaction, but with money rather clearly the senior partner in longer-run movements and in major cyclical movements, and more nearly an equal partner with money income and prices in shorter-run and milder movements—this is the generalization suggested by our evidence [p. 695].

But how does one respond to propositions of this character?

Clearly not by referring to bodies of evidence other than those considered by Friedman and Schwartz, for they have already covered this flank in a prefatory acknowledgment (p. xxii):

A full-scale economic and political history would be required to record at all comprehensively the role of money in the United States in the past century. Needless to say, we have not been so ambitious. Rather, we have kept in the forefront the initial aim: to provide a prologue and background for a [later] statistical analysis of the secular and cyclical behavior of money in the United States, and to exclude any material not relevant to that purpose.

Might one not then respond that to express firm judgments on the basis of such a limited range of evidence is to draw "over-hasty" conclusions? Again the answer must be qualified: first, because most of Friedman and Schwartz's judgments are advanced as "tentative hypotheses"; second, because a glance at the materials actually used to document major analytical themes in the *History* suffices to show that Friedman and Schwartz have spoken disingenuously about "not being so ambitious." Any young historian who managed to display a comparable "lack of ambition" could be certain of immediate professional recognition and renown upon his first venture into print!

Thus one is driven finally to resort to analytical dialectics—to oppose Friedman and Schwartz's judgments by saying that they picture the economic system as "a ship of income afloat on a sea of money." (The simile is not inapt; ocean waves not only influence but are influenced by the motions of a ship, but the ocean is clearly the "senior partner" in long and violent storms.) One can then pour scorn on this view of the world as presupposing that trading is perfectly synchronized in all markets of the economy at every instant of time and that all markets "clear" automatically even over relatively short time intervals. But alas, except that Friedman and Schwartz display a moderate antipathy to Keynesian economics (see pp. 533–534, 626–627) and nowhere worry seriously about possible direct effects of current market transactions on current demand and supply conditions, this line of argument cannot be sustained either—except by gross prejudice. The *shading* of the argument is in the direction claimed, but the *substance* is not.

I need go no further. My conclusion is that Friedman and Schwartz's conjectures deserve to be taken very seriously indeed. Their book does not pretend to be a definitive account of the monetary experience of the United States (though in fact it comes close to being just that). However, their historical judgments about this history are based on painstaking examination of a fantastically large body of evidence and on thorough, honest, and closely reasoned analysis of its implications. My guess is that subsequent researches, provoked by Friedman and Schwartz's pronouncements, will overturn some of their bolder judgments,[32] but that is another story.

---

[32] For example, a recent analysis by George Horwich casts serious doubt on the correctness of Friedman and Schwartz's explanation of the persistence of "excess reserves" during the period 1933–1939 (*History*, pp. 534 ff.); also on their interpretation of the 1937 contraction (*ibid.* pp. 543–545). See George Horwich, "Effective Reserves, Credit, and Causality in the Banking System of the Thirties," in *Banking and Monetary Studies*, D. Carson, ed. (Homewood, Ill.: D. Irwin, 1963).

In a more general vein, Ando and Modigliani have shown (in a forthcoming paper) that changes in autonomous expenditure, suitably defined, are as closely correlated with changes in income and consumption as are changes in the stock of money, thus casting doubt on the causal significance of the money-income relation on which Friedman and Schwartz place so much emphasis. For background on this, see Friedman and Meiselman, "Monetary Velocity," and Franco Modigliani, "The Monetary Mechanism and Its Interaction with Real Phenomena," *Review of Economics and Statistics*, XLV (Feb. 1963 suppl.). 79–107 (esp. pp. 102 ff.).

# 3 | THE MONETARY INTERPRETATION OF HISTORY*

JAMES TOBIN
*Yale University*

This monumental "monetary history of the United States"[1] since the Civil War is at the same time a critical history of monetary events, institutions, and policies and a monetary interpretation of the general economic—and even political—history of the century. I shall discuss these two aspects of the work in turn, although it is impossible to keep them entirely separate. In a sense the first aspect is the determination of the stock of money, $M$, while the second concerns the stability of the velocity of money, $V$. In the third and final section I shall review some of the judgments of the authors concerning particular episodes in the history of monetary policy.

## I. The Stock of Money

Milton Friedman and Anna Schwartz (F&S henceforth) provide a statistical account of the stock of money in the United States since 1867. Much of this is new, the product of long and painstaking statistical research. The profession is greatly indebted to them for constructing monetary series homogeneous in concept and definition over so long a span of time. The numerical account is dexterously and gracefully interwoven with a history of monetary institutions, legislation, policies, personalities, and politics. The resulting narrative is fascinating and absorbing, and it is written in a consistently lucid and lively style.

WHAT IS MONEY? The "money" whose stock F&S trace and explain consists of currency and commercial bank deposits held outside the federal government and the banks. The main questions raised by this definition are these: Why are time and savings deposits in commercial banks, which are not means of payment, included? If they are included, why are similar claims on other financial institutions—notably deposits in mutual savings banks and shares in savings and loan associations—excluded?

On the first question, a decisive practical answer is that it is evidently impossible to distinguish time from demand deposits in commercial banks prior to 1914. But F&S do not stand on this answer. They do not think that their inability to exclude deposits not subject to check impairs the utility or relevance of their series for the stock of money. They cannot contend, of course, that their $M$ measures the stock of means of payment, but they do not regard this as a defect.

More basic, in their view, is a concept of money as "a temporary abode of purchasing power enabling the act of purchase to be separated from the act of sale" (p. 650). I am not sure what this means; on its face

* Reprinted from *The American Economic Review*, vol. 55 (June, 1965) pp. 646–685, by permission of the author and the American Economic Association.

[1] Milton Friedman and Anna Jacobson Schwartz, *A Monetary History of the United States 1867-1960*. National Bureau of Economic Research, Studies in Business Cycles, No. 12. Princeton: Princeton University Press, 1963. Pp. xxiv, 860.

the concept seems to allow all forms of wealth, all stores of value, to qualify as money. Clearly purchasing power can find temporary abodes other than currency and commercial bank deposits, for example in other savings institutions.

F&S recognize that, once the means-of-payment criterion is dropped, drawing the lines that define "money" is a matter of expediency. What statistical quantity works best? That is, what measure bears the closest and most predictable relationship to measures of economic activity? This is fair enough scientific procedure. But such open-minded pragmatism in the concept and definition of money is an unconvincing prelude to policy conclusions which stress the overriding importance of providing money in precisely the right quantity. Sometimes Friedman and his followers seem to be saying: "We don't know what money is, but whatever it is, its stock should grow steadily at 3 to 4 per cent per year."

F&S are entitled to use words the way they please, and their "money" is a very worthwhile magnitude to measure. Being an aggregative economist by nature myself, I am not as disposed as many critics might be to point out how much information any particular aggregate conceals. All global measures do conceal information. That is their virtue as well as their vice, and the task of science, in economics as elsewhere, is to find and devise aggregates which retain mostly essential information and discard mainly irrelevant information.

Nevertheless the central place which F&S give their money stock in theoretical analysis, historical interpretation, and policy recommendation invites critical scrutiny. Imagine a balance sheet expressing on one side the financial claims of the rest of the economy on the federal government (including the Federal Reserve) and the commercial banking system and on the other side the debts of the public to the government and the banks. (The balancing item is that amount of private net worth represented by the net debt of the central government to the public.) Both the government and the commercial banks have demand liabilities to the public, currency and demand deposits. Both have time liabilities to the public, securities and deposits. The total on which F&S focus is the sum of the government's demand liabilities to the public and all of the commercial banking system's deposit liabilities, time as well as demand. In their view, this seems to be the only feature of the consolidated balance sheet which matters.

Do F&S really think that the composition of this magnitude is of no consequence? Do they, for example, expect the velocity of a given $M$ to be the same after a shift from demand to time deposits? And is their answer to this question the same whether such a shift is the autonomous result of a change in preferences or the induced effect of an increase in time-deposit interest rates? In special cases they recognize that compositional shifts are not neutral. They argue, for example, that shift to currency induced by bank failures will raise velocity—that is, it will reduce the demand for money because currency is an imperfect substitute for the safe deposits it replaces. But this attention to special cases suggests that there may be general and systematic compositional effects which the authors have ignored. I shall return to this question in Part II in discussing the stability of velocity.

What about the liabilities omitted from $M$, the interest-bearing government debt held by the public? Are its size and composition of no monetary consequences? F&S tend to take an extreme either/or black-or-white view. Generally they do not regard this debt as money or as affecting the significance for economic activity of the liabilities that are money. But there is an important exception. In 1942-51, Federal Reserve support of government security prices made them the equivalent of money, indeed of high-powered money. The true money stock should include these securities, valued at their support prices. By the same logic the 1951 Accord would abruptly shrink money to its usual constituents.[2]

I think most readers will agree with me that this is farfetched. There is uncertainty about government security prices in normal times, but it does not prevent them from being good substitutes for bank deposits. This is especially true of short maturities, but it is true of any maturities the holders

2 "The support program converted all securities into the equivalent of money" (p. 563) The authors are more cautious in discussing, on page 598 and page 625, the consequences of the Accord.

can match with their own future-payments schedules. Uncertainty was doubtless reduced, but it was not eliminated, by the Fed's wartime support commitment. There was considerable doubt, justified in the event, that the policy would be permanently continued. There is no evidence—either in interest rates on government obligations or in velocity figures—of such radical and abrupt revisions of public attitude towards government securities.

Moreover, I cannot see the logic which makes F&S so anxious to assimilate completely to money marketable government securities temporarily supported at par, and so reluctant to assimilate to money the liabilities of thrift institutions which are always "supported at par."

Finally, are F&S justified in neglecting the asset side of the consolidated balance sheet of the government and the commercial banking system? The authors are strongly opposed to giving attention to "credit" as against "money." The word "credit" in this dichotomy has a host of meanings, whose only common bond is concern for features of bank operations and financial markets other than the quantity of money. In Federal Reserve history, credit policy was long associated with the real-bills fallacy written into its very charter. According to this doctrine, the Federal Reserve could and should enable the banking system to meet the legitimate needs of trade and industry to finance productive activity, so long as its credit was not used for speculation or for unsound accumulation of inventories. This hardy tradition survives to this day insofar as the state of confidence or anxiety over the quality and direction of credit influences general monetary policy. F&S are properly critical of this tradition and of the surprisingly complete neglect of the quantity of money in prewar Federal Reserve theory.

The real-bills "credit" tradition also neglects interest rates. For example, the credit situation is judged satisfactory if all borrowers of good credit standing are being accommodated, regardless of the rates and other terms prevailing in the market. All that matters is equality of supply and demand, the absence of queues, regardless of the price and quantity at which the market is cleared.

I stress this point because F&S lump under the same heading—that of excessive attention to "credit" all concerns with the interest-rate effects of monetary measures. Indeed they blame Keynes for elevating "credit" above "money" because of the role of the long-term interest rate in the *General Theory*—even though the only way to get at the interest rate in the Keynesian model is to manipulate $M$.

Personally I think that interest rates rank high among the gauges that measure the impact of monetary policies and conditions on economic activity, and that central bankers surely ought to consider the interest-rate effects of their policies. But whether this view is right or wrong, it is certainly not cut from the same cloth as the real-bills and credit-quality fallacies.

Interest rates aside, does the composition of bank assets make no difference? Will the effect on economic activity be the same whether a given increase in the money stock reflects (a) commercial loans by banks to private-business borrowers, or (b) exchange of bank certificates of deposit for Treasury bills previously held by the public? The monetization of commercial loans (or really indirectly of the inventories of goods which they finance) seems to me to be alchemy of much deeper significance than semimonetization of Treasury bills. By this I mean simply that I would expect (a) to stimulate more spending on GNP than does (b). If so, the same $M$ packs a bigger wallop if it is the counterpart of operations like (a) than if it is the result of asset swaps like (b). You will never detect the difference if you confine your attention to the liabilities of the banking system.

THE PROXIMATE DETERMINANT OF THE STOCK OF MONEY. F&S explain the irregular growth of the stock of money, $M$, in terms of three "proximate determinants": (1) the stock of high-powered money, $H$, i.e., currency and Federal Reserve deposit liabilities held outside the federal government; (2) the ratio $D/C$ of the public's commercial bank deposits, $D$, to the public's holdings of currency, $C$; and (3) the ratio $D/R$ of deposits owned by the public, $D$, to the total high-powered money reserves, $R$, of the commercial banking system. It is purely arithmetic tautology to express the stock of money in terms of these three factors and to explain its development over time by variations in these "proximate determinants." Since $M = D + C$ and $H = R + C$,

$$M = H\left[\frac{\frac{D}{R}\left(1+\frac{D}{C}\right)}{\frac{D}{R}+\frac{D}{C}}\right]$$

F&S breathe life into this tautology as they trace the three factors over the century.

The concept of "high-powered money" is indispensable to understanding a monetary and banking system like that of the United States. The essential feature of the system is the commitment of the banks, with only fractional reserves of currency, to maintain convertibility at par and on demand between their deposit liabilities and currency. Since 1914 the major portion of bank reserves has not been literally in the form of currency but rather in deposits in Federal Reserve Banks. But this difference of form is inconsequential, because the Federal Reserve maintains for banks two-way convertibility between these deposits and currency.

In the United States today the government—i.e., the Treasury and the Federal Reserve together—determines the quantity of high-powered money. The behavior of the public and the banks determines how much of this stock is in circulation as currency and how much serves as reserves for multiple creation of deposits by the banking system. The authors do not say so explicitly, but the logic of the three "proximate determinants" evidently is this: the stock of high-powered money is determined by the government, the deposit-currency ratio by the public, and the deposit-reserve ratio by the banks. Of course this is an oversimplification, because each of the three sectors can, at least indirectly, affect all of the determinants. For example, the government, by determining reserve requirements, strongly influences the deposit-reserve ratio which the banks seek and achieve. Nevertheless I agree that this is an illuminating way to discuss the determination of the stock of money.

For the Federal Reserve era, I would find it more illuminating, and more in keeping with the spirit of the scheme, to exclude from high-powered money reserves borrowed by member banks from the Federal Reserve Banks. Then member-bank decisions to use the discount window would affect the deposit-reserve ratio rather than the stock of high-powered money. The amount of borrowing is of course influenced by Federal Reserve policy in setting the discount rate and administering the discount window. But the initiative is the banks', and it seems to me more natural to regard decisions to borrow reserves in the same light as decisions to hold smaller excess reserves. This, however, is a matter of taste and analytical convenience rather than of principle.

THE STOCK OF HIGH-POWERED MONEY. The federal government's control—even its proximate control—over the stock of high-powered money was considerably tightened by the establishment of the Federal Reserve System in 1914. In earlier times national banks could expand the supply of high-powered money on their own initiative by issuing national bank notes; they never exploited their note-issue privilege to the legal maximum permitted. (Since note issue appears to have been profitable, the authors frankly say that this is a puzzle they cannot explain [p. 23].) Private gold transactions provided another gap in government control of high-powered money. Banks needing reserves, for example, could buy gold in London. For the system as a whole this expedient was limited by the "gold points" in periods when the United States was on the gold standard. But in the greenback period, before 1879, the banks could in effect increase their high-powered money reserves by depreciating the dollar relative to gold and sterling. I am indebted to F&S for these points, but I do not think they stress sufficiently their implications—i.e., the government's control over the stock of high-powered money was relatively loose over much of the period which they cover.

Governmental actions to increase the stock of high-powered money have been of three kinds: (1) purchase and monetization of gold, (2) printing or coining of currency to meet other government expenditure, including the purchase of silver, and (3) the extension of Federal Reserve credit through open-market purchases of securities, purchases of acceptances from banks, or discounting of paper for member banks. The reverse actions, of course, diminish the stock. Although these various sources of high-powered money are arithmetically equivalent, given the values of the two ratios, in their effects on the stock of money, I think it is misleading to regard them as economically equivalent.

In some cases high-powered money is created as a by-product of income-generating expenditures by the government or by foreign purchases of U.S. exports. In others, high-powered money arises simply from exchanges of assets between the government or central bank and private banks or individuals. In the former cases, the new high-powered money also reflects additions to private net worth; in the latter cases, it does not. Some of the expansionary economic consequences of growth in high-powered money may be due to income and wealth directly generated. These cannot be duplicated by purely monetary policy, which is confined to the third of the three ways of engineering increases in high-powered money. You cannot repeat the consequences for employment, income, and spending of purchasing a million dollars of newly mined gold by purchasing a million dollars of old government securities—even though both operations increase high-powered money by a million dollars.

THE DEPOSIT-CURRENCY RATIO. Over the long run this ratio reflects the habits, institutions, and preferences of the community with respect to the use of currency and bank deposits. Over most of the short runs in this history, variations in the ratio reflect the fluctuating confidence of the public in banks' ability to maintain convertibility of their deposits into currency.

Secularly, banks gained steadily and dramatically at the expense of currency until 1929, although most of the gains after 1915 were in time deposits rather than in the ratio of demand deposits to currency in public use. But the banks have never restored the position they lost in the Great Depression and World War II. Although heavier income taxation has presumably promoted the use of currency, the success of deposit insurance and the general growth of income and wealth should have favored the use of banks. Bankers might well ask themselves why their liabilities are not as preferred a medium of exchange as they were thirty-five or forty years ago. Could service charges be a factor?

Much monetary history concerns the maintenance of convertibility between deposits and currency, and it is a dismal record of panics, crises, failures, and lessons never learned. The worst episode was of course that of 1930-33. The Federal Reserve System, established precisely to defend the monetary and banking structure against an "internal drain," failed utterly to do so. F&S make a convincing case that a better job would have been done without the Fed. Following earlier precedent, the banks would have stayed open while the conversion of deposits into currency was temporarily restricted. This would have been done, the authors think, as early as 1930; and this timely therapy would have prevented the subsequent disastrous scrambles for liquidity.

However this may be, the authors are surely right to regard federal deposit insurance as the real remedy, and therefore as the most important banking reform since the National Banking Act nationalized the issue of currency. Ironically enough, deposit insurance was stubbornly opposed as unsound by the banking fraternity it has so greatly benefited.

The deposit-currency ratio is broadly descriptive of the community's balance of preference between currency and deposits and of the state of confidence in banks. It is often used in another sense, as a parameter in calculation of the increase in money stock to be expected from a dollar's increase in high-powered money. I have doubts about this use of the ratio. It implies behavior that does not seem plausible, namely that currency and deposits are rigidly complementary—for every $X$ dollars the community adds to its deposits, it will acquire also one dollar of currency. It is more likely that the demand for stocks of currency varies in the short run with money income, or more precisely with the volume of retail and wage transactions in which currency is used. If so, an increase in deposits will bring in its wake an increase in demand for currency only to the extent that it increases economic activity. Likewise increases in activity against an unchanged volume of deposits will tend to increase the demand for currency and to pull down the deposit-currency ratio. This hypothesis is borne out by the cyclical behavior of the ratio, so far as this can be divorced from fluctuations of confidence in banks. The ratio tends to fall prior to cyclical peaks, and thanks to the "return flow" of currency to banks to rise prior to troughs.

THE DEPOSIT-RESERVE RATIO. This ratio reflects both legal reserve requirements and voluntary precautions against deposit withdrawal. I should perhaps repeat the authors' warning that both the numerator and denominator of the ratio exclude interbank deposits. Hence the use of correspondent balances as required or voluntary reserves tends to raise the ratio, and their replacement by high-powered money (as for reserves required of all Federal Reserve member banks) to lower it. In a sense the ratio measures the degree of protection the banking system as a whole has against withdrawals of currency. But this is so only on the assumption, contrary to fact, that in an emergency reserves would not be immobilized by legal requirements. It would have been better if the authors could have provided statistical series distinguishing between required and excess reserves, but evidently this was not technically possible.

Much of the short-run variation in this ratio, as in the previous one, is connected with the state of public confidence in banks. When confidence weakened, banks sought to protect themselves by increasing their reserves. Here was another element in the inherent instability of the system prior to deposit insurance. In classic banking crises banks and public joined in a mad scramble for high-powered money. There was never enough to go round.

Banks' demand for excess reserves—and banks' willingness to borrow reserves—depend on their assessments of the risks of deposit withdrawals, their appraisals of the possibilities and costs of obtaining reserves in emergency, and the earning opportunities on nonreserve uses of funds. F&S are not inclined to stress the importance of interest rates in the liquidity preferences of banks—or, as we shall see later, in the liquidity preferences of the public.

The issue is clearly posed by the excess reserves of the banks after 1933. These reached $2.5 billion, 42 per cent of total reserves, in 1936. Even after the doubling of reserve requirements in 1936-37, excess reserves were $1.2 billion, 18 per cent of total reserves. And they grew again to $6.3 billion, 48 per cent of total reserves, in 1940. On one common interpretation, this accumulation meant that the banks were "loose," in the sense that gains or losses of reserves, over a considerable range, would affect very little or not at all their holdings of nonreserve assets. F&S, on the other hand, believe that the banks were about as "tight" as ever. True, their demand for excess reserves had greatly increased as a result of of the 1930-33 experience; but it was just as important to satisfy this demand as it had been to satisfy the more modest reserve demands of the previous decade. Banks would respond to losses of reserves by reducing their other assets and their deposits, and to gains in reserves by significant increases in loans and investments and deposits.

Another way to put this difference of opinion is as follows: According to the first, or Keynesian, interpretation, banks were by the mid-'thirties moving along a fairly flat liquidity preference curve. Having invested in short-term Treasury and commercial paper until the rates were virtually zero, they would hold in cash any further accretions of reserves. The more high-powered money, the lower the deposit-reserve ratio —and these two proximate determinants certainly do show strong negative correlation in this period. (It is, of course, not at all inconsistent with this interpretation to agree with F&S that the unhappy events of the early 1930's had also moved the banks' liquidity preference curves bodily to the right [Chart 44, p. 537].)

According to the authors' interpretation, this correlation is a coincidence. The decline in the deposit-reserve ratio is due much more to shifts of the banks' cash preference schedule than to movements along it. While shifting, the schedule remained steep. One shift was a result of the 1930-33 experience, the bank runs and the demonstration that the Federal Reserve was no help. A second shift in the same direction was the result of the 1936-37 increases in reserve requirements, reinforced by the 1937 economic contraction. This shift reflected not just the increase in required reserves but, more important and more permanent, an increase in demand for excess reserves to hold against the possibility that the Fed might again raise requirements. F&S believe that these shifts proceeded at their own pace, largely independent of the growth of the stock of high-powered money. The banks and the money supply were never out of the control of the Fed. By changing the supply of reserves, or reserve requirements, the Fed could at any time alter the deposits and earning assets of the banks by the usual multiple-expansion process.

For these reasons F&S regard gold sterilization, failure to engage in open-market operations, and the raising of reserve requirements as disastrous errors of policy. On the other interpretation, they were mistakes all right, but relatively harmless ones.

I find the interpretation of F&S unconvincing. I do not see why shifts in preference resulting from discrete events should proceed so smoothly, and in particular with such striking negative correlation with the growth of high-powered money. Did bankers never take heart again, even when the deposit-currency ratio was rising and bank runs seemed to be a thing of the past? It may be that the introduction of variation of reserve requirements into the Federal Reserve's tool kit occasioned an increase in the demand for excess reserves. If so, it would be more reasonable to expect this to occur in 1935 when the legislation was passed but the powers were yet to be used, rather than after 1937 when requirements were already at, or very near, the maximum permitted by Congress.

No doubt the depression led to an increase in banks' demand for safe short-term assets, whether excess cash reserves or Treasury bills. As banks' excess cash spilled into short-term securities, short-term rates were driven almost to zero. In these circumstances Federal Reserve open-market purchases of bills were useless—almost like trading cash for cash. Surely there is this much truth, at least, in the Keynesian interpretation. Long-term rates and commercial loan rates were sticky, and it might have been hoped that banks' accumulation of excess reserves and low-yielding short-term securities would eventually put pressure on these other rates. But their differentials above short-term rates stubbornly reflected the lessons of the depression regarding risks of illiquidity and default. In spite of the substantial liquidity of the banks and the public, they did not give way until war altered the whole economic climate. Open-market purchases of long-term securities might have helped to depress their rates and to push banks and other financial institutions into more private lending. As it was, the gold-sterilization policy kept these institutions supplied with safe income from government bonds during much of this period. The Federal Reserve Board does not deserve the scorn with which F&S treat their statement that in the circumstances of 1939 open-market purchases were more important for their direct effects on the capital market than for their influence on member-bank reserves (p. 534).[3]

## II. The Velocity of Money

THE TREND IN INCOME VELOCITY OF MONEY. Before World War II, the income velocity of F&S money showed a sharp downward trend. Actually velocity did not begin its decline until after 1880, when it reached a record high of 4.97. It had fallen to 1.91 by 1914. No trend is apparent from 1914 to 1929. Velocity generally declined from 1929 to 1946. There were wartime bulges in 1918-19 and 1942-44. Since 1946 the trend has been upward, but $V$ remains lower than in the 1920's or in 1914.

F&S believe that the normal trend of velocity is down. The reason is that the services of money stocks are a luxury, with income elasticity greater than one. As its per capita income rises, society devotes an increasing fraction of its income to purchase

[3] In an interesting statistical study of the period, George Horwich has compared the responsiveness of bank earning assets to external loan demand, represented by personal income, on the one hand, and to effective reserves, on the other. His results, which are the more convincing because a similar test comes out the other way round for the 'fifties, support the "Keynesian" rather than the F&S interpretation of the 'thirties. "Effective Reserves, Credit, and Causality in the Banking System of the Thirties," in D. Carson, ed., *Banking and Monetary Studies*, Homewood, Ill. 1963, pp. 80–100.

of the services of stocks of money. That is, society increases its holdings of money relative to money income.

Irving Fisher would be surprised to read this theory and history of velocity. He would have expected an account of the demand for money to be closely tied to its function as means of payment. He would have wished to hear about the frequency and timing of wage payments and bill settlements, the speed and cost of communications, the trend of industrial integration, the scope of the barter and subsistence economy relative to the money economy, the volume of total transactions relative to income-generating transactions, and so on.

F&S provide no such discussion, and not even an excuse for omitting it. Partly, I suppose, this is because their money includes time deposits, which are not means of payment. Mainly, I think, it is because they don't regard the properties of money as particularly relevant to an explanation of the demand for money. Here is a consumer good much like any other. Empirically, it turns out—but for reasons that have almost nothing to do with the distinctive properties of money—that this commodity is a luxury, i.e., has an income elasticity greater than one. Like butter, or automobile mileage, or cameras. The big difference is that the supply of money does not respond to changes in income in accordance with its income elasticity, but instead makes income dance to its tune.

The treatment of money as a luxury consumer durable good seems to me a strained analogy. For one thing, it does not apply very easily to business firms, which hold most of the money stock. In any case, there are no identifiable services yielded by ownership of a stock of money. I don't believe F&S are referring to the joys of numismatics or to the satisfactions of a miser. The services of a stock of money are indirect. They can be measured only by comparing the implications of holding on average large stocks of money and small stocks of other assets with the alternative policy of holding on average smaller stocks of money and larger stocks of other assets. Possible advantages of the first policy over the second are smaller costs in effort or in fees and smaller risks of loss when it is necessary or expedient to make payments. The disadvantages of the first policy are the sacrifice of earnings when alternative assets yield more than monetary assets. Individuals and business firms presumably adjust their money holdings until these advantages and disadvantages balance at the margin.

It is certainly not obvious why this process should lead to a secular decline in velocity. If this is the model F&S have in mind, then they should tell us how time and the growth of incomes have altered the relevant costs, risks, and yields. But then they would have to assign much greater importance to interest-rate differentials as a determinant of velocity than they are prepared to do. They prefer to leave the alleged downward trend in velocity unexplained—for saying that money is a luxury is just another way of saying that its velocity declines with income.

This inadequacy of theory would not be so damaging if the empirical evidence for the downward trend were more convincing. On F&S's interpretation of the series, there is a downward trend from 1869 to 1946. This leaves the period since 1946 as the principal aberration to be explained; but it also leaves the 1920's as a disconcertingly long period during which the trend was interrupted. For the most recent period, the authors' hypothesis is that the demand for money has been reduced by the favorable postwar experience of economic stability.[4] Another *ad hoc* shift in preferences! Since adaptation to this experience will sooner or later be complete, the authors expect a resumption of the normal downward trend.

To me it seems strange to rely on a trend which regards the 1930's and 1940's as normal and the 1920's and 1950's as abnormal. The only convincing trend evident in the velocity series is 1880-1915. Since 1915 the series is dominated by fluctuations associated with wars and depression. Latané has shown that the velocity of money excluding time deposits since 1909 can be explained by interest rates, independent of the trend of real income.[5] F&S state that the two velocity series differ since 1915 only in

[4] F&S recognize that this interpretation must be "highly tentative" and "await further evidence" (p. 675).

[5] H. A. Latané, "Income Velocity and Interest Rates—A Pragmatic Approach," *Rev. Econ. Stat.*, Nov. 1960, pp. 445–449.

**TABLE 1. REGRESSIONS OF VELOCITY**

Dependent Variables: $V_1$ Velocity of F&S Money, Which Includes Time Deposits, $V_2$ Velocity of F&S Money Less Time Deposits

| Regression number | Period | Dependent variable | Constant term | Coefficients (and Their Ratio to Their Standard Errors) of | | | | Proportion of variance of $V$ explained | Standard error of residual |
|---|---|---|---|---|---|---|---|---|---|
| | | | | Year − 1914 | Rate of change of money income | Short-term interest rate | Long-term interest rate | | |
| | | | 1 | $t$ | $\Delta Y/Y$ | $R_1$ | $R_2$ | $R^2$ | |
| 1.1 | 1869–1959 | $V_1$ | 2.43 | −.035 (−20.5) | | | | .82 | .42 |
| 1.2 | 1869–1959 | $V_1$ | 2.38 | −.034 (−20.2) | −.220 (−0.5) | | | .82 | .42 |
| 1.3 | 1869–1959 | $V_1$ | 2.44 | −.034 (−14.6) | −.221 (−0.5) | −.000 (−0.0) | | .82 | .43 |
| 1.4 | 1869–1959 | $V_1$ | 1.74 | −.030 (−14.0) | −.005 (−0.0) | | +.175 (3.0) | .84 | .41 |
| 1.5 | 1869–1914 | $V_1$ | 1.70 | −.064 (−22.3) | | | | .92 | .26 |
| 1.6 | 1869–1914 | $V_1$ | 2.18 | | | +.192 (2.1) | | .10 | .87 |
| 1.7 | 1869–1914 | $V_1$ | 0.13 | | | | +.707 (8.0) | .60 | .58 |
| 1.8 | 1915–1959 | $V_1$ | 2.06 | −.016 (−6.7) | | | | .51 | .21 |
| 1.9 | 1915–1959 | $V_1$ | 1.35 | | | +.121 (+7.4) | | .56 | .20 |
| 1.10 | 1915–1959 | $V_1$ | 0.83 | | | | +.235 (+5.9) | .45 | .22 |
| 1.11 | 1915–1959 | $V_1$ | 2.06 | −.016 (−6.6) | −.009 (−0.0) | | | .51 | .21 |

**TABLE 1.** *(Continued)*

| Regression number | Period | Dependent variable | Constant term | Coefficients (and Their Ratio to Their Standard Errors) of | | | | Proportion of variance of $V$ explained | Standard error of residual |
|---|---|---|---|---|---|---|---|---|---|
| | | | | Year – 1914 | Rate of change of money income | Short-term interest rate | Long-term interest rate | | |
| | | | 1 | $t$ | $\Delta Y/Y$ | $R_1$ | $R_2$ | $R^2$ | |
| 1.12 | 1915–1959 | $V_1$ | 1.59 | –.009 (–3.7) | +.438 (+2.0) | +.096 (+5.5) | | .72 | .16 |
| 1.13 | 1915–1959 | $V_1$ | 1.43 | –.010 (–2.7) | +.224 (0.8) | | +.130 (+2.2) | .56 | .20 |
| 2.8 | 1915–1959 | $V_2$ | 3.26 | –.034 (–11.3) | | | | .64 | .33 |
| 2.9 | 1915–1959 | $V_2$ | 1.81 | | | +.241 (+8.9) | | .65 | .33 |
| 2.10 | 1915–1959 | $V_2$ | 0.49 | | | | +.551 (+10.1) | .70 | .31 |
| 2.11 | 1915–1959 | $V_2$ | 3.32 | –.034 (–9.9) | –.932 (–2.5) | | | .70 | .30 |
| 2.12 | 1915–1959 | $V_2$ | 2.59 | –.022 (–6.5) | –.207 (–0.6) | +.150 (6.0) | | .83 | .24 |
| 2.13 | 1915–1959 | $V_2$ | 1.70 | –.018 (–3.8) | –.293 (–0.8) | | +.335 (+4.3) | .78 | .27 |

SOURCES: $V_1$ and $V_2$, F&S Table A-5, p. 774. $\Delta Y/Y$ derived from F&S money income series, described on page 775. $R_1$ (commercial paper rate) and $R_2$ (basic yield on long-term corporate bonds) are series charted and described in F&S, pp. 640–641. I am grateful to the authors for providing me with the series $Y$, $R_1$ and $R_2$.,

periods when identifiable special circumstances affected the demand for time deposits. So it is not the difference in the denominators of the two velocity ratios which is at issue. F&S object that interest rates cannot explain low velocity in 1932-33 and in 1946. But given the wealth of particular explanations their own book provides for abnormally high demands for money in those years, this criticism of Latané's results does not seem very damaging. F&S are left, therefore, with the assertion that Latané and other "Keynesians" cannot explain, via interest rates, the downward trend in velocity before 1915.

Actually, the long-term interest rate "explains" 60 per cent of the variation of velocity from 1869-1914 (Table 1, regression 1.7). It is true that simple trend explains much more (92 per cent, regression 1.5). After 1914, trend explains only 51 per cent; short-term interest rate 56 per cent; long-term interest rate 45 per cent (regressions 1.8, 1.9, 1.10). The introduction of either interest rate into a multiple regression (regressions 1.12 and 1.13) lowers the absolute size of the trend coefficient.

The interest-rate explanation, although it succeeds well enough so that the authors have no right to dismiss it, is at a disadvantage in respect to the velocity of F&S money. For F&S money includes time deposits, which bear an interest rate that can be expected to be correlated with market rates. The proper variable would be the differential of the market rate from the rate on time deposits. It is not surprising that interest rates are more closely related to the velocity of money exclusive of time deposits (regressions 2.9, 2.10, 2.12, 2.13).

You have your choice. The F&S income-luxury theory seems to work up to World War II but has to rely on considerable *ad hoc* explanation since. The Keynes-Latané interest rate theory of velocity seems to work since 1909 or so, but needs help for the preceding period.

This help is not hard to find. The downward trend in velocity coincided with a strong upward trend in the public's holdings of deposits relative to currency, the deposit-currency ratio already discussed. Neither trend started until about 1880. The correlation between these two variables before 1915 is .90.[6] The trend toward deposits, after interruption during World War I, seems to have continued until 1930, thanks to growth of time deposits. During the same period 1880-1915, commercial bank deposits grew relative to mutual savings banks. Mutual savings banks were almost as important as commercial banks around 1880, when the decline in velocity began. Their deposits were 80 per cent as large as those in commercial banks in 1877, 60 per cent as large in 1880, only 25 per cent as large as their rivals in 1915. During these years, of course, the territory covered by mutual savings banks became a smaller part of the continental economy.

I suspect, therefore, that over this period there was a considerable thrift element in the accumulation of commercial bank deposits. The character of F&S money changed radically as currency became less important. Some deposits replaced currency as stocks of means of payment. Other deposits replaced mutual savings deposits; commercial banks became the principal available savings institutions.

Perhaps 1880-1915 was the great day for commercial banking, and the decline in velocity reflects its successful spread. Similarly savings and loan associations have been the spectacular success of the period since World War II. Their spread has helped to increase the velocity of money, just as the spread of commercial banks increased the velocity of currency. To the extent, however, that the spread of SLA's has also taken business from the security markets, the velocity of money-plus-SLA shares has declined, just as the velocity of currency-plus-bank deposits did before 1915.

The regressions of Table 1 include both a cyclical variable $\Delta Y/Y$ and interest rates. They indicate that the association of velocity with interest rates is not due simply to

---

[6] In this correlation for 1869-1914, the velocity series is from F&S (Table A-5, p. 774). The series for $D/C$ is given in Table B-3, pp. 799–801. For years after 1907, where monthly observations are given, the observation for the year is the average of the 12 months. For previous years, for which observations are available for only one or two months a year, estimates were made for missing months by linear interpolation, and yearly estimates by averaging the resulting monthly series.

the fact that both are pro-cyclical. Inclusion of interest rates invariably reduces or eliminates the apparent significance of the cyclical variable. In the case of $V_2$, the velocity of money without time deposits, the cyclical variable $\Delta Y/Y$ has a negative coefficient. This suggests that the pro-cyclical behavior of $V_1$, the velocity of F&S money, is wholly due to time deposits. Most of it is in any case explained by one or the other interest rate. More generally, in boom times deposits lose out to other thrift accounts, to securities, including equities, and to real investments, while in recessions these alternatives become relatively less attractive. When a phenomenon is so simply explained, is it necessary to construct an elaborate theory, in which estimates of unobserved variables like permanent income and permanent prices are invested with an altogether spurious reality?

CYCLICAL FLUCTUATIONS IN VELOCITY. Whatever its secular trend, velocity increases in cyclical expansions and declines in contractions. Several interpretations are consistent with this observation. One is that the cycle is nonmonetary: Money income is driven along its cyclical course by exogenous factors, the money supply is sluggish, and the cyclical behavior of velocity is the arithmetic result. F&S present convincing narrative evidence that at least on some crucial occasions this has not been true.

A second interpretation (not necessarily at odds with the first) is that velocity follows the pro-cyclical movement of interest rates. This has the scientific virtue of providing a unified theoretical and statistical (see, for example, the findings of Latané previously discussed) explanation of both trend and cycle in velocity.

A third explanation is Friedman's. The demand for real balances in the form of money grows with *permanent* real income—indeed, as we have already seen, more than proportionately. Measured incomes run ahead of permanent incomes in cyclical upswings, making the velocity statistic high, and behind in downswings, making it low. Some day perhaps Friedman will tell us what transient income is used for. We know from his work on the consumption function that none of it is consumed. We now know that none of it is saved in monetary form. Does it all go into the stock market? A priori I should have thought that money balances were a likely repository of windfalls. After all, didn't F&S define money as a "temporary abode of purchasing power . . ."?

The trend-cycle explanation of velocity leaves many episodes unexplained, and F&S provide a fascinating account of the special forces operating on the demand for money from time to time. A recurrent favorite is price expectations. When the public expects prices to fall, their demand for money will be increased.

This is F&S's explanation of one of the most puzzling phenomena in their narrative, the extraordinarily high demand for money, and for other liquid assets, between 1946 and the Korean conflict. (The low velocity of money in those years is the more surprising to F&S because they believe that their figures *over*state the true velocity. They overstate it for a reason I have already commented upon, namely that in their view "money" ought to include marketable government obligations during the period the Fed was committed to support their prices.) It is easy to forget that before Korea the economy had apparently reached a noninflationary equilibrium with a high degree of liquidity and interest rates on government securities not exceeding 2½ per cent.

I am inclined to agree with F&S's interpretation of the 1946-50 period, the more so because there is survey evidence, thanks to George Katona, that the public actually held the expectations attributed to it. There are other instances as well in which the imputation of price expectations up or down seems a reasonable way to make sense of otherwise puzzling movements of velocity. But F&S bring in these expectations only when they are obviously needed, leaving the reader with the uneasy feeling that their introduction at other times might be embarrassing. More important, I find it hard to reconcile their attention to price expectations with their neglect of explicit interest rates.

The real rate of return on money consists of two parts: the gain or loss in purchasing power due to change in prices, and the nominal or own-rate of return, zero for currency and interest net of service charges for deposits. A similar real rate of return can be computed for other assets. From a theoretical standpoint it is hard to understand why F&S are attributing such strategic importance to the first component of real rate of return and so little to the second. Inflationary or deflationary expectations affect the real rate of return on money, but no differently than they affect the real rate of return on a host of other assets fixed in ultimate money value. (Incidentally F&S refer to inflation—presumably unanticipated inflation—as a tax on money. In fact it is a tax on all fixed-money-value assets, and a subsidy on all fixed-money-value debts. The excess of the first over the second is not identical with the stock of money except by accident.) However, these other fixed-money-value assets differ from money in the flexibility of their nominal yields. These can and do rise or fall to compensate at least partially for generally held inflationary or deflationary expectations. Nominal yields on monetary assets, even time deposits, respond more slowly, if at all, because of institutional and legal ceilings.

Consequently, inflationary expectations will affect the demand for money differently, depending on the extent to which nominal yields on other fixed-money-value assets rise to compensate for these expectations.

In 1946-50, for example, interest rates on government bonds did not decline as a result of deflationary expectations. The Fed simply had to make fewer purchases in order to keep rates at the support levels. The public's demand for bonds was greater, and its demand for money less, than if interest rates had been free to adjust downward to expectations of postwar deflation.

THE STABILITY AND INDEPENDENCE OF VELOCITY. The main conclusion of F&S is that although the stock of money has been determined by a variety of forces in the nine decades they review, its relationship to other economic variables has been stable. Has this been so? The annual percentage change in the money supply explains only 31 per cent of the variation in the annual percentage change in money income.[7]

Has velocity been stable and predictable? F&S point out (p. 682) that the year-to-year change in velocity was less than 10 per cent in 78 of the 91 years and that velocity fell within 90-110 per cent of trend in 53 of 92 years. Since a 10 per cent difference in money income is the difference between inflation and recession, these figures are not very reassuring. I have regressed F&S velocity against the factors they use to explain it: time trend, and percentage increase in money income, the latter representing a cyclical variable. The residual standard deviation of velocity is .42, one-sixth of its mean value (regression 1.2, Table 1).

But no one, even the most skeptical of the importance of monetary factors, is surprised to find a fairly close statistical relationship between the course of economic activity and the money stock. The direction of influence in this correlation is something else again. For example, F&S cite the contractions of money stock that have accompanied major business contractions. We know, however, that some events—e.g., loss of foreign demand for U.S. products—could contribute both to business contraction and to monetary contraction. Furthermore, business contractions themselves set in motion forces which reduce the money stock—banks, business borrowers, and depositors all become more cautious. The same may be true historically of the monetary authorities, reacting, however mistakenly, in response to "needs of trade" or defending the dollar against external drain. An inspection of F&S's own figures will show that it is adverse changes in the two ratios, deposit-reserves and deposit-currency, more than changes in high-powered money, which are proximately responsible for contracting the money stock. So the sins of the monetary authorities are generally ones of omission rather than commission.

Of course, F&S are aware of the two-way nature of the relationship between money and economic activity. They say:

> Apparently, the forces determining the long-run rate of growth of real income are largely inde-

[7] Regression of $\Delta Y/Y$ on $\Delta M/M$, 1869-1959, where $Y$ is F&S money income series (derivation described p. 775), and $M$ is F&S money (series given in Table A-1, pp. 704–720). Annual observations of $M$ are averages of monthly figures. Monthly figures are not provided for all months prior to May 1907. They were estimated by linear interpolation between the months for which observations are given.

pendent of the long-run rate of growth of the stock of money, so long as both proceed smoothly. But marked instability of money is accompanied by instability of economic growth [p. 678].

Changes in the money stock are therefore a consequence as well as an independent source of change in money income and prices, though, once they occur, they produce still further effects on income and prices. Mutual interaction, but with money rather clearly the senior partner in longer-run movements and in major cyclical movements, and more nearly an equal partner with money income and prices in shorter-run and milder movements—this is the generalization supported by our evidence [p. 695].[8]

F&S's monetary interpretation of history requires not simply that monetary contractions and major business contractions are statistically associated, but two further propositions: Preventing monetary contraction would have prevented these business contractions, and nothing else would have done so. The authors require also, of course, the corresponding propositions regarding marked expansions of money income.

I believe that this amounts to saying that velocity is independent of autonomous, policy-engineered alterations in stock of money. For if such an increase in the stock of money would, by lowering interest rates or otherwise, result in a systematic reduction of velocity, then the linkage of money and business activity is much weaker than F&S think. And the historically observed correlation is much less comfort to the monetary authorities. Results like those of Latané, already cited, relating velocity to interest rates are therefore of the greatest importance.

I do not wish to be misunderstood. F&S cite some convincing examples of monetary changes that were clearly independent of contemporary or immediately preceding economic events: the increased gold production in 1897-1914 and the sharp increases in the Federal Reserve discount rate in 1920 and again in 1931. I am willing to agree that these monetary events contributed in important degree to the economic events which followed.

Consider the following three propositions: Money does not matter. It does too matter. Money is all that matters. It is all too easy to slip from the second proposition to the third, to use reasoning and evidence which support the second to claim the third. In this book F&S have ably and convincingly marshaled evidence for the proposition that money matters. They have put to rout the neo-Keynesian, if he exists, who regards monetary events as mere epiphenomena, postscripts added as afterthoughts to the nonmonetary factors that completely determine income, employment, and even prices. But in their zeal and exuberance Friedman and his followers often seem to go—though perhaps less in this book than elsewhere—beyond their own logic and statistics to the other extreme, where the stock of money becomes the necessary and sufficient determinant of money income. Much as I admire their work, I cannot follow them there.

Remember that the difference between the propositions "Money matters" and "Money is all that matters" is also the difference between the propositions "Fiscal policy matters" and "Fiscal policy doesn't matter." If there is a tight linkage, at any moment of time, between money income and the stock of money, then pure fiscal policy —e.g., bond-financed government spending—cannot raise money income. But if the income-velocity of money is flexible, in response to interest rates, the stock of money itself, or other variables, then expansionary fiscal policy can raise both velocity and money income.[9] When F&S minimize or blur the distinction between the weak and strong propositions concerning the importance of money, they do not warn the reader how crucial are the issues of policy involved.

8 Elsewhere the authors have summarized their position as follows: "For major movements in [money] income, we concluded that there is an extremely strong case for the proposition that sizable changes in the rate of change in the money stock are a necessary and sufficient condition for sizable changes in the rate of change in money income. For minor movements, we concluded that, while the evidence was far less strong, it is plausible to suppose that changes in the stock of money played an important independent role, though certainly the evidence for these minor movements does not rule out other interpretations." Friedman and Schwartz, "Money and Business Cycles," *Rev. Econ. Stat.*, Feb. 1963, Supplement, p. 63.

9 This is a well-understood point of macroeconomic theory, explained among other places in my article "Liquidity Preference and Monetary Policy," *Rev. Econ. Stat.*, May 1947, pp. 124–131.

## III. Judgments on Monetary Policy

Enough of the parochial disputes of monetary theorists. The notorious disagreements among economists are a source of great comfort to practical men in business, finance, and government. When the experts differ the policymaker can in better conscience do what he would have done anyway. By reputation monetary economists are especially prone to mutually cancelling differences of opinion. Many controversies on monetary theory and policy pit Friedman and his followers against the rest of the profession. But consensus among Friedman's opponents generally extends no further than the proposition that Friedman is wrong. In the course of their narrative F&S frequently pause to point out error and to allege harm resulting from Keynesian ways of thinking.

But as F&S led me through the major decisions of monetary politics and monetary policy of the past century, I did not find their Monday morning quarterbacking very controversial. I think that economists today—though they differ sharply in theoretical approach and political color—would agree very widely on the major practical and operational issues of these nine decades.

I prefer to end with this note of operational agreement rather than with theoretical discord. Laymen should not be too disheartened, or heartened, by strife among academic monetary theorists. Economists are likely to show a united front when the occasion arises to second guess the decisions of men of affairs. Friedman and Schwartz—believing so strongly in the powers for good or evil of monetary policy—are even more critical of the use of these powers than other economists.

I will give some examples, working more or less backward in time.

*1.* As already noted, F&S condemn the Federal Reserve and the Treasury for restrictive policy from 1933 to 1941. Many economists would assign to monetary factors much less weight than F&S do in explaining the course of economic activity in those years, in particular the recession of 1937. But few would, I think, dispute the authors' retrospective practical conclusions. The monetary authorities should have tried harder to promote expansion in 1933-1936 and 1937-1940—nothing would have been lost and something might have been gained. The 1936-1937 increases in reserve requirements, whether or not they caused the recession, were too drastic. Throughout the period the authorities were too little concerned with deflationary risks immediately at hand and too much concerned to forestall the hypothetical future dangers of excess liquidity. Incidentally I note with some dismay that at least some members of the central banking fraternity wished to use monetary policy to keep a rein on fiscal policy. One of the reasons given for immobilizing reserves in a Federal Reserve Bank of New York memorandum (quoted by F&S, p. 523) was to remove the temptation easy money gives national, state, and local governments to "over-borrow." The same memorandum offers as another reason for restrictive policy the danger that "large excess reserves may, by causing foreign expectation of favorable conditions for speculative investment, accentuate the gold *in*flow" (my italics). It appears that no matter which gold problem we may have, tighter money is the remedy.

*2.* Economists will differ also in the weights they assign monetary factors in the origins, severity, and length of the Great Contraction of 1929-1933. But from today's vantage point no one will defend the passive acquiescence of the Fed in the monetary contraction and banking collapse. The Fed's failure to undertake an aggressive policy of open-market purchases seems incredible. Even when open-market purchases were finally carried out in the spring and summer of 1932, it was less for economic reasons than to forestall unsound inflationary actions by the Congress. The System's indifference to domestic crisis stands in contrast to its classic reflex to the U.K. devaluation in 1931; the Fed raised the discount rate two points. Even so French balances didn't stay in New York very much longer.

The traditional excuse for Federal Reserve passivity in this period has been a technical one, the alleged shortage of "free gold." The Federal Reserve Banks were required to hold gold reserves of 35 per cent against their deposit liabilities and 40 per cent against their note liabilities. The other 60 per cent of Federal Reserve Notes had to be backed either by "eligible paper" or by gold. When banks stopped discounting during the contraction, the Federal Reserve Banks ran short of eligible paper; correspondingly Federal Reserve Notes had to be covered by gold more than 40 per cent. The problem was finally resolved by the Glass-Steagall Act of February 1932, which permitted government securities to serve in place of eligible paper as collateral for notes.

F&S find no evidence that free gold was in fact an important constraint on Federal Reserve action or a central consideration in discussions within the System at the time. If it had been an effective constraint, they point out, there were several avenues of escape that could have been tried, including earlier request for corrective legislation. In fact the Administration rather than the Fed asked for the legislation, and its enactment was not followed by a change in Federal Reserve policy until six weeks later.[10]

*3.* Perhaps there would be less agreement among economists with F&S's verdict that monetary policy was too tight in 1928-1929. A speculative stock market boom during a period of stable noninflationary economic growth presented the System with a difficult and cruel dilemma. A policy tight enough to curb the stock market would inevitably make credit costly or unavailable to ordinary business and agricultural borrowers. In a sense, of course, inflated stock prices themselves spelled easy money and encouraged real investment, but only for businesses legally and institutionally prepared to issue new equities. There were not enough of these, in the short run at least, to offset the restrictive effects of tight bank credit on businesses dependent on debt finance. Personally I agree with the judgment of F&S that in 1928-1929 the System should have ignored the stock market in arriving at its general credit policy and concentrated instead on easing money sufficiently to promote the continued expansion of the economy. But given this judgment, F&S are unduly doctrinaire in rejecting out of hand the use of moral suasion or selective controls against stock market credit.

*4.* Economists of all schools would, I think, agree with F&S that the Fed was too slow to raise the discount rate after World War I and then contributed to a drastic deflation in 1920 by raising the rate from 4 to 7 per cent in six months.

*5.* Preservation or restoration of the gold value of the dollar has on several occasions been accorded undeserved primacy as a goal of monetary policy, at severe cost to the domestic economy. Concerning the 1879 resumption of gold-dollar convertibility at the pre-Civil War rate, F&S's judgment in retrospect is that, given that a gold standard was to be reestablished, it would have been preferable to have resumed at a parity that gave a dollar-pound exchange rate somewhere between the pre-Civil War rate and the rate at the end of the war. However, they point out that the progress of real output does not appear to have been set back by the severe and painful price deflations which preceded and followed resumption.

Similarly, F&S have some sympathy for the silver agitation prior to 1897. But they are not, of course, for bimetallism; and they recognize also that silver agitation, so long as it led to uncertainty about the country's commitment to gold, made the gold standard even more deflationary than it would have been otherwise. The dilemma between gold standard and internal stability recurred in 1932-33, and F&S clearly would have put internal stability first. They point out that the Fed and Treasury played the gold standard game asymmetrically; gold inflows were sterilized before 1929 and after 1933, but gold outflows were not sterilized in the intervening years. To a certain extent they think this has also happened during the most recent decade.

*6.* I have left until last F&S's views on recent monetary policies and controversies.

[10] In their historical research on Federal Reserve policy-making in this and other eras, the authors were limited to the materials available in the private papers of Federal Reserve officials, principally those of George L. Harrison (an official of the New York Bank 1920-1940 and its governor or president 1928-1940), Charles L. Hamlin (a member of the Board 1914–1936), and E. A. Goldenweiser (director of research and statistics for the Board 1926-1945). Now, thanks to the constructive action of the present Board of Governors in making available past minutes of the Board and the Open Market Committee, scholars will be able to provide a more definitive history of Federal Reserve policy-making. It is entirely possible that future research will alter the interpretations to which the available evidence led Friedman and Schwartz.

Federal Reserve policy since World War II gets fairly good marks from F&S. They condemn the continuation of the bond price support policy after the war, but find that it did little harm until the Korean inflation. They also condemn the 4¼ per cent interest rate ceiling on government bonds. They cannot get excited about the "bills only" controversy, partly because they agree with the policy's advocates in stressing "monetary" rather than "credit" effects, partly because such policy need not prevent the Treasury-cum-Federal Reserve from achieving any desired maturity distribution of debt held outside the government. They applaud the Fed's discovery of the quantity of money and of the principle that it should keep pace with the real growth of the economy. The period as a whole has been one of unusual stability in the rate of change of the stock of money, but the authors detect a growing variability and attribute it in part to increased self-assurance on the part of the monetary managers. So far as month-to-month anticyclical policy is concerned, the authors find little to criticize. They feel the Fed reacted too late and too strongly at times, but they praise the shifts to ease that occurred before the cyclical peaks of 1953 and 1960.

CONCLUSIONS: I have not done justice to the scope of this book. History presents the theoretically minded scholar with one challenge after another. Here these are met with the brilliance and finesse one would expect. Examples are: the determination of the exchange rate and gold premium during the greenback era, the economics of the 1879 resumption; the silver question; balance-of-payments pressure and adjustments in the 1890's; FDR's gold purchase policy; the mechanics of Federal Reserve bond support policy during and after World War II. The reader is advised in no event to omit the footnotes, which contain many gems of monetary theory: on Gresham's law; purchasing power parity; the prohibition and regulation of interest on commercial bank deposits; the significance of the "free reserve" position of member banks; the monetary mechanics of shifts among currency, demand deposits, time deposits, and other thrift accounts.

This is one of those rare books that leave their mark on all future research on the subject.

# B Contemporary Hypotheses

# 4 MONEY, INTEREST RATES, AND ECONOMIC ACTIVITY: THEIR INTERRELATIONSHIP IN A MARKET ECONOMY*

PAUL A. SAMUELSON
*Massachusetts Institute of Technology*

## Real and Monetary Determinants of the Interest Rate Structure

### *Classical Real Theory: Statics*

Although interest appears superficially as a percentage yield on money values, to the classical economist it represents at the deeper level the real productivity of roundabout, time-consuming production embodied in machines, industrial plants, and unfinished goods in process. Capital goods are limited in amount, and their scarcity can be relieved only by sacrificing current consumption—transferring resources from them to enhanced capital formation. More roundabout processes may be more productive, but it takes *waiting* by consumers to get them going. The disutility of labor was thought to keep labor scarce and its productive wage high, and thus the wage can in a sense be called the reward for sweat. In the same way, the disutility of *abstaining* from current consumption and of engaging in further waiting is what keeps capital instruments scarce and productive. Thus, interest can be regarded as the reward for abstinence or waiting, the price needed to overcome this natural human impatience to consume now and not in the future.

The classical view regards interest as determined by demand and supply—the productivity of capital goods providing the main elements of demand (albeit reinforced by consumer-loans demand on the part of especially needy and impatient borrowers), and the supply of capital being limited by the reluctance to abstain from current consumption and do more saving, resulting in cumulative capital formation.

What follows from this classical model of interest as being determined solely by real factors? Here are some consequences.

*1.* Though interest is paid in money terms on money loans and assets, *the level of interest has nought to do with the level of money and with the price level.* If metal coins form the currency, and if their supply is much augmented by, say, past mining discoveries of precious metals, the only effect is to raise the level of *all* prices proportionately. Thus, if money $M$ doubles, so will be doubled the prices of tea, cloth, lumber, machinery, and land. The dividends of stocks and the coupons of bonds will, in the new equilibrium, be exactly doubled, but so too will the principal values of these assets be exactly doubled—with the result that the percentage ratio of money yield to money principal will work out to exactly the same

* Reprinted from *Proceedings of a Symposium on Money, Interest Rates, and Economic Activity*, New York, American Bankers Association, 1967, pp. 45–57, by permission of the author and the American Bankers Association.

interest rate. (David Ricardo and Knut Wicksell were nineteenth-century writers who clearly insisted on this classical fact.)

*2.* Commercial banks are mere *conduits* for the more efficient channelling of savings into the best investment outlets. Except for transitional states in which the system moves from one long-run equilibrium to another, the banks do not affect the level of interest rates.

*3.* Suppose banks can issue currency in the form of bank notes or checkable bank deposits which the people treat as the equivalent to holding currency. Then laissez faire in banking can *not* be counted on to lead to equilibrium with stable price levels. In particular, a basic notion underlying the founding of the Federal Reserve System in 1913 is quite false; providing for an "elastic" total supply of money and credit by enabling banks to create new money whenever they can lend to manufacturers, merchants, and farmers on genuine productive assets (to finance inventories, permit production maintenance and expansion, et cetera), will *not* be conducive to stability of the price level and of general business activity.

At what levels of interest are the "legitimate" demands of production and trade to be met? If market interest rates prevail below the real equilibrium levels set by the classical quasi-barter model, the total money supply will grow, thus creating demand-pull inflation. Lending against real goods (the so-called real-bills doctrine) is *not* guaranteed to produce an enhanced supply of goods that will quench (at unchanged prices) the manufactured increase of new $M$ (and the resulting increased flow of its $MV$ spending).

Although the level of the money supply and prices cannot affect the interest rate in the crudest classical system, classical writers are correct to insist that there must be some limitation on the total supply of money set by the Government if the price level is to be determinate. And if there can be expected to be a steady growth of population and productivity, leading to a steady growth of real output—and if there can be expected to emerge a generally constant level of interest rates, as the result of cancelling out innovations of a capital-saving- and labor-saving-type in comparison with any capital accumulation relative to labor supply—then a desire for a generally stable level of prices can only be achieved if the Government contrives that there be a rise in the supply of money commensurate with the changes in real output.

### *Dynamic Modifications of the Crude Classical System*

The above real system abstracts from innumerable factors known to be of importance in any economy that actually exists, whether it be the Victorian model of England in the nineteenth century or the mixed economies of the present. Thus, its postulates leave no room for a Great Depression with mass unemployment on a lasting basis; its postulates throw no light on the fluctuations of business conditions as they have been studied by the National Bureau of Economic Research for this country and for the major industrial nations. The classical model that I have caricatured above operates upon the premise of quixotic flexibility of prices. The 25 per cent rate of unemployment that prevailed both in the United States and in Germany in the 1930s could not have happened if downward flexibility of prices and wages existed. So, at a low enough wage level all the unemployed could find willing employers (whose effective demand had not, because of the "Pigou effect," been undetermined by the hyperdeflation itself). On the inflationary side, the classical model has no room within its postulates for cost-push inflation, such as many observers claim to have observed in many mixed economies of the post-World War II generation.

However, within the classical system itself, we can discern some systematic theorizing about dynamic transitional states between states of stable equilibrium. Since the time of David Hume, two centuries ago, classicists noted that unforeseen inflation could be expected to favor debtors at the expense of creditors, to favor entrepreneurial profit-seekers at the expense of *rentiers* and contractual wage earners, and to favor vigorous high-employment conditions at the expense of more stagnant conditions.

After the 1890s Wicksell, the great Swedish neoclassical economist, kept insisting that practical men were right to think that lowering the market interest rate in the short run, by having the banks create and lend out money, would indeed raise prices and expand business activity. Wicksell insisted, however, that once the system was at full employment such expansion of money would lead only to an increase in price tags; and each impulse of new-money creation by the banks would be followed by a tendency for all prices to rise, including those of the rents from capital goods and the market values of those goods—so, ultimately, the interest rate would tend to move back to its real classical level. Indeed, once the market rate of interest was set by the central bank back at that classical real level, there would cease to be an increase in the money supply and in the price level. But, if the central bank persisted in keeping the market rate of interest below the true real rate, it would thereby give rise to a more or less permanent rate of money creation and price inflation (adding to the real interest rate a percentage price-increase allowance).

We may summarize thus: *The independence of the interest rate from the behavior of money and banks that is posited in the statical classical theory disappears in considerable part once dynamic assumptions are made about the creation of money growth as a result of mines, banks, or governments.*

By the early 1930s there had grown up the so-called neo-Wicksellian view[1] that the real supply-and-demand curves determining interest rates should have added to them a component of the supply of saving which is associated with the creation of new money, or $M$. According to this view banks have a great deal to do in the short run with increasing the flow of capital formation and reducing the market rates of interest. If banks are able to create new $M$, which they lend out to would-be investors in new construction, inventory, and equipment, they change the mix of gross national product toward capital formation and away from current consumption; and they are able to "force" this money on the system only by lowering the explicit interest rate, or diminishing the effective stringency of rationing, and thereby implicitly lowering the interest costs of borrowing. The rest of the community, even if it wants to save the same fraction of its incomes as before, undergoes "forced saving" in consequence of the fact that the banks have created inflation of the price level; and by the time the community comes to spend its incomes, it buys less in the way of real goods.

Moreover, in our day when the Government is committed to following a militant fiscal policy of its own, involving budget surpluses and deficits at different levels of total taxation and spending, we recognize that fiscal policy interacts with monetary policy in shaping the behavior of interest rates, capital supplies, price levels, and intensity of unemployment.

For example, if fiscal policy is chronically expansionary—in the sense of involving high levels of public expenditure with low levels of tax receipts so that large budget deficits continuously take place—and if monetary policy is chronically tight—so that interest rates are kept high enough and the rate of growth of $M$ slow enough to hold down investment and consumer-durable spending to a level low enough to wipe out demand-pull inflationary gaps—then the community will evolve with less capital formation than would otherwise have taken place. It will evolve with higher short-term and higher long-term interest rates than would otherwise be the case.

The last two cases involved maintenance of full employment and assumed no cost-push inflation problem. If we consider mixed economies that are characterized by price-wage inflexibilities and which display chronically different degrees of unemployment and underemployment, different policies by the Fed can lead to different levels of achieved employment and production. Expansionary monetary policies that keep investment spending higher than would otherwise be the case lead initially to lower money rates of interest and ultimately to lower real-productivity yields on the enhanced stock of physical capital equipment. But they achieve this not at all at the expense of current consumption, for consumption too is higher than would otherwise be the case. Both capital formation and con-

[1] See Gottfried Von Haberler, *Prosperity and Depression; A Theoretical Analysis of Cyclical Movements* (originally published by the League of Nations in 1937; later postwar editions available), Chapter 3, for an exposition of the writings of F. Hayek and other similar writers.

sumption can be increased by utilizing resources that would otherwise be dissipated in mass unemployment and industrial excess capacity.

### *The Extreme Keynesian Case*

A few years after J. M. Keynes wrote his 1936 *General Theory of Employment, Interest and Money*, there grew up the strong notion that the interest rate is purely a monetary phenomenon. Passages can be found in the *General Theory* claiming that interest is merely the difference between the yield on safe money and risk-involving securities, and therefore interest is merely the price for giving up the liquidity of holding money. Statements like these can be harmless if nothing is read into them. They can be misleading if we read into them the view that the real productivity of capital has nought to do with the short- or long-run levels of interest, or infer that current thrift has nought to do with interest rates, or that shifts in the marginal efficiency of capital cannot affect the rate of interest as it can in the classical system. And if we look critically at the actual properties of the system of relations in the *General Theory*, we find they are usually in agreement with the results previously mentioned.

For example, if banks are given extra reserves and use them to bid down the yields of loans and bonds, that increase in $M$ leads, in the Keynesian system, to lower interest rates, more investment, and greater total dollar spending. If employment was not previously full and still falls short of full employment, there is no reason why the increase in $M$ should cause a proportional increase in prices generally.

If businessmen discover new investment opportunities, that will, with total $M$ fixed, raise interest rates and the level of dollar GNP. If people save less out of current incomes, that will depress money GNP and interest rates. In short, if one reads the *General Theory* rigorously, one ends up with conclusions not too different from those of an eclectic neoclassical monetary theorist.

Nevertheless, in times like those which prevailed in, say, 1938 when most disciples were just mastering the *General Theory*, banks held considerable excess reserves and short-term interest rates on Treasury Bills were often down to ⅜ of ⅜ of 1 per cent.[2] Hence, massive changes in $M$ have little effect even on short-term interest rates, and, a fortiori, cause little change in employment, production, or capital formation. Moreover, in times of deep depression, such as in 1932 when existing plants were operating at losses and idle capacity was everywhere, even if one could contrive by monetary policy a substantial change in short- and long-term interest rates, little new investment could be coaxed out by such monetary policies. And, since we are discussing conventional central bank operations which merely involve buying existing assets with $M$ (old bonds and Treasury Bills), there is no significant change in the *net worth* of the public generally. Investors have no incentive to spend more on capital formation, and consumers have no new incentive to spend more on consumption. In consequence, Federal Reserve operations of $N$ billion dollars then involve less than their normal potency.[3]

### *The Neoclassical Synthesis*

As I have insisted upon in the recent editions of my ECONOMICS, once we introduce systematically into a post-Keynesian system treatment of stocks of assets, monetary and real, and take into account fluctuating levels of real unemployment, there remain no inconsistencies between the classical system and the Keynesian system. The synthesis of common content emerges with an eclectic position on the interplay of real and monetary factors in determining the structure and levels of interest rates.

In the short run, changes in the money supply contrived by conventional Federal Reserve open-market operations produce opposite effects upon the level of interest rates. Within limits, changes in the compo-

---

[2] On occasions the yield was zero or even negative, a fact to be accounted for presumably in terms of personal property tax exemptions and subscription rights. Often, Treasury Bills were not cashed in at maturity. When I then asked a Government official why, he said to me, "Do you know a better way to hold a million dollars?"

[3] In this model we have one of those rare cases in which a contrived increase in $M$ can be predictably expected to induce an opposing change in velocity of circulation $V$, with the product $MV$ little increased.

sition of Fed purchases as between short bills and long bonds can slightly influence the shape of the yield differentials between long- and short-term assets. But apparently only within narrow limits unless massive "twists" are indulged in.

In the longer run, if expanded credit achieves a restoration of full employment and beyond, there tends to be a permanent bidding up of all prices, and there reemerges a strong tendency for interest rates to revert to their real level. This is the continuing kernel of truth in the classical crude "quantity theory."

Fiscal policy changes can produce substantial changes in total GNP or $MV$ magnitudes. If $M$ is not changed concomitantly, this can be expected to produce changes in the interest rate (and opposing changes in $V$).[4]

[4] The valid core of the "quantity theory" that is implied by neoclassical reasoning does not require constancy of the velocity of circulation, $V$. It requires only that a balanced change in *all* prices should itself have no effect on $V$. Moreover, it is only a quirk of law that keeps banks from paying interest on demand deposits. In eras when the market would determine a high, short-term interest rate, free competition would permit us to use as our circulating medium interest-bearing bank deposits. When fiats prevent banks from paying interest on checkable accounts, nature ordains that competitive substitutes will flourish, time deposits will in fact require no notice, they will pay daily interest, they will become negotiable, and institutional arrangements will be made so that they can serve as a close money substitute for most exchange purposes. As soon as the liquid assets that we use to perform the function of money begin to pay interest, an entirely new pattern of velocity is to be expected from a rational man. That is why I should not expect $V$ to be constant in the future, even if it had been more constant in the past than it actually has been.

Furthermore, along with the noninterest-bearing public debt that we call money, there is the interest-bearing public debt. This too acts like an "outside asset" making the community feel richer than it really is. As soon as we realize this, we see that there is substantive difference between an increase in $M$ resulting from *past* gold mining or greenback financed war expenditure and an equal increase in $M$ resulting from an open-market purchase. The gold and greenbacks result in a permanent increase in the net worth as envisaged by the typical person. The $M$ created by open-market purchase takes from people some of their net worth embodied in bonds, and in return gives them some net worth in the form of $M$.

## How Monetary Policy Affects the Level of Economic Activity

### *Scope of Monetary Policy*

By monetary policy we mean primarily Federal Reserve actions designed to affect the tightness and easiness of credit conditions, and the behavior of the total supply of money and money substitutes (that is, the supply of currency, checkable bank deposits, various categories of time deposits, and other liquid instruments).

The chief weapon of the Federal Reserve in doing all this is its *open-market purchases and sales of Government securities.* But intermittently, as last month, changes in the *legal reserve requirement ratios* that must be held against various categories of demand and time deposits have effects like those of open-market operations. Furthermore, *raising or lowering the discount rate* at which banks can borrow from the Federal Reserve can reinforce or offset the effects of open-market operations. And aside from the quoted rate at which discount borrowing is permitted to take place, *the manner in which access to the discount window is administered* can have powerful effects upon the actual volume of such borrowing and hence on the reserves of the banking system.

*Moral suasion*, by which I mean the whole atmosphere in which banking is carried on —including letters to the banks like that of last year which urged them to go easy in making loans, and including voluntary programs of foreign lending by the banks—is constantly being pooh-poohed by many economists as a factor of any quantitative importance for monetary policy. But in my judgement, it is often a significant variable and, as in so many countries abroad, it will become an increasingly important variable in the future.

Although I have mentioned these five weapons of the Federal Reserve, the first is by all odds the most important. And in principle, by more vigorous use of open-market operations alone in both the downward and upward direction, we could achieve most of the same goals that can be achieved by all five weapons. (This is only approximately true and is not meant as a recommendation for a monistic reform.)

I am purposely defining monetary policy broadly to include attention to credit conditions as well as to the supply of money. I am thus explicitly rejecting the view that it should be concerned only with achieving some desired pattern of behavior in some defined magnitude of "money," such as currency plus demand deposits or the latter plus certain categories of time deposits. Like fiscal and other macroeconomic policies, monetary policy is concerned with achieving the desired total of gross national product spending; and if one writes GNP as the product of some defined $M$ and its implicitly defined $V$, then the neoclassical position which I have already expounded militates against considering the factor $M$ independently of the $V$ in $MV$. Moreover, one cannot stipulate in advance that a modern mixed economy will be indifferent to the composition of the GNP, as for example between residential construction and other forms of investment. And hence the central bank, as an important and indispensable arm of the modern state, has a responsibility in conducting overall macroeconomic activities to take into account alternative effects upon sectors. Ours is a pluralistic society, and properly so. In a pluralistic society it makes no sense to set up institutions with a monistic function and then have to set up new superagencies to coordinate them.

Hence, although it is the principal function of the Federal Reserve to deal with overall credit conditions, it must also perform many selective functions. The Board and the System are not now so overworked that this will negate accomplishment of their principal function, and if the System were to shrink back from these duties, that would only create a political vacuum into which other agencies would rush. I do not think it would be a good thing to have competing central banks in this country, one dealing primarily with residential real estate, one with farm problems, and so forth.

From the broad way in which I have defined monetary policy, it will be evident that the Federal Reserve is merely the chief instrument of such policies, not the exclusive instrument. In particular, the United States Treasury, in connection with the way that it floats and refunds debt—using at one time long-term and at other times short-term instruments, selling at one time to its Trust Funds and at another to the open market—is also powerfully affecting monetary and credit conditions. And within the sector of finance, commercial banks which are outside of the Federal Reserve are of some importance in just the way that mutual savings and savings and loan institutions are important in affecting the overall pattern of monetary conditions and GNP aggregates. Because financial intermediaries both initiate and reinforce changes in credit conditions, they too come within the province of my broad definition of monetary policy.[5]

### *How Federal Reserve Policy Affects GNP*

We may concentrate upon the open-market purchases and sales of the Federal Reserve. If the Fed were to print bank notes or write checks in order to provide free current services for the people (weather forecasting, national defense, research and development) or to give people transfer incomes every month (Social Security payments, relief, et cetera), that would be quite another thing from what it actually does. Instead, it buys and sells existing assets—not used cars or factories, but Government securities of all durations. Like any bidder or seller of Government bonds, it has a direct effect on the market price of those bonds and an opposite effect upon the bonds' yields. Indeed, only by bidding up or down the yields of existing bonds can the Fed persuade people and banks to let it consummate its open-market operations. It has no powers of eminent domain or fiat.

DIRECT EFFECTS ON INTEREST RATES AND CREDIT AVAILABILITY. Whenever anybody bids up or down the yields on Government bonds, that automatically has an effect upon the

[5] Fiscal policy questions, such as whether there should be an increase in personal income tax rates, affect directly the flow of income and would be distinguishable from monetary policy actions. But policies that call for earlier payments of accruing tax obligations are definitely akin to monetary policies. Some authorities would even try to draw the line between monetary and fiscal policy actions by means of the functional criterion: Does the policy act primarily upon a *stock* (the stock of money, of outstanding bonds, of liquid money substitutes, of less-liquid housing assets, et cetera); or does it act primarily upon a *flow* (as in the case of a reduced tax rate on current incomes or increased expenditure on current public services)?

supply-and-demand bids that determine the pattern of yields on corporate bonds and other securities that are alternatives to Government bonds. There is, thus, a direct effect upon the structure of interest rates from open-market purchases by the Fed. Such purchases directly lower the yields on the issues bought and (with attenuation) tend to lower the yields on Governments of other maturities and the yield of corporate bonds. Since bonds are substitutes, albeit not terribly close ones, for other forms of investment such as mortgage loans, the lowering of bond yield tends to channel funds into mortgages and to lower their yield, at the same time making mortgage loans somewhat more available, and more available with lower down payments and longer amortization periods.

INDIRECT EFFECTS ON INTEREST AND CREDIT CONDITIONS. What has been already described would be the whole story if ours was not a fractional reserve banking system. Because the Fed's purchase has increased the cash of someone in the system, and because that someone is likely to hold most of that cash in some bank, there is now an increase in the investable reserves of the banking system. These will generally not be left in the form of excess reserves, but instead will encourage the banks to make new loans or acquire other securities. We thus have a repetition and reinforcement of the bidding down of the yields of the whole spectrum of assets in the community, and concomitantly this increases the availability of loans to borrowers at the same time that costs of borrowing are being bid down. There is nothing mechanical about the process; it takes place at each stage of the game in terms of people being motivated to make new supply-and-demand bids. It rests on the multilateral willingness of people to leave their money in banks, of banks to make loans or buy bonds, and of the rest of the community to borrow money and to issue new securities or give up old ones in favor of holding demand or time deposits. Although not mechanical, the process is in normal times highly predictable. A certain fraction of the Fed's created reserves will go into currency holdings, a certain fraction into repayment of discounts, a certain fraction into holding of deposits, a certain (normally very small) fraction into extra excess reserves; and in consequence we can predict that there has been created somewhere in the system several times as much of new bank deposits for each dollar of open-market purchase.[6]

DIRECT AND INDIRECT EFFECTS ON NET WORTHS. When Federal Reserve open-market purchases achieve some lowering of interest yields, they produce some increase in the capitalized value of assets people own. My 20-year bonds now sell for $103 instead of $100, and I may somewhat increase my consumption spending on food, travel, TV sets. My home may sell for a bit more, and it may be regarded by me as more easily sellable and hence a bit more liquid. This may increase my consumption and depress my current saving rate. The same is true of business enterprises—their balance-sheet assets may be bid up in price and be of increased liquidity, and this could be one of the determinants of their spending more on new investments.

In sum, open-market purchase creation of *M* has some upward effects on total community net worth, and therefore some direct effects upon increasing current consumption and investment spending. But this is not a strong effect by itself. The new *M* is not burning a hole in someone's pocket and aching to be spent at the old velocity of circulation. On the contrary, we have got hold of this new *M* in exchange for selling liquid securities; if they were not burning a hole in our pockets, neither will the new *M*, particularly since our securities have been bid up just enough by this process to make us content to forego them and instead hold cash as an asset.

I do not wish to be misunderstood. In a moment I shall trace through how the direct and indirect lowering of interest rates coaxes out more spending on investment goods

[6] In deep depression when short-term yields had already been bid down to a fraction of a per cent, and when everybody was pessimistic about the marginal profitability of additions to inventory, plant, and equipment, the predictable results would be quite different from that in normal times. Conceivably, the only effect would be to exchange near-*M* for *M* and to bid up slightly the existing value of long-term securities. Existing excess reserves would be added to in such times.

and creates an increased flow of current income and employment. That has a powerful effect on total spending. But it is the much smaller effects on saving through the channel of increased net worths that I am now trying to evaluate.

To make my point, imagine an unrealistic experiment. Suppose rationing on capital formation kept the Fed's open-market purchase from inducing any increased inventory spending or plant and equipment spending. Suppose that consumers' durable finance was already copiously available at rates that could be brought down very little, even if the Treasury Bill rate were negligible. Then where would a substantial increase in the current flow of spending come from? The $M$ itself does not represent any increase in net worth for the banks and public; it is only the rise in securities prices that it created in coming into existence (that is, in coming out of the Fed in exchange for bonds that go into the Fed) that raises net worth. Undoubtedly, under my bizarre rationing of investment, the resulting drop in interest rate from the open-market purchase would be all the larger; prices for existing bonds would be bid up a lot before people would be content to hold the zero-earning new $M$. Only if you have what I regard as an unrealistic theory for the functional relationship between velocity and interest rates will you conclude that net worths in the community will be bid up to whatever gigantic levels are needed to get all the new-$M$ spending on consumption at the old rate of turnover.[7]

In any case when we trace through realistically the *modus operandi* of an expansion of credit, we find that it works only slightly through direct increases in net worth; instead it works primarily through inducing new investment spending (including in the term "investment spending," spending on consumers' durables in excess of their being used up). It is to this vital link that I now turn.

**INCREASE IN INVESTMENT SPENDING INDUCED BY LOWER-COST AND MORE AVAILABLE CREDIT.** Now comes the most important step in the process by which monetary policy works to affect business activity. When banks and lenders generally have more funds to lend, and when the interest yields of investments have been bid down, the result will tend to be an increase in lending and borrowing activity. It does not matter in the first instance whether the increase in business spending on inventory, plant, or equipment comes from a lowered interest cost of finance which makes projects pay that previously did not pay; or whether the increased investment spending comes because the investor is able to arrange for financing that was previously just not available to him. In either case, there follows an increase in investment spending which gives jobs to someone and which directly increases production in the form of capital formation or investment. The incomes received in these new lines of activity are spent by their recipients in considerable measure by the familiar propensity-to-consume mechanisms. Hence, the primary expansion in investment, induced by credit-easing, results in a secondary chain of consumption respending in accordance with familiar multiplier sequence.

Nor is this all. With production higher, the profitability of existing capital goods is enhanced; there is both an extra desire for additions to capacity and also an extra cash and income flow available to would-be investors to finance such activity. So, along with secondary consumption respending, the multiplier chain sets off a tertiary flow of acceleration-principle investment spending. This in turn begins another multiplier-accelerator chain. I do not imply that the process leads to perpetual expansion. Far from it; in most circumstances any particular once-and-for-all open-market purchase leads to a subsequent increment of spending that is finite in total amount, and which reaches a maximum effect within a finite time (perhaps one or two quarters) and then tails off to insignificance.

It should be understood that this induced investment leads to the creation of real capital and adds to the lasting net worths of people and businesses. While it is generating the higher flow of incomes, it also leads to a desire for the holding of more cash for transaction purposes, and thus transiently to a higher velocity of circulation than would be the case without the income increase; and it thus leads tran-

[7] See the equation on page 59.

siently to less of a fall in the interest rate than will ultimately take place after the induced expansion of production subsides.

All the above is premised upon the postulate that the open-market purchase impinged upon a system which was at underemployment and which was capable of increase in production and employment. If industry is already operating at capacity, and if the labor market is already so tight as to be nonexpandable, the induced increase in investment demand will serve merely to produce an inflationary gap. At preexisting prices, there will be a demand-pull gap and there will tend to result a bidding up of commodity prices generally, and through derived demand, a bidding up of wages. Although money wages will be observed to be growing faster than the growth in physical productivity, there is no need to conclude that any cost-push inflation is going on. It could be—and as I am describing it, would be—all demand-pull inflation. As long as this is going on, there is being generated an enhanced need for cash balances for purely transactional purposes.

If the price level ultimately rises by as great a percentage as the increase in the $M$ created by the open-market purchase, there can emerge a new equilibrium with the interest rate back to where it was in the beginning. In this particular case, the effect of the open-market purchase has been to raise prices and nothing else. Only in the transitional stages have there been real effects. Here we have a case, often envisaged by economists like Marshall, where an initial decrease in the interest rate leads ultimately to a restoration of the old interest rate at a higher price level. And indeed if we envisage a dynamic system with some momentum in it which generates psychological and other self-reinforcing mechanisms, we should not be surprised to meet a model in which an initial lowering of interest rates by open-market $M$ creation leads penultimately to raising the interest rates above the *ex ante* level. If the system is ultimately stable, this penultimate state would, in its turn, subside.

For the specialist, symbolism may clarify. Let *net worth* equal the sum of *money* plus *Government bonds* (mostly short-term) plus *value of capital goods.*

$$\begin{aligned} NW &= M + B + K \\ &= M + \pi(i)(b + k) \\ &= NW(a_1 + a_2 + a_3) \end{aligned}$$

where $\pi\ (i)$ represents the capitalization factor that depicts a bidding up of prices of existing machines or face-value bonds when the interest rate drops; and where $(a_i)$ represents the respective fractions of $NW$ represented by the three kinds of assets. An open-market purchase represents an increase in $M$ matched by a decrease in $b$; except that this would involve a lowering of $i$ and a (slight) increase in $\pi\ (i)$, the drop in $b$ would equal the rise in $M$. Writing $Y$ for money income and assuming for expositional simplicity that the price level of consumption, $C$, and investment goods, $I$, remains constant until full employment is reached, our simplest system becomes—

$$Py = PC\left(\frac{Y}{P}, \frac{NW}{P}; a_2, a_3\right) + PI\left(i, \frac{Y}{P}, k\right) \quad (1)$$

$$\frac{M}{P} = L\left(i, \frac{\pi(i)\,b + \pi(i)\,k}{P}, \frac{Y}{P}\right) \quad (2)$$

with the usual properties—

$$\frac{\partial C}{\partial y} > 0, \quad \frac{\partial C}{\partial (NW/P)} > 0, \quad \frac{\partial I}{\partial i} < 0,$$

$$\frac{\partial I}{\partial y} > 0, \quad \frac{\partial I}{\partial k} < 0$$

$$\frac{\partial L}{\partial i} < 0, \quad \frac{\partial L}{\partial (\pi b)} > 0, \quad \frac{\partial L}{\partial y} > 0$$

The first row above is noncontroversial. The second row relations would be challenged by those who believe that $L$ is a constant, a view that I respect but differ with. Particularly at a low $i$, such constancy seems doubtful to me. In (1), an increase in $a_2$ and $a_3$, at the expense of $M$'s share of net worth, I judge to be, at most, a mild depressant on C; that is, $\partial C/\partial a_i < 0$, but small in magnitude.

For this model, an increase in $M$ through an open-market operation that lowers $b$ will slightly decrease $i$, slightly raise $NW$, significantly raise $I$, and thereby $Y$ and $C$. After full employment is reached (and assuming no cost-push Phillips-curve problem), increases in $M$ will tend to result ultimately in rises in $P$ with small ultimate further changes in $i$ or $y$. If $k/y$ is increased in the transition by the positive $M$, $k$ and $y$ will be permanently higher and $i$ lower.

## Availability of Credit as a Factor Different from the Cost of Credit

My argument thus far can be briefly summarized: Central bank open-market operations produce their primary effects on the economic system *by lowering or raising the spectrum of interest rates,* thereby increasing or decreasing the flow of investment and durable-goods spending, which leads in turn to expansion or contraction in the aggregate of GNP flow. How the change in dollar spending is divided into real output or price-level changes depends upon the amount of slack in the system and upon the institutional factors that make for price-wage inflexibility or for cost-push rises in prices and wages.

In using the expression "spectrum of interest rates," I wish to make room explicitly for various intensities of rationing of credit. Loans are not auctioned off in perfect markets so that the scarcity of funds can be accurately measured by a quoted market rate of interest. Loans and securities are negotiated in a great variety of retail and wholesale markets. Often interest rates are like administered prices—the rates quoted are changed, but infrequently. However, the unavailability of funds at these rates changes markedly and in sympathy with the movement of market interest rates.

Thus, when the Treasury Bill rate is rising from 4 to 5 per cent, when the long-term bond yields on corporate and Government securities are rising from 5 to 5½ per cent, and when the discounts are growing on mortgages quoted in the secondary markets, you will find your friendly banker less friendly. No longer will he press funds on you. If you ask for a $50,000 loan for six months, he may agree only to $30,000 for four months. And although he may stick by the 6 per cent rate he has long been charging you, there may now be an insistence that you maintain at least 30 per cent in the form of compensating balances instead of the usual 10 per cent (a shift which already raises 6 per cent effectively to almost 8 per cent). Moreover, many people who have been relying on such 6 per cent bank loans will now be turned down and will have to go to a finance company and pay 7 per cent or more. Hence, even though each posted interest rate may seem to change little, the effective interest rates at which people really borrow will have gone up much by virtue of the concomitant changes in the severity of rationing of credit.

How important is this factor of rationing? And (since it seems to operate in the same direction as changes in market interest rates) does the subject matter? I think that practical men exaggerate the importance of the rationing factor, and academic men underestimate—its short-run effectiveness. Aside from those who deny that rationing plays any important role, there exist two schools. Both agree it is important, but one insists that this is a dreadful phenomenon which is in fact responsible for giving bankers such a bad name and which leads to serious distortions and inequities as between small and large business, new and old businesses, and different sectors of the economy. The other school congratulates monetary policy on its potency and effectiveness that stems from the alleged importance of induced credit availability conditions.

Lending and borrowing and evaluation of securities must from their nature involve uncertainties and different degrees of imperfection of knowledge and information. From its nature, therefore, we must expect the banking and investment business to be peculiarly vulnerable to Chamberlinian imperfections of competition. In such markets we expect to encounter somewhat inflexible administered prices with hidden or open departures from those quoted rates. And even in a steady state where there are no changes in overall money supply or market rates of interest, the lenders must always be forming judgments about credit-worthiness so that a decision process involving rationing of credit is inevitable. Nevertheless, the longer changed credit conditions prevail, the more will differences in degree of rationing tend to be replaced by differences in stated rates. If funds are scarce, the efficient way of allocating them is to change their market prices; and it is increasingly to the self-interest of parties on both sides of the market to push in that direction. Why should the banks throw a gift in the direction of those firms lucky enough to qualify for loans in terms of credit stringency? And why penalize the refused firms? Moreover, what good are low rates to a firm that can not get a loan? The excluded firms will, one way or another, try to bribe the providers of funds into meeting their needs; that is, meeting them at a price.

Some might say that we live in the best of all possible worlds. It is precisely in the short run that economists would expect the demands for investable funds to be inelastic, thereby reducing the dollar-for-dollar potency of central bank operations. And it is in this short run that highly effective (if inequitable and distorting) elements of rationing prevail. Then in the longer run, just when rationing is dissipating its effects and spreading into differences in the cost rather than mere availability of credit, we can expect lowering of interest rates to coax out new long-term projects, and raising of interest rates to discourage such projects.

Before leaving the subject of credit rationing, I ought to mention some transitional frictions that also help to increase the short-run potency of Federal Reserve credit policy.

NEW-ISSUE BOTTLENECKS. When interest rates are hardening, new securities issues often go to a discount in the period when the underwriters are bringing them out. Since underwriters are subject to the tremendous risks involved in their extreme leveraging, one or two debacles of this type can discourage them from bidding and can dry up the effective supplying of any new issues.[8]

BOTTLENECKS FROM INHERITED NOTIONS OF NORMAL RATES. If long-term interest rates have been at one level for some time, and if the Federal Reserve engineers a tightening of them, many localities and states will drop out of the new-issue market completely. By law or custom they may be restricted from borrowing at the higher rate. By psychological belief that they can do better if they wait until rates are not so high, they may desist from borrowing. Often such phenomena have been observed. Of course, in the longer run, should the high-rate trend continue, many borrowers will be forced to come into the market willy-nilly later on, paying a penalty for their mistaken delay. And, to the degree that some canny borrowers correctly appraise the beginning of a rising trend of interest rates, they may overborrow in the early stages of a period of credit contraction. This can lead to a frictional weakening, rather than enhancing, of the short-term potency of monetary policy.[9]

---

[8] Analytically, a high level of $i$ discourages new investment, but so does a transitional large positive value of $di/dt$.

[9] When the Federal Reserve is trying to ease credit conditions, correct anticipation by speculators can speed up and amplify the decline in market interest rates. Although $di/dt$ is negative, juicy capital gains are to be earned from buying bonds (but, unfortunately, this could lead to a high level of yield inclusive of capital gains and thus temporarily raise the attractiveness of alternative to real investment in new brick and cogs).

# 5 | A NEO-KEYNESIAN VIEW OF MONETARY POLICY*

WARREN L. SMITH
*University of Michigan*

Those of us who take an essentially Keynesian view in macroeconomics are often accused, somewhat unjustly, I believe, of minimizing the importance of monetary forces. That contention was probably true 20 years ago for a variety of historical and institutional reasons. But much water has passed over the dam since that time, and I believe it would now be difficult to find an example of the popular stereotype of the Keynesian economist who thinks fiscal policy is all-important and monetary policy is of no consequence. After all, in Keynesian analysis the power of monetary policy depends on the values of certain parameters, and if one is open-minded, he must be prepared to alter his views as empirical evidence accumulates. In some respects, this process has already proceeded quite far—some of the simulations performed with the FRB-MIT model, which is decidedly Keynesian in spirit, show monetary policy having very powerful effects indeed, albeit operating with somewhat disconcerting lags.

Thus, there is nothing inherent in the Keynesian view of the world that commits its adherents to the belief that monetary policy is weak. What is, it seems to me, distinctive about Keynesianism is the view that fiscal policy is capable of exerting very significant independent effects—that there are, broadly speaking, two instruments of stabilization policy, fiscal policy and monetary policy, and that the mix of the two is important. Indeed, I suppose most Keynesians would assign primacy to fiscal policy, although even this need not inevitably be the case. But in a certain fundamental sense, I believe the issue separating the Keynesians and the so-called Monetarist School relates more to fiscal than to monetary policy, since some Monetarists seem to deny that fiscal policy is capable of exerting any significant independent effects. In addition, the neo-Keynesian view seems to differ significantly from that of the Monetarists with respect to the role played by the stock of money in the process by which monetary policy affects the economy.

In this paper, I shall attempt to sketch what I would describe as a neo-Keynesian view of the process by which monetary and fiscal policy produce their effects on the economy and to evaluate some aspects of the recent controversy regarding stabilization policy in the context of this view. I shall then advance some suggestions concerning the conduct of monetary policy.

## I. The Transmission Mechanism of Monetary Policy

There appear to be several elements involved in the mechanism by which the effects of changes in monetary policy are transmitted to income, employment, and prices.

### *Portfolio Adjustments*

The major advance in monetary theory in recent years has been the development of a

* Reprinted from *Controlling Monetary Aggregates*, Boston, Federal Reserve Bank of Boston, 1969, pp. 105–117, by permission of the author and the Federal Reserve Bank of Boston.

systematic theory of portfolio adjustments involving financial and physical assets. This theory of portfolio adjustments fits very comfortably within a Keynesian framework and indeed greatly enriches Keynesian analysis and increases its explanatory power. The *General Theory,* itself, embodied a rudimentary theory of portfolio adjustments: the way in which the public divided its financial wealth between bonds and speculative cash balances depended on "the" rate of interest. The interest rate then affected investment expenditure, but Keynes failed to incorporate the stock of real capital into his analysis and relate it to the flow of investment spending. Indeed, many of the undoubted shortcomings of the *General Theory* stem from the failure to take account of capital accumulation.

The way in which monetary policy induces portfolio adjustments which will, in due course, affect income and employment may be described briefly as follows: A purchase of, say, Treasury bills by the Federal Reserve will directly lower the yield on bills and, by a process of arbitrage involving a chain of portfolio substitutions will exert downward pressure on interest rates on financial assets generally. Moreover—and more important—the expansion of bank reserves will enable the banking system to expand its assets. If the discount rate is unchanged, the banks can be expected to use some portion of the addition to their reserves to strengthen their free reserve position by repaying borrowings at the Federal Reserve and perhaps by adding to their excess reserves. But the bulk of the addition to reserves will ordinarily be used to make loan accommodation available on more favorable terms, and to buy securities, thereby exerting a further downward effect on security yields.

With the expected yield on a unit of real capital initially unchanged, the decline in the yields on financial assets, and the more favorable terms on which new debt can be issued, the balance sheets of households and businesses will be thrown out of equilibrium. The adjustment toward a new equilibrium will take the form of a sale of existing financial assets and the issuance of new debt to acquire real capital and claims thereto. This will raise the price of existing units of real capital—or equity claims against these units—relative to the (initially unchanged) cost of producing new units, thereby opening up a gap between desired and actual stocks of capital, a gap that will gradually be closed by the production of new capital goods. This stock adjustment approach is readily applicable, with some variations to suit the circumstances, to the demands for a wide variety of both business and consumer capital—including plant and equipment, inventories, residential construction, and consumer durable goods.

### *Wealth Effects*

Since monetary policy operates entirely through voluntary transactions involving swaps of one financial asset for another, it does not add to wealth by creating assets to which there are no corresponding liabilities. Nevertheless, monetary policy does have wealth effects, which may be of considerable importance. An expansionary monetary policy lowers the capitalization rates employed in valuing expected income streams, thereby raising the market value of outstanding bonds as well as real wealth and equity claims thereto. In part, this strengthens the impact on economic activity of the portfolio adjustments, already referred to, by increasing the size of the net portfolios available for allocation. In addition, the increase in household wealth may significantly stimulate consumption. Indeed, in a recent version of the FRB-MIT model, the effect on consumption resulting from the induced change in the value of common stock equities held by households accounts for 35 to 45 percent of the initial impact of monetary policy in some simulations.

### *Credit Availability Effects*

The portfolio and wealth effects appear to constitute the basic channels through which monetary policy has its initial impact on economic activity. In addition, however, the institutional arrangements for providing financing to certain sectors of the economy may be such as to give monetary policy a special leverage over the availability of credit to these sectors, thereby affecting their ability to spend. It is perhaps most illuminating to discuss changes in credit availability in the context of a restrictive monetary policy.

No doubt changes in credit availability affect many categories of expenditures to some degree. But the sector in which they are most clearly of major importance is homebuilding. Even in the absence of the rather unique institutional arrangements for its financing, housing demand might be significantly affected by monetary policy as changes in mortgage interest rates altered the desired housing stock. But as postwar experience has repeatedly shown, most dramatically in the "credit crunch" of 1966, changes in mortgage credit availability may greatly strengthen the impact of restrictive monetary policy on homebuilding and cause the effects to occur much more rapidly than the stock-adjustment mechanism would imply. There are three different ways in which mortgage credit availability may be affected by a restrictive monetary policy.

First, commercial banks may raise interest rates on consumer-type time deposits to attract funds to meet the demands of their customers. If savings and loan associations do not raise the rates paid to their depositors or raise them less than the banks raise their rates, households may rechannel their saving flows away from the savings and loan associations and toward the banks—or may even withdraw existing savings from savings and loan associations and shift them to banks. Even if, as has recently been the case, the Regulation Q ceilings are used to prevent the banks from attracting household saving away from savings and loan associations, a rise in short- and intermediate-term open-market interest rates may set in motion a process of "disintermediation," with savers channelling their funds away from fixed-value redeemable claims generally and directly into the securities markets. Either of these processes which cut down the flows of funds to savings and loan associations can have, of course, a powerful effect on housing activity. With frozen portfolios of older mortgages made at lower interest rates than currently prevail, these institutions may find it difficult to pay substantially higher interest rates to attract or hold funds even if the Home Loan Bank Board will allow them to.

Second, when commercial banks feel the effects of credit restraint, they normally reduce their mortgage lending in order to be able to accommodate the needs of their business borrowers.

Third, as interest rates rise, yields on corporate bonds typically rise relative to mortgage interest rates, and some institutional investors, such as life insurance companies, shift the composition of their investment flows away from mortgages and toward corporate bonds, which, in any case, have investment properties which make them more attractive than mortgages at equivalent yields. This tendency may be exacerbated by unrealistically low interest rate ceilings on FHA and VA mortgages and by State usury laws applicable to conventional mortgages.

The way in which mortgage credit availability impinges on homebuilding has changed with the passage of time. In the 1950's, when FHA and VA financing was more important than it has been recently and when the FHA and VA interest rate ceilings were more rigid than they are now, restrictive monetary policy affected housing mainly by diverting the flows of funds coming from investors having diversified portfolios away from mortgages and toward corporate securities. That is, the third effect listed above was the most important. In 1966, when homebuilding was drastically curtailed by monetary restraint, all of the effects were operating, but the first—the drain of funds away from savings and loan associations—was by far the most important. In 1968 and 1969, interest rates have risen sufficiently to arouse concern about a repetition of the 1966 experience. But while housing seems currently to be feeling the effects of tight money, it has proved to be much less vulnerable than was generally expected. There are several reasons for this, but the one most worthy of mention is the adoption by the Federal Reserve and the various Federal housing agencies of a number of measures designed to cushion or offset the effects of high interest rates on housing activity.

### *Secondary Effects*

Working through portfolio effects, wealth effects, and credit availability effects, the initial impacts of monetary policy will generate additional income, and this will further increase the demand for consumer nondurable goods and services. It will also expand the demand for the services of durable goods, thereby giving a further boost to the desired stocks of these goods. Thus, the familiar magnification of demand through multiplier and accelerator effects comes into play. It is often overlooked that the sharp reduction in the multiplier since the 1930's as a result of the greatly increased income-sensitivity of the tax-transfer system has presumably had important effects on the working of monetary as well as fiscal policy. Indeed, I would judge this increase in "built-in stability" through the fiscal system to be a major factor making monetary policy less potent today than in earlier times.

A further chain of secondary effects is set in motion as the rise in income increases demands for demand deposits and currency for transactions purposes, thereby reversing the initial decline in interest rates. This induced rise in interest rates will exert a dampening effect on the expansion by a partial reversal of the forces that initially triggered the rise in income. Whether or not this secondary effect will carry interest rates all the way back to their initial level (or higher) is an open question, concerning which I shall have some comments later on in this paper.

### *Effects on Real Output vs. Prices*

I think almost all economists of a Keynesian persuasion would accept the proposition that the way in which the effect of an increase in demand is divided between output response and price-level response depends on the way it impinges on productive capacity. Thus, expansion caused by monetary policy is generally no more or no less inflationary than expansion caused by fiscal policy (or, for that matter, by an autonomous increase in private demand). This statement needs to be qualified in a couple of minor respects. First, monetary expansion might be less inflationary than an equivalent amount of fiscal expansion over the longer run if it resulted in more investment, thereby causing labor productivity to increase more rapidly. Second, the impacts of monetary policy are distributed among sectors in a different way from those of fiscal policy; and, with less than perfect mobility of resources, the inflationary effect might depend to some degree on this distribution.

## II. Some Controversial Issues

I would now like to discuss several of the issues that seem to be at the heart of the recent controversy regarding monetary and fiscal policy.

### *The Effectiveness of Fiscal Policy*

For the purpose of isolating the effects of fiscal policy from those of monetary policy, I believe a "pure" fiscal policy action should be defined as a change in government expenditures or a change in tax rates without any accompanying change in the instruments of monetary policy. Under our present institutional set-up, the instruments of monetary policy are open-market operations, changes in reserve requirements, and changes in the Federal Reserve discount rate. Open-market operations may be viewed as governing unborrowed reserves plus currency, with defensive operations offsetting undesired changes in this total that would result from erratic variations in float, gold stock, etc.

An increase in government purchases of goods and services, with tax rates constant, would affect the economy by three different routes. First, there would be a direct expansionary *income effect* resulting from the purchase of output by the government. Second, there would be an expansionary *wealth effect* as the private sector, experiencing an increment to its wealth entirely in the form of net claims against the government, increased its demand for real capital in an effort to diversify its portfolios.[1] These income and wealth effects would set off a multiplier-accelerator process of economic expansion. This expansion, in turn, would activate a partially offsetting monetary effect as the rise in income increased the demand for money. If the dial settings of the monetary instruments remained un-

[1] For an extensive theoretical treatment of the wealth effect, see James Tobin, "An Essay on the Principles of Debt Management," in *Fiscal and Debt Management Policies* (Englewood Cliffs, N.J.: Prentice-Hall, Inc., 1963), pp. 142–218.

changed, this would drive up interest rates. The rise in interest rates would cause some reductions in those types of expenditures that were sensitive to interest rates through portfolio, wealth, and availability effects.

The wealth effect of fiscal policy may be quite powerful, particularly because it is cumulative—that is, it continues to operate until the budget has been brought back into balance, thereby shutting off the increase in net claims against the government. But, unfortunately, no effort that I know of has been made to incorporate it in an empirical model; consequently there is no way to formulate even a crude estimate of its importance.

If we neglect the wealth effect simply because we do not know how much weight to give it, we are left with the income effect and the offsetting monetary effect. The monetary effect will be greater (a) the greater the proportion of expenditures in GNP that are affected by interest rates, (b) the greater (in absolute value) is the average interest elasticity of these expenditures, (c) the greater is the income elasticity of demand for money, (d) the smaller (in absolute value) is the interest elasticity of demand for money and (e) the smaller is the interest elasticity of the supply of money.[2]

Only if the interest elasticities of both the demand for and supply of money are zero will the monetary effect completely cancel out the income effect.[3] That is, there will be some leeway for fiscal policy to increase income if a rise in interest rates either induces economization in the use of demand deposits and currency or causes the supply of such monetary assets to expand (for example, by inducing banks to increase their borrowings at the Federal Reserve). Since the empirical evidence is overwhelming that both money demand and money supply possess some degree of interest elasticity, it seems clear that fiscal policy is capable of exerting an independent effect on income. This conclusion is heavily supported by evidence derived from large structural models of the U.S. economy. For example, while there is no unique multiplier for fiscal policy in the FRB-MIT model, a number of simulations with that model show fiscal policy to have very substantial independent effects on economic activity.

It is often pointed out, especially by those who emphasize the role of money in the economy, that the effect produced by a stimulative fiscal action is dependent on the way in which the resulting deficit is financed. This is in a sense true, but this way of putting it is somewhat misleading. For example, it is sometimes stated that, in order to achieve the full Keynesian multiplier effect, the entire deficit must be financed by creating money—some statements even say high-powered money. What is necessary to achieve this result is to create enough money to satisfy the demand for money at the new higher level of income and the initial level of interest rates.

Ordinarily, the required increase in the supply of money will be only a fraction of the deficit, and the required increase in high-powered money will be an even smaller fraction. Moreover, there is a serious stock-flow problem. When income reaches its new equilibrium in a stable economy, the in-

[2] It is possible to derive a more elaborate version of the static Keynesian multiplier incorporating the monetary effect. The following is such a multiplier equation.

$$\frac{dY}{dG} = \frac{1}{1 - e + \dfrac{\frac{I}{Y}\eta_{Ir}\eta_{LY}}{\eta_{Lr} - \eta_{Mr}}}$$

Here Y is GNP; G is government purchases; e is the marginal propensity to spend out of GNP; I/Y is the proportion of GNP that is sensitive to interest rates; $\eta_{Ir}$ ($< 0$) is the average interest elasticity of interest-sensitive expenditures; $\eta_{Lr}$ ($< 0$) is the interest elasticity of demand for money; $\eta_{Mr}$ ($> 0$) is the interest elasticity of supply of money; and $\eta_{LY}$ ($> 0$) is the income elasticity of demand for money. The usual simple Keynesian multiplier without allowance for monetary effect is $1/(1 - e)$. The monetary effect is incorporated in the third term (taking the form of a fraction) in the denominator of the equation above. Since this term is positive, its presence reduces the size of the multiplier. The statement in the text above regarding the factors determining the size of the monetary effect is based on this expression.

[3] In this case, the supply of money may be regarded as exogenously determined. If the demand for money depends only on income, income will have to change sufficiently to eliminate any discrepancies that arise between the demand for and supply of money. Thus, money controls income, and fiscal policy is incapable of affecting it. The reader will note that if both $\eta_{Mr}$ and $\eta_{Lr}$ are zero, the multiplier for fiscal policy given in footnote 2 above becomes zero.

creased deficit (a flow) will be financed out of the excess of saving over investment generated by the rise in income. Additional demand deposits and currency are needed to meet the increased transaction demand at the higher income level, but this requires only a single increase in the money stock. In reality, there may be further complexities that require a modification of this principle—for example, if the demand for money depends on wealth as well as income or if the price level is determined by a Phillips Curve mechanism so that prices are not merely higher but are increasing more rapidly at higher levels of income.

Nevertheless, the principle is, I believe, basically correct. Rather than saying that the multiplier depends on how the deficit is financed, I think it is more accurate to say that it depends on the kind of monetary policy that accompanies the fiscal action. If monetary policy is such as to hold interest rates approximately constant, something analogous to the full Keynesian multiplier (with no monetary feedback) will be realized; if it allows interest rates to rise, the multiplier will be somewhat smaller; if it causes interest rates to fall, the multiplier will be somewhat greater.[4]

### *The Role of Money*

Although I have used the term "money" in my discussion above, I am not sure the term is a very useful or meaningful one. Money (in the sense of means of payment) has two components, demand deposits and currency. Those two components are not, however, perfect substitutes—they are held, by and large, by different kinds of spending units; demand for them responds in different ways to different stimuli; and, because they are subject to markedly different reserve requirements, shifts between them alter the total amount of credit that can be supplied by the financial system. They are best regarded as two different financial assets and treated as such.

Moreover, there is no apparent reason why "money"—whether in the form of currency or demand deposits—is more or less important than any of the myriad other financial assets that exist. It is now generally agreed that the demands for demand deposits and currency depend on the yields available on alternative assets and on income or related measures (and possibly, but by no means certainly, on wealth). Thus, the quantities of currency and demand deposits held by the public are generally agreed to be endogenous variables determined in a general equilibrium setting along with the prices and quantities of other financial and real assets.

Nor is there any appreciable evidence that money—whether in the form of demand deposits or currency—affects peoples' spending on goods and services directly. Such empirical evidence as there is suggests that people change their expenditures on goods and services because (a) their income changes; (b) their wealth changes; (c) their portfolios are thrown out of equilibrium by changes in relative yields on real and financial assets by actions taken by the monetary or fiscal authorities; (d) credit availability changes for institutional reasons altering in one direction or the other their ability to finance expenditures they want to make; or (e) their propensities to spend or their preferences for different kinds of assets change for essentially exogenous reasons, such as changes in tastes, changes in technology, and so on. That changes in the stock of money *per se* would affect spending seems to me highly improbable.

Of course, if changes in stocks of demand deposits and currency—or the combination of the two—were tightly linked to those changes in yields, in wealth, and in credit availability through which monetary policy operates, changes in the stocks of these monetary assets might be highly useful measures of the thrust of policy even

[4] If fiscal policy has a wealth effect working through changes in the public's holdings of net claims against the government, it seems quite likely that the magnitude of this effect will depend on the form taken by the change in net claims. For example, a change in public holdings of short-term debt may have a larger effect on aggregate demand than an equal change in holdings of long-term debt. To the extent that this is the case, debt management policies which change the maturity composition of the public's holdings of government debt may have important economic effects. But there is no reason to focus special attention on the composition of increments to the debt resulting from deficits, since the increment to the debt in any year is only a tiny fraction of the total debt to be managed. In any case, as indicated earlier, we are entirely neglecting the wealth effect because in the present state of knowledge there is no way of forming a judgment concerning its importance.

though they played no part in the causal nexus. But this, too, I think is unlikely. In a highly sophisticated financial system such as ours, in which new financial instruments and practices are constantly being introduced, it seems highly improbable that the demands for monetary assets are simple and stable functions of a few unchanging variables.

The many empirical studies of the demand for money that have been made in recent years have generally proved incapable of differentiating among alternative hypotheses. Consequently, one is free to choose among a variety of possible theories of the demand for money. The one that appeals to me is the hypothesis that money (i.e., demand deposits and currency) is dominated by time deposits and very short-dated securities, with the result that it is not a significant portion of permanent portfolios. This leaves the demand for monetary assets as an interest-elastic transactions demand along the lines postulated by Baumol and by Tobin.[5]

Such an explanation, however, makes sense only for relatively large business firms and wealthy individuals. It does not seem applicable to smaller units. Among such units, I suspect that the general rise in interest rates that has been going on for the past two decades has pushed these rates successfully above the thresholds of awareness of different groups of people, causing them to abandon their careless habit of foregoing income by holding excessive cash balances. If I am right, this behavior is probably not readily reversible if interest rates should fall. It seems to me that there is still a substantial element of mystery about the demand for monetary assets—mystery that will probably be resolved, if at all, only on the basis of extensive study of the behavior of the cash-holdings of micro-units.

### *Relationship Between Changes in Money and Changes in Income*

None of the above should be taken to mean that there is no relation between changes in demand deposits and currency and changes in income. Indeed, I believe there are three such relationships, which are very difficult to disentangle.

First, an expansionary monetary policy that stimulated increased spending and income through portfolio effects, wealth effects, and credit availability effects would bring in its wake an increase in supplies of demand deposits and currency. This would be a sideshow rather than the main event, but it would nevertheless occur. But the size of the increase associated with a given stimulus might vary considerably from one situation to another.

Second, a rise in income caused by fiscal policy or by an autonomous shift of private demand, with the monetary dials unchanged, would react back on the money supply in three different ways.[6] (1) The rise in interest rates caused by the rise in income would cause the banks to increase their borrowings from the Federal Reserve and perhaps to economize on excess reserves. (2) The rise in market interest rates would cause investors to shift funds from time deposits and similar claims into securities if, as is likely, the interest rates on these claims did not rise fully in pace with market rates. This would cause the quantity of demand deposits to increase as investors withdrew funds from time accounts and paid them over to sellers of securities for deposit in demand accounts. (3) If banks and related institutions raised rates on time-deposit type claims, some holders of noninterest-bearing demand deposits would be induced to shift funds to time accounts. To the extent that issuers of these claims held cash reserves against them, the amount of reserves available to support demand deposits would be reduced, requiring a contraction in these deposits. Effects (1) and (2) would cause the money supply to increase, while effect (3) would cause it to fall. It seems likely that (1) and (2) would outweigh (3), leading to an increase in the supply of monetary assets. The probability of this outcome would be

[5] See W. J. Baumol, "The Transactions Demand for Cash: An Inventory Theoretic Approach," *Quarterly Journal of Economics*, LXVI, November 1952, pp. 545–556; James Tobin, "The Interest Elasticity of the Transactions Demand for Cash," *Review of Economics and Statistics*, XXXVIII, August 1956, pp. 241–247.

[6] This discussion is based on an analysis developed in W. L. Smith, "Time Deposits, Free Reserves, and Monetary Policy," in Giulio Pontecoroo, R. P. Shay, and A. G. Hart (eds.), *Issues in Banking and Monetary Analysis* (New York: Holt, Rinehart and Winston, Inc., 1967), pp. 79–113.

increased if the Federal Reserve was laggard in adjusting Regulation Q ceilings. Indeed, a rigid Regulation Q ceiling would completely immobilize effect (3) while maximizing the size of effect (2).

Third, under the rubric of "meeting the needs of trade" or "leaning against the wind," the Federal Reserve has, at times, adjusted the supply of reserves to accommodate, or partially accommodate, changes in the demand for money brought about by changes in income, thereby creating a third chain of causation running from income to money supply.

With perhaps three relations between money and income present at the same time —one running from money to income and two running from income to money—it is likely to be almost impossible to tell what is going on by direct observation. And, as Tobin has shown, in such a complex dynamic situation, it is almost impossible to infer anything conclusive about causation by studying the lags.[7]

[7] James Tobin, "Money and Income: Post Hoc Propter Hoc?" (mimeographed); also W. C. Brainard and James Tobin, "Pitfalls in Financial Model Building," *American Economic Review*, LVIII, May 1968, pp. 99–122.

# 6 A MONETARIST MODEL OF THE MONETARY PROCESS*

DAVID I. FAND
*Wayne State University*

## Introduction

Important differences in stabilization policy have emerged in recent years between those who seek to stabilize the economy through discretionary fiscal policies, and those who favor a stabilization framework defined in terms of guidelines (or rules) for the money stock. For lack of better terms, I shall refer to these two points of view as the Monetarist and Fiscalist schools. Fiscalists are those who follow the Income-Expenditure theory and place chief reliance on the government's taxing and spending powers to stabilize the economy, while Monetarists follow the Quantity theory and emphasize the central banking system's control of the money stock.[1,2]

A popular view of the two schools stresses the following differences: Monetarists define stabilization policy in terms of the

* Reprinted from *The Journal of Finance,* vol. 25 (May, 1970) pp. 275–289, by permission of the author and the American Finance Association.

[1] The term Fiscalist is not a particularly good one. It is intended to cover the large group of modern Keynesians ranging from the neo-stagnationists to the neo-classicists, who advocate fiscal policies on theoretical growths, but also including some who may favor fiscal policy for pragmatic reasons. Note too that the Keynesian neo-classicists are, in many analytical respects, closer to the Monetarists than to the neo-stagnationists. Nevertheless, in spite of these obvious limitations, the term Fiscalist does probably convey the range of views we are trying to analyze. The term Monetarist is intended to cover the group who base their macro-economic policies on the modern Quantity theory.

[2] For influential statements of the Fiscalist position as applied to the U.S. economy in the early 1960's see Council of Economic Advisers, *The American Economy in 1961: Problems and Policies* (Washington, 1961), and P. A. Samuelson, *Stability and Growth in the American Economy,* 1962 Wicksell Lectures (Stockholm, 1962). For an articulate statement of the "New Economics" Fiscalist approach to stabilization emphasizing discretionary changes in the full-employment surplus, see W. W. Heller, *New Dimensions of Political Economy* (Norton, 1966). See also W. W. Heller (ed), *Perspective on Economic Growth* (Random House, 1968), and A. Okun, *The Political Economy of Prosperity* (Brookings, 1970). For a cogent statement of the neo-classical synthesis and its application to stabilization policy in the U.S. in the early 1960's, see J. Tobin, *The Intellectual Revolution in U.S. Economic Policy Making* (The University of Essex, 1966).

The classic statement of the pre-Keynesian Monetarist theory is, of course, in I. Fisher, *The Purchasing Power of Money* (Macmillan, 1911). For statements of the modern Quantity theory see L. W. Mints, *History of Banking Theory* (Chicago, 1945) and *Monetary Policy in a Competitive Society* (McGraw-Hill, 1951). See also Clark Warburton's selected papers for 1945–1953 in *Depression, Inflation, and Monetary Policy* (Johns Hopkins Press, 1966); M. Friedman (ed) *Studies in the Quantity Theory of Money* (Chicago, 1958); M. Friedman, *A Program for Monetary Stability* (Fordham, 1959); M. Friedman and A. Schwartz, *A Monetary History of the United States* (Princeton, 1963); and M. Friedman, *The Optimum Quantity of Money* (Aldine, 1969); D. Patinkin, *Money Interest and Prices,* 2nd ed. (Harper 1965); and H. G. Johnson, *Essays in Monetary Economics* (Harvard, 1967).

money stock, favor either fixed rules or a set of guidelines for the monetary aggregates, and seemingly uphold extremist views that "only money matters"; Fiscalists implement stabilization policy in terms of the full-employment surplus, take a more positive view of discretionary budgetary changes, and emphasize—and possibly exaggerate—the short run stabilization potentials of temporary changes in taxes and expenditures. This summary does not point to any analytical basis for their different views; it therefore leaves open the possibility that their respective stabilization policies may reflect differences in temperament, emphasis, judgment, or political affiliation.

In this paper we shall argue that the stabilization differences between Monetarists and Fiscalists reflect substantially different models of the monetary process, and is not just a question of emphasis, judgment, or temperament. We shall also suggest that a classification of monetary theories in terms of "does money matter" or "only money matters" does not highlight the distinctive analytical aspects of these monetary models. We illustrate some of these aspects by considering the following substantive features of the modern Quantity theory—the Monetarists' model of the monetary process: the Monetarist distinction between nominal money, a policy variable, and real cash balances, an endogenous variable; the Monetarist distinction between high and rising interest rates, and between nominal and real interest rates; and the Monetarist distinction between *ceteris paribus* and *mutatis mutandis* fiscal effects—defined in terms of the monetary growth rates. In our concluding section we summarize some essential features of the Monetarists' model.

## I. The Classification of Monetary Theories: Monetary Extremism Re-examined

In a recent paper on "The Role of Money in National Economic Policy", Samuelson states that monetarism is "the central issue that is debated these days in connection with macro-economic aggregate demand—whether there will be unemployment, whether there will be inflation—is money, $M_1$ or $M_2$, and more specifically, perhaps, its various rates of change." He adds that if we can define a spectrum of remarks from "money doesn't matter," to "money alone matters," monetarism is somewhere between "money matters most" to "money alone matters"—at the right end of the spectrum.[3]

This view of monetarism has some validity: Monetarists do attribute the Great Depression, and the subsequent terrible debacle of the 1930's, to the precipitous fall (between 25-35 per cent) in the money stock—explaining these great disasters in terms of erratic money stock behavior. Finding few exceptions to this generalization, they accept the hypothesis that the money stock is the key policy variable for avoiding inflations and for preventing severe depressions. The Fiscalist, in contrast, seeking to explain the twin scourges of depressions and inflations, is apt to be more eclectic and highlights either fundamental (or structural) changes in the economy, or overpowering external forces, such as a war. Monetarists thus often do appear either as extremists—in asserting that a major disaster such as the Great Depression could be averted by good monetary policy—or as naive in overlooking, or dismissing, many of the fundamental changes in the real economy emphasized by the Fiscalists.

If we move on to consider the impact of monetary policy on economic growth, there is a significant change in their respective views. Many Fiscalists believe that the central bank can stimulate capital formation and the growth rate of real output by adopting a monetary-fiscal policy mix of easy money and tight budgets. Monetarists, in contrast, are more inclined to the view that changes in monetary policy affect prices rather than interest rates and rates of return. One could therefore argue that the Fiscalists may be taking an extreme position and exaggerating the monetary impact on the real rate of interest, on rates of return, on capital formation, and on economic growth.

"Monetary extremism" may serve as a mnemonic symbol for calling attention to the strategic role assigned by the Monetarists to money policy in avoiding deep

[3] See P. A. Samuelson's "The Role of Money in National Economic Policy" in *Controlling Monetary Aggregates* (Federal Reserve Bank of Boston, 1969), pp. 7–13.

depressions and inflations; it may also highlight the Fiscalists' position that monetary policy may play a key role in facilitating capital formation and economic growth. But it does not focus on the theoretical basis for the policies recommended by Monetarists and Fiscalists for dealing with ordinary business cycle fluctuations, with mild inflations, or with the sluggish performance of the American economy in the late 1950's.

Theories said to contain extreme views of money are, in effect, being classified with respect to singular, and very specific, issues. Accordingly, this is meaningful if we limit analysis to deep depressions or galloping inflations, to the so-called "Keynesian Case" (absolute liquidity preference and zero elasticities) where "Money doesn't matter," to "Radcliffe" type theories where "money hardly matters," and to the contribution of easy money policies to economic growth. Barring these special cases, both the Monetarist and Fiscalist schools clearly believe that "money matters," and neither school believes that "only money matters." Far more important are the substantive differences between Monetarists and Fiscalists concerning the precise manner in which money matters—the theory of the transmission mechanism explaining how changes in the nominal money stock may affect real output, employment, the price level, capital formation, and economic growth.[4]

The monetary models used by the Monetarists and Fiscalists contain substantively different assumptions with respect to the following technical questions: Can the Federal Reserve control the (nominal) money stock within fairly close limits, or should we treat it as an endogenous variable?[5] Is it possible for the Federal Reserve, acting through the FOMC, to lower (or raise) interest rates if such a change is thought to be either desirable or necessary? Should the Federal Reserve formulate the directive to the account manager in terms of the monetary aggregates and scrap its present money market strategy?[6] And would the stabilization performance of recent years have been better if the authorities were required by statute to keep monetary growth within a given set of guidelines?[7]

Substantive differences in the monetary models used by Monetarists and Fiscalists led, in turn, to substantially different conclusions concerning the following policy issues: Is the post-1965 inflation the result of extraordinary expansion in the monetary aggregates, or of an excessively lax, and inappropriate, fiscal policy? Is the transmission mechanism, as conceived in the income theory, too restrictive or may changes in the nominal money stock *directly* affect private expenditures, aggregate demand, and the price level? Does the theory of

[4] The statement that a theory is extreme is always somewhat arbitrary, and depends partly on the classification principle that it used. Thus, a theory with any new result, whether the result is important substantively, or is merely a trivial addition to previous results, can be viewed as an extremist theory, if all theories are classified on the basis of whether they contain this new result.

[5] See D. I. Fand, "Some Issues in Monetary Economics", *Banca Nazionale del Lavoro Quarterly Review,* 90, September 1969, and *Review,* Federal Reserve Bank of St. Louis, January 1970.

[6] For an explanation of the Federal Reserve's money market strategy, and an interpretation of the proviso clause as a device for correcting errors in the projected relation between money market variables and the monetary aggregates, see the recent paper by Governor Sherman Maisel, "Controlling Monetary Aggregates" in Federal Reserve Bank of Boston, *Controlling Monetary Aggregates* (September 1969) [reprinted in this volume]. See J. M. Guttentag, "The Strategy of Open Market Operations", *Quarterly Journal of Economics* (February 1966) [reprinted in this volume]. See also the paper by A. Meltzer and the joint paper by G. Horwich and P. Hendershott on "The Appropriate Indicators of Monetary Policy" in *Savings and Residential Financing,* 1969 Conference Proceedings (U.S. League, 1969) [reprinted in this volume].

[7] M. Friedman, "The Role of Monetary Policy", *American Economic Review,* March 1968 [reprinted in this volume]; P. Hendershott, *The Neutralized Money Stock—An Unbiased Measure of Federal Reserve Policy Actions* (Richard D. Irwin, 1968); the Joint Economic Committee *Hearings on Standards for Guiding Monetary Action* (Washington, 1968); D. I. Fand, "Comment: The Impact of Monetary Policy in 1966", *Journal of Political Economy,* August 1968; the House Committee on Banking and Currency *Compendium on Monetary Policy Guidelines and Federal Reserve Structure* (Washington, 1968); T. Mayer, *Monetary Policy in the United States* (Random House, 1968); K. Brunner (ed), *Targets and Indicators of Monetary Policy* (Chandler Publishing Co., 1969).

fiscal policy often assume an elastic (or accommodating) monetary policy, and does it therefore fail to distinguish between a pure fiscal deficit excluding any money stock effects (a *ceteris paribus* effect) and an increase in the monetary aggregates accompanied by a fiscal deficit (a *mutatis mutandis* effect)?[8] And do temporary changes (discretionary or automatic) in the full-employment surplus have quantitatively predictable effects on aggregate demand?[9]

Differences in the assumptions implicit in the monetary models used by Monetarists and Fiscalists help explain some of their substantive differences on policy issues. And until we are able to clarify and resolve these differences, the controversy over the relative merits of monetary and fiscal policy, as it is emerging in the current dialogue, will necessarily continue. We shall now take up three distinctive features of the Monetarists' model: their theory of money, their theory of interest rates and prices, and their analysis of fiscal policy.

8 See L. Andersen and J. Jordan, "Monetary and Fiscal Actions: A Test of Their Relative Importance in Economic Stabilization", November 1968 issue of the *Review*, Federal Reserve Bank of St. Louis [reprinted in this volume]; the Comment by F. DeLeeuw and J. Kalchbrenner, and Reply by Andersen and Jordan in the April 1969 *Review* of the Federal Reserve Bank of St. Louis; M. Levy, "Monetary Pilot Policy Growth and Inflation", and W. Lewis, "Money is Everything Economics—A Tempest in a Teapot" in the *Conference Board Record* for January and April 1969; R. Davis, "How Much Does Money Matter? A Look at Some Recent Evidence" in the June 1969 *Monthly Review*, Federal Reserve Bank of New York [reprinted in this volume]; and L. C. Andersen, "The Influence of Economic Activity on the Money Stock: Some Additional Evidence", August 1969 issue of the *Review*, Federal Reserve Bank of St. Louis.

9 The American Enterprise Institute's symposium volume, *Fiscal Policy and Business Capital Formation* (Washington, 1967) contains an informed discussion of this subject. See especially the papers by P. McCracken, C. Harriss, S. Fabricant, and R. Musgrave, and the comments by G. Haberler and N. Ture.
The key stabilization role assigned to changes in the full-employment surplus is critically reviewed by G. Terborgh in his *The New Economics* (MAPI, 1968). For a discussion of the stabilization roles to be assigned to monetary and fiscal policy see the Friedman-Heller dialogue, *Monetary vs. Fiscal Policy* (Norton, 1969).

## II. A Monetarist View of Money: Nominal Money vs. Real Balances

The Monetarist position is often misunderstood, and they are often interpreted as advocating extremist views about money. This failure to communicate effectively may be due to the fact that Monetarists seem to be advocating two contradictory propositions at the same time: on the one hand, their theoretical analysis views the nominal money stock as a kind of veil (as in the classical tradition) and stresses real variables as opposed to nominal variables; on the other hand, their historical and applied analysis suggests that movements in the money stock are the key to curbing inflation and to preventing depressions. As we move from monetary theory into the analysis of stabilization policy, the money stock is somehow transformed from an innocuous veil into an extremely powerful force for determining income, employment, and the price level. Monetarists may have experienced difficulties in obtaining a wider understanding of their model, and in communicating the theoretical basis of their monetary theory because it seems to include, in one category, both the money veil of theory and the extremely potent high-powered money of stabilization policy.[10]

There is an apparent paradox, striking some as a contradiction, between the theoretical proposition that the quantity of nominal money will not, substantially, affect any of the real endogenous variables, and a policy recommendation to impose either fixed rules or policy guidelines on monetary growth, in order to stabilize the economy. The first proposition implies that monetary changes will only affect nominal variables; the second, that monetary policy is, in fact, the key to obtaining the desired values for the important real endogenous variables of macro-economics (i.e., the real wage, employment, real output, and the rate of economic growth).

10 In saying that Monetarists view nominal money as a veil we do not wish to rule out the possibility that in a growth model context, alternative policies with respect to nominal money may affect some of the equilibrium values of the endogenous variables in the real economy. But even with this property, nominal money is still almost like a veil in a comparative static sense.

The puzzle may be resolved by noting first that the nominal money stock may affect nominal variables while exerting very little *direct* influence on the real variables. Thus, when an increase in nominal money raises money income, the level of money wages and the price level, without affecting any of the real endogenous variables—when nominal money stock changes affect only nominal variables — money is properly viewed as a veil. Second, nominal money stock changes may significantly affect the real endogenous variables, in an economy where output can easily expand and where quantities adjust faster than prices. The money veil of theory can become an extremely powerful stimulus to increase real output and employment in the world of stabilization policy. Third, in an economy where output can no longer expand and where prices adjust rather than quantities, control of the nominal money stock is the key to controlling the rise in prices. And it is in these latter cases the Monetarists focus on the growth rate of nominal money as the key policy for preventing both depressions and inflations.

To emphasize this distinction between the money veil of monetary theory and the potent money of stabilization policy, Monetarists distinguish between nominal money —a supply-determined policy variable—and the real (value of the) money stock—a demand-determined endogenous variable. Monetarists treat the quantity of nominal money as a variable determined primarily by the supply condition, postulating a fairly close link between the monetary base (or high-powered money) supplied by the central bank, and the quantity of nominal money available to the public. In contrast, the real money stock is an endogenous variable, determined by the interaction of the financial and real sectors, and satisfying the demand function for real balances. Thus, while the nominal money stock may be varied as a policy variable, the real money stock is an endogenous variable with an equilibrium solution value, given by the demand function for real balances.[11]

The Monetarist therefore postulates (1) that the nominal money stock can be controlled by the monetary authorities and used for policy purposes, (2) that the real money stock is determined by the general equilibrium of the real and monetary sectors, and cannot generally be controlled by the authorities. This model therefore implies (3) that the authorities cannot increase real balances by printing nominal money, and that they will ultimately fail and serve only to raise prices, unless there is a substantial volume of unused resources. The relation between money and prices in (3) serves to emphasize (4) that an increase in nominal money will generally bring about permanently higher prices, rather than lower interest rates. The Monetarists' linking of nominal money with prices contrasts sharply with the Fiscalists' linking of nominal money with interest rates.

The sharp distinction drawn between the nominal money stock, treated as a supply-determined policy variable, and the real money stock, treated as a demand-determined endogenous variable (with an equilibrium solution value), is a striking feature of monetarism. It is also a paradoxical feature, since the Monetarists' model allows the authorities effective control over the nominal stock, while simultaneously severely limiting the circumstances where they influence the stock of real balances.[12]

The Monetarist emphasis on the endogenity of real cash balances, suggesting a close relation between nominal money and the price level, is the basis for their rejection of the liquidity preference theory as a general theory of money and interest rates. We shall now consider the Monetarist theory relating money and prices with nominal and real interest rates.

[11] The proposition that the quantity of nominal money is determined by conditions of supply is not intended to rule out the possibility that the money supply function has some interest elasticity, or that some variation in the quantity of money may result from shifts in the demand for money. What it does say is that through its control over the monetary base the central bank can exercise effective control over the nominal money stock.

[12] The Fiscalist does not usually distinguish between nominal and real balances. The Fiscalist model may allow the authorities less control over nominal balances and greater control over real balances, as compared to the Monetarists' model.

## III. A Monetarist View of Money, Interest Rates and Prices

The Income-Expenditure theory of the Fiscalists adopts a particular transmission mechanism to analyze the effects of a change in the money stock (or its growth rate) on the real economy. It assumes that money changes will affect output or prices only through its effect on a set of conventional yields—on the market interest rate of a small group of financial assets, such as government or corporate bonds. A given change in the money stock will have a calculable effect on these interest rates (this set of conventional yields) given by the liquidity preference analysis, and the interest rate changes are then used to derive the change in investment spending, the induced effects on income and consumption, etc.

Monetarists, following the Quantity theory, do not accept this transmission mechanism and this liquidity preference theory of interest rates for several reasons: First, they suggest that an increase in money may directly affect expenditures, prices, and a wide variety of implicit yields on physical assets, and need not be restricted to a small set of conventional yields on financial assets.[13] Second, they view the demand for money as determining the desired quantity of real balances, and not the level of interest rates. Third, and most fundamentally, they reject the notion that the authorities can change the stock of real balances — an endogenous variable — and thereby bring about a permanent change in interest rates, except for very special circumstances.[14]

Monetarists reject the liquidity preference interest rate theory because it applies only as long as we can equate an increase in nominal money with a permanent increase in real balances. This suggests that the liquidity preference theory may be useful as a theory of the short run interest rate changes — the liquidity effect — associated with the impact effects of nominal money changes. But Monetarists also insist that this liquidity effect is temporary and will disappear as aggregate demand, output, and/or prices rise. Monetarists therefore depart from the Income theory and conclude that the liquidity effect will spend itself, and that market interest rates will return to their former level. They argue that the rise in income increases the demand for money, causing market interest rates to rise, and that any tendency for prices to rise with output will lower the real value of the money stock, and thus hasten the return of interest rates to their former level. The income and the price level effects thus reinforce each other to raise interest rates, offsetting the initial decline due to the liquidity effect. Some recent estimates suggest that market rates will, on the average, return to their initial level within a year, so that a one-time increase in nominal money

13 Monetarists favor a transmission mechanism in which an increase in money may directly affect expenditures, prices, and implicit yields on physical assets. They suggest that money may be substituted not only for bonds but also for other assets, and that individuals may re-establish portfolio equilibrium by purchasing either a financial or a physical asset. Note that when money is used to acquire physical assets the interest rate effect no longer proceeds the price effect, since it is only through an increase in the price of assets that the reduction in yield is effectuated. Moreover, if we define assets to include consumer durables (e.g., cars, appliances) it would be reasonable to suppose that these expenditures—which are now classified as consumption—can be directly stimulated by an increase in money. In a period of rising prices, inflationary expectations raise the cost of holding money and the public has an incentive to reduce the quantity of desired real balances by increasing expenditures. The link between money and prices is likely to be strengthened during an inflation. See D. I. Fand, "A Monetary Interpretation of the Post-1965 Inflation in the U.S.", *Banca Nazionale del Lavoro Quarterly Review*, 89, June 1969. See also W. J. Yohe and D. S. Karnosky, "Interest Rates and Price Level Changes", December 1969 *Review*, Federal Reserve Bank of St. Louis [reprinted in this volume].

14 Thus, if prices are given in the short run, and if real and nominal balances do move together, the money demand function may be used as a liquidity preference function to analyze the initial *changes* in the level of interest rates. Moreover, if an increase in real balance does not affect aggregate demand, income, and prices, the initial effect is also the total effect on interest rates. See D. I. Fand, "Keynesian Monetary Theories, Stabilization Policy and the Recent Inflation", *Journal of Money, Credit and Banking*, August 1969.

will have no lasting effect on the level of interest rates.[15]

An additional price expectation effect may also become operative if accelerated monetary growth generates *rising* prices, and if the public expects the price rise to continue. Anticipated price increases—inflationary expectations — may indeed cause market interest rates to rise above their initial level, if the rate of monetary growth is sufficiently large to bring in the price expectation effect. When this occurs, market rates will rise above their initial level.[16]

Monetarists and Fiscalists both acknowledge that an increase in nominal money may have a permanent effect on output, on prices, on interest rates, or on some combination of these. Monetarists, nevertheless, emphasize the permanent effects on the price level and/or output, while Fiscalists emphasize the effect on interest rates and/or output, and treat the initial liquidity effect as if it were the permanent interest rate effect. Monetarists thus envision the price level as equilibrating the demand for, and supply of, real balances, so that the nominal money stock is a determinant of the price level; Fiscalists view the interest rate as equilibrating the demand for, and supply of, money and explain the price level in terms of money wages, unit labor costs, markup factors, etc.[17]

The interest rate and price level theories of the Monetarists and the Fiscalists are thus mutually exclusive: if an increase (or accelerated growth) in nominal money permanently lowers interest rates and/or raises output, its effect on prices is lessened; alternatively, if its permanent effect is to raise prices and/or output, its effect on real interest rates is lessened. The transmission mechanism of the Income theory in which an increase in nominal money directly affects interest rates but not prices is thus a crucial link in developing the negative *ceteris paribus* association between money and interest rate movements. The opposite assumption, that the real value of the money stock is an endogenous variable—relating the stock of nominal money and the absolute price level—is the basis for rationalizing a positive relation between money and interest rates. The historical association between interest rates and prices may be interpreted as a *mutatis mutandis* relation, where the initial liquidity effect of an increase in nominal money is subsequently offset by the induced income and price expectation effects.[18]

---

[15] See W. Gibson, "Effects of Money on Interest Rates", Federal Reserve *Staff Economic Studies #43,* January 1968; P. Cagan, "The Channels of Monetary Effects on Interest Rates" (M.S., 1966); W. Gibson and G. Kaufman, "The Sensitivity of Interest Rates to Changes in Money and Income", *Journal of Political Economy,* May 1968; M. Friedman, "Factors Affecting the Level of Interest Rates" in *Savings and Residential Financing,* 1968 Conference Proceedings (U.S. League, 1968); P. Cagan and A. Gandolfi, "The Lag in Monetary Policy as Implied by the Time Pattern of Monetary Effects on Interest Rates", *American Economic Review,* May 1969.

[16] The Keynesian liquidity effect is the permanent interest rate effect if, and only if, there are no offsetting income, price level, and price expectations effects. But this requires an economy in which money does not affect aggregate demand, real output or prices—an extreme case that would be rejected by both Monetarists and Fiscalists.

[17] The price level theory incorporated in the FRB-MIT model is described as follows: Prices are assumed to be a variable markup over wages, with excise taxes completely shifted onto consumers. The variables determining the markup are the productivity trend which allows producers to maintain profit shares even though wages rise faster than prices, farm and import prices, which measure other costs, and the ratio of unfilled orders to shipments, which indicates demand shifts.

See F. DeLeeuw and E. Gramlich, "The Channels of Monetary Policy," *Federal Reserve Bulletin,* June 1969 [reprinted in this volume].

[18] The statement that the Fiscalists have a monetary theory of the interest rate and a nonmonetary theory of the price level needs to be modified somewhat when we consider the large scale econometric models. But while the larger models do allow for some feedback from money to prices, they still retain the negative association between money and interest rates, even allowing for the price level effects. Thus, in the FRB-MIT model, an increase in money will lower interest rates and these rates do not return to their former level even in simulation that extend for several years (20 quarters). In this sense even the large scale models retain the main features of the simpler Fiscalist models, and do not approximate the more classical results. See G. Kaufman and R. Laurent, "Simulating Policy Strategies on the FRB-MIT Model Under Two Alternative Monetary Policy Regimes", *Quarterly Review of Economics and Business,* Winter 1970.

The Monetarist theory of interest rates utilizes the close link between nominal money and prices to rationalize the positive association between monetary growth and the level of market rates. It helps motivate the distinction emphasized by the Monetarists between *high* and *rising* rates, that has become increasingly relevant in recent years. In a fully anticipated inflation, we expect that market interest rates will be high, reflecting the rate of inflation, even if *real* rates (or rates of return) remain constant. Thus, if the real rate, r, is 5 per cent and stays at that level, and if the rate of inflation, i, is expected to continue indefinitely at a 20 per cent annual rate, the market rate, m, should start to rise. It will continue to rise for an indefinite period until the rate of inflation is fully anticipated, when it will settle at 26%, as shown in equation (1):

$$m = r + i + ri \qquad (1)$$

This important distinction between high (low) rates and rising (falling) interest rates, and their relation to rising (falling) prices was developed by Irving Fisher in the 1890's.

Fisher's theory, relating monetary growth, price level changes, and market interest rates helps rationalize the puzzling, though well documented, empirical association between high interest rates and high prices—the Gibson Paradox. The Fisher model postulates: that market rates are high (low) when prices are rising (falling); that market rates lag behind price level changes; that market rates are highly correlated with a weighted average of past price level changes. Gibson's empirical finding that *high* rates accompany *high* prices and *low* rates accompany *low* prices may then be explained if there is a fairly long lag between interest rates and prices. The Fisher theory thus clearly suggests a sequence in which (excessive) growth in the money stock causes first a rise in prices and, ultimately, higher market rates (nominal interest rates).[19]

Monetarists following the Fisher model thus relate monetary expansion, rising prices, with rising (and high) market interest rates. They distinguish therefore among the following concepts: (1) *rising* rates, when inflationary expectations have not yet caught up with the actual rise in prices; (2) *high* (though stable) rates, when inflation is fully anticipated; (3) market rates, nominal interest rates incorporating inflationary expectations; and (4) real rates, interest rates corrected for the rate of inflation. Monetarists therefore postulate a sequence of monetary expansion, rising prices, and high interest rates, distinguish between nominal and real rates, and introduce a price expectation variable in order to rationalize a rise in market rates (relative to the real rate) when prices are rising.

Fiscalists, following the liquidity preference theory, abstract (1) from any direct link of monetary growth on prices, (2) from any direct link of rising prices on rising (or high) market rates, and (3) from the resulting divergence between market rates (nominal interest rates) and real rates. They do not distinguish between *rising* rates and *high* rates, between market rates (nominal interest rates) and real rates, and do not accept the Fisher rationalization of the *mutatis mutandis* positive association between monetary expansion and high (or rising) interest rates. Accordingly, to explain empirical data suggesting a positive association of interest rates and prices, they must necessarily assume increases in the demand for money—or an increase in the natural rate relative to the market rate—causing market rates to rise; and in the

[19] For an analysis of the Gibson Paradox see I. Fisher, *Appreciation and Interest* (Macmillan, 1930); *The Theory of Interest* (Macmillan, 1930); J. M. Keynes, *A Treatise on Money* (Macmillan, 1930); D. Meiselman, "Bond Yield and the Price Level: The Gibson Paradox Regained" in D. Carson (ed) *Banking and Monetary Studies* (Irwin, 1963), and his "Money and Factor Proportions" (M.S. 1964). See also the summary of the Wicksell and Keynes Analysis in P. Cagan's *Determination and Effect of Changes in the Stock of Money* (Columbia University Press, 1965); M. Friedman and A. Schwartz, *Trends in Money, Income and Prices* (M.S.); and D. I. Fand, "Keynesian Monetary Theories, . . .", *op. cit.*

W. J. Yohe and D. S. Karnosky in their comprehensive article on "Interest Rates and Price Level Changes 1952–1969", *op. cit.*, provide a succinct statement of the Fisher theory and an illuminating discussion of the theoretical aspects of the Gibson Paradox. They summarize their experiments with several weighting patterns for the price expectation effect, derive alternative estimates of the real rate, and relate this analysis to explain interest rate movements in recent years.

absence of monetary growth would leave market rates at even higher levels.

The implications of the Monetarists' theory is best seen if we consider the consequences of the Fiscalists' reluctance to distinguish between market rates and real rates, and to bring in a price expectations variable in the analysis of interest rate movements. This has two subtle, but important and far reaching, consequences: first, they must postulate successive upward shifts in the demand for money—or in the natural rate—in order to explain a continuing rise in market interest rates since they are reluctant, *ex hypothesi,* to explain rising (or high) market rates in terms of rising prices and price expectations; second, by assuming that the variability in market rate movements corresponds to changes in real rates, the Fiscalists' theory necessarily carries an implication that real interest rates, or rates of return, the marginal productivity of capital, and the real sector of the economy are highly volatile. But this substantively important conclusion about the instability of the real economy is clearly inappropriate if market rates are responding to, and reflecting, past and present price level changes.

The significance of the Monetarist theory, explaining the association of rising rates with inflation, of high rates with high prices, and of high rates with excessive monetary growth —a rationalization not available to the Fiscalists—is thus clear. The Fiscalist, seeking to explain the positive association of interest rates and prices, must hypothesize shifts in the demand for money, or increases in the natural rate, to explain rising market rates. The assumption that the variability in market rates corresponds to the volatility of real rates, and the far reaching implications concerning the instability of the real economy, are therefore directly related to the Fiscalists' analytical framework—his liquidity preference theory of interest rates. They serve, therefore, to highlight and emphasize the extraordinary contribution of Fisher's theory relating money and prices to interest rates.

## IV. A Monetarist View of Fiscal Policy

Monetarists and Fiscalists disagree, by definition, on the relative roles of monetary and fiscal policy in stabilization: Monetarists analyze the taxing and spending decisions in the budget—in older pre-Keynesian public-finance tradition—as having their primary effect on the allocation of resources from the private to the public sectors, and conclude that budget policy should not be the major instrument for stabilizing aggregate demand. This is, of course, in sharp contrast to the Fiscalists—in the post-Keynesian tradition —who emphasize fiscal policy as the key variable in controlling aggregate demand.

Monetarists are sometimes interpreted as denying that fiscal surpluses (or deficits)— e.g., a rise (or cut) in taxes holding government expenditures constant—have any substantial effects on aggregate demand. This inference is, in my opinion, incorrect. Monetarists must surely acknowledge that an increase in taxes, with constant government expenditures, will certainly depress private expenditures if the Treasury impounds the revenue. They will also agree that an increase in taxes, with both government expenditures and the monetary aggregates (or their rate of growth) constant, will also depress aggregate demand. The rise in taxes will raise the surplus (or reduce the deficit), causing interest rates to fall, and bring about a reduction in private spending if desired real money balances respond to changes in interest rates. What the Monetarists do question is whether a *mutatis mutandis* increase in taxes, allowing both government expenditures and the monetary aggregates to rise, will necessarily reduce either private spending or aggregate demand.

A Monetarist—focussing on the monetary aggregates—distinguishes between a *mutatis mutandis* increase in taxes, where both government expenditures and the money stock may vary, and a *ceteris paribus* tax action, where government expenditure and monetary growth are held constant. That an increase in taxes, matched by an equivalent increase in expenditures, will be stimulative rather than restrictive is, of course, an accepted theorem in the Fiscalist theory, and they take account of this by measuring fiscal policy changes in terms of the full-employment surplus. But while the full-employment surplus nets out the taxes against the expenditures, it does not specify any requirements for the money stock, nor is it adjusted for the size of the real GNP, or for price level changes.

The notion that fiscal restraint can be offset by easy money is not unique to the Monetarist. What may be unique about the Monetarist view is his further statement that this offset will occur even if market interest rates are rising. To the Monetarist, the thrust of monetary policy is defined by the aggregate rather than by market rates, and easy money (accelerated growth in the monetary aggregates) is not necessarily inconsistent with rising interest rates. The admitted failure of the Revenue and Control Act of June 1968 to cool down the economy seems to support the Monetarist view. It has brought about greater agreement, if not a consensus, that an increase in the monetary aggregates may be expansionary and offset a rise in taxes, even if market interest rates are rising. But this is all that the Monetarist needs to question about fiscal policy, and it is surely not equivalent to saying that fiscal policy actions do not affect aggregate demand. To deny any short run stabilization effects to fiscal actions, one must be prepared to argue that surpluses (or deficits), irrespective of magnitude, have no direct effect on spending through changes in disposable income; and that they have no indirect effect through changes in desired real money balances or desired liquidity, and on velocity. But this can be true only in the exceptional case of a completely (interest) inelastic demand for money.

The Monetarist analysis of the stabilization effects of fiscal actions is directly related to calibration of the posture of monetary policy in terms of monetary aggregates, and which, as recent events have indicated, may differ substantially from the Fiscalist calibration based on interest rates.[20] The Fiscalist calibration of monetary policy will therefore associate tight money with high (or rising) interest rates, stable monetary policy with stable rates, etc. As a consequence, a fiscal deficit, accompanied by stable interest rates, is accordingly defined as a *ceteris paribus* action—as a fiscal stimulus with monetary policy constant. On this calibration it is natural to attribute the entire rise in income to the deficit. But a fiscal deficit with stable interest rates implies money creation (financing through the banking system), and (accelerated) growth in the monetary aggregates. Using the Monetarist calibration, this very same action is necessarily defined as a monetary stimulus—an expansive monetary action. The *ceteris paribus* fiscal stimulus, when interest rates serve to define the posture of monetary policy, is thus necessarily a (*mutatis mutandis*) monetary stimulus, when the monetary aggregates serve to define the monetary posture.

Because deficits are associated with money creation and surpluses with decelerated monetary growth, much of the evidence can be rationalized by both the Income theory as well as the Quantity theory.[21] On the basis of experience in the 1930's and 1950's, Fiscalists have accepted the multiplier analysis of the Income theory; accordingly, they focus on the full-employment surplus as the key to controlling aggregate demand, and de-emphasize the allocative function of the budget relative to its stabilization function. This approach to budget policy assumes that

---

20 The relevance of this point is apparent when we consider the June 1968 tax action where fiscal restraint was accompanied by rising interest rates. To a Fiscalist this is a case of a *joint* action, since the increase in the full-employment surplus—fiscal restraint—was compounded by high interest rates—monetary restraint. The combination of high interest rates, together with the rise in the full-employment surplus, helps rationalize the articulated fears of overkill in the summer of 1968 and constitute a case of an offsetting action, since the increase in the full-employment surplus—fiscal restraint—was associated with an accelerated growth in the money stock—monetary ease. Moreover, the offsetting monetary action was, apparently, stronger than the enacted, and presumed massive, dose of fiscal restraint.

21 Deficits (and surpluses) are usually associated with acceleration (deceleration) in money stock growth, and it is therefore possible for Fiscalists and Monetarists to cite the same evidence to support their respective views. Fiscal deficits associated with rising income, employment and prices, seem to support the Multiplier theory of Fiscalists. But when a period of fiscal stimulus is characterized by monetary expansion—e.g., the 1964 tax cut—it also supports the Monetarist theory. It is only when movements in the money stock and in the full-employment surplus go in opposite directions, as in 1966 and in 1968, that we can get any real test of their relative effects. See D. I. Fand, "Some Issues in Monetary Economics", *op. cit.*

monetary policy cannot serve effectively as a major instrument of stabilization, a view that was widespread among Fiscalists until very recently.[22]

Monetarists have challenged the interpretation of the 1930's and of the 1950's which played such a major role in shaping the stabilization theories of the Fiscalists; and their re-examination of the evidence leads them to conclude that the Fiscalists' earlier pessimism is unjustified, and that monetary policy can indeed play a major, and decisive, role in stabilization.[23] Monetarists have also challenged the Fiscalist stabilization theory and the key role assigned to the full-employment surplus. They question whether discretionary fiscal policy actions will affect private spending without a fairly long lag, whether these spending effects do come about very quickly, and whether temporary budget changes have effects that are dependable, and easily predictable. They question whether the multiplier theory and the econometric estimates of the multiplier adequately distinguishes between the *ceteris paribus* and *mutatis mutandis* fiscal effects; they also question whether the important priorities implied by the budget decisions—the determination of the relative size and the resources allocated to the public sector—should be constrained with short run stabilization goals. Taken together, these questions raise doubts whether discretionary fiscal policy can, in fact, serve effectively as a short run stabilization tool.

The Monetarist concludes that discretionary budgetary changes are not an efficient means for short run stabilization purposes, and that fiscal policy changes are likely to have permanent effects on the relative sizes of the private and public sectors. Accordingly, they stress the crucial importance of a stabilizing monetary policy. Monetarists do not deny that discretionary fiscal policy actions may affect aggregate demand in the short run, although their analysis of these effects may differ from the Fiscalist analysis. Perhaps the most fundamental difference between Monetarists and Fiscalists is in choosing those policies which are most likely to succeed in keeping the economy on a course of high employment with stable prices. Monetarists believe that stable monetary growth is the most effective policy for stabilizing the economy, while Fiscalists place their hopes on discretionary changes in the full-employment surplus.[24]

## Conclusion

This paper assesses the Monetarists' model of money, emphasizing those analytical aspects which differentiate it from the Fiscalists' monetary model. Although these two

[22] Although the stagnationist fears of the 1930's receded somewhat in the early fifties, the revival of monetary policy was interrupted when it appeared ineffective in stopping the mild inflations of the 1950's. Many Fiscalists concluded that the monetary policy was ineffective in dealing with mild inflations associated with wage or cost push, markup, administered price, demand shift, and sectoral inflation. The Fiscalist's interpretation of our recent history, as manifest in the early 1960's, seem to conclude that monetary policy was not only ineffective in the deep depression of the 1930's, but almost equally ineffective in dealing with the mild inflations experienced by the advanced industrialized countries in the 1950's. For a useful summary of these views see the Joint Economic Committee *Staff Report on Employment, Growth, and Price Level* (Washington, 1959).

[23] A recent study concludes with the following comments:

> A historical investigation of the past fifty years reveals that in every case where the monetary variable and the fiscal variable moved in opposite directions, economic activity moved in the direction of the monetary variable and opposite in direction to the fiscal variable. Every cyclical movement in the money stock since 1919 has been followed by a proportional cyclical movement in economic activity.
>
> Both the statistical results and the historical investigation provide strong support for the case that monetary influences have a significant impact on economic activity over the business cycle. An important implication of these results is that monetary policy should be given a central role in any economic stabilization program.

See M. W. Keran, "Monetary and Fiscal Influences on Economic Activity—The Historical Evidence", November 1969 *Review* Reserve Bank of St. Louis.

[24] The monetary lag surfaced in the 1950's before the relatively recent (post-1968 tax action) discovery of a possible similar lag in fiscal policy. Differences between Monetarists and Fiscalists based on, or at least presuming, the non-existence of a fiscal lag, may disappear in time. See J. M. Duesenberry, "Tactics and Targets of Monetary Policy" in *Controlling Monetary Aggregates.*

models are sometimes categorized in terms of "money matters" or "only money matters," this mnemonic classification does not highlight the analytical distinctiveness of their respective monetary theories. To obtain a better understanding of the Monetarists' model we also need to distinguish the money veil of theory and the extremely potent, and high-powered, money of stabilization policy, and between nominal money and the real money stock.

The monetary model (Quantity theory) of the Monetarists incorporates a theory of money, prices and interest rates that differs substantially from the liquidity preference analysis of interest rates of the Fiscalists. Monetarists have a monetary theory of the price level, a non-monetary theory of the (real) interest rate, and a theory relating rising (or high) market rates (nominal interest rates) to rising prices: they postulate, following Fisher, a sequence leading from monetary expansion to rising prices and high market rates; they distinguish, therefore, between rising rates and high rates, and between market rates and real (interest) rates; and they rationalize a rise in market rates (relative to real rates) by introducing a price expectation variable in their model to capture the impact of rising prices on nominal interest rates. The Fiscalists, in contrast, have a monetary theory of the interest rate, a non-monetary theory of the price level, and do not distinguish either between rising and high rates or between nominal and real rates: they assume that high (or rising) market rates reflect corresponding changes in real rates; and they associate the variability of market rates with volatility in real rates. The implication concerning the instability of the real economy is, in this sense, related to this particular analytical framework.[25]

The Monetarists' view of fiscal policy may also be somewhat misunderstood, because it is closely tied to the manner in which they calibrate and measure the posture of monetary policy. An action defined by Fiscalists as one of fiscal stimulus may also be defined by Monetarists as one of monetary stimulus, so that clear-cut discriminating tests of the two theories are not readily available. Thus, it is only when movements in the money stock and in the full-employment surplus go in opposite directions—as in 1966 and in 1968—that we get any real tests of their relative effects.

The Monetarist advocacy of stable monetary growth does not necessarily imply that discretionary fiscal policy actions have no short run aggregate demand effects. It is sufficient for Monetarists to argue that the effects of temporary budgetary changes are uncertain, that they have long and variable lags, that they are not superior (and may be inferior) to monetary actions in terms of effectiveness, and that budgetary changes should be instituted primarily for their important allocative effects. The post-1968 experiences, and the discovery that some fiscal effects may also be subject to a lag, should serve to re-open theoretical and policy discussions of the relative roles of Monetary and Fiscal policy in stabilization.

25 The income-expenditure theory of money, interest rates and prices may explain several of the troublesome features of recent stabilization policy: a tendency to use market interest rates as an indicator of monetary policy; a tendency to minimize the price level consequences of excessive monetary growth; a tendency to abstract from the impact of inflationary expectations on market interest rates; a tendency to treat nominal variables as if they were real quantities; and a tendency to explain the rising market interest rates in the U.S. since 1965 as reflecting an increased demand for money, and not as the result of accelerated growth in the monetary aggregates.

## C. *Contemporary Evidence*

# 7 THE ROLE OF THE MONEY SUPPLY IN BUSINESS CYCLES*

RICHARD G. DAVIS
*Federal Reserve Bank of New York*

Most, if not quite all, economists are agreed that the behavior of the quantity of money makes a significant difference in the behavior of the economy—with "money" usually defined to include currency in circulation plus private demand deposits, but sometimes to include commercial bank time deposits as well.[1] Most economists, for example, setting out to forecast next year's gross national product under the assumption that the money supply would grow by 4 per cent, would probably want to revise their figures if they were to change this assumption to a 2 per cent decrease.

In the past five to ten years, however, there has come into increasing prominence a group of economists who would like to go considerably beyond the simple assertion that the behavior of money is a significant factor influencing the behavior of the economy. It is not easy to characterize with any precision the views of this group of economists. As is perhaps to be expected where complex issues are involved, their statements about the importance of monetary behavior in determining the course of business activity encompass a variety of individual positions, positions which may themselves be undergoing change. Moreover these positions are rarely stated in quantitative terms. More frequently, the importance of money as a determinant of business conditions will be characterized as "by far the major factor," "the most important factor," "a primary factor," and by similar qualitative phrases inescapably open to various interpretations.

Of course as one moves from the stronger phrases to the weaker, one comes closer and closer to the view that money is simply "a significant factor," at which point it becomes virtually impossible to distinguish their views from those of the great majority of professional opinions. In order to bring a few of the issues into sharper focus, this article will take a look at some evidence for the "money supply" view of business fluctuations in one of its more extreme forms. Without necessarily implying that all the following positions are held precisely as stated by any single economist, an extreme form of the money supply view can perhaps be characterized somewhat as follows: The behavior of the rate of change of the money supply is the overriding determinant of fluctuations in business activity. Government spending, taxing policies, fluctuations in the rate of technological innovation, and similar matters have a relatively small or even negligible in-

* Reprinted from *Monthly Review*, Federal Reserve Bank of New York, vol. 50 (April, 1968), pp. 63–73, by permission of the author and the Federal Reserve Bank of New York.

[1] More rarely, other types of liquid assets such as mutual savings bank deposits are also included in the definition of money.

fluence on the short-run course of business activity. Hence, to the extent that it can control the money supply, a central bank, such as the Federal Reserve System, can control ups and downs in business activity. The influence of money on business operates with a long lag, however, and the timing of the influence is highly variable and unpredictable. Thus attempts to moderate fluctuations in business activity by varying the rate of growth of the money supply are likely to have an uncertain effect after an uncertain lag. They may even backfire, producing the very instability they are designed to cure. Consequently, the best policy for a central bank to follow is to maintain a steady rate of growth in the money supply, year in and year out, at a rate which corresponds roughly to the growth in the economy's productive capacity.

The implications of these views are obviously both highly important and strongly at variance with widely held beliefs. Thus they deny the direct importance of fiscal policy (except perhaps in so far as it may influence monetary policy), while they attribute to monetary policy a virtually determining role as regards business fluctuations. At the same time, they deny the usefulness of discretionary, countercyclical monetary policy. The issues involved are highly complex and cannot possibly be adequately treated in their entirety in a single article.[2] The present article, therefore, confines itself to examining the historical relationship between monetary cycles and cycles in general business. The article concludes that the relationship between these two kinds of cycles does not, in fact, provide any real support for the view that the behavior of money is the predominant determinant of fluctuations in business activity. Moreover, the historical relationship between cycles in money and in business cannot be used to demonstrate that monetary policy is, in its effects, so long delayed and so uncertain as to be an unsatisfactory countercyclical weapon.

The first section shows how proponents of the money supply view have measured cycles in money and examines the persistent tendency of turning points in monetary cycles, so measured, to lead turning points in general business activity. It argues that these leads do not necessarily point to a predominant causal influence of money on business. A second section suggests that the cyclical relationship of money and business activity may be as much a reflection of a reverse influence of business on money as it is of a direct causal influence running from money to business. A third section indicates why, for some periods at least, the tendency for cycles in money to lead cycles in business may reflect nothing more than the impact on money of a countercyclical monetary policy. Next, the relative amplitudes of monetary contractions and their associated business contractions are examined. Again it is argued that these relative amplitudes fail to provide any clear evidence for a predominant causal influence of money. A fifth section examines the timing of turning points in money and in business for evidence that the influence of money operates with so long and variable a lag as to make countercyclical monetary policy ineffective. A final section suggests that there may well be better ways to evaluate the causal influence of money on business than through the examination of past cyclical patterns.

## Cycles in Money and Cycles in Business Activity

As already implied, proponents of the money supply school have argued that the historical relationship between cycles in money and cycles in general business activity provides major support for their views on the causal importance of money in the business cycle. For the most part, these economists have delineated cycles in the money supply in terms of peaks and troughs in the percentage rate of change of money (usually including time deposits), while cycles in business have been defined in terms of peaks and troughs in the *level* of business activity as marked off, for instance, by the so-called "reference cycles" of the National Bureau of Economic

[2] Among the many interesting and relevant issues not discussed are the advantages and disadvantages of the money supply as an immediate target of monetary policy or as an indicator of the effects of policy, the proper definition of the money supply, and the nature and stability of the demand for money.

Research NBER).[3] They have argued that virtually without exception every cycle in the level of business activity over the past century of United States experience can be associated with a cycle in the rate of growth of the money supply. The exceptions that are observed occurred during and just after World War II—although the events of 1966-67 may also be interpreted as an exception, since an apparent cyclical decline in monetary growth was not followed by a recession but only by a very brief slowdown in the rate of business expansion.[4] The money supply school also finds that cycles in business activity have lagged behind the corresponding cycles in the rate of growth of the money supply, with business peaks and troughs thus following peaks and troughs in the rate of monetary change.

While the evidence supporting these generalizations is derived from about a century of United States data, the nature of the measurements and some of the problems of interpretation can be illustrated from the postwar experience represented in Chart 1. The chart shows monthly percentage changes in the money supply, defined here to include currency in the hands of the public plus commercial bank private demand and time deposits, on a seasonally adjusted daily average basis.[5] The shaded areas represent periods of business recession as determined by the NBER. The first point to note is the highly erratic nature of month-to-month movements in the rate of change of the money supply. Indeed, the reader might be excused if he found it difficult to see any clear-cut cyclical pattern in the chart. The erratic nature of the money series, which partly reflects short-run shifts of deposits between Treasury and private accounts, does make the precise dating of peaks and troughs in the money series somewhat arbitrary. This introduces a corresponding degree of arbitrariness in measuring timing relationships relative to turning points in business activity. Waiving this difficulty, however, peaks and troughs in the money series as dated in one well-known study of the problem are marked on the chart for the 1947-60 period.[6] As can be seen, each monetary peak occurs during the expansion phase of the business cycle and thus leads the peak in business. Similarly, there is a monetary trough marked during three of the four postwar recessions acknowledged by the NBER. A fourth monetary trough, however, in February 1960 occurs somewhat before the onset of recession three months later.

---

[3] See, for example, Milton Friedman and Anna J. Schwartz, "Money and Business Cycles", *Review of Economics and Statistics* (February 1963, supplement), pages 34–38. While the procedure of these economists in comparing percentage rates of growth of money with levels of business activity can certainly be defended, it is by no means obvious that this is the most appropriate approach, and there are many possible alternatives. Thus, for example, cycles in the rate of growth of money could be compared with cycles in the rate of growth, rather than the level, of business activity. For some purposes the choice among these alternatives makes a considerable difference, as is noted later in connection with measuring the length of the lags of business-cycle turning points relative to turning points in the monetary cycle.

[4] Granting the difficulties of dating specific cycle turning points for series as erratic as the rate of growth of the money supply, a peak (for the definition of money that includes time deposits) seems to have occurred in October 1965, with a trough in October 1966. While there was a slowdown in the rate of growth of business activity in the first half of 1967, there was clearly no business cycle peak corresponding to the peak in the money series. Indeed, the current dollar value of GNP moved ahead in the first two quarters of 1967, although at a reduced rate. The 1965-66 decline in the rate of growth in the money supply was relatively short (twelve months). In amplitude it was clearly among the milder declines, but it was nevertheless still nearly twice as steep as the mildest of past contractions in the rate of monetary growth (November 1951 to September 1953). In any case, the 1965-66 decline does appear to represent a specific cycle contraction for the rate of monetary change under the standard NBER definition. See Arthur F. Burns and Wesley C. Mitchell, *Measuring Business Cycles* (National Bureau of Economic Research, 1946), pages 55–66.

[5] While, as noted, many analysts would prefer to define the money supply to exclude commercial bank time deposits, such an exclusion would not materially affect the general picture, at least not for the period illustrated by the chart.

[6] The dates used are essentially those presented in Milton Friedman and Anna J. Schwartz, *op. cit.*, page 37, Table I. Minor modifications of the Friedman-Schwartz dates have been made when these seemed obviously dictated by revisions in the data subsequent to publication of their work.

**CHART 1** Changes in money supply plus time deposits (month-to-month percentage changes; compound annual rates). *Percentage changes are based on seasonally adjusted data. Shaded areas represent recession periods, according to National Bureau of Economic Research Chronology. (Source: Board of Governors of the Federal Reserve System.)*

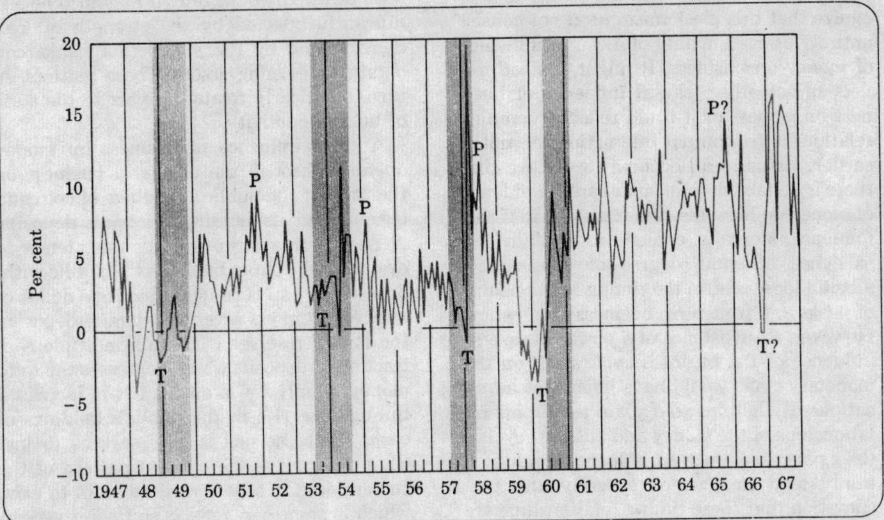


The leads of the peaks in the money series with respect to the subsequent peaks in business activity are, it should be emphasized, quite variable, ranging from twenty months to twenty-nine months for the period covered in the chart and from six months to twenty-nine months for the entire 1870 to 1961 period. The corresponding range of leads of money troughs relative to subsequent troughs in business cycles varies from three months to twelve months for the charted period and up to twenty-two months for the longer period.

The significance, if any, of these leads in assessing the importance of cycles in money in causing cycles in business is highly problematical. Firstly, chronological leads do not, of course, necessarily imply causation. It is perfectly possible, for example, to construct models of the economy in which money has *no* influence on business but which generate a consistent lead of peaks and troughs in the rate of growth of the money supply relative to peaks and troughs in general business activity.[7] Secondly, the extreme variability of the length of the leads would seem to suggest, if anything, the existence of factors other than money that can also exert an important influence on the timing of business peaks and troughs. Certainly even if a peak or trough in the rate of growth of the money supply could be identified around the time it occurred, this would be of very little, if any, help in predicting the timing of a subsequent peak or trough in business activity. Thirdly, there is a real question as to whether anything at all can be inferred from the historical record about the influence of money on business if, as is argued in the next section, there is an important reverse influence exerted by the business cycle on the monetary cycle itself.

## The Influence of Business on Money

Although the persistent tendency of cycles in monetary growth rates to lead business activity does not, as noted, necessarily imply a predominant causal influence of money on business, this tendency has nevertheless seemed to the money supply economists to be highly suggestive of such an influence. Certainly the consistency with which these

[7] See James Tobin, "Money and Income: Post Hoc Propter Hoc?" *Quarterly Journal of Economics,* May 1969.

leads show up in cycle after cycle is rather striking and does suggest that cycles in money and cycles in business are related by some mechanism, however loose and unreliable. Nevertheless, it is important to recognize that this mechanism need not consist entirely or even mainly of a causal influence of money on business. It might, instead, reflect principally a causal influence of business on money, or it could reflect a complex relationship of mutual interaction. As noted earlier, virtually all economists believe that there is, in fact, at least *some* causal influence of money on business, and it may be that this influence alone is enough to explain the existence of some degree of consistency, albeit a loose one, in the timing relationships of peaks and troughs in business and money. However, the existence of a powerful reverse influence of the business cycle itself on the monetary cycle would have important implications. By helping to explain the timing relationships of the money and business cycles, the existence of such an influence would certainly tend to question severely any presumption that these timing relationships are themselves evidence for money as the predominant cause of business cycles.

There are, in fact, a number of important ways in which changing business conditions can affect, and apparently have affected, the rate of growth of the money supply over the 100 years or so covered by the available data. First, the state of business influences decisions by the monetary authorities to supply reserves and to take other actions likely to affect the money supply—as is discussed in detail in the next section. Business conditions can also have a direct impact on the money supply, however. For example, they may affect the balance of payments and the size of gold imports or exports. These gold movements, in turn, may affect the size of the monetary base—the sum of currency in the hands of the public and reserves in the banking system. Various official policies have tended to reduce or offset this particular influence of business on money, but at least prior to the creation of the Federal Reserve System it may have been of considerable significance.

Second, business conditions may influence the money stock through an influence on the volume of member bank borrowings at the Federal Reserve. While the size of such borrowings is, of course, importantly conditioned by the terms under which loans to member banks are made, including the level of the discount rate, it may also be significantly affected by the strength of loan demand and by the yields that banks can obtain on earning assets. These matters, in turn, are clearly related in part to the state of business activity.

A third influence of business on money operates through the effects of business on the ratio of the public's holdings of coin and currency to its holdings of bank deposits. A rise in this ratio, for example, tends to drain reserves from banks as the public withdraws coin and currency. Since one dollar of reserves supports several dollars of deposits, the loss of reserves leads to a multiple contraction of deposits which depresses the total money supply by more than it is increased through the rise in the public's holdings of cash. While no one is very sure as to just what determines the cyclical pattern of the currency ratio, a pattern does seem to exist which in some way reflects shifts in the composition of payments over the business cycle as well as, in the historically important case of banking panics, fluctuations in the public's confidence in the banks themselves.[8]

A final avenue of influence of business on money is through the influence of business conditions on the ratio of bank excess reserves to deposits. When the ratio of excess reserves to deposits is relatively high, other things equal, the money supply will be relatively low since banks will not be fully utilizing the deposit-creating potential of the supply of reserves available to them. Business conditions can affect the reserve ratio in various ways. Thus they can influence bank desires to hold excess reserves through variations in the strength of current and prospective loan demand, through variations in the yields on the earning assets of banks, and through variations in banker expectations.

[8] It might be noted that while the Federal Reserve has for many years routinely offset the reserve effects of short-term movements in coin and currency, such as occur around holidays, for example, the ratio of coin and currency in the hands of the public to deposits has apparently continued to show some mild fluctuations of a cyclical nature.

When business is rising, loan demand is apt to be strengthening, yields on earning assets are apt to be rising, and banker confidence in the future is likely to be increasing. Thus excess reserves are apt to decline, with the reserve ratio rising and thereby exerting an upward influence on the money supply.

The influence of business on money—acting through its influence on the growth of the monetary base, the currency ratio, and the excess reserve ratio—is extremely complex and is not necessarily stable over time. The cyclical behavior of the monetary base and the currency and reserve ratios have in fact varied from cycle to cycle. Moreover the relative importance of these three factors in influencing the cyclical behavior of money has varied over the near 100-year period for which data are available. In part, these variations have reflected the effects of the creation and evolution of the Federal Reserve System. A detailed examination of the behavior of the monetary base, the currency and reserve ratios, and the role of business conditions in fixing their cyclical patterns is beyond the scope of this article. Recently, however, a very thorough analysis of the problem has been done for the NBER by Professor Phillip Cagan of Columbia University. He finds that "although the cyclical behavior of the three determinants [of the money stock] is not easy to interpret, it seems safe to conclude that most of their short-run variations are closely related to cyclical fluctuations in economic activity. . . . Such effects provide a plausible explanation of recurring cycles in the money stock whether or not the reverse effect occurred."[9]

The fact that the business cycle itself has an important role in determining the course of the monetary cycle seriously undermines the argument that the timing relationships of monetary cycles and business cycles point to a dominant influence of money on business. By the same token, ample room is left for the possibility that many other factors, such as fiscal policy, fluctuations in business investment demand, including those related to changes in technology, fluctuation in exports, and replacement cycles in consumer durable goods, may also exert important independent influences on the course of business activity.

## Monetary Policy and the Cyclical Behavior of Money

One important, though perhaps indirect, influence of business on money requires special mention, namely the influence it exerts via monetary policy. The relevance of monetary policy to the behavior of monetary growth during the business cycle was perhaps especially clear during the period beginning around 1952 and extending to the very early 1960's. In this period, policy was more or less able to concentrate on the requirements of stabilizing the business cycle relatively (but not entirely) unimpeded by considerations of war finance, the balance of payments, and possible strains on particular sectors of the capital markets. The ultimate aim of stabilizing the business cycle is, of course, to prevent or moderate recessions and to forestall or limit inflation and structural imbalances during periods of advance. The tools available to the Federal Reserve, however, such as open market operations and discount rate policy, influence employment and the price level only through complex and indirect routes. Hence, in the short run, policy must be formulated in terms of variables which respond more directly to the influence of the System. Some possibilities include, in addition to the rate of growth of the money supply, the growth of bank credit, conditions in the money market and the behavior of short-term interest rates, and the marginal reserve position of banks as measured, for example, by the level of free reserves or of member bank borrowings from the Federal Reserve. It is clear that the money supply need not always be the immediate objective of monetary policy, and indeed it was not by any means always such during the 1950's. Given this fact, the behavior of the rate of growth of the money supply during the period cannot be assumed to be simply and directly the result of monetary policy decisions alone.

Nevertheless, it is clear that the current and prospective behavior of business strongly influenced monetary policy decisions, given the primary aim of moderating the cycle, and that these decisions, in turn, influenced the

---

[9] Phillip Cagan, *Determinants and Effects of Changes in the Stock of Money, 1875–1960* (National Bureau of Economic Research, 1965), page 261.

behavior of the rate of growth of the money supply. Thus, for example, as recoveries proceeded and threatened to generate inflationary pressures, monetary policy tightened to counteract these pressures. Regardless of what particular variable the System sought to control—whether the money supply itself, conditions in the money market, or bank marginal reserve positions—the movement of any of these variables in the direction of tightening would, taken by itself, tend to exert a slowing influence on the rate of monetary expansion. In this way, the firming of monetary policy in the presence of cumulating expansionary forces would no doubt help to explain the tendency of the rate of monetary growth to peak out well in advance of peaks in the business cycle. Similarly, the easing of policy to counteract a developing recession would help to produce an upturn in the rate of monetary growth in advance of troughs in business activity.

In addition to the feedback from business conditions to policy decisions and thence from policy to the money supply, there are circumstances in which developments in the economy can react on the money supply even with monetary policy unchanged. Consider, for example, a situation in which the focus of policy is on maintaining an unchanged money market "tone"—a phrase that has been interpreted to imply, among other things, some rough stabilization of the average level of certain short-term interest rates such as the rate on Federal funds. Now a speedup in the rate of growth in economic activity would ordinarily accelerate the growth of demand for bank credit and deposits. This, in turn, would normally result in upward pressure on the money market and on money market interest rates. Maintaining the stability in money market tone called for by such a policy would require, however, under the assumed circumstances, supplying more reserves to the banks in order to offset the upward pressures on money market rates. Thus, with unchanged policy, an acceleration in the rate of business expansion could generate an acceleration in the rate of growth of reserves, and thence in the money supply. Similarly, a tapering-off in the rate of business expansion could, in these circumstances, generate a tapering-off in the rate of monetary expansion well before an absolute peak in business activity occurred. It should be emphasized that unchanged monetary policy could be perfectly consistent with countercyclical objectives under these conditions if the slowdown (or speedup) in the rate of business advance either were expected to be temporary or were regarded as a healthy development.

The reaction of monetary policy to changing business conditions and the reaction of the money supply to monetary policy undoubtedly help explain the tendency of peaks and troughs in the rate of growth of the money supply to precede peaks and troughs in the level of economic activity during this period. The resulting monetary leads, however, cannot then be interpreted as demonstrating a dependence of cycles in business on cycles in monetary growth. These leads would very likely have existed even if the influence of money on business were altogether negligible.

### Severity of Cyclical Movements

Apart from matters of cyclical timing, some proponents of the money supply school have also regarded the relationship between the severity of cyclical movements in money and the severity of associated cyclical movements in business as suggesting a predominant causal role for money. They argue, perhaps with some plausibility, that, if the behavior of money were the predominant determinant of business fluctuations, the relative sizes of cyclical movements in business and roughly contemporaneous cyclical movements in money should be highly correlated. For example, the severity of a cyclical decline in the rate of growth of the money supply should be closely related to the severity of the associated business recession or depression. The evidence for such a correlation, however, is actually rather mixed.

Cyclical contractions in the monetary growth rate can be measured by computing the decline in the rate of monetary growth from its peak value to its trough value.[10] On the basis of these computations, monetary contractions can be ranked in order of severity. Similarly, the severity of business

[10] Generally, three-month averages centered on the specific cycle turning point months have been used to reduce the weight given to especially sharp changes in the peak and trough months themselves.

contractions can be ranked by choosing some index of business activity and computing its decline during each business contraction recognized and dated by the NBER. If the resulting rankings of monetary contractions are compared with the rankings of their associated business declines for eighteen nonwar business contractions from 1882 to 1961, the size of monetary and business contractions proves to be moderately highly correlated.[11] It turns out, however, that this correlation depends entirely on the experience of especially severe cyclical contractions. Among the eighteen business contractions experienced during the period, six are generally recognized as having been particularly deep. They include three pre-World War I episodes and the contractions of 1920-21, 1929-33, and 1937-38. In the latter three declines, the Federal Reserve Board's industrial production index fell by 32 per cent, 52 per cent, and 32 per cent, respectively, compared with a decline of only 18 per cent for the next largest contraction covered by the production index (1923-24).

These six most severe contractions were in fact associated with the six most severe cyclical declines in the rate of growth of the money supply, though the rankings within the six do not correspond exactly. As was argued earlier, business conditions themselves exert a reverse influence on the money supply, and it seems probable that particularly severe business declines may tend to accentuate the accompanying monetary contractions. Thus, for example, the wholesale default of loans and sharp drops in the value of securities that accompanied the 1929-33 depression helped lay the groundwork for the widespread bank failures of that period. These failures were in part caused by, but also further encouraged, large withdrawals of currency from the banking system by a frightened public. By contracting the reserve base of the banking system, in turn, these withdrawals resulted in multiple contractions of the deposit component of the money supply.

Developments of this type help to explain the association of major monetary contractions with major depressions but do not seem to account fully for it.[12] Thus it may be that catastrophic monetary developments are in fact a pre-condition for catastrophic declines in business activity. In any case, for more moderate cyclical movements, the association between the severity of monetary contractions and the severity of business contractions breaks down completely. There is virtually no correlation whatever between the relative rankings of the twelve nonmajor contractions in the 1882-1961 period and the rankings of the associated declines in the rate of monetary growth.[13] Certainly this finding does not support the theory that changes in the rate of monetary growth are of predominant importance in determining business activity.

## Measuring Lags in the Influence of Money on Business

Despite their belief in the crucial role of the money supply in determining the cyclical course of business activity, some members of the money supply school nevertheless argue, as suggested at the beginning of this article, that discretionary monetary policy is a clumsy and even dangerous countercyclical weapon. The starting point for this view is again the fact that peaks and troughs in the level of business activity tend to lag behind peaks and troughs in the rate of change of the money supply—in particular the fact that these lags have tended to be quite long on average and highly variable from one cycle to another. Thus long average lags of about sixteen months for peaks and twelve months for troughs have suggested to these economists that the impact of monetary policy is correspondingly delayed, with actions taken to moderate a boom, for example, having their primary impact during the subsequent recession when precisely the opposite influence is needed. Moreover, the great variability from cycle to cycle of the lags as

[11] The Spearman rank correlation, for which satisfactory significance tests apparently do not exist when medium-sized samples ($10 < n < 20$) are involved, is .70. The Kendall rank correlation coefficient, adjusted for ties, is .53 and is significant at the 1 per cent level. Rankings of business contractions are based on the Moore index. See Friedman and Schwartz, *op. cit.*, Table 3, page 39.

[12] See Phillip Cagan, *op. cit.*, pages 262–68.

[13] The Kendall coefficient for the twelve nonmajor contractions is a statistically insignificant .03, while the corresponding Spearman coefficient is .01.

measured by the money supply school has suggested that the timing of the impact of monetary policy is similarly variable and unpredictable. For this reason, they argue, it will be impossible for the monetary authorities to gauge when their policy actions will take effect and therefore whether these actions will turn out to have been appropriate.

It is true, of course, that monetary policy affects the economy with a lag. The full effects of open market purchases on bank deposits and credit, for example, require time to work themselves out. More important, additional time must elapse before businessmen and consumers adjust their spending plans to the resulting changes in the financial environment. For this reason, the pattern of spending at any given time will to some degree reflect the influence of financial conditions as they existed several months or quarters earlier. Hence it is certainly possible, for example, that some of the effects of a restrictive monetary policy would continue to be felt during a recession even though the current posture of monetary policy were quite expansionary.

The fact that such lags do exist, however, shows only that monetary policy cannot be expected to produce immediate results. Like fiscal policy, its effectiveness depends in part on the ability to anticipate business trends so that policy actions taken today will be appropriate to tomorrow's conditions. Of course the longer the lags in the effects of policy prove to be, the further out in time must such anticipations be carried and the greater is the risk that policy actions will prove to be inappropriate. Moreover, if the lengths of the lags are highly variable and thus perhaps unpredictable, the risks of inappropriate policy decisions are obviously increased and the need for continuous adjustments in policy is apt to arise.

The timing of cycles in money and cycles in business, however, provides absolutely no basis for believing that the lags in the effects of monetary policy are so long or so variable as to vitiate the effectiveness of a countercyclical policy. First, there are many reasons for doubting that the lag in the effects of monetary policy should be measured by comparing the timing relationships between cyclical turns in money and in business. It has been argued, for example, that other variables more directly under the control of policy makers, such as member bank nonborrowed reserves, or variables more clearly related to business decisions, such as interest rates, must also be taken into account. Yet, even if the behavior of the money supply be accepted as the indicator of policy, there are many alternative ways in which "the lag" between monetary and business behavior can be measured, and it makes a great deal of difference which measure is used. If, for example, the rate of change in the money supply is replaced by deviations in the level of the money supply from its long-run trend, the average lag between monetary peaks so measured and peaks in general business apparently shrinks from the sixteen months previously cited to a mere five months.[14] Alternatively, it can be plausibly argued that the appropriate measure is the lag between the rate of change in the money supply, and the *rate of change,* rather than the level, of some measure of business activity such as gross national product (GNP) or industrial production. When peaks and troughs for money and business are compared on this basis, the lead of money over business appears to be quite short.[15] The near simultaneity, in most cases, of peaks and troughs in the rates of change of the money supply and of GNP during the post-World War II period can be seen in Chart 2. To be sure, movements in the two series are quite irregular, so that the decision on whether to treat a particular date as a turning point is sometimes rather arbitrary. Nevertheless, the lead of peaks and troughs in the rate of growth of money over peaks and troughs in the rate of growth of GNP appears to average about one quarter or less.[16]

---

[14] This estimate is presented by Milton Friedman in "The Lag Effect in Monetary Policy", *Journal of Political Economy,* October 1961, page 456.

[15] See John Kareken and Robert Solow, "Lags in Monetary Policy", *Stabilization Policies* (Commission on Money and Credit, 1963), pages 21–24.

[16] When quarterly dollar changes in the money supply are correlated with quarterly dollar changes in GNP experimenting with various lags, the highest correlation is achieved with GNP lagged two quarters behind money. (For the 1947–II to 1967–III period the $R^2$ is .34.) The correlation with a one quarter lag is almost exactly as high, however ($R^2$ = .33). When percentage changes in the two series are used instead, the correlation virtually disappears, no matter what lag is used.

**CHART 2** Changes in gross national product and in money supply plus time deposits (quarter-to-quarter percentage changes; compound annual rates). *Percentage changes are based on seasonally adjusted data. (Sources: Board of Governors of the Federal Reserve System; United States Department of Commerce.)*

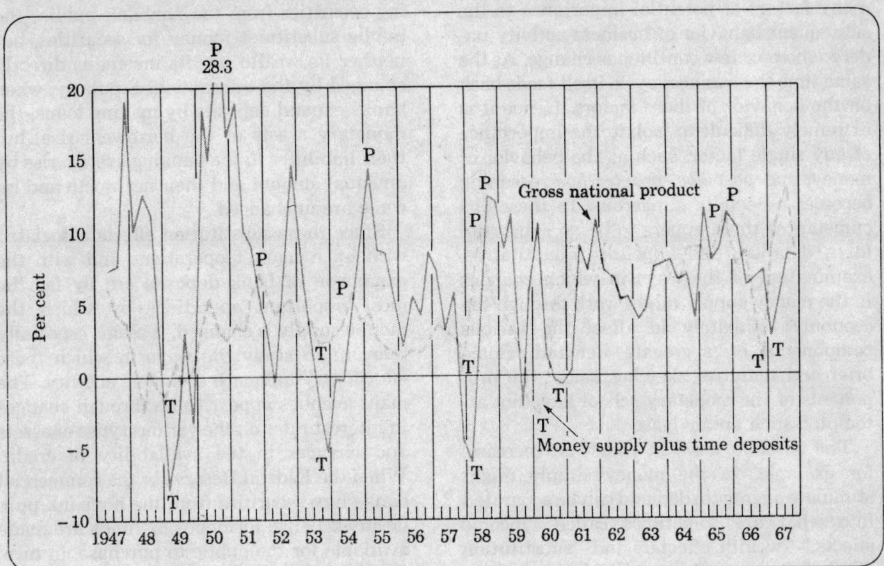


The point of these various comparisons is not to prove that the lag in monetary policy is necessarily either very long or very short, but rather to illustrate how hard it is to settle the matter through the kind of evidence that has been offered by the money supply school. Similar difficulties, as well as others, beset attempts to measure the *variability* of the lag in the influence of money on business by comparisons of cyclical peaks and troughs in the two. However the turning points are measured, the resulting estimates may seriously overstate the true variability of the lag in the influence of money on business. The reason is that observed differences from cycle to cycle in the timing of turning points in money relative to turning points in business are bound to reflect a number of factors over and beyond any variability in the influence of money on business.[17] These "other" sources of variability include purely statistical matters such as errors in the data and the arbitrariness involved in assigning precise dates to turning points in money and in business. More fundamentally, the fact that there exists a reverse influence of business on money, an influence that is probably uneven from one cycle to the next, imparts a potentially serious source of variability to the observed lags. Moreover, if there are important influences on the general level of business activity other than the behavior of money, these factors would also increase the variability of the observed timing relationships between turning points in money and in business. Taking all these possibilities into account, it seems fair to say that whatever the true variability in the impact of money on business, its size is overstated when it is measured in terms of the variability of the lags in cyclical turning points.

[17] Other sources of variability are discussed in some detail by Thomas Mayer in "The Lag in the Effect of Monetary Policy: Some Criticisms", *Western Economic Journal* (September 1967), pages 335–42.

## Ways in Which Money May Influence Business

If there is a broad conclusion to be drawn from a study of the historical pattern of relationships between cycles in money and cycles in business, it is that there are distinct limits to what can be learned about the influence of money on business from this kind of statistical analysis. Perhaps this should not be surprising. During the business cycle many factors of potential importance to the subsequent behavior of business activity undergo more or less continuous change. At the same time the business cycle itself feeds back on the behavior of these factors. Hence it is extremely difficult to isolate the importance of any single factor, such as the behavior of money, and *post hoc, propter hoc* reasoning becomes especially dangerous. In these circumstances there appers to be no substitute for a detailed, and hopefully quantitative, examination of the ways in which changes in the money supply might work through the economy ultimately to affect the various components of aggregate demand. Some brief and tentative sketches aside, the proponents of the monetary school have not attempted such an analysis.

The possible ways in which an increase, for example, in the money supply might stimulate aggregate demand can be separated into what are sometimes called "income effects," "wealth effects," and "substitution effects." Income effects exist when the same developments that produce an increase in the quantity of money also add directly to current income. Examples would be increases in bank reserves and deposits resulting from domestically mined gold or an export surplus. Similarly, a wealth effect occurs when a process increasing the money supply also increases the net worth of the private sector of the economy. A Treasury deficit financed by a rundown of Treasury deposit balances might be regarded as an example of such a process, since the resulting buildup of private deposits would represent an increase in private wealth.

Far more important than the income or wealth effects in the present-day United States economy are substitution effects such as result when the Federal Reserve engages in open market operations and banks expand loans and investments.[18] When the Federal Reserve buys Government securities from the nonbank public, the public of course acquires deposits and gives up the securities. There is no direct change in the public's net worth position,[19] or in its income; rather there is a substitution of money for securities in the public's balance sheet. The same is true when the banks expand the money supply by buying securities from the nonbank public: the public substitutes money for securities, but neither its wealth nor its income is directly changed by the transaction. Similarly, when banks expand deposits by making loans, the monetary assets of the borrowers rise, but their liabilities to the banking system rise by an equal amount and their net worth and income are unchanged.

Since these substitution effects associated with open market operations and with the expansion of bank deposits are by far the most important operations by which the money supply is changed, it seems especially relevant to study the ways in which these effects may influence economic activity. The main avenues appear to be through changes in interest rates on the various types of assets and changes in the availability of credit. When the Federal Reserve or the commercial banks buy securities from the nonbank public in exchange for deposits, funds are made available for the public to purchase, in turn, a wide variety of private securities such as mortgages, corporate bonds, or bankers' acceptances.[20] The increased demand for these

[18] These substitution effects are sometimes also known as "portfolio balance" or "liquidity" effects.

[19] This statement has to be modified to the extent that the Federal Reserve's buying activity bids up the market value of the public's holdings of Government securities. The significance of this wealth effect is probably minimal and is further limited in its consequences by the tendency of many holders to value Governments at original purchase price or at par rather than at current market value.

[20] The newly created deposits may of course in principle be used immediately to buy goods rather than financial assets, thus tending directly to stimulate business activity. Even in this case, however, the effects of the money-creating operations work through and depend upon reactions to interest rates. When the Federal Reserve or the commercial banks enter the market to buy securities, their bids add to total market demand, making market prices for securities higher (and yields lower) than they otherwise would have been. Indeed it is these relatively higher prices (lower yields) that induce the nonbank public to give up securities in exchange for deposits. If the deposits are in fact immediately used to purchase goods, then the process can be regarded as one in which lower market interest rates on securities stemming from bids by the Federal Reserve or the commercial banks have

securities tends to push rates on them down. And with borrowing costs down, business firms may be induced to expand outlays on plant and equipment or inventory while consumers may increase spending on new homes. In most cases, the effects of lower interest rates on capital spending probably stem from the fact that external financing has become cheaper. In some cases, however, lower market yields on outstanding government and private securities might induce business holders to sell such assets in order to purchase higher yielding capital goods and thus, in effect, to make direct substitution of physical capital for financial assets in their "portfolios." Finally, lower interest rates on securities may reduce consumer incentives to acquire and hold financial assets while tempting them to make more use of consumer credit, thereby reducing saving out of current income and increasing consumption purchases.[21]

With regard to bank lending, open market purchases of Government securities increase bank reserves and may ease the terms on which banks are willing to make loans. Changes in lending terms other than interest rates, which include repayment procedures, compensating balance requirements, and the maximum amount a bank is willing to lend to a borrower of given credit standing, are often bracketed as changes in "credit availability." Such changes are regarded by many analysts as being more important influences on many types of spending than are changes in interest rates. Moreover, changes in credit availability related in part to changes in the money supply are not confined to lending by commercial banks, as was dramatically illustrated in 1966 with regard to nonbank mortgage lenders. In any case, an increased availability of funds permits and encourages potential borrowers to increase their loan liabilities, thereby providing funds which can be used to build up financial assets (perhaps mainly money market instruments) or to purchase physical assets in the form of business capital goods, inventories, or consumer durables. Stepped-up purchases of financial assets add to downward pressures on interest rates, stimulating spending through the processes already described, while additional demand for physical assets stimulates business activity directly.

Studies of the influence of changes in interest rates and the availability of credit on spending in the various sectors of the economy have appeared with increasing frequency in the post-World War II period, especially within the past few years. Some of these studies have taken the form of interviews of businessmen and consumers with regard to the influence of credit cost and availability conditions on their spending decisions. Other studies have employed modern statistical and computer technology in an attempt to extract such information from data on past behavior.[22] With regard to spending on housing, there has been general agreement that the cost and availability of credit are highly important. A number of studies have also found varying degrees of influence on business spending for plant and equipment

induced the public to give up securities in exchange for goods. The extent to which such switching will occur obviously depends upon the sensitivity to interest rates of business and consumer demands for goods.

21 While there is little general agreement that such direct effects on consumption are important, a recent study of the problem has in fact found a significant influence of interest rates on consumer demand for automobiles and other durables. (See Michael J. Hamburger, "Interest Rates and the Demand for Consumer Durable Goods", *American Economic Review,* December 1967.) In general, proponents of the monetary school feel that analyses of the role of interest rates in consumer demand undertaken to date have neglected to take into account certain important factors. In particular, they think that the most relevant interest rates may not be the ones usually studied, namely the rates on financial instruments, but rather the interest rates "implicit" in the prices of the durable goods themselves —i.e., where the value of the services yielded by a consumer durable, such as an auto or a washing machine, is treated as analogous to the coupon or dividend yielded by a bond or stock. The obvious difficulties of defining and measuring the value of such services have probably been responsible for the notable dearth of research into this possibility, however, and the issue must be regarded as completely unsettled.

22 For a summary of some of these studies, see Michael J. Hamburger, "The Impact of Monetary Variables: A Selected Survey of the Recent Empirical Literature" (Federal Reserve Bank of New York, July 1967). Copies of this paper are available on request from Publications Services, Division of Administrative Services, Board of Governors of the Federal Reserve System, Washington, D.C. 20551.

and for inventories as well as on consumer spending for durable goods such as autos and appliances. All these studies, however, have also found factors other than cost and availability of credit to be highly important. Moreover, a large degree of disagreement exists with regard to the exact quantitative importance of the financial factors.

Given the serious technical problems that surround these studies, major areas of disagreement are virtually certain to exist for some time to come. Nevertheless, studies of the type referred to here appear to offer the hope at least that firmly grounded and widely accepted conclusions on the importance of money in the business cycle may ultimately be reached. Of particular interest are large-scale econometric models which attempt to provide quantitative estimates of the timing and magnitude of the effects of central bank actions on the money supply and other financial magnitudes and the subsequent effects, in turn, of these variables on each of the various major components of aggregate demand. One such model is currently under construction by members of the Federal Reserve Board staff in cooperation with members of the Economics Department of the Massachusetts Institute of Technology.[23] Granting the major technical problems still unresolved, projects of this kind appear promising as a means of eventually tracking down the importance of money in explicit, quantitative terms.

---

[23] Some preliminary results of this work are discussed in "The Federal Reserve-MIT Econometric Model" by Frank deLeeuw and Edward Gramlich, *Federal Reserve Bulletin* (January 1968), pages 9–40.

# 8 | THE ROLE OF MONEY AND MONETARY POLICY*

KARL BRUNNER
*The Ohio State University*

The development of monetary analysis in the past decade has intensified the debate concerning the role of money and monetary policy. Extensive research fostered critical examinations of the Federal Reserve's traditional descriptions of policy and of the arrangements governing policymaking. Some academic economists and others attribute the cyclical fluctuations of monetary growth and the persistent problem concerning the proper interpretation of monetary policy to the established procedures of monetary policy and the conceptions traditionally guiding policymakers.

The critique of established policy procedures, which evolved from this research into questions concerning the monetary mechanism, is derived from a body of monetary theory referred to in this paper as the Monetarist position. Three major conclusions have emerged from the hypotheses put forth. First, monetary impulses are a major factor accounting for variations in output, employment and prices. Second, movements in the money stock are the most reliable measure of the thrust of monetary impulses. Third, the behavior of the monetary authorities dominates movements in the money stock over business cycles.

A response to the criticisms of existing monetary policy methods was naturally to be expected and is welcomed. Four articles which defend present policy procedures have appeared during the past few years in various Federal Reserve publications.[1] These articles comprise a countercritique which argues that monetary impulses are neither properly measured nor actually transmitted by the money stock. The authors reject the Monetarist thesis that monetary impulses are a chief factor determining variations in economic activity, and they contend that cyclical fluctuations of monetary growth cannot be attributed to the behavior of the Federal Reserve authorities. These fluctuations are claimed to result primarily from the behavior of commercial banks and the public.

The ideas and arguments put forth in these articles deserve close attention. The controversy defined by the critique of policy in professional studies and the countercritique appearing in Federal Reserve publications bears on issues of fundamental importance to public policy. Underlying all the fashionable words and phrases is the fundamental question: What is the role of monetary policy and what are the requirements of rational policymaking?

* Reprinted from *Review,* Federal Reserve Bank of St. Louis, vol. 50 (July, 1968), pp. 9–24, by permission of the author and the Federal Reserve Bank of St. Louis.

[1] Lyle Gramley and Samuel Chase, "Time Deposits in Monetary Analysis," Federal Reserve *Bulletin,* October 1965 [reprinted in this volume]. John H. Kareken, "Commercial Banks and the Supply of Money: A Market Determined Demand Deposit Rate," Federal Reserve *Bulletin,* October 1967. J. A. Cacy, "Alternative Approaches to the Analysis of the Financial Structure, *Monthly Review,* Federal Reserve Bank of Kansas City, March 1968. Richard G. Davis, "The Role of the Money Supply in Business Cycles," *Monthly Review,* Federal Reserve Bank of New York, April 1968 [reprinted in this volume].

The following sections discuss the major aspects of the countercritique. These rejoinders may contribute to a better understanding of the issues, and the resulting clarification may remove some unnecessary disputes. Even though the central contentions of the controversy will remain, the continuous articulation of opposing points of view plays a vital role in the search for greater understanding of the monetary process.

### A Summary of the Countercritique

The four articles relied on two radically different groups of arguments. Gramley-Chase, Kareken and Cacy exploit the juxtaposition "New View versus Traditional View" as the central idea guiding their countercritique. The analytical framework developed by the critique is naturally subsumed for this purpose under the "Traditional View" label. On the other hand, Davis uses the analytical framework developed by the critique in order to organize his arguments.

Gramley-Chase describe their general argument in the following words:

> (New) developments have reaffirmed the bankers' point of view that deposits are attracted, not created, as textbooks suggest. In this new environment, growth rates of deposits have become more suspect than ever as indicators of the conduct of monetary policy. . . . A framework of analysis [is required] from which the significance of time deposits and of changing time deposits can be deduced. Traditional methods of monetary analysis are not well suited to this task. The "New View" in monetary economics provides a more useful analytical framework. In the new view, banks—like other financial institutions—are considered as suppliers of financial claims for the public to hold, and the public is given a significant role in determining the total amount of bank liabilities. . . . Traditional analysis . . . fails to recognize that substitution between time deposits and securities may be an important source of pro-cyclical variations in the stock of money even in the face of countercyclical central bank policy.[2]

This general argument guided the construction of an explicit model designed to emphasize the role of the public's and the banks' behavior in the determination of the money stock, bank credit and interest rates.

Kareken's paper supplements the Gramley-Chase arguments. He finds "the received money supply theory" quite inadequate. His paper is designed to improve monetary analysis by constructing a theory of an individual bank as a firm. This theory is offered as an explanation of a bank's desired balance sheet position. It also appears to form the basis of a model describing the interaction of the public's and the banks' behavior in the joint determination of the money stock, bank credit and interest rates. The whole development emphasizes somewhat suggestively the importance of the public's and banks' behavior in explanations of monetary growth. It is also designed to undermine the empirical hypotheses advanced by the Monetarist position. This is achieved by means of explicit references to specific and "obviously desirable" features of the model presented.

Cacy's article develops neither an explicit framework nor a direct critique of the basic propositions advanced by the Monetarist thesis. However, he provides a useful summary of the general position of the countercritique. The Monetarist analysis is conveniently subsumed by Cacy under a "Traditional View" which is juxtaposed to a "New View" of monetary mechanisms: "The new approach argues . . . that there is no essential difference between the manner in which the liabilities of banks and nonbank financial institutions are determined. Both types of institutions are subject in the same way to the portfolio decisions of the public."[3] The new approach is contrasted with the Traditional View, which "obscures the important role played by the public and overstates the role played by the central bank in the determination of the volume of money balances."[4] The general comparison developed by Cacy suggests quite clearly to the reader that the Traditional View allegedly espoused by the Monetarist position cannot match the "realistic sense" of the New View advocated by the countercritique.

In the context of the framework developed by the critique, Davis questions some basic propositions of the Monetarist position:

> In the past five to ten years, however, there has come into increasing prominence a group of

[2] Gramley-Chase, pp. 1380, 1381, 1393.

[3] Cacy, pp. 5 & 7.

[4] Ibid., p. 7.

economists who would like to go considerably beyond the simple assertion that the behavior of money is a significant factor influencing the behavior of the economy. . . . In order to bring a few of the issues into sharper focus, this article will take a look at some evidence for the "money supply" view. . . .
It confines itself to examining the historical relationship between monetary cycles and cycles in general business. The article concludes that the relationship between these two kinds of cycles does not, in fact, provide any real support for the view that the behavior of money is the predominant determinant of fluctuations in business activity. Moreover, the historical relationship between cycles in money and in business cannot be used to demonstrate that monetary policy is, in its effects, so long delayed and so uncertain as to be an unsatisfactory countercyclical weapon.[5]

## An Examination of the Issues

A careful survey of the countercritique yielded the following results. The Gramley-Chase, Kareken, and Cacy papers parade the New View in order to question the status of empirical theories used by the Monetarist critique in its examination of monetary policy. The Davis paper questions quite directly, on the other hand, the existence and relevance of the evidence in support of the Monetarist position, and constitutes a direct assault on the Monetarist critique. The others constitute an indirect assault which attempts to devalue the critique's analysis, and thus to destroy its central propositions concerning the role of money and monetary policy.

The indirect assault on the Monetarist position by Gramley-Chase, Kareken and Cacy requires a clarification concerning the nature of the New View. A program of analysis must be clearly distinguished from a research strategy and an array of specific conjectures.[6] All three aspects are usually mixed together in a general description. It is important to understand, however, that neither research strategy nor specific empirical conjectures are logical implications of the general program. The explicit separation of the three aspects is crucial for a proper assessment of the New View.

Section A examines some general characteristics of the countercritique's reliance on the New View. It shows the New View to consist of a program acceptable to all economists, a research strategy rejected by the Monetarist position, and an array of specific conjectures advanced without analytical or empirical substantiation. Also, not a single paper of the countercritique developed a relevant assessment of the Monetarist's empirical theories or central propositions.

In Sections B and C detailed examinations of specific conjectures centered on rival explanations of cyclical fluctuations of monetary growth are presented. The direct assault on the Monetarist position by Davis is discussed in some detail in Section D. This section also states the crucial propositions of the Monetarist thesis in order to clarify some aspects of this position. This reformulation reveals that the reservations assembled by Davis are quite innocuous. They provide no analytical or empirical case against the Monetarist thesis. Conjectures associated with the interpretation of monetary policy (the "indicator problem") are presented in Section E.

### *A. The New View*

The countercritique has apparently been decisively influenced by programmatic elaborations originally published by Gurley-Shaw and James Tobin.[7] The program is most faithfully reproduced by Cacy, and it also shaped the arguments guiding the model construction by Kareken and Gramley-Chase. The New View, as a program, is a sensible response to a highly unsatisfactory state of monetary analysis inherited in the late 1950's. A money and banking syndrome perpetuated by textbooks obstructed the application of economic analysis to the financial

[5] Davis, pp. 63–64.

[6] These three aspects of the New View will subsequently be elaborated more fully. Their program of analysis refers to the application of relative price theory to analysis of financial markets and financial institutions. Their research strategy refers to a decision to initiate analysis in the context of a most general framework. Their specific conjectures refer to propositions concerning the causes of fluctuation of monetary growth and propositions about proper interpretation of policy.

[7] John G. Gurley and Edward F. Shaw, *Money in a Theory of Finance,* (Washington: Brookings Institute, 1960). James Tobin, "Commercial Banks as Creators of Money," *Banking and Monetary Studies,* ed. Deane Carson (R. D. Irwin, 1963).

sector. At most, this inherited literature contained only suggestive pieces of analysis. It lacked a meaningful theory capable of explaining the responses of the monetary system to policy actions or to influences emanating from the real sector. The New View proposed a systematic application of economic analysis, in particular an application of relative price theory, to the array of financial intermediaries, their assets and liabilities.

This program is most admirable and incontestable, but it cannot explain the conflict revealed by critique and countercritique. The Monetarist approach accepted the general principle of applying relative price theory to the analysis of monetary processes. In addition, this approach used the suggestions and analytical pieces inherited from past efforts in order to develop some specific hypotheses which do explain portions of our observable environment. The New Viewers' obvious failure to recognize the limited content of their programmatic statements only contributes to maintenance of the conflict.

A subtle difference appears, however, in the research strategy. The New View was introduced essentially as a generalized approach, including a quite formal exposition, but with little attempt at specific structuring and empirical content. The most impressive statements propagated by the New View were crucially influenced by the sheer formalism of its exposition. In the context of the New View's almost empty form, little remains to differentiate one object from another. For instance, in case one only admits the *occurrence* of marginal costs and marginal yields associated with the actions of every household, firm, and financial intermediary, one will necessarily conclude that banks and non-bank financial intermediaries are restricted in size by the same economic forces and circumstances. In such a context there is truly no essential difference between the determination of bank and non-bank intermediary liabilities, or between banks and non-bank intermediaries, or between money and other financial assets.

The strong impressions conveyed by the New View thus result from the relative emptiness of the formulation which has been used to elaborate their position. In the context of the formal world of the New View, "almost everything is almost like everything else." This undifferentiated state of affairs is not, however, a property of our observable world. It is only a property of the highly formal discussion designed by the New View to overcome the unsatisfactory state of monetary analysis still prevailing in the late 1950's or early 1960's.[8]

Two sources of the conflict have been recognized thus far. The Monetarists' research strategy was concerned quite directly with the construction of empirical theories about the monetary system, whereas the New View indulged, for a lengthy interval, in very general programmatic excursions. Moreover, the New Viewers apparently misconstrued their program as being a meaningful theory about our observable environment. This logical error contributed to a third source of the persistent conflict.

The latter source arises from the criticism addressed by the New Viewers to the Monetarists' theories of money supply processes. Three of the papers exploit the logically dubious but psychologically effective juxtaposition between a "New View" and a "Tra-

[8] Adequate analysis of the medium of exchange function of money, or of the conditions under which inside money becomes a component of wealth, was obstructed by the programmatic state of the New View. The useful analysis of the medium-of-exchange function depends on a decisive rejection of the assertion that "everything is almost like everything else." This analysis requires proper recognition that the marginal cost of information concerning qualities and properties of assets differs substantially between assets, and that the marginal cost of readjusting asset positions depends on the assets involved. The analysis of the wealth position of inside money requires recognition of the marginal productivity of inside money to the holder. Adequate attention to the relevant differences between various cost or yield functions associated with different assets or positions is required by both problems. The blandness of the New View's standard program cannot cope with these issues. The reader may consult a preliminary approach to the analysis of the medium of exchange function in the paper by Karl Brunner and Allan H. Meltzer, in the *Journal of Finance*, 1964, listed in footnote 9. He should also consult for both issues the important book by Boris Pesek and Thomas Saving, *Money, Wealth and Economic Theory*, The Macmillan Company, New York, 1967, or the paper by Harry Johnson, "Inside Money, Outside Money, Income, Wealth and Welfare in Monetary Theory," *The Journal of Money, Credit and Banking*, December 1968.

ditional View." In doing this they fail to distinguish between the inherited state of monetary system analysis typically reflected by the money and banking textbook syndrome and the research output of economists advocating the Monetarist thesis. This distinction is quite fundamental. Some formal analogies misled the New Viewers and they did not recognize the logical difference between detailed formulations of empirical theories on the one side and haphazard pieces of unfinished analysis on the other side.[9]

A related failure accompanies this logical error. There is not the slightest attempt to assess alternative hypotheses or theories by systematic exposure to observations from the real world. It follows, therefore, that the countercritique scarcely analyzed the empirical theories advanced by the Monetarist critique and consequently failed to understand the major implications of these theories.

For instance, they failed to recognize the role assigned by the Monetarist view to banks' behavior and the public's preferences in the monetary process. The objection raised by the New View that "the formula [expressing a basic framework used to formulate the hypothesis] obscures the important role played by the public" has neither analytical basis nor meaning. In fact, the place of the public's behavior was discussed in the Monetarist hypotheses in some detail. Moreover, the same analysis discussed the conditions under which the public's behavior dominates movements of the money stock and bank credit.[10] It also yielded information about the response of bank credit, money stock and time deposits to changes in ceiling rates, or to changes in the speed with which banks adjust their deposit-supply conditions to evolving market situations. Every single aspect of the banks' or the public's behavior emphasized by the countercritique has been analyzed by the Monetarist's hypotheses in terms which render the results empirically assessable. Little remains, consequently, of the suggestive countercritique assembled in the papers by Gramley-Chase, Kareken and Cacy.[11]

---

[9] As examples of the empirical work performed by the Monetarists, the reader should consult the following works: Milton Friedman and Anna Jacobson Schwartz, *A Monetary History of the United States, 1867–1960,* (Princeton: Princeton University Press, 1963). Philip Cagan, *Determinants and Effects of Changes in the Stock of Money,* (Columbia: Columbia University Press, 1965). Karl Brunner and Allan H. Meltzer, "Some Further Investigations of Demand and Supply Functions for Money," *Journal of Finance,* Volume XIX, May 1964. Karl Brunner and Allan H. Meltzer, "A Credit-Market Theory of the Money Supply and an Explanation of Two Puzzles in U.S. Monetary Policy," *Essays in Honor of Marco Fanno,* 1966, Padova, Italy. Karl Brunner and Robert Crouch, "Money Supply Theory and British Monetary Experience, *Methods of Operations Research III—Essays in Honor of Wilhelm Krelle,* ed. Rudolf Henn (Published in Meisenheim, Germany, by Anton Hain, 1966). Karl Brunner, "A Schema for the Supply Theory of Money," *International Economic Review,* 1961. Karl Brunner and Allan H. Meltzer, "An Alternative Approach to the Monetary Mechanism," *Subcommittee on Domestic Finance, Committee on Banking and Currency, House of Representatives,* August 17, 1964.

[10] The reader will find this analysis in the following papers: Karl Brunner and Allan H. Meltzer, "Liquidity Traps for Money, Bank Credit, and Interest Rates," *Journal of Political Economy,* April 1968. Karl Brunner and Allan H. Meltzer, "A Credit-Market Theory of the Money Supply and an Explanation of Two Puzzles in U.S. Monetary Policy," *Essays in Honor of Marco Fanno,* Padova, Italy, 1966.

[11] The reader is, of course, aware that these assertions require analytic substantiation. Such substantiation cannot be supplied within the confines of this article. But the reader could check for himself. If he finds, in the context of the countercritique, an analysis of the Monetarists' major hypotheses, an examination of implication, and exposure to observations, I would have to withdraw my statements. A detailed analysis of the banks' and the public's role in the money supply, based on two different hypotheses previously reported in our papers will be developed in our forthcoming books. This analysis, by its very existence, falsifies some major objections made by Cacy or Gramley-Chase. Much of their criticism is either innocuous or fatuous. Gramley-Chase indulge, for instance, in modality statements, i.e. statements obtained from other statements by prefixing a modality qualifier like "maybe" or "possibly." The result of qualifying an empirical statement always yields a statement which is necessarily true, but also quite uninformative. The modality game thus yields logically pointless but psychologically effective sentences. Cacy manages, on the other hand, some astonishing assertions. The New View is credited with the discovery that excess reserves vary over time. He totally disregards the major contributions

## B. A Monetarist Examination of the New View's Money Supply Theory

Three sources of the conflict have been discussed thus far. Two sources were revealed as logical misconstruals, involving inadequate construction and assessment of empirical theories. A third source pertains to legitimate differences in research strategy. These three sources do not explain all major aspects of the conflict. Beyond the differences in research strategy and logical misconceptions, genuinely substantive issues remain. Some comments of protagonists advocating the New View should probably be interpreted as conjectures about hypotheses to be expected from their research strategy. It should be clearly understood that such conjectures are not logical implications of the guiding framework. Instead, they are pragmatic responses to the general emphasis associated with this approach.

A first conjecture suggests that the money stock and bank credit are dominated by the public's and the banks' behavior. It is suggested, therefore, that cyclical fluctuations of monetary growth result primarily from the responses of banks and the public to changing business conditions. A second conjecture naturally supplements the above assertions. It is contended that the money stock is a thoroughly "untrustworthy guide to monetary policy."

Articles by Gramley-Chase and Kareken attempt to support these conjectures with the aid of more explicit analytical formulations allegedly expressing the general program of the New View. The paper contributed by Gramley-Chase has been critically examined in detail on another occasion,[12] and only some crucial aspects relevant for our present purposes will be considered at this point. Various aspects of the first conjecture are examined in this and the next section. The second conjecture is examined in Sections D and E.

A detailed analysis of the Gramley-Chase model demonstrates that it implies the following reduced form equations explaining the money stock (M) and bank credit (E) in terms of the extended monetary base ($B^e$),

$$\begin{aligned} M &= g(B^e, Y, c) \qquad g_1 > 0 < g_2 \\ E &= h(B^e, Y, c) \qquad h_1 > 0 > h_2 \\ &\qquad\qquad\qquad \text{and } h_1 > g_1 \end{aligned}$$[13]

the level of economic activity expressed by national income at current prices (Y), and the ceiling rate on time deposits (c).[14]

The Gramley-Chase model implies that monetary policy does affect the money stock and bank credit. It also implies that the money stock responds *positively* and bank credit *negatively* to economic activity. This model thus differs from the Monetarist hypotheses which imply that both bank credit and the money stock respond *positively* to economic activity. The Gramley-Chase model also implies that the responses of both the money stock and bank credit to monetary actions are independent of the general scale of the public's and the banks' interest elasticities. Uniformly large or small interest elasticities yield the same response in the

to the analysis of excess reserves emanating from the Monetarists' research. A detailed analysis of excess reserves was developed by Milton Friedman and Anna Schwartz in the book mentioned in footnote 9. The reader should also note the work by George Morrison, *Liquidity Preferences of Commercial Banks,* (Chicago: University of Chicago Press, 1966), and the study by Peter Frost, "Banks' Demand for Excess Reserves," an unpublished dissertation submitted to the University of California at Los Angeles, 1966. The classic example of an innocuous achievement was supplied by Cacy with the assertion: ". . . the actual volume of money balances determined by competitive market forces may or may not be equal to the upper limit established by the central bank" (p. 8). Indeed, we knew this before the New View or Any View, just as we always knew that "it may or may not rain tomorrow." The reader should note that similar statements were produced by other authors with all the appearances of meaningful elaborations.

12 The reader may consult my chapter "Federal Reserve Policy and Monetary Analysis" in *Indicators and Targets of Monetary Policy,* ed. by Karl Brunner (Chandler House Publishing Co., San Francisco, 1969). This book also contains the original article by Gramley-Chase. Further contributions by Patric H. Hendershott and Robert Weintraub survey critically the issues raised by the Gramley-Chase paper.

13 In the Gramley-Chase model, $g_3$ and $h_3$ are indeterminant.

14 This implication was demonstrated in my paper listed in footnote 12. The monetary base is adjusted for the accumulated sum of reserves liberated from or impounded into required reserves by changes in requirement ratios.

money stock or bank credit to a change in the monetary base.

A detailed discussion of the implications derivable from a meaningfully supplemented Gramley-Chase model is not necessary at this point. We are foremost interested in the relation between this model and the propositions mentioned in the previous paragraph. The first proposition can be interpreted in two different ways. According to one interpretation, it could mean that the marginal multipliers $g_i$ and $h_i$ $(i = 1, 2)$ are functions of the banks' and the public's response patterns expressing various types of substitution relations between different assets. This interpretation is, however, quite innocuous and yields no differentiation relative to the questioned hypotheses of the Monetarist position.

A second interpretation suggests that the growth rate of the money stock is dominated by the second component (changes in income) of the differential expression:

$$\Delta M = g_1 \, \Delta B^e + g_2 \, \Delta Y$$

This result is not actually implied by the Gramley-Chase model, but it is certainly consistent with the model. However, in order to derive the desired result, their model must be supplemented with special assumptions about the relative magnitude of $g_1$ and $g_2$, and also about the comparative cyclical variability of $\Delta B^e$ and $\Delta Y$. This information has not been provided by the authors.

Most interesting is another aspect of the model which was not clarified by the authors. Their model implies that policymakers could easily avoid procyclical movements in $\Delta M$. This model exemplifying the New View thus yields little justification for the conjectures of its proponents.

A central property of the Gramley-Chase model must be considered in the light of the programmatic statements characterizing the New View. Gramley-Chase do not differentiate between the public's asset supply to banks and the public's demand for money. This procedure violates the basic program of the New View, namely, to apply economic analysis to an array of financial assets and financial institutions. Economic analysis implies that the public's asset supply and money demand are distinct, and not identical behavior patterns. This difference in behavior patterns is clearly revealed by different responses of desired money balances and desired asset supply to specific stimuli in the environment. For instance, an increase in the expected real yield on real capital *raises* the public's asset supply but *lowers* the public's money demand. It follows thus that a central analytical feature of the Gramley-Chase model violates the basic and quite relevant program of the New View.

Kareken's construction shares this fundamental analytical flaw with the Gramley-Chase model, but this is not the only problem faced by his analysis. The Kareken analysis proceeds on two levels. First, he derives a representative bank's desired balance sheet position. For this purpose he postulates wealth maximization subject to the bank's balance sheet relation between assets and liabilities, and subject to reserve requirements on deposits. On closer examination, this analysis is only applicable to a monopoly bank with no conversion of deposits into currency or reserve flows to other banks. In order to render the analysis relevant for a representative bank in the world of reality, additional constraints would have to be introduced which modify the results quite substantially. It is also noteworthy that the structural properties assigned by Kareken to the system of market relations are logically inconsistent with the implications one can derive from the author's analysis of firm behavior developed on the first level of his investigation.

This disregard for the construction of an economic theory relevant for the real world is carried into the second level of analysis where the author formulates a system of relations describing the joint determination of interest rates, bank credit, and money stock. A remarkable feature of the Kareken model is that it yields no implications whatsoever about the response of the monetary system to actions of the Federal Reserve. It can say nothing, as it stands, about either open market operations or about discount rate and reserve requirement actions. This model literally implies, for instance, that the money stock and the banking system's deposit liabilities do not change as a result of any change in reserve requirement ratios.

None of the conjectures advanced by the countercritique concerning the behavior of the money stock and the role of monetary policy find analytical support in Kareken's analysis. To the extent that anything is implied, it would imply that monetary policy operating directly on bank reserves or a mysterious rate of return on reserves dominates the volume of deposits—a practically subversive position for a follower of the New View.[15]

### C. *Alternative Explanations of Cyclical Fluctuations in Monetary Growth*

The examination thus far in this article has shown that even the most explicit formulation (Gramley-Chase) of the countercritique, allegedly representing the New View with respect to monetary system analysis, does assign a significant role to monetary policy. This examination also argued that the general emphasis given by the New View to the public's and the banks' behavior in determination of the money stock and bank credit does not differentiate its product from analytical developments arising from the Monetarist approach. It was also shown that the only explicit formulation advanced by the New Viewers does not provide a sufficient basis for their central conjectures. It is impossible to derive the proposition from the Gramley-Chase model that the behavior of the public and banks, rather than Federal Reserve actions, dominated movements in the money supply. But the declaration of innocence by the countercritique on behalf of the monetary authorities with respect to cyclical fluctuations of monetary growth still requires further assessment.

The detailed arguments advanced to explain the observed cyclical fluctuations of monetary growth differ substantially among the contributors to the countercritique. Gramley-Chase maintain that changing business conditions modify relative interest rates, and thus induce countercyclical movements in the time deposit ratio. These movements in demand and time deposits generate cyclical fluctuations in monetary growth. On the other hand, Cacy develops an argument used many years ago by Wicksell and Keynes, but attributes it to the New View. He recognizes a pronounced sensitivity of the money stock to variations in the public's money demand or asset supply. These variations induce changes in credit market conditions. Banks, in turn, respond with suitable adjustments in the reserve and borrowing ratios. The money stock and bank credit consequently change in response to this mechanism.

Davis actually advances two radically different conjectures about causes of cyclical fluctuations of monetary growth. The first conjecture attributes fluctuations of monetary growth to the public's and banks' responses. Changing business conditions modify the currency ratio, the banks' borrowing ratio, and the reserve ratio. The resulting changes generate the observed movements in money. His other conjecture attributes fluctuations in monetary growth to Federal Reserve actions: "the state of business influences decisions by the monetary authorities to supply reserves and to take other actions likely to affect the money supply."[16]

The various conjectures advanced by

[15] Two direct objections made to the Brunner-Meltzer analysis by Kareken should be noted. He finds that the questioned hypotheses do not contain "a genuine supply function" of deposits. Accepting Kareken's terminology, this is true, but neither does the Gramley-Chase model contain such a supply function. But the objection has no evidential value anyway. If a hypothesis were judged unsatisfactory because some aspects are omitted, all hypotheses are "unsatisfactory." Moreover, the cognitive status of an empirical hypothesis does not improve simply because an "analytical underpinning" has been provided. Kareken also finds fault with our use of the term "money supply function." Whether or not one agrees with his terminological preferences surely does not affect the relation between observations and statements supplied by the hypothesis. And it should be clear that the status of a hypothesis depends only on this relation, and not on names attached to statements.

[16] Davis, p. 66. One argument about monetary policy in the same paper requires clarification. Davis asserts on p. 68 that the money supply need not be the objective of policy, and "given this fact, the behavior of the rate of growth of the money supply during the period cannot be assumed to be simply and directly the result of monetary policy decisions alone." This quote asserts that the money supply is "simply and directly the result of policy alone" whenever policy uses the money supply as a target. This is in a sense correct. But the quote could easily be misinterpreted due to the ambiguity of the term "policy." This term is frequently used to designate a strategy guiding the adjustment of policy variables. It is also frequently used to refer to the behavior of the policy variables or directly to the variables as such. The quote is quite acceptable in the first sense of "policy," but thoroughly unacceptable in the second sense.

Gramley-Chase, Cacy, and Davis in regard to causes of movements in money and bank credit can be classified into two groups. One set of conjectures traces the mechanism generating cyclical fluctuations of monetary growth to the responses of banks and the public; the behavior of monetary authorities is assigned a comparatively minor role. The other group of conjectures recognizes the predominant role of the behavior of monetary authorities.

In the following analysis the framework provided by the Monetarist view will be used to assess these conflicting conjectures. The emphasis concerning the nature of the causal mechanisms may differ between the various conjectures regarding sources of variations in money, but the following examination will be applied to an aspect common to all conjectures emphasizing the role of public and bank behavior.

In the context of the Monetarist framework, the money stock (M) is exhibited as a product of a multiplier (m) and the monetary base (B), (such that M = mB). This framework, without the supplementary set of hypotheses and theories bearing on the proximate determinants of money summarized by the multiplier and the base, is completely neutral with respect to the rival conjectures; it is compatible with any set of observations. This neutrality assures us that its use does not prejudge the issue under consideration. The Monetarist framework operates in the manner of a language system, able to express the implications of the competing conjectures in a uniform manner.

The first group of conjectures advanced by the countercritique (behavior of the public and banks dominates movements in money) implies that variations in monetary growth between upswings and downswings in business activity are dominated by the variations in the monetary multiplier. The second group (behavior of monetary authorities dominates movements in money) implies that, in periods with unchanged reserve requirement ratios and ceiling rates on time deposits, variations in the monetary base dominate cyclical changes in monetary growth. The movements of the monetary multiplier which are strictly attributable to the changing of requirement ratios can be separated from the total contribution of the multiplier and combined with the monetary base. With this adjustment, the second group of conjectures implies that the monetary base, supplemented by the contribution of reserve requirement changes to the multiplier, dominates variations in the money stock.

In this examination of contrasting explanations of monetary fluctuations, values of the money stock (M), the multiplier (m), and the monetary base adjusted for member bank borrowing (B) are measured at the initial and terminal month of each half business cycle (i.e., expansions and contractions) located by the National Bureau of Economic Research. We form the ratios of these values and write:

$$\frac{M_1}{M_0} = \frac{m_1}{m_0}\frac{B_1}{B_0}; \text{ or } \mu = \alpha\beta$$

The subscript 1 refers to values of the terminal month and the subscript 0 to values of the initial month. These ratios were measured for each half cycle in the period March 1919 to December 1966. They were computed for two definitions of the money stock, inclusive and exclusive of time deposits, with corresponding monetary multipliers.

Kendall's rank correlation coefficients between the money stock ratios ($\mu$) and the multiplier ratios ($\alpha$), and between ($\mu$) and the monetary base ratio ($\beta$) were computed. We denote these correlation coefficients with $\rho(\mu, \alpha)$ and $\rho(\mu, \beta)$. The implications of the two rival conjectures can now be restated in terms of the two coefficients. The first group of conjectures implies that $\rho(\mu, \alpha) > \rho(\mu, \beta)$; while the second group implies that in periods of unchanged reserve requirement ratios and ceiling rates on time deposits, the coefficient $\rho(\mu, \beta)$ exceeds the coefficient $\rho(\mu, \alpha)$. The second group implies nothing about the relation of the two coefficients in periods of changing reserve requirements and ceiling rates on time deposits. It follows, therefore, that observations yielding the inequality $\rho(\mu, \beta) > \rho(\mu, \alpha)$ disconfirm the first group and confirm the second group.

The correlations obtained are quite unambiguous. The value of $\rho(\mu, \beta)$ is .537 for the whole sample period, whereas $\rho(\mu, \alpha)$ is only .084. The half-cycle from 1929 to 1933 was omitted in the computations, because movements in the money stock and the multiplier were dominated by forces which do not discriminate between the rival conjectures under consideration. The sample period, including 1929 to 1933, still yields a substantially larger value for $\rho$ $(\mu, \beta)$. The same pattern also holds for other subperiods. In particular, computations based on observations for 1949 to 1966 confirm the pattern observed for the whole sample period. The results thus support the second group of conjectures but not the first group. These results also suggest, however, that forces operating through the multiplier are not quite negligible. The surprisingly small correlation $\rho$ $(\mu, \alpha)$ does not adequately reveal the operation of these forces. Their effective operation is revealed by the correlation $\rho$ $(\mu, \beta)$, which is far from perfect, even in subperiods with constant reserve requirement ratios. This circumstance suggests that the behavior of the public and banks contributes to the cyclical movements of monetary growth. The main result at this stage is, however, the clear discrimination between the two groups of conjectures. The results are quite unambiguous on this score.

Additional information is supplied by Table 1. For each postwar cycle beginning with the downswing of 1948-49, the average annual growth rate of the money stock was computed. The expression M = mB was then used to compute the contribution to the average growth rate of money from three distinct sources: (i) the behavior of monetary authorities (i.e., the monetary base and reserve requirement ratios), and the public's currency behavior, (ii) the time deposit substitution process, and (iii) the variations in the excess reserve and borrowing ratios of commercial banks (Wicksell-Keynes mechanism).

**TABLE 1. A COMPARISON OF ALTERNATIVE CONTRIBUTIONS TO THE AVERAGE ANNUAL GROWTH RATE OF THE MONEY STOCK AND BANK CREDIT**

| | Rank Correlations | |
|---|---|---|
| Contribution made by: | Money | Bank credit |
| Public's currency and authorities' behavior | .905 | .333 |
| Time deposit substitution mechanism | .048 | .381 |
| Wicksell-Keynes mechanism | .143 | −.333 |

Remarks: The figures listed state the rank correlation between the average growth rate of the money stock and bank credit with three different contributing sources.

The rank correlations between each contribution, and the average growth rate of the money stock over all postwar half-cycles clearly support the conclusion of the previous analysis that cyclical movements in the money stock are dominated by Federal Reserve actions.

Table 1 also presents the results of a similar examination bearing on causes of movements in bank credit. The reader should note the radical difference in the observed patterns of correlation coefficients. The behavior of monetary authorities, supplemented by the public's currency behavior, does not appear to dominate the behavior of bank credit. The three sources contributing to the growth rate of money all exerted influences of similar order on bank credit. It appears that bank credit is comparatively less exposed to the push of Federal Reserve actions than was the money stock. On the other hand, the money stock is less sensitive than bank credit to the time-deposit substitution mechanism emphasized by Gramley-Chase, and the Wicksell-Keynes mechanism suggested by Cacy. Most astonishing, however, is the *negative* association between the average growth rate of bank credit and the Wicksell-Keynes mechanism emphasized by Cacy.

It should also be noted that the average growth rate of money conforms very clearly to the business cycle. Such conformity does not hold for bank credit over the postwar half-cycles. This blurring occurred particularly in periods when the ceiling rate on time deposits was increased. These periods exhibit relatively large contributions to the growth rate of bank credit emanating from the time deposit substitution mechanism.

A regression analysis (Table 2) of the reduced form equations derived from the Gramley-Chase model confirms the central role of the monetary base in the money supply process. Estimates of the regression coefficient relating money to income are highly unstable among different sample periods, relative to the coefficient relating money to the monetary base. Furthermore, estimates of regression coefficients relating money to income occur in some periods with signs which contradict the proposition of Gramley-Chase and Cacy, or exhibit a very small sta-

TABLE 2. REGRESSIONS OF THE MONEY SUPPLY ON THE MONETARY BASE AND GROSS NATIONAL PRODUCT*

| | Regression Coefficients for: | | | |
|---|---|---|---|---|
| | Monetary Base | | Gross National Product | |
| Cycle | First differences | Log first differences | First differences | Log first differences |
| IV/48 | 2.03 | .77 | .04 | .11 |
| to | (9.80) | (10.02) | (3.12) | (3.39) |
| II/53 | .92 | .93) | .62 | .65 |
| II/53 | 1.75 | .63 | .02 | .07 |
| to | (1.89) | (1.96) | (1.02) | (1.23) |
| III/57 | .44 | .45 | .26 | .30 |
| III/57 | 4.59 | 1.66 | .06 | .19 |
| to | (11.76) | (11.81) | (5.10) | (5.34) |
| II/60 | .97 | .97 | .86 | .67 |
| II/60 | 2.76 | 1.08 | −.01 | −.03 |
| to | (7.56) | (8.54) | (−.33) | (−.27) |
| III/65 | .87 | .89 | −.08 | −.07 |

*The monetary base was adjusted for reserve requirement changes and shifts in deposits. All data are quarterly averages of seasonally adjusted figures. The first entry in a column for each cycle is the regression coefficient, t-statistics are in parentheses, and partial correlation coefficients are below the t-statistics.

tistical significance. These diverse patterns of coefficients do not occur for the estimates of coefficients relating money and the monetary base. It is also noteworthy that the average growth rate of the monetary base (adjusted for changes in reserve requirement ratios), over the upswings, exceeds without exception the average growth rate of adjacent downswings. This observation is not compatible with the contention made by Gramley-Chase that policy is countercyclical.

Additional information is supplied by Table 3, which presents some results of a spectral analysis bearing on the monetary base and its sources. Spectral analysis is a statistical procedure for decomposing a time series into seasonal, cyclical, and trend movements. After such an analysis was conducted on the monetary base and its sources, a form of correlation analysis was run between movements in the monetary base and movements in its various sources. The results of this procedure (Table 3) indicate

TABLE 3. SPECTRAL CORRELATION BETWEEN THE MONETARY BASE, FEDERAL RESERVE CREDIT AND OTHER SOURCES OF THE BASE

| | Special Correlation between | |
|---|---|---|
| Period in months | Monetary base and Federal reserve credit | Monetary base and other sources of the base |
| ∞ | .65 | .24 |
| 120 | .69 | .61 |
| 60 | .74 | .71 |
| 40 | .74 | .45 |
| 30 | .73 | .25 |
| 24 | .71 | .18 |
| 20 | .60 | .11 |
| 17.14 | .43 | .11 |
| 15 | .51 | .07 |
| 13.33 | .82 | .48 |
| 12 | .94 | .71 |
| 6 | .91 | .21 |
| 4 | .92 | — |
| 3 | .90 | — |

Remarks: The monetary base equals Federal Reserve Credit plus other sources of the base. The spectral analysis is based on first differences between adjacent months. The data used were not seasonally adjusted.

that movements in Federal Reserve credit dominate seasonal and cyclical movements in the monetary base.

In summary, preliminary investigations yield no support for the contention that the behavior of banks and the public dominates cyclical movements in the money stock. The conjectures advanced by Gramley-Chase or Cacy are thus disconfirmed, whereas Davis' second conjecture that fluctuations in monetary growth may be attributed to Federal Reserve actions seems substantially more appropriate. However, further investigations are certainly useful.

### *D. Relevance of Money and Monetary Action With Respect to Economic Activity*

At present, a broad consensus accepts the relevance of money and monetary policy with respect to economic activity. But this consensus concerning the relevance of money emerges from two substantially different views about the nature of the transmission mechanism. One view is the Keynesian conception (not to be confused with Keynes' view), enshrined in standard formulations of the income-expenditure framework. In this view, the interest rate is the main link between money and economic activity. The other view rejects the traditional separation of economic theory into parts: national income analysis (macro economics) and price theory (micro economics). According to this other view, output and employment are explained by a suitable application of relative price theory. With regard to discussions of the impact of money and monetary actions on economic activity, this latter view has been termed the Monetarist position. This position may be divided into the weak Monetarist thesis and the strong Monetarist thesis. In a sense, both the New View and the Monetarist extension of the "traditional view" are represented in the weak Monetarist position.

The following discussions develop the weak and the strong Monetarist thesis. The weak thesis is compared with some aspects of the income-expenditure approach to the determination of national economic activity. The strong thesis supplements the weak thesis with special assumptions about our environment, in order to establish the role of monetary forces in the business cycle.

1. THE WEAK MONETARIST THESIS. According to the weak Monetarist thesis, monetary impulses are transmitted to the economy by a relative price process which operates on money, financial assets (and liabilities), real assets, yields on assets and the production of new assets, liabilities and consumables. The general nature of this process has been described on numerous occasions and may be interpreted as evolving from ideas developed by Knut Wicksell, Irving Fisher, and John Maynard Keynes.[17]

The operation of relative prices between money, financial assets, and real assets may be equivalently interpreted as the working of an interest rate mechanism (prices and yields of assets are inversely related). Monetary impulses are thus transmitted by the play of interest rates over a vast array of assets. Variations in interest rates change relative prices of existing assets, relative to both yields and the supply prices of new production. Acceleration or deceleration of monetary impulses are thus converted by the variation of relative prices, or interest rates, into increased or reduced production, and subsequent revisions in the supply prices of current output.

This general conception of the transmission mechanism has important implications which conflict sharply with the Keynesian interpretation of monetary mechanisms expressed by standard income-expenditure formulations.[18] In the context of standard income-expenditure analysis, fiscal actions are considered to have a "direct effect" on economic activity, whereas monetary actions are considered to have only an "indirect effect." Furthermore, a constant budget deficit has no effect on interest rates in a Keynesian framework, in spite of substantial accumulation of outstanding government debt when a budget deficit continually occurs. And lastly, the operation of interest rates on investment decisions has usually been rationalized with the aid of considerations based on the effects of borrowing costs.

These aspects of the income-expenditure approach may be evaluated within the framework of the weak Monetarist thesis. The effects of fiscal actions are also transmitted

[17] The reader may consult the following studies on this aspect: Milton Friedman and David Meiselman, "The Relative Stability of Monetary Velocity and the Investment Multiplier in the United States, 1897–1958," in *Stabilization Policies*, prepared by the Commission on Money and Credit, Englewood Cliffs, 1963. The paper listed in footnote 21 by James Tobin should also be consulted. Harry Johnson, "Monetary Theory and Policy," *American Economic Review*, June 1962. Karl Brunner, "The Report of the Commission on Money and Credit," *The Journal of Political Economy*, December 1961. Karl Brunner, "Some Major Problems of Monetary Theory," *Proceedings of the American Economic Association*, May 1961. Karl Brunner and Allan H. Meltzer, "The Role of Financial Institutions in the Transmission Mechanism," *Proceedings of the American Economic Association*, May 1963. Karl Brunner, "The Relative Price Theory of Money, Output, and Employment," unpublished manuscript based on a paper presented at the Midwestern Economic Association Meetings, April 1967.

[18] The paper on "The Effect of Monetary Policy on Expenditures in Specific Sectors of the Economy," presented by Dr. Sherman Maisel at the meetings organized by the American Bankers Association in September 1967, exemplifies very clearly the inherited Keynesian position. The paper is in the *Journal of Political Economy*, vol. 76 (July/August, 1968) pp. 796–814 [reprinted in this volume].

by the relative price mechanism. Fiscal impulses, i.e., Government spending, taxing, and borrowing, operate just as "indirectly" as monetary impulses, and there is no *a priori* reason for believing that their speed of transmission is substantially greater than that of monetary impulses. The relative price conception of the transmission mechanism also implies that a constant budget deficit exerts a continuous influence on economic activity through persistent modifications in relative prices of financial and real assets. Lastly, the transmission of monetary impulses is not dominated by the relative importance of borrowing costs. In the process, marginal costs of liability extension interact with marginal returns from acquisitions of financial and real assets. But interest rates on financial assets not only affect the marginal cost of liability extension, but also influence the substitution between financial and real assets. This substitution modifies prices of real assets relative to their supply prices and forms a crucial linkage of the monetary mechanisms; this linkage is usually omitted in standard income-expenditure analysis.

The description of monetary mechanisms in Davis' article approaches quite closely the notion developed by the weak Monetarist thesis. This approximation permits a useful clarification of pending issues. However, the criticisms and objections advanced by Davis do not apply to the weak Monetarist position. They are addressed to another thesis, which might be usefully labeled the *strong Monetarist thesis.*

2. THE STRONG MONETARIST THESIS. If the theoretical framework of the weak Monetarist thesis is supplemented with additional and special hypotheses, the *strong Monetarist thesis* is obtained. An outline of the strong thesis may be formulated in terms of three sets of forces operating simultaneously on the pace of economic activity. For convenience, they may be grouped into monetary forces, fiscal forces, and other forces. The latter include technological and organizational innovation, revisions in supply prices induced by accruing information and expectation adjustments, capital accumulation, population changes and other related factors or processes.

All three sets of forces are acknowledged by the strong thesis to affect the pace of economic activity via the relative price process previously outlined. Moreover, the strong Monetarist point of view advances the crucial thesis that the variability of monetary forces (properly weighted with respect to their effect on economic activity) exceeds the variability of fiscal forces and other forces (properly weighted). It is argued further that major variabilities occurring in a subset of the other forces (e.g., expectations and revisions of supply prices induced by information arrival) are conditioned by the observed variability of monetary forces. The conjecture thus involves a comparison of monetary variability with the variability of fiscal forces and independent "other forces." According to the thesis under consideration, the variability of monetary impulses is also large relative to the speed at which the economy absorbs the impact of environmental changes. This predominance of variability in monetary impulses implies that pronounced accelerations in monetary forces are followed subsequently by accelerations in the pace of economic activity, and that pronounced decelerations in monetary forces are followed later by retardations in economic activity.

The analysis of the monetary dynamics, using the relative price process, is accepted by both the weak and the strong Monetarist theses. This analysis implies that the regularity of the observed association between accelerations and decelerations of monetary forces and economic activity depends on the relative magnitude of monetary accelerations (or decelerations). The same analysis also reveals the crucial role of changes in the rate of change (second differences) of the money stock in explanations of fluctuations in output and employment. It implies that any pronounced deceleration, occurring at any rate of monetary growth, retards total spending. It is thus impossible to state whether any particular monetary growth, say a 10 per cent annual rate, is expansionary with respect to economic activity, until one knows the previous growth rate. The monetary dynamics of the Monetarist thesis also explains the simultaneous occurrence of permanent price-inflation and fluctuations in output and employment observable in some countries.

The nature and the variability of the "Friedman lag" may also be analyzed within the framework of the Monetarist thesis. This lag measures the interval between a change in sign of the *second* difference in the money stock and the subsequent turning point located by the National Bureau. In general, the lag at an upper turning point will be shorter, the greater the absorption speed of the economy, and the sharper the deceleration of monetary impulses relative to the movement of fiscal forces and other forces. Variability in the *relative* acceleration or deceleration of monetary forces necessarily generates the variability observed in the Friedman lag.

What evidence may be cited on behalf of the strong Monetarist thesis? Every major inflation provides support for the thesis, particularly in cases of substantial variations of monetary growth. The attempt at stabilization in the Confederacy during the Civil War forms an impressive piece of evidence in this respect. The association between monetary and economic accelerations or decelerations has also been observed by the Federal Reserve Bank of St. Louis.[19] Observations from periods with divergent movements of monetary and fiscal forces provide further evidence. For instance, such periods occurred immediately after termination of World War II, from the end of 1947 to the fall of 1948, and again in the second half of 1966. In all three cases, monetary forces prevailed over fiscal forces. The evidence adduced here and on other occasions does not "prove" the strong Monetarist thesis, but does establish its merit for serious consideration.

Davis' examination is therefore welcomed. His objections are summarized by the following points: (a) observations of the persistent association between money and income do not permit an inference of causal direction from money to income; (b) the timing relation between money and economic activity expressed by the Friedman lag yields no evidence in support of the contention that variations in monetary growth cause fluctuations in economic activity; (c) the correlation found in cycles of moderate amplitude between magnitudes of monetary and economic changes was quite unimpressive; (d) the length of the Friedman lag does not measure the interval between emission of monetary impulse and its ultimate impact on economic activity. Furthermore, the variability of this lag is due to the simultaneous operation and interaction of monetary and non-monetary forces.

Davis' first comment (a) is of course quite true and well known in the logic of science. It is impossible to derive (logically) causal statements or any general hypotheses from observations. But we can use such observations to confirm or disconfirm such statements and hypotheses. Davis particularly emphasizes that the persistent association between money and income could be attributed to a causal influence running from economic activity to money.

Indeed it could, but our present state of knowledge rejects the notion that the observed association is essentially due to a causal influence from income on money. Evidence refuting such a notion was presented in Section C. The existence of a mutual interaction over the shorter-run between money and economic activity, however, must be fully acknowledged. Yet, this interaction results from the conception guiding policymakers which induces them to accelerate the monetary base whenever pressures on interest rates mount, and to decelerate the monetary base when these pressures wane. Admission of a mutual interaction does not dispose of the strong Monetarist thesis. This interaction, inherent in the weak thesis, is quite consistent with the strong position and has no disconfirming value. To the contrary, it offers an explanation for the occurrence of the predominant variability of monetary forces.

The same logical property applies to Davis' second argument (b). The timing relation expressed by the Friedman lag, in particular the chronological precedence of turning points in monetary growth over turning points in economic activity, can probably be explained by the influence of business conditions on the money supply. Studies in money supply theory strongly suggest this thesis and yield evidence on its behalf. The cyclical pattern of the currency ratio, and the strategy typically pursued by monetary policymakers explain this lead of monetary growth. And again, such explanation of the timing relation does not bear negatively on the strong conjecture.

The objection noted under Davis' point

[19] *U.S. Financial Data,* Federal Reserve Bank of St. Louis, week ending February 14, 1968. Also see "Money Supply and Time Deposits, 1914–1964" in the September 1964 issue of this *Review.*

(c) is similarly irrelevant. His observations actually confirm the strong thesis. The latter implies that the correlation between amplitudes of monetary and income changes is itself correlated with the magnitude of monetary accelerations or decelerations. A poor correlation in cycles of moderate amplitude, therefore, yields no discriminating evidence on the validity of the strong thesis. Moreover, observations describing occurrences are more appropriate relative to the formulated thesis than correlation measures. For instance, observations tending to disconfirm the strong Monetarist thesis would consist of occurrences of pronounced monetary accelerations or decelerations which are *not followed* by accelerated or retarded movements of economic activity.

Point (d) still remains to be considered. Once again, his observation does not bear on the strong Monetarist thesis. Davis properly cautions readers about the interpretation of the Friedman lag. The variability of this lag is probably due to the interaction of monetary and non-monetary forces, or to changes from cycle to cycle in the relative variability of monetary growth. But again, this does not affect the strong thesis. The proper interpretation of the Friedman lag, as the interval between reversals in the rate of monetary impulses and their prevalence over all other factors simultaneously operating on economic activity, usefully clarifies a concept introduced into our discussions. This clarification provides, however, no relevant evidence bearing on the questioned hypotheses.

In summary, the arguments developed by Davis do not yield any substantive evidence against the strong Monetarist thesis. Moreover, the discussion omits major portions of the evidence assembled in support of this position.[20]

### E. Countercyclical Policy and the Interpretation of Monetary Policy

The usual assertion of the New View, attributing fluctuations of monetary growth to the public's and the banks' behavior, assumed a strategic role in the countercritique. The countercritique denied, furthermore, that monetary actions have a major impact on economic activity. With the crumbling of these two bastions, the monetary policymakers' interpretation of their own behavior becomes quite vulnerable. In a previous section, the substantial contribution of the monetary base to the fluctuations of monetary growth has been demonstrated. These facts, combined with repeated assertions that monetary policy has been largely countercyclical, suggest the existence of a pronounced discrepancy between actual behavior of the monetary authorities and their interpretation of this behavior.

A crucial question bearing on this issue pertains to the proper measure summarizing actual behavior of the monetary authorities. Two major facts should be clearly recognized. First, the monetary base consists of "money" directly issued by the authorities, and every issue of base money involves an action of the monetary authorities. This holds irrespective of their knowledge about it, or their motivation and aims. Second, variations in the base, extended by suitable adjustments to incorporate changing reserve requirement ratios, are the single most important factor influencing the behavior of the money stock. And this second point applies irrespective of whether Federal Reserve authorities are aware of it or wish it to be, or whatever their motivations or aims are. Their actual behavior, and not their motivations or aims, influences the monetary system and the pace of economic activity. Thus, actual changes in the monetary base are quite

[20] Milton Friedman's summary of the evidence in the *Forty-fourth Annual Report of the National Bureau of Economic Research* is important in this respect. Davis overlooks in particular the evidence accumulated in studies of the money supply mechanism which bears on the issue raised by point (a) in the text. A persistent and uniform association between money and economic activity, in spite of large changes in the structure of money supply processes, yields evidence in support of the Monetarist theses.

The reader should also consult Chapter 13 of the book by Milton Friedman and Anna Schwartz listed in footnote 9; *Studies in the Quantity Theory of Money*, edited by Milton Friedman, University of Chicago Press, 1956; and a doctoral dissertation by Michael W. Keran, "Monetary Policy and the Business Cycle in Postwar Japan," Ph.D. thesis at the University of Minnesota, March 1966, to be published as a chapter of a book edited by David Meiselman.

**TABLE 4. THE ASSOCIATION BETWEEN POLICYMAKERS' INTERPRETATION OF POLICY, CHANGES IN THE MONETARY BASE AND CHANGES IN FREE RESERVES**

| Periods | Cumulative scores of policymakers' interpretation over the period | Changes in free reserves over the period in $ million | Changes in the monetary base over the period in $ million |
|---|---|---|---|
| 11/49 - 5/53 | −4.75 | −1030 | +5216 |
| 6/53 - 11/54 | +2.63 | + 286 | +1321 |
| 12/54 - 10/55 | −3.37 | − 818 | + 345 |
| 11/55 - 7/56 | +1.12 | + 352 | + 399 |
| 8/56 - 7/57 | −1.00 | − 44 | + 657 |
| 8/57 - 7/58 | +3.50 | +1017 | +1203 |
| 7/58 - 6/59 | −2.12 | −1059 | + 531 |
| 7/59 - 12/60 | +2.62 | +1239 | − 53 |
| 1/61 - 12/62 | − .63 | − 428 | +3288 |

meaningful and appropriate measures of actual behavior of monetary authorities.[21]

The information presented in Table 4 supports the conjecture that monetary policymakers' interpretation of their own behavior has no systematic positive association with their actual behavior. Table 4 was constructed on the basis of the scores assigned to changes in policies, according to the interpretation of the Federal Open Market Committee.[22] Positive scores were associated with each session of the FOMC which decided to make policy easier, more expansionary, less restrictive, less tight, etc., and negative scores indicate decisions to follow a tighter, less expansionary, more restrictive course. The scores varied between plus and minus one, and expressed some broad ordering of the revealed magnitude of the changes.

An examination of the sequence of scores easily shows that the period covered can be naturally partitioned into subperiods exhibiting an overwhelming occurrence of scores with a uniform sign. These subperiods are listed in the first column of Table 4. The second column cumulated the scores over the subperiods listed in order to yield a very rough ranking of the policymakers' posture according to their own interpretation.

Table 4 reveals that the FOMC interpreted the subperiods from August 1957 to July 1958, and from July 1959 to December 1960 as among the most expansionary policy periods. The period from November 1949 to May 1953 appears in this account as a phase of persistently tight or restrictive policy. The next two columns list the changes of two important variables during each subperiod. The third column describes changes in free reserves, and the fourth column notes changes in the monetary base. A cursory examination of the columns immediately shows substantial differences in their broad association. The rank correlation between the various columns is most informative for our purposes.

These rank correlations are listed in Table 5. The results expose the absence of any positive association between the policymakers' own interpretation or judgement of their stance and their actual behavior, as indicated by movements in the monetary base.

**TABLE 5. RANK CORRELATION BETWEEN CHANGES IN THE MONETARY BASE, CHANGES IN FREE RESERVES AND THE CUMULATED SCORES OF POLICYMAKERS' INTERPRETATIONS**

| | |
|---|---|
| Cumulated scores and base | −.09 |
| Cumulated scores and free reserves | +.70 |
| Free reserves and base | −.26 |

[21] The reader may also be assured by the following statement: ". . . monetary policy refers particularly to determination of the supply of (the government's) demand debt . . ." This demand debt coincides with the monetary base. The quote is by James Tobin, a leading architect of the New View, on p. 148 of his contribution to the Commission on Money and Credit, "An Essay on Principles of Debt Management," in *Fiscal and Debt Management Policies,* Prentice Hall, Englewood Cliffs, 1963.

[22] The scores were published as Appendix II to "An Alternative Approach to the Monetary Mechanism." See footnote 9.

The correlation coefficient between the monetary base and cumulated scores has a *negative* value, suggesting that a systematic divergence between stated and actual policy (as measured by the monetary base) is probable. On the other hand, the correlation between the policymakers' descriptions of their posture, and the movement of free reserves, is impressively close. This correlation confirms once again that the Federal Reserve authorities have traditionally used the volume of free reserves as an indicator to gauge and interpret prevailing monetary policies. Yet little evidence has been developed which establishes a causal chain leading from changes in free reserves to the pace of economic activity.

Another observation contained in Table 4 bears on the issue of policymakers' interpretation of their own behavior. Changes in the cumulated scores and free reserves between the periods listed always move together and are perfect in terms of direction. By comparison, the co-movement between cumulated scores and changes in the monetary base is quite haphazard; only three out of eight changes between periods move together. This degree of co-movement between cumulated scores and the monetary base could have occurred by pure chance with a probability greater than .2, whereas the probability of the perfect co-movement between cumulated scores and free reserves occurring as a matter of pure chance is less than .004. The traditional selection of free reserves or money market conditions as an indicator to interpret prevailing monetary policy and to gauge the relative thrust applied by policy, forms the major reason for the negative association (or at least random association) between stated and actual policy.

Attempts at rebuttal to the above analysis often emphasize that policymakers are neither interested in the monetary base, nor do they attach any significance to it. This argument is advanced to support the claim that the behavior of the monetary base is irrelevant for a proper examination of policymakers' intended behavior. This argument disregards, however, the facts stated earlier, namely, movements in the monetary base are under the direct control and are the sole responsibility of the monetary authorities. It also disregards the fact that actions may yield consequences which are independent of motivations shaping the actions.

These considerations are sufficient to acknowledge the relevance of the monetary base as a measure summarizing the actual behavior of monetary authorities. However, they alone are not sufficient to determine whether the base is the most reliable indicator of monetary policy. Other magnitudes such as interest rates, bank credit, and free reserves have been advanced with plausible arguments to serve as indicators. A rational procedure must be designed to determine which of the possible entities frequently used for scaling policy yields the most reliable results.

This indicator problem is still very poorly understood, mainly because of ambiguous use of economic language in most discussions of monetary policy. The term "indicator" occurs with a variety of meanings in discussions, and so do the terms "target" and "guide." The indicator problem, understood in its technical sense, is the determination of an optimal scale justifying interpretations of the authorities' actual behavior by means of comparative statements. A typical statement is that policy X is more expansionary than policy Y, or that current policy has become more (or less) expansionary. Whenever we use a comparative concept, we implicitly rely on an ordering scale.

The indicator problem has not been given adequate treatment in the literature, and the recognition of its logical structure is often obstructed by inadequate analysis. It is, for instance, not sufficient to emphasize the proposition that the money supply can be a "misleading guide to the proper interpretation of monetary policy." This proposition can be easily demonstrated for a wide variety of models and hypotheses. However, it establishes very little. The same theories usually demonstrate that the rate of interest, free reserves, or bank credit can also be very misleading guides to monetary policy. Thus, we can obtain a series of propositions about a vast array of entities, asserting that each one can be a very misleading guide to the interpretation of policy. We only reach a useless stalemate in this situation.

The usual solution to the indicator problem at the present time is a decision based on mystical insight supplemented by some impressionistic arguments. The most frequently advanced arguments emphasize that central banks operate directly on credit markets where interest rates are formed, or that the interest mechanism forms the centerpiece of the transmission process. Accordingly, in both cases market interest rates should "obviously" emerge as the relevant indicator of monetary policy.

These arguments on behalf of market interest rates are mostly supplied by economists. The monetary authorities' choice of money market conditions as an indicator evolved from a different background. But in recent years a subtle change has occurred. One frequently encounters arguments which essentially deny either the existence of the indicator problem or its rational solution. A favorite line asserts that "the world is very complex" and consequently it is impossible or inadmissible to use a single scale to interpret policy. According to this view, one has to consider and weigh many things in order to obtain a "realistic" assessment in a complicated world.

This position has little merit. The objection to a "single scale" misconstrues the very nature of the problem. Once we decide to discuss monetary policy in terms of comparative statements, an ordinal scale is required in order to provide a logical basis for such statements. A multiplicity of scales effectively eliminates the use of comparative statements. Of course, a single scale may be a function of multiple arguments, but such multiplicity of arguments should not be confused with a multiplicity of scales. Policymakers and economists should therefore realize that one either provides a rational procedure which justifies interpretations of monetary policy by means of comparative statements, or that one abandons any pretense of meaningful or intellectually honest discussion of such policy.

Solution of the indicator problem in the technical sense appears obstructed on occasion by a prevalent confusion with an entirely different problem confronting the central banker—the target problem. This problem results from the prevailing uncertainty concerning the nature of the transmission mechanism and the substantial lags in the dynamics of monetary processes.

In the context of perfect information, the indicator problem becomes trivial and the target problem vanishes. But perfect information is the privilege of economists' discourse on policy; central bankers cannot afford this luxury. The impact of their actions are both delayed and uncertain. Moreover, the ultimate goals of monetary policy (targets in the Tinbergen-Theil sense) appear remote to the manager executing general policy directives. Policymakers will be inclined under these circumstances to insert a more immediate target between their ultimate goals and their actions. These targets should be reliably observable with a minimal lag.

It is quite understandable that central bankers traditionally use various measures of money market conditions, with somewhat shifting weights, as a target guiding the continuous adjustment of their policy variables. This response to the uncertainties and lags in the dynamics of the monetary mechanism is very rational indeed. However, once we recognize the rationality of such behavior, we should also consider the rationality of using a particular target. The choice of a target still remains a problem, and the very nature of this problem is inadequately understood at this state.

This is not the place to examine the indicator and target problem in detail. A possible solution to both problems has been developed on another occasion.[23] The solutions apply decision theoretic procedures and concepts from control theory to the determination of an optimal choice of both indicator and target. Both problems are in principle solvable, in spite of the "complexity of the world." Consequently, there is little excuse for failing to develop rational monetary policy procedures.

## Conclusion

A program for applying economic analysis to financial markets and financial institutions is certainly acceptable and worth pursuing. This program suggests that the public and banks interact in the determination of bank credit, interest rates, and the money stock, in

[23] The reader may consult the chapter by Karl Brunner and Allan H. Meltzer on "Targets and Indicators of Monetary Policy," in the book of the same title, edited by Karl Brunner, published by Chandler House Publishing Co., Belmont, California, 1969.

response to the behavior of monetary authorities. But the recognition of such interaction implies nothing with respect to the relative importance of the causal forces generating cyclical fluctuations of monetary growth. Neither does it bear on the quality of alternative empirical hypotheses, or the relative usefulness of various magnitudes or conditions which might be proposed as an indicator to judge the actual thrust applied by monetary policy to the pace of economic activity.

The Monetarist thesis has been put forth in the form of well structured hypotheses which are supported by empirical evidence. This extensive research in the area of monetary policy has established that: (i) Federal Reserve actions dominate the movement of the monetary base over time, (ii) movements of the monetary base dominate movements of the money supply over the business cycle, and (iii) accelerations or decelerations of the money supply are closely followed by accelerations or decelerations in economic activity. Therefore, the Monetarist thesis puts forth the proposition that actions of the Federal Reserve are transmitted to economic activity via the resulting movements in the monetary base and money supply, which initiate the adjustments in relative prices of assets, liabilities, and the production of new assets.

The New View, as put forth by the countercritique, has offered thus far neither analysis nor evidence pertaining relevantly to an explanation of variations in monetary growth. Moreover, the countercritique has not developed, on acceptable logical grounds, a systematic justification for the abundant supply of statements characterizing policy in terms of its effect on the economy. Nor has it developed a systematic justification for the choice of money market conditions as an optimal target guiding the execution of open market operations.

But rational policy procedures require both a reliable interpretation and an adequate determination of the course of policy. The necessary conditions for rational policy are certainly not satisfied if policies actually retarding economic activity are viewed to be expansionary, as in the case of the 1960-61 recession, or, if inflationary actions are viewed as being restrictive, as in the first half of 1966.

The major questions addressed to our monetary policymakers, their advisors and consultants remain: How do you justify your interpretation of policy, and how do you actually explain the fluctuations of monetary growth? The major contentions of the academic critics of the past performance of monetary authorities could possibly be quite false, but this should be demonstrated by appropriate analysis and relevant evidence.

# 9 MONETARY AND FISCAL ACTIONS: A TEST OF THEIR RELATIVE IMPORTANCE IN ECONOMIC STABILIZATION*

LEONALL C. ANDERSEN
and
JERRY L. JORDAN
*Federal Reserve Bank of St. Louis*

High employment, rising output of goods and services, and relatively stable prices are three widely accepted national economic goals. Responsibility for economic stabilization actions to meet these goals has been assigned to monetary and fiscal authorities. The Federal Reserve System has the major responsibility for monetary management. Fiscal actions involve Federal Government spending plans and taxing provisions. Governmental units involved in fiscal actions are the Congress and the Administration, including the Treasury, the Bureau of the Budget, and the Council of Economic Advisers.

This article reports the results of recent research which tested three commonly held propositions concerning the relative importance of monetary and fiscal actions in implementing economic stabilization policy. These propositions are: The response of economic activity to fiscal actions relative to that of monetary actions is (I) greater, (II) more predictable, and (III) faster. Specific meanings, for the purposes of this article, of the broad terms used in these propositions are presented later.

This article does not attempt to test rival economic theories of the mechanism by which monetary and fiscal actions influence economic activity. Neither is it intended to develop evidence bearing directly on any causal relationships implied by such theories. More elaborate procedures than those used here would be required in order to test any theories underlying the familiar statements regarding results expected from monetary and fiscal actions. However, empirical relationships are developed between frequently used measures of stabilization actions and economic activity. These relationships are consistent with the implications of some theories of stabilization policy and are inconsistent with others, as will be pointed out.

A brief discussion of the forces influencing economic activity is presented first. Next, with this theory as a background, specific measures of economic activity, fiscal actions, and monetary actions are selected. The results of testing the three propositions noted above, together with other statements concerning the response of economic activity to monetary and fiscal forces, are then presented. Finally, some implications for the conduct of stabilization policy are drawn from the results of these tests.

## A Theoretical View of Economic Activity

Our economic system consists of many markets. Every commodity, service, and financial

* Reprinted from *Review*, Federal Reserve Bank of St. Louis, vol. 50 (November, 1968), pp. 11–24, by permission of the authors and the Federal Reserve Bank of St. Louis.

assset is viewed as constituting an individual market in which a particular item is traded and a price is determined. All of these markets are linked together in varying degrees, since prices in one market influence decisions made in other markets.

About a century ago, Leon Walras outlined a framework for analyzing a complex market economy. Such an analysis includes a demand and a supply relationship for every commodity and for each factor of production. Trading in the markets results in prices being established which clear all markets, i.e., the amount offered in a market equals the amount taken from the market. According to this analysis, outside occurrences reflected in shifts in demand and supply relationships cause changes in market prices and in quantities traded. These outside events include changes in preferences of market participants, in resource endowments, and in technology. Financial assets were not viewed as providing utility or satisfaction to their holders and were therefore excluded from the analysis.

Later developments in economic theory have viewed financial assets as providing flows of services which also provide utility or satisfaction to holders. For example, a holder of a commercial bank time deposit receives liquidity service (ease of conversion into the medium of exchange), store of value service (ability to make a future purchase), risk avoidance service (little risk of loss), and a financial yield. According to this later view, economic entities incorporate choices among goods, services, *and* financial assets into their decision-making processes.

The fact that economic entities make choices in both markets for goods and services and markets for financial assets requires the addition of demand and supply relationships for every financial asset. Market interest rates (prices of financial assets) and changes in the stocks outstanding of most financial assets are determined by the market process along with prices and quantities of goods and services.

These theoretical developments have enlarged the number of independent forces which are regarded as influencing market-determined prices, interest rates, quantities produced of commodities, and stocks outstanding of financial assets. Government and monetary authorities are viewed as exerting independent influences in the market system.

**EXHIBIT 1 CLASSIFICATION OF MARKET VARIABLES**

**Dependent Variables**

Prices and quantities of goods and services.
Prices and quantities of factors of production.
Prices (interest rates) and quantities of financial assets.
Expectations based on:
- a. movements in dependent variables.
- b. expected results of random events.
- c. expected changes in fiscal and monetary policy.

**Independent Variables**

Slowly changing factors:
- a. preferences.
- b. technology.
- c. resources.
- d. institutional and legal framework.

Events outside the domestic economy:
- a. change in total world trade.
- b. movements in foreign prices and interest rates.

Random events:
- a. outbreak of war.
- b. major strikes.
- c. weather.

Forces subject to control by:
- a. fiscal actions.
- b. monetary actions.

These influences are called fiscal and monetary policies or actions. Random events, such as the outbreak of war, strikes in key industries, and prolonged drought, exert other market influences. Growth in world trade and changes in foreign prices and interest rates, relative to our own, influence exports and therefore are largely an outside influence on domestic markets.

Market expectations have also been assigned a significant factor in markets, but these are not viewed as a distinctly independent force. Expectations result from market participants basing their decisions on movements in market-determined variables, or they are derived from market responses to the expected results of random events, such as the outbreak of a war or the anticipation of changes in fiscal or monetary policy.

These dependent and independent market variables are summarized in Exhibit 1. The dependent variables are determined by the interplay of market forces which results from changes in the independent variables. Market-determined variables include prices and quantities of goods and services, prices and quantities of factors of production, prices (interest rates) and quantities of financial assets, and expectations. Independent variables consist of slowly changing factors, forces from outside our economy, random events, and forces subject to control by fiscal and monetary authorities. A change in an independent variable (for example, a fiscal or a monetary action) causes changes in many of the market-determined (dependent) variables.

## Measures of Economic Activity and of Monetary and Fiscal Actions

Three theoretical approaches have been advanced by economists for analyzing the influence of monetary and fiscal actions on economic activity. These approaches are the textbook Keynesian analysis derived from economic thought of the late 1930's to the early 1950's, the portfolio approach developed over the last two decades, and the modern quantity theory of money. Each of these theories has led to popular and familiar statements regarding the direction, amount, and timing of fiscal and monetary influences on economic activity. As noted earlier, these theories and their linkages will not be tested directly, but the validity of some of the statements which purport to represent the implications of these theories will be examined. For this purpose, frequently used measures of economic activity, monetary actions and fiscal actions are selected.

### *Economic Activity*

Total spending for goods and services (gross national product at current prices) is used in this article as the measure of economic activity. It consists of total spending on final goods and services by households, businesses, and governments plus net foreign investment. Real output of goods and services is limited by resource endowments and technology, with the actual level of output, within this constraint, determined by the level of total spending and other factors.

### *Monetary Actions*

Monetary actions involve primarily decisions of the Treasury and the Federal Reserve System. Treasury monetary actions consist of variations in its cash holdings, deposits at Federal Reserve Banks and at commercial banks, and issuance of Treasury currency. Federal Reserve monetary actions include changes in its portfolio of Government securities, variations in member bank reserve requirements, and changes in the Federal Reserve discount rate. Banks and the public also engage in a form of monetary actions. Commercial bank decisions to hold excess reserves constitute a monetary action. Also, because of differential reserve requirements, the public's decisions to hold varying amounts of time deposits at commercial banks or currency relative to demand deposits are a form of monetary action, but are not viewed as stabilization actions. However they are taken into consideration by stabilization authorities in forming their own actions. Exhibit 2 summarizes the various sources of monetary actions related to economic stabilization.

The monetary base[1] is considered by both the portfolio and the modern quantity theory schools to be a strategic monetary variable. The monetary base is under direct control of the monetary authorities, with major control exerted by the Federal Reserve System. Both of these schools consider an increase in the monetary base, other forces constant, to be an expansionary influence on economic activity and a decrease to be a restrictive influence.

The portfolio school holds that a change in the monetary base affects investment spending, and thereby aggregate spending, through changes in market interest rates relative to the supply price of capital (real rate of return on capital). The modern quantity theory holds that the influence of the monetary base works through changes in the

[1] The monetary base is derived from a consolidated monetary balance sheet of the Federal Reserve and the Treasury. See Leonall C. Andersen and Jerry L. Jordan, "The Monetary Base: Explanation and Analytical Use," in the August 1968 issue of this *Review*. Since the uses of the base are bank reserves plus currency held by the public, it is often called "demand debt of the Government." See James Tobin, "An Essay on Principles of Debt Management," in *Fiscal and Debt Management Policies*, The Commission on Money and Credit, Prentice-Hall, Inc., Englewood Cliffs, N.J., 1963. In some analyses, Tobin includes short-term Government debt outstanding in the monetary base.

EXHIBIT 2. STABILIZATION ACTIONS AND THEIR MEASUREMENT

| Stabilization Actions | Frequently Used Measurements of Actions |
|---|---|
| **1. Monetary actions** | **1. Monetary actions** |
| Federal Reserve System | Monetary base* |
| a. open market transactions. | Money stock, narrowly defined* |
| b. discount rate changes. | Money plus time deposits |
| c. reserve requirement changes. | Commercial bank credit |
| | Private demand deposits |
| Treasury | |
| a. changes in cash holdings. | **2. Fiscal actions** |
| b. changes in deposits at Reserve banks. | High-employment expenditures.* |
| c. changes in deposits at commercial banks. | High-employment receipts.* |
| d. changes in Treasury currency outstanding. | High-employment surplus.* |
| | Weighted high-employment expenditures. |
| | Weighted high-employment receipts. |
| | Weighted high-employment surplus. |
| **2. Fiscal actions** | National income account expenditures. |
| Government spending programs. | National income account receipts. |
| Government taxing provisions. | Autonomous changes in Government tax rates. |
| | Net Government debt outside of agencies and trust funds. |

* Tests based on these measures are reported in this article. The remaining measures were used in additional tests. These results are available on request.

money stock which in turn affect prices, interest rates, and spending on goods and services. Increases in the base are reflected in increases in the money stock which in turn result directly and indirectly in increased expenditures on a whole spectrum of capital and consumer goods. Both prices of goods and interest rates form the transmission mechanism in the modern quantity theory.

The money stock is also used as a strategic monetary variable in each of the approaches to stabilization policies, as the above discussion has implied. The simple Keynesian approach postulates that a change in the stock of money relative to its demand results in a change in interest rates. It also postulates that investment spending decisions depend on interest rates, and that growth in aggregate spending depends in turn on these investment decisions. Similarly, in the portfolio school of thought changes in the money stock lead to changes in interest rates, which are followed by substitutions in asset portfolios; then finally, total spending is affected. Interest rates, according to this latter school, are the key part of the transmission mechanism, influencing decisions to hold money versus alternative financial assets as well as decisions to invest in real assets. The influence of changes in the money stock on economic activity, within the modern quantity theory framework, has already been discussed in the previous paragraph.[2]

The monetary base, as noted, plays an important role in both the portfolio and the modern quantity theory approaches to monetary theory. However, there remains considerable controversy regarding the role of money in determining economic activity, ranging from "money does not matter" to "money is the dominant factor." In recent years there has been a general acceptance that money, among many other influences, is important. Thomas Mayer, in a recent book, summarizes this controversy. He concludes:

> All in all, much recent evidence supports the view that the stock of money and, therefore, monetary policy, has a substantial effect. Note, however, that this reading of the evidence is by no means acceptable to all economists. Some, Professor Friedman and Dr. Warburton for example, argue that changes in the stock of money

[2] Also see Leonall C. Andersen and Jerry L. Jordan, "Money in a Modern Quantity Theory Framework" in the December 1967 issue of this *Review*. For an excellent analysis of these three monetary views see David I. Fand, "Keynesian Monetary Theories, Stabilization Policy and the Recent Inflation," *Journal of Money, Credit and Banking*, vol. 1, no. 3, August, 1969, pp. 556–587.

do have a dominant effect on income, at least in the long run, while others such as Professor Hansen believe that changes in the stock of money are largely offset by opposite changes in velocity.[3]

The theories aside, changes in the monetary base and changes in the money stock are frequently used as measures of monetary actions. This article, in part, tests the use of these variables for this purpose. Money is narrowly defined as the nonbank public's holdings of demand deposits plus currency. Changes in the money stock mainly reflect movements in the monetary base; however, they also reflect decisions of commercial banks to hold excess reserves, of the nonbank public to hold currency and time deposits, and of the Treasury to hold demand deposits at commercial banks. The monetary base reflects monetary actions of the Federal Reserve, and to a lesser extent, those of the Treasury and gold flows. But changes in the base have been found to be dominated by actions of the Federal Reserve.[4]

Other aggregate measures, such as money plus time deposits, bank credit, and private demand deposits, are frequently used as monetary indicators (Exhibit 2). Tests using these indicators were also made. The results of these tests did not change the conclusions reached in this article; these results are available on request. Market interest rates are not used in this article as strategic monetary variables since they reflect, to a great extent, fiscal actions, expectations and other factors which cannot properly be called monetary actions.

### *Fiscal Actions*

The influence of fiscal actions on economic activity is frequently measured by Federal Government spending, changes in Federal tax rates, or Federal budget deficits and surpluses. The textbook Keynesian view has been reflected in many popular discussions of fiscal influence. The portfolio approach and the modern quantity theory suggest alternative analyses of fiscal influence.

The elementary textbook Keynesian view concentrates almost exclusively on the direct influence of fiscal actions on total spending. Government spending is a direct demand for goods and services. Tax rates affect disposable income, a major determinant of consumer spending, and profits of businesses, a major determinant of investment spending. Budget surpluses and deficits are used as a measure of the net direct influence of spending and taxing on economic activity. More advanced textbooks also include an indirect influence of fiscal actions on economic activity through changes in market interest rates. In either case, little consideration is generally given to the method of financing expenditures.

The portfolio approach as developed by Tobin attributes to fiscal actions both a direct influence on economic activity and an indirect influence. Both influences take into consideration the financing of Government expenditures.[5] Financing of expenditures by issuance of demand debt of monetary authorities (the monetary base) results in the full Keynesian multiplier effect. Financing by either taxes or borrowing from the public has a smaller multiplier effect on spending. Tobin views this direct influence as temporary.

The indirect influence of fiscal actions, according to Tobin, results from the manner of financing the Government debt, that is, variations in the relative amounts of demand debt, short-term debt, and long-term debt. For example, an expansionary move would be a shift from long-term to short-term debt or a shift from short-term to demand debt. A restrictive action would result from a shift in the opposite direction. As in the case of monetary actions, market interest rates on financial assets and their influence on investment spending make up the transmission mechanism.

The modern quantity theory also suggests that the influence of fiscal actions depends on the method of financing Government expenditures. This approach maintains that financing expenditures by either taxing or borrowing from the public involves a transfer of command over resources from the public to

---

[3] Thomas Mayer, *Monetary Policy in the United States,* Random House, N. Y., 1968, pp. 148–149.

[4] For a discussion of these points, see: Karl Brunner, "The Role of Money and Monetary Policy," in the July 1968 issue of this *Review* [reprinted in this volume].

[5] Tobin, pp. 143–213.

the Government. However, the net influence on total spending resulting from interest rate and wealth changes is ambiguous. Only a deficit financed by the monetary system is necessarily expansionary.[6]

High-employment budget concepts have been developed as measures of the influence of fiscal actions on economic activity.[7] In these budget concepts, expenditures include both those for goods and services and those for transfer payments, adjusted for the influence of economic activity. Receipts, similarly adjusted, primarily reflect legislated changes in Federal Government tax rates, including Social Security taxes. The net of receipts and expenditures is used as a net measure of changes in expenditure provisions and in tax rates. These high-employment concepts are used in this article as measures of fiscal actions (Exhibit 2). Tests were also made alternatively using national income account Government expenditures and receipts, a series measuring autonomous changes in Government tax rates, a weighted high-employment expenditure and receipt series, and a series of U. S. Government debt held by the public plus Federal Reserve holdings of U. S. Government securities. These tests did not change the conclusions reached in this article. Results of these tests are available on request.

[6] The importance of not overlooking the financial aspects of fiscal policy is emphasized by Carl F. Christ in "A Simple Macroeconomic Model with a Government Budget Restraint," *Journal of Political Economy*, vol. 76, no. 1, January/February 1968, pp. 53–67. Christ summarizes (pages 53 and 54) that "the multiplier effect of a change in government purchases cannot be defined until it is decided how to finance the purchases, and the value of the multiplier given by the generally accepted analysis [which ignores the government budget restraint] is in general incorrect . . . [the] multiplier effect of government purchases may be greater or less than the value obtained by ignoring the budget restraint, depending on whether the method of financing is mainly by printing money or mainly by taxation."

[7] See Keith M. Carlson, "Estimates of the High-Employment Budget: 1947–1967," in the June 1967 issue of this *Review*. The high-employment budget concept was used in the *Annual Report of the Council of Economic Advisors* from 1962 to 1966. For a recent analysis using the high-employment budget, see "Federal Fiscal Policy in the 1960's," *Federal Reserve Bulletin*, September 1968, pp. 701–718. According to this article, "the concept does provide a more meaningful measure of the Federal budgetary impact than the published measures of actual Federal surplus or deficit taken by themselves."

### *Other Influences*

Measures of other independent forces which influence economic activity are not used in this article. Yet this should not be construed to imply that these forces are not important. It is accepted by all economists that the non-monetary and non-fiscal forces listed in Exhibit 1 have an important influence on economic activity. However, recognition of the existence of these "other forces" does not preclude the testing of propositions relating to the relative importance of monetary and fiscal forces. The analysis presented in this study provides indirect evidence bearing on these "other forces." The interested reader is encouraged to read the technical note presented in the Appendix to this article before proceeding.

## Testing the Propositions

This section reports the results of testing the three propositions under consideration. First, the concept of testing a hypothesis is briefly discussed. Next, the results of regression analyses which relate the measures of fiscal and monetary actions to total spending are reported. Finally, statistics developed from the regression analyses are used to test the specific propositions.

### *The Concept of Testing a Hypothesis*

In scientific methodology, testing a hypothesis consists of the statement of the hypothesis, deriving by means of logic testable consequences expected from it, and then taking observations from past experience which show the presence or absence of the expected consequences. If the expected consequences do not occur, then the hypothesis is said to be "not confirmed" by the evidence. If, on the other hand, the expected consequences occur, the hypothesis is said to be "confirmed."

It is important to keep the following point in mind. In scientific testing, a hypothesis (or conjecture) may be found "not confirmed" and therefore refuted as the explanation of the relationship under examination.

However, if it is found to be "confirmed," the hypothesis cannot be said to have been proven true. In the latter case, however, the hypothesis remains an acceptable proposition of a real world relationship as long as it is found to be "confirmed" in future tests.[8]

The results presented in this study all bear on what is commonly called a "reduced form" in economics. A reduced-form equation is a derivable consequence of a system of equations which may be hypothesized to represent the structure of the economy (i.e., a so-called structural model). In other words, all of the factors and causal relations which determine total spending (GNP) are "summarized" in one equation. This reduced-form equation postulates a certain relationship over time between the independent variables and the dependent variable—total spending. Using appropriate statistical procedures and selected measures of variables, it is possible to test whether or not the implications of the reduced-form equation have occurred in the past. If the implied relationships are not confirmed, then the relationship asserted by the reduced-form equation is said to have been refuted. However, not confirming the reduced form does not necessarily mean that the whole "model," and all of the factors and causal relations contained in it, are denied. It may be only that one or more of the structural linkages of the model is incorrect, or that the empirical surrogates chosen as measures of monetary or fiscal influence are not appropriate.[9]

Frequently one encounters statements or conjectures regarding factors which are asserted to influence economic activity in a specific way. These statements take the form of reduced-form equations, and are sometimes attributed to various theories of the determination of economic activity. As stated previously, this study does not attempt to test the causal linkages by which fiscal and monetary actions influence total spending, but is concerned only with the confirmation or refutation of rival conjectures regarding the strength and reliability of fiscal and monetary actions based on frequently used indicators of such actions.

### *Measuring the Empirical Relationships*

As a step toward analyzing the three propositions put forth earlier, empirical relationships between the measures of fiscal and monetary actions and total spending are established. These relationships are developed by regressing quarter-to-quarter changes in GNP on quarter-to-quarter changes in the money stock (M) and in the various measures of fiscal actions: high-employment budget surplus (R-E), high-employment expenditures (E), and high-employment receipts (R). Similar equations were estimated where changes in the monetary base (B) were used in place of the money stock.

Changes in all variables were computed by two methods. Conventional first differences were calculated by subtracting the value for the preceding quarter from the value for the present quarter.[10] The other method used is an averaging procedure used by Kareken and Solow called central differences.[11] The structure of lags present in the regressions was estimated with use of the Almon lag technique.[12] The data are seasonally adjusted quarterly averages for the

[8] For a detailed discussion of testing hypotheses in reference to monetary actions, see Albert E. Burger and Leonall C. Andersen, "The Development of Testable Hypotheses for Monetary Management," *Southern Journal of Business*, vol. 4, no. 4, October 1969, pp. 140–164.

[9] A more specific statement relating to these considerations is presented in the Appendix.

[10] Changes in GNP, R and E are quarterly changes in billions of dollars measured at annual rates, while changes in M and B are quarterly changes in billions of dollars. Changes in GNP, R and E are changes in flows, whereas changes in M and B are changes in a stock. Since all of the time series have strong trends, first differences tend to increase in size over time. Statistical considerations indicate that per cent first differences would be more appropriate. On the other hand, regular first differences provide estimates of multipliers which are more useful for the purposes of this study. Test regressions of relative changes were run and they did not alter the conclusions of this article.

[11] John Kareken and Robert M. Solow, "Lags in Monetary Policy" in *Stabilization Policies* of the research studies prepared for the Commission on Money and Credit, Prentice-Hall, Inc., 1962, pp. 18–21.

[12] Shirley Almon, "The Distributed Lag Between Capital Appropriations and Expenditures," *Econometrica*, vol. 33, no. 1, January 1965, pp. 178–196.

period from the first quarter of 1952 to the second quarter of 1968.[13]

As discussed previously, statements are frequently made from which certain relationships are expected to exist between measures of economic activity on the one hand and measures of monetary and fiscal actions on the other hand. Such relationships consist of a direct influence of an action on GNP and of an indirect influence which reflects interactions among the many markets for real and financial assets. These interactions work through the market mechanism determining the dependent variables listed in Exhibit 1. The postulated relationships are the total of these direct and indirect influences. Thus, the empirical relationship embodied in each regression coefficient is the *total* response (including both direct and indirect responses) of GNP to changes in each measure of a stabilization action, assuming all other forces remain constant.

The results presented here do not provide a basis for separating the direct and indirect influences of monetary and fiscal forces on total spending, but this division is irrelevant for the purposes of this article. The interested reader is referred to the Appendix for further elaboration of these points.

Using the total response concept, changes in GNP are expected to be positively related to changes in the money stock (M) or changes in the monetary base (B). With regard to the high-employment surplus (receipts minus expenditures), a larger surplus or a smaller deficit is expected to have a negative influence on GNP, and conversely. Changes in high-employment expenditures (E) are expected to have a positive influence and changes in receipts (R) are expected to have a negative influence when these variables are included separately.

Considering that the primary purpose of this study is to measure the influence of a few major forces on changes in GNP, rather than to identify and measure the influences of all independent forces, the results obtained are quite good (Table 1). The $R^2$ statistic, a measure of the percent of the variance in changes in GNP explained by the regression equation, ranges from .53 to .73; these values are usually considered to be quite good when first differences are used rather than levels of the data. All of the estimated regression coefficients for changes in the money stock or the monetary base have the signs implied in the above discussion (equations 1.1 to 2.4 in Table 1) and have a high statistical significance in most cases. The estimated coefficients for the high-employment measures of fiscal influence do not have the expected signs in all cases and generally are of low statistical significance. These regression results are discussed in greater detail below.

MONEY AND THE MONETARY BASE. The total response of GNP to changes in money or the monetary base distributed over four quarters is consistent with the postulated relationship (i.e., a positive relationship), and the coefficients are all statistically significant. The coefficients of each measure of monetary action may be summed to provide an indication of the overall response of GNP to changes in monetary actions. These summed coefficients are also statistically significant and consistent with the postulated relationships. The results obtained for measures of monetary actions were not affected significantly when measures of fiscal actions other than those reported here were used in the regressions.

HIGH-EMPLOYMENT BUDGET SURPLUS. As pointed out previously, the high-employment surplus or deficit is often used as a measure of the direction and strength of fiscal actions. Equation 1.1 summarizes the total response of GNP to changes in money and changes in the high-employment surplus. The coefficients of the high-employment surplus estimated for the contemporaneous and first lagged quarter have the expected sign, but the coefficients are of very low statistical significance and do not differ significantly from zero. The signs of the coefficients estimated for the second and third lagged quarters are opposite to the expected signs. The sum of

---

[13] As a test for structural shifts, the test period was divided into two equal parts and the regressions reported here were run for each sub-period and for the whole period. The Chow test for structural changes accepted the hypothesis that the sets of parameters estimated for each of the sub-periods were not different from each other or from those estimated for the whole period, at the five per cent level of significance. As a result, there is no evidence of a structural shift; consequently, the whole period was used.

TABLE 1. REGRESSION OF CHANGES IN GNP ON CHANGES IN MONETARY AND FISCAL ACTIONS

| First Differences | (Equation 1.1) | | (Equation 1.2) | | | (Equation 1.3) | | (Equation 1.4) | | |
|---|---|---|---|---|---|---|---|---|---|---|
| | ΔM | Δ(R-E) | ΔM | ΔE | ΔR | ΔM | ΔE | ΔB | ΔE | ΔR |
| t | 1.57* (2.17) | –.15 (.65) | 1.51* (2.03) | .36 (1.15) | .16 (.53) | 1.54* (2.47) | .40 (1.48) | 1.02 (.49) | .23 (.67) | .52 (1.68) |
| t-1 | 1.94* (3.60) | –.20 (1.08) | 1.59* (2.85) | .53* (2.15) | –.01 (.03) | 1.56* (3.43) | .54* (2.68) | 5.46* (3.37) | .37 (1.36) | .02 (.07) |
| t-2 | 1.80* (3.37) | .10 (.55) | 1.47* (2.69) | –.05 (.19) | –.03 (.10) | 1.44* (3.18) | –.03 (.13) | 6.48* (4.10) | –.21 (.84) | –.17 (.64) |
| t-3 | 1.28 (1.88) | .47* (1.95) | 1.27 (1.82) | –.78* (2.82) | .11 (.32) | 1.29* (2.00) | –.74* (2.85) | 3.05 (1.54) | –.93* (3.10) | .14 (.39) |
| Sum | 6.59* (7.73) | .22 (.45) | 5.84* (6.57) | .07 (.13) | .23 (.32) | 5.83* (7.25) | .17 (.54) | 16.01* (5.67) | –.54 (.89) | .51 (.67) |
| Constant | 1.99* (2.16) | | 2.10 (1.88) | | | 2.28* (2.76) | | 1.55 (1.22) | | |
| $R^2$ | .56 | | .58 | | | .60 | | .53 | | |
| S. E. | 4.24 | | 4.11 | | | 4.01 | | 4.35 | | |
| D-W | 1.54 | | 1.80 | | | 1.78 | | 1.71 | | |

TABLE 1. *(Continued)*

| Central Differences | (Equation 2.1) | | (Equation 2.2) | | | (Equation 2.3) | | (Equation 2.4) | | |
|---|---|---|---|---|---|---|---|---|---|---|
| | ΔM | Δ(R-E) | ΔM | ΔE | ΔR | ΔM | ΔE | ΔB | ΔE | ΔR |
| t | 1.50<br>(1.84) | −.24<br>(.91) | 1.58*<br>(2.01) | .53<br>(1.52) | .32<br>(1.05) | 1.54*<br>(2.45) | .63*<br>(2.21) | .61<br>(.28) | .28<br>(.73) | .87*<br>(2.55) |
| t-1 | 2.11*<br>(3.61) | −.23<br>(1.16) | 1.57*<br>(2.78) | .60*<br>(2.44) | −.04<br>(.17) | 1.63*<br>(3.57) | .59*<br>(2.61) | 5.42*<br>(3.16) | .50<br>(1.87) | −.07<br>(.27) |
| t-2 | 1.89*<br>(3.18) | .15<br>(.81) | 1.41*<br>(2.45) | −.15<br>(.60) | −.11<br>(.47) | 1.43*<br>(3.16) | −.16<br>(.71) | 6.87*<br>(3.92) | −.27<br>(1.04) | −.33<br>(1.31) |
| t-3 | 1.06<br>(1.36) | .52<br>(1.90) | 1.26<br>(1.72) | −.96*<br>(3.15) | .18<br>(.48) | 1.13<br>(1.71) | −.86*<br>(3.07) | 3.51<br>(1.71) | −1.26*<br>(3.65) | .35<br>(.87) |
| Sum | 6.56*<br>(8.16) | .21<br>(.47) | 5.80*<br>(7.57) | .02<br>(.04) | .34<br>(.54) | 5.74*<br>(8.45) | .19<br>(.77) | 16.41*<br>(6.95) | −.75<br>(1.37) | .82<br>(1.16) |
| Constant | 2.02*<br>(2.48) | | 2.00*<br>(2.14) | | | 2.30*<br>(3.55) | | 1.24<br>(1.14) | | |
| $R^2$ | .66 | | .72 | | | .73 | | .67 | | |
| S. E. | 3.35 | | 3.03 | | | 2.97 | | 3.26 | | |
| D-W | .88 | | 1.14 | | | 1.13 | | 1.05 | | |

NOTE: Regression coefficients are the top figures, and their "t" values appear below each coefficient enclosed by parentheses. The regression coefficients marked by an asterisk (*) are statistically significant at the 5 per cent level. $R_2$ are adjusted for degrees of freedom. S.E. is the standard error of the estimate, and D-W is the Durbin-Watson statistic.

the coefficients (total response distributed over four quarters) is estimated to have a positive sign (opposite the postulated sign) but is not statistically significant. These results provide no empirical support for the view that fiscal actions measured by the high-employment surplus have a significant influence on GNP. In principle, these results may have occurred either because the high-employment surplus was not a good measure of fiscal influence, or because fiscal influence was not important during the sample period.[14]

EXPENDITURES AND RECEIPTS. Simple textbook Keynesian models of income determination usually demonstrate, theoretically, that changes in tax rates exert a negative influence on economic activity, while changes in Government expenditures exert a positive influence. Equations 1.2 and 1.3 provide tests of these propositions. The signs of the coefficients estimated for tax receipts are the same as the hypothesized signs for only the first and second lagged quarters. However, since these coefficients (individually and the sums) are of low statistical significance, no importance can be attached to this variable. Inclusion of changes in receipts ($\Delta R$) in equation 1.2 does not improve the overall results, in terms of $R^2$ and the standard error of estimate, compared with equation 1.3 from which receipts are excluded.

These results provide no support for theories which indicate that changes in tax receipts due to changes in tax rates exert an overall negative (or any) influence on economic activity. The results are consistent with theories which indicate that if the alternative to tax revenue is borrowing from the public in order to finance Government spending, then the influence of spending will not necessarily be greater if the funds are borrowed rather than obtained through taxation. They are also consistent with the theory that consumers will maintain consumption levels at the expense of saving when there is a temporary reduction in disposable income.

The signs of the coefficients estimated for high-employment expenditures in equations 1.2 and 1.3 indicate that an increase in Government expenditures is mildly stimulative in the quarter in which spending is increased and in the following quarter. However, in the subsequent two quarters this increase in expenditures causes offsetting negative influences. The overall effect of a change in expenditures distributed over four quarters, indicated by the sum, is relatively small and not statistically significant. These results are consistent with modern quantity theories which hold that Government spending, taxing and borrowing policies would have, through interest rate and wealth effects, different impacts on economic activity under varying circumstances.[15]

### *Three Propositions Tested*

The empirical relationships developed relating changes in GNP to changes in the money stock and changes in high-employment expenditures and receipts are used to test the three propositions under consideration. The results of testing the propositions using changes in the money stock are discussed in

[14] It was suggested to the authors that a weighted high-employment budget surplus might be a better measure of fiscal influence than the usual unweighted series. For an elaboration of such a weighed series, see Edward M. Gramlich, "Measures of the Aggregate Demand Impact of the Federal Budget," in *Staff Papers of the President's Commission on Budget Concepts,* U.S. Government Printing Office, Washington, D.C., October 1967. Gramlich provided weights from the FRB-MIT model of the economy for constructing a weighted series. It was further suggested that the level of the high-employment budget surplus was a more appropriate measure of fiscal actions. Coefficients of fiscal influence were estimated using both changes in the weighted series, and levels of the high-employment surplus. The results did not change any of the conclusions of this article.

[15] John Culbertson points out that in a financially constrained economy (i.e., no monetary expansion to finance Government expenditures), expenditures by the Government financed in debt markets in competition with private expenditures can very possibly "crowd out of the market an equal (or conceivably even greater) volume that would have financed private expenditures." He asserts that it is possible to have a short-lived effect of Government spending on total spending if the financial offsets lag behind its positive effects. The results obtained for $\Delta E$ in this article are consistent with his analysis. See John M. Culbertson, *Macroeconomic Theory and Stabilization Policy,* McGraw-Hill Inc., New York, 1968, pp. 462–463.

TABLE 2. MEASUREMENTS OF THE RELATIVE IMPORTANCE OF MONETARY AND FISCAL ACTIONS

First Differences (Equations 1.2 and 1.4)

| | Beta Coefficients | | | | | | Partial Coefficients of Determination | | | | | |
|---|---|---|---|---|---|---|---|---|---|---|---|---|
| Quarter | ΔM | ΔE | ΔR | ΔB | ΔE | ΔR | ΔM | ΔE | ΔR | ΔB | ΔE | ΔR |
| t | .24 | .14 | .05 | .06 | .09 | .16 | .07 | .02 | .01 | * | .01 | .05 |
| t-1 | .26 | .20 | * | .31 | .14 | .01 | .14 | .08 | * | .18 | .03 | * |
| t-2 | .24 | −.02 | −.01 | .37 | −.08 | −.05 | .12 | * | * | .24 | .01 | .01 |
| t-3 | .20 | −.30 | .03 | .17 | −.36 | .04 | .06 | .13 | * | .04 | .16 | * |
| Sum | .94 | .02 | .07 | .91 | −.21 | .16 | .45 | * | * | .38 | .02 | .01 |

Central Differences (Equations 2.2 and 2.4)

| | Beta Coefficients | | | | | | Partial Coefficients of Determination | | | | | |
|---|---|---|---|---|---|---|---|---|---|---|---|---|
| Quarter | ΔM | ΔE | ΔR | ΔB | ΔE | ΔR | ΔM | ΔE | ΔR | ΔB | ΔE | ΔR |
| t | .26 | .20 | .09 | .04 | .11 | .25 | .07 | .04 | .02 | * | .01 | .11 |
| t-1 | .26 | .23 | −.01 | .31 | .19 | −.02 | .13 | .10 | * | .16 | .06 | * |
| t-2 | .23 | −.06 | −.03 | .40 | −.10 | −.09 | .11 | .01 | * | .23 | .02 | .03 |
| t-3 | .20 | −.36 | .05 | .20 | −.47 | .10 | .05 | .16 | * | .05 | .21 | .01 |
| Sum | .95 | .01 | .10 | .95 | −.27 | .24 | .53 | * | .01 | .49 | .04 | .03 |

*Less than .005.

detail in this section. Similar results are reported in the accompanying tables using changes in the monetary base instead of the money stock. Conclusions drawn using either measure of monetary actions are similar.

*Proposition I* states that fiscal actions exert a larger influence on economic activity than do monetary actions. A test of this proposition involves an examination of the size of the regression coefficients for high-employment expenditures relative to those for money and the monetary base.[16] Proposition I implies that the coefficients for ΔE would be larger, without regard to sign, than those for ΔM and ΔB.

The coefficients presented in Table 1 are not appropriate for this test because the variables have different time dimensions and are a mixture of stocks and flows. An appropriate measure is developed by changing these regression coefficients to "beta coefficients" which eliminate these difficulties (Table 2). These coefficients take into consideration the past variation of changes in each independent variable relative to the past variation of changes in GNP.[17] The size of beta coefficients may be, therefore, directly compared as a measure of the relative contribution of each variable to variations in GNP in the test period.

According to Table 2, the beta coefficients for changes in money are greater than those for changes in high-employment expenditures for the quarter in which a change occurs and during the two following quarters. The coefficients for changes in the monetary base are greater for the two quarters immediately following a change in the base. In the lagged quarters in which the beta coefficients for ΔE are largest, a negative sign is associated with the regression coefficient, indicating a lagged contractionary effect of increased expenditures. As a measure of the total contribution over the four quarters, the sum of the beta coefficients for changes in money and the monetary base are much greater than those for changes in expenditures.

Proposition I may also be tested by the use of partial coefficients of determination. These statistics are measures of the percent of variation of the dependent variable remaining after the variation accounted for by all other variables in the regression has been subtracted from the total variation. Proposition I implies that larger coefficients should be observed for fiscal actions rather than for monetary actions. Table 2 presents the partial coefficients of determination for the variables under consideration. For the quarter of

16 Since little response of GNP to ΔR was found, further discussions consider only ΔE.

17 Arthur S. Goldberger, *Econometric Theory*. John Wiley & Sons, Inc., December 1966, New York, New York, pp. 197–200.

TABLE 3. SIMULATED RESPONSE OF AN INCREASE IN GOVERNMENT EXPENDITURES FINANCED BY MONETARY EXPANSION (millions of dollars)

| | Increase in Government Expenditures | | | Required Increase in Money | | | Total Response in GNP | |
|---|---|---|---|---|---|---|---|---|
| Quarter | Change in expenditures | Impact effect on GNP | Cumulative effect on GNP | Change in money stock | Impact effect on GNP | Cumulative effect on GNP | Impact effect on GNP | Cumulative effect on GNP |
| 1 | $1000 | $400 | $400 | $250 | $ 385 | $ 385 | $ 785 | $ 785 |
| 2 | 0 | 540 | 940 | 250 | 775 | 1160 | 1315 | 2100 |
| 3 | 0 | − 30 | 910 | 250 | 1135 | 2295 | 1105 | 3205 |
| 4 | 0 | −740 | 170 | 250 | 1458 | 3753 | 718 | 3923 |
| 5 | −1000 | −400 | −230 | 0 | 1072 | 4825 | 672 | 4595 |
| 6 | 0 | −540 | −770 | 0 | 682 | 5507 | 142 | 4737 |
| 7 | 0 | 30 | −740 | 0 | 323 | 5830 | 353 | 5090 |
| 8 | 0 | 740 | 0 | 0 | 0 | 5830 | 740 | 5830 |

a change and the subsequent two quarters, these coefficients for $\Delta M$ are much greater than those for $\Delta E$. With regard to $\Delta B$, the coefficients are about equal to those for $\Delta E$ in the first quarter and are much greater in the two subsequent quarters. The partial coefficients of determination for the total contribution of each policy variable to changes in GNP over four quarters may be developed. Table 2 shows that the partial coefficients of determination for the over-all response of $\Delta GNP$ to $\Delta M$ and $\Delta B$ range from .38 to .53, while those for $\Delta E$ are virtually zero.

Other implications of the results presented in Table 1 may be used to test further the relative strength of the response of GNP to alternative government actions under conditions where "other things" are held constant. Three alternative actions are assumed taken by stabilization authorities: (1) the rate of government spending is increased by $1 billion and is financed by either borrowing from the public or increasing taxes; (2) the money stock is increased by $1 billion with no change in the budget position; and (3) the rate of government spending is increased by $1 billion for a year and is financed by increasing the money stock by an equal amount.

The impact on total spending of the first two actions may be measured by using the sums of the regression coefficients presented for equation 1.3. A billion dollar increase in the rate of government spending would, after four quarters, result in a permanent increase of $170 million in GNP. By comparison, an increase of the same magnitude in money would result in GNP being $5.8 billion permanently higher after four quarters.

The results of the last action are presented in Table 3.[18] The annual rate of government spending is assumed to be increased by $1 billion in the first quarter and held at that rate for the following three quarters. This would require an increase in money of $250 million during each of the four quarters to finance the higher level of expenditures. Since we are interested only in the result of financing the original increase in expenditures by monetary expansion, expenditures must be reduced by $1 billion in the fifth quarter. If expenditures were held at the higher rate, money would have to continue to grow $250 million per quarter. According to Table 3, GNP would rise to a permanent level $5.8 billion higher than at the beginning. This increase in GNP results entirely from monetary expansion.

According to these three tests, the regression results implied by Proposition I did not occur. Therefore, the proposition that the response of total demand to fiscal actions is greater than that to monetary actions is not confirmed by the evidence.

*Proposition II* holds that the response of economic activity to fiscal actions is more predictable than the response to monetary

[18] The authors wish to give special thanks to Milton Friedman for suggesting this illustration and Table 3. However, the formulation presented here is the sole responsibility of the authors.

TABLE 4. MEASUREMENT OF RELIABILITY OF THE RESPONSE OF GNP TO MONETARY AND FISCAL ACTIONS ("t-values" of Regression Coefficients[1])

| | First Differences | | | | | |
|---|---|---|---|---|---|---|
| Quarter | ΔM | ΔE | ΔR | ΔB | ΔE | ΔR |
| t | 2.03 | 1.15 | 0.53 | 0.49 | 0.67 | 1.68 |
| t-1 | 2.85 | 2.15 | 0.03 | 3.37 | 1.36 | 0.07 |
| t-2 | 2.69 | 0.19 | 0.10 | 4.10 | 0.84 | 0.64 |
| t-3 | 1.82 | 2.82 | 0.32 | 1.54 | 3.10 | 0.39 |
| Sum | 6.57 | 0.13 | 0.32 | 5.67 | 0.89 | 0.67 |
| | **Central Differences** | | | | | |
| Quarter | ΔM | ΔE | ΔR | ΔB | ΔE | ΔR |
| t | 2.01 | 1.52 | 1.05 | 0.28 | 0.73 | 2.55 |
| t-1 | 2.78 | 2.44 | 0.17 | 3.16 | 1.87 | 0.27 |
| t-2 | 2.45 | 0.60 | 0.46 | 3.92 | 1.04 | 1.31 |
| t-3 | 1.72 | 3.15 | 0.48 | 1.71 | 3.65 | 0.87 |
| Sum | 7.57 | 0.04 | 0.54 | 6.95 | 1.37 | 1.16 |

[1] t-values associated with equations 1.2, 1.4, 2.2 and 2.4 in Table 1.

influence. This implies that the regression coefficients relative to their standard errors (this ratio is called the "t-value"), relating changes in E to changes in GNP, should be greater than the corresponding measures for changes in M and in B. The greater the t-value, the more confidence there is in the estimated regression coefficient, and hence, the greater is the reliability of the estimated change in GNP resulting from a change in the variable. These t-values are presented in Table 4.

An examination of this table indicates greater t-values for the regression coefficients of the two monetary variables than for the fiscal variable, except for the third quarter after a change. Also, the t-values for the sum of the regression coefficients for ΔM and ΔB are large, while those for ΔE are not statistically significant from zero. Since the regression results implied by Proposition II did not appear, the proposition is not confirmed.

*Proposition III* states that the influence of fiscal actions on economic activity occurs faster than that of monetary actions. It is tested by examining the characteristics of the lag structure in the regressions. Proposition III implies that beta coefficients for ΔE should be greater than those for ΔM in the quarter of a change and in those immediately following. It also implies that the main response of GNP to fiscal actions occurs within fewer quarters than its response to monetary actions.

The beta coefficients are plotted in Chart 1.[19] A change in the money stock induces a large and almost equal response in each of the four quarters. The largest response of GNP to changes in the monetary base occurs in the first and second quarters after a change. The beta coefficients for changes in M are greater than those for changes in E for the quarter of a change and the following quarter, indicating comparatively smaller response of GNP to fiscal actions in these first two quarters. Moreover, the largest coefficient for ΔE occurs for the third quarter after a change.

The expected regression results implied by Proposition III were not found. Therefore, the proposition that the major impact of fiscal influence on economic activity occurs within a shorter time interval than monetary influence is not confirmed.

[19] The Almon lag structure was developed by using a fourth degree polynomial and constraining the coefficients for t-4 to zero. The regressions indicate that four quarters constitute an appropriate response period for both fiscal and monetary actions. Equations using up to seven lagged quarters were also estimated, but there was little response in GNP to fiscal and monetary actions beyond the three quarter lags reported.

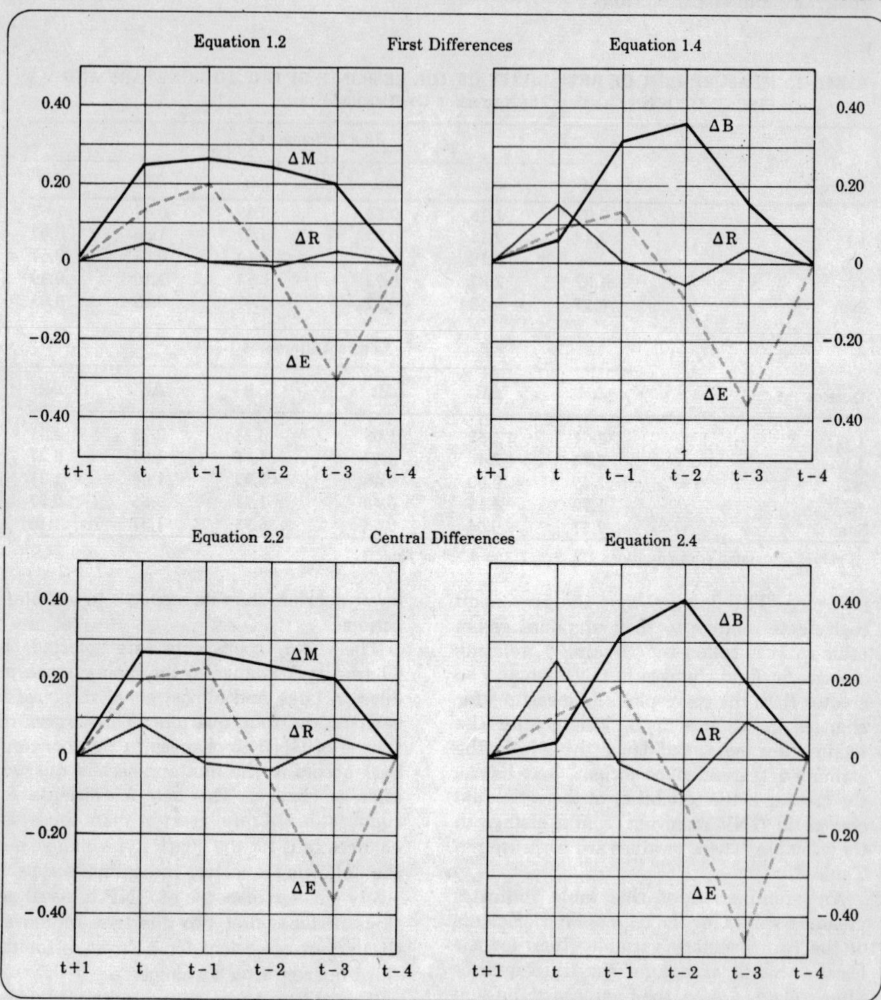


**CHART 1** Measures of lag response. *Beta coefficients are for changes in the money stock* (ΔM), *the monetary base* (ΔB), *high-employment expenditures* (ΔE), *and high-employment receipts* (ΔR). *These beta coefficients are calculated as the products of the regression coefficient for the respective variables times the ratio of the standard deviation of the variable to the standard deviation of GNP.*

SUMMARY. This section tested the propositions that the response of economic activity to fiscal actions relative to monetary actions is (I) larger, (II) more predictable, and (III) faster. The results of the tests were not consistent with any of these propositions. Consequently, either the commonly used measures of fiscal influence do not correctly indicate the degree and direction of such influence, or there was no measurable net fiscal influence on total spending in the test period.

The test results are consistent with an alternate set of propositions. The response of economic activity to monetary actions compared with that of fiscal actions is (I′) larger, (II′) more predictable, and (III′) faster. It should be remembered that these alternative propositions have not been proven true, but this is always the case in scientific testing of hypothesized relationships. Nevertheless, it is asserted here that these alternative propositions are appropriate for the conduct of stabilization policy until evidence is presented proving one or more of them false.

There is a major qualification to these statements. Since the propostions were tested using the period first quarter 1952 to second quarter 1968, it is implicitly assumed in making these statements that the general environment prevailing in the test period holds for the immediate future.

### *Implications for Economic Stabilization Policy*

Rejection of the three propositions under examination and acceptance of the alternatives offered carry important implications for the conduct of economic stabilization policy. All of these implications point to the advisability of greater reliance being placed on monetary actions than on fiscal actions. Such a reliance would represent a marked departure from most present procedures.

The finding that statements which assert that changes in tax rates have a significant influence on total spending are not supported by this empirical investigation suggests that past efforts in this regard have been overly optimistic. Furthermore, the finding that the response of total spending to changes in Government expenditures is small compared with the response of spending to monetary actions strongly suggests that it would be more appropriate to place greater reliance on the latter form of stabilization action.

Finding of a strong empirical relationship between economic activity and either of the measures of monetary actions points to the conclusion that monetary actions can and should play a more prominent role in economic stabilization than they have up to now. Furthermore, failure to recognize these relationships can lead to undesired changes in economic activity because of the relatively short lags and strong effects attributable to monetary actions.

Evidence was found which is consistent with the proposition that the influence of monetary actions on economic activity is more certain than that of fiscal actions. Since monetary influence was also found to be stronger and to operate more quickly than fiscal influence, it would appear to be inappropriate, for stabilization purposes, for monetary authorities to wait very long for a desired fiscal action to be adopted and implemented.

Evidence found in this study suggests that the money stock is an important indicator of the total thrust of stabilization actions, both monetary and fiscal. This point is argued on two grounds. First, changes in the money stock reflect mainly what may be called discretionary actions of the Federal Reserve System as it uses its major instruments of monetary management—open market transactions, discount rate changes, and reserve requirement changes. Second, the money stock reflects the joint actions of the Treasury and the Federal Reserve System in financing newly created Government debt. Such actions are based on decisions regarding the monetization of new debt by Federal Reserve actions, and Treasury decisions regarding changes in its balance at Reserve banks and commercial banks. According to this second point, changes in Government spending financed by monetary expansion are reflected in changes in the monetary base and in the money stock.

A number of economists maintain that the major influence of fiscal actions results only if expenditures are financed by monetary expansion. In practice, the Federal Reserve does not buy securities from the Government. Instead, its open market operations and other actions provide funds in the markets in which both the Government and private sectors borrow.

The relationships expressed in Table 1 may be used to project the expected course of GNP, given alternative assumptions about monetary and fiscal actions. Such projections necessarily assume that the environment in the period used for estimation and the average relationships of the recent past hold in the future. The projections are not able to take into consideration the influences of other independent forces; therefore, they are not suitable for exact forecasting purposes. However, they do provide a useful measure of monetary and fiscal influences on economic activity.

An example of such projections using equa-

TABLE 5. PROJECTED CHANGE IN GNP WITH ALTERNATIVE RATES OF CHANGE IN MONEY STOCK[1]

| | Assumed Rates of Change in Money Stock[2] | | | |
|---|---|---|---|---|
| Quarter | 2% | 4% | 6% | 8% |
| 1968/III[3] | 17.9 | 17.9 | 17.9 | 17.9 |
| IV | 14.6 | 16.0 | 17.5 | 19.0 |
| 1969/I | 12.0 | 15.0 | 18.0 | 20.7 |
| II | 11.0 | 15.2 | 19.4 | 23.7 |
| III | 6.8 | 12.3 | 18.0 | 23.4 |
| IV | 8.0 | 13.7 | 19.4 | 25.2 |

[1]First differences of quarterly data. All variables are in billions of dollars. Projections are based on coefficients of equation 1.3 in Table 1.

[2]Assumed alternative rates of change in the money stock from III/68 to IV/69.

[3]Preliminary estimate by the Department of Commerce.

tion 1.3 is presented in Table 5. Equation 1.3 related quarter-to-quarter changes in GNP to changes in the money stock and changes in high-employment expenditures, both distributed over four quarters.

Assumptions used in computing the projections of quarterly changes in GNP reported in Table 5 include: (a) high-employment expenditures were projected through the second quarter of 1969 under the assumption that Federal spending in fiscal 1969 will be about 5 per cent (or $10 billion) greater than fiscal 1968; (b) Federal spending was assumed to continue increasing at a 5 to 6 per cent rate in the first two quarters of fiscal 1970; and (c) quarter-to-quarter changes in the money stock were projected from III/68 to IV/69 for four alternative constant annual growth rates for money: 2 per cent, 4 per cent, 6 per cent, and 8 per cent.

The highest growth rate of the money stock (8 per cent) indicates continued rapid rates of expansion in GNP during the next five quarters. The slowest growth rate of money (2 per cent) indicates some slowing of GNP growth in the fourth quarter of this year and further gradual slowing throughout most of next year.

The projections indicate that if the recent decelerated growth in the money stock (less than 4 per cent from July to October) is continued, and growth of Government spending is at about the rate indicated above, the economy would probably reach a non-inflationary growth rate of GNP in about the third quarter of 1969 and would then accelerate slightly. These projections, of course, make no assumptions regarding the Vietnam war, strikes, agricultural situations, civil disorders, or any of the many other noncontrollable exogenous forces.

## Appendix[1]

The specific hypothesis underlying the analysis in this study is expressed by the following relation:

$$Y = f(E, R, M, Z) \quad (1)$$

where: Y = total spending; E = a variable summarizing government expenditure actions; R = a variable summarizing government taxing actions; M = a variable summarizing monetary actions; Z = a variable summarizing all other forces that influence total spending.[2]

Expressing this relation in terms of the changes of each variable yields:

$$\Delta Y = f(\Delta E, \Delta R, \Delta M, \Delta Z) \quad (2)$$

If this relation (2) were empirically estimated, the following would be obtained:[3]

$$\Delta Y = \alpha_1 \Delta E + \alpha_2 \Delta R + \alpha_3 \Delta M + \alpha_4 \Delta Z \quad (3)$$

where the values for $\alpha_1$, $\alpha_2$, $\alpha_3$, and $\alpha_4$ are estimated by regression of the observed values of $\Delta Y$ on the observed values of $\Delta E$, $\Delta R$, $\Delta M$ and $\Delta Z$. In (3) the value of the coefficients ($\alpha$'s) are the total response of $\Delta Y$ to changes in each of the four independent variables.

As discussed in the text, time series for E, R and M have been selected on the basis of frequently used indicators or measures of fiscal and monetary actions. The purpose of this study was to test some frequently encountered rival conjectures regarding the influence of fiscal and monetary forces on eco-

1 The authors would like to give special thanks to Karl Brunner for useful discussion regarding the points made in this note.

2 See Exhibit 1 for a listing of "other forces" which influence total spending.

3 For purposes of this note the lags of the independent variables are ignored.

nomic activity, not to quantify all forces influencing our economy. Therefore, attention here has been directed toward estimating the magnitude and statistical reliability of the response of $\Delta Y$ to $\Delta E$, $\Delta R$, and $\Delta M$. However, $\Delta Z$ cannot be simply ignored.

The reader will note that there is no constant term in equation (3) since the effect of "all other forces" influencing spending are summarized by $\alpha_4 \Delta Z$. However, in the results reported in Table 1 of this study, a constant term is reported for each equation. These constant terms are an estimate of $\alpha_4$ times the average autonomous non-monetary and non-fiscal forces summarized in Z.

In a complex market economy, it is possible for monetary and fiscal actions to exert an indirect as well as a direct influence on $\Delta Y$. This indirect influence would operate through $\Delta Z$. One form of the relation between $\Delta Z$ and monetary and fiscal forces is shown by:

$$\Delta Z = b_0 + b_1 \Delta E + b_2 \Delta R + b_3 \Delta M \quad (4)$$

The empirical values of $\alpha_1$, $\alpha_2$, and $\alpha_3$, which were estimated by regression analysis and reported in this study, embody both the direct and the indirect responses of total spending to monetary and fiscal actions. Using $\Delta E$ as an example, the expression $(a_1 + b_1 a_4)$ is an estimate of $\alpha_1$, the total response of $\Delta Y$ to $\Delta E$. The direct response is $a_1$ and the indirect response is $b_1 a_4$. Consequently, the equation estimated and reported in this study (for example, equation 1.2 in Table 1) is:

$$\Delta Y = b_0 a_4 + (a_1 + b_1 a_4)\Delta E + (a_2 + b_2 a_4)\Delta R + (a_3 + b_3 a_4)\Delta M \quad (5)$$

where $b_0 a_4$ is the "constant" reported in Table 1. If it were known that $b_1$, $b_2$ and $b_3$ are zero, it could be concluded that there are no indirect effects of monetary and fiscal forces operating through Z on Y, only direct effects which are measured by $a_1$, $a_2$ and $a_3$. Since this cannot be established conclusively, it cannot be ruled out that $\Delta Z$ may include some indirect monetary and fiscal forces influencing economic activity.

The constant term is estimated to be quite large and statistically significant. This provides indirect evidence that $\Delta Z$ is explained to some extent by factors other than $\Delta E$, $\Delta R$, and $\Delta M$. The value of $b_0 a_4$ is a measure of the average effect of "other forces" on $\Delta Y$, which operate through $\Delta Z$.

As another test of the independence of $\Delta Z$ from monetary and fiscal forces, the total time period was divided into two subsamples and the equations were estimated for these sub-samples. The Chow test (see text) was applied to the sets of regression coefficients estimated from the sub-samples compared to the whole sample; the hypothesis that there were no structural shifts in the time period could not be rejected, implying no change in the size of $b_0 a_4$. If there was a significant indirect influence of $\Delta E$, $\Delta R$ and $\Delta M$ operating through $\Delta Z$, $b_0 a_4$ would change along with changes in these independent variables. Since this intercept was found to be stable over the test period, this provides further evidence that $\Delta Z$ is influenced by factors other than monetary and fiscal forces.

The results from the sub-samples indicate that there were differences in the relative variability of the independent variables between the two sub-samples. This tends to strengthen the conclusions of this article since the response of $\Delta$GNP to $\Delta M$ or $\Delta B$ was greater even in the first sub-sample (I/53 to I/60) in which the variability of $\Delta M$ and $\Delta B$ was smaller than the variability of $\Delta E$ and $\Delta R$.

# 10 HOW MUCH DOES MONEY MATTER? A LOOK AT SOME RECENT EVIDENCE*

RICHARD G. DAVIS
*Federal Reserve Bank of New York*

The air has been filled of late with signs of upheaval in long-established patterns of thinking regarding monetary and fiscal policy and, more generally, regarding the role of money in the economy. The basic framework used for years by most of us in analyzing these matters has come under serious challenge. Signs of intellectual disarray are evident all over, among public officials, in the business press, and among academics. Indeed, the current sense of confusion may well exceed anything witnessed since the early 1930's. Obviously the questions of "how much does money matter?" and "in what way does money matter?" are central issues underlying many specific problems of policy making, forecasting, and business-cycle analysis that are currently up for reexamination.

The change in atmosphere has been a very recent phenomenon. Only two or three years ago, there was rather general agreement that a wide variety of factors could produce fluctuations in business activity. Monetary developments were but one item in the list and, in the minds of many, by no means the most important. Money was assumed to operate through its effects on financial interest rates and through changes in the degree of credit rationing impinging on certain types of borrowers operating in imperfect capital markets.

The view that "only money matters" or, perhaps more accurately, that "mainly money matters" was the province of an obscure sect with headquarters in Chicago. For the most part, economists regarded this group—when they regarded it at all—as a mildly amusing, not quite respectable collection of eccentrics. The number of serious attempts to grapple with the Friedman view on the role of money until recently has been remarkably small. A 1960 paper by John Culbertson,[1] some work by Kareken and Solow on Friedman's approach to measuring lags,[2] and the papers surrounding the controversy over the Friedman-Meiselman work[3] comprise a nearly exhaustive list of the pre-

* Reprinted from *Monthly Review*, Federal Reserve Bank of New York, vol. 51 (June, 1969) pp. 119–31, by permission of the author and the Federal Reserve Bank of New York.

[1] See his "Friedman on the Lag Effect of Monetary Policy," *Journal of Political Economy* (December 1960), pages 617–21. See also Friedman's reply, "The Lag Effect of Monetary Policy" in the October 1961 issue of the same *Journal* (pages 447–66) as well as Culbertson's rejoinder in the same issue (pages 467–77).

[2] John Kareken and Robert Solow, "Lags in Monetary Policy," in *Stabilization Policies* (Commission on Money and Credit, 1963), pages 14–96.

[3] Milton Friedman and David Meiselman, "The Relative Stability of Monetary Velocity and the Investment Multiplier in the United States," in *Stabilization Policies* (Commission on Money and Credit, 1963), pages 165–268. See also Donald Hester, "Keynes and the

1968 literature. The fact is that the view held by Friedman and a few others on the predominant importance of money was just not given serious attention by most economists.

This whole situation has been changing of late with a rather startling abruptness. Indeed as far as the general public is concerned, much of the change in atmosphere has occurred within the last six to nine months. There can be no doubt that the principal explanation for this development has been the surprisingly exuberant behavior of the economy since the tax surcharge was enacted last June. Most forecasters who, like myself, have used the usual techniques of short-term projecting, hopefully with at least average skill, have consistently and fairly substantially underestimated the strength of the economy in the past nine months. Now of course these forecasting mistakes may not have been due to any overestimate of the potency of fiscal policy or an underestimate of the importance of the monetary growth rate. Many other explanations are possible. Nevertheless, it has been distinctly unsettling to see the projected slowdown recede further and further into the future, month after month and quarter after quarter. It is the sort of experience to make one reexamine one's "maintained hypotheses"—and perhaps such a reexamination is really in order.

The failure of conventional forecasting techniques in the wake of fiscal restraint would not, of course, necessarily send one running to the money supply for an explanation were there not a large body of research on the importance of money already waiting in the wings. This research needed only the right historical moment to bring it forth into the limelight. The post-surcharge experience has provided such a moment. Looking at the evidence in behalf of a dominant role for money presented in most of this research, however, it is not too difficult to understand why it achieved relatively little acceptance for the monetary view—on its own merits, so to speak, and without the psychological benefit of the post-surcharge trauma.

### Evidence for the Monetary Position

By far the largest mass of evidence consisted of the Friedman-Schwartz measurement and comparison of specific cycles in the monetary growth rate with reference cycles using the standard National Bureau techniques.[4] The consistency with which cycles in the monetary growth rate were found to lead reference cycles was so nearly perfect that it seemed scarcely possible that it could be due to chance alone. The existence of these timing leads was interpreted by Friedman and Schwartz to mean a dominant causal role for money, while their length and variability was taken as meaning a corresponding length and variability in the lags with which the money supply exerts its influence on business activity.

It is probably fair to say that relatively few not already in the fold were converted by these arguments. The main problem is that the evidential value of the monetary leads in trying to demonstrate a dominant causal role for money, as well as a long and variable lag in its timing, is gravely compromised by the possibility of a reverse influence of business on money. This point was made back in 1960 by Culbertson in the article mentioned earlier. At the time he wrote, little work had been done on the supply side of the money problem. Hence the existence of important reverse effects of business on money could really only be put forward as a plausible hypothesis. This situation was changed in 1965 with the publication of Phillip Cagan's book, *The Determinants and Effects of Changes in the Stock of Money.* While Cagan's book appears to be very much in the Friedman tradition, it seems to me that its results in fact tend to undercut that tradition. Cagan's work suggests rather clearly that the characteristic cyclical timing relationships between monetary rates of change and the business cycle are very im-

Quantity Theory: A Comment on the Friedman-Meiselman CMC Paper," and the Friedman-Meiselman reply in the *Review of Economics and Statistics* (November 1964). In addition, see Albert Ando and Franco Modigliani, "Velocity and the Investment Multiplier"; Michael dePrano and Thomas Mayer, "Autonomous Expenditures and Money"; and replies by Friedman and Meiselman plus rejoinders by Ando-Modigliani and dePrano-Mayer, all in the *American Economic Review* (September 1965), pages 693–792.

[4] Their major results are summarized in Milton Friedman and Anna Schwartz, "Money and Business Cycles," *Review of Economics and Statistics* (February 1963 Supplement), pages 32–64.

portantly determined by the influence of business on money. The case is made even stronger if one takes explicit account—as Cagan does not—of the impact of the Federal Reserve's attempts at countercyclical policy. Federal Reserve behavior alone may be sufficient to explain the characteristic lead of cycles in the monetary growth rate ahead of business-cycle turning points during the postwar period without the need to posit any influence of money on business whatever. If Cagan's work is correct, then the massive evidence gathered by Friedman and Schwartz for leads in the turning points of monetary cycles seems distinctly questionable as evidence for a dominant causal role for money.

The second sort of evidence in behalf of the "mainly money matters" position, as of last June, was the so-called "reduced-form" equations turned up in the famous Friedman-Meiselman paper. As will be recalled, Friedman and Meiselman regressed first the money supply against consumption and then what they called "autonomous" spending against consumption. They regarded their results as "strikingly one-sided"[5] in support of the money multiplier over their version of the Keynesian multiplier.

Again, however, it seems unlikely that many outside the fold were converted by the Friedman-Meiselman evidence. As the mass of correlation coefficients computed by the various combatants began to pile up, it became increasingly obvious that the controversy would never be able to produce a clear and decisive verdict. Results turned out to depend very much on the definition of "autonomous" spending and on the years for which the computations were made. Using definitions of autonomous spending much more akin to those of the usual textbook versions of Keynes than the one adopted by Friedman and Meiselman, little difference between the money multiplier and the autonomous spending multiplier could be discerned. Moreover, interpretation of all the results was complicated by the extreme simplicity of the "models" chosen to be tested, as well as by the inability of correlation techniques to distinguish an influence of money on business from an influence of business on money. To me, at least, the whole thing was a washout, proving nothing and making the Friedman position seem not one jot more plausible than it had seemed before.

Thus those economists, journalists, and public officials who began to take a hard look at the evidence for the monetarist position in the wake of the apparent failure of the tax surcharge found a rather mixed bag. On the one hand, Friedman and his colleagues had established beyond question a very substantial gross association between the money supply and business activity. On the other hand, the monetarists had failed to convince the majority of their professional colleagues that their claims for the importance of money had been adequately demonstrated. The reasons for their failure lay mainly in relatively esoteric matters of statistical methodology and economic theory. Such problems have obviously made much less impression on the lay public than has the simple fact of the gross association between money and business itself.

### The St. Louis Equation

Under these circumstances, a new study of the importance of the money supply, and its importance relative to fiscal policy, was certain to be welcome. The paper by Leonall Andersen and Jerry Jordan published last November[6] in the St. Louis Federal Reserve Bank's *Review* has understandably created a good deal of interest. Their approach consists of regressing current changes in gross national product (GNP) on current and lagged changes in the money supply and in fiscal variables. Certainly their procedure is very simple but not, for that reason, necessarily invalid. My own feeling is that, right or wrong, the St. Louis article is a distinctly worthwhile contribution to the literature on the importance of money. It deserves to be taken seriously and, by the same token, it deserves careful scrutiny. I propose to use the remainder of this paper to examine the claims made by Andersen and Jordan.

The first thing I want to note about the St. Louis equation is that it portrays a world in several respects sharply at variance with the expectations of most of us.

[5] Friedman and Meiselman, *op. cit.*, page 166.

[6] "Monetary and Fiscal Actions: A Test of Their Relative Importance in Economic Stabilization," Federal Reserve Bank of St. Louis *Review* (November 1968), pages 11–24 [reprinted in this volume].

**TABLE 1. THE FISCAL MULTIPLIERS IN THE BOARD-MIT AND ST. LOUIS MODELS**

| Elapsed time | Board-MIT | | St. Louis | |
|---|---|---|---|---|
| | Spending | Taxes | Spending | Taxes |
| After 1 quarter | 2.0 | 1.1 | 0.4 | 0.2 |
| After 2 quarters | 2.5 | 2.2 | 0.9 | 0.2 |
| After 4 quarters | 3.4 | 3.2 | 0.1 | 0.2 |
| After 12 quarters | 3.2 | 4.7 | 0.1 | 0.2 |

NOTE: Figures for the Board-MIT model are estimates made from the simulation presented in Charts 8 and 9 on pages 28 and 29 of the January 1968 *Federal Reserve Bulletin*. The tax simulations in the Board-MIT model are actually in terms of percentage point changes in tax rates, but it is noted on page 23 of the *Bulletin* that the .02 percentage point change used for the simulations was equivalent to about $4 billion during the period for which the simulations were conducted.

*1.* The fiscal multipliers in the St. Louis world are virtually zero. The fiscal multipliers for spending and taxes taken directly from the St. Louis equation are shown in Table 1. At no point do these multipliers rise above unity, and after four quarters they have returned essentially to zero. Multipliers taken from the recent Federal Reserve Board staff-Massachusetts Institute of Technology structural econometric model are shown in the same Table 1. These multipliers, by contrast, correspond roughly to expectations, rising to over 3 after a year.

*2.* Current and lagged changes in $M_1$ (private holdings of demand deposits and currency) explain a remarkably high proportion of the variance of quarterly changes in GNP. For the 1952-68 period used by St. Louis, about 50 percent of the variance of changes in GNP is "explained" by changes in money. This leaves the remaining 50 percent to be accounted for by every other pos-

Quarterly changes in gross national product. *"Predicted" data derived from* $\Delta GNP = +2.70\ \Delta M - 0.09\ \Delta M_{-1} + 2.20\ \Delta M_{-2} + 1.10\ \Delta M_{-3} + 2.19$.

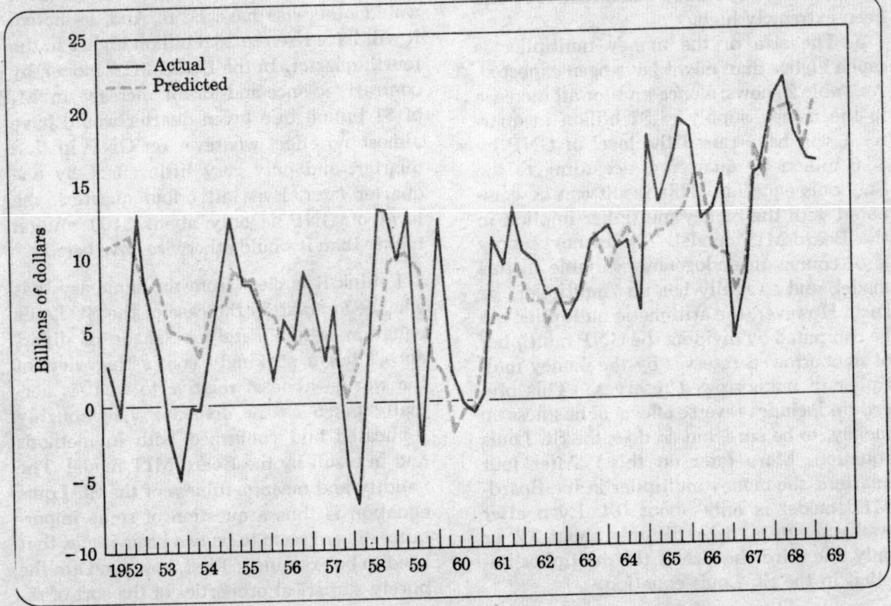

**TABLE 2. THE MONEY MULTIPLIER IN THE BOARD-MIT AND ST. LOUIS MODELS**

| Elapsed time | Board-MIT | | | St. Louis multiplier |
|---|---|---|---|---|
| | $\Delta M_1$ | $\Delta$GNP | Multiplier | |
| | (1) | (2) | (3) | (4) |
| After 1 quarter | +2.5 | + 0.5 | 0.2 | 1.6 |
| After 2 quarters | +3.5 | + 1.3 | 0.4 | 3.5 |
| After 4 quarters | +4.3 | + 2.0 | 0.4 | 6.6 |
| After 12 quarters | +5.0 | +11.0 | 2.2 | 6.6 |

NOTE: Changes in $M_1$ and GNP were estimated from charts presented on page 27 of the January 1968 *Federal Reserve Bulletin*. These charts show results for the Board-MIT model in which the effects of a $1.0 billion increase in nonborrowed reserves are simulated. The implied "money multiplier" shown in column 3 is computed by dividing the change in GNP (column 2) by the change in money (column 1). Actually only effects for demand deposits are shown—currency effects are thus assumed to be comparatively small.

The money multiplier shows the change in the level of GNP after the time period specified associated with a once-and-for-all increase in the level of the money supply of $1.0 billion. Estimates of the money multiplier for the St. Louis equation are obtained simply by summing coefficients over the appropriate number of quarters.

sible determinant of the course of business activity! Just how well money does is illustrated in the chart. The equation used here differs from the St. Louis equation only in omitting the fiscal variables and in having an unconstrained lag structure. When it is kept in mind that the chart shows *changes* in GNP, I think the closeness is visually reasonably impressive. The only prolonged period of really serious errors is from the beginning of 1952 to about mid-1954. On the other hand, the equation's accuracy since mid-1967 has been extremely high.

*3.* The size of the money multiplier is much higher than might have been expected. As Table 2 shows, a once-and-for-all increase in the money supply of $1 billion in quarter 1 will have raised the level of GNP by $6.6 billion by quarter 4, according to the St. Louis equation. This result can be compared with the money multiplier implicit in the Board-MIT model. The money supply is of course an endogenous variable in this model, and so really has no "multiplier" as such. However, the arithmetic multiplier can be computed by dividing the GNP multiplier of nonborrowed reserves by the money multiplier of nonborrowed reserves. (This procedure includes reverse effects of business on money, to be sure, but so does the St. Louis equation. More later on this.) After four quarters, the money multiplier in the Board-MIT model is only about 0.4. Even after twelve quarters, it is still only about 2.2, or only one third the size of the multiplier implicit in the St. Louis equation.

*4.* To me, the most surprising thing about the world of the St. Louis equation is not so much the force, but rather the speed with which money begins to act on the economy. This can also be seen in the results presented in Table 2. If the level of the money supply undergoes a $1 billion once-and-for-all increase in a given quarter, it will already raise GNP by $1.6 billion in that very same quarter. In the next quarter, the level of GNP will have risen to $3.5 billion above what it would otherwise have been. And, as noted, it will have risen to $6.6 billion higher in the fourth quarter. In the Board-MIT model, by contrast, a once-and-for-all increase in $M_1$ of $1 billion in a given quarter would have almost no effect whatever on GNP in that quarter, and only very little effect by one quarter later. Even after four quarters, the level of GNP is only about $400 million higher than it would otherwise have been.

I think it is clear from the summary that what is at stake in the case of the St. Louis equation is not merely a "shade of difference," but a strikingly contrasting view of the world—at least relative to what is normally taken as the orthodox view roughly replicated and confirmed both in methods and in result by the Board-MIT model. The validity and meaningfulness of the St. Louis equation is thus a question of some importance. There seem to be two basic issues that need to be examined: First, how good are the purely statistical properties of the sort of relationship presented by Andersen and Jordan? Second, how much of the relationship they find is due to a reverse influence of business on money, the problem that has plagued all previous attempts to buttress the so-called "strong monetarist position?"

Before turning to these questions, I should note that I have concentrated all my attention in what follows on the question of the importance of money. I will have virtually nothing to say on the seeming unimportance of the fiscal variables. This latter problem is of course also of great interest, but there has simply not been time to give adequate attention to both issues.

## Other St. Louis-Type Equations

Table 3 presents a number of St. Louis-type equations covering differing time periods and using different techniques for estimating the lag structure. The first line of figures contains the original St. Louis results for their 1952 to 1968-II period. The second line reproduces these results with two differences: (1) the fiscal variables were not included and (2) a second degree polynomial was used for the Almon lag rather than St. Louis' fourth degree. (This later adjustment was made solely to accommodate programming limitations.) A comparison of these two equations reveals

TABLE 3. CHANGES IN GNP REGRESSED ON CURRENT AND LAGGED CHANGES IN $M_1$ (QUARTERLY CHANGES)

| Period | $R^2$<br>SE of est. | Sum of Coefficients | t | t-1 | t-2 | t-3 |
|---|---|---|---|---|---|---|
| | The St. Louis Equation† Almon Lag with Fourth Degree Polynomial | | | | | |
| 1. 1952-68* | .56<br>4.2 | 6.6 | 1.6<br>(2.2) | 1.9<br>(3.6) | 1.8<br>(3.4) | 1.3<br>(1.9) |
| | Equations Using Almon Lag with Second Degree Polynomial‡ | | | | | |
| 2. 1952-68* | .48<br>4.6 | 5.6 | 1.6<br>(3.0) | 1.7<br>(7.6) | 1.4<br>(4.3) | 0.9<br>(3.0) |
| 3. 1952-60 | .18<br>5.1 | 3.6 | 1.7<br>(1.7) | 1.1<br>(2.6) | 0.6<br>(1.1) | 0.2<br>(0.5) |
| 4. 1961-68* | .62<br>3.2 | 5.3 | 0.8<br>(1.6) | 1.6<br>(6.4) | 1.7<br>(5.4) | 1.2<br>(4.5) |
| | Equations Using Unconstrained Lag Coefficients‡ | | | | | |
| 5. 1952-68* | .50<br>4.6 | 5.9 | 2.7<br>(3.3) | −0.1<br>(−0.1) | 2.2<br>(2.0) | 1.1<br>(1.3) |
| 6. 1952-60 | .18<br>5.3 | 3.7 | 1.9<br>(1.1) | 0.6<br>(0.3) | 1.2<br>(0.5) | − .05<br>(−) |
| 7. 1961-68* | .68<br>3.0 | 5.7 | 2.0<br>(2.8) | −0.3<br>(−0.3) | 2.6<br>(2.8) | 1.4<br>(2.0) |

NOTE: Values of "t" statistics are indicated in parentheses.
*Through the second quarter of 1968.
†Fiscal variables included but not shown.
‡No fiscal variables included.

that neither omission of the fiscal variables nor reduction of the degree of the polynomial has any substantial effect on the results for the monetary variables.

Concentrating on this second set of equations in Table 3 using the second degree polynomial, the following observations seem pertinent. First, the coefficients for the two subperiods are quite clearly different, but they are not drastically different. The overall money multiplier after four quarters is 3.6 for the earlier period and 5.3 for the later period. Both are strikingly larger than the 0.4 one-year multiplier of the Board-MIT model. The St. Louis equation does pass the Chow test for the two subperiods at the 5 percent level.

Second, the explanatory power of the monetary variables is quite low in the first half of the period ($R^2 = .18$)[7] and quite high ($R^2 = .62$) in the second half of the period. What is the reason for this difference? One possible answer is a strong common time trend in changes in $M_1$ and in GNP present in the 1960's but not in the earlier period. Such a trend beginning around the early 1960's is readily visible in the chart referred to earlier. (The $R^2$ of time alone on changes in GNP is .38 in the later period, virtually zero for the earlier period and .36 for the entire 1952 to 1968-II period.)

Now of course the mere existence of a common time trend in the 1960's does not necessarily mean that the close relationship between money and GNP is spurious. One could argue that we have had relatively steady rises in quarterly GNP increments because we have had relatively steady rises in quarterly money increments. Some equations including time as an explicit variable suggest that there may have been a reasonably strong association between GNP and current and lagged changes in $M_1$ during the 1960's even after time is allowed for. Nevertheless, the fact remains that the degree of association between GNP and current and lagged money supply would have looked very different to Andersen and Jordan had they done their work in 1961 instead of 1968. Given an $R^2$ as low as prevailed in the 1952-60 period, it may be doubted that they would have felt it worthwhile to pursue the matter further.

Finally, I would like to point out the bottom three equations shown on Table 3. These are simply unconstrained multiple regressions of changes in GNP on current and lagged changes in $M_1$. Comparison with the other lines in the table shows the extent to which imposition of Almon lags changes the results. The lag pattern present in the unconstrained equations is, of course, infected with multi-collinearity. Nevertheless, it is interesting to note that the one-period lag coefficient for the entire 1952-68 period, which is the *largest* for the Almon lags, actually becomes the *lowest* in the unconstrained equation.

[7] $R^2$ is the square of the multiple correlation coefficient.

## Problem of Two-Way Causation

I now want to turn to the problem of two-way causation. That there is a high "gross" association between money and business, however measured, has long been apparent from the work of Friedman-Schwartz and Friedman-Meiselman, as noted earlier. The St. Louis results generally confirm this finding—at least for the 1960's. As I noted, however, the possibility of important influences running from business to money seem to weaken substantially the evidential value of the work done by Friedman and his collaborators in trying to establish a dominant *causal* role for money. The question now is, does the St. Louis study suffer from the same fatal defect?

In a critique of the St. Louis work published in the April issue of the St. Louis Bank's *Review*, Frank de Leeuw, one of the principal architects of the Board-MIT model, and John Kalchbrenner take note of the two-way causation problem.[8] They note that the "reduced-form" approach used by St. Louis requires that the variables on the right-hand side be truly exogenous. If they are not, biased coefficient estimates may result. Conceivably, such bias could account for the surprisingly powerful and quick-acting effects of money seemingly indicated by the coefficients of the St. Louis equation. De Leeuw and Kalchbrenner believe that Andersen and Jordan recognized the vulnerability of the money supply as an exogenous variable and that it was for this reason that they constructed an alternative version of their equation. In this alternative version, current and lagged changes in $M_1$ are replaced with cur-

[8] Frank deLeeuw and John Kalchbrenner, "Comment," St. Louis Reserve Bank *Review* (April 1969), pages 6–11.

TABLE 4. CHANGES IN GNP REGRESSED ON VARIOUS MEASURES OF CURRENT AND LAGGED CHANGES IN THE MONETARY BASE OR NONBORROWED RESERVES (QUARTERLY CHANGES)

| Period | $R^2$ SE of est. | Sum of Coefficients | t | t-1 | t-2 | t-3 |
|---|---|---|---|---|---|---|
| | **The St. Louis Equation–Total Monetary Base Almon Lag with Fourth Degree Polynomial†** | | | | | |
| 1. 1952-68* | .53 4.4 | 16.0 | 1.0 (0.5) | 5.5 (3.4) | 6.5 (4.1) | 3.1 (1.5) |
| | **Total Monetary Base Almon Lag with Second Degree Polynomial‡** | | | | | |
| 2. 1952-68* | .45 4.8 | 14.8 | 3.5 (1.8) | 4.4 (7.1) | 4.1 (3.5) | 2.7 (2.5) |
| | **Nonborrowed Monetary Base Almon Lag with Second Degree Polynomial‡** | | | | | |
| 3. 1952-68* | .32 5.3 | 10.8 | −0.1 (−0.1) | 3.2 (5.2) | 4.4 (4.7) | 3.3 (4.0) |
| 4. 1952-60 | .07 5.5 | − 3.4 | −4.1 (−1.6) | −1.0 (−0.6) | 0.7 (0.4) | 1.1 (0.8) |
| 5. 1960-68* | .33 4.2 | 9.2 | −1.0 (−0.5) | 2.8 (3.0) | 4.2 (3.5) | 3.2 (3.3) |
| | **DeLeeuw-Kalchbrenner–Nonborrowed Monetary Base Almon Lag with Fourth Degree Polynomial†** | | | | | |
| 6. 1952-68* | .45 4.5 | 10.4 | n.a. | n.a. | n.a. | n.a. |
| | **DeLeeuw-Kalchbrenner–Nonborrowed Reserves Almon Lag with Fourth Degree Polynomial†** | | | | | |
| 7. 1952-68* | .42 4.7 | 2.4 | n.a. | n.a. | n.a. | n.a. |

NOTE: Values of "t" statistics are indicated in parentheses.
*Through the second quarter of 1968.
†Fiscal variables included but not shown.
‡No fiscal variables included.

rent and lagged changes in the monetary base *(adjusted for changes in reserve requirements)*.[9] This alternative version of the St. Louis equation is reproduced on the top line of Table 4. The explanatory power is similar to that of the money supply equation. The size of the multiplier, however, is naturally much larger since it represents the combined effect of the base-to-money multiplier and the money-to-GNP multiplier. The second line of figures on Table 4 contains a reesti-

[9] The monetary base consists of total member bank reserves plus currency in circulation outside banks.

mate of the parameters of line 1, this time with no fiscal variables included and with the second degree polynomial rather than the St. Louis fourth degree polynomial.

The problem with the St. Louis equations using the monetary base is that, while the latter may be more exogenous than the money supply, its own "exogeneity" is still far from beyond question. In other words, a good case can be made for the view that the two-way causation problem is still present in the monetary base. First, the monetary base includes borrowed reserves. While the Federal Reserve sets the conditions for borrowing and the discount rate, actual borrowings take place at the initiative of the member banks themselves. Certainly current business conditions, interest rates, and the state of loan demand influence the demand for borrowed reserves. Second, the base includes currency. The volume of currency the public wishes to hold is an endogenous variable. The banks supply the public with currency on demand, and, during the period of the 1950's and 1960's, the Federal Reserve has more or less automatically replenished the reserves lost by the banking system through currency drains. Hence a strong case can also be made that the currency component of the base is endogenous too. In a rejoinder to de Leeuw and Kalchbrenner, Andersen and Jordan dispute the contention that borrowed reserves and currency should be subtracted from the base to obtain a more "exogenous" variable.[10] While I remain unconvinced by their rejoinder, I will not say anything more about this "exogeneity" issue since I want to pursue a somewhat different tack.[11]

The remaining equations in Table 4 show the results of stripping away, successively, borrowed reserves and currency from the total monetary base. As can be seen from the table, $R^2$ falls and the standard error rises noticeably when the sole independent variables are the current and lagged *nonborrowed* monetary base. (Compare lines 2 and 3.) Furthermore, breaking the entire period into the two subperiods used earlier, we find no significant relationship whatever between the nonborrowed monetary base and GNP in the earlier period ended in 1960. Indeed, the overall multiplier is actually negative.

The first de Leeuw and Kalchbrenner equation shown in Table 4 also uses the nonborrowed monetary base, but differs from mine in that it includes fiscal variables. The inclusion of the latter accounts for an $R^2$ higher than the one in my equation. Otherwise, the results are similar to mine. (Compare lines 3 and 6.)

The second de Leeuw-Kalchbrenner equation reported in Table 4 eliminates both borrowed reserves and currency from the monetary base, thus leaving nonborrowed member bank reserves. As these authors note, the effect of leaving out currency is to reduce the multiplier drastically. Indeed, the multiplier of 2.4 obtained for this equation is not very different from the 2.0 multiplier of nonborrowed reserves onto GNP obtained from the Board-MIT model (see Table 2). As a result, de Leeuw and Kalchbrenner conclude that the coefficients of the St. Louis equation are in fact heavily distorted by simultaneous equations bias. Once this is removed, they

[10] St. Louis Reserve Bank *Review* (April 1969), pages 12–16.

[11] Andersen and Jordan find a negative correlation between changes in borrowed reserves and changes in nonborrowed reserves (*op. cit.*, page 15). From this they conclude that the Federal Reserve System automatically offsets the effects on total reserves of endogenous changes in borrowed reserves and that total reserves, rather than the nonborrowed component, should therefore be treated as exogenous. However, a negative correlation would also be found if the System used either nonborrowed reserves or borrowed reserves (or some other related money market variable such as free reserves or the Federal funds rate) as an operational target. Thus a deliberate increase in nonborrowed reserves would tend to make banks pay off borrowings. Similarly, a deliberate increase in the level of borrowed reserves would have to be engineered by a subtraction of nonborrowed reserves. In neither of these cases would total reserves or the total monetary base be the appropriate exogenous variable. Similarly, Andersen and Jordon conclude that automatic System accommodation of currency drains implies a nonborrowed reserves target; that the System has not in fact followed a nonborrowed reserves target; and, therefore, that currency cannot be endogenous (*op. cit.*, page 13). This chain of reasoning is invalid, if only because many targets other than a nonborrowed reserve target involve automatic System accommodation of currency drains, including free reserve and other money market targets.

argue, the results closely resemble the sort of world most of us have always believed in.

I certainly agree with de Leeuw and Kalchbrenner that, while the total monetary base is statistically superior to the money supply as an exogenous variable, it probably is not exogenous enough. Moreover, I agree that the similarity of the results for nonborrowed reserves to the Board-MIT structural model is interesting. Nevertheless, I can't help feeling that this is not quite the end of the story. Even if one were wholly satisfied that nonborrowed member bank reserves are the proper exogenous monetary variable, it must nevertheless be kept in mind that what is at stake is not a member-bank-nonborrowed-reserves theory of the economy, but rather a money supply theory of the economy. There is a substantial gap between member bank nonborrowed reserves and the money supply. The problem with the computations presented in Table 4 is that they short-circuit a two-stage chain of relationships consisting of the relationship between the nonborrowed base or nonborrowed reserves and money, on the one hand, and the relationship between money and GNP, on the other. Let us suppose that the money supply *does* exert a powerful and quick-acting influence on GNP. Let us suppose also that the influence of GNP on the money supply is minimal. One might nevertheless get a rather weak and slow-acting influence of the nonborrowed base or of nonborrowed reserves on GNP simply because the relationship between the base, or reserves, and money was relatively weak. Moreover, the lag between the base, or reserves, and GNP would represent the sum of the lags in the two links of the chain. In other words, it is possible that, even though the regressions proposed by de Leeuw and Kalchbrenner and myself may be more statistically "pure" in terms of the "reduced-form" rationale of the St. Louis equations, these regressions may nevertheless fail to do justice to the real power, stability, and promptness of the causal influence of money on business.

This possibility puts us in a new dilemma. On the one hand, we can't accept the St. Louis equations at face value because neither money nor the total reserve base may be suf-

**TABLE 5. CHANGES IN $M_1$ REGRESSED ON CURRENT AND LAGGED CHANGES IN THE NONBORROWED MONETARY BASE ($\Delta B$) (QUARTERLY CHANGES)**

| Period | $R^2$ | $\Delta B$ | $\Delta B_{-1}$ | $\Delta B_{-2}$ | $\Delta B_{-3}$ |
|---|---|---|---|---|---|
| | | | **Unconstrained Lag Structure** | | |
| 1952–68* | .54 | .67<br>(2.6) | .80<br>(2.8) | .55<br>(1.9) | .27<br>(1.0) |
| 1952–60 | .37 | .23<br>(0.6) | .85<br>(2.3) | .56<br>(1.5) | .90<br>(2.6) |
| 1961–68* | .58 | 1.37<br>(3.4) | .64<br>(1.4) | .83<br>(1.8) | −.43<br>(−1.0) |
| | | | **Almon Lag–Second Degree Polynomial** | | |
| 1952–68* | .53 | .73<br>(3.6) | .67<br>(8.4) | .56<br>(4.6) | .33<br>(3.1) |
| 1952–60 | .34 | .29<br>(0.9) | .74<br>(3.8) | .84<br>(4.1) | .59<br>(3.7) |
| 1961–68* | .54 | 1.31<br>(4.4) | .76<br>(5.1) | .36<br>(1.9) | .11<br>(0.7) |

NOTE: Values of "t" statistics are indicated in parentheses.
*Through the second quarter of 1968.

ficiently exogenous. On the other hand, the equations using the nonborrowed base or reserves may understate the causal influence of money for the reasons just given. To separate out the influence of money on business from the influence of business on money, one would seem to need a complete structural model. But this is precisely what the "reduced-form" approach, originated by Friedman and Meiselman and carried on by Andersen and Jordan, seeks to avoid!

## Reduced-Form Equations for Money

One possible way out of this mess is to examine reduced-form equations for money itself. If the relationship between the nonborrowed monetary base and money is not very tight, this will explain some of the relative looseness of the relationship between the nonborrowed base and GNP. Moreover, by adding current and lagged GNP to the instrument variables of policy, it may be possible to get some qualitative idea of how much of the gross relationship between money and GNP reflects a direct causal influence of money on GNP and how much of it reflects a reverse influence of GNP on money.

Some reduced-form equations for quarterly changes in $M_1$ using current and lagged values of the nonborrowed monetary base are presented in Table 5. Current and lagged changes in the nonborrowed monetary base (which, it should be recalled, has been adjusted for changes in reserve requirements) explain about 54 percent of the variance of quarterly changes in $M_1$. What is more to the point for present purposes is that the nonborrowed base *fails* to explain fully 46 percent of the variance. Hence there is considerable looseness in the relationship between the nonborrowed base and $M_1$. Again, such a looseness is especially evident in the first half of the period. Moreover, the coefficients in Table 5 suggest that the influence of the base on $M_1$ does operate with a distributed lag that would contribute to the total lag of the influence of the base on GNP. Thus the results of Table 5 lend some support to the contention that the regressions of GNP on the nonborrowed monetary base *under*state (implicitly) the closeness of the association between money and GNP and the size of the money multiplier operating on GNP within any given period of elapsed time.[12]

If something in the neighborhood of one half the variance of quarterly changes in $M_1$ is left unexplained by the nonborrowed base, what accounts for the *remainder* of this variance? One factor would be the other instrument variables of policy, i.e., changes in the discount rate and in the Regulation Q ceiling. In addition, there could be various factors operating from within the banking sector of the economy, such as shifts in bank demand schedules for excess and borrowed reserves. Finally, there would be all the remaining factors summed up in the expression "the influence of business on money." Only part of the influence of business on money would be represented as an influence of, specifically, *GNP* on money. Other parts would perhaps be represented by movements in the composition of GNP, interest rates, and the various categories of credit demands.

How large a part of the unexplained variance does reflect an influence of GNP, as such, on money is the question that Table 6 attempts to answer. The first equation presented for each time period covered in the table attempts to show the influence of the nonborrowed base and other policy instrument variables on changes in $M_1$. Actually, the only difference between these equations and those in Table 5 is the addition of changes in the discount rate—which does not, in fact, make much difference. As noted earlier, changes in reserve requirements are accounted for in the measure of the base. The remaining instrument variable of policy, changes in the Q ceiling, is simply not included. Some experiments on time periods when no change in the Q ceiling occurred showed essentially the same results. Hence it seemed better to omit it and save the degrees of freedom.

On balance, the results presented in Table 6 do not seem to show any very strong

[12] Essentially the same conclusions apply if member bank nonborrowed reserves are used instead of the nonborrowed reserve base. However, $R^2$'s are of course lower since nonborrowed reserves make no attempt to explain, or to allow for, changes in the currency component of $M_1$. Using an unconstrained lag structure, nonborrowed reserves gives an $R^2$ of .34 for the full period with a total multiplier of 3.2. For the 1952–60 subperiod, the $R^2$ is .30, while it is .39 for the 1961 to 1968-II subperiod.

**TABLE 6. CHANGES IN $M_1$ REGRESSED ON CURRENT AND LAGGED CHANGES IN GNP, THE NONBORROWED MONETARY BASE, AND THE DISCOUNT RATE (QUARTERLY CHANGES)**

| Period | Δ GNP | Δ GNP-1 | Δ GNP-2 | Δ GNP-3 | Δ B | Δ $B_{-1}$ | Δ $B_{-2}$ | Δ $B_{-3}$ | Δ Rd | $R^2$ | $\bar{R}^2$ † |
|---|---|---|---|---|---|---|---|---|---|---|---|
| 1952-68* | | | | | .78 (3.0) | .85 (3.0) | .47 (1.6) | .17 (0.6) | .73 (2.1) | .57 | .53 |
| | .08 (3.9) | .01 (0.3) | – (–) | – (–) | | | | | | .32 | .27 |
| | .03 (1.7) | .01 (0.3) | – (–) | – .04 (–2.3) | .95 (3.7) | .79 (2.8) | .38 (1.4) | .02 (0.1) | .56 (1.4) | .64 | .58 |
| 1952-60 | | | | | .46 (1.1) | .93 (2.5) | .61 (1.6) | .88 (2.6) | .49 (1.1) | .39 | .29 |
| | .05 (1.9) | – .01 (–0.4) | .01 (0.2) | – .04 (–1.7) | | | | | | .23 | .13 |
| | .05 (2.2) | .01 (0.5) | .03 (1.1) | – .02 (–0.9) | .70 (1.7) | .91 (2.5) | .64 (1.7) | .73 (2.3) | – .12 (–0.2) | .55 | .39 |
| 1961-68* | | | | | 1.39 (3.8) | .86 (2.0) | .46 (1.0) | – .59 (–1.5) | 1.54 (2.5) | .66 | .59 |
| | .09 (2.0) | .01 (0.3) | – .03 (–0.6) | .02 (0.4) | | | | | | .21 | .08 |
| | .06 (1.7) | .03 (0.9) | – .05 (–1.4) | – .03 (–1.1) | 1.61 (4.3) | .90 (1.8) | .21 (0.5) | – .64 (–1.6) | .86 (1.3) | .77 | .67 |

NOTE: Values of "t" statistics are indicated in parentheses.
*Through the second quarter of 1968.
†Adjusted $R^2$.

feedback from GNP to money—which, it should be emphasized again is *not* the same thing as a feedback from "business" to money. To be sure, current and lagged changes in GNP "explain" about 32 percent of the variance of changes in $M_1$ over the whole 1952 to 1968-II period and a bit over 20 percent in each of the two subperiods. However, most of this impact appears to occur in the current quarter, when the direction of causation is of course ambiguous. The lagged changes in GNP contribute almost nothing.

Similarly, the addition of current and lagged GNP variables contributes almost nothing to explaining changes in $M_1$, once current and lagged monetary "policy" variables have already been included. For the period as a whole, the adjusted $R^2$ of .53 for the policy variables rises only .05 to .58 when current and lagged changes in GNP are added. In contrast, the addition of the *policy* variables to the GNP variables raises $R^2$ substantially, from .27 to .58. As to the subperiods, GNP does make a noticeable contribution in the earlier period. In the 1960's, however, current and lagged GNP variables give an adjusted $R^2$ of only .08 by themselves. When the policy variables are added, this rises to fully .67. This is an interesting result in view of the especially close relationship between changes in GNP and current and lagged changes in $M_1$ during the 1960's, as noted earlier.

The impression that the influence of "policy" variables on the money supply dominates any feedback from GNP to the money supply has to be modified, but only somewhat, if nonborrowed member bank reserves are used in place of the nonborrowed monetary base. The reason is, of course, that nonborrowed reserves make no allowance for the currency component of the money supply and therefore explain less of the variance of changes in $M_1$ than does the nonborrowed base. For the entire 1952 to 1968-II period, changes in nonborrowed member bank reserves (adjusted for reserve requirements) and in the discount rate have an adjusted $R^2$ with respect to changes in $M_1$ of .39. Addition of current and lagged changes in GNP raises this to .50. For the 1952-60 subperiod, the "policy" variables, so defined, give an adjusted $R^2$ of .20 alone, with $R^2$ rising to .21 when the GNP variables are added. For the 1961 to 1968-II subperiod, the "policy" variables give an adjusted $R^2$ of .38, which rises to .50 when GNP is included. While these results using nonborrowed reserves are less clearly one-sided than those using the nonborrowed monetary base, the conclusion that the feedback from changes in GNP to changes in $M_1$ may be relatively modest still seems warranted.

## Summary of Major Statistical Issues

At this point a brief general summary of the major statistical issues for and against the St. Louis equation may be useful.

*(1)* The equation shows very little explanatory power when fitted to the 1952-60 data. It seems to fit the data well only in the 1960's. Coincidentally or not, there was a significant trend in the first differences of money and GNP in the 1960's that was not present in the 1950's. In rejoinder, St. Louis might note that the period 1952-60 happens to be about the worst possible subperiod from the entire 1952 to 1968-II period. The $R^2$ for this subperiod, as noted earlier, is .18. For the still shorter subperiods, 1952-57 and 1955-60, it is about .32 in each case. Personally, this rejoinder does not seem very impressive to me. Consequently, I would regard the poor performance of the St. Louis equation in the 1952-60 subperiod as a distinct embarrassment.

*(2)* In the St. Louis equation's favor is the fact that the coefficients are reasonably stable over time, even though the two halves of the 1952-68 period show such different $R^2$'s.

*(3)* If the nonborrowed monetary base or nonborrowed member bank reserves are used as the exogenous variable, rather than the money supply or the total monetary base, explanatory power drops rather substantially. So do the sizes of the multipliers. Indeed, there is no significant relationship at all between the nonborrowed base, current and lagged, and GNP in the 1952-60 subperiod. In defense of the St. Louis equation, however, one may argue that the total base is in fact a more appropriate "exogenous" variable than the nonborrowed base. Again, I myself am not at all satisfied with the St. Louis rejoinder on this point cited earlier. Nevertheless, I freely confess that the problem of identifying a suitable exogenous monetary variable does not seem to have an entirely obvious solution.

*(4)* I would prefer a somewhat different defense of the St. Louis equation. This would be along the lines that the relatively poor relationship between the nonborrowed base (or reserves) and GNP does not deal directly with the question of the relationship between money itself and GNP. To deal with this question, it is worthwhile to attempt to determine how much of the relationship between changes in money and changes in GNP is a feedback relationship from GNP to money.

*(5)* The available evidence suggests that current and lagged changes in the nonborrowed base (or nonborrowed reserves) and other monetary policy variables leave a substantial amount of the variance in monetary changes unexplained. This therefore leaves a large potential role for all the influences wrapped up under the general rubric of "business conditions."

*(6)* The specific variable GNP, however, seems to contribute rather little extra to explaining the variance in monetary changes beyond what is explained by the policy variables. Hence, only a relatively modest part of the gross relationship between money and GNP exhibited in the St. Louis equation may reflect a feedback effect from GNP to money. Much of the powerful influence of "business" on money found by Cagan must be reflected by variables other than GNP (such as interest rates)—or perhaps the cyclical behavior of the monetary growth rate is simply a very different sort of variable than quarterly dollar changes in $M_1$.

On balance it would seem fair to say that the St. Louis equation has not been devastated by the critical scrutiny to which it has been subjected. On the other hand, I think it is equally obvious that some distinctly troublesome questions exist regarding the equation. The equation's merits do not seem to me sufficient to compel by themselves our acceptance of the world it portrays. This being the case, it seems appropriate in closing to put aside regression results and consider briefly some of the underlying economic issues.

## Transmission Mechanism

The St. Louis equation says that a $1 billion increase in the money supply this quarter will raise GNP in this same quarter by $1.6 billion and that, by the next quarter, money will have raised GNP by $3.5 billion. This is somewhat over half its ultimate influence. If the money supply were increased by means of Government handouts of newly printed dollar bills, this sort of quick, sharp reaction would certainly seem reasonable. The actual process of money creation is of course quite different, however. It works primarily through central bank open market operations and through asset purchases by commercial banks. It involves no direct effects on private income or wealth of any great magnitude.

Most people now seem to agree that monetary impulses must work their effects on GNP primarily through a chain of substitution relationships. This chain most often begins when the Trading Desk at the New York Reserve Bank makes a bid over the phone to a group of Government securities dealers who are persuaded by the terms of the offer to exchange part of their portfolio of Governments for demand deposits. Relative interest rates change and portfolio balance is disturbed. Thus further substitutions are made. Deposits are exchanged for private securities, and the rates on these securities are bid down. Ultimately, wealth holders must be persuaded that they should substitute into physical assets (whether producers' goods or consumers' durables). It is at this stage that GNP begins to be affected.

The crucial point is that, if there are no important income or wealth effects stemming from the process of money creation, then this final substitution into goods can only take place as a result of the shifts in relative interest rates that are set in motion by the monetary process. If wealth holders' net worth is unchanged, and if their income is unchanged, they will be induced to try to shift into more extensive holdings of real assets only if their demand for such assets is sensitive to the changes in relative yields. If there are no income and wealth effects whatever, the impact of monetary changes on the real economy can be no swifter or more powerful than is permitted by the interest-rate responsiveness of the demand for real capital.

As far as I can tell, incidentally, these conclusions depend in no way on the length of the chain of transactions between the original money-creating transaction and the first transaction involving nonfinancial assets.

Some argue that the initial money-creating transaction may lead immediately to an increased demand for goods and that, in such cases, the interest rate elasticity of the demand for goods is irrelevant. This seems quite wrong to me. Suppose an individual is induced to exchange with the Federal Reserve some of his Government securities for deposits because the Fed's bid in the market makes such an exchange attractive to him. At this point in time, his income and wealth are unchanged, but the rate on Governments is lower. If his equilibrium portfolio composition now involves, say, fewer Governments and more of both cash and goods, it can only be because his desired holdings of both cash and of goods are sensitive to the changed yield on Governments. Given an unchanged utility function, there is simply no other possible explanation.

To the extent that the monetary process depends upon portfolio composition effects induced by changes in relative interest rates, the monetary impulses in the St. Louis equation seem to me to influence GNP with an implausible rapidity. We are, after all, not wholly devoid of information on the response of business fixed investment, inventories, and consumer durables to changes in interest rates. Indeed, we have a large body of econometric and interview-type studies accumulated over the years on these matters. Certainly these studies are open to a variety of interpretations, and they are by no means unanimous in their findings. Nevertheless, I think there can be little question that their tenor is overwhelmingly against the sort of large short-period multipliers found in the St. Louis equation. The Board-MIT model incorporates a fairly representative sample of such econometric research, and its multipliers are much closer to what this research had in the past led us to expect.

On the other hand, it is possible that the conventional studies of the interest-elasticity of demand of the different categories of capital goods, as well as the traditional interview approach to this subject, are leaving out major elements of the transmission mechanism. The omission of these elements may explain the divergence of the St. Louis world from the world seemingly implied by the more traditional sort of research. I can think of at least three possible factors that may not be adequately accounted for in the more traditional studies.

First, the money creation process itself—and the subsequent shifting of financial portfolios—does involve bidding up the prices of a variety of financial assets, Government and private. Obviously a rise in the market price of outstanding private financial instruments has no effect on real private wealth. However, there may be a sort of "pseudo-wealth," or "distribution" effect stemming from such price rises. This could occur if private financial assets were valued by their holders at market value while the issuers valued their liabilities at maturity value or at some conventional par. How important such distributional effects may be we do not know. Certainly I would not expect that the effects of rising market prices for debt instruments related to the monetary expansion process would be of much significance. For one thing, holders of these instruments often do not value their holdings at market prices. To this extent, net worth positions as perceived by their owners would not be changed by changing market prices. When one considers rises in the price of equities, however, the possibility of a significant secondary wealth effect on the demand for goods and services seems much more real.

A second possible source of transmission from monetary changes to the real sector that may not have been given sufficient attention in the traditional empirical research is availability effects. We know that the capital market is structured so that some potential borrowers simply cannot obtain all the funds they want by raising their bid in the market. To the extent that a money supply increase is associated with a direct increase in the funds made available to these borrowers, it could have a direct, swift-acting, and powerful effect on real spending. That there exists availability effects of this kind is beyond question; that they are important enough to account for the very high short-run multipliers in the St. Louis equation is less clear.

A third possible deficiency of the conventional research may be its treatment, or lack of treatment, of the implicit rates of return on real capital. Friedman and others have argued for years that existing research on the importance of interest rates in the demand for capital goods was wholly inadequate because it failed to include own-rates of return on real capital, including rates of return on consumer durable goods. It is of course possible that a more adequate treatment of implicit real rates would turn up a much sharper and more rapid response to interest rates than has been found in past studies. At the moment, however, this is totally unexplored territory.

## Concluding Comment

In conclusion, I can summarize my overall reaction to the St. Louis equation about as follows. Andersen and Jordan have produced a monetarist equation that holds up rather better than I would have thought likely. In particular, it does not seem easy to dispose of the association between changes in money and changes in GNP by showing that it is primarily or largely a matter of "reverse causation." On the other hand, the reduced-form approach they use, which at first looks so seductively easy, turns out on closer inspection to be itself fraught with difficulties. In this particular case, it leads to an equation that produces a much quicker monetary response than seems consistent with a large part of existing research on the nature of the monetary transmission mechanism. At the moment, I find it very difficult to believe in the St. Louis equation: I just don't quite see how things could work that way. On the other hand, I am ready to concede at least the possibility that proper allowance for various secondary wealth effects, credit availability effects, and a broader treatment of interest rates *might,* in principle, be able to make the St. Louis world seem plausible.

I think the onus is now clearly on the monetarists to spell out in detail precisely how they think the transmission process works. Moreover, this description must be translated into an econometric model with a reasonable degree of structural detail. Certainly the rest of us would like to see just exactly how such a model would differ from the Board-MIT model, for example. We need to see precisely how money is supposed to produce the results it appears to produce in the Andersen-Jordan equation. I suspect that only after such a project is carried out, and carried out successfully, will most economists really be prepared to believe that money matters as much and as fast as it seems to in St. Louis.

# 11 THE CHANNELS OF MONETARY POLICY*

FRANK DE LEEUW
*The Urban Institute*

EDWARD M. GRAMLICH
*Board of Governors of the Federal Reserve System*

One of the most perplexing questions in macroeconomics is the importance of financial variables in influencing the real economy. Opinions on this question have varied greatly from decade to decade, and still vary from economist to economist. Whereas classical economists felt that monetary forces were quite important—indeed the only long-run determinant of the price level—the standard Keynesian view during and after the Great Depression tended to deemphasize the role of money. The period since World War II has seen a definite revival of interest in monetary phenomena, but this revival has by no means generated a consensus on the importance of money in influencing economic activity.

A basic reason for differences of opinion on the importance of money has been the difficulty in obtaining convincing empirical evidence on the sensitivity of aggregate demand to exogenous monetary and fiscal forces. Historical evidence suggests that such autonomous monetary forces as gold discoveries and reserve requirement decisions played an important role in such major economic swings as the inflation of 1900-10, the Great Depression, and the contraction of 1936-37. These findings are buttressed by the studies of Friedman-Meiselman, the staff of the Federal Reserve Bank of St. Louis, and others who find monetary variables to be much more important than fiscal variables in explaining subsequent movements in gross national product. On the other hand, the evidence from several of the large econometric models—the Wharton School model, the Commerce Department model, the Michigan model, and to a lesser extent the Brookings model—is that monetary forces are rather unimportant in influencing total demand.

Behind different assessments of the role of monetary factors lie differences of opinion regarding the number and significance of the channels through which monetary forces operate. Many econometric models include only one channel: namely, the effects of financial yields on the opportunity cost of holding durable goods and structures, with the cost in turn influencing tangible investment. Even within this one channel there is room for a wide range of empirical estimates of the strength of the forces at work, and further research is still urgently needed. At the same time, however, the possibility should be investigated that the conflict stems partly from the existence of other channels through which monetary forces work, channels which have been either inadequately treated or completely ignored in previous econometric work.

* Reprinted from *Federal Reserve Bulletin,* vol. 55 (June, 1969) pp. 472–491, by permission of the authors and the Board of Governors of the Federal Reserve System.

The Federal Reserve—MIT econometric model project attempted to examine these ideas. The aim was to build a model which, though not necessarily larger than most other existing models, would focus more intensively on monetary forces and how they affect the economy. The format of an econometric model was chosen because it seemed to be the best way to take advantage of recent work in areas such as household and producer behavior, financial behavior, and price-wage determination; of recent econometric advances in techniques for dealing with distributed lags, autocorrelation, and constraints on parameters; and of advances in computer technology that make possible rapid estimation and solution of large nonlinear systems. It was also felt that only through a model could one surmount problems involving the large number of exogenous monetary and fiscal variables, variable policy multipliers and time lags, and other difficulties which the one-equation approach to explaining GNP necessarily oversimplifies or ignores.

This article concentrates on the channels through which monetary forces influence the real economy. Previous reports have dealt with other aspects of the model—its over-all structure, its theoretical innovations, the characteristics of its multiplier-accelerator mechanism—and we will touch on these points to only a minor extent.[1] An Appendix —available on request in mimeographed form—gives a current listing of the model along with mention of the equations which have been altered since our earlier report.[2]

The paper first sets out the theoretical and institutional bases for the three channels of monetary policy currently represented in the model. Cost-of-capital influences constitute one channel, affecting single- and multifamily housing, plant and equipment, State and local construction, and investment in consumer durable goods. The transmission of rates of return on bonds to the value of wealth held in the form of equities constitutes a second channel, one that affects household net worth and consumption. Finally, credit rationing constitutes a third channel which we have so far found to be important only in the housing market. As yet, we have found that neither the cost of capital nor credit rationing is important for inventory investment, though we have tested these possibilities extensively.

Next the paper presents estimates of the quantitative importance of each channel. Simulation of different groups of equations of the model and of the full model under varying sets of initial conditions illustrates direct effects and complete-system effects of monetary policy alone and in comparison with fiscal policy. The results of these simulations are still subject to large uncertainties, and we will make changes as work on the model continues. For what they are worth, however, the current results imply 1- or 2-year fiscal policy effects that are roughly comparable to results for other models and monetary policy effects that are appreciably larger than results for other models though smaller than what a simple quantity theory of money would imply. Financial variables are seen to operate with a somewhat longer lag than fiscal variables, and both monetary and fiscal multipliers vary depending on the initial state of the economy.

## I. The Channels of Monetary Policy

The three channels of monetary policy represented in the model are as follows:

### *The Cost of Capital*

A general formula showing the conditions under which a potential investor would be indifferent about renting or buying a capital good is

$$\frac{PR\,(1 - vt)}{P\,(1 - u)} = D\,(1 - wt) + R\,(1 - xt) + TP\,(1 - yt) - G\,(1 - zt) \qquad \text{(A.1)}$$

where $PR$ = rental price (explicit or implicit) of a unit of capital services; $P$ = price of the capital equipment; $D$ = physical rate of depreciation; $R$ = the appropriate rate of interest, or time discount; $TP$ = property tax rate; $G$ = expected rate of capital gains; $t$ = the income tax rate; $u$ = the rate of investment credit; $v$, $z$

[1] See (2), (6), (11), and (14). [References appear at the end of this reading.]

[2] Requests should be addressed to: *Publications Services, Division of Administrative Services, Board of Governors of the Federal Reserve System, Washington, D.C. 20551.*

= proportions of $PR$ and $G$ which are taxable; and $w, z, y$ = proportions of $D, R$, and $TP$ which can be deducted from taxable income.

This equation, from Jorgenson,[3] shows that the gross rate of return on an investment should cover its physical depreciation plus an appropriate interest rate plus the rate of taxation on gross value less expected capital gains, with all terms adjusted for income tax treatment. In a world of profit-maximizing investors and competitive capital markets, the expression for the rental price implied by equation A.1 determines the way in which interest rates would interact with prices of capital goods and tax rates to affect investment decisions.

We make use of this cost-of-capital formula for four categories of final demand: equipment, plant, single-family housing, and multifamily housing. In addition, we use simple approximations to the formula for State and local construction spending and investment in consumer durable goods. In each case, of course, differences in tax rates, depreciation rates, and other variables in the formula, as well as differences in data availability, make things work out somewhat differently.

In each case we allow for uncertainty and delayed reactions by adding a risk discount in the derivation of $R$, by allowing for flexible distributed lags in the equating of costs and returns, and by allowing for separate lags—and hence separate mechanisms through which expectations are formed—for the different important variables in equation A.1. The extensive use of flexible lag distributions is also important from another standpoint; in the absence of good empirical proxies for such difficult-to-measure phenomena as credit rationing and postponement effects, examination of the lag pattern can convey at least some information on how different categories of spending react to monetary effects. If postponement effects and credit rationing are important, or if expectations are regressive, the response to a change in interest rates will be shifted toward the beginning, whereas the reverse is true if expectations are extrapolative.

[3] Jorgenson (9). The Jorgenson formulation does not include property taxes or investment tax credits, but it is easily modified to take account of them.

PRODUCERS' INVESTMENT. The model assumes that producers take as exogenous wage rates and variables that determine the cost of capital. They set prices of their own products largely as an oligopolistic mark-up on costs, and the prices of their products, in conjunction with other demand influences on the public, determine their sales. Plant and equipment investment decisions—the subject of this section—are made so as to maximize expected future profits given product prices, the cost of capital, and expected future output.

*Equipment.* The equations for producers' durable equipment expenditures are taken from the work of Charles Bischoff (4). Equation A.1 is solved for the implicit quasi-rent which is substituted into a production function to give the optimal, or cost-minimizing, capital/output ratio for new capacity. The capital/output ratio and output itself are then combined to determine the demand for new orders, with the lag patterns differing for the two variables because producers' equipment is found to be substitutable for other factors of production before but not after the order is placed. The final step in this process explains current equipment expenditures as a result of current and past orders, with high backlogs of orders postponing the lag.

In the derivation of the implicit rent relevant to equipment investment decisions, terms such as the asset price, tax rates, and the rate of investment credit can be taken directly from available data. The $TP$ and $G$ terms are ignored, though there is some allowance for capital gains in that $R$ is assumed to be a linear function of a monetary interest rate and the stock market yield, with the relative weights determined empirically by the investment function. An important role for capital gains would be reflected in a high weight for the stock market yield, which is a better approximation to a real (inflation-adjusted) interest rate, but in fact Bischoff did not find this to be true for producers' equipment. Since all returns from producers' equipment are taxable, $v$ is unity, but $w$ is greater than 1 because of accelerated depreciation, and $x$ is less than 1 because most investment is financed out of internal funds where interest opportunity costs cannot be deducted from taxable income.

The final expression for the implicit rent for new equipment is:

$$P_{QE} = \frac{P_{PD}\,(.01\,R_E + .16)\,(1 - t_c Z_e - Z_k)}{1 - t_c} \quad \text{(A.2)}$$

The entire interest-rate term (that is, $R(1 - xt)$ in equation A.1) is estimated as

$$R_E = (1 - .2t_c)\,(-1.30 + .629R_{CBI} + .216R_D) \quad \text{(A.3)}$$

where $P_{QE}$ = implicit quasi-rent for equipment ($PR$ in equation A.1); $P_{PD}$ = price deflator, producers' durable equipment ($P$ in equation A.1); $Z_k$ = rate of investment tax credit ($u$ in equation A.1); $t_c$ = corporate tax rate ($t$ in equation A.1); 0.16 = estimated rate of depreciation ($D$ in equation A.1); $Z_e$ = present value of depreciation deduction (approximately

$$\frac{wD}{D + (1 - ut)(R)});$$

0.2 = average debt-asset ratio for corporations ($x$ in equation A.1); $R_{CBI}$ = industrial bond rate, percentage; $R_D$ = dividend-price ratio on common stock, percentage.

In the equation for new orders for equipment (equation 28 in the Appendix), this expression appears with a long distributed lag. In part, the lag represents the fact that rapid additions to the stock of equipment tend to be much more costly than gradual additions. In part, the lag is believed to represent the "putty-clay" nature of equipment investment; that is, the apparent fact that it is much more costly to change the capital intensity of equipment once it has been installed than to choose the desired degree of capital intensity of newly ordered equipment. As Bischoff explains, a putty-clay model implies a much slower response of investment to changes in the cost of capital—much of the response occurring only as old equipment wears out—than it does to changes in output.

*Structures.* The general framework of the relationships for producers' structures is similar to those for producers' durables. Again equation A.1 is solved for the implicit quasi-rent, which is again substituted into the production function to give the optimal capital/output ratio. Since there are no readily usable statistics on orders for structures, the equations are fit directly for investment expenditures without going through the intermediate stage of orders.

For structures, the manipulation of equation A.1 is exactly the same as for equipment except that the rate of investment credit is absent because the investment credit does not apply. The specific expression for the implicit quasi-rent is

$$P_{QS} = \frac{P_{PS}\,(.01\,R_S + .06)\,(1 - t_c Z_S)}{(1 - t_c)} \quad \text{(A.4)}$$

where $R_S = (1 - .2t_c)\,(-1.833 + .026 R_{CBI} + .726R_D)$; $P_{PS}$ = price deflator, producers' structures; 0.06 = estimated rate of depreciation; and $Z_S$ = present value of depreciation deduction. (A.5)

We notice that here the physical rate of depreciation is lower than for equipment and, interestingly, that the stock market rate of return is estimated to be much more important than the monetary interest rate. The importance of the stock market either could reflect the fact that waves of optimism and pessimism—which strongly influence the stock market—are more important for structures than for equipment or could imply that the real interest rates—which are more closely approximated by stock yields than by bond yields—are more important. Perhaps the higher past rate of price increase for structures than for equipment has taught investors that it is more costly to delay purchases if prices are rising.

Estimation of the structures equation (equation 33 in the Appendix) suggested that producers' structures seem to behave according to a "putty-putty" model, where factor proportions are variable after as well as before installation. Part of the difference between structures and equipment in this respect can be explained by physical attributes—structures are not generally built to be manned by a fixed amount of labor as machines are—but the difference could also be due to the fact that a producer can more readily sell a structure and reinvest at the new desired capital/output ratio than he can sell a specialized piece of equipment. In any event, net investment in structures, in contrast to equipment, has similar lags for output and for the cost of capital, responding to both only so long as the capital stock is out of equilibrium.

RESIDENTIAL CONSTRUCTION. In the residential construction market we depart from one of our general assumptions about business behavior. As noted earlier, we have assumed that, because of oligopolistic market structures, business output prices are a mark-up on costs and are not directly determined by rates of return on other assets. For residential structures, there is very active trading by owners in the existing asset stock and there are a great many small producers. Consequently, the housing equations incorporate the notion that asset prices ($P$ in equation A.1) respond directly to rates of return on other assets. Changes in income and population may also affect prices through their effect on implicit or explicit rents.

From this difference in price behavior there follows a difference in the way we view investment behavior in equipment and plant on the one hand and in housing on the other. Whereas shifts in demand and rates of return on other assets affect investment by producers directly, in the housing market these factors set up a disequilibrium between prices and costs which then indirectly stimulates building. A construction boom in response to a rise in house prices will expand the capital stock, which in turn will depress rents and prices and eventually reduce construction back to its old level.

*One- and Two-family Units.* In the actual empirical relationships for single-family housing—defined here as one- and two-unit structures—we lack quarterly observations for both an implicit rental rate and the asset price. We are therefore forced to fall back on a chain of theoretical assumptions and algebraic manipulation before arriving at an equation we can estimate.

We first assume that the rental rate is determined by the market for single-unit housing space. The demand for this space depends on permanent income, population, and relative prices, while the supply is proportional to the actual single-unit stock. Equating demand and supply in per capita terms gives

$$\frac{K_{H1R}}{N_1} = e^{a_0}\left(\frac{C_{TR}}{N}\right)^{a_1}\left(\frac{P_{R1}}{P_C}\right)^{-a_2} \tag{A.6}$$

where $K_{H1R}$ = real single-family housing stock; $N_1$ = adult population (aged 25-65) expected to live in single-family structures; $C_{TR}$ = total real consumption, a proxy for permanent income[4]; $N$ = total population; $P_{R1}$ = implied price for single-family housing space; and $P_C$ = price deflator for personal consumption expenditures.

Next, the implicit equilibrium asset price for houses is found by using equation A.1. The appropriate interest rate is a weighted average of the mortgage rate and the corporate bond rate, with the weights determined by the average mortgage/value ratio on new houses. Since purchase of a house usually involves buying land, the rates of depreciation and capital gains are weighted averages of postwar rates on single-family houses and on land. There is some indication that using a constant postwar rate to measure expected capital gains fails to capture a shift in expectations in the 1960's, and though the data for land prices are very fragmentary, we are currently attempting to improve this treatment of capital gains. Finally there are the adjustments of equation A.1 for the effect of taxes: $x$ and $y$ are unity because the personal tax law allows deduction of interest costs and property taxes, and $v$, $w$, and $z$ are zero because imputed rent and capital gains generally are

[4] Our consumption variable includes estimates of the value of services yielded by stocks of durable goods instead of expenditures on new durables. It is therefore related to a longer-run concept of income than would be the case for quarterly consumer spending.

not taxable and depreciation generally is not deductible.

Inserting this information in equation A.1 gives

$$100 \frac{\hat{P}_{R1}}{P_{H1}} = -1.14 + (1 - t_h)$$
$$(.7R_M + .3R_C + t_p) = R_{H1} \quad \text{(A.7)}$$

where $\hat{P}_{R1}$ = implicit rental on single-family housing derived by solving equation A.6 for $P_{R1}$; $P_{H1}$ = implied asset price of single-family houses; $t_h$ = personal tax rate; $t_p$ = effective property tax rate, percentage[5]; $R_M$ = mortgage rate, percentage; $R_C$ = corporate Aaa rate, percentage (a proxy for the rate on own financing); 0.7, 0.3 = appropriate weights for mortgage rate and other rates based on average loan/value ratios for new houses; $-1.14 = D - G$[6]; and $R_{H1}$ = cost of capital, single-family houses, percentage.

Finally, housing starts are taken to depend on the ratio of the asset price to housing construction costs. We substitute for the asset price in this relationship by solving equation A.7 for $P_{H1}$—a process which requires substituting for $P_{R1}$ from equation A.6. Here starts in value terms are divided by a trend that approximates the capacity of the economy, thus allowing a larger response to the price ratio signal as the economy grows larger. There is also an additional credit rationing variable (to be discussed under "Credit Rationing") which measures the ease of obtaining mortgage financing. The housing starts relationship is thus

$$\frac{HS_1}{N_1 P_{HC}} \Big/ K^* e^{r(time)} = e^{b_0} \left(\frac{\hat{P}_{H1}}{P_{HC}}\right)^{b_2} \left(D'\right)^{b_2} \quad \text{(A.8)}$$

where $HS_1$ = one- and two-unit housing starts times in value terms; $\hat{P}_{H1}$ = implicit housing price derived by solving equations A.7 and A.6; $P_{HC}$ = price deflator for housing construction costs adjusted for productivity; $D'$ = credit rationing variable; $K^* e^{r(time)}$ = real per capita capacity, single-family housing industry; and $r$ = quarterly rate of growth of real per capita capacity, taken to be 0.5 per cent per quarter (consistent with a growth in real full employment GNP of 4 per cent per year).

In the estimation of equation A.8 we fix the permanent income elasticity of demand for housing space ($a_1$) to be unity in accordance with the results of other studies.[7] We transpose the arbitrary constant to the right side, where it is part of the regression's constant term. Finally, since it is likely that patterns of reaction and of expectations are entirely different for prices and interest rates, we allow separate flexible lags for $R_{H1}$ and $P_C/P_{HC}$. The estimated lag distributions imply that adjustment to a change in interest rates is very fast, indicating postponement effects or regressive expectations; the adjustment to a change in prices is delayed, indicating extrapolative expectations.[8]

The single-family housing sector is completed by an identity which explains the single-family stock and construction expenditures from past housing starts, additions and alterations, and the rate of depreciation. When the entire sector is put together, a change in either prices or income first changes the asset price, then housing starts,

[5] This rate was computed by dividing annual State and local property tax receipts by the estimated current dollar value of the housing stock plus land.

[6] The annual rates of depreciation are assumed to be 2.7 per cent for houses and 0 for land. The annual expected rates of capital gains are assumed to be 1.6 per cent for houses and 10 per cent for land. The composite value for $D - G$ was then computed by assigning the weights 0.8 for houses and 0.2 for land.

[7] See especially (13) and (15).

[8] By regressive expectations we mean that an observed change sets up expectations of a return back toward the old level. Expectations of this sort make it advantageous to postpone purchases of a good when the price goes up, in addition to any long-run response to the price change. The postponement effect therefore makes the lag in response to a price change shorter than the long-run response lag alone. Extrapolative expectations, or expectations of a further change in the same direction as the observed one, lead to a speeding up of purchases in response to a price change—to avoid paying still higher prices later—and make the lag greater than the long-run response lag alone.

then the stock of housing. The change in the stock of housing changes the rental space price, and hence the asset price, in a direction counter to the initial movement—thus giving rise to a stock-adjustment mechanism (a "putty-putty" model) in response to changes in both prices and income.

*Three-or-more-family Units.* The multifamily sector works in much the same way as the single-family sector except for differences due to institutional phenomena and available data series. There is, for example, a published rental space index for multifamily housing, and an equation for this index can be estimated directly instead of substituting for it in deriving the multifamily housing starts equation 39 in the Appendix. In addition, we have added a nonlinear trend term to equation 39 to reflect a learning process which most experts consider to have been of great importance in the multifamily housing boom of the early 1960's.

The cost of capital for multiunit structures is derived in the same manner as for single-family units. The interest-rate term is again a weighted average of the mortgage rate and the corporate bond rate, with the weight of the mortgage rate being higher because the typical loan/value ratio is higher for multiunit structures. The estimated rate of capital gains for multiunit structures is the same as for single-family structures, but the estimated rate of physical depreciation is slightly smaller. The parameters $x$ and $y$ are still equal to 1, as are $v$ and $z$ because rental income and capital gains for multiunits are monetary and reportable, but $w$ is greater than 1 because of accelerated depreciation. The appropriate cost of capital expression for multiunit housing is then

$$100\,\frac{P_{R3}}{P_{H3}} = -2.44 + .95\,R_M + .05\,R_C + t_p = R_{H3} \qquad \text{(A.9)}$$

where $R_{H3}$ = cost of capital, multifamily houses, percentage; $P_{H3}$ = implied asset price, multifamily houses; $P_{R3}$ = price deflator for apartment rental space, component of consumer price index; 0.95, 0.05 = appropriate weights for mortgages and other rates; and $-2.44$ =

$$D\left(\frac{1 - wt}{1 - t}\right) - G.^{9}$$

The multifamily housing starts equation is of the form

$$\frac{HS_3}{N_3 P_{HC}} \Big/ K^{*} e^{r(time)} = e^{d_0} \left(\frac{P_{H3}}{P_{HC}}\right)^{d_1} \left(D'\right)^{d_2} e^{-\left(\frac{d_4}{K_{H3R} - d_5}\right)} \qquad \text{(A.10)}$$

where the subscript "3" designates the appropriate variable for the multiunit sector. It is similar to equation A.8 except for the logistic term which accounts for the growth in multiunit starts in the 1960's. The value of $d_5$ was chosen to place this growth as nearly as possible in the early 1960's. As before, separate lags were estimated for the cost of capital and the price ratio, and these lags again show regressive expectations for interest rates and extrapolative expectations for prices.

Just as in the single-unit housing sector, the starts determined in equation A.10 enter the capital stock. An increase in the stock reduces the rental price—the equation is not shown here—and therefore depresses both the implicit price and the housing investment, implying the same kind of stock-adjustment mechanism as for single-family housing.

CONSUMPTION. Financial conditions affect consumption mainly through the wealth effect (discussed under "The Wealth Effect"), but the cost of capital also plays a role. Total consumption, defined and crudely measured so as to include the consumption of services yielded by durable goods instead of expenditures on these goods, is determined by current and lagged disposable income and by net worth. This consumption is then allocated between nondurable goods and services and consumption of the services of durable

[9] The $D$ and $G$ terms were computed exactly as in footnote 8, except that the annual rate of depreciation of multiunit structures was taken to be 2.0 per cent. The tax rate $t$ was equal to a weighted average of personal and corporate rates (about .33), and $w$ was assumed equal to 2.

goods depending on population, the initial stock of durable goods, and the relative costs of durable and nondurable goods. This last term is the channel through which the opportunity cost of holding durable goods affects consumer behavior. The consumption sector is closed by an identity relating consumption on durables to the initial stock and to durable goods expenditures, which is the quantity that (along with consumption of nondurables and services) is included in GNP. Since a change in either prices or incomes first alters expenditures on durable goods, then the stock, and this stock dampens future expenditures, consumer durables too follow a stock-adjustment mechanism in response to changes in both prices and incomes.

To represent the relative cost term for consumer durable goods we use a linear function of the relative price and past interest rates on corporate bonds. We ignore capital gains, property taxes, personal income taxes, and depreciation rates—the last two on the ground that the imputed rent on consumer durables is nontaxable and depreciation expenses are nondeductible. The distributed lag of corporate bond rates serves as a proxy for unobserved rates and other credit terms on consumer installment contracts.

The allocation of total consumption is thus equation A.11.

In accordance with the identity that $C_{TR}$ equals the sum of its parts, equation A.11

$$\begin{pmatrix} \dfrac{C_{NR}}{C_{TR}} \\ \dfrac{C_{AR}}{C_{TR}} \\ \dfrac{C_{DR}}{C_{TR}} \end{pmatrix} = AZ \qquad \text{(A.11)}$$

where $C_{NR}$ = real consumption of nondurable goods and services, annual rates; $C_{AR}$ = real implied consumption, autos and parts, annual rates; $C_{DR}$ = real implied consumption, other durable goods, annual rates; $C_{TR}$ = total real consumption, by definition equal to $C_{NR} + C_{AR} + C_{DR}$; $A$ = a $3 \times 6$ matrix of coefficients; $Z$ = a $6 \times 1$ matrix of allocating variables which includes (a) 1 (to give the constant); (b) $(R_C)$, in distributed lag form; (c) $P_{CN}/P_{CD}$ ($P_{CN}$ is the price deflator for nondurable goods and services and $P_{CD}$ is the price deflator for durable goods); (d) $K_{AR}/C_{TR}$ ($K_{AR}$ is the start-of-period real stock of autos); (e) $K_{DR}/C_{TR}$ ($K_{DR}$ is the start-of-period real stock of other durables); and (f) $N/C_{TR}$.

was estimated so that the sum of the three constants $(a_{11} + a_{21} + a_{31})$ is unity, but the sum of all other columns of coefficients is zero. This means that if a change in, say, relative prices affects the consumption of nondurables in one way, it affects the consumption of durables in an exactly offsetting way; thus total consumption remains unchanged. Since the signs in equation A.11 were all as expected, a rise either in the relative price of durables or in interest rates permanently reduces the consumption of durable goods, resulting in a magnified temporary drop in expenditures on durable goods and permanently increases the consumption of nondurable goods and services.

STATE AND LOCAL GOVERNMENT EXPENDITURES. The remaining way in which the cost of capital goods affects final demand is through the construction expenditures of State and local governments. The capital stock that these governments wish to hold is assumed to be a function of relative prices, interest rates, output, and demographic variables. Construction expenditures then depend upon the relation of actual and desired capital stock, together with the matching grants-in-aid of the Federal Government. These expenditures affect the capital stock, hence generating the back pressure which eventually shuts off the expenditure response to a stimulus.[10]

The property tax term in equation A.1 can be ignored because we would hardly expect State and local governments to tax their own structures. For similar reasons, $v$, $w$, $x$, $y$,

[10] Other State and local expenditures, which are mainly wage payments but also include purchases of nondurable goods and transfer payments, are explained by a different mechanism. These other expenditures are assumed to behave more like consumption goods than investment goods, and the latest versions of these equations find the interest-rate effect to be quite unimportant.

and $z$ are all zero—the Federal Government neither taxes States and local governments nor allows tax deductions. The interest-rate term is measured by the rate on State and local bonds, and the rate of depreciation is assumed to be a constant. Capital gains are measured by a long distributed lag on past rates of change of the State and local price deflator; these governments seldom realize capital gains, but the expected rate of price increase is nevertheless important for State and local construction because it measures the cost of postponing construction.

The appropriate expression for the cost of capital under these conditions is:

$$P_{RS} = P_{SL}\left[D + R_{SL} - 100\left(\frac{\Delta P_{SL}}{P_{SL}}\right)^e\right] \tag{A.12}$$

where $P_{RS}$ = implicit quasi-rent, State and local structures; $P_{SL}$ = price deflator, State and local purchases; $R_{SL}$ = State and local bond rate, percentage; and $\left(\frac{\Delta P_{SL}}{P_{SL}}\right)^e$ = expected rate of change in $P_{SL}$.

Dividing through by the price of all goods to get the relative price for States and localities and approximating $\left(\frac{\Delta P_{SL}}{P_{SL}}\right)^e$ by a distributed lag on past rates of change of $P_{SL}$, we get equation A.13

$$\frac{P_{RS}}{P_Y} = \frac{P_{SL}}{P_Y}\left[D + R_{SL} - 100 \sum_i w_i \left(\frac{\Delta P_{SL}}{P_{SL}}\right)_{-i}\right] \tag{A.13}$$

where $P_Y$ = GNP deflator.

Because the deflator for State and local purchases is heavily influenced by State and local wage rates, which could introduce an irrelevant trend into the response to interest rates and expected price changes, we decompose the right side into one term in $P_{SL}/P_Y$, one in $R_{SL}$, and one in $\frac{\Delta P_{SL}}{P_{SL}}$. The construction equation 55 in the Appendix uses these variables, all fitted with separate lags, along with income, demographic variables, matching grants, and capital stock. It turns out that the lag on the interest rate is quite short, indicating that postponement effects are predominant, whereas the lag on price changes is very long. Coefficients indicate that a 1 per cent change in the annual rate of inflation has about half the effect of a 1 per cent change in the rate of interest.

### *The Wealth Effect*

The second channel of monetary policy is through the net worth of consumers. There are two key relationships here: the link between household net worth—of which one component is the value of common stock equities—and consumption; and the link between financial rates of return and the stock market rate of return, and hence the value of equities.

The link between household net worth and consumption has a long tradition in macroeconomics, culminating in the life-cycle hypothesis as formulated by Modigliani, Brumberg, and Ando (3) and (5). The basic idea is that consumers allocate consumption over their entire lifetime, given initial net worth, a rate of time preference, and expectations regarding labor income. Since labor income is a recurring flow during a consumer's working years, the propensity to consume this income will be reasonably high, but it will be less than unity because of the need to save for retirement years. At the same time, since net worth at any point in time is an addition to the consumers' resources, it will have a positive coefficient, but the coefficient will be small because net worth is an exhaustible stock and consumption out of this stock must be spread over many years.

The life-cycle hypothesis leads to a consumption function in which total consumption as defined earlier in "The cost of capital" depends on current and lagged disposable labor income and net worth. In the model we use a transformation to substitute total disposable income for labor income to avoid the difficulty of allocating national accounts' disposable income between its labor and nonlabor components. The lag for disposible income is due to the fact that it takes consumers time to change expectations about future income. For our purposes the important point is that net worth is defined to include capital gains along with accumulation due to past saving, and in the U.S. economy the predominant source of capital gains has been the stock market. Although the marginal propensity to consume out of net worth is quite small—less than 0.04 in the consumption function we are presently using—since consumption is so important in total final expenditures, even this response is large enough for stock market swings to have an important effect on the economy.

The value of equities in consumer net worth which determines capital gains in the stock market follows from the capitalization identity

$$ST = 100\left(\frac{Y_{CD}}{R_D}\right)$$

where $ST$ = value of common stock in net worth; $Y_{CD}$ = corporate dividend payments; and $R_D$ = dividend-price ratio on common stock, percentage.

Dividend payments are determined by current and lagged corporate cash flows through a model similar to Lintner's (10), thus leaving the dividend-price ratio as the vehicle through which monetary forces influence equity values.

The theory behind determination of the rate of return in the stock market is similar to the theory developed above for deriving the rate of return on tangible assets. Since equities are a substitute for bonds, changes in the long-term bond rate change the rate at which the stock market capitalizes dividend payments and hence the value of equities in net worth. In equilibrium we would expect the total rate of return on common stocks, which equals the dividend-price ratio plus the expected rate of growth of stock prices, to equal the interest rate plus a risk premium. Inflation can be viewed either as something that leads to larger expected rate of growth of stock prices given interest rates, or as meaning that the total rate of return on stocks should equal a real interest rate plus a risk premium. If we adopt the latter convention, we can write

$$R_D + G^e = R_C - 100\left(\frac{\Delta P_C}{P_C}\right)^e + \pi \tag{B.1}$$

where $R_D$ = dividend-price ratio, common stock, percentage; $G^e$ = measure of expected change in stock prices; $R_C$ = corporate bond rate, percentage; $(\Delta P_C/P_C)^e$ = expected rate of change of the price deflator for consumption expenditures; and $\pi$ = risk premium.

In something as volatile as the stock market, it is not easy to measure either the risk premium or the expected rate of change of prices. For the expected rate of change of consumer prices we have had some luck with a long distributed lag on past rates of change of consumer prices, though the long-run effect of this variable is only 10 per cent of what we would expect if real interest rates were the appropriate measure of the opportunity cost of holding equities. For the expected rate of change of stock prices, we tried without success a similar long distributed lag on past rates of change of dividends (both gross and per share). The best results substitute a downward time trend for the combination of expected change in stock prices and risk premium—since apparently the riskiness in holding equities is adjudged to be a good deal less now than in the early postwar period—along with a dummy ($DU_{ST}$) for the 1962 crisis of confidence in the stock market. The stock market equation is thus of the form

$$R_D = a_1 R_C - a_2 \sum_i w_i \left(\frac{\Delta P_C}{P_C}\right)_{-i} - a_3\,(\text{time}) + a_4\, DU_{ST} + a_5 \tag{B.2}$$

The steady-state coefficient for the past annual percentage rates of consumer price change should be 1 but is only 0.10. The average lag on $R_C$ is 2.3 quarters and on past price changes is seven quarters. This result is similar to that obtained in the housing and State and local construction equations, where interest-rate changes seem to be accepted as permanent much sooner than changes in the rate of price increase. The time trend is constructed so that the downward drift in the dividend-price ratio is substantially over by the late 1960's.

One implication of this group of equations is that a change in interest rates changes the dividend-price ratio, changes the valuation of equities and net worth, and is responsible for a permanent change in consumption expenditures for both durable and nondurable goods and services. A further implication is that some of the difficulty in predicting per-

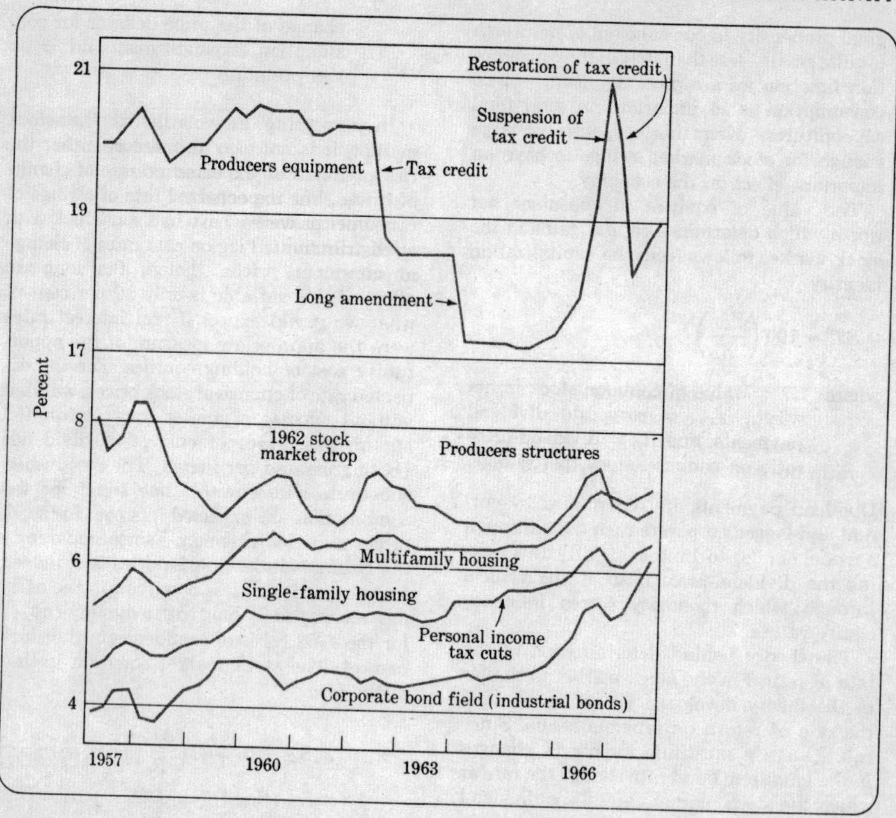


**CHART 1** Measures of the cost of capital.

sonal saving rates can be attributed to difficulties in predicting stock prices.

*Credit Rationing*

A third channel of monetary policy is credit rationing. We use credit rationing to refer to the failure of interest rates on loans to adjust rapidly enough to clear financial markets, so that lenders ration credit by various nonprice terms.[11] Since the specific details of this nonprice rationing—changes in downpayment terms, requirements for collateral balances, or outright denials—are often not recorded, it is difficult to measure and identify credit rationing and so indirect means must be used to represent it. Possibly this explains why in the present version of the model we have evidence of the presence of credit rationing only in the housing sector, although we tested various indicators of it in the commercial loan market and for plant and equipment and inventory investment.

The most widely noted case of credit rationing in recent years is the link between savings institutions and the housing market. The rates paid to depositors and charged to mortgage lenders by savings institutions are found to be quite sluggish, possibly due to oligopolistic market structure, possibly due to the costliness of changing advertised rates frequently, and at times due to governmental ceilings. Since at least part of the deposit inflows to these institutions is found to be sensitive to interest-rate spreads, savings institutions experience large fluctuations in their deposit flows when market rates change

[11] A careful theoretical treatment with applications to the bank commercial loan market is developed in (7) and (8).

rapidly. On the asset side, these institutions are forced, again by governmental regulation, to invest a very high portion of their portfolio in long-term, low-turnover mortgages. The combination of volatile deposits, fixed-commitment mortgages, and sluggish mortgage rates increases the risk exposure of savings institutions in times of rising market interest rates, and this combination of circumstances is assumed to cause nonprice rationing—at least for new mortgages. The credit rationing variable in the housing starts equations (A.8 and A.10), following this line of causation, is taken to be the ratio of actual deposit flows to the deposit flows that might have been expected, with the latter measured by the average—adjusted for growth—over the preceding 3 years. When actual flows are low relative to expected flows, savings institutions are forced to ration new mortgage loans and thereby restrict new housing starts.

The prerequisites for credit rationing—sluggish lending and deposit rates, little predictability of deposit flows, little short-run control over asset composition—are by far more prevalent in the mortgage-housing area than in most other credit markets. Nevertheless, we are not convinced that they are unimportant in other markets, and we feel further work on representing and testing for rationing effects might prove fruitful.

*Summary*

Chart 1 plots the cost of capital in real percentage terms for plant and equipment investment and for single- and multifamily housing quarterly from 1957-67.[12] All four time series are heavily influenced by the basic pattern of long-term interest rates, but there are some interesting differences. The cost of capital for equipment is basically much higher than the others because of the relatively high depreciation rate for equipment. It dropped sharply with the introduction of the investment credit in 1962 and again with the Long Amendment in 1964.[13]

The cost of capital for structures has neither of these effects, but there are sharp changes in this variable during periods of stock price fluctuations such as the drop in 1962. The housing costs are similar to each other in pattern except in 1964 and 1965 when personal tax rates changed. The lowering of personal tax rates in the first quarters of 1964 and of 1965 reduced the differential advantage given to single-family houses by the tax law and raised the single-family cost of capital relative to the multifamily cost.

The flow diagram [p. 160] exhibits the direct effects of monetary policy. Financial yields shown at the left affect the various categories of final demand on the right through the three channels—cost of capital, wealth effect, and credit rationing. Cost-of-capital variables affect all categories of expenditure listed on the right. The combination of these cost-of-capital linkages, the effect of financial yields on net worth and consumption, and the effect of the credit rationing variable in housing cause for the entire model a very complicated response to monetary forces. Section II estimates the quantitative importance and timing pattern of this response by simulation experiments.

## II. Some Empirical Results

For this report we are using a version of the Federal Reserve–MIT econometric model which contains 75 behavioral equations, identities for 35 other endogenous variables, and 70 exogenous variables. Many of the equations are nonlinear, many depend importantly on initial conditions, and many have complicated internal dynamics. The response patterns of the entire model are thus quite complex, with a great many oscillatory and nonoscillatory mechanisms superimposed on each other. The following results are designed to illustrate just the essential elements of the response of aggregate demand to monetary and fiscal policy measures.

The properties of this large and complicated model are best illustrated by simulation experiments. We made a series of such experiments that measured the effects of step changes in key policy variables by computing differences between two simulation runs. The first run in every case is a dynamic simulation of the model over some time period. By dynamic we mean that, while we use

---

12 The variables plotted are $100\frac{P_{QE}}{P_{PD}}$ for equipment, $100\frac{P_{QS}}{P_{PS}}$ for structures, $R_{H1}$ for single-family housing, and $R_{H3}$ for multifamily housing.

13 The Long Amendment allowed the entire cost of an equipment investment to qualify for depreciation deductions. Previously only the cost net of investment credit could qualify.

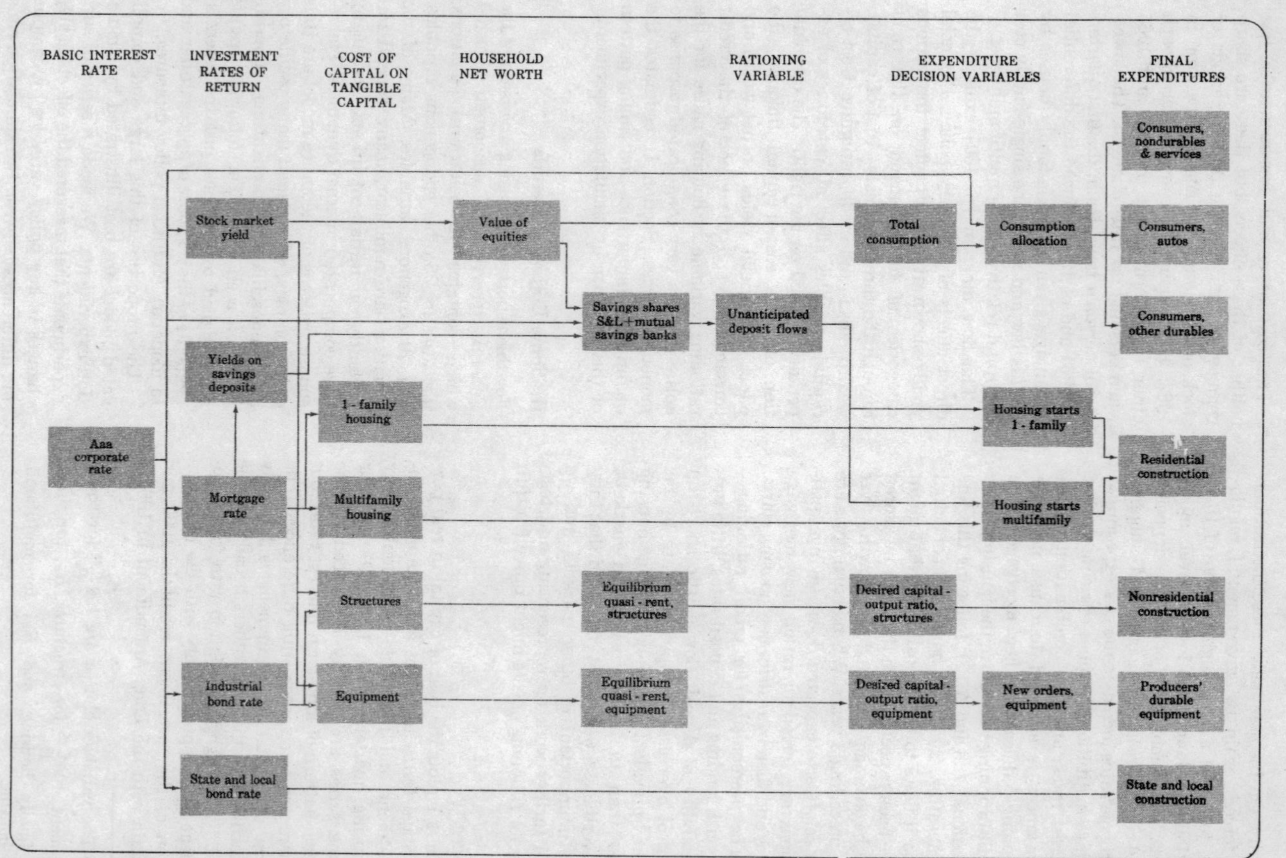


First-round effects of monetary policy.

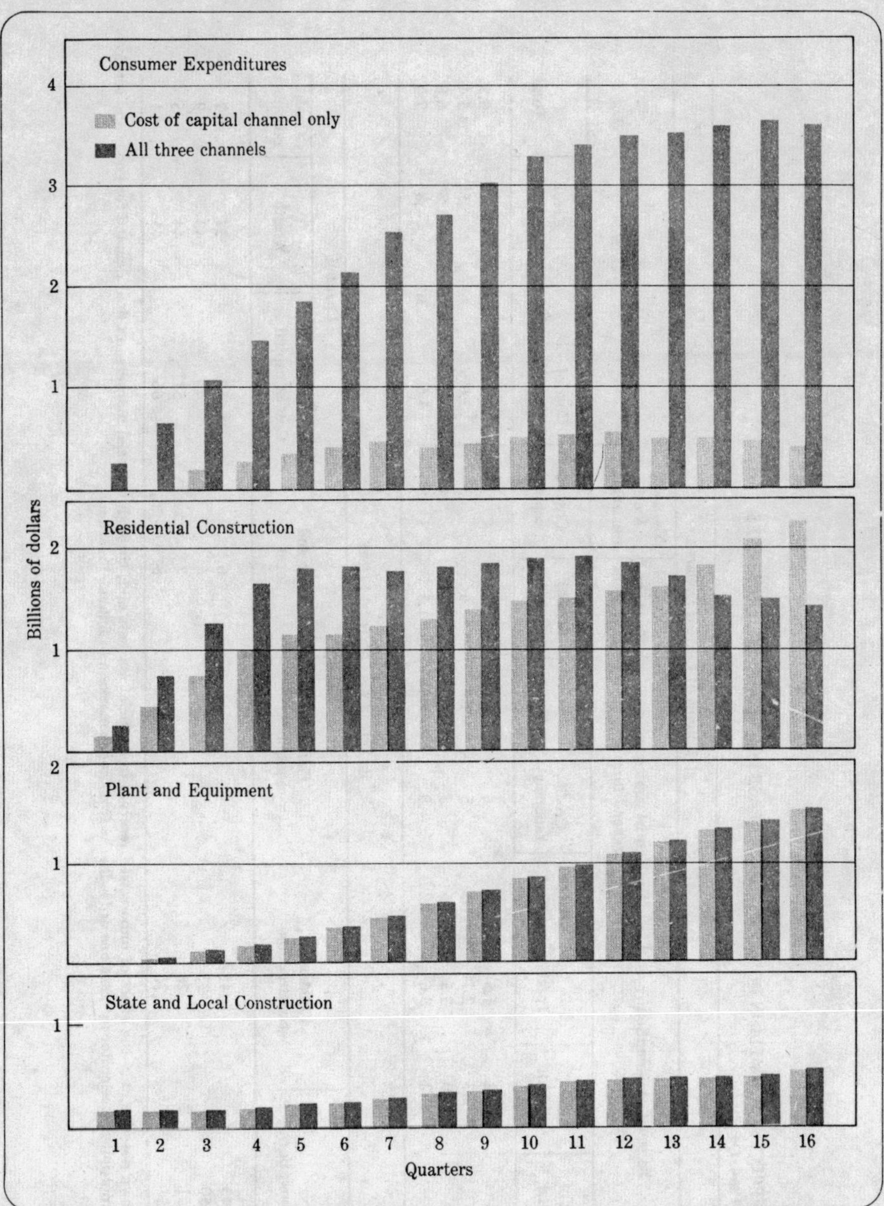


**CHART 2** Direct effects on final demand of a billion-dollar step increase in unborrowed reserves, initial conditions of 1964, Q1.

actual values for all current and lagged exogenous variables, we use only initial actual values for endogenous variables. The model generates solutions for the endogenous variables during the first simulation period, then uses these in generating solutions for the second period, and so forth for each succeeding period. The second run in each ex-

**TABLE 1. DIRECT EFFECTS OF A BILLION-DOLLAR STEP INCREASE IN UNBORROWED RESERVES**
**Initial Conditions of 1964, Q1**

a. Billions of Current Dollars

| Quarter | Personal consumption expenditures | | | Residential construction expenditures | | | Plant and equipment | State and local construction | Total | | | |
|---|---|---|---|---|---|---|---|---|---|---|---|---|
| | Cost of capital | Wealth | Total | Cost of capital | Credit rationing | Total | Cost of capital | Cost of capital | Cost of capital | Wealth | Credit rationing | Total |
| 4 | .3 | 1.2 | 1.5 | 1.0 | .6 | 1.6 | .2 | .2 | 1.7 | 1.2 | .6 | 3.5 |
| 8 | .4 | 2.3 | 2.7 | 1.3 | .5 | 1.8 | .6 | .3 | 2.6 | 2.3 | .5 | 5.4 |
| 12 | .5 | 3.0 | 3.5 | 1.5 | .3 | 1.8 | 1.1 | .4 | 3.5 | 3.0 | .3 | 6.8 |
| 16 | .4 | 3.2 | 3.6 | 2.2 | –.8 | 1.4 | 1.5 | .5 | 4.6 | 3.2 | –.8 | 7.0 |

b. Percentages of Total Effect

| Quarter | Consumption | Residential construction | Plant and equipment | State and local | Channel | | |
|---|---|---|---|---|---|---|---|
| | | | | | Cost of capital | Wealth | Credit rationing |
| 4 | 43 | 45 | 6 | 6 | 49 | 34 | 17 |
| 8 | 50 | 33 | 11 | 6 | 48 | 43 | 9 |
| 12 | 51 | 26 | 16 | 7 | 51 | 44 | 5 |
| 16 | 51 | 20 | 21 | 8 | 66 | 45 | –11 |

NOTE: The results shown describe only the effect of unborrowed reserves in financial markets and, through financial markets, on final demand for goods and services. They do not include multiplier-accelerator interactions or feedbacks from goods markets to financial markets.

periment is another dynamic simulation that is identical to the first in all respects except that one of the policy variables is altered by a specified amount beginning in a specified quarter and continuing for all subsequent quarters of the simulation period. The final step—computing differences between the control and experimental simulations—gives the response of endogenous variables in the model to the specified maintained change in the policy variable.

### *Monetary Policy Simulations*

Two simulations of monetary policy were made.

DIRECT EFFECTS OF MONETARY POLICY. We measure the effect of our central monetary policy instrument—unborrowed reserves—by examining the response of the model to a maintained reserve increase of $1 billion. That is, we assume that the Federal Reserve made $1 billion more unborrowed reserves available than the actual historical amount in the initial quarter and maintained the billion-dollar excess over historical amounts in each succeeding quarter. While actual monetary policy changes rarely follow this step-change pattern, nevertheless it is a useful experiment because it enables us to compute the multiplier over time for this policy change.

We first conduct this experiment for a subset of the equations of the model including only the financial sector and demand equations for categories of goods and services affected directly by monetary policy. This simulation gives us only the direct effects of monetary policy on financial markets and—through financial markets—on final spending, uncomplicated by feedbacks of output and prices back to the financial sector or by multiplier-accelerator responses within nonfinancial markets. The results are presented in Chart 2 and summarized in Table 1.

The table shows that the direct effect of the $1 billion open market operations is to stimulate final demand by $3.5 billion by the end of 1 year, by $5.4 billion after 2 years, and on up to $7.0 billion after 4 years. These amounts are appreciably smaller than the total effect over the first few years including the multiplier-accelerator mechanism and the feedback from the real sector to the financial sector.

Table 1b shows that while residential construction is responsible for much of the early effect, its importance gradually declines over time. This pattern can be attributed largely to the rationing channel. In periods immediately following the policy change, market rates of interest fall relative to the sluggish deposit rates of savings institutions. There follows a sharp rise in savings deposit inflows, which in turn stimulates housing starts and expenditures. Thus the credit-rationing channel alone comprises 17 per cent of the total direct monetary effect by the end of four quarters. But as time goes on, the normal relation between deposit rates and market rates is restored and savings inflows fall relative to their recent high levels. As this happens, the importance of the rationing effect is reduced. In fact, by the end of 4 years deposit rates have adjusted completely, savings funds are returning to their pre-policy-change allocation, and a reverse credit-rationing process is at work. In the longer run, this process too dies out as deposit inflows settle down to a steady rate of growth.

The cost of capital channel operates strongly throughout the 4-year simulation period. Initial effects are important for housing and ultimate effects both for housing and for plant and equipment. As mentioned earlier, cost-of-capital effects on expenditures last only until actual capital stocks have reached their desired levels; in the model this process is not complete by the end of 4 years. One reason for this long lag is the time it takes short-term market interest rates to affect long-term rates. The simulations in Table 1 are not carried on for a long enough period to see expenditures induced by changes in the cost of capital recede towards zero. The beginnings of this pattern are visible for consumer durables, but investment in plant and equipment, multifamily housing, and State and local construction is still building up after 4 years.

The wealth effect also operates strongly throughout the period. Since the change in wealth affects consumption promptly, this wealth effect accounts for 35 per cent of the total effect by the end of the first year. It builds up gradually to 45 per cent by the end of 4 years, and in the very long run when the other channels fade out of the picture—

TABLE 2. EFFECTS OF A BILLION-DOLLAR STEP INCREASE IN UNBORROWED RESERVES, FULL MODEL EFFECTS
Initial Conditions of 1964, Q1. In Percentage Points Unless Otherwise Indicated

| Quarter | Real GNP (billions of 1958 dollars) | GNP deflator | Money GNP (billions of current dollars) | Corporate Aaa bond rate | Unemployment rate |
|---|---|---|---|---|---|
| 1 | .7 | ... | .8 | −.27 | ... |
| 2 | 2.0 | ... | 2.3 | −.14 | −.1 |
| 3 | 3.6 | .1 | 4.3 | −.12 | −.2 |
| 4 | 5.4 | .1 | 6.6 | −.16 | −.3 |
| 5 | 7.0 | .2 | 8.9 | −.19 | −.4 |
| 6 | 8.3 | .3 | 11.1 | −.22 | −.5 |
| 7 | 9.3 | .4 | 13.2 | −.22 | −.6 |
| 8 | 10.0 | .6 | 15.1 | −.24 | −.6 |
| 9 | 10.5 | .8 | 16.9 | −.25 | −.7 |
| 10 | 10.7 | .9 | 18.6 | −.26 | −.7 |
| 11 | 10.3 | 1.2 | 19.9 | −.24 | −.7 |
| 12 | 9.4 | 1.4 | 20.6 | −.25 | −.6 |
| 13 | 7.9 | 1.7 | 20.6 | −.25 | −.6 |
| 14 | 6.1 | 1.9 | 20.1 | −.23 | −.5 |
| 15 | 3.9 | 2.1 | 19.0 | −.23 | −.3 |
| 16 | 1.4 | 2.2 | 17.2 | −.23 | −.2 |

aside from the permanent replacement effect of the cost of capital—the wealth effect would comprise the entire direct monetary effect.

FULL-MODEL EFFECTS OF MONETARY POLICY. We turn now to the full-model effects of a change in unborrowed reserves. These are different from the direct effects we have described earlier because we now allow these direct effects to set in motion a multiplier-accelerator process and because we also permit the real sector to feed back into the monetary sector. The former inclusion expands the effects of monetary policy changes in early years, whereas the latter inclusion, by allowing the rise in money income to increase interest rates and partially reverse initial rate movements, gradually dampens the long-run effects.

The results of the full-model simulation beginning in the first quarter of 1964 are shown in Table 2. Here the effects on real GNP build up to $5.4 billion in 1 year and $10.0 billion in 2 years, but after that they decline so rapidly that by the end of 4 years there is scarcely any effect on real income. The 4-year effect of the monetary change on money GNP is thus almost entirely in the form of higher prices. For the first 2 years the full-system response for real GNP is much larger than the direct effect shown in Table 1 because of the multiplier-accelerator mechanism. But after that the full system real response dies out because of the oscillations inherent in the accelerator system as well as because of the rises in interest rates stimulated by the rise in money GNP. By way of illustration of this interest-rate feedback, in the direct-effect simulations underlying Table 1, the corporate Aaa rate declined by 46 basis points after 4 years, whereas in the full-model simulations underlying Table 2 the corporate rate declined by only 23 basis points.

EFFECT OF INITIAL CONDITIONS. We now compare full-model multipliers for different initial conditions and different directions of policy change. For one set of simulations we start in the first quarter of 1964 and raise unborrowed reserves—these are the simulations described already—and for the other set we begin in the second quarter of 1958 and lower unborrowed reserves.

The obvious difference between these two initial periods is the difference in inflationary potential. The quarters during and after

**TABLE 3. EFFECTS OF A BILLION-DOLLAR STEP DECREASE IN UNBORROWED RESERVES, FULL MODEL EFFECTS**

**Initial Conditions of 1958, Q2. In Percentage Points Unless Otherwise Indicated**

| Quarter | Real GNP (billions of 1958 dollars) | GNP deflator | Money GNP (billions of current dollars) | Corporate Aaa bond rate | Unemployment rate |
|---|---|---|---|---|---|
| 1 | −.5 | . . . | −.5 | .27 | . . . |
| 2 | −1.3 | −.1 | −1.5 | .14 | .1 |
| 3 | −2.7 | −.1 | −2.9 | .13 | .2 |
| 4 | −4.2 | −.1 | −4.6 | .17 | .3 |
| 5 | −5.4 | −.2 | −6.1 | .20 | .4 |
| 6 | −6.5 | −.2 | −7.5 | .24 | .5 |
| 7 | −7.3 | −.3 | −8.8 | .27 | .6 |
| 8 | −7.9 | −.4 | −9.8 | .28 | .7 |
| 9 | −8.3 | −.5 | −10.7 | .29 | .7 |
| 10 | −8.5 | −.6 | −11.5 | .29 | .7 |
| 11 | −8.6 | −.7 | −12.1 | .29 | .7 |
| 12 | −8.4 | −.8 | −12.5 | .30 | .7 |
| 13 | −8.1 | −.9 | −12.8 | .30 | .7 |
| 14 | −7.7 | −1.0 | −13.1 | .30 | .7 |
| 15 | −7.2 | −1.1 | −13.2 | .30 | .6 |
| 16 | −6.6 | −1.2 | −13.4 | .29 | .6 |

1964 were ones of fairly high resource utilization, and the expansion of reserves at this time would be expected to stimulate price increases promptly. On the other hand, there was substantial excess capacity in 1958 and the decrease in reserves at that time could be expected to have a minimal short-run effect on prices. The Appendix includes a discussion and listing of the nonlinear "Phillips curve" equation (No. 96) which largely accounts for this result in the model.

Another, perhaps less obvious difference between the two periods which affects the simulation results is the difference in initial stock market conditions. It will be recalled that the value of common stock in net worth is given by the capitalization identity

$$ST = 100\left(\frac{Y_{CD}}{R_D}\right)$$

The response of stock prices to a unit change in $R_D$, it follows, is equal to $\left(\frac{ST}{R_D}\right)$. If the dividend-price ratio changes by a constant absolute amount, therefore, the absolute change in the value of stock—and hence net worth and consumption—will be greater the lower is the initial level of this dividend-price ratio and the higher the initial level of stock prices. In a sense, the dividend-price ratio has greater leverage the lower it is. In 1958 the dividend-price ratio was 4.1 per cent, and the first-year rise of 14 basis points induced by the restrictive monetary change reduced the value of common stock equities by only $14 billion. But by 1964 the secular fall in dividend-price ratio had reduced it to 3.0 per cent, stock values had more than doubled, and the decline induced by the monetary expansion, again 14 basis points, increased the value of common stock by $37 billion. Since the coefficient of net worth in the consumption function is 0.04, this difference alone directly stimulated almost $1 billion of added consumption.

These differences are illustrated by Tables 2 and 3. We see that initial real income effects in the 1964 simulation are moderately larger than in the 1958 simulation, mainly because of the greater impact of the dividend-price ratio. The price response is substantially higher in 1964, even allowing for the bigger initial real income response, be-

**TABLE 4. EFFECTS OF THREE EXPANSIONARY POLICIES**

**Initial Conditions of 1964, Q1. In Percentage Points Unless Otherwise Indicated**

| Quarter | Real GNP (billions of 1958 dollars) | | | GNP deflator | | | Money GNP (billions of current dollars) | | | Corporate Aaa bond rate | | | Unemployment rate | | |
|---|---|---|---|---|---|---|---|---|---|---|---|---|---|---|---|
| | A | B | C | A | B | C | A | B | C | A | B | C | A | B | C |
| 1 | .7 | 6.6 | 1.4 | ... | ... | ... | .8 | 7.3 | 1.6 | −.27 | .06 | .03 | ... | −.2 | ... |
| 2 | 2.0 | 8.3 | 2.9 | ... | ... | ... | 2.3 | 9.4 | 3.4 | −.14 | .05 | .02 | −.1 | −.5 | −.2 |
| 3 | 3.6 | 8.7 | 3.6 | .1 | .2 | .1 | 4.3 | 10.3 | 4.4 | −.12 | .05 | .02 | −.2 | −.6 | −.2 |
| 4 | 5.4 | 8.9 | 4.0 | .1 | .2 | .1 | 6.6 | 11.2 | 5.2 | −.16 | .06 | .03 | −.3 | −.6 | −.3 |
| 5 | 7.0 | 9.0 | 4.5 | .2 | .4 | .2 | 8.9 | 12.0 | 6.1 | −.19 | .08 | .04 | −.4 | −.6 | −.3 |
| 6 | 8.3 | 8.7 | 4.8 | .3 | .4 | .2 | 11.1 | 12.4 | 6.8 | −.22 | .09 | .05 | −.5 | −.6 | −.3 |
| 7 | 9.3 | 8.0 | 5.0 | .4 | .6 | .3 | 13.2 | 12.6 | 7.6 | −.23 | .10 | .06 | −.6 | −.6 | −.3 |
| 8 | 10.0 | 7.9 | 5.2 | .6 | .7 | .4 | 15.1 | 13.5 | 8.5 | −.24 | .12 | .07 | −.6 | −.6 | −.3 |
| 9 | 10.4 | 7.6 | 5.3 | .8 | .9 | .5 | 16.9 | 14.1 | 9.3 | −.25 | .14 | .09 | −.7 | −.5 | −.4 |
| 10 | 10.7 | 6.8 | 5.4 | .9 | 1.0 | .6 | 18.6 | 14.3 | 10.1 | −.26 | .16 | .10 | −.7 | −.5 | −.4 |
| 11 | 10.3 | 6.1 | 5.4 | 1.2 | 1.1 | .7 | 19.9 | 14.5 | 10.9 | −.24 | .17 | .12 | −.7 | −.4 | −.4 |
| 12 | 9.4 | 5.6 | 5.2 | 1.4 | 1.3 | .8 | 20.6 | 15.2 | 11.6 | −.25 | .19 | .14 | −.6 | −.4 | −.3 |
| 13 | 7.9 | 5.8 | 4.7 | 1.7 | 1.4 | .9 | 20.6 | 16.5 | 11.8 | −.25 | .20 | .14 | −.6 | −.4 | −.3 |
| 14 | 6.1 | 6.2 | 3.9 | 1.9 | 1.6 | 1.1 | 20.1 | 18.2 | 11.7 | −.23 | .22 | .15 | −.5 | −.4 | −.3 |
| 15 | 3.9 | 5.7 | 2.8 | 2.1 | 1.8 | 1.2 | 19.0 | 18.8 | 11.3 | −.23 | .24 | .16 | −.3 | −.4 | −.2 |
| 16 | 1.4 | 5.0 | 1.6 | 2.2 | 1.9 | 1.2 | 17.2 | 19.2 | 10.6 | −.23 | .25 | .18 | −.2 | −.3 | −.2 |

NOTE: A indicates step increase in unborrowed reserves of $1.0 billion; B indicates step increase in real Federal wage payments of $5.0 billion; and C indicates step decrease in personal tax rate of .02 (about $4.5 billion in revenue).

cause of the lower initial unemployment rate. But it is interesting to note that the much higher 1964 money GNP response leads to a greater reversal of initial interest-rate movements; this means that by the end of 4 years the real GNP response is much less in the 1964 simulations. In the very long run of, say, 15 or 20 years, the real GNP response would die out in both cases—but this happens more quickly the faster prices respond.

### *Comparison of Monetary and Fiscal Policy Multipliers*

Finally these monetary policy multipliers are compared with multipliers for common fiscal policy stabilization tools. The comparisons are given in Table 4, which shows the full-model response to a $1 billion increase in unborrowed reserves, a $5 billion increase in real Federal compensation of employees, and a 0.02 decrease in the personal income tax rate. The last implies an initial revenue loss of $4.5 billion at levels in the first quarter of 1964.

The size of these policy changes, and hence of the real GNP and price results, is arbitrary; there is nothing "natural" about comparing a $1 billion reserve change with a $5 billion expenditure change or any other specific amount. Of interest are the dynamic paths—which show a much more rapid approach to peak real GNP effects for Federal spending than for monetary policy—and tax rates in between the two. We have noted before that these findings imply that it is difficult for monetary and fiscal authorities to conduct "fine-tuning" stabilization policy operations, though stabilization operations could be successful against more persistent exogenous swings.[14]

Monetary policy works more slowly than fiscal policy in our model because it takes time for the open market operations to be reflected in changes in long-term interest rates and even more time for these rate changes to be reflected in investment decisions. The latter delay can be attributed to the putty-clay behavior of equipment investment expenditures and the long decision lag for producers' and State and local construction expenditures. If we had found these decision lags to be shorter, or if we had found the more quick-acting credit rationing and wealth effects of monetary policy to be more important in the first year, the model would have implied a more rapid operation of monetary policy.

Comparisons of these results with those of other models reveal a mixture of similarities and differences. Although the fiscal policy multipliers in Table 4 roughly agree with those of other econometric models, the monetary multipliers are much larger. On the other hand, the monetary multipliers are appreciably smaller than those obtained by the staff of the St. Louis Federal Reserve Bank recently in a regression of GNP on monetary and fiscal variables. In addition, the timing patterns and the effect of fiscal policy computed by the two studies are radically different.[15]

We would like, in conclusion, to encourage the use of the Federal Reserve–MIT model as a framework for resolving these puzzling differences among estimates of monetary and fiscal policy effects. Most of the estimates suggest properties of the economy which can be translated into assertions about equations and parameters in our model. The structure of the model is flexible enough to permit monetary policy to be either a dominant or a rather minor force and to permit the income-expenditure approach with its implication of important fiscal policy effects to be either completely overshadowed or largely valid. Monetary policy is permitted to work through a number of channels, including carefully developed measures of the cost of capital, wealth effect, and credit rationing. We have presented one set of estimates of the model in this paper, suggesting important roles for a wide range of policy instruments. Further work on the specification and estimation of the model should be a useful way to analyze and ultimately reconcile different views about how our major fiscal and monetary policy tools operate.

## References

1. ANDERSEN, L., and JORDAN, J. "Monetary and Fiscal Actions: A Test of Their Relative Importance in Economic Stabilization," Federal Reserve Bank of St. Louis, *Monthly Review*, November 1968 [reprinted in this volume].

14 (6), p. 27.

15 See (1), particularly equation 4.

2. ANDO, A., and MODIGLIANI, F. "Econometric Analysis of Stabilization Policies." Paper presented at the December 1968 meetings of the American Economic Association.

3. ———. "The 'Life Cycle' Hypothesis of Saving: Aggregate Implications and Tests," *American Economic Review,* March 1963.

4. BISCHOFF, C. W. *A Study of Distributed Lags and Business Fixed Investment.* Doctoral dissertation, Massachusetts Institute of Technology, 1968.

5. DE LEEUW, F., and GRAMLICH, E. "The Federal Reserve–MIT Econometric Model," *Federal Reserve Bulletin,* January 1968.

6. JAFFEE, D. *Credit Rationing and the Commercial Loan Market.* Doctoral dissertation, Massachusetts Institute of Technology, 1968.

7. JAFFEE, D., and MODIGLIANI, F. "A Theory and Test of Credit Rationing." To be published.

8. JORGENSON, D. "Anticipations and Investment Behavior," in *The Brookings Quarterly Econometric Model of the United States.* Edited by Duesenberry *et al.* Chicago: Rand McNally, 1965.

9. LINTNER, J. "Distribution of Incomes of Corporations Among Dividends, Retained Earnings, and Taxes," *American Economic Review,* May 1956.

10. MODIGLIANI, F. "Econometric Models of Stabilization Policy." Presented at the Far Eastern Meeting of the Econometric Society, June 1968.

11. MODIGLIANI, F., and BRUMBERG, R. "Utility Analysis and the Consumption Function: An Interpretation of Cross-Section Data," *Post-Keynesian Economics.* Edited by K. Kurihara. Rutgers University Press, 1954.

12. MODIGLIANI, F., and SUTCH, R. "Innovations in Interest Rate Policies," *American Economic Review,* May 1966.

13. MUTH, R. "The Demand for Non-Farm Housing," in *The Demand for Durable Goods.* Edited by Harberger. University of Chicago Press, 1960.

14. RASCHE, R., and SHAPIRO, H. "The F.R.B.–MIT Econometric Model: Its Special Features," *American Economic Review,* May 1968.

15. REID, M. *Housing and Income.* University of Chicago Press, 1962.

# D. *Limitations of Monetary Policy*

## 12 | THE ROLE OF MONETARY POLICY*

MILTON FRIEDMAN
*University of Chicago*

There is wide agreement about the major goals of economic policy: high employment, stable prices, and rapid growth. There is less agreement that these goals are mutually compatible or, among those who regard them as incompatible, about the terms at which they can and should be substituted for one another. There is least agreement about the role that various instruments of policy can and should play in achieving the several goals.

My topic for tonight is the role of one such instrument—monetary policy. What can it contribute? And how should it be conducted to contribute the most? Opinion on these questions has fluctuated widely. In the first flush of enthusiasm about the newly created Federal Reserve System, many observers attributed the relative stability of the 1920s to the System's capacity for fine tuning—to apply an apt modern term. It came to be widely believed that a new era had arrived in which business cycles had been rendered obsolete by advances in monetary technology. This opinion was shared by economist and layman alike, though, of course, there were some dissonant voices. The Great Contraction destroyed this naive attitude. Opinion swung to the other extreme. Monetary policy was a string. You could pull on it to stop inflation but you could not push on it to halt recession. You could lead a horse to water but you could not make him drink. Such theory by aphorism was soon replaced by Keynes' rigorous and sophisticated analysis.

Keynes offered simultaneously an explanation for the presumed impotence of monetary policy to stem the depression, a nonmonetary interpretation of the depression, and an alternative to monetary policy for meeting the depression and his offering was avidly accepted. If liquidity preference is absolute or nearly so—as Keynes believed likely in times of heavy unemployment—interest rates cannot be lowered by monetary measures. If investment and consumption are little affected by interest rates—as Hansen and many of Keynes' other American disciples came to believe—lower interest rates, even if they could be achieved, would do little good. Monetary policy is twice damned. The contraction, set in train, on this view, by a collapse of investment or by a shortage of investment opportunities or by stubborn thriftiness, could not, it was argued, have been stopped by monetary measures. But there was available an alternative—fiscal policy. Government spending could make up for insufficient private investment. Tax reductions could undermine stubborn thriftiness.

The wide acceptance of these views in the economics profession meant that for some two decades monetary policy was believed by all but a few reactionary souls to have been rendered obsolete by new economic knowl-

* Presidential address delivered at the Eightieth Annual Meeting of the American Economic Association, Washington, D.C., December 29, 1967. Reprinted from *The American Economic Review*, vol. 58 (March, 1968) pp. 1–17, by permission of the author and the American Economic Association.

edge. Money did not matter. Its only role was the minor one of keeping interest rates low, in order to hold down interest payments in the government budget, contribute to the "euthanasia of the rentier," and maybe, stimulate investment a bit to assist government spending in maintaining a high level of aggregate demand.

These views produced a widespread adoption of cheap money policies after the war. And they received a rude shock when these policies failed in country after country, when central bank after central bank was forced to give up the pretense that it could indefinitely keep "the" rate of interest at a low level. In this country, the public denouement came with the Federal Reserve-Treasury Accord in 1951, although the policy of pegging government bond prices was not formally abandoned until 1953. Inflation, stimulated by cheap money policies, not the widely heralded postwar depression, turned out to be the order of the day. The result was the beginning of a revival of belief in the potency of monetary policy.

This revival was strongly fostered among economists by the theoretical developments initiated by Haberler but named for Pigou that pointed out a channel—namely, changes in wealth—whereby changes in the real quantity of money can affect aggregate demand even if they do not alter interest rates. These theoretical developments did not undermine Keynes' argument against the potency of orthodox monetary measures when liquidity preference is absolute since under such circumstances the usual monetary operations involve simply substituting money for other assets without changing total wealth. But they did show how changes in the quantity of money produced in other ways could affect total spending even under such circumstances. And, more fundamentally, they did undermine Keynes' key theoretical proposition, namely, that even in a world of flexible prices, a position of equilibrium at full employment might not exist. Henceforth, unemployment had again to be explained by rigidities or imperfections, not as the natural outcome of a fully operative market process.

The revival of belief in the potency of monetary policy was fostered also by a reevaluation of the role money played from 1929 to 1933. Keynes and most other economists of the time believed that the Great Contraction in the United States occurred despite aggressive expansionary policies by the monetary authorities—that they did their best but their best was not good enough.[1] Recent studies have demonstrated that the facts are precisely the reverse: the U.S. monetary authorities followed highly deflationary policies. The quantity of money in the United States fell by one-third in the course of the contraction. And it fell not because there were no willing borrowers—not because the horse would not drink. It fell because the Federal Reserve System forced or permitted a sharp reduction in the monetary base, because it failed to exercise the responsibilities assigned to it in the Federal Reserve Act to provide liquidity to the banking system. The Great Contraction is tragic testimony to the power of monetary policy—not, as Keynes and so many of his contemporaries believed, evidence of its impotence.

In the United States the revival of belief in the potency of monetary policy was strengthened also by increasing disillusionment with fiscal policy, not so much with its potential to affect aggregate demand as with the practical and political feasibility of so using it. Expenditures turned out to respond sluggishly and with long lags to attempts to adjust them to the course of economic activity, so emphasis shifted to taxes. But here political factors entered with a vengeance to prevent prompt adjustment to presumed need, as has been so graphically illustrated in the months since I wrote the first draft of this talk. "Fine tuning" is a marvelously evocative phrase in this electronic age, but it has little resemblance to what is possible in practice—not, I might add, an unmixed evil.

It is hard to realize how radical has been the change in professional opinion on the role of money. Hardly an economist today accepts views that were the common coin some two decades ago. Let me cite a few examples.

In a talk published in 1945, E. A. Goldenweiser, then Director of the Research Division of the Federal Reserve Board, described the primary objective of monetary policy as being to "maintain the value of Government bonds. . . . This country" he wrote, "will have to adjust to a 2½ per cent interest rate as the

[1] In (2), I have argued that Henry Simons shared this view with Keynes, and that it accounts for the policy changes that he recommended. [Numbers in parentheses refer to References at the end of this reading.]

return on safe, long-time money, because the time has come when returns on pioneering capital can no longer be unlimited as they were in the past" (4, p. 117).

In a book on *Financing American Prosperity,* edited by Paul Homan and Fritz Machlup and published in 1945, Alvin Hansen devotes nine pages of text to the "savings-investment problem" without finding any need to use the words "interest rate" or any close facsimile thereto (5, pp. 218-27). In his contribution to this volume, Fritz Machlup wrote, "Questions regarding the rate of interest, in particular regarding its variation or its stability, may not be among the most vital problems of the postwar economy, but they are certainly among the perplexing ones" (5, p. 466). In his contribution, John H. Williams—not only professor at Harvard but also a long-time adviser to the New York Federal Reserve Bank—wrote, "I can see no prospect of revival of a general monetary control in the postwar period" (5, p. 383).

Another of the volumes dealing with postwar policy that appeared at this time, *Planning and Paying for Full Employment,* was edited by Abba P. Lerner and Frank D. Graham (6) and had contributors of all shades of professional opinion—from Henry Simons and Frank Graham to Abba Lerner and Hans Neisser. Yet Albert Halasi, in his excellent summary of the papers, was able to say, "Our contributors do not discuss the question of money supply. . . . The contributors make no special mention of credit policy to remedy actual depressions. . . . Inflation . . . might be fought more effectively by raising interest rates. . . . But . . . other anti-inflationary measures . . . are preferable" (6, pp. 23-24). *A Survey of Contemporary Economics,* edited by Howard Ellis and published in 1948, was an "official" attempt to codify the state of economic thought of the time. In his contribution, Arthur Smithies wrote, "In the field of compensatory action, I believe fiscal policy must shoulder most of the load. Its chief rival, monetary policy, seems to be disqualified on institutional grounds. This country appears to be committed to something like the present low level of interest rates on a long-term basis" (1, p. 208).

These quotations suggest the flavor of professional thought some two decades ago. If you wish to go further in this humbling inquiry, I recommend that you compare the sections on money—when you can find them—in the Principles texts of the early postwar years with the lengthy sections in the current crop even, or especially, when the early and recent Principles are different editions of the same work.

The pendulum has swung far since then, if not all the way to the position of the late 1920s, at least much closer to that position than to the position of 1945. There are of course many differences between then and now, less in the potency attributed to monetary policy than in the roles assigned to it and the criteria by which the profession believes monetary policy should be guided. Then, the chief roles assigned monetary policy were to promote price stability and to preserve the gold standard; the chief criteria of monetary policy were the state of the "money market," the extent of "speculation" and the movement of gold. Today, primacy is assigned to the promotion of full employment, with the prevention of inflation a continuing but definitely secondary objective. And there is major disagreement about criteria of policy, varying from emphasis on money market conditions, interest rates, and the quantity of money to the belief that the state of employment itself should be the proximate criterion of policy.

I stress nonetheless the similarity between the views that prevailed in the late 'twenties and those that prevail today because I fear that, now as then, the pendulum may well have swung too far, that, now as then, we are in danger of assigning to monetary policy a larger role than it can perform, in danger of asking it to accomplish tasks that it cannot achieve, and, as a result, in danger of preventing it from making the contribution that it is capable of making.

Unaccustomed as I am to denigrating the importance of money, I therefore shall, as my first task, stress what monetary policy cannot do. I shall then try to outline what it can do and how it can best make its contribution, in the present state of our knowledge—or ignorance.

## I. What Monetary Policy Cannot Do

From the infinite world of negation, I have selected two limitations of monetary policy to discuss: (1) It cannot peg interest rates for more than very limited periods; (2) It cannot peg the rate of unemployment for more than very limited periods. I select these because the contrary has been or is widely believed, because they correspond to the two main unattainable tasks that are at all likely to be assigned to monetary policy, and because essentially the same theoretical analysis covers both.

### *Pegging of Interest Rates*

History has already persuaded many of you about the first limitation. As noted earlier, the failure of cheap money policies was a major source of the reaction against simple-minded Keynesianism. In the United States, this reaction involved widespread recognition that the wartime and postwar pegging of bond prices was a mistake, that the abandonment of this policy was a desirable and inevitable step, and that it had none of the disturbing and disastrous consequences that were so freely predicted at the time.

The limitation derives from a much misunderstood feature of the relation between money and interest rates. Let the Fed set out to keep interest rates down. How will it try to do so? By buying securities. This raises their prices and lowers their yields. In the process, it also increases the quantity of reserves available to banks, hence the amount of bank credit, and, ultimately the total quantity of money. That is why central bankers in particular, and the financial community more broadly, generally believe that an increase in the quantity of money tends to lower interest rates. Academic economists accept the same conclusion, but for different reasons. They see, in their mind's eye, a negatively sloping liquidity preference schedule. How can people be induced to hold a larger quantity of money? Only by bidding down interest rates.

Both are right, up to a point. The *initial* impact of increasing the quantity of money at a faster rate than it has been increasing is to make interest rates lower for a time than they would otherwise have been. But this is only the beginning of the process not the end. The more rapid rate of monetary growth will stimulate spending, both through the impact on investment of lower market interest rates and through the impact on other spending and thereby relative prices of higher cash balances than are desired. But one man's spending is another man's income. Rising income will raise the liquidity preference schedule and the demand for loans; it may also raise prices, which would reduce the real quantity of money. These three effects will reverse the initial downward pressure on interest rates fairly promptly, say, in something less than a year. Together they will tend, after a somewhat longer interval, say, a year or two, to return interest rates to the level they would otherwise have had. Indeed, given the tendency for the economy to overreact, they are highly likely to raise interest rates temporarily beyond that level, setting in motion a cyclical adjustment process.

A fourth effect, when and if it becomes operative, will go even farther, and definitely mean that a higher rate of monetary expansion will correspond to a higher, not lower, level of interest rates than would otherwise have prevailed. Let the higher rate of monetary growth produce rising prices, and let the public come to expect that prices will continue to rise. Borrowers will then be willing to pay and lenders will then demand higher interest rates—as Irving Fisher pointed out decades ago. This price expectation effect is slow to develop and also slow to disappear. Fisher estimated that it took several decades for a full adjustment and more recent work is consistent with his estimates.

These subsequent effects explain why every attempt to keep interest rates at a low level has forced the monetary authority to engage in successively larger and larger open market purchases. They explain why, historically, high and rising nominal interest rates have been associated with rapid growth in the quantity of money, as in Brazil or Chile or in the United States in recent years, and why low and falling interest rates have been associated with slow growth in the quantity of money, as in Switzerland now or in the United States from 1929 to 1933. As an empirical matter, low interest rates are a sign that monetary policy *has been* tight—in the sense that the quantity of money has grown slowly; high interest rates are a sign that monetary policy *has been* easy—in the sense that the quantity of money has grown rapidly. The broadest facts of experience run in precisely the opposite direction from that which the financial community and academic economists have all generally taken for granted.

Paradoxically, the monetary authority

could assure low nominal rates of interest—but to do so it would have to start out in what seems like the opposite direction, by engaging in a deflationary monetary policy. Similarly, it could assure high nominal interest rates by engaging in an inflationary policy and accepting a temporary movement in interest rates in the opposite direction.

These considerations not only explain why monetary policy cannot peg interest rates; they also explain why interest rates are such a misleading indicator of whether monetary policy is "tight" or "easy." For that, it is far better to look at the rate of change of the quantity of money.[2]

### *Employment as a Criterion of Policy*

The second limitation I wish to discuss goes more against the grain of current thinking. Monetary growth, it is widely held, will tend to stimulate employment; monetary contraction, to retard employment. Why, then, cannot the monetary authority adopt a target for employment or unemployment—say, 3 per cent unemployment; be tight when unemployment is less than the target; be easy when unemployment is higher than the target; and in this way peg unemployment at, say 3 per cent? The reason it cannot is precisely the same as for interest rates—the difference between the immediate and the delayed consequences of such a policy.

Thanks to Wicksell, we are all acquainted with the concept of a "natural" rate of interest and the possibility of a discrepancy between the "natural" and the "market" rate. The preceding analysis of interest rates can be translated fairly directly into Wicksellian terms. The monetary authority can make the market rate less than the natural rate only by inflation. It can make the market rate higher than the natural rate only by deflation. We have added only one wrinkle to Wicksell—the Irving Fisher distinction between the nominal and the real rate of interest. Let the monetary authority keep the nominal market rate for a time below the natural rate by inflation. That in turn will raise the nominal natural rate itself, once anticipations of inflation become widespread, thus requiring still more rapid inflation to hold down the market rate. Similarly, because of the Fisher effect, it will require not merely deflation but more and more rapid deflation to hold the market rate above the initial "natural" rate.

This analysis has its close counterpart in the employment market. At any moment of time, there is some level of unemployment which has the property that it is consistent with equilibrium in the structure of *real* wage rates. At that level of unemployment, real wage rates are tending on the average to rise at a "normal" secular rate, i.e., at a rate that can be indefinitely maintained so long as capital formation, technological improvements, etc., remain on their long-run trends. A lower level of unemployment is an indication that there is an excess demand for labor that will produce upward pressure on real wage rates. A higher level of unemployment is an indication that there is an excess supply of labor that will produce downward pressure on real wage rates. The "natural rate of unemployment," in other words, is the level that would be ground out by the Walrasian system of general equilibrium equations, provided there is imbedded in them the actual structural characteristics of the labor and commodity markets, including market imperfections, stochastic variability in demands and supplies, the cost of gathering information about job vacancies and labor availabilities, the cost of mobility, and so on.[3]

You will recognize the close similarity between this statement and the celebrated Phillips Curve. The similarity is not coincidental. Phillips' analysis of the relation between unemployment and wage change is deservedly celebrated as an important and original contribution. But, unfortunately, it contains a basic defect—the failure to distinguish between *nominal* wages and *real* wages—just as Wicksell's analysis failed to distinguish be-

[2] This is partly an empirical not theoretical judgment. In principle, "tightness" or "ease" depends on the rate of change of the quantity of money supplied compared to the rate of change of the quantity demanded excluding effects on demand from monetary policy itself. However, empirically demand is highly stable, if we exclude the effect of monetary policy, so it is generally sufficient to look at supply alone.

[3] It is perhaps worth noting that this "natural" rate need not correspond to equality between the number unemployed and the number of job vacancies. For any given structure of the labor market, there will be some equilibrium relation between these two magnitudes, but there is no reason why it should be one of equality.

tween *nominal* interest rates and *real* interest rates. Implicitly, Phillips wrote his article for a world in which everyone anticipated that nominal prices would be stable and in which that anticipation remained unshaken and immutable whatever happened to actual prices and wages. Suppose, by contrast, that everyone anticipates that prices will rise at a rate of more than 75 per cent a year—as, for example, Brazilians did a few years ago. Then wages must rise at that rate simply to keep real wages unchanged. An excess supply of labor will be reflected in a less rapid rise in nominal wages than in anticipated prices,[4] not in an absolute decline in wages. When Brazil embarked on a policy to bring down the rate of price rise, and succeeded in bringing the price rise down to about 45 per cent a year, there was a sharp initial rise in unemployment because under the influence of earlier anticipations, wages kept rising at a pace that was higher than the new rate of price rise, though lower than earlier. This is the result experienced, and to be expected, of all attempts to reduce the rate of inflation below that widely anticipated.[5]

To avoid misunderstanding, let me emphasize that by using the term "natural" rate of unemployment, I do not mean to suggest that it is immutable and unchangeable. On the contrary, many of the market characteristics that determine its level are man-made and policy-made. In the United States, for example, legal minimum wage rates, the Walsh-Healy and Davis-Bacon Acts, and the strength of labor unions all make the natural rate of unemployment higher than it would otherwise be. Improvements in employment exchanges, in availability of information about job vacancies and labor supply, and so on, would tend to lower the natural rate of unemployment. I use the term "natural" for the same reason Wicksell did—to try to separate the real forces from monetary forces.

Let us assume that the monetary authority tries to peg the "market" rate of unemployment at a level below the "natural" rate. For definiteness, suppose that it takes 3 per cent as the target rate and that the "natural" rate is higher than 3 per cent. Suppose also that we start out at a time when prices have been stable and when unemployment is higher than 3 per cent. Accordingly, the authority increases the rate of monetary growth. This will be expansionary. By making nominal cash balances higher than people desire, it will tend initially to lower interest rates and in this and other ways to stimulate spending. Income and spending will start to rise.

To begin with, much or most of the rise in income will take the form of an increase in output and employment rather than in prices. People have been expecting prices to be stable, and prices and wages have been set for some time in the future on that basis. It takes time for people to adjust to a new state of demand. Producers will tend to react to the initial expansion in aggregate demand by increasing output, employees by working longer hours, and the unemployed by taking jobs now offered at former nominal wages. This much is pretty standard doctrine.

But it describes only the initial effects. Because selling prices of products typically respond to an unanticipated rise in nominal demand faster than prices of factors of production, real wages received have gone down —though real wages anticipated by employees went up, since employees implicitly evaluated the wages offered at the earlier price level. Indeed, the simultaneous fall *ex post* in real wages to employers and rise

[4] Strictly speaking, the rise in nominal wages will be less rapid than the rise in anticipated nominal wages to make allowance for any secular changes in real wages.

[5] Stated in terms of the rate of change of nominal wages, the Phillips Curve can be expected to be reasonably stable and well defined for any period for which the *average* rate of change of prices, and hence the anticipated rate, has been relatively stable. For such periods, nominal wages and "real" wages move together. Curves computed for different periods or different countries for each of which this condition has been satisfied will differ in level, the level of the curve depending on what the average rate of price change was. The higher the average rate of price change, the higher will tend to be the level of the curve. For periods or countries for which the rate of change of prices varies considerably, the Phillips Curve will not be well defined. My impression is that these statements accord reasonably well with the experience of the economists who have explored empirical Phillips Curves.

Restate Phillips' analysis in terms of the rate of change of real wages—and even more precisely, anticipated real wages—and it all falls into place. That is why students of empirical Phillips Curves have found that it helps to include the rate of change of the price level as an independent variable.

*ex ante* in real wages to employees is what enabled employment to increase. But the decline *ex post* in real wages will soon come to affect anticipations. Employees will start to reckon on rising prices of the things they buy and to demand higher nominal wages for the future. "Market" unemployment is below the "natural" level. There is an excess demand for labor so real wages will tend to rise toward their initial level.

Even though the higher rate of monetary growth continues, the rise in real wages will reverse the decline in unemployment, and then lead to a rise, which will tend to return unemployment to its former level. In order to keep unemployment at its target level of 3 per cent, the monetary authority would have to raise monetary growth still more. As in the interest rate case, the "market" rate can be kept below the "natural" rate only by inflation. And, as in the interest rate case, too, only by accelerating inflation. Conversely, let the monetary authority choose a target rate of unemployment that is above the natural rate, and they will be led to produce a deflation, and an accelerating deflation at that.

What if the monetary authority chose the "natural" rate—either of interest or unemployment—as its target? One problem is that it cannot know what the "natural" rate is. Unfortunately, we have as yet devised no method to estimate accurately and readily the natural rate of either interest or unemployment. And the "natural" rate will itself change from time to time. But the basic problem is that even if the monetary authority knew the "natural" rate, and attempted to peg the market rate at that level, it would not be led to a determinate policy. The "market" rate will vary from the natural rate for all sorts of reasons other than monetary policy. If the monetary authority responds to these variations, it will set in train longer term effects that will make any monetary growth path it follows ultimately consistent with the rule of policy. The actual course of monetary growth will be analogous to a random walk, buffeted this way and that by the forces that produce temporary departures of the market rate from the natural rate.

To state this conclusion differently, there is always a temporary trade-off between inflation and unemployment; there is no permanent trade-off. The temporary trade-off comes not from inflation per se, but from unanticipated inflation, which generally means, from a rising rate of inflation. The widespread belief that there is a permanent trade-off is a sophisticated version of the confusion between "high" and "rising" that we all recognize in simpler forms. A rising rate of inflation may reduce unemployment, a high rate will not.

But how long, you will say, is "temporary"? For interest rates, we have some systematic evidence on how long each of the several effects takes to work itself out. For unemployment, we do not. I can at most venture a personal judgment, based on some examination of the historical evidence, that the initial effects of a higher and unanticipated rate of inflation last for something like two to five years; that this initial effect then begins to be reversed; and that a full adjustment to the new rate of inflation takes about as long for employment as for interest rates, say, a couple of decades. For both interest rates and employment, let me add a qualification. These estimates are for changes in the rate of inflation of the order of magnitude that has been experienced in the United States. For much more sizable changes, such as those experienced in South American countries, the whole adjustment process is greatly speeded up.

To state the general conclusion still differently, the monetary authority controls nominal quantities—directly, the quantity of its own liabilities. In principle, it can use this control to peg a nominal quantity—an exchange rate, the price level, the nominal level of national income, the quantity of money by one or another definition—or to peg the rate of change in a nominal quantity—the rate of inflation or deflation, the rate of growth or decline in nominal national income, the rate of growth of the quantity of money. It cannot use its control over nominal quantities to peg a real quantity—the real rate of interest, the rate of unemployment, the level of real national income, the real quantity of money, the rate of growth of real national income, or the rate of growth of the real quantity of money.

## II. What Monetary Policy Can Do

Monetary policy cannot peg these real magnitudes at predetermined levels. But monetary policy can and does have important effects on these real magnitudes. The one is in no way inconsistent with the other.

My own studies of monetary history have made me extremely sympathetic to the oft-quoted, much reviled, and as widely misunderstood, comment by John Stuart Mill. "There cannot . . .," he wrote, "be intrinsically a more insignificant thing, in the economy of society, than money; except in the character of a contrivance for sparing time and labour. It is a machine for doing quickly and commodiously, what would be done, though less quickly and commodiously, without it: and like many other kinds of machinery, it only exerts a distinct and independent influence of its own when it gets out of order" (7, p. 488).

True, money is only a machine, but it is an extraordinarily efficient machine. Without it, we could not have begun to attain the astounding growth in output and level of living we have experienced in the past two centuries—any more than we could have done so without those other marvelous machines that dot our countryside and enable us, for the most part, simply to do more efficiently what could be done without them at much greater cost in labor.

But money has one feature that these other machines do not share. Because it is so pervasive, when it gets out of order, it throws a monkey wrench into the operation of all the other machines. The Great Contraction is the most dramatic example but not the only one. Every other major contraction in this country has been either produced by monetary disorder or greatly exacerbated by monetary disorder. Every major inflation has been produced by monetary expansion—mostly to meet the overriding demands of war which have forced the creation of money to supplement explicit taxation.

The first and most important lesson that history teaches about what monetary policy can do—and it is a lesson of the most profound importance—is that monetary policy can prevent money itself from being a major source of economic disturbance. This sounds like a negative proposition: avoid major mistakes. In part it is. The Great Contraction might not have occurred at all, and if it had, it would have been far less severe, if the monetary authority had avoided mistakes, or if the monetary arrangements had been those of an earlier time when there was no central authority with the power to make the kinds of mistakes that the Federal Reserve System made. The past few years, to come closer to home, would have been steadier and more productive of economic well-being if the Federal Reserve had avoided drastic and erratic changes of direction, first expanding the money supply at an unduly rapid pace, then, in early 1966, stepping on the brake too hard, then, at the end of 1966, reversing itself and resuming expansion until at least November, 1967, at a more rapid pace than can long be maintained without appreciable inflation.

Even if the proposition that monetary policy can prevent money itself from being a major source of economic disturbance were a wholly negative proposition, it would be none the less important for that. As it happens, however, it is not a wholly negative proposition. The monetary machine has gotten out of order even when there has been no central authority with anything like the power now possessed by the Fed. In the United States, the 1907 episode and earlier banking panics are examples of how the monetary machine can get out of order largely on its own. There is therefore a positive and important task for the monetary authority—to suggest improvements in the machine that will reduce the chances that it will get out of order, and to use its own powers so as to keep the machine in good working order.

A second thing monetary policy can do is provide a stable background for the economy—keep the machine well oiled, to continue Mill's analogy. Accomplishing the first task will contribute to this objective, but there is more to it than that. Our economic system will work best when producers and consumers, employers and employees, can proceed with full confidence that the average level of prices will behave in a known way in the future—preferably that it will be highly stable. Under any conceivable institutional arrangements, and certainly under those that now prevail in the United States, there is only a limited amount of flexibility in prices and wages. We need to conserve this flexibility to achieve changes in relative prices and wages that are required to adjust to dynamic changes in tastes and technology. We should not dissipate it simply to achieve changes in the absolute level of prices that serve no economic function.

In an earlier era, the gold standard was relied on to provide confidence in future monetary stability. In its heyday it served that function reasonably well. It clearly no longer does, since there is scarce a country in the world that is prepared to let the gold standard reign unchecked—and there are persuasive reasons why countries should not do so. The monetary authority could operate as a surrogate for the gold standard, if it pegged exchange rates and did so exclusively by altering the quantity of money in response to balance of payment flows without "sterilizing" surpluses or deficits and without resorting to open or concealed exchange control or to changes in tariffs and quotas. But again, though many central bankers talk this way, few are in fact willing to follow this course—and again there are persuasive reasons why they should not do so. Such a policy would submit each country to the vagaries not of an impersonal and automatic gold standard but of the policies—deliberate or accidental—of other monetary authorities.

In today's world, if monetary policy is to provide a stable background for the economy it must do so by deliberately employing its powers to that end. I shall come later to how it can do so.

Finally, monetary policy can contribute to offsetting major disturbances in the economic system arising from other sources. If there is an independent secular exhilaration—as the postwar expansion was described by the proponents of secular stagnation—monetary policy can in principle help to hold it in check by a slower rate of monetary growth than would otherwise be desirable. If, as now, an explosive federal budget threatens unprecedented deficits, monetary policy can hold any inflationary dangers in check by a slower rate of monetary growth than would otherwise be desirable. This will temporarily mean higher interest rates than would otherwise prevail—to enable the government to borrow the sums needed to finance the deficit—but by preventing the speeding up of inflation, it may well mean both lower prices and lower nominal interest rates for the long pull. If the end of a substantial war offers the country an opportunity to shift resources from wartime to peacetime production, monetary policy can ease the transition by a higher rate of monetary growth than would otherwise be desirable—though experience is not very encouraging that it can do so without going too far.

I have put this point last, and stated it in qualified terms—as referring to major disturbances—because I believe that the potentiality of monetary policy in offsetting other forces making for instability is far more limited than is commonly believed. We simply do not know enough to be able to recognize minor disturbances when they occur or to be able to predict either what their effects will be with any precision or what monetary policy is required to offset their effects. We do not know enough to be able to achieve stated objectives by delicate, or even fairly coarse, changes in the mix of monetary and fiscal policy. In this area particularly the best is likely to be the enemy of the good. Experience suggests that the path of wisdom is to use monetary policy explicitly to offset other disturbances only when they offer a "clear and present danger."

## III. How Should Monetary Policy Be Conducted?

How should monetary policy be conducted to make the contribution to our goals that it is capable of making? This is clearly not the occasion for presenting a detailed "Program for Monetary Stability"—to use the title of a book in which I tried to do so [3]. I shall restrict myself here to two major requirements for monetary policy that follow fairly directly from the preceding discussion.

The first requirement is that the monetary authority should guide itself by magnitudes that it can control, not by ones that it cannot control. If, as the authority has often done, it takes interest rates or the current unemployment percentage as the immediate criterion of policy, it will be like a space vehicle that has taken a fix on the wrong star. No matter how sensitive and sophisticated its guiding apparatus, the space vehicle will go astray. And so will the monetary authority. Of the various alternative magnitudes that it can control, the most appealing guides for policy are exchange rates, the price level as defined by some index, and the quantity of a monetary total—currency plus adjusted demand deposits, or this total plus commercial bank time deposits, or a still broader total.

For the United States in particular, exchange rates are an undesirable guide. It might be worth requiring the bulk of the economy to adjust to the tiny percentage consisting of foreign trade if that would guarantee freedom from monetary irresponsibility—as it might under a real gold standard. But it is hardly worth doing so simply to adapt to the average of whatever policies monetary authorities in the rest of the world adopt. Far better to let the market, through floating exchange rates, adjust to world conditions the 5 per cent or so of our resources devoted to international trade while reserving monetary policy to promote the effective use of the 95 per cent.

Of the three guides listed, the price level is clearly the most important in its own right. Other things the same, it would be much the best of the alternatives—as so many distinguished economists have urged in the past. But other things are not the same. The link between the policy actions of the monetary authority and the price level, while unquestionably present, is more indirect than the link between the policy actions of the authority and any of the several monetary totals. Moreover, monetary action takes a longer time to affect the price level than to affect the monetary totals and both the time lag and the magnitude of effect vary with circumstances. As a result, we cannot predict at all accurately just what effect a particular monetary action will have on the price level and, equally important, just when it will have that effect. Attempting to control directly the price level is therefore likely to make monetary policy itself a source of economic disturbance because of false stops and starts. Perhaps, as our understanding of monetary phenomena advances, the situation will change. But at the present stage of our understanding, the long way around seems the surer way to our objective. Accordingly, I believe that a monetary total is the best currently available immediate guide or criterion for monetary policy—and I believe that it matters much less which particular total is chosen than that one be chosen.

A second requirement for monetary policy is that the monetary authority avoid sharp swings in policy. In the past, monetary authorities have on occasion moved in the wrong direction—as in the episode of the Great Contraction that I have stressed. More frequently, they have moved in the right direction, albeit often too late, but have erred by moving too far. Too late and too much has been the general practice. For example, in early 1966, it was the right policy for the Federal Reserve to move in a less expansionary direction—though it should have done so at least a year earlier. But when it moved, it went too far, producing the sharpest change in the rate of monetary growth of the postwar era. Again, having gone too far, it was the right policy for the Fed to reverse course at the end of 1966. But again it went too far, not only restoring but exceeding the earlier excessive rate of monetary growth. And this episode is no exception. Time and again this has been the course followed—as in 1919 and 1920, in 1937 and 1938, in 1953 and 1954, in 1959 and 1960.

The reason for the propensity to overreact seems clear: the failure of monetary authorities to allow for the delay between their actions and the subsequent effects on the economy. They tend to determine their actions by today's conditions—but their actions will affect the economy only six or nine or twelve or fifteen months later. Hence they feel impelled to step on the brake, or the accelerator, as the case may be, too hard.

My own prescription is still that the monetary authority go all the way in avoiding such swings by adopting publicly the policy of achieving a steady rate of growth in a specified monetary total. The precise rate of growth, like the precise monetary total, is less important than the adoption of some stated and known rate. I myself have argued for a rate that would on the average achieve rough stability in the level of prices of final products, which I have estimated would call for something like a 3 to 5 per cent per year rate of growth in currency plus all commercial bank deposits or a slightly lower rate of growth in currency plus demand deposits only.[6] But it would be better to have a fixed

[6] In "The Optimum Quantity of Money" [in Milton Friedman, *The Optimum Quantity of Money and Other Essays,* Chicago, Aldine Publishing Company, 1969, 1–50] I conclude that a still lower rate of growth, something like 2 per cent for the broader definition, might be better yet in order to eliminate or reduce the difference between private and total costs of adding to real balances.

rate that would on the average produce moderate inflation or moderate deflation, provided it was steady, than to suffer the wide and erratic perturbations we have experienced.

Short of the adoption of such a publicly stated policy of a steady rate of monetary growth, it would constitute a major improvement if the monetary authority followed the self-denying ordinance of avoiding wide swings. It is a mater of record that periods of relative stability in the rate of monetary growth have also been periods of relative stability in economic activity, both in the United States and other countries. Periods of wide swings in the rate of monetary growth have also been periods of wide swings in economic activity.

By setting itself a steady course and keeping to it, the monetary authority could make a major contribution to promoting economic stability. By making that course one of steady but moderate growth in the quantity of money, it would make a major contribution to avoidance of either inflation or deflation of prices. Other forces would still affect the economy, require change and adjustment, and disturb the even tenor of our ways. But steady monetary growth would provide a monetary climate favorable to the effective operation of those basic forces of enterprise, ingenuity, invention, hard work, and thrift that are the true springs of economic growth. That is the most that we can ask from monetary policy at our present stage of knowledge. But that much—and it is a great deal—is clearly within our reach.

### References

1. ELLIS, H. S., ed. *A Survey of Contemporary Economics*, Philadelphia 1948.

2. FRIEDMAN, MILTON. "The Monetary Theory and Policy of Henry Simons," *Jour. Law and Econ.*, Oct. 1967, 10:1-13.

3. ———. *A Program for Monetary Stability*, New York 1959.

4. GOLDENWEISER, E. A. "Postwar Problems and Policies," *Fed. Res. Bull.*, Feb. 1945, 31: 112-21.

5. HOMAN, P. T., AND MACHLUP, FRITZ, eds. *Financing American Prosperity*, New York 1945.

6. LERNER, A. P., AND GRAHAM, F. D., eds. *Planning and Paying for Full Employment.* Princeton 1946.

7. MILL, J. S. *Principles of Political Economy*, Bk. III, Ashley ed. New York 1929.

# II THE DEFINITION of MONEY

When investigators wish to develop evidence on the direction and strength of monetary influences on other variables in the economy, the theoretical concept of money must be given empirical content. As some of the selections in part I suggest, writers are not in complete agreement on what assets correspond to the concept of money. The problem is to pick some collection of assets which the public in fact views as money. For this problem, the theoretical properties of money must first be specified, and then the empirical aggregate must be found which corresponds to that concept. If the monetary authorities operate on the wrong aggregate, monetary policy can, for instance, be misdirected when the controlled aggregate is changed in one direction while the "true" money stock moves in the opposite direction.

The definition of a measure of money is by no means fixed and unchanging over time; economic usage and customs change, and the problem is to define what corresponds to this usage. Since the emergence of economics as a discipline, there has never been unanimity among writers about how money should be defined.[1] It is, however, generally agreed that over the past two centuries the aggregate commonly used as money has been expanded from gold and silver coins to include, progressively, bank notes and bank deposits subject to check. At issue at present is whether the aggregate that is called money should be expanded to include other assets—among which time deposits at commercial banks, mutual savings bank deposits, and savings and loan shares are perhaps the most eligible but far from the only candidates for inclusion. As an empirical matter, the competing monetary aggregates by and large move together in direction and degree, so that one usually reaches the same conclusions about monetary policy no matter which of several aggregates he examines. But the correlations of the series are not perfect, and at times they display divergent movements. At such times one is interested in knowing in which direction the "true" money stock is moving, and he needs some criteria to select among the alternative measures. The usefulness of alternative selection criteria forms the substance of the controversy over the definition of money.

The search for a satisfactory definition of money has proceeded along two general lines. One approach has concentrated on developing a theoretical concept of money and including those financial assets that appear to possess characteristics consistent with the concept. Two such

[1] Milton Friedman and Anna J. Schwartz survey early attempts to define money in their recent book *Monetary Statistics of the United States*, New York: National Bureau of Economic Research, 1970.

concepts have been money as a means of payment and money as a temporary abode of purchasing power. The other approach has been to investigate financial assets empirically and to define as money those assets whose characteristics satisfy one or more criteria of similarity in behavior. To these investigators, money is what money does.[2] The criteria imposed by empirical definitions include stability of demand for a grouping of financial assets, high degree of substitutability among these financial assets, and ability of the grouping of financial assets to explain statistically variations in real sector variables of policy concern.

Laidler reviews and describes a number of approaches to the definition of money. In particular, he emphasizes definitions that choose among competing monetary aggregates by selecting that one for which the "best" empirical demand function can be developed. "Best" in this context denotes the function's ability to predict much of the variation in the aggregate under consideration with a limited number of independent variables. In addition, it is desired that the aggregate permit the construction of a demand function which is "stable" over time; that is, the quantity demanded is not susceptible to large variations as a result of temporal movements in variables not included in the demand function.

Another approach compares empirical relationships between monetary aggregates and other variables, such as income, output, or prices, with postulated theoretical relationships between money and these same variables. For instance, if theory suggests a very close positive relation between money and income, one chooses the monetary aggregate most closely correlated with income. Defining money in this way aids monetary policy analysis if the aim of policy is to vary money so as to influence income. This approach to delineating a measure of money might be convincing if the theoretical relationships between money and other variables used were universally agreed upon. But as the readings in part II suggest, complete unanimity is yet lacking. Kaufman finds that more than one grouping of assets satisfies the criterion of a close relationship with income. In addition, he finds little evidence for including currency in this optimum set of assets. Timberlake and Fortson follow another procedure and find that variations in commercial bank time deposits affect income quite differently than do variations in demand deposits. Lastly, Chetty adopts the idea first proposed by Gurley that the appropriate aggregation of financial assets to delineate money might include weighting the assets by their relative moneyness. Chetty determines the weights by first estimating a utility function for financial assets.

---

[2] *Ibid.*, p. 137. Friedman and Schwartz have stated the rationale for this approach succinctly, arguing that ". . . the definition of money is to be sought for not on grounds of principle but on grounds of usefulness in organizing our knowledge of economic relationships. 'Money' is that to which we choose to assign a number by specified operations: it is not something in existence to be discovered, like the American continent; it is a tentative scientific construct to be invented, like 'length' or 'temperature' or 'force' in physics."

# 13 THE DEFINITION OF MONEY*

DAVID LAIDLER
*University of Manchester*

## I. Introduction

Changes in the money supply can affect the economy by two distinct mechanisms. First, they may change the level of real wealth held by the community and, by way of the influence of the level of wealth on aggregate demand, they can change the levels of income, employment, and prices. Second, even if changes in the money supply leave the level of real wealth unchanged, as is usually assumed when dealing with an economy in which money is largely the liability of a privately owned banking system, these changes nevertheless alter the composition of portfolios, and hence the rates of return at which existing stocks of assets will be held.[1] In this case, it is changes in these rates of return that influence the level of aggregate demand.

However, whether money supply changes work primarily by way of a wealth effect or a substitution effect, before the monetary authorities in any actual economy can hope to influence behaviour in a predictable way by manipulating the money supply there are a number of preconditions that must be met. Among the most important of these necessary (but not sufficient) conditions are that the authorities must be able to control the volume of that set of assets that most closely corresponds to the "money stock" of standard macroeconomics; at the same time the demand function for this stock of assets must be stable enough for the consequences of changing its volume to be predictable with a high degree of reliability.

Whether or not these preconditions are met is a matter of the specific economy with which one is dealing and as far as the United States is concerned there has been a great deal of debate on these issues. The once quite widely held view that the demand for money would be highly unstable due to the vicissitudes of speculative behaviour is not stressed very much in recent literature. However, the question as to whether the United States monetary authorities have control over the relevant stock of assets is one that has come in for a good deal of attention, both at the theoretical and at the empirical level.

One may distinguish three broad views of what is "money" in the United States economy. First there are those who cling to the traditional concept of currency in the hands of the public and demand deposits at commercial banks, and second, there are those who argue that time deposits at commercial banks are such a close substitute for demand deposits that they should be included in the quantity of money which the authorities must manipulate in attempting to influence the level of economic activity. Proponents of both of these points of view are broadly agreed that current institutional arrangements permit the authorities to control the

* Reprinted from *Journal of Money, Credit and Banking,* vol. 1 (August, 1969), pp. 508–525, by permission of the author and the Ohio State University Press.

1 Though Pesek and Saving (21) argue for the existence of a wealth effect even in these circumstances. cf. below Part II. [Numbers in parentheses refer to literature cited at the end of this reading.]

relevant stocks of assets as far as monetary policy is concerned, and find themselves opposed to those who argue that the liabilities of certain non-bank financial intermediaries, particularly savings and loan associations and mutual savings banks, are such close substitutes for commercial bank liabilities as to require their inclusion in the "money stock." The latter group argue that these other institutions must also be brought under the control of the monetary authorities before one can expect useful results from monetary policy.[2]

As we shall see, the empirical element in the debate has tended to center on the question of whether a useful definition of money should include time deposits at commercial banks, or whether the more traditional concept is adequate. One suspects that this issue of time deposits has taken the center of the stage, not so much because it is obviously a more important question than the one which asks whether the liabilities of such institutions as mutual savings banks and savings and loan associations are not also money, but rather because Milton Friedman (7), in using this slightly broader money concept in a pioneering and influential piece of empirical work, obtained results, particularly about the apparent insensitivity of the demand for money to the interest rate, which were quite contrary to what most would have expected, and which appeared to stem largely from the definition of money he had employed.

Whatever the historical reason for its existing as an issue, it is not unreasonable to give the question of the inclusion of time deposits in the definition of money some sort of priority in the present context because the arguments that would lead to the inclusion of Saving and Loan Association shares and the like in the definition of money all point to currency plus demand deposits being an inadequate concept. If the traditional notion proves adequate in competition with a money concept that includes time deposits, the issues raised by the other arguments mentioned above are virtually settled by default and in favour of a traditional view of what is money, a view that implies that the monetary authorities can control its quantity under present institutional arrangements. Even if the traditional definition of money fails in such tests, their outcome can still throw light on the question as to whether it might be desirable to include the liabilities of non-bank financial intermediaries in the definition of money. If it turns out that a stable demand function for money, defined to exclude these assets, can be identified, then there would appear to be no pressing need to introduce them into the definition of money. Thus, even if the basic issue is a broader one, it still makes sense to pay particular attention to the question of whether or not the introduction of time deposits into the definition of money noticeably improves empirical results, because the evidence on this question is capable of throwing light on the more fundamental issue.

## II. Some Theoretical Issues

Two sets of theoretical arguments, one virtually as old as monetary economics, and the other almost brand new, are relevant to the issue of what constitutes the money stock. The first argument, in its modern form, says that the theory of the demand for money is a theory of the demand for an asset that is a generally acceptable means of exchange and also happens to be a store of value. It goes on to argue that, unlike demand deposits which are readily transferable by cheque, time deposits, savings deposits and so forth are not means of exchange. From these premises it inexorably follows that demand deposits are money and these other assets are not.[3]

The second argument, due to Pesek and Saving (21), says that demand deposits, even though they are the liabilities of commercial banks whose owners are members of the economy, represent net wealth to the community, while time deposits and the liabilities of other financial institutions do not represent net wealth. It is argued that the

[2] One may find the case for the first of these views put in Teigen (22) and Feige (4), while the secondary view is of course that of Friedman (6, 7). The third position stems from the work of Gurley and Shaw (9).

[3] This type of reasoning goes back at least as far as the monetary debates of the Napoleonic wars in which one of the principal issues was whether or not any assets other than coin and banknotes were money.

principal means by which monetary policy works is the wealth effect and that the proper empirical definition of money is confined to currency plus demand deposits, since it is only changes in the real quantity of these assets that represent changes in the community's wealth.

Both of these arguments seem to me to be unsatisfactory. Consider the first of them; though its logic is faultless its premises may be questioned. It is simply not true that economists generally accept the proposition that the theory of the demand for money is the theory of the demand for a means of exchange. The theory of the transactions demand for money fits this description well enough, but the theory of the speculative demand for money does not. The latter, both in its original Keynesian form and in its more recent manifestations [cf. Tobin (23)], is a theory of the demand for an asset whose capital value does not fluctuate with the rate of interest. Time deposits are just as good as demand deposits from this point of view, as indeed are deposits at mutual savings banks and savings and loan association shares. The question as to how to define money overlaps heavily with another important issue in monetary economics, namely whether transactions motives alone are sufficient to enable one to produce an adequate theory of the demand for money. One is hardly going to be able to settle this issue if it is prejudged by defining money in such a way as to be inherently incompatible with non-transactions approaches to monetary theory.[4]

There is more to be said on this count, for the tradition of dealing with the demand for money in terms of careful analysis of the motives that prompt its being held does not exhaust the approaches that may be taken to the problem. It is possible to take a simpler but not outright contradictory approach: to observe that it is convenient to hold assets in order to bridge the gap between the receiving and making of payments and to note that there is a wide variety of assets that could be used for this purpose.[5] Money then comes to be defined as that asset or set of assets which is best adapted for this purpose in the sense that it is easy to store, cheap to realize and relatively riskless as far as its market value is concerned.[6] Though it is readily granted that time deposits and demand deposits are not perfect substitutes in these respects, neither are currency and demand deposits. If one is willing to treat the latter pair as sufficiently close substitutes to make it worthwhile to ignore the differences between them for some problems, he must immediately admit that it is an empirical question as to how close is the substitutability between demand and time deposits, and an empirical issue to which the answer is not a foregone conclusion.

The implicit question involved here is whether the cost involved in the transformation of a time deposit into a demand deposit before a transfer of funds can be made is sufficiently great to make the former unsuitable for use as a temporary abode of purchasing power. Quite apart from the fact that banking institutions in the United States as they stand at present do in fact lead to costs being imposed upon demand deposit holders over and above the fees for the actual transfer of funds when certain classes of demand deposits are used for making payments, and quite apart from the fact that certain time deposits are *de facto* if not *de jure* subject to cheque, so that the distinction between demand deposits and time deposits is not quite the same thing as the distinction between those liabilities of banks that are a means of exchange and those that are not, it is hard to see how this issue could be settled without

[4] Though it is sometimes argued that monetary theory is properly confined to dealing only with the transactions motive since other motives affect the demand for a far wider class of assets than anyone would think of classifying as money. There is more than a trace of this view in Sir John Hicks' recent work [(11), chaps. i–iii].

[5] This is of course the approach of the so-called "Chicago School" and is thoroughly dealt with in Friedman (6).

[6] Riskless here should not be confused with stable. It is the ease with which the future value of an asset can be predicted rather than the constancy of that value that helps make the asset suitable as a temporary abode of purchasing power. Hence, people continue to hold money, though in smaller amounts, in even very rapid inflations so long as the rate of price change can be anticipated.

some reference to facts.[7] Similar arguments can be made about the liabilities of other institutions of course, for all these arguments rest on an empirical judgement about the costs of transforming such assets into means of exchange.

The foregoing discussion, I believe, summarizes the well known theoretical background to much of the empirical debate on the question of the most appropriate definition of money. However, before going on to deal with the relevant empirical evidence it is worthwhile to digress in order to consider the second view mentioned above, namely, that one must distinguish between demand deposits and other financial assets because the former represent net wealth to society while the latter do not.

This argument is presented by Pesek and Saving (21) as following from their important insight that the introduction even of so-called "inside" money into an economy enables its members to reach a higher level of utility than they would otherwise be able, an argument that seems to be analogous to the one that states that opening a closed economy to trade enables a higher level of welfare to be achieved with no expansion in the available supplies of productive resources.[8] Pesek and Saving argue that demand deposits are held for the flow of amenities that they yield while time deposits and other assets are held solely for the interest they bear. Since the interest on time deposits is the liability of the banks that must pay it while the amenity flow from demand deposits is not provided at the expense of banks, except inasmuch as they must hold reserves to ensure that they may fulfill their obligations under what Pesek and Saving call the "instant repurchase clause" involved in the issue of demand deposits, it is argued that the public's gain from holding time deposits is just offset by the banker's loss in having them outstanding, while there is no such offset involved as far as demand deposits are concerned. Hence the latter represent net wealth to the community.

It seems to me, if I have understood and stated the argument correctly, that the initial insight mentioned above is the only valid element in this chain of reasoning, which otherwise seems to rest on a failure to distinguish carefully between average, total and marginal values of variables. In the first place, it seems wrong to argue, as Pesek and Saving implicitly do, that the introduction of time deposits and other financial assets into an economy has no net effect on its welfare. If this were the case it is hard to see how these assets would ever come into being. Abstracting from the matter of liquidity premiums and such, it is only from the marginal unit of such assets that there is no net gain, for it is only the marginal unit that is held solely for the interest it bears.[9] All intramarginal units presumably yield a flow of amenities to their holders in addition to the interest they carry. If they did not it would not be possible for an institution to intermediate between borrowers and lenders by issuing such assets. This, though, seems to put time deposits and other such financial assets on the same footing as demand deposits, and seems to show that the non-interest bearing characteristics of the latter, on which Pesek and Saving put so much weight, is a red herring.[10] This is perhaps just as well for it is

[7] Commercial banks sometimes permit time deposit holders to overdraw their demand deposits without notice, and this is hard to distinguish from permitting cheques to be drawn on the time deposit. At the same time reduced charges are made against demand deposit accounts that continually have certain *minimum* balances. If the balance falls below that minimum the reduced charge privilege is lost for the whole month regardless of the length of time for which the account is deficient. This is to impose a cost on the owner of the account for subjecting part of it to transfer by cheque, hence making the amount held in the account, up to the minimum balance, take on some of the characteristics of a time deposit.

[8] Most of the issues dealt with in the next few pages are also dealt with in Johnson (13), a paper to which my attention was drawn only after the first draft of this one had been completed. It was, however, a most useful reference in the redrafting of these few pages.

[9] Liquidity premiums are of course a price paid for a special amenity flow yielded by certain assets. It is as important here, as in any other context, to distinguish between the average and the marginal value that is attached to the "liquidity" possessed by any particular asset. For a more detailed discussion of this, see Meiselman (18), pp. 57–59.

[10] The confusion in Pesek and Saving's book over the matter of marginal and total values of a variable, and the difficulties it leads them into on the matter of interest-bearing demand deposits is pervasive. The following passage will serve as an illustration: "When demand

fairly clear that in fact the prohibition of interest payments on demand deposits in the United States has merely caused them to be made implicitly and in kind, in the form of free bookkeeping services and the like, instead of explicitly and in cash.

In a perfectly competitive banking system demand deposits would bear the market rate of interest and the parallel between them, time deposits, and the liabilities of other intermediaries as far as the wealth position of the community is concerned would be perfect. Interest payments would represent a gain to the owners of demand deposits and a cost to their emitters, and these would cancel out only on the marginal unit of demand deposits, there being a net gain to the community in the shape of an amenity flow on all intra-marginal units. The correct implication of Pesek and Saving's initial insight is that the introduction of any new debt instrument that the community is found to be willing to hold must enable it to reach a higher level of utility than before and in this sense represents an increase in wealth. Far from showing up a critical difference between demand deposits and other liquid assets, their arguments, correctly presented, would appear to stress a similarity between these various assets.

The above reasoning would seem to undermine Pesek and Saving's view that changes in the quantity of money operate primarily by way of a wealth effect. In a competitive banking system, initially in equilibrium, changes in the real quantity of money would lead to a fall in the public's utility whether they were positive or negative. In the case of an increase in the quantity of money the value of the interest payments that demand deposits bear would just be offset by the interest rate paid to the banks on the extra bonds they would be holding, while the amenity flow to the public from the extra deposits would be negative. In the case of a fall in demand deposits, interest payments would again cancel out and there would be a loss of amenity flow on the money taken out of the system. In either case the public would try to readjust their balance sheets to get back to equilibrium. It is precisely this readjustment of balance sheets that is usually called "the substitution effect."

If the banking system is not completely competitive and does not pay the appropriate market interest rate on its liabilities, then changes in the quantity of real demand deposits, or real time deposits for that matter, will increase the community's wealth in just the same sense as an increase in the output of anything whose marginal social cost of production is below the marginal social benefit it provides increases the community's wealth. As far as the non-bank public is concerned, the substitution effect will operate as described above. The amenity flow from extra demand deposits, plus the interest (if any) they bear, will not compensate the public for the extra interest payments made to the banks, and the public will attempt to adjust its balance sheet to restore equilibrium. However, in this case, the wealth of bank owners will change because the increase in their in-

---

deposit money starts to pay the market rate of interest, the price of this money is reduced to zero. This may be seen best by considering a consumer who wishes to borrow twenty dollars' worth of demand deposits. Before the introduction of interest payments, such a loan would cost him one dollar per annum (at a market interest rate of 5 per cent) and this expense would be justified by the imputed income (also equal to $1 according to Pesek and Saving). After the introduction of interest payments, this item will now also yield one dollar per year in interest payments so that the net cost of borrowing it has been reduced to zero; thus the price of it has been reduced to zero. Need one add that, as long as this item continues to serve as money, a source of purchasing power, the demand for it will be insatiable?" Pesek and Saving (21), pp. 107–108.

First, it should be obvious that it is only on the marginal unit of demand deposits that the return must be equal to the market rate of interest, so that the imputed income to twenty dollars of cash balances will exceed $1 when the market rate of interest is 5 per cent. Second, the confusion in this passage between the marginal utility of the services of money on the one hand and the price of money on the other hand should be self-evident, as should the fatal ambiguity of the conclusion that the marginal utility of the services of demand deposits can only reach zero if the "item" ceases to serve as money. It is only the marginal unit of demand deposits that will cease to yield any return as a means of exchange, not demand deposits in general. Pesek and Saving here confuse the price of the *flow* of services of money with the price of a unit of the *stock* of money. The former is equal to the market rate of interest and the latter is defined as the inverse of the general price level. Johnson (13), deals with this point in some detail.

terest liabilities on demand deposits will be less than the increase in the income from the assets they hold. Bank owners' behaviour will presumably be influenced by a wealth effect then, but to make such an effect the centerpiece of the analysis of the way in which monetary policy works seems to me to put far too much emphasis on the consequences of a market imperfection. In any event, it provides no basis for distinguishing between demand deposits and time deposits as far as the definition of money is concerned.

The analysis of the substitution effect still appears to be the most fruitful way of understanding the way in which monetary policy works, and if this conclusion is correct, the issues involved in finding the "right" definition of money are still what they were before the appearance of Pesek and Saving's book and still require empirical solution. I will deal with the available evidence in the next section of this paper.

## III. Empirical Evidence

The issues at stake are as follows. First, are time deposits sufficiently close substitutes for demand deposits to warrant treating them as the same asset? Second, if the answer to the first question is yes, is it also the case that the liabilities of other financial intermediaries are sufficiently close substitutes for those of commercial banks to warrant treating them as the same asset? Now one can only define what is meant by a "sufficiently close substitute" if he will specify the problem with which he wishes to deal, and as far as the definition of money is concerned the most important issue has been the identification and measurement of a stable aggregate demand for money function.

As was noted earlier, it is important to know about the aggregate demand for money function if one wishes to influence the level of economic activity by manipulating the money supply, for though it is not the only relationship involved in the transmission of the effects of monetary policy, it is clearly an important one. A "more stable demand function" is precisely one that permits the consequences of shifting the supply of money to be more easily and accurately predicted.

In a deterministic world, in which the arguments of all functions, and their parameters, were known and unchanging, there would be no problem of this sort. One could, for example, define money to include time deposits and worry about the determination of its velocity, or define money to exclude time deposits and introduce time deposits in their role as a close substitute for money as something that might influence velocity. In either case one would get the same results. However, in a stochastic world, with less than perfect knowledge, to get a given degree of accuracy in prediction, one approach might require knowledge of fewer parameters and the values of fewer variables than another, and hence be simpler to employ.

The problem of the "right" definition of money is, in this sense, fundamentally empirical. A "more stable demand for money function" may be taken to be one that requires knowledge of fewer variables and their parameters in order to predict the demand for money with a given degree of accuracy, or, which amounts to the same thing, one that yields parameter estimates that are less subject to variation when the same arguments are included in the function and hence enables more accurate predictions of the demand for money to be made.[11]

That time deposits be substitutes for demand deposits is a necessary condition for a money concept that includes them to be more stably related than a narrower definition to market rates of interest and some appropriate constraint variable, such as for example permanent income, but it is not a sufficient condition. The same argument obviously holds as far as the inclusion of the liabilities of other financial intermediaries in the definition of money is concerned, and most of the empirical work that has been done on the question of the definition of money has therefore concentrated on investigating the stability of the demand for money function under different definitions of money. Some work,

[11] It is worth pointing out that $R^2$ and $R$ are not appropriate statistics for comparing the stability of functions having different dependent variables. This writer (15) has not been alone in misusing them in this way. When log-linear regression is employed the standard error of the estimate has the particularly attractive characteristic of measuring the *amount* of the percentage variation (as opposed to its proportion in the case of $R^2$ and $R$) that is left unexplained by the independent variables and hence may be used to measure the relative stability of functions using different dependent variables.

however, has been done on directly measuring the degree of substitutability of one potential component of the money stock for another and, as we shall see below, the results of these two types of test are not altogether consistent.

It will be convenient to begin the account of the relevant evidence with Friedman's paper (7), because the results of this study, as far as other important issues in monetary economics are concerned, have often been erroneously interpreted as depending critically upon his inclusion of time deposits at commercial banks in the definition of money he used. First of all, Friedman found an elasticity of demand for money with respect to permanent income of about 1.8. Second, he was unable to produce any evidence that the rate of interest was an important variable in the demand for money function. Both of these results struck many economists as anomalous, and the inclusion of time deposits in the money definition employed was held largely, though not solely, responsible for them. It was held responsible for the high permanent income elasticity of demand for money because, it was argued, theory suggested that the demand for money would rise less than in proportion to income. This prediction was based on an inventory approach to the demand for a means of exchange pure and simple. [Cf. Baumol (1).] The demand for time deposits, these not being a means of exchange, was not expected to follow this prediction, and hence their inclusion in the definition of money was held responsible for the results of Friedman's test contradicting it. As to the evidence concerning the rate of interest, it was argued that, since time deposits were interest-bearing assets, variations in the demand for them in response to changes in the rate of interest they bore could mask the responsiveness of the demand for demand deposits to rates of interest in general. Thus the inclusion of time deposits in the definition of money automatically resulted in an underestimate of the importance of the role of interest rates in the function. Both of these arguments are now known to be false.[12]

Numerous studies have shown quite explicitly that the rate of interest, whatever the actual series that might be used to measure it, has a statistically significant negative effect on the demand for money, however defined. One study, by the present writer, even suggests that the inclusion of time deposits in the definition of money improves the stability of the relationship. [Cf. Laidler (16) pp. 551-54.] The same study also shows clearly that Friedman's inability to find a close relationship between the demand for money and the rate of interest is a result of the test procedure he followed, for it is possible to find such a relationship using Friedman's own data and with only a slight variation on his test.[13] As to the permanent income elasticity of demand for money of 1.8, this would appear from subsequent evidence to be partly the result of omitting the rate of interest from the function fitted, but also the product of Friedman's using a time series that goes back as far as 1869.

Meltzer's study (19), using data going back only to 1900, finds an elasticity of demand for money with respect to non-human wealth, a variable that is very highly correlated with permanent income, of just a little greater than unity for both concepts of money. This writer (16) found, for the years 1892 to 1916, a permanent income elasticity of demand for broadly defined money in the region of 1.6, but over the period 1919 to 1960 this parameter seems to have been somewhere between unity and 1.3, appearing to fall below unity in the years following the second world war. The results for the post-1919 period are not changed if a narrow definition of money is employed, so that while they present us with the problem of explaining why there might have been a fall over

[12] No one writer is responsible for all of these arguments. However, some aspects of them appear in Feige (4), Meltzer (19), and Teigen (22), to give but three examples.

[13] Friedman's error was to leave the rate of interest out of the initial cycle average regression he performed. Since the rate of interest is slightly negatively correlated with permanent income over the long-run this led to his obtaining an erroneous estimate of the relationship between permanent income and the demand for money. His elasticity estimate of 1.8 was too high. For a full account, cf. Laidler (16), pp. 545–46. It is worth pointing out that the complaint sometimes voiced that total inelasticity of the demand for money with respect to the rate of interest means that monetary policy cannot work by way of changing interest rates is analytically wrong. It is perfect elasticity with respect to this variable that causes this problem.

time in the permanent income (or wealth) elasticity of demand for money, they also rule out the explanation being found in any eccentricity of the definition of money employed.[14]

In general, there is a great deal of evidence showing that the answers to questions about what arguments belong in the demand for money function do not seem to be very sensitive to the actual definition of money employed. The importance of rates of interest is now unchallenged, while the conclusions drawn by Friedman in 1959 as to the inadequacy of measured income as an argument in the function are amply confirmed by subsequent work, the only disagreement remaining being whether wealth defined to exclude human wealth, or a more inclusive definition proxied by permanent income, is the more appropriate replacement.[15] Brunner and Meltzer's results (3) point to the former conclusion while some results of my own (15) tend to favour permanent income. However, both of these conclusions are independent of the definition of money used in the tests upon which they are based. The differences here arise from the different time periods used and the different test procedures applied to the data. In any event they do not seem to this writer to be of such great importance for, as Meltzer argues (19), the basic debate is between wealth and income as determinants of the demand for money, with choice between non-human wealth and permanent income being one between alternative ways of measuring wealth.

All the evidence suggests that a highly stable demand for money function can be identified whether time deposits are included in the definition of money or not. Functions using wealth and an interest rate, regardless of the precise series chosen, show a high degree of explanatory power with respect to variations in the demand for money defined on either concept, whether this explanatory power is judged on the basis of the T-values of the coefficients of the arguments, the amount by which these coefficients vary when the function is fitted to independent subperiods, the amount of variation in the dependent variable that the function leaves unexplained, or the accuracy with which the function predicts variations in the dependent variable when that function is extrapolated beyond the period over which it is fitted. Moreover, the differences that do exist between the results attained with different money definitions do not consistently favour one definition or another, and are not, in this writer's judgement, large enough to furnish a firm basis for deciding whether time deposits should be included in or excluded from the definition of money.

However, these functions are stable enough to warrant the conclusion that over the period for which they have been fitted the liabilities of other institutions do not appear to have been such close substitutes for the liabilities of commercial banks to warrant any special attention. One must be careful though about extrapolating this judgement, which is inevitably about the way things were in the past, to deal with the present. There is some evidence that circumstances have been changing. Apart from a brief but rapid period of growth in the 1920's, institutions such as savings and loan associations have been important only in the years since the second world war, and as far as these years are concerned there is some doubt about the stability of demand for money relationships that ignore this factor. Not only did the velocity of circulation rise in the late 1940's and 1950's in a fashion that was not predictable on the basis of pre-war experience, but the performance of functions fitted separately to

[14] The reader might note that for years before the setting up of the Federal Reserve System in 1913 it is not really possible to distinguish between which liabilities of banks were demand deposits in the modern sense and which were time deposits. There must always be some doubt about the reliability of empirical evidence on the demand for narrowly defined money when it is based on data that include observations taken before 1913. Friedman's inclusion of time deposits in the definition of money is to some extent motivated by the fact that it enables a consistent time series going back to 1869 to be constructed.

[15] I base this conclusion largely on results dealt with in Brunner and Meltzer (3), Meltzer (19), and Laidler (15). Good results obtained with measured income have usually come from functions having a lagged value of the dependent variable in them, as for example, Teigen (22) and Bronfenbrenner and Mayer (2), and such functions cannot easily be distinguished analytically from those employing permanent income as usually defined. Recent work by Feige (5) has shown that the permanent income interpretation of such functions is more likely to be correct.

data for these years also frequently leaves something to be desired.

Results already mentioned [Laidler (16)] suggest that the permanent income elasticity of demand for money fell to a value of less than unity in the post-war period, a statistical reflection of the fact that variations in market interest rates alone are not enough to account for the post-war rise in velocity, and that the stability of the demand function, as measured by the T-statistics attaching to its arguments, is noticeably less than for earlier periods. Similarly, Motley (20), when dealing with the household sector's demand for money, found a marked difference in both the value and the stability of the parameters of the function he fitted for the pre- and post-war periods. All this suggests that the relationship between the demand for money and the arguments usually used to explain it was in the process of shifting in this post-World War II period, and Johnson's suggestion (12) that these results might have something to do with the growth of importance of non-bank intermediaries is certainly borne out by Lee's (17) results for the period since 1951. Lee found the demand for money to be more stably related to the rate of return on savings and loan association shares than to the market interest rates more frequently used when fitting demand for money functions and in fact used in the studies alluded to above. The rate of return on savings and loan association shares appears from Lee's results to have acquired in recent years a more stable influence on the demand for money, whether money is defined to include or exclude time deposits, than either of the more frquently used short-term commercial paper rates and long-term corporate bond yields.[16]

One must be a little careful with Lee's results because, during the period they cover, variation in the rate of return on savings and loan association shares has taken the form of an almost continuous upward trend so that it can be argued that almost any variable following such a time path might have performed as well in his tests.[17] However, it is precisely an upward trend in velocity that needs explaining, and it is certainly plausible to suggest that a rising rate of return on savings and loan association shares has been responsible for it. Moreover, results recently reported by Hamburger [(10), pp. 104-106] for quarterly data over the period 1952-62, suggest that the household sector's demand for time deposits at commercial banks and its demand for the liabilities of other savings institutions (savings and loan associations, mutual savings banks, and credit unions) are more sensitive to the rate of return on the other asset than to bond yields. These results lend a little more weight to the conclusion that the activities of non-bank financial intermediaries have, in recent years, become more important as far as the demand for the liabilities of commercial banks is concerned. All in all the picture that emerges is of a demand function for money whose stability is largely independent of whether money is defined to include or exclude time deposits, but whose form has perhaps changed somewhat over time as the available substitutes for money have changed. In particular, it would appear that the activities of non-bank intermediaries can now affect the public's desire to hold the liabilities of commercial banks, but, to judge from Lee's and Hamburger's evidence, in a predictable way so that there seems to be no strong case for including the liabilities of these institutions in one's notion of money.[18] This is certainly a

[16] The actual interest variable used by Lee is the interest differential between money and savings and loan association shares. There can be no objection to this when time deposits are included in the definition of money, for a reasonably accurate series on the interest paid on these deposits does exist. However, there are serious difficulties in appropriately measuring the rate of return on demand deposits, and Lee's solution, which is to use the ratio of bank charges to total demand deposits, is open to serious objections which are gone into below in the context of Feige's work. It seems more likely to this writer that Lee's surprising conclusion that time deposits are not such close substitutes for demand deposits as are savings and loan association shares is due to the unsatisfactory way in which he measured the rate of return on demand deposits rather than that it reflects an empirical truth about the United States economy.

[17] I am grateful to both Philip Cagan and Thomas Mayer for drawing my attention to this argument.

[18] It is worth noting that Friedman and Schwartz (8) consider at some length the possibility that savings and loan associations have exercised an important influence on the demand for money in the post-war period and reject it on the grounds that there is no evidence of

plausible picture, and it is disconcerting to find that the most careful study [Feige (4)] so far carried out of the issues that are being dealt with here would lead us to conclude that it is false. One must choose between the evidence already dealt with, and Feige's results, and I would tentatively suggest that there are sufficient problems with the latter to justify a preference for the rival set of conclusions.

Feige finds that there is no close degree of substitutability between demand deposits, time deposits, savings and loan association shares and mutual savings bank deposits and hence concludes that a narrow definition of money is not only useable but preferable, while he also concludes that the activities of other intermediaries need have no effect on the demand for money. His basic technique is to take observations on household ownership of various liquid assets (demand deposits, time deposits, mutual savings bank deposits and savings and loan association shares) for each state for the years 1949 to 1959, to treat each year's observations as a different sample, and to attempt to relate household ownership of each of these assets to the rates of return on all of them and permanent personal income. Each state in each year then constitutes a different observation, and a different set of regressions was performed for each year.[19] Feige found that the ownership of each of these assets was quite sensitive to its own rate of return but not to that on other assets.

There are at least three problems which might lead us to suspect these results. In the first place, though Feige's tests ideally require data on household ownership of assets, the only available information on a state-by-state basis is for the aggregate ownership of the relevant assets by households, partnerships, and corporations. The latter two groups are of course particularly important as far as demand deposit ownership is concerned. The details of Feige's method of adjusting his data to deal with this problem need not concern us here, but he himself concludes that there is no way of assessing how satisfactory it is. [Cf. Feige (4) pp. 18-19.] There is thus no way of knowing how this data problem might have affected the outcome of his tests.

The second problem arises because, instead of having data for assets owned by residents of each state, Feige seems to have data on assets in each state owned by residents of all states. These will be the same if there is no asset ownership across state lines, but not otherwise. Even if out-of-state ownership was not large, one might expect people who own assets across state lines to be more sophisticated portfolio managers than the average household, and hence more sensitive to alternative rates of return in their asset choice. If this is the case, then by failing to include rates of return in other states as determinants of the demand for assets in any particular state, Feige has left out of his regression equations potentially important determinants of the demand for any asset. Again this opens the reliability of his results to question.

These problems affect Feige's results as far as all assets are concerned, but the third difficulty is particularly relevant to his demand deposits results. It arises from his method of measuring the rate of return on demand deposits. Interest is usually paid on demand deposits in the form of deductions from the bookkeeping charges that banks levy on their customers. If the latter charges were otherwise proportional to the quantity of demand deposits held, then any variation in their ratio to deposits held would reflect variations in the interest rate paid on demand deposits. It is this ratio that Feige uses to measure the (negative) rate of return on demand deposits.

There are two difficulties with doing so. In the first place, it at best measures variations in the average interest rate on demand deposits and, given that the prohibition of explicit interest payments gives banks scope for price discrimination, it is not clear that movements in such an average rate accurately reflect movements in the more relevant marginal rate, or rates, to which asset holders

similar influence in the 1920's when these institutions underwent a similar period of spectacular growth. It may be, however, that differences in the regulations governing the activities of commercial banks in the two periods explain this difference, for the banks are certainly less able freely to meet competition from other institutions now than they were in the 1920's. There seems to be an important unsettled question in monetary history here, and one that would be well worth investigating further.

[19] Feige also included variables for such items as the number of savings and loan association offices in the state, advertising expenditures, dummies for various regions, and so forth.

are responding. Second, the ratio of bank charges to deposits may not remain a constant in the absence of changes in the interest rate on demand deposits. For a given volume of payments, this ratio might be expected to rise as the quantity of demand deposits falls, for it should be related to the rate of deposit turnover. Bank charges are primarily bookkeeping charges and are related to the rate of flow of payments made by cheque rather than to the stock of demand deposits in existence. If the volume of cheque payments is roughly related to the level of permanent income, one would expect a negative relationship to hold between the ratio of bank charges to deposits and the level of demand deposits held, given the level of permanent income, a relationship such as Feige finds. It would arise from variations in the rate of turnover of deposits implied by their being held in different ratios to permanent income. This relationship though would reflect the nature of bank charges and not the influence of the rate of return on demand deposits. At least one of the rates of return that Feige uses then probably measures the true variable very inaccurately indeed, but apart from noting that this measure is likely to be inversely correlated with holdings of demand deposits, given the level of permanent income, there is nothing very definite that can be said about its likely effect on the results Feige gets.

Now it would be fruitless to speculate as to how seriously Feige's results are affected by any of these problems just as it would be wrong to imply that the studies I dealt with earlier are without blemish. The only point I am at pains to make here is that even though Feige's study is addressed directly to the problem that I am dealing with in this paper, and even though it is carried out with great care, there are good grounds for doubting its conclusions, grounds that might be considered strong enough to warrant our asking for more evidence before we reject the intuitively more plausible conclusions that may be drawn from other studies.

## IV. Summary and Conclusions

The problem posed by this paper is that of whether the stock of assets over which the monetary authorities have control may be regarded as corresponding to what is called "money" in macroeconomics. The issue is of course an empirical one, but it nevertheless has proved worthwhile to go into the theoretical elements of the question, both to sort out sensible theoretical arguments from some which seem, to this writer at least, to be erroneous, and also to formulate more precisely the type of empirical questions to be asked.

The basic empirical question is one of rates of substitution between assets, and there appear to be three a priori defensible positions that may be held. First it may be argued that demand deposits and currency are sufficiently differentiated from their closest substitute to make it desirable to treat them as a separate asset. This view is grounded on these assets' role as a means of exchange, while the view that time deposits and the liabilities of other financial intermediaries are also money seems to be based primarily on the view that the demand for money is to an important degree the demand for an asset whose capital value does not vary with the rate of interest. The intermediate view, that time deposits, but not the liabilities of other financial institutions, should be treated as money appears to stem from a judgement that time deposits are substantially cheaper assets to use as a "temporary abode of purchasing power" than are these others.

Strong a priori cases can be made out on all sides of the argument and the empirical evidence is also to some degree in conflict. It would appear to be the case that stable demand functions for money defined both to include and to exclude time deposits at commercial banks may be identified for the United States economy. However, there does seem to have been some change over time, particularly since the second world war, in the assets to whose rate of return the demand for money however defined is most sensitive. The apparent importance of savings and loan associations in recent years is particularly noteworthy. These conclusions must, however, be treated with care, since they are contradicted by Feige's important study (4).

With the evidence we have at the moment, then, it is possible to come to only tentative conclusions about what set of assets the monetary authorities should attempt to manipulate in carrying out monetary policy. These conclusions are as follows: As far as the liabilities of commercial banks are concerned it does not seem to matter much whether the authorities confine their efforts to controlling the volume of demand deposits alone, or whether they seek to control the volume of demand and time deposits together. The demand function for money defined in either way seems stable enough for changes in the supply of the appropriate set of assets to have predictable affects on the variables that appear in the demand function, given that the influence of other factors on these variables is taken into account. It would appear though, if we overlook Feige's results, that important among these "other factors" must be the activities of such institutions as savings and loan associations.

However, even Lee's and Hamburger's results do not enable us to make out any strong case for extending the regulatory powers of the monetary authorities to non-bank intermediaries. The liabilities of these institutions have perhaps become important substitutes for money, but the substitution relationship involved appears to be stable, so that, provided that the activities of these institutions are taken into account, the demand for the liabilities of commercial banks seems to be no more difficult to predict than it was in the years when, for example, short-term commercial paper seems to have been an important substitute for money. The case for controlling savings and loan associations and the like, inasmuch as it rests on the substitutability of their liabilities for those of commercial banks, is no stronger than was the case in earlier years for controlling the emitters of short-term commercial bills. Of course there are more elements to the case than this, for the regulations under which commercial banks operate undoubtedly make it more difficult for them to compete *qua* financial intermediary with other institutions; there is certainly a case to be made on grounds of equity for either reducing the amount of control the authorities exercise over commercial banks or for increasing their control over other institutions. To go into this issue any further would take us far beyond the scope of this paper, but its relevance to some of the questions at hand should not be ignored for that reason.[20]

To return to the main problem, however, the evidence suggests that existing institutional arrangements are adequate as far as the exercise of monetary policy is concerned. It further suggests that which particular aggregate of commercial bank liabilities the authorities try to manipulate is a question which must be settled on other grounds, for example, which aggregate it is easier to control, than those discussed in this paper. As far as the demand function for money is concerned there seems to be nothing to choose between the alternatives considered.

[20] The interested reader will find these issues taken up in Johnson (14).

## Literature Cited

1. BAUMOL, W. J. "The Transactions Demand for Cash—an Inventory Theoretic Approach," *Quarterly Journal of Economics,* 66 (1952), 545–56.

2. BRONFENBRENNER, M., AND MAYER, T. "Liquidity Functions in the American Economy," *Econometrica,* 28 (1960), 810–34.

3. BRUNNER, KARL, AND MELTZER, ALLAN H. "Predicting Velocity: Implications for Theory and Policy," *Journal of Finance,* 18 (1963), 319–54.

4. FEIGE, EDGAR. *The Demand for Liquid Assets: A Temporal Cross Section Analysis.* Englewood Cliffs, N.J.: Prentice-Hall, 1964.

5. ———. "Expectations and Adjustments in the Monetary Sector," *American Economic Review,* 57 (Papers and Proceedings, 1967), 462–73.

6. FRIEDMAN, MILTON. "The Quantity Theory of Money, a Restatement," in *Studies in the Quantity Theory of Money,* ed. M. Friedman, Chicago, Ill.: University of Chicago Press, 1956.

7. ———. "The Demand for Money—Some Theoretical and Empirical Results," *Journal of Political Economy,* 67 (1959), 327–51.

8. ———, AND SCHWARTZ, A. J. *A Monetary History of the United States 1867–1960.* Princeton, N.J.: Princeton University Press (for the National Bureau of Economic Research), 1963.

9. GURLEY, J., AND SHAW, E. *Money in a Theory of Finance.* Washington, D.C.: Brookings Institute, 1960.

10. HAMBURGER, MICHAEL. "Household Demand for Financial Assets," *Econometrica,* 36 (1968), 97–118.

11. HICKS, SIR J. R. *Critical Essays in Monetary Theory,* London, Oxford University Press, 1967.

12. JOHNSON, H. G. "A Quantity Theorist's Monetary History of the United States," *Economic Journal,* 75 (June 1965) pp. 388–96.

13. ———. "Inside Money, Outside Money, Income, Wealth, and Welfare in Monetary Theory," Paper read at the 1968 meeting of the Association of University Teachers of Economics held at York, *Journal of Money, Credit and Banking,* 1 (1969), 30–45.

14. ———. "Problems of Efficiency in Monetary Management," *Journal of Political Economy,* Forthcoming.

15. LAIDLER, DAVID. "Some Evidence on the Demand for Money," *Journal of Political Economy,* 74 (February 1966), pp. 55–68.

16. ———. "The Rate of Interest and the Demand for Money—Some Empirical Evidence," *Journal of Political Economy,* 74 (December 1966), pp. 545–55.

17. LEE, T. H. "Alternative Interest Rates and the Demand for Money: The Empirical Evidence," *American Economic Review,* 57 (December 1967), pp. 1168–81.

18. MEISELMAN, DAVID. *The Term Structure of Interest Rates,* Englewood Cliffs, N.J., Prentice-Hall, 1963.

19. MELTZER, ALLAN H. "The Demand for Money: The Evidence from the Time Series," *Journal of Political Economy,* 71 (June 1963), pp. 219–46.

20. MOTLEY, B. "A Demand-for-Money Function for the Household Sector—Some Preliminary Findings," *Journal of Finance,* 22 (September 1967), pp. 405–18.

21. PESEK, B. P., AND SAVING, T. R. *Money, Wealth, and Economic Theory,* New York, Macmillan, 1967.

22. TEIGEN, R. "Demand and Supply Functions for Money in the United States," *Econometrica,* 32, No. 4 (October 1964), pp. 477–509.

23. TOBIN, JAMES. "Liquidity Preference as Behaviour Towards Risk," *Review of Economic Studies,* 25 (February 1958), pp. 65–86.

# 14 | MORE ON AN EMPIRICAL DEFINITION OF MONEY*

GEORGE G. KAUFMAN
*University of Oregon*

There is considerable disagreement among economists on the appropriate definition of money. Definitions based on apparently reasonable but empirically unsubstantiated hypotheses concerning the use of financial assets as media of exchange are neither precise nor universally accepted. A number of attempts have been made in recent years to define money empirically. Of these, three techniques appear most promising: (1) Definition by cross-elasticity of substitution of financial assets [1]; (2) Definition by discriminant analysis of time series characteristics [6]; and (3) Definition by ability to explain statistically aggregate nominal income [2]. Without evaluating the relative merits of these techniques, this paper presents additional evidence on the definition of money that best explains aggregate nominal income.

In their study for the Commission on Money and Credit, Milton Friedman and David Meiselman (F-M) used two criteria in selecting sets of financial assets to be included in the money supply: (1) the highest correlation of the sum of these assets with income and (2) higher correlation of the sum with income than of any of the components separately [2, p. 181]. The second criterion is included to ensure that an increase in correlation is attributed to the inclusion of a component in the money supply concept and not to the association between income and the particular component alone.[1]

F-M apply these dual criteria to three alternative definitions of money. They find that the set of assets including currency, demand deposits, and time deposits at commercial banks only satisfies the criteria better than either a narrower concept, including only currency and demand deposits, or a broader concept, including also savings-type accounts at mutual savings banks, savings and loan associations, and post offices [2, pp. 242-46].[2] The correlation for the narrower concept is consistently lower for the periods examined. The correlation for the broader concept is sometimes greater, but it is attributed to a still greater correlation between income and the additional savings-type accounts alone.

The tests described here pertain to a larger number of money supply components than considered by F-M, including a separation of currency and demand deposits. The tests also apply the F-M criteria to alternative money supply concepts observed before and after corresponding income observations as well as

* Reprinted from *The American Economic Review*, vol. 59 (March, 1969), pp. 78–87, by permission of the author and the American Economic Association.

[1] This procedure implicitly assumes some preconceived ordering of the components and does not represent a "pure" empirical test. See Robert H. Strotz [7, pp. 306–10]. I am indebted to Robert Laurent for initially calling my attention to this point. In a subsequent manuscript, Milton Friedman details his ordering procedure more clearly [3].

[2] F-M assign each component equal weight in summing. In contrast, John G. Gurley has proposed that the components be weighed by their degree of "moneyness" [4].

TABLE 1. SIMPLE CORRELATION COEFFICIENTS BETWEEN Δ GNP AND Δ MONEY SUPPLY COMPONENTS IN PRECEDING, SYNCHRONOUS, AND LATER PERIODS

| | Quarters Money Component Leads GNP | | | | | | |
|---|---|---|---|---|---|---|---|
| | +4 | +3 | +2 | +1 | 0 | −1 | −2 |
| | | | | A. 1953–66 | | | |
| *C* | −.01 | −.05 | .05 | .20 | .39 | .41 | .42 |
| *DD* | −.01 | .24 | .40 | .49 | .44 | .19 | −.01 |
| $TD_B$ | .36 | .35 | .32 | .20 | −.09 | −.24 | −.17 |
| *MSB* | .14 | .25 | .21 | .17 | .10 | −.08 | −.09 |
| *SC* | −.19 | −.19 | −.18 | −.17 | −.21 | −.24 | −.31 |
| *SB* | .23 | .32 | .39 | .38 | .25 | .13 | .04 |
| *US* | −.31 | −.46 | −.39 | −.23 | .15 | .42 | .50 |
| *SAV* | .34 | .35 | .30 | .16 | −.14 | −.32 | −.28 |
| | | | | B. 1953–59 | | | |
| *C* | −.43 | −.58 | −.36 | −.06 | .36 | .55 | .46 |
| *DD* | −.24 | .03 | .33 | .68 | .64 | .24 | −.14 |
| $TD_B$ | .19 | .17 | .17 | .03 | −.38 | −.58 | −.49 |
| *MSB* | −.14 | −.00 | .19 | .10 | .06 | −.22 | −.26 |
| *SC* | −.05 | −.07 | .03 | .07 | .06 | −.02 | −.10 |
| *SB* | −.08 | .07 | .24 | .30 | .22 | .01 | −.16 |
| *US* | −.22 | −.62 | −.63 | −.41 | .08 | .51 | .67 |
| *SAV* | .18 | .19 | .24 | .10 | −.32 | −.58 | −.52 |
| | | | | C. 1960–66 | | | |
| *C* | .35 | .35 | .30 | .34 | .42 | .29 | .41 |
| *DD* | .32 | .57 | .58 | .37 | .20 | .07 | .06 |
| $TD_B$ | .53 | .52 | .43 | .27 | .02 | −.19 | −.16 |
| *MSB* | .53 | .64 | .36 | .33 | .15 | .01 | −.00 |
| *SC* | −.16 | −.13 | −.22 | −.22 | −.35 | −.34 | −.43 |
| *SB* | .61 | .62 | .55 | .41 | .09 | −.01 | −.07 |
| *US* | −.55 | −.17 | .21 | .48 | .58 | .36 | .13 |
| *SAV* | .53 | .53 | .34 | .17 | −.10 | −.27 | −.30 |

KEY TO FIGURES AND TABLES

$C$ = Currency outside banks
$DD$ = Demand deposits at commercial banks
$TD_B$ = Time deposits at commercial banks
$MSB$ = Deposits at mutual savings banks
$SC$ = Share capital at savings and loan associations
$SB$ = U.S. government savings bonds plus deposits in postal savings system
$US$ = Private nonbank holdings of U.S. government marketable securities maturing within one year
$GNP$ = Gross national product in current dollars
$SAV = (TD_B + MSB + SC)$
$M_1 = (DD + C)$
$M_2 = (M_1 + TD_B)$
$M_3 = (M_2 + MSB + SC)$
$M_4 = (M_3 + SB)$
$M_5 = (M_4 + US)$
$n$ = Number of quarters money leads GNP (negative values denote lags)

NOTE: The minimum significant $r$ at the .05 level for the entire 1953–66 period is .25; for the subperiods the minimum significant $r$ is .33.

concurrently with income.[3] The latter tests are conducted because a considerable body of doctrine suggests that money is most

[3] These tests also differ from those conducted by R. Timerlake, Jr. and J. Fortson in another recent reexamination of the F-M analysis [8]. By considering the same components of the money supply as F-M but over differing observation periods, Timberlake and Fortson conclude that little is gained by including time deposits at commercial banks in the definition of money.

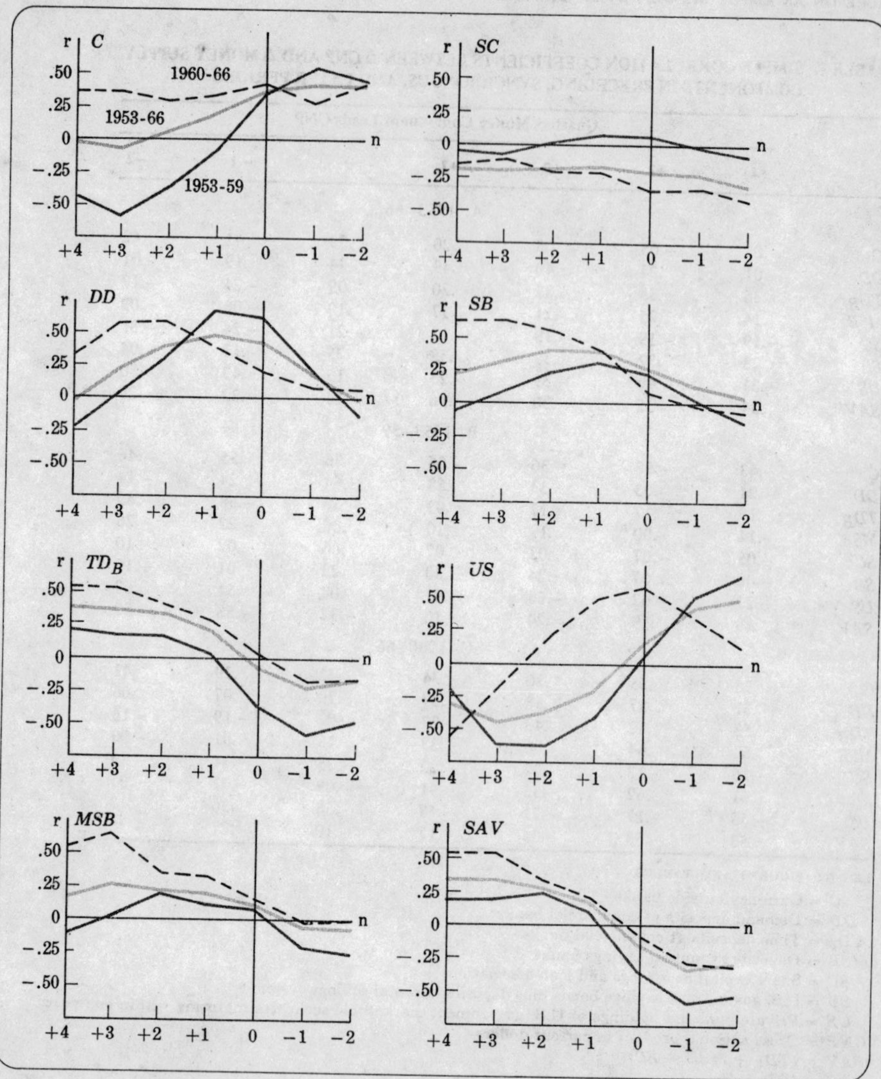


**FIGURE 1** Simple correlation coefficients between Δ GNP and Δ money supply components.

closely related to income in periods other than the concurrent period.[4]

[4] Although the chief proponents of a theory relating money to income in succeeding periods, F-M test for the definition of money using only concurrent observations. The highest correlation definition is then correlated with income in subsequent periods to estimate the lags.

All the data are seasonally adjusted quarterly first differences of logarithmic magnitudes. Income data are observations of nominal gross national product for the 1953-66 post-accord period. Money supply components are those included in the Federal Reserve Board's series on liquid assets and are observed for a slightly longer time period to maintain a fixed number of income observations in the lead-lag analysis.[5] The period is also divided into two equal subperiods (1953-59 and 1960-66) to permit examination of the stability of the estimates.

The simple correlation coefficients between income and each money component are shown in Table 1 and plotted in Figure 1 for observations of money from four quarters before the accompanying income observation through two quarters after. Marked differences among the correlation coefficients and among the correlation time patterns are readily discernible. Currency is correlated best with income in concurrent and earlier periods, and the correlation declines sharply as currency is observed before income. On the other hand, the correlation between demand deposits and income is highest when deposits precede income by a quarter and the correlation declines slowly on either side of the peak. Time deposits at commercial banks also tend to be most closely correlated with income in later periods. The highest correlations are obtained when time deposits precede income by two to four quarters. The correlation turns negative when time deposits are related to concurrent or earlier income observations.[6]

Deposits at mutual savings banks show approximately the same pattern as commercial bank time deposits, although the correlations are both lower and less stable. The correlation between savings and loan share capital and income tends to be small for almost all observations and frequently is negative. Similar to bank deposits, holdings of U.S. savings bonds are most highly correlated with income in later periods and only weakly correlated with income in earlier periods. The relationship between private nonbank holdings of marketable short-term Treasury securities and income differs from the patterns of the other financial assets and is noticeably more unstable. The pattern for the first subperiod shows these securities to be negatively correlated with income when income observations lag and positively related when income observations are concurrent or leading. The pattern for the 1960-66 subperiod indicates positive correlations except when income is observed three or more quarters later. The last panel in Figure 1 shows the correlation coefficients when time deposits at commercial banks, deposits at mutual savings banks, and share capital at savings and loan associations are combined to form a total depository savings concept. The correlation pattern of this series closely resembles that of commercial bank time deposits alone, being highest when income is observed in later periods and inversely related to income in concurrent and earlier periods.

The individual components are progressively aggregated according to the ordering in Table 1 to form the more common alternative definitions of money. These definitions are correlated with income in the same, earlier, and later periods. The resulting correlation coefficients are shown in Table 2 and plotted in Figure 2. The correlation patterns are dominated by both demand and time deposits at commercial banks. For example, the pattern for the narrow definition of money—currency and demand deposits—resembles that for demand deposits alone, although the average time span by which the concept leads income is slightly briefer. The addition of time deposits both increases the correlation coefficients and lengthens the peak correlation to between one and two quarters preceding income. The subsequent addition of other savings-type deposits or savings bonds neither greatly increases the correlation of the resulting money supply concepts nor greatly changes the correlation pattern. The inclusion of marketable short-term Treasury securities yields a money supply concept clearly inferior to most narrower concepts.

This evidence suggests that satisfaction of the best-fit criterion—a necessary but not sufficient condition for the satisfaction of the dual F-M criteria—depends not only on the money supply components considered but also on the range of time periods between

5 Data for money supply components are averages of figures for the last Wednesday of the three months in the quarter and the preceding month. These data for currency, demand deposits, and time deposits differ slightly from the corresponding daily average data which are unavailable for the other money supply components considered.

6 Although not shown, the coefficients also decline when time deposits at commercial banks are correlated with income five or more quarters later. Interestingly enough, the introduction and rapid growth of negotiable CDs in the second subperiod do not appear to have altered the correlation pattern greatly although, unlike other forms of time deposits, few of these deposits are owned by individuals.

TABLE 2. SIMPLE CORRELATION COEFFICIENTS BETWEEN Δ GNP AND Δ ALTERNATIVE DEFINITIONS OF MONEY IN PRECEDING, SYNCHRONOUS, AND LATER PERIODS

| | Quarters Money Definition Leads GNP | | | | | | |
|---|---|---|---|---|---|---|---|
| | +4 | +3 | +2 | +1 | 0 | −1 | −2 |
| | | | A. 1953-66 | | | | |
| $C$ | −.01 | −.05 | .05 | .20 | .39 | .41 | .42 |
| $M_1 = DD + C$ | −.01 | .20 | .37 | .49 | .49* | .28 | .09 |
| $M_2 = M_1 + TD_B$ | .25 | .36* | .44* | .45 | .30 | .09 | .03 |
| $M_2 + MSB$ | .25 | .37* | .44 | .45 | .30 | .08 | .02 |
| $M_3 = M_2 + MSB + SC$ | .26 | .38* | .44 | .44 | .27 | .04 | −.04 |
| $M_4 = M_3 + SB$ | .28 | .40* | .46* | .45 | .29 | .09 | −.00 |
| $M_5 = M_4 + US$ | .00 | .01 | .12 | .25 | .37 | .38 | .37 |
| | | | B. 1953-59 | | | | |
| $C$ | −.43 | −.58 | −.36 | −.06 | .36 | .55 | .46 |
| $M_1 = DD + C$ | −.33 | −.11 | .24 | .65 | .69* | .32 | −.07 |
| $M_2 = M_1 + TD_B$ | −.13 | .06 | .35* | .57 | .29 | −.13 | −.34 |
| $M_2 + MSB$ | −.14 | .06 | .36* | .56 | .28 | −.15 | −.35 |
| $M_3 = M_2 + MSB + SC$ | −.12 | .09 | .41* | .61 | .33 | −.13 | −.35 |
| $M_4 = M_3 + SB$ | −.11 | .12 | .45* | .66 | .37 | −.10 | −.34 |
| $M_5 = M_4 + US$ | −.34 | −.63 | −.45 | −.09 | .32 | .47 | .45 |
| | | | C. 1960-66 | | | | |
| $C$ | .35 | .35 | .30 | .34 | .42 | .29 | .41 |
| $M_1 = DD + C$ | .36* | .57 | .57 | .40* | .28 | .14 | .15 |
| $M_2 = M_1 + TD_B$ | .53 | .63* | .58 | .42* | .24 | .05 | .11 |
| $M_2 + MSB$ | .54* | .64 | .57 | .42 | .24 | .05 | .10 |
| $M_3 = M_2 + MSB + SC$ | .54 | .65* | .54 | .35 | .12 | −.08 | −.09 |
| $M_4 = M_3 + SB$ | .56 | .65 | .55 | .38 | .13 | −.05 | −.07 |
| $M_5 = M_4 + US$ | .13 | .48 | .65* | .58* | .39 | .15 | .03 |

*Coefficient exceeds those of any of the respective definition's components separately.

corresponding observations of money and income. F-M's definition of money $(C+DD+TD_B)$ meets this criterion better than the narrower definition only for observations two or more quarters before income, although it is not necessarily superior to broader concepts even in these periods. The narrow definition for money explains income better when observed one quarter before income through two quarters after income, although for lagging observations, currency alone is clearly superior.

The effects on the correlation coefficient of including additional money supply components to form consecutively broader concepts of money are also clearly discernible from Figures 3 and 4. Figure 3 shows the correlation pattern for each lead-lag relationship as components are progressively added to currency. The failure of components beyond time deposits at commercial banks to increase the correlation coefficients greatly becomes more evident. The unique relationship of currency is also more evident. Currency contributes little explanatory power when money leads income and almost all the explanatory power when money is observed concurrently or after income. In Figure 4, currency is added last, rather than first. The correlations here are affected less by the progressive inclusion of additional components. For the entire period, the highest correlations are obtained when demand deposits alone are observed one quarter before income and when broader concepts are observed two quarters before income. These leads are uniformly only one quarter in the 1953-59 subperiod and, except for demand deposits alone, three quarters in the 1960-66 subperiod.

Introduction of the second of the two F-M criteria—that the correlation of the particular money supply concept with income is greater than the correlation of any of the

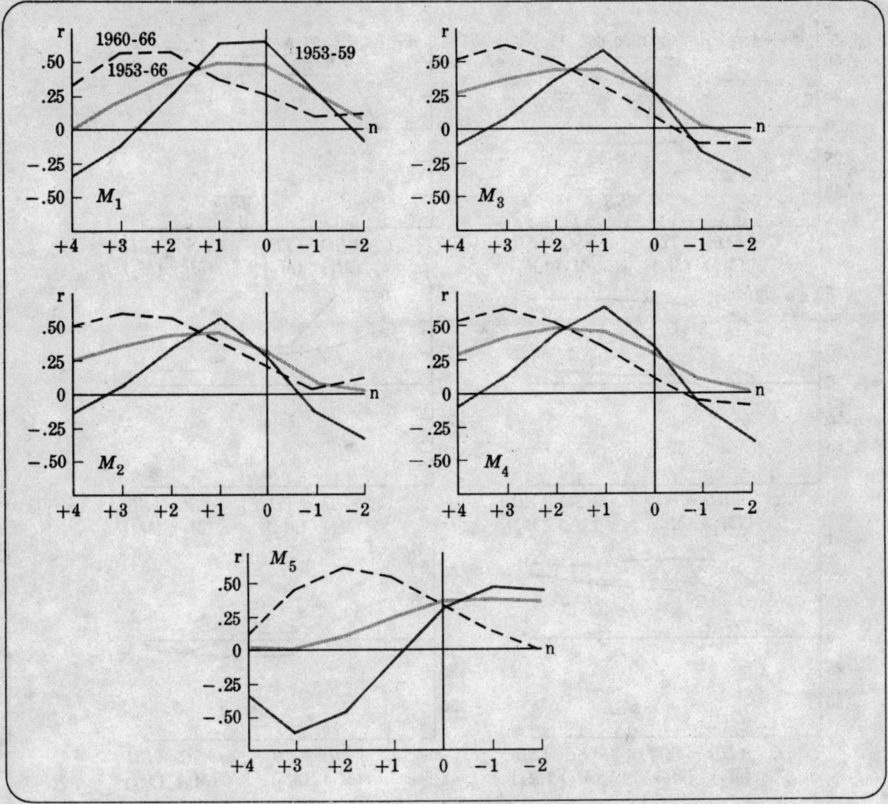


**FIGURE 2** Simple correlation coefficients between Δ GNP and Δ alternative definitions of money.

components alone—changes the "best" definition of money derived from satisfaction of only the highest correlation criterion. A survey of Tables 1 and 2 reveals that only a limited number of definitions satisfy the second criterion. (Coefficients associated with definitions for which the income correlation exceeds that of any of its parts are marked with an asterisk in Table 2.) Concurrent observations of the narrow definition of money supply best satisfy the dual criteria for the period as a whole. Second-best solutions are obtained for a number of broader definitions of money when observed two or three quarters before income. Of these, the highest correlations are obtained for definitions that include, in addition to currency and demand deposits, time deposits at commercial banks and those that also include all depository savings plus savings bonds.

These findings do not differ greatly for the two subperiods. Concurrent observations of the narrow definition of money satisfy the dual criteria best in the 1953-59 subperiod. However, this definition performs less well in the 1960-66 subperiod. In that period, concepts including a broader spectrum of financial assets yield the highest correlations. In addition, the time span by which the best-fit money observations precede income observations is longer in this period. Observations of the highest-correlation money concepts lead income by three quarters and observations of narrow money, by one quarter.

Although the narrow definition of money supply yields the best overall result, this definition satisfies both criteria less often than alternative concepts when the lead-lag relationships are considered individually.

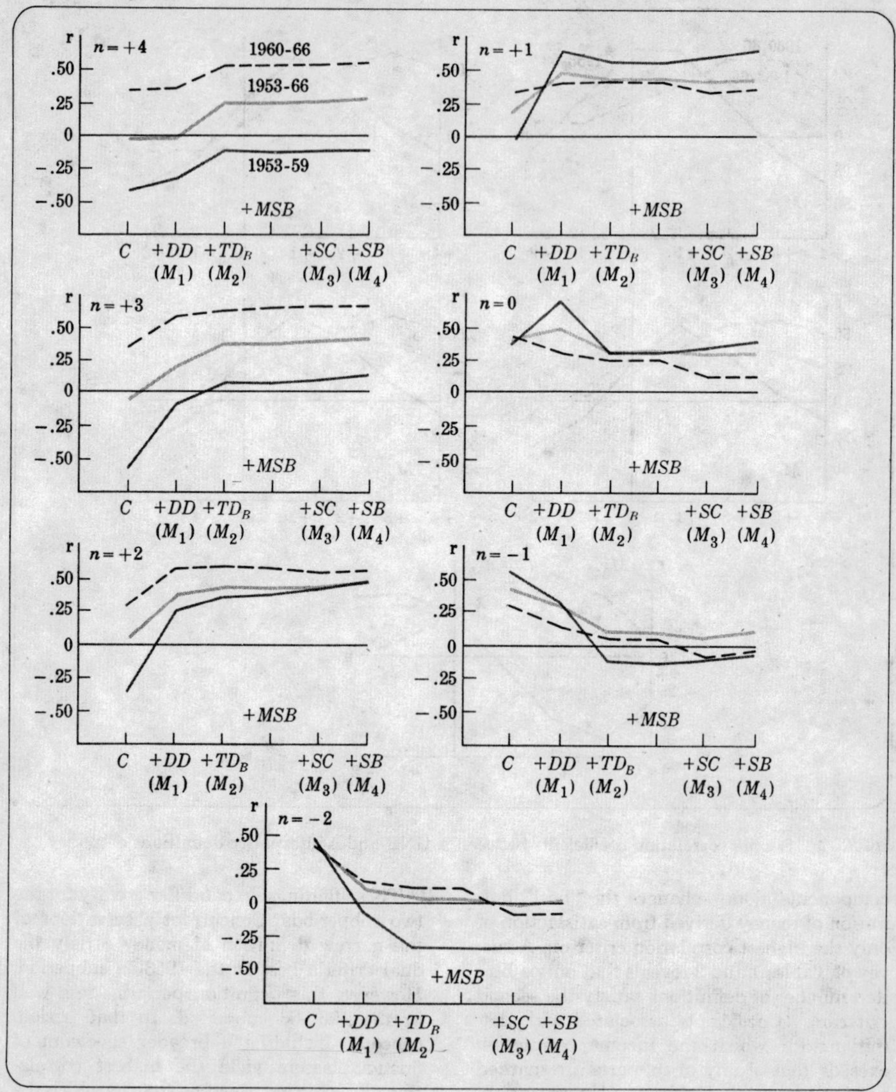


**FIGURE 3** Simple correlation coefficients between Δ GNP and Δ progressively broader concepts of money (currency specified first).

For the entire 1953-66 period, the narrow definition yields the best results only for concurrent observations and fails to satisfy the criteria for any other time relationships. The definition encompassing all depository savings and savings bonds in addition to currency and demand deposits performs best when money supply is observed either two or three quarters before income. In the 1953-59 subperiod, narrow money again satisfies the criteria for concurrent observations and a broader concept for observations preceding income by two quarters. In the 1960-66 subperiod, the narrow definition fails to satisfy the criteria in any of the lead-lag observation periods, while broader concepts satisfy the criteria in each of the periods for which their observa-

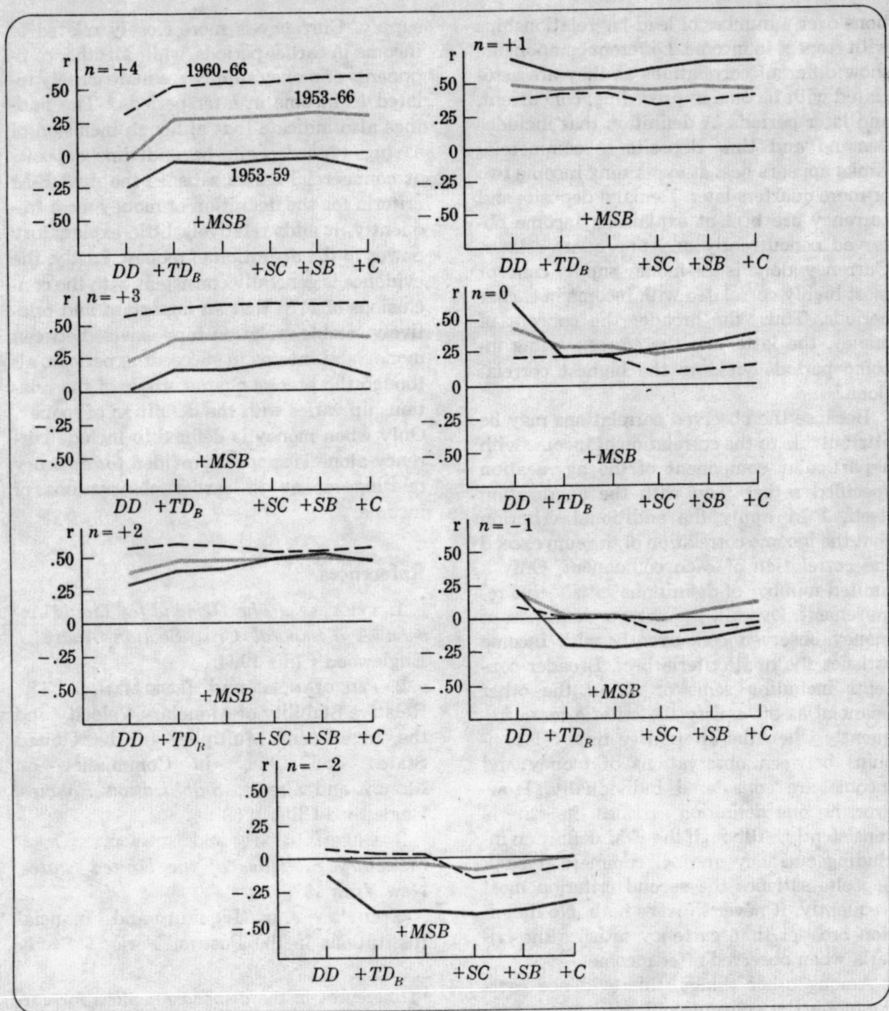


**FIGURE 4** Simple correlation coefficients between Δ GNP and Δ progressively broader concepts of money (currency specified last).

tions precede those of income. Nevertheless, no single concept consistently satisfies both criteria. At times when a number of definitions satisfy the second criterion, the broadest concept generally satisfies both criteria best even though the explanatory power of the definitions is increased only slightly by the inclusion of the additional financial assets. Thus, although the F-M definition satisfies the second criterion more often than any of the other concepts, it never satisfies both. At no time do any definitions satisfy the F-M dual criteria when they are observed after the corresponding income observation.

## Conclusions

The evidence developed in this study indicates that defining money according to the dual criteria established by F-M involves not only tests of alternative groupings of financial assets but also tests of alternative definitions over a number of lead-lag relationships with respect to income. Different components show different correlations as they are associated with income in preceding, concurrent, and later periods. A definition that includes demand and time deposits at commercial banks appears best at explaining income two or more quarters later. Demand deposits and currency are best at explaining income observed concurrently and one quarter later. Currency alone is the money supply concept most highly correlated with income in earlier periods. Thus, the broader the concept of money, the latter are the corresponding income periods yielding the highest correlations.[7]

Because the observed correlations may be attributable to the correlation of income with a particular component of the aggregation specified rather than with the aggregation itself, F-M apply the additional criterion that the income correlation of the sum exceed the correlation of each component. Only a limited number of definitions satisfy this requirement. Overall, the narrow definition of money observed concurrently with income satisfies the dual criteria best. Broader concepts including some or all of the other financial assets satisfy the criteria more frequently when the alternative time relationships between observations of money and income are considered individually. However, no one definition satisfies the criteria consistently. Although the F-M definition including currency and all commercial bank deposits satisfies the second criterion most frequently, it never satisfies both. No definition broader than currency satisfies the criteria when observed after income.

Among other things, this evidence casts doubt on the conventional wisdom of automatically including both currency and demand deposits in any definition of money supply. Currency is more closely related to income in earlier periods, while all other components of money supply are more closely related to income in later periods.[8] The findings also indicate that although inclusion of savings-type deposits beyond time deposits at commercial banks satisfies the dual F-M criteria for the definition of money most frequently, it adds relatively little explanatory power to the definition of money. Lastly, the evidence is generally consistent with the conclusions of F-M that an important and relatively stable relationship exists between money and income in succeeding periods, although the precise characteristic of the relationship varies with the definition of money. Only when money is defined to include currency alone is support provided for a theory relating money to earlier observations of income.

## References

1. FEIGE, E. L. *The Demand for Liquid Assets: A Temporal Cross-Section Analysis,* Englewood Cliffs 1964.

2. FRIEDMAN, M., and MEISELMAN, D. "The Relative Stability of Monetary Velocity and the Investment Multiplier in the United States, 1897–1958," in Commission on Money and Credit, *Stabilization Policies,* Englewood Cliffs 1963.

3. FRIEDMAN, M., and SCHWARTZ, A. J. *Monetary Statistics of the United States,* New York 1970.

4. GURLEY, J. G. "Liquidity and Financial Institutions in the Postwar Period," Study

[7] These findings are not seriously altered by estimates for the earlier pre-accord 1948–52 period. Indeed, the correlation patterns are surprisingly stable, although the correlation values tend to be lower on the whole. Of the components, demand deposits are most highly correlated with income, particularly when the two series are observed concurrently. Currency again is most highly correlated with income one quarter earlier. The various savings-type funds are most highly correlated with income substantially later, but the correlations are very low.

[8] Differences in the demand functions for currency and demand deposits have been noted before. For example, see James Tobin [9], and George G. Kaufman [5]. Some observers have suggested that currency may be a closer substitute for time deposits than demand deposits. The above analysis indicates, however, that the correlation patterns of currency and time deposits differ substantially more than between currency and demand deposits.

This finding has similar implications for combining currency and member bank reserves to form high powered money or the monetary base. Reserves alone tend to be most highly correlated with income in later periods. Moreover, while currency accounts for less than one-quarter of the narrow money supply and even less of broader concepts, it represents over one-half of the monetary base.

Paper No. 14, *Study of Employment, Growth, and Price Levels,* Joint Economic Committee, 86th Cong., 1st sess., Washington 1960.

5. KAUFMAN, G. G. *The Demand for Currency,* Board of Governors of the Federal Reserve System, Staff Economic Studies, Washington 1966.

6. MC KIM, B. T. *Income Velocity and Monetary Policies in the United States: 1951–60.* Unpublished doctoral dissertation, Univ. Iowa, 1962.

7. STROTZ, R. H. "Empirical Evidence on the Impact of Monetary Variables and Aggregate Demand," in G. Horwich, ed., *Monetary Process and Policy: A Symposium,* Homewood 1967.

8. TIMBERLAKE, R. H., JR., and FORTSON, J. "Time Deposits in the Definition of Money," *Am. Econ. Rev.,* March 1967, *57,* 190–93 [reprinted in this volume].

9. TOBIN, J. "Monetary Interpretation of History," *Am. Econ. Rev.,* June 1965, *55,* 464–85 [reprinted in this volume].

# 15 | TIME DEPOSITS IN THE DEFINITION OF MONEY*

RICHARD H. TIMBERLAKE, JR.,
AND
JAMES FORTSON
*University of Georgia*

The original study by Milton Friedman and David Meiselman (3)[1] on the competitive abilities of a stock of money and autonomous expenditures to predict money income in the United States has been subjected recently to an intensive reappraisal and review (1) (2) (4). The essence of the arguments seems to be that the accuracy of autonomous expenditures in predicting money income or consumption depends critically on the definition of autonomous expenditures chosen as a predictor. To a lesser extent this same issue can be raised about the various possible inclusions made in constructing "the" quantity of money used for testing purposes. Essentially, the question boils down to the "moneyish" influence time deposits exert on the "narrow" stock of money (currency and demand deposits).

The analysis presented below purports to develop a pragmatic answer to this question by allowing annual first differences in three diverse stocks of money to compete at predicting annual changes in money income. In order to check the results of the simple correlations, annual first differences in the narrow stock of money and annual first differences in all time deposits are then structured in the form of a multiple correlation to estimate annual changes in money income. The multiple correlation analysis also tests the data for a significant coefficient of moneyness in time deposits.

The raw data for currency, demand deposits, and time deposits may be used to construct an infinite number of money stocks. Each stock would include the first two of these items plus some percentage (weight) of all time deposits. F-M chose to include in their money stock the percentage of time deposits in commercial banks. Both expediency and logic recommended this choice. It is expedient because reliable estimates for this definitional stock of money can be obtained for a much longer time period than can be obtained for other money stocks;[2] and it is logical because of the distinct possibility that time deposits and demand deposits may be held as close substitutes for each other when they are claims against the same commercial bank. However, the case can also be made that the narrow stock of money is the only one that can be used for transactions and is, therefore, the only stock that influences spending.[3] Yet another and contrary view sees all *time* deposits generating liquidity in

* Reprinted from *The American Economic Review*, vol. 57 (March, 1967) pp. 190–194, by permission of the authors and the American Economic Association.

[1] Hereafter, references to the work of these authors is abbreviated to "F-M." [Numbers in parentheses refer to References at the end of this reading.]

[2] Reliable data for *all* deposits in commercial banks are available back to 1875, but accurate breakdowns of these data into time and demand components are available only from 1914.

[3] This argument is tantamount to assigning irrelevant monetary influence to financial assets that are not transactive.

TABLE 1. SIMPLE CORRELATIONS OF FIRST DIFFERENCES IN THREE CONCEPTUAL STOCKS OF MONEY ON FIRST DIFFERENCES IN NOMINAL MONEY INCOME, THE PER CENT OF ALL TIME AND SAVINGS DEPOSITS IN COMMERCIAL BANKS, AND COEFFICIENTS FOR A MULTIPLE REGRESSION OF FIRST DIFFERENCES IN NARROW MONEY AND TIME DEPOSITS ON FIRST DIFFERENCES IN NOMINAL MONEY INCOME

| Period annually (1) | $r_{Y \cdot M1}$ (Narrow) (2) | $r_{Y \cdot M^a2}$ (F – M) (3) | $r_{Y \cdot M3}$ (All time) (4) | Per cent all time deposits in commercial banks (average for period) (5) | $b_1$ (6) | $b_2$ (7) | $b_2/b_1$ (8) | $R_{Y \cdot M1}$ (9) | $R_{Y \cdot M1,T}$ (10) |
|---|---|---|---|---|---|---|---|---|---|
| 1897–1908 | b | .890 | .820 | b | b | b | b | b | b |
| 1903–1913 | b | .788 | .813 | b | b | b | b | b | b |
| 1908–1921 | b | .766 | .726 | b | b | b | b | b | b |
| 1913–1920 | .796 | .786 | .727 | 63 | 3.086 | –1.131 | – .3664 | .796 | .803 |
| 1920–1929 | .775 | .700 | .702 | 70 | 4.939 | –1.035 | – .2096 | .775 | .779 |
| 1921–1933 | .883 | .801 | .772 | 68 | 6.922 | –1.128 | – .1630 | .883 | .894 |
| 1929–1939 | .891 | .882 | .865 | 58 | 3.170 | .4467 | .1409 | .891 | .893 |
| 1933–1938 | .785 | .766 | .865 | 53 | 1.224 | 9.791 | 7.997 | .902[c] | .987 |
| 1938–1953 | .028 | .006 | –.145 | 63 | .3812 | –1.620 | –4.249 | –.419[c] | .471 |
| 1939–1948 | –.019 | –.009 | –.171 | 63 | .3681 | –1.660 | –4.510 | –.410[c] | .458 |
| 1948–1960 | .495 | .408 | .285 | 64 | 1.162 | – .4902 | – .3032 | .496 | .514 |
| 1953–1965 | .667 | .609 | .633 | 68 | 1.919 | .2903 | .1521 | .667 | .692 |
| 1929–1960 | .398 | .501 | .427 | 62 | .8945 | –1.146 | –1.281 | .401[c] | .504 |
| 1897–1960 | b | .573 | .517 | 54 | 1.004 | .7277 | .7251 | b | .518 |

SOURCES: Original data for $M_1$ and $T$ to 1957 were taken from: U.S. Bureau of the Census, *Historical Statistics of the United States, Colonial Times to 1957*, Washington, D. C., 1960, Series X, p. 646. Data for $M_2$ and $Y$ to 1957 were taken from (3, pp. 259–60, Table II-B). Data for the period 1953–1965 were obtained from current issues of the *Survey of Current Business* and the *Federal Reserve Bulletin*. Percentages in Column (5) were computed by the authors.

[a]Most of these values correspond to ones given by $F—M$ in (5, p. 375, Table I).

[b]Separate estimates for demand and time deposits in commercial banks before 1913 are not reliable.

[c]These values are for the correlation coefficient of *time* deposits on income. The computer kicks out only the higher of the two values in a multiple correlation (without regard to sign). To compare the simple coefficient of the narrow stock of money on income, see Column (2).

the monetary system, and thus making more efficacious the spendability of the narrow money stock. Each of these concepts is logical, and each has intuitive plausibility. The choice, however, must be made in terms of the empirical relevance shown by the various stocks in predicting money spending.[4]

The groundwork for this study required time series data of the three most relevant stocks of money: the narrow stock, $M_1$, the F-M stock, $M_2$, and the narrow stock plus all time deposits in commercial and savings banks, $M_3$. Data for money income from the spending side, $Y$, were taken from the original work by F-M and supplemented to 1965 using their definition. Annual first differences in the various money stocks were then correlated with annual first differences in money income for the reference cycle periods defined in the original F-M study.[5] The results of this series of tests are summarized in the first four columns of Table 1.

The correlation values shown here make possible some interesting inferences that are obscured when only the values for longer periods are computed. First, the correlation coefficients for all the money stocks in most of the subperiods covered show extremely high degrees of association between changes in money and changes in income. Second, while the F-M money stock, $M_2$, has the highest correlation value over the entire period, the narrow money stock, $M_1$, has higher values in more of the years than either $M_2$ or $M_3$. This seeming anomaly results from the inclusion of data from the war years (1942-46) in the tests, and the much poorer performance of $M_1$ in that period. Third, time deposits improve the correlation values only in the 1933-38 period.

The first inference—that any of the stocks of money influences spending—needs no interpretation beyond that given by F-M. Second, the irregular values for the periods embracing the war years obviously result from biases in the raw data and confirm Donald Hester's observation on the original F-M study, viz: "Indeed it is remarkable that the monetary model failed to reflect these conditions [in the 1942-46 period] more vividly" (6, p. 367).[6] The raw data associations for the various money stocks and money income do not reflect wartime discrepancies because of the dominance of trend in the series. First difference correlations do emphasize the warpings of normal spending relationships by abstracting trend. Price controls, rationing, much higher taxes, and exhortations not to spend, dammed up money in peoples' pockets or caused "under the table" spending, the effects of which could not be measured. This alteration continued to some degree through most of the Korean War. The 1953-65 correlation values indicate a gradual return to more normal relationships.

Third, the better performance of $M_3$ during 1933-38 can be attributed to two "real" factors also not measurable cardinally. First, very low interest rates on time deposits discouraged their attractiveness as investments and encouraged their use as quasi-transaction balances. Probably more important, however, was the influence of the bank debacle in the early 1930s on deposit holdings. Demand deposits lost some of their moneyness due to the additional risk imputed to them by depositors after the monetary blood-letting of 1932-33. Time deposits seemed less risky to both banks and their depositors, so the deduction reasonably can be made that moneyness was lost by demand deposits and gained by time deposits.

To test these conclusions further, and also to test for a significant monetary coefficient of time deposits, a multiple regression analysis was conceived using first differences in the narrow stock of money, $M_1$, and in all time deposits, $T$, to predict changes in money income, $Y$.[7] The form of the testing equation is:

$$\Delta Y = a + b_1 \Delta M_1 + b_2 \Delta T \qquad (1)$$

or

$$\Delta Y = a + b_1[\Delta M_1 + b_2/b_1 \Delta T] \qquad (2)$$

[4] This methodological postulate is the one adopted by F-M and not seriously challenged by anyone so far.

[5] First difference correlations for the whole period are mentioned in the original study and are computed in a later investigation by one of the authors of this paper (Timberlake, 7), but only for the whole period (1897–1960) and the two half-periods (1897–1929) and (1930–1960).

[6] F-M's effort to include *all* data in their original study is commendable, but surely they leaned too far when they included monetary and income data for 1942–46.

[7] We are indebted to Milton Friedman for suggesting this method.

If time deposits have some degree of moneyness, the ratio $(b_2/b_1)$ should be greater than zero but less than one. A value of one for this fraction would imply that time deposits had moneyness equal in degree to the items in the narrow stock of money. A negative value for $(b_2/b_1)$ implies that time deposits serve more in the nature of investments: that people actively reduce their transactions balances to "buy" time deposits.

As can be seen from Table 1, the fraction $(b_2/b_1)$ is between $-1$ and 0 except for the period 1933-38. In this period the ratio jumps up to 7.997! Furthermore, bringing time deposits into the picture as a multiple correlate to the narrow stock of money does not add significantly to the simple correlation coefficient in any of the periods except 1933-38. [See Columns (9) and (10).] But in this period first differences in time deposits are better predictors of changes in money income than are changes in the narrow money stock, and the multiple correlation coefficient becomes a whopping .987! Such dramatic results confirm the supposition that time deposits gained appreciably in moneyness due to the depreciation in confidence people had in demand deposits.

The value for $(b_2/b_1)$ then becomes large and negative for the periods that include the war years, emphasizing the efforts of people to keep purchasing power they were enjoined from spending in a form that obtained some return. Only in the last 12 years does the ratio of $(b_2/b_1)$ become a positive fraction of a magnitude that would give some credence to the theory of moneyness in time deposits, and even in this case the additional predictability gained from including time deposits in the analysis is insignificant (.667 to .692).

## References


1. ANDO, A., and MODIGLIANI, F. "The Relative Stability of Monetary Velocity and the Investment Multiplier," *Am. Econ. Rev.*, Sept. 1965, *55*, 693–728.

2. DEPRANO, M., and MAYER, T. "Tests of the Relative Importance of Autonomous Expenditures and Money," *Am. Econ. Rev.*, Sept. 1965, *55*, 729–52.

3. FRIEDMAN, M., and MEISELMAN, D. "The Relative Stability of Monetary Velocity and the Investment Multiplier in The United States, 1897–1958," Commission on Money and Credit, *Stabilization Policies*, Englewood Cliffs 1963, pp. 165–268.

4. ——— ———. "Reply to Ando and Modigliani and to DePrano and Mayer," *Am. Econ. Rev.*, Sept. 1965, *55*, 753–85.

5. ——— ———. "Reply to Donald Hester," *Rev. Econ. Stat.*, Dec. 1964, *46*, 369–76.

6. HESTER, D. "Keynes and the Quantity Theory. A Comment on the Friedman Meiselman CMC Paper," *Rev. Econ. Stat.*, *46*, Dec. 1964, 364–68.

7. TIMBERLAKE, R., JR. "The Stock of Money and Money Substitutes," *So. Econ. Jour.*, Jan. 1964, *30*, 253–60.

# 16 ON MEASURING THE NEARNESS OF NEAR-MONEYS*

V. KARUPPAN CHETTY
*Columbia University*

Monetary economists have long been concerned about the substitutability of the liabilities of various financial institutions for money. Knowledge of the degree of substitutability of such liquid assets for money is essential for many reasons. For example, if these assets are close substitutes for money, then the financial intermediaries can, in principle, reduce the effectiveness of any given monetary action. This is, in fact, the position taken by Gurley and Shaw (11) (12) (13) (14). They argue that the monetary authorities did not succeed in reducing the liquidity in the economy during the postwar period due to the rapid growth of liabilities of financial intermediaries. There has been some theoretical discussion about the relevance of Gurley and Shaw's arguments, but as pointed out by Johnson (16) and Cagan (5), in a slightly different context, this issue cannot be resolved by theoretical arguments. In order to determine whether consumers regard the various liquid assets as substitutes for money or not, one has to look at their market behavior. The question is essentially an empirical one.

Recently, Feige (9), Hamburger (15), and Lee (20) attempted to test empirically the validity of Gurley and Shaw's hypothesis. Not surprisingly, these econometric studies are not in agreement about the substitutability of liquid assets for money. Feige (9), using temporal cross-section data of liquid asset holdings by states in the United States for the period 1949-59, found that the yields on nonbank intermediary liabilities did not affect the demand for money, defined as demand deposits plus currency. Hence he concluded that these assets are not substitutes for money. Lee (20), using Feige's and other types of data, concluded that savings and loan association shares are much better substitutes for money than time deposits. Hamburger (15), using U.S. time series data, found that the predictive power of the demand function for money did not increase significantly when the definition of money was expanded to include other liquid assets. For reasons given in the next section, the methods used by Feige (9) and Lee (20) are better than that of Hamburger (15).

In order to determine whether the public regards various liquid assets as substitutes for money, one has to determine empirically the shape of consumers' indifference curves for money and other liquid assets. In the present paper, a utility function which generates a variety of indifference curves is used to estimate directly the elasticity of substitution between money and other liquid assets. In the past, monetary economists attempted to test substitutability hypotheses by estimating the various (cross) interest elasticities of demand for money. In this paper, the various elasticities of substitution are used to test the same hypothesis. In theory, one would expect the two methods to lead to the

---

* Reprinted from *The American Economic Review,* vol. 59 (June, 1969), pp. 270–281, by permission of the author and the American Economic Association.

NOTE: Numbers in parentheses refer to References at the end of this reading.

same conclusion. However, the empirical results of our paper differ to a great extent from the findings of others and seem to be more reasonable in terms of our a priori expectations.

Furthermore, knowledge of these elasticities of substitution will be useful in answering many other questions in monetary economics. For instance, suppose one finds, as Lee (20) does, that some liquid assets are substitutes for money. In what ways can a monetary theorist, interested in controlling the liquidity of the economy, use these findings for policy purposes? If, for example, the supply of these liquid assets increases, other things being equal, their prices will fall. Using the demand function for money, the monetary theorist will determine the amount by which the demand for money will go down and recommend an appropriate policy measure for reducing the quantity of money. Thus policy action is taken only after the effect of the increases in other liquid assets shows up in the yields of these assets, which, of course, takes some time. On the other hand, using the elasticity of substitution approach one can immediately find the money equivalent of the change in other liquid assets and determine the amount by which the money supply should be reduced to maintain the same level of liquidity in the economy. This will avoid some delay in taking appropriate monetary measures which is certainly desirable, since many economists in the past have argued that there is considerable lag between the time a policy measure is taken and the time its effect is realized.

Another related problem, which has attracted the attention of monetary economists for many years, is the definition of money. The commonly used definition classifies demand deposits and currency as money. Friedman and Meiselman (10) and Cagan (5) define money as demand deposits, currency, and time deposits in commercial banks. One of the reasons for inclusion of time deposits is that they can not be meaningfully separated from demand deposits until the 1930's. Friedman and Meiselman also argue that "they are such close substitutes for other monetary items that it is preferable to treat them as if they were *perfect substitutes* than to omit them."

In reality, the various liquid assets may not be regarded as perfect substitutes for money nor can they be treated as completely unrelated to money. Hence the all-or-nothing approach in defining money does not seem to be very useful. Gurley (11), in this context, points out, "If the degree of substitutability between each type of monetary asset and money were known, liquid assets could be weighted in such a way that the constancy of this weighted amount would imply constant interest rates, other things the same." For illustrative purposes, Gurley used a definition which assigned weights of one to currency and demand deposits and weights of one-half to other liquid assets. It has been pointed out by several writers that the "best" set of weights can be derived using canonical correlation techniques or the method of principal components. This will give the "best" definition of money in some statistical sense, like maximum correlation or maximum variance, but it is difficult to give economic interpretation to these weights. Instead, in this paper, we suggest a method of aggregating the liquid assets, using the elasticities of substitution and other economically meaningful parameters.

Another related and controversial issue in monetary theory is concerned with the choice of the appropriate interest rate or rates to explain the demand for money. Some economists, such as Eisner (8) and Latane (19) maintain, following the Keynesian tradition of relating income and investment to long rates, that the relevant rate is that on long-term bonds. Bronfenbrenner and Mayer (4), Laidler (17), and a few others advocate the use of short-term interest rates, since this reflects the opportunity cost of holding money. Gurley and Shaw (11) (12) (13) (14), naturally, argue for their candidate, the yield on nonbank intermediary liabilities. Lee (20) has recently presented empirical evidence for the superiority of the yield on saving and loan association shares over others but his conclusions are questionable for reasons pointed out in the sections that follow. Christ (6) and Lee (20) have used the relative quantities of these assets to form a weighted average of the various interest rates.

Regarding the choice of the interest rate, Turvey (22) remarked, "Their relative importance depends upon the relative substitutability of long-term and short-term paper assets for money and upon their relative quantities. The former is unknown (hence all the argument), while the latter is measurable. . . ." Since the elasticities of substitution of various assets for money are estimated in the present paper, they are used to construct an index of interest rates as suggested by Turvey (22). Since the demand for money in theory is a function of a number of highly correlated interest rates, it seems appropriate to use economically meaningful weights to come up with an average, rather than trying to choose *the* interest rate using some statistical criterion, like standard errors.

The plan of the paper is as follows. In Section I, the method of estimating the various elasticities of substitution, aggregation of the liquid assets, and construction of the interest rate index are discussed when assets are taken two at a time. Empirical estimates are presented for U.S. time series data for the period 1945-66. A more general method to handle all the assets simultaneously and the empirical results are presented in Section II. A new series based on the new definition of money and an index of interest rates are computed, and a velocity series based on the new definition of money is calculated and compared with other velocity series. Concluding remarks are made in Section III.

## I. A Model for Estimating the Elasticity of Substitution

Throughout this paper, the term money ($M$) will be used to denote hand-to-hand currency plus demand deposits in commercial banks. To start with, it is assumed that there is one other financial asset, namely time deposits ($T$). Following the new approach to consumer demand theory, as developed by Becker (3) and Lancaster (18), let us assume that the consumer combines money and time deposits to produce various characteristics like liquidity, store of value, etc. We assume that the consumer combines $M$ and $T$ such that, for any given budget, he maximizes his satisfaction. The possibility of substituting $T$ for $M$ arises for two reasons: (1) $M$ and $T$ may have some common characteristics; (2) even if they have no characteristics in common, there may be substitution between different characteristics. The indifference curves between $M$ and $T$ may assume various possible shapes ranging from straight lines, in the case of perfect substitutes, to right angle curves, when they are consumed in fixed proportions. The degree of curvature of these indifference curves is a measure of substitutability of money and time deposits. To answer this question, we need a utility function, which generates a variety of indifference curves with different degrees of substitution and whose parameters can be estimated with the use of observed variables like quantities and prices. One such function which generates a variety of indifference curves, but has only few parameters, is the constant elasticity of substitution production function introduced by Arrow, *et al.* (2). The CES function was introduced to study the degree of substitution between capital and labor, but we can make use of this function to study the substitutability of money and other financial assets. The utility function of the consumer can be written as

$$U = (\beta_1 M^{-\rho} + \beta_2 T^{-\rho})^{-(1/\rho)}$$

where $M$ and $T$ represent money holdings and money value of time deposits in the next period, respectively. Since this is a fairly general function, it can be assumed that it will provide an adequate approximation to the true utility function. Since only ordinal utility is used, $\beta_1$ can be assumed to be equal to 1 without loss of generality. This normalization is adopted throughout this paper. The implications of this normalization for the aggregation procedure are discussed later.

Suppose the consumer has cash holdings of $M_0$ dollars and wants to allocate them between $M$ and $T$. If $T$ represents the cash value of time deposits in the *next* period and if $i$ is the rate of interest on time deposits of the current period, then the budget constraint of the consumer can be written as

$$M_0 = M + \frac{T}{1+i} \tag{1}$$

The slope of the budget line is $-(1+i)$. Hence $(1+i)$ can be considered as the ratio of the prices of money to time deposits.[1]

[1] Alternatively, one can assume that the consumer maximizes $U[T(1+i), M]$, subject to the constraint $M+T=M_0$, where $T$ now represents the amount of time deposits in the *current* period. In both cases, the marginal conditions are the same. Also if one assumes that the consumer maximizes $U(Ti, M)$ subject to $M+T=M_0$, one obtains very similar results empirically, since the form of $U$ is quite general.

When the utility function is maximized subject to the budget constraint (1), the following marginal conditions are obtained:

$$\frac{\partial U}{\partial M} = \lambda \tag{2}$$

$$\frac{\partial U}{\partial T} = \lambda/(1+i) \tag{3}$$

$$M_0 = M + \frac{T}{(1+i)} \tag{4}$$

where $\lambda$ is the Lagrange multiplier. Dividing (2) by (3) we have

$$\frac{\beta_1}{\beta_2}\left(\frac{M}{T}\right)^{-\rho-1} = 1+i$$

Taking logarithms on both sides, rearranging terms, and adding a disturbance term, we have the regression model

$$\log\frac{M}{T} = -\frac{1}{1+\rho}\log\frac{\beta_2}{\beta_1} + \frac{1}{1+\rho}\log\frac{1}{1+i} + e \tag{5}$$

Using data relating to $M$, $T$, and $i$, and making the usual assumptions about the disturbance term, we can estimate $1/1+\rho$ and the intercept term using least squares methods. From the intercept term, an estimate of $\beta_2/\beta_1$ can be obtained, and using a normalization rule $\beta_1$ and $\beta_2$ can then be estimated. The elasticity of substitution between money and time deposits is given by $\sigma=1/1+\rho$. Thus whether any particular financial asset is a substitute or not can be directly tested using this regression.

This model has some similarities to the one used by Christ (6), since he regressed ratios of various stocks on interest rates and income, but his regression equations were not derived from any specific model like the one set out in this paper.

In our model,[2] the ratio of prices of $M$ and $T$ is $1+i$. There are alternative ways of specifying the price of holding a dollar of $M$ or $T$. If one takes the alternative cost approach, the price of holding a dollar of $M$ will be the alternative income forgone. If, for example, the interest rate on corporate bonds, $i_\beta$, represents the alternative income, then the price ratio of $T$ and $M$ is given by $(i_\beta-i_T)/i_\beta=1-i_T/i_\beta$, where $i_T$ is the interest rate on time deposits. If this price ratio is used in equation (5) this would imply that $M/T$ will not change for a given percentage change in both $i_T$ and $i_\beta$. This does not seem reasonable.

The empirically determined indifference curves can now be used to aggregate money and time deposits. The aggregation procedure is illustrated in Figure 1. For a given set of $M_1$ and $T_1$, we find the indifference curve that passes through that point. This is the maximum satisfaction that can be produced with this combination. From the same figure, we also find that the same satisfaction

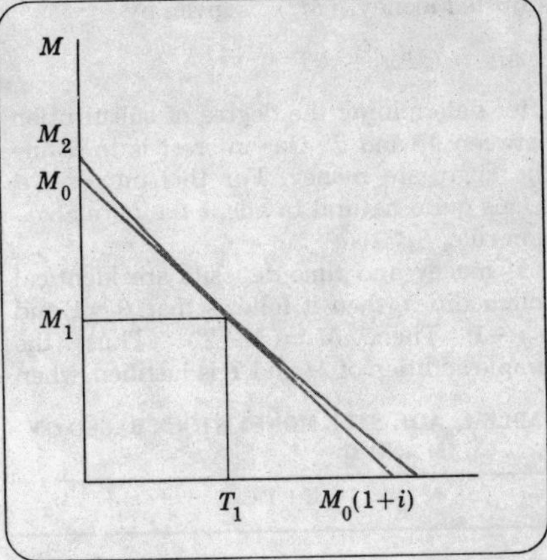


**FIGURE 1** Indifference curve betwen $M$ and $T$.

[2] Milton Friedman, in a personal communication, pointed out to me that the price ratio has units of time in it and hence the estimated elasticity substitution will depend on the arbitrary choice of the time unit. To get around this difficulty, we should maximize the utility function subject to one more constraint on the flow of income from these assets. Where we have three or more assets, this can be done. If $\mu$ is the lagrangean multiplier for the new constraint, then the regressions will be of the form $\log M/T=a+b\log(1+\mu i/\lambda)$. $\mu i$ is now independent of the units of time. Here $T$ is the amount of time deposits in the current period. Since $\mu/\lambda$ is the same for all regressions, $b$ will be affected in the same manner in all regressions when $i$ is small. Hence we can still run the same regression. Discussions with Gary Becker on this point have been very useful.

can be produced by using $M_2$ units of money alone. Hence adding $T_1$ units of time deposits to $M_1$ is equivalent to adding $(M_2 - M_1)$ units of money to $M_1$. Determination of such an $M_2$ is possible whenever the indifference curves intersect or are tangent to the $M$-axis. This measure of aggregate liquid assets *is exactly* the normalized utility function with $\beta_1=1$.

Friedman and Meiselman (10), in this context, point out that one should find out the moneyness of other liquid assets and use that to give an extended definition of money. Our aggregation procedure is along the same lines. In order to use this procedure, one need not determine completely the indifference curve that passes through a given $M$ or $T$. Instead, if we assume that $\beta_1=1$, then the adjusted money, $(M_a)$, is given by

$$M_a = (M^{-\rho} + \beta_2 T^{-\rho})^{-1/\rho}$$

after determining the degree of substitution between $M$ and $T$. Our interest is to define the aggregate money. For this purpose, it seems quite natural to adopt the normalization rule, $\beta_1=1$.

If money and time deposits are identical commodities, then it follows that $\beta_2=1$ and $\rho=-1$. Then, $M_a=(M+T)$. Thus, the simple addition of $M$ and $T$ is justified, when $M$ and $T$ are identical. Of course, we do not have to make use of a CES function to reach this obvious conclusion. The fact, however, that the aggregation procedure reduces to a reasonable method under simple conditions increases our confidence in the procedure.

**TABLE 1. ADJUSTED MONEY STOCK BASED ON M AND T**

| $M$ | $M+T$ | $M_a$ |
|---|---|---|
| 102.3 | 132.4 | 133.5 |
| 110.0 | 143.8 | 145.0 |
| 113.6 | 148.8 | 150.1 |
| 111.6 | 147.4 | 148.6 |
| 111.2 | 147.3 | 148.5 |
| 117.7 | 154.0 | 155.3 |
| 124.5 | 162.0 | 163.8 |
| 129.0 | 169.7 | 171.2 |
| 130.5 | 174.2 | 175.8 |
| 134.4 | 181.2 | 182.9 |
| 138.2 | 186.6 | 188.4 |
| 139.7 | 190.3 | 192.4 |
| 138.6 | 194.7 | 196.9 |
| 144.2 | 207.4 | 209.8 |
| 145.6 | 212.2 | 214.8 |
| 144.7 | 216.8 | 219.7 |
| 149.4 | 212.2 | 214.4 |
| 151.6 | 248.3 | 252.1 |
| 157.3 | 268.3 | 272.6 |
| 164.0 | 289.2 | 294.0 |
| 172.0 | 317.2 | 322.8 |
| 175.8 | 335.4 | 341.9 |

The methods discussed above were used to estimate the elasticity of substitution between money and commercial bank time deposits using time series data for the United States for the period 1945-66.[3]

$$\log M/T = 1.510 + \underset{(1.569)}{34.69} \log 1/(1+i)$$

$$R^2 = .981$$
$$D.W. = .57$$

The elasticity of substitution between money and time deposits is significantly different from zero at the 5 percent level and considerably large. Hence we can treat $M$ and $T$ as very good substitutes for each other. Since there is evidence of auto-correlation among the disturbances, the standard error has been corrected using Wold's (24) method. When the logarithm of the current income is used as an additional explanatory variable, it turned out to be insignificant at the conventional levels. This is in agreement with our theoretical formulation, since our utility function implies that $M/T$ will not depend on $M_0$ or income for given $i$. The implied estimate of $\beta_2$ is found to be

$$\beta_2 = \exp(-1.510/34.69) = .957.$$

The adjusted stock of money is given by

$$M_a = (M^{.971} + .957T^{.971})^{1.03}$$

An indifference curve between $M$ and $T$ is shown in Figure 1. This looks almost like a straight line, supporting Friedman's hypothesis that $M$ and $T$ are perfect substitutes.

The series relating to $M$, $M+T$, and $M_a$ are shown in Table 1. It can be seen from columns (2) and (3) that there is not much difference between $M+T$ and $M_a$. Hence if we are interested in including $T$, we can simply add $T$ to $M$.

[3] The money stock and time deposits in commercial banks are from various issues of the *Federal Reserve Bulletin* (*FRB*). Interest rates on time deposits are from Cagan (5) for 1945–60 and from various issues of the *FRB* for 1961–66. Current income figures are from various issues of *Survey of Current Business*.

Similar regressions were run to estimate the elasticities of substitution between money and the liabilities of savings and loan association ($SL$) and deposits in mutual savings banks ($MS$) for the period 1945-66.[4] The estimated equations are

$$\log M/SL = \underset{}{4.612} + \underset{(8.900)}{101.851} \log 1/(1 + i_{SL})$$
$$\bar{R}^2 = .946, \quad D.W. = .510$$
$$\log M/MS = 2.297 + \underset{(1.354)}{27.637} \log 1/(1 + i_{MS})$$
$$\bar{R}^2 = .980, \quad D.W. = .829$$

$i_{SL}$ and $i_{MS}$ are yields on $SL$ and $MS$ respectively. The elasticity of substitution between $M$ and $SL$ is 101.851, the highest among the three assets. These findings strongly support Gurley and Shaw's (14) hypothesis and the findings of Lee (20) that savings and loan association shares are good substitutes for money. Hence we join Lee (20) in rejecting the conclusion of Feige (9) and Hamburger (15). Feige, in fact, found that savings and loan shares are likely to be complementary to money.

Lee also found that, in the presence of the yield on nonbank intermediary liabilities, the yields on other assets, like time deposits, turn out to be statistically insignificant explanatory variables in the demand function for money. Hence this implies that time deposits are not substitutes for money while savings and loan association shares are. This conclusion is somewhat questionable because the yields on various assets are highly correlated and hence the standard errors become unreliable. So one cannot conclude on the basis of "$t$" values which asset is a substitute and which is not.[5] Also Hamburger (15) reports that inclusion of other financial assets in $M$ does not increase the $R^2$, but sometimes decreases it. But this is small wonder because the variance of $(M+T)$ is different from the variance of $M$. Since the dependent variables are different in the two regressions, $R^2$ can not be reliably used as a basis of comparison.

A weakness in our approach in estimating the degree of substitution is that we consider only one asset, in addition to $M$, at a time. The movements of $M/T$ may reflect a shift between $M$ and $T$ or between one of them and other financial assets. Hence our estimates of the coefficients are likely to be biased. To remove this difficulty, we have to introduce all the assets simultaneously in our model and estimate the parameters. This is done in the next section. Briefly the results are: (1) The elasticity of substitution between $T$ and $M$ remains the same as before. (2) The substitutability of savings and loan association shares becomes somewhat weaker than before, but still they remain substitutes for money. (3) Deposits in mutual savings banks are also substitutes for money.

## II. Some Extensions of the Model

We now assume that there are more than two financial assets. Let the utility function be

$$U = f(X_1, X_2, X_3 \cdots X_n),$$

where $X_1, X_2, \cdots, X_n$ are the various assets. We must now specify the form of the utility function. The purpose of our study will be defeated if we use the CES function for $n$ inputs as generalized by Uzawa (23), since the partial elasticity of substitution between any two inputs is the same. The generalized CES function of Mukerjee (21) and Dhrymes and Kurz (7) does not assume that the partial elasticities are the same. Hence we assume that the utility function is given by equation (8). We assume that the budget constraint is given by equation (9) where $Y$ is income and the $r$'s are the yields on the various assets.

If the utility function is maximized subject to equation (9), we have the following first order conditions.

$$\frac{\partial U}{\partial M} - \lambda = 0 \tag{10}$$

$$\frac{\partial U}{\partial X_j} - \lambda/(1 + r_j) = 0 \quad (j = 1, 2, \cdots, n) \tag{11}$$

where $\lambda$ is a Lagrangian multiplier.

[4] Savings and loan association shares and time deposits in mutual savings banks and their yields are from the *Savings and Loan Fact Book*, 1967.

[5] Lee has used the differentials between yields on liquid assets and the yield on money in his regressions to avoid the problem of collinearity. Michael J. Hamburger told me that when he recomputed the regressions after introducing the yield on money explicitly, instead of using the differentials, the interest elasticities for $SL$ go down considerably.

The parameters of the utility function can be estimated using these conditions along the lines suggested by Dhrymes and Kurz (7). Dividing equation (10) by (11) and manipulating as before, we have equation (12). If we substitute (12) in (9), we get an implicit relation between the interest rates, $M$, and $Y$. This relation can now be solved for $M$. Let the explicit relation between $M$, interest rates, and $Y$ be given by

$$M = f(r_1, r_2, \cdots, r_n, Y)$$

Assuming log $M$ has a valid Taylor series

$$U = (\beta M^{-\rho} + \beta_1 X_1^{-\rho_1} + \beta_2 X_2^{-\rho_2} \cdots + \beta_n X_n^{-\rho_n})^{-1/\rho} \quad (8)$$

$$M_0 = f(Y, r_1, r_2, \cdots, r_n) = M + \frac{X_1}{1+r_1} + \frac{X_2}{1+r_2} + \frac{X_n}{1+r_n} \quad (9)$$

$$\log X_i = \frac{-1}{\rho_i + 1} \log \frac{\beta\rho}{\beta_i\rho_i} - \frac{1}{\rho_i+1} \log \frac{1}{1+r_i} + \frac{\rho+1}{\rho_i+1} \log M \quad (12)$$

$$\log M = a_0 + \sum_{j=1}^{n} a_j \log (1+r_j) + a_{n+1} \log Y \quad (13)$$

expansion in terms of log $r_j$ and log $Y$, we can write this expansion as equation (13).

When the disturbance terms are introduced in equations (12) and (13), the parameters of the system can be estimated using two-stage least squares. First, log $M$ is estimated as a function of $Y$ and the $r_j$'s, which are assumed to be exogenous. The estimate of log $M$ is then inserted in (12) and each equation is estimated individually. The estimates obtained in the second stage are consistent and can be used to determine the implied estimates of the parameters of the production function. Also the asymptotic variances of these estimates can be calculated using standard methods of large sample distribution theory.[6] These estimates can then be used to calculate the partial elasticity of substitution between $M$ and other assets defined as:

$$\sigma_{M,X_i} = \frac{d \log (M/X_i)}{d \log \left(\frac{\partial U/\partial M}{\partial U/\partial X_i}\right)} = \frac{1}{(1+\rho) + (\rho_i - \rho) \Big/ \left[1 + \frac{\beta_i \rho_i X_i^{-\rho_i}}{\beta\rho M^{-\rho}}\right]} \quad (14)$$

This is the Hicks-Allen (1) direct partial elasticity of substitution.

Here income and interest rates may not be strictly exogenous variables[7] and hence the two-stage least squares may not be consistent for equation (12). Thus the ordinary least squares may be no worse than the two-stage least squares as far as the inconsistency is concerned. Using the least squares method, one can simply estimate (12) and omit equation (13) and the Taylor series approximation altogether. Both the methods were tried in estimating the regression. Since the estimates of the parameters were almost identical, only the ordinary least squares estimates are given below.

The estimated regression equations for time deposits, savings and loan association shares, and mutual savings bank deposits are given in equation (15), where $P_j = 1/(1+r_j)$.

$$\begin{aligned} \log T &= .118 - \underset{(2.69)}{40.384} \log P_T + \underset{(.19)}{.649} \log M & R^2 &= .991, & D.W. &= .87 \\ \log SL &= -15.398 - \underset{(10.25)}{52.346} \log P_{SL} + \underset{(.49)}{3.517} \log M & R^2 &= .983, & D.W. &= .49 \quad (15) \\ \log MS &= -3.517 - \underset{(3.32)}{24.105} \log P_{MS} + \underset{(.197)}{1.217} \log M & R^2 &= .992, & D.W. &= .84 \end{aligned}$$

$$M_a = [M^{.954} + 1.020T^{.975} + .880MS^{.959} + .615SL^{.981}]^{1.026} \quad (16)$$

[6] Dhrymes and Kurz (7) suggest a method of constructing the confidence interval for $\rho_i$, given the confidence interval for $1/(\rho_i - 1)$. This is incorrect because if $1/(\rho_i - 1)$ has a "$t$" distribution, the moments of $\rho_i$ will not in general exist for finite samples. Hence only asymptotic variance can be used. Also in this case, the distribution of $1/(\rho_i - 1)$, a two-stage least squares estimate, is not known for finite samples.

[7] This was pointed out to me by a referee.

TABLE 2. ADJUSTED MONEY STOCK BASED ON $M$, $T$, $SL$ AND $MS$.

| | $M_a$ | $M_a'$ | $V_1 = Y/M$ | $V_2 = Y/M+T$ | $V_3 = Y/M_a$ | $i$ (percent) |
|---|---|---|---|---|---|---|
| 1945 | 144.75 | 150.42 | 2.09 | 1.61 | 1.47 | 1.56 |
| 1946 | 157.67 | 163.81 | 1.92 | 1.47 | 1.33 | 1.48 |
| 1947 | 164.16 | 170.49 | 2.06 | 1.57 | 1.42 | 1.48 |
| 1948 | 164.38 | 170.36 | 2.32 | 1.76 | 1.57 | 1.53 |
| 1949 | 160.20 | 171.97 | 2.32 | 1.75 | 1.55 | 1.59 |
| 1950 | 173.91 | 180.21 | 2.42 | 1.85 | 1.63 | 1.66 |
| 1951 | 183.96 | 190.69 | 2.64 | 2.03 | 1.78 | 1.74 |
| 1952 | 194.69 | 201.40 | 2.69 | 2.04 | 1.78 | 1.94 |
| 1953 | 203.33 | 209.69 | 2.80 | 2.10 | 1.79 | 2.03 |
| 1954 | 215.01 | 221.22 | 2.70 | 2.00 | 1.68 | 2.13 |
| 1955 | 225.02 | 231.16 | 2.88 | 2.13 | 1.68 | 2.19 |
| 1956 | 233.78 | 239.52 | 3.00 | 2.20 | 1.78 | 2.36 |
| 1957 | 243.53 | 248.36 | 3.18 | 2.26 | 1.80 | 2.67 |
| 1958 | 262.37 | 266.84 | 3.07 | 2.13 | 1.68 | 2.76 |
| 1959 | 272.71 | 276.58 | 3.32 | 2.27 | 1.76 | 2.96 |
| 1960 | 284.23 | 286.94 | 3.47 | 2.31 | 1.76 | 3.20 |
| 1961 | 306.57 | 308.51 | 3.47 | 2.24 | 1.68 | 3.32 |
| 1962 | 333.52 | 333.97 | 3.76 | 2.26 | 1.67 | 3.62 |
| 1963 | 364.39 | 363.70 | 3.73 | 2.28 | 1.60 | 3.76 |
| 1964 | 396.45 | 394.81 | 3.86 | 2.19 | 1.58 | 3.85 |
| 1965 | 433.73 | 431.15 | 3.98 | 2.16 | 1.56 | 4.00 |
| 1966 | 457.43 | 453.85 | 4.23 | 2.22 | 1.60 | 4.34 |
| Mean velocity | | | $\overline{V}_1$=2.99 | $\overline{V}_2$=2.03 | $\overline{V}_3$=1.65 | |
| Coefficient of Variation | | | 21.77 | 12.1 | 7.6 | |

The partial elasticities of substitution between $M$ and other assets at their mean values are calculated using (14). We have the following results:

$$\sigma_{M,T} = 30.864$$
$$\sigma_{M,SL} = 35.461$$
$$\sigma_{M,MS} = 23.310$$

The partial elasticities of substitution, $\sigma_{MT}$ and $\sigma_{M},M_S$ are similar to those obtained in the previous section. The partial elasticity of substitution between $M$ and $SL$ is 35.461, compared to 101.851 obtained before. Our second estimate of $\sigma_{M,SL}$=35.461 seems more reasonable than 101.851, since the former is close to $\sigma_{M,T}$ and $\sigma_{M,MS}$. Also it is free from the bias due to the single equation approach mentioned earlier. There is no reason why $\sigma_{M,SL}$ alone should be considerably different from those of other financial assets. Also in view of the larger standard errors associated with the regression equation relating to $SL$, one cannot conclude that the liabilities of savings and loan association are the best substitutes for money. The conclusion that can be drawn from these regressions is that $T$, $SL$, and $MS$ are all good substitutes for money. Thus, we have provided empirical evidence for Gurley and Shaw's hypothesis.

Also the utility function in equation (8) can be used to determine the adjusted money stock as before. The adjusted stock of money in this case is given by equation (16). It is interesting to observe that all the exponents are very close to one. Also the coefficient of time deposits is approximately 1, which again supports Friedman's definition. Approximately we can write $M$ as

$$M_a' = M + T + .880MS + .615SL$$

On the basis of the coefficients of various assets we can probably rank the assets in the decreasing order of closeness to money as follows: $T$, $MS$, and $SL$. Thus our conclusions are different from those of Lee (20).

It is comforting to find that the weights for $T$, $MS$, and $SL$ are in the range (0,1). Since the estimates are derived from a least squares regression with the unrestricted coefficients, the results are really amazing. We believe it is only fair to remark that it is not a very common event in econometrics to find the estimated coefficients within the relevant range. The weight for $T$ is slightly greater than 1; but in view of the standard error of the coefficients of the regression relating to $T$ and $M$, this is not bad. Also, if $T$ is almost as good as money, as Friedman and others suspect, we would even expect the weight to be slightly greater than 1, since it yields a positive rate of return.

Since we have estimates of substitution and other parameters, we can define an index of interest rates. The exponents in the equation for $M_a$ are very close to 1, and we will just use the marginal rates of substitution between $M$ and other assets, namely 1, .88, and .615. Hence the interest rate index is given by

$$i_a = (i_T + .88i_a + .615i_{SL}) \div (1 + .88 + .615)$$

The adjusted money stock series $M_a$ and $M'_a$, the interest index, $i_a$, and velocities based on various definitions of money are given in Table 2. It can be seen that there is not much difference between $M_a$ and $M'_a$. The correlation coefficient between $M_a$ and $M+T$ is .999. This does not mean that one definition is as good as the other for all purposes. The mean and standard deviation of $M+T$ are 202.67 and 57.73, respectively, while the mean and standard deviation of $M_a$, are respectively, 253.72 and 93.07. There is considerable difference between the standard deviations. Hence for purposes of controlling or explaining money supply or demand, the two series will have different implications. But if one is using money stock to predict some other variable, say national income, then $M+T$ is as good as $M'_a$, or for that matter as $M$.

Also it can be seen from Table 2 that velocity based on $M'_a$ is virtually a constant, while the other velocities vary to a considerable extent. The coefficient of variation is about one-third of that based on the traditional definition of money and about one-half of that based on Friedman's definition of money. Thus, as Gurley and Shaw and others have argued, we can attribute the postwar rise in velocity (based on the traditional definition of money) to the increased availability of money substitutes.

## III. Summary

In this paper, some methods of estimating the degree of substitution between money and other financial assets are set out and used to test the substitution hypothesis of Gurley and Shaw using U.S. time series data for the period 1945-66. Also a method of aggregating the various liquid assets and interest rates using the elasticities of substitution and other economically meaningful parameters is presented. The empirical findings of this paper are: (1) Time deposits and savings and loan association shares are also very good substitutes for money and can be ranked in decreasing or order of closeness to money as follows: $T$, $MS$, and $SL$. (2) Our empirical results lead to the following definition of money:

$$M'_a = M + T + .880MS + .615SL$$

(3) Velocity, based on the new definition of money, has been virtually a constant since 1951.

## References

1. ALLEN, R. G. D., and HICKS, J. R. "A Reconsideration of the Theory of Value, II," *Economica*, May 1934, *1*, 196–219.

2. ARROW, K. J., CHENERY, H. B., MINHAS, B. S., and SOLOW, R. M. "Capital-Labor Substitution and Economic Efficiency," *Rev. Econ. Stat.*, Aug. 1961, *63*, 225–50.

3. BECKER, G. S. "A Theory of the Allocation of Time," *Econ. Jour.*, Sept. 1965, *75*, 493–517.

4. BRONFENBRENNER, M., and MAYER, T. "Liquidity Functions in the American Economy," *Econometrica*, Oct. 1960, *28*, 810–34.

5. CAGAN, P. *Determinants and Effects of Changes in the Stock of Money, 1875–1960*, New York, 1965.

6. CHRIST, C. F. "Interest Rates and Portfolio Selection among Liquid Assets in the U.S., *Measurement in Economics: Studies in Mathematical Economics and Econometrics in Memory of Yehuda Grunfeld*, Stanford 1963.

7. DHRYMES, P. J., and KURZ, M. "Technology and Scale in Electricity Generation," *Econometrica*, July 1964, *32*, 287–315.

8. EISNER, R. "Another Look at Liquidity Preference," *Econometrica*, July 1963, *31*, 531–38.

9. FEIGE, E. L. *The Demand for Liquid Assets: A Temporal Cross-Section Analysis*. Englewood Cliffs 1964.

10. FRIEDMAN, M., and MEISELMAN, D. "The Relative Stability of Monetary Velocity and the Investment Multiplier in the United States, 1897–1958," in Commission on Money and Credit, *Stabilization Policies*, Englewood Cliffs 1963.

11. GURLEY, J. G. "Liquidity and Financial Institutions in the Postwar Economy," U.S. Congress, Joint Economic Committee, *Study of Employment, Growth and Price Levels*, Study paper No. 14, Jan. 1960.

12. GURLEY, J. G., and SHAW, E. S. "Financial Aspects of Economic Development," *Am. Econ. Rev.*, Sept. 1955, *45*, 515–38.

13. ———. "Financial Intermediaries and the Saving-Investment Process," *Jour. Fin.*, May 1956, *11*, 257–76.

14. ———. *Money in a Theory of Finance*. Washington, D.C. 1960.

15. HAMBURGER, M. J. "The Demand for Money by Households, Money Substitutes, and Monetary Policy," *Jour. Pol. Econ.*, Dec. 1966, *74*, 600–23.

16. JOHNSON, H. G. "Monetary Theory and Policy," *Am. Econ. Rev.*, June 1962, *52*, 335–84.

17. LAIDLER, D. "Some Evidence on the Demand for Money—Some Empirical Evidence," *Jour. Pol. Econ.*, Dec. 1966, *74*, 543–55.

18. LANCASTER, K. J. "A New Approach to Consumer Theory," *Jour. Pol. Econ.*, April 1966, *74*, 132–57.

19. LATANE, H. A. "Cash Balances and the Interest Rate—A Pragmatic Approach," *Rev. Econ. Stat.*, Nov. 1954, *36*, 456–60.

20. LEE, T. H. "Alternative Interest Rates and the Demand for Money: The Empirical Evidence," *Am. Econ. Rev.*, Dec. 1967, *57*, 1168–81.

21. MUKERJEE, V. "A Generalized S.M. A.C. Function with Constant Ratios of Elasticity of Substitution," *Rev. Econ. Stud.*, Oct. 1963, *30*, 233–36.

22. TURVEY, R. "On the Demand for Money," *Econometrica*, April 1965, *33*, 459–60.

23. UZAWA, H. "Production Functions with Constant Elasticities of Substitution," *Rev. Econ. Stud.*, Oct. 1962, 291–99.

24. WOLD, H. *Demand Analysis*. New York 1953.

# 17 | BIOLOGICAL ANALOGIES FOR MONEY: A CRUCIAL BREAKTHROUGH*

ALFRED MARTIAL†
*Unemployed*

During the seventeenth century, economists of the Mercantilist School gained insight into the functioning of the aggregate economy by exploring evident similarities between the *Body Politic* and the *Body Natural.* However, in the wake of Adam Smith's refutation of the Mercantilist position, this method has fallen into almost total disuse. One might say that the Body was thrown out with the Bathwater. Increasingly, mathematized physical analogies have replaced biological ones, until today Rostow's vision of the developing economy as passing through the life cycle of a bird stands as the only instance of a biological analogy that has achieved contemporary success.

This dissertation seeks phoenix-like to resuscitate the time-honored method of biological analogy by settling once and for all what constitutes the proper biological analogue for money. As Milton Friedman and Robert Keale ("Love doth much, but money doth all," 1615) both hold, money plays a critical role in the determination of the level of economic activity. It follows that, until someone solves the conundrum of money's biological analogue, biological models of the aggregate economy will lack proper focus.

The problem is approached in two ways. First, we examine the various analogues proposed by seventeenth-century theorists. It could be that in the profession's rush to physical (mathematical) models a valid prior solution has been overlooked.[1] Then, we focus on the essential functions and attributes of money to determine precisely what Bodily Organ, Principle, or Substance performs parallel functions in the Body Natural.

Our review of the literature reveals no fully satisfactory solutions, but does uncover five near-misses:

*1. Money is fat.*
Money is but the Fat of the Body-Politick, whereof too much doth as often hinder its Agility, as too little makes it sick. 'Tis true that as Fat lubricates the motion of the Muscles, feeds in want of Victuals, fills up uneven Cavities, and beautifies the Body, so doth Money in the State quicken its Action, feeds from abroad in the time of Dearth at Home; even accounts by reason of its divisibility, and beautifies the whole, altho more especially the particular persons that have it in plenty. (William Petty, 1665.)

*2. Money is spirit.*
Money is the *vitall spirit of trade* and if the spirits faile, needs must the Body faint. (Edward Misselden, 1622.)

* Abstract of a dissertation completed at the Neoplastic Institute of Technology in 1968. Reprinted from *The Journal of Finance,* vol. 24 (March, 1969) pp. 111–112, by permission of the author and the American Finance Association.

† By painstaking research we have discovered that Dr. Martial is in reality Edward J. Kane (Boston College), who acknowledges the generous assistance of Michael Rothschild of Harvard University and of a number of other friends and colleagues.

[1] Although this is not a particularly promising hypothesis, a dissertation must review the literature in any case.

*3. Money is blood.*

[Money is] . . . as useful in the Body Politick as Blood in the Veins of the Body Natural, dispersing itself and giving Life and Motion to every Part thereof. (Samuel Lamb, 1659.)

*4. Money is muck.*

Money is like Muck, not good except it be spread. (Thomas Manley, 1625.)

*5. Money is Muscle (specifically, the "sinews of war").*

. . . War is become rather an expense of money than men, and success attends those that can most and longest spend money: whence it is that princes' armies in Europe are become more proportionable to their purses than to the number of their people. (James Whiston, 1693.)

These analogies stress the role of money in economic circulation, but they ignore certain of its other important attributes. In particular, none of these analogies are consistent with the fact (proved for the first time in this thesis) that national currencies show a statistically significant tendency to be *green.*

On the other hand, recognizing this fact (and ignoring the almost equally significant incidence of red monies[2] virtually solves our problem. *Money must be Bile.*[3] This is a substance of the proper color and one which plays a critical role in the production of Fat, Muscle and Muck, as well as in the circulation of the Blood. Moreover, when Bile ceases to flow, the Spirit must "faile."

While identifying money with Bile is only the first step on a long analogical-analytical road, its implications are decidedly anti-Keynesian. Whereas Keynes (in the last sentence of his *Essays in Persuasion*) views economists as dentists, we hold that economists do the work of internists: an insight that may well touch off a Martiallian Revolution.

---

[2] We reject the hypothesis that money is red because of that color's recessive (in the Mendelian sense) connotations: (1) not all money is "hot"; (2) not all money is injected via expenditure deficits; and (3) monetary theory assumes free-world institutions.

[3] This finding has important policy implications. First, close reading of the literature on international monetary reform indicates that the overriding obstacle to agreement on an international reserve currency has been the selection of an appropriately persuasive acronym. Our work suggests that units of this currency should be termed Basic International Liquidity Effusions (*Base Internationale Liquide d'Effusions*).

Second, the central bank rather than being an inflationary engine is now seen to be the liver of the economy, so that instead of speaking of an *overheated* economy macroeconomists should use the more precise term *choleric.*

# III FEDERAL RESERVE CONTROL OF THE MONEY STOCK

The two previous parts of this volume considered whether and how money and monetary policy affect economic activity and the appropriate definition of money. Part III discusses the Federal Reserve's ability to control the stock of money. The importance of this ability depends crucially upon the effects of money (however defined) on economic activity. If money has an insignificant or unpredictable impact, there would be little justification for controlling money. The monetary authorities would be well advised to direct their attentions to other more important financial variables such as interest rates. If, however, money is considered to have a significant and predictable impact, then policy control of the money supply is important. In brief, problems concerning the importance of money on economic activity relate primarily to the specification and stability of the demand function for money. Problems concerning the control of money relate primarily to the specification and stability of the supply function for money.

Many writers have assumed that the Federal Reserve could exercise effective control over the money stock and have generated theories and policy recommendations on this basis. Others have argued that such control is not sufficiently complete to permit reliance on the money stock as the intermediate target of monetary policy. Members of this latter group in turn include writers of many different approaches. One group views money stock determination as a part of a simultaneous solution for all variables in the financial sector. That is, the Federal Reserve changes the tools under its control—such as bank reserves, the discount rate, reserve requirements, etc.—and these actions affect the rates and volumes in all financial markets simultaneously, not simply in the market for money. Thus the resulting money stock depends not only upon the Federal Reserve's actions but also upon the responses in other asset markets and is not subject to close Federal Reserve control. This tends to be the process envisioned by proponents of the "New View."[1] To them a Federal Reserve policy action is only one of a number of important factors affecting the stock of money. These writers also argue, however, that even if the Federal Reserve could control the money stock, this control would not by itself permit adequate stabilization policy because money may not have a strong and predictable effect on real variables. Another group considers the money stock to be importantly influenced not only by other financial markets but also by the real sector. That is, while money tends

[1] See Donald Hester and James Tobin (eds.), *Financial Markets and Economic Activity,* Cowles Foundation Monograph 21, New York, John Wiley and Sons, 1967.

to influence real variables, these real variables are themselves changing, and they exert strong contemporaneous effects on the money stock itself. For this analysis, all variables are endogenous except those specifically under the Federal Reserve control. Consequently, this group also doubts the Federal Reserve's ability to control the money stock.

Those who dispute the Federal Reserve's ability to closely control the money stock—due to the effects of either financial or financial and real variables on money—argue against use of the money stock as the intermediate target of monetary policy. Rather they favor conducting policy by affecting those variables or tools over which the Federal Reserve has total control, such as member bank reserves, high-powered money, the discount rate, reserve requirements, or Federal Reserve securities holdings, rather than by affecting the money stock.

All economists tend to agree that given enough time there will be influences in both directions between money and income. That is, monetarists do not deny that the financial and real sectors influence the money stock. The issue then between the monetarists and nonmonetarists is essentially empirical: How important are the forces affecting the money stock which cannot be directly controlled by the Federal Reserve, and how stable and predictable are the behavior patterns of the public and the banking system?

The relationship between banks' reserves and the supply of money is fundamental to Federal Reserve control of the money supply through the reciprocal of the reserve requirement ratio. However, many non-policy variables affect the dollar volume of reserves. For example, while the Federal Reserve can affect the dollar volume of reserves by buying and selling Treasury securities, it has no control over other variables that also affect the volume of reserves, such as gold flows, float, and Treasury balances at Federal Reserve Banks. At the same time both currency and time deposits, whether or not included in the definition of money, absorb different amounts of reserves than an equal dollar volume of demand deposits and thus affect the reserve-money multiplier. Similar variations in the multiplier result from changes in excess reserves and Treasury deposits at commercial banks.

The ability of the Federal Reserve to control the stock of money effectively depends on its ability to predict changes in the variables not subject to its immediate control, that is, on the stability of the functions explaining the behavior of these non-controlled variables. The greater the predictability, the greater is Federal Reserve control of the money supply.

The selections in part III reflect differing views on the desirability of Federal Reserve control of the money stock and the ability of the Federal Reserve to do so. Holmes, who as manager of the Federal Open Market Desk has day-to-day responsibility for trading activity, argues that there is insufficient knowledge of the factors affecting both reserves and the reserve-money multiplier in the short run to achieve close day-to-day control of the money supply. Moreover, even if such knowledge were available, it might be undesirable to attempt day-to-day control. Inherent "lumpiness" through time in the demand for loanable funds produces abrupt and undesirable movements in short-term interest rates that should be offset. This lumpiness in the demand for funds is believed to result from large and abrupt temporary shifts in the uses of funds, e.g., the floating of a new security issue by the U.S. Treasury or a large corporation. Holmes' views are shared by Maisel, a member of the Board of Governors of the Federal Reserve System, who expands on the operational difficulties of controlling the money stock and emphasizes the magnitude of the forces outside Federal Reserve control. Accommodation of many of these forces is considered a legitimate and desirable activity of the central bank. Jordan identifies the variables affecting the reserve-money multiplier and discusses the implications of changes in these variables. Although he does not empirically test for stability of the multipliers, the results of such tests are reported by Brunner in his selection in part I. Building on the work of Tobin,[2] the leading proponent of the New View, Gramley and Chase construct a model stressing the close substitutability among financial assets and

---

[2] James Tobin, "Commercial Banks as Creators of 'Money,'" in Deane Carson (ed.) *Banking and Monetary Studies*, Homewood, Ill., Richard D. Irwin, Inc., 1963, pp. 408–419.

derive negative implications for Federal Reserve control of the money stock. They argue that actions by the central bank have a broad impact on all financial assets, not only money, narrowly defined. The existence of close money substitutes loosens the link between monetary policy actions and the money stock. In their framework, the nominal money stock is almost entirely determined by the desires of the public rather than the central bank. Thus, the money stock is a poor guide for central bank actions. Fand develops a framework for testing alternative hypotheses of the supply of money. His preliminary findings indicate that all the functions examined are reasonably stable with respect to a limited number of arguments. Thus, contrary to Gramley and Chase, Fand believes that the presence of other financial assets does not loosen the linkage between central bank actions and the narrowly defined money stock.

# 18 OPERATIONAL CONSTRAINTS ON THE STABILIZATION OF MONEY SUPPLY GROWTH*

ALAN R. HOLMES
*Federal Reserve Bank of New York*

The debate over whether the Federal Reserve should rely exclusively on the money stock—somehow defined—as an indicator or a target of monetary policy, or both, continues unabated. While the debate has shed some light on the role of money in monetary policy and the role of monetary policy in the overall mix of policies that affect the real economy, there has been perhaps as much heat as light. And the light that is being generated from the many research studies that have stemmed from the debate is very often dim indeed.

This paper does not attempt to contribute to the controversy. Instead it tries to sketch out briefly current practices of the FOMC in establishing guidelines for the conduct of open market operations—guidelines that involve a blend of interest rates and monetary aggregates. It then turns to the operational constraints and problems that would be involved if the Federal Reserve were to rely exclusively on the money supply as the guideline for day-to-day operations.

The approach taken in the paper is essentially practical rather than theoretical. The views expressed should be taken as those of the author, and not as representative of the Federal Reserve System. It will probably not come as much of a surprise, however, that the conclusions find much in favor of current FOMC practices and procedures.

## Current FOMC Practices

The Federal Reserve has frequently been accused of money market myopia. This is a false charge usually made by economists affected in some degree by a peculiar myopia of their own. The charge stems, or so it seems to me, in the first instance from a confusion between monetary policy decisions *per se* and the operational instructions given by the FOMC for the day-to-day conduct of open market operations.

The Federal Reserve has always maintained that money matters just as it believes that interest rates matter too, particularly given the institutional framework of our financial system In reaching policy decisions, the Committee not only pays attention to the real economy—to current and prospective developments in employment, prices, GNP and the balance of payments—but it also considers a broad range of interest rates and monetary measures. Among the monetary measures, there are the various reserve measures—total reserves, nonborrowed reserves, excess reserves, and free or net borrowed reserves. Next are the measures of money ranging from $M_1$ on out. Finally, there are the credit measures, bank credit, the credit proxy—ranging on out to total credit in the economy and the flow of funds.

Is the Federal Reserve wrong in its eclectic approach? Is it wrong to consider a broad

* Reprinted from *Controlling Monetary Aggregates,* Boston, Federal Reserve Bank of Boston, 1969, pp. 63–77, by permission of the author and the Federal Reserve Bank of Boston.

range of interest rates and aggregates and to reach a judgment as to the combination of rates and aggregates (and the resultant impact of that mix on market psychology and the expectations of consumers, savers, and investors) that is compatible with desirable movements in the real economy and the balance of payments? Should it instead adopt a single aggregate variable—the money supply—and devote its entire attention to stabilizing that variable no matter what happens to other aggregates or to interest rates?

Despite the empirical claims of the monetary school, there appears to be little conclusive evidence to support their case that such a course of action would give the desired overall economic results. Both the St. Louis equations and correlation analysis at the Federal Reserve Bank of New York, for example, give slightly better marks to bank credit than to money supply. Moreover, the analyses suggest that significantly different results can be attained by relatively small changes in the time period covered.

While I do not believe that research results to date justify adopting an operating policy designed solely to stabilize the monetary growth rate, I nevertheless believe that the research efforts stimulated by the monetary school have a real value. Out of it all, there is bound to develop a better understanding of the relationships between monetary aggregates, interest rates, and the real economy. I suspect, however, that the underlying relationships are so complex that no simple formula can be found as an unerring guide to monetary policy. The psychology and expectations involved in private decision making are probably too complicated to compress into any such simple formula.

Thus, I think, the FOMC is right in paying attention to a broad range of reserve, money, and credit aggregates; in trying to understand why they are behaving as they are; and in assessing the implications of their past and prospective behavior for employment, prices, and GNP. Further, I think the Federal Reserve is right in not restricting itself to a single theory of money, and in choosing the best from a number of theories.

In reaching a policy decision, the Committee pays close attention to a wide spectrum of interest rates, ranging from the Federal funds rate, through the short and intermediate term rates, out to rates in the long-term capital markets. One obvious problem with interest rates as either an indicator or target of monetary policy is that they may be measuring not only the available supply of money and credit but also the demand for money and credit. Obviously, a policy aimed at stabilizing interest rates in the face of rising demand will give rise to greater increases in the monetary aggregates than would be the case if demand were stable. Interest rates can also be misleading indicators of underlying conditions at times of special short-lived supply and demand relationships—of some fiscal policy development or of prospects for war or peace in Vietnam, to take some recent examples. But interest rates have the decided advantage of being instantaneously available, and they can often be excellent indicators that estimates of monetary aggregates, particularly reserve estimates, are wrong. The judicious use of interest rates as correctors of poor aggregative forecasting should not be underestimated.

Thus, when the FOMC reaches a policy decision, it is not thinking exclusively in terms of rates or of monetary aggregates, but of a combination of the two. A move towards a tighter policy would normally involve a decline in the rate of growth of the aggregates and an increase in rates. And a move towards an easier policy would normally involve an increase in aggregate growth rates and a decline in interest rates.

But, unfortunately, given the nature of our commercial banking system, money and credit flows cannot be turned off and on instantaneously. At any given point in time, banks have on their books a large volume of firm commitments to lend money. Also, potential borrowers may, if they surmise that the Federal Reserve is tightening policy, decide *en masse* to take down loans in anticipation of future needs. Hence there may be, for a time, an undeterred growth in bank credit and the money supply. But this, in turn, should involve a more rapid and larger rise in interest rates than would otherwise have been the case. The point is that the Federal Reserve is always making a trade-off between aggregates and rates. It has, and takes, the opportunity at its FOMC meetings every three or four weeks to assess what has developed, what the impact has been on the real economy and on private expectations of the future, and to determine whether another turn of the screw—towards tightness or ease—is called for.

The moral of the story, if there is one, is that Federal Reserve policy should not be judged exclusively in terms of interest rates or in terms of monetary aggregates but by the combination of the two—and by the resultant impact of this combination on market psychology and expectations about the future and, ultimately, on the real economy. The weights placed on aggregates and rates, including those placed on individual components of either group, can and do vary from time to time. It is important to recognize that there is nothing in the present framework of Federal Reserve policymaking, or policy implementation, that would prevent placing still greater weight on aggregates if that should be considered desirable. I think it is obvious that aggregate measures of money and credit are getting their full share of attention at the present time.

Rates and aggregates, along with real economic developments and prospects, are the basic ingredients of any FOMC policy decision. They are also involved in the instructions that the FOMC gives to the Federal Reserve Bank of New York for the day-to-day conduct of operations in the interval between Committee meetings. Obviously, it would make little sense for the Committee to issue directives to the Desk in terms of the real economy with which it is basically concerned. Not only are open market operations in the very short run unlikely to have a major impact on the real economy, but adequate measures of economic change are unavailable in the short time span involved.

Thus the Committee, in its instructions to the Manager, focuses on a set of money market conditions—a blend of interest rates and rates of growth of various reserve and credit measures—the Committee believes is compatible with its longer run goals. At each FOMC meeting, the Committee has before it staff estimates of ranges for the Federal funds rate, the Treasury bill rate, bank borrowings from the Federal Reserve, and net borrowed reserves that the Staff believes compatible with an overall policy of no change, or of greater tightness or ease, as the case may be. Additionally, the Staff prepares estimates of the money supply and the bank credit proxy that it believes likely to correspond to a given set of money market conditions. Needless to say, these forecasting techniques fall short of being an exact science, but their existence tends to focus attention on the vital interrelationships between interest rates and aggregates that will ensue from any policy decision.

As is well known, since the spring of 1966 the Open Market Committee has usually included in the directive a proviso clause with an explicit reference to one aggregate measure—the bank credit proxy—with specific instructions to modify open market operations if the proxy is tending to move outside a predicted or desired range. Thus the Committee expects to see money market conditions moving to the tighter end of the scale if the proxy is expanding too rapidly, or towards the easier end of the scale if the proxy is falling short.

How does this all work out in practice? First of all, the money and capital markets send out a constant stream of signals of interest rate developments that we can and do measure from day-to-day and hour-to-hour. If there are deviations from past patterns or levels (or from anticipated patterns or levels) of interest rates, we can usually find out a good deal about the source and meaning of the deviations.

Second, we have forecasts of the factors affecting bank reserves apart from open market operations—estimates of float, currency in circulation, gold and foreign exchange operations, and the level of Treasury balances at the Federal Reserve. These factors can and do supply or absorb hundreds of millions in bank reserves from day-to-day or week-to-week. The estimates are made at the Board and at the New York bank for the current statement week and for three weeks ahead, and they are revised daily on the basis of the inflow of reserve information available within the System each day.

Third, we have available an estimate once a week (on Friday) of the bank credit proxy and of the money supply for the current month; and, as we get towards the middle of the month, for the next month as well. And this estimate can be revised—at least informally—by the middle of a calendar week, after there has been time to analyze weekend deposit performance at Reserve City banks and a weekly sample of deposit data at country banks. We can then use these aggregate data—available less frequently and with a greater time lag than interest rate or reserve data—to modify subsequent open market operations with an impact on interest rates and the reserve supply.

I should add that we are fairly cautious about over-interpreting any short-run wriggle in the credit proxy. While forecasts of the proxy have generally proved to be more stable than money supply forecasts—perhaps mainly because the proxy avoids the large and erratic shifts between Treasury deposits in commercial banks and private demand deposits—they, too, have proved to be somewhat undependable on a week-to-week basis. Thus we have felt it desirable—particularly early in the month when firm data are scant—to wait for some confirmation of any suggested movement of the proxy before beginning to shade operations towards somewhat greater firmness or ease.

Nevertheless, the proxy has been a useful adjunct to the directive, modifying reserve and rate objectives on a number of occasions and tending to flag aggregate problems for the Committee's attention at subsequent FOMC meetings.

It should, of course, be noted that, at times like the present, when Regulation Q ceilings are pressing hard on bank CD positions, the credit proxy loses much of its value as a continuous series. It does not, however, necessarily lose its value as a short-run guide—provided that it is understood that much lower growth rates may be required to allow for the shift of intermediate credit away from the commercial banking system. Despite all the talk about disintermediation and intermediation, we need to know much more about the process and its implications for monetary policy. The problem is that commercial banks are at the same time creators of money and credit and intermediaries between savers and borrowers in competition with other nonbank financial institutions. Worthwhile research remains to be done in this area, particularly in light of the dramatic changes that are occurring in our financial institutions.

In summary, there are four main points that I would like to draw from this abbreviated review of monetary policy formulation and implementation. First, monetary policymakers have always paid close attention to monetary aggregates—along with interest rates—in the formulation of policy decisions. It has been the interaction of the two on the real economy—on employment, prices, the GNP, and the balance of payments—that has been the focus of concern. Reluctance to adopt money supply as the sole guide to policy decisions has not stemmed from lack of concern about money but from the lack of evidence that the adoption of such a guide would give the desired results. Empirical research to date does not supply that evidence.

Second, it is incorrect to characterize monetary policy in terms of money supply alone. A rise in money supply—outside some specified range—does not necessarily mean easy money nor a decline of tight money. Policy has to be judged by a combined pattern of interest rates and monetary aggregates—and money supply is only one of those aggregates.

Third, since the spring of 1966 the FOMC has included an aggregate measure—the bank credit proxy—in its directive covering day-to-day open market operations. While use of the aggregates to shape interest rates and reserve measures has probably not been as aggressive as the monetarists would like to see (and, besides, it is the wrong aggregate according to some of them), it has been a useful adjunct to the directive.

Fourth, information on the performance of monetary aggregates (e.g., credit proxy and money supply) is available only with a time lag, and week-to-week forecasts of monthly data have tended to be erratic. This suggests that, in the short run, interest rate movements may provide a very useful indication of forecasting errors. It further suggests that aggregates can contribute more to the process of policy formulation—when there are opportunities to take a long-range view—than to the process of policy implementation as exemplified by the second paragraph of the directive. But current procedures for both policy formulation and policy implementation provide room for as much attention to monetary aggregates as may be required, and it is apparent that the aggregates are receiving a full measure of attention at the present time.

## Operational Problems in Stabilizing Money Supply

In the absence of a concrete proposal, there are major difficulties in attempting to isolate the operational problems that would be involved in stabilizing the monetary growth rate to some targeted level. Much would depend on the definition of the money supply used, the time span over which the growth rate was to be stabilized, and whether the money supply was to be the sole indicator and/or target of monetary policy or mainly a primary indicator or target.

It obviously makes a great deal of difference whether the proposal is for a rigid monetary rule or whether there is room—and how much—for discretion. Some of the proposals for moving to the money supply as a target and indicator have been coupled with the complete abandonment of so-called "defensive" open market operations—a suggestion that raises a host of other problems that are not relevant to the main point at issue.

There is, of course, a strong temptation to pick and choose among the various suggestions, and to erect a money supply target as a "straw man" that can be readily demolished. I shall try to resist that temptation and consider in more general terms the operational problems that would be involved if the FOMC were to move to money supply as the principal indicator of policy or target for open market operations.

But before setting straw men aside, it might be worthwhile to consider the proposition that open market operations should be limited to the injection of a fixed amount of reserves at regular intervals—say $20 million a week. So-called defensive operations—the offsetting of net reserve supply or absorption through movements in float, currency in circulation, gold or foreign exchange operations, etc.—would be abandoned, leaving the banking system to make its own adjustments to these outside movements. While such a system would certainly reduce the level of operations at the Trading Desk, it has never been quite clear how the banking system would make the adjustments to the huge ebb and flow of reserves stemming from movements in the so-called market factors. Either banks would have to operate with excess reserves amounting to many billion dollars at periods of maximum reserve supply by market factors, or they would have to have practically unlimited access to the discount window. Neither possibility seems very desirable, if one is really interested in maintaining a steady growth rate in some monetary aggregate.

There is no reason to suppose that banks would, in fact, hold idle excess reserves in the amounts required. At times of reserve supply by market factors, attempts to dispose of excesses through the Federal funds market would drive the Federal funds rate down and generally lower dealer borrowing costs and the interest rate level. At other times, the reverse would happen. As a result, there would be either feast or famine in the money market, inducing changes in bank loan and investment behavior that would make it impossible to achieve the steady growth of financial aggregates that was presumably desired to begin with. The resultant uncertainty would undermine the ability of the money and capital markets to underwrite and to provide a means of cash and liquidity adjustment among individuals and firms.

The opening of the discount window, on the other hand, runs the risk that reserves acquired at the initiative of the commercial banks would be used to expand the total supply of money and credit and not solely to meet the ebb and flow of reserves through movement of market factors. As a result, the Federal Reserve would have to institute the same controls—in a decentralized fashion—at the various discount windows to limit the supply of reserves that are now provided in a more impersonal way through open market operations.

Consequently, it would appear wise to disassociate the debate over money supply from the problem of so-called defensive open market operations. There seems to be no reason why a seasonal movement of currency, a random movement of float, or a temporary bulge in Federal Reserve foreign currency holdings should automatically be allowed to affect the money market or bank reserve positions. There would seem to be no point in consciously reducing our efficient and integrated money and capital markets to the status of a primitive market where the central bank lacks the means and/or the ability to prevent sharp fluctuations in the availability of reserves—in the misguided attempt to hold "steady" the central bank's provision of reserves.

But the point remains that the ebb and flow of reserves through market factors is very large. While defensive operations are generally successful in smoothing out the impact of these movements on reserves, even a 3 percent margin of error in judging these movements would exceed a $20 million reserve injection in many weeks. Hence the small, regular injection of reserves, week by week, is not really a very practical approach.

The idea of a regular injection of reserves—in some approaches at least—also suffers from a naive assumption that the banking system only expands loans after the System (or market factors) have put reserves in the banking system. In the real world, banks extend credit, creating deposits in the process, and look for the reserves later. The question then becomes one of whether and how the Federal Reserve will accommodate the demand for reserves. In the very short run, the Federal Reserve has little or no choice about accommodating that demand; over time, its influence can obviously be felt.

In any given statement week, the reserves required to be maintained by the banking system are predetermined by the level of deposits existing two weeks earlier. Since excess reserves in the banking system normally run at frictional levels—exceptions relate mainly to carryover excess or deficit positions reached in the previous week or errors by banks in managing their reserve positions—the level of total reserves in any given statement week is also pretty well determined in advance. Since banks have to meet their reserve requirements each week (after allowance for carryover privileges), and since they can do nothing within that week to affect required reserves, that total amount of reserves has to be available to the banking system.

The Federal Reserve does have discretion as to how the banks can acquire this predetermined level of needed reserves. The reserves can be supplied from the combination of open market operations and the movement of other reserve factors, or they can come from member bank borrowing at the discount window. In this context, it might be noted that the suggestion that open market operations should be used in the short run to prevent a rise in total reserves through member bank borrowing is completely illogical. Within a statement week, the reserves have to be there; and, in one way or another, the Federal Reserve will have to accommodate the need for them.

This does not mean that the way that reserves are supplied makes no difference, nor that aggregate indicators cannot be used to influence the decision as to whether reserves will be supplied through open market operations or whether banks will be required to use the discount window. A decision to provide less reserves through open market operations in any given week, thereby forcing banks to borrow more at the window, could be triggered by a prior FOMC decision (based partly on a review of aggregate money and credit measures) to move to tighter money market conditions, or it might be occasioned by the implementation of the proviso clause if the bank credit proxy was exhibiting a tendency to expand more rapidly than the Committee deemed to be warranted.

No individual bank, of course, has unlimited access to the discount window. Borrowing from the Federal Reserve involves the use of adjustment credit that is limited in both amount and in frequency of use. Eventually, as the aggregate level of borrowing is built up, the discount officers' disciplinary counseling of individual banks that have made excessive use of the window will force the banks to make the necessary asset adjustments. Other banks, desirous of maintaining their access to the discount window intact for use in their own emergency situations, will try to avoid use of the window by bidding up for Federal funds or by making other adjustments in their reserve positions. In the process, interest rates, spreading out from the Federal funds rate, will have been on the rise. As pressure on the banks is maintained or intensified, the banking system as a whole is forced to adjust its lending and investment policies with corresponding effects on money and credit—and eventually on the real economy.

A switch to money supply as the target of monetary policy would, of course, make no difference in the process through which open market operations work on the banking system to affect monetary aggregates. But, depending on the time span over which it was desired to stabilize the rate of monetary growth and on whether money were to become the exclusive indicator and/or target, there would be a significant difference in the rate of interest rate variations. How great that variation might be would be a matter of concern for the Federal Reserve in the conduct of open market operations. I would like to return to that subject in just a few minutes.

First, however, it may be worthwhile to touch on the extensively debated subject whether the Federal Reserve, if it wanted to, could control the rate of money supply growth. In my view, this lies well within the power of the Federal Reserve to accomplish provided one does not require hair-splitting precision and is thinking in terms of a time span long enough to avoid the erratic, and largely meaningless, movements of money supply over short periods.

This does not mean that the money supply could be used efficiently as a target for day-to-day operations. Given the facts that adequate money supply data are not available without a time lag and that there may be more statistical noise in daily or weekly figures than evidence of trend, we would be forced to rely on our monthly estimates for guidance in conducting day-to-day operations. Projections of money supply—and other monetary aggregates—are, of course, an important ingredient of monetary policy-making. While I believe we have made considerable progress in perfecting techniques, forecasting is far from an exact science. Money supply forecasting is especially hazardous because of the noise in the daily data and because of the massive movements in and out of Treasury Tax and Loan accounts at commercial banks.

Let me illustrate the sort of problem that might be faced by citing some numbers representing successive weekly forecasts of annual rates of money supply growth for a recent month—admittedly not a good month for our projectors. The projections cited begin with the one made in the last week of the preceding month and end with the projection made in the last week of the then current month. The numbers are: −0.5 percent, +4 percent, +9 percent, +14 percent, +7 percent and +4.5 percent. I might also note that, in the middle of that then-current month, the projections for the following month were for a 14 percent rate of growth. By the end of the month, the projection was −2.5 percent.

Assuming that the Desk had been assigned a target of a 5 percent growth rate for money supply, it seems quite obvious that, at mid-month, when the forecast was for a 14 percent growth rate for both the current and the following month, we would have been required to act vigorously to absorb reserves. Two weeks later, on the other hand, if the estimates had held up, we would have been required to reverse direction rather violently.

The foregoing should suggest that short-run measures of monetary growth do not provide a good target for the day-to-day conduct of open market operations. Use of such a target runs the serious risk that open market operations would be trying to offset random movements in money supply, faulty short-run seasonal adjustments, or errors of forecasting. In the process, offensive open market operations might have been increased substantially—and I have the uneasy feeling that financial markets might find such operations offensive in more than one sense.

While short-term measures of money supply growth appear to be too erratic to use as a primary target of open market operations, there are times when cumulative short-term evidence begins to build up—even between meetings of the FOMC—that strongly suggests that a deviation from past trends has gotten under way. Such evidence could of course be used, if interpreted cautiously, to modify operations in much the same way that the bank credit proxy is now used.

To return to the question of interest rate variation, there appears to be general agreement that variations would be greater with money supply as a guideline than they have been while the System was using multiple guidelines involving both monetary aggregates and interest rates. How great interest rate variations would be, would depend very much on how rigid the guideline was and how short the time horizon in which it was supposed to operate might be. The question of how great variations might be can probably never be resolved in the absence of any concrete experience.

Some exponents of the monetary school, however, seem to imply that interest rate variations make no difference at all—somehow the market is supposed to work everything out. It seems to me that there are serious risks in the assumption that the financial markets of the real world—in contrast to the markets of a theoretical model—can readily handle any range of interest rate variation. Pushing too hard on money supply control in the face of rapid interest rate adjustment could wind up by destroying the very financial mechanism which the monetary authority must use if it expects to have any impact on the real economy. Psychology and expectations play too great a role in the operations of these markets to permit the monetary authority to ignore the interpretations that the market may place on current central bank operations.

Thus, in the real world of day-to-day open market operations — theoretical considerations aside—the use of money supply as a target would appear to be too mechanistic and, in the short run, too erratic to be of much use. The use of money market conditions—a blend of interest rates and reserve and credit measures—is a more realistic short-run guide, providing opportunities for trade-offs between interest rates and aggregates in the light of market psychology and expectations. Aggregate measures, including the money supply, are, of course, indispensable indicators for the monetary authorities as they reach policy decisions. But exclusive reliance on—or blind faith in—any single indicator does not appear justified by the current state of the arts.

# 19 CONTROLLING MONETARY AGGREGATES*

SHERMAN J. MAISEL
*Board of Governors of the Federal Reserve System*

It sometimes appears that many people have a basic misunderstanding of the manner in which the Federal Reserve attempts to implement monetary policy. Much discussion attributes the exact amount of a week's or month's movements in the monetary aggregates—whether the narrowly defined money supply, bank reserves, or bank credit—to a specific plan or action of the Federal Reserve. Many statements, which describe how the Fed increases or decreases reserves to fix the amount of money, seem derived from an incorrect interpretation of what the Federal Reserve does based upon the highly oversimplified elementary textbook explanations of the procedure by which banking systems create money and credit.

Too few statements recognize that in any period the amount of money or bank credit created is the joint result of a complex interaction among households, commercial and industrial corporations, financial institutions, the Treasury, and the Federal Reserve. In addition, there appears to be a failure to recognize that the changes in money or credit as reported in the weekly or monthly statistics can differ greatly from the true situation. There are large random forces and estimating errors present in most short-period adjusted data. There are very few weeks—frequently even months—in which much of the reported movement in monetary aggregates is not primarily the result of statistical "noise."

What I propose to do in this paper is first to explain my understanding of how the Federal Reserve attempts to implement monetary policy. Then I shall discuss the large amount of noise which exists in the weekly or monthly published data. Finally I will give some idea of the orders of magnitude of the reserve movements which would have to be forecast or offset in any attempt to control the narrowly defined money supply in a short period if operations attempted to control the amount of demand deposits or money by fixing the reserves available as a base for deposit creation.

## The Federal Reserve Money Market Strategy

It is clear that as a matter of fact the Federal Reserve does not attempt to increase the money supply by a given amount in any period through furnishing a fixed amount of reserves on the assumption that they would be multiplied to result in a given increase in money. (The multiplier, it is recognized, would not be a constant but would vary from period to period depending on relative interest rates and the actions of groups other than the monetary authorities. Sophisticated advocates of a policy based on highly con-

* Reprinted from *Controlling Monetary Aggregates,* Boston, Federal Reserve Bank of Boston, 1969, pp. 152–174, by permission of the author and the Federal Reserve Bank of Boston. [Revised by the author.]

trolled reserve generation recognize that monetary action must also be taken either to anticipate changes in the multiplier or to determine it.)

Instead, the Federal Reserve follows what has been termed a money market strategy:[1]

1. The operational directives of the Open Market Committee specify values (within a range) of money market variables that the manager of the Account is to attempt to maintain. It is expected that he can do so by altering the margin between required reserves and the amount of reserves furnished by the System and by the form his market operations take. These margins are considered significant in their direct impact on bank operations, but probably more important, they influence the interest rates on money market instruments.

2. The amount of marginal reserves to be furnished and the money market rates sought are picked so as to influence the direction and rate of change of a more remote intermediate monetary variable.

3. The desired rate of change in the intermediate monetary variable is that judged to be the most effective in aiding the economy to move toward its ultimate optimum goals.

A possible side advantage of this strategy is that it can be followed even though it might be impossible to get agreement among the members of the FOMC either as to ultimate goals, or to the form or level of an intermediate monetary variable, or as to how to define what strategy is being followed.

Each decision-maker may believe one or the other of the following types of variables is most significant at a given time.

*Intermediate Monetary Variables*

(*1*) Monetary or credit aggregates such as: the money supply narrowly or broadly defined; deposits of financial institutions; member bank liabilities or credit; broader concepts of credit flows, liquid assets, wealth, and lending.

(*2*) Relative and absolute real or nominal interest rates.

(*3*) The general atmosphere of the credit markets and banking as reflected in expectations; demand for credit; the amount of credit being supplied; rates of change.

Because significant relationships exist among all these variables, influencing one will move others in the same direction although not necessarily to the same degree. As a result, if there is an agreement as to the operational variables the manager is directed to follow, there need be no meeting of minds with respect to which intermediate monetary variables should be controlled or as to the proper degree of control.

The movements of these intermediate variables can be influenced by a change in the level of any of the policy instrument variables within the power of the Fed. These are primarily:

*Policy Instrument Variables*

(*1*) The purchase or sale of open market securities.

(*2*) Repurchase agreements on securities.

(*3*) The discount rate.

(*4*) Regulation Q ceilings.

(*5*) Required reserve ratios.

A change in an instrument variable reacts with other forces in the credit markets and the economy to shift the demand and supply for funds. At each Open Market Committee meeting, estimates are made as to the effect changes in particular instrument variables will have on those money market variables which respond most clearly to Federal Reserve policy, namely:

*Money Market Variables*

(*1*) Borrowings of member banks from the Federal Reserve.

(*2*) Net free reserves.

(*3*) The Federal funds rate.

(*4*) Call money rates to government bond dealers.

(*5*) The three-month bill rate.

The expected movements in the money market variables are accompanied by esti-

[1] For those interested in more detailed statements of some of the concepts and problems, cf., J. M. Guttentag, "The Strategy of Open Market Operations," *Quarterly Journal of Economics,* Vol. LXXX, No. 1 (February 1966), pp. 1–38; and P. H. Hendershott, *The Neutralized Money Stock* (Homewood, Illinois: Richard D. Irwin, Inc., 1968), 159 pp.

The present discussion is my personal construct. As indicated in the text, many and even most members of the FOMC might disagree with my construct. They would build entirely different ones of their own to express their views of what are obviously identical operations.

mates of growth in the intermediate monetary variables. Each possible setting of the money market variables, given the projected state of the economy, the banking system, Treasury operations, etc., is expected to lead to a unique growth rate for an intermediate monetary variable with the realization, however, that in the short run fluctuations will occur in the variables around their trend for the period.

Debates may occur with respect to desired goals; desired movements of the intermediate financial variables; the importance of specific instrument variables; or as to the correctness or errors in the judgment models—which are used to estimate changes in the economy, as well as the changes in the intermediate variables, and the money market results of shifting the instrument variables.

All these considerations are summed up when the manager of the Open Market Account is instructed to buy or sell securities in order to achieve specific (within a range) values for the money market variables. The manager of the Account operates in the securities markets accordingly. At times, because of outside influences, the specified relationships for all variables cannot be achieved simultaneously. When this occurs, the manager uses his discretion in an attempt to achieve those settings which he believes are most consistent with the goals of the Committee.

This intent to control intermediate monetary variables through the money market variables is shown by the inclusion in most directives of a proviso clause. The manager is provided the growth rate for the bank credit proxy (within a range) expected to result from the directed settings of the money market variables. If the proxy moves outside the projected limits, he is instructed to operate in the open market so as to alter the money market variables in order to influence the credit proxy toward its projected path. The proviso clause is an attempt to correct for errors which may arise if the relationships among the money market variables and the intermediate monetary variables have not been projected correctly, or if errors were made in projecting the other financial and economic variables which also influence the proxy's growth.

This picture of operations can be expressed symbolically:

Where IMV = Intermediate monetary variable
$R_b$ = Borrowed reserves
$R_f$ = Free reserves
Q = Q ceiling
$r_b$ = Treasury bill rate
$r_f$ = Federal funds rate
$r_c$ = Call money rate to dealers
GNP = Economic activity
L = Liquidity preference of corporations, banks, financial institutions, etc.
T = Treasury cash management
$r_d$ = Discount rate
RR = Required reserves
S = Open market operations

Then

$$\Delta IMV = M\,(R_b, R_f, Q, r_b, r_f, r_c, GNP, L, T) \quad (1.0)$$

$$r_b;\ r_f;\ r_c = r\,(r_d, R_b, R_f, GNP, L, T) \quad (2.0)$$

The change in the intermediate monetary variable, however defined, is determined by the interaction of the Federal Reserve controlled variables; certain money market rates strongly influenced by the Federal Reserve; changes in output and prices; movements in the financial sector and liquidity functions; and the Treasury as in (1.0).

The Federal Reserve action may influence directly the IMV. It also will influence money market rates as in (2.0).

$$\Delta RR_{T+2} \cong \Delta IMV \quad (3.0)$$

$$R_b;\ R_f = R\,(\Delta RR, S) \quad (4.0)$$

The change in the intermediate monetary variable approximately determines the change in required reserves two weeks later (3.0). Given the change in required reserves, the manager of the Open Market Account can (within the limits of his operating misses) determine exactly the level of net free reserves (4.0). The banking system, given a level of net free reserves, determines its own level of borrowings and excess reserves simultaneously.

When the manager is directed to influence

the money market variables and through them intermediate monetary variables, he cannot at the same time control the changes in total reserves. Most reserves additions will follow directly from the previous changes in the IMV (credit proxy). The manager will operate so as to furnish slightly more or less than the change in required reserves (4.0) so as to interact with the market (2.0) to obtain the settings he is attempting to achieve. This means in most cases, he will furnish most (say, 90 per cent or more) of the changes in required reserves which have been previously determined by the various market interactions.

## Technical Operations

Let us express this in terms of actual weekly operations. At the start of a week, the manager has a report of borrowings and an estimate of excess reserves, and, therefore, of net borrowed reserves for the previous week.

The manager also knows the amount by which required reserves will change for the week since they depend upon changes in deposits two weeks previously. He has projections of movements expected in certain so-called technical factors which will increase or decrease the amount of reserves available to member banks in the current week. These include float, currency in circulation, Treasury deposits at Federal Reserve Banks, gold and foreign accounts, Federal Reserve foreign currency holdings, and all other items.

He sums these projections. By comparing them to the changes in required reserves, he can estimate the amount that banks would have to add or subtract from the free reserves of the week before if he takes no action to increase or decrease reserves by Federal Reserve security operations. For example, assume during week No. 1, banks borrowed $600 million and had net borrowed reserves of $500 million. If the total change in required reserves and the technical factors indicate an increased requirement of $500 million, he knows—if his projections are correct—that if he does not change his security accounts, banks will have $1 billion of net borrowed reserves in week No. 2. They will have to borrow somewhere in the vicinity of $1.1 billion, but borrowings will vary somewhat because banks can alter the amount of excess reserves that they carry as a whole during the week.

At this point, the manager can determine a tentative program of open market operations in order to meet his instructions from the FOMC with respect to the desired range of money market variables he is to attempt to achieve. During the course of the week, he receives five types of information:

*1.* The changes in interest rates reported in the market.

*2.* Borrowings at Federal Reserve Banks.

*3.* New estimates of changes occurring from technical factors as the week progresses.

*4.* Background information on supply and demand in the money markets.

*5.* Changed projections of movements in the monetary aggregates including the credit proxy, $M_1$, and $M_2$. These changes arise from revisions of prior weeks information, and from data on current deposit movements in a sample of banks.

As the week progresses, the manager performs open market operations in an attempt to achieve the constellation of borrowings and rates shown in his instructions from the FOMC. If one or another of the variables differs from the expected relationship, the manager must use his background information and his judgment in determining the operations which will best meet the Committee's objectives. If the projections for the intermediate monetary variables move outside the range projected for the Committee, the manager will alter his operations so as to change the money market variables in the direction deemed likely to influence the IMV's in the desired direction.

The manager will not be able to meet his exact objectives in any week. The projections of technical operations may be in error. Banks may or may not borrow reserves after it is too late for him to operate. Because of sudden changes, he may not be able to accomplish his desired operations. Finally, the estimates of the monetary aggregates may be in error.

## "Noise" in the Monetary Aggregates

Reported changes in the monetary aggregates can vary from the basic underlying trend of monetary policy. As one would expect, the longer the period under consideration the smaller the impact of the nonpolicy-determined movements. Still, even over a quarter these other movements are large.

The movements are actually of two very different types. The first, which I have labeled "noise," consists of: operating misses; errors in estimating the actual data at the time that operations for a period end; shifting seasonals; and irregular movements which are temporary and the product of special factors. The second type arise from two facts already noted: (a) under the current money market strategy the Fed reserves are a dependent variable only partly controlled by the Fed; (b) furthermore, even if the Fed did fix the exact rate of reserve increments, large variations in money and credit could still occur because the banks and the market determine how total reserves are divided among the bases supporting different types of deposits.

Operating misses arise either because of errors in reporting, errors in sampling, or information not available when operations must be ended. For some time, the size of misses has been decreasing steadily. The misses are small compared to the totals, but large compared to weekly or monthly changes.

The seasonal factors are large. In addition, they are dominated by irregular forces, particularly over short periods. In many cases, it is hard to determine by analysis of historical data what corrections should be made in the figures if the objective is to arrive at a true measure of the changes in the monetary aggregates required to measure either the underlying trend of monetary policy or those movements expected to influence spending or prices and quantities.

The demand for money will vary greatly depending on the day of the week in which a month, quarter, or year ends. The same is true of the day on which traditional dividend and tax dates fall. The change in tax collection dates and percentages has been important in most recent years. The day on which the Treasury borrows and the form of its borrowings are critical. While estimates are made currently as to the impacts of these factors, they still confuse the judgment of seasonal variation, particularly as observed at the time operations take place.

The irregular elements include seemingly minor factors such as the financing of a corporate take-over bid, a breakdown of a bank computer, or a snow storm. Each of these may cause even weekly average changes to vary by over 100 per cent or more. As an example of such movements, examine pages A17 and A18 of the January 1969 Federal Reserve Bulletin. Each carries an estimate for the December 1968 change in the narrowly defined money supply. In one case the increase is reported as $1.2 billion which translates to an annual rate of growth of 7.5 per cent. In the second case the increase is estimated at $8.4 billion, or at an annual rate of 53 per cent. Neither figure is in error. The first weights the extremely unusual end-of-year changes in one way, the second in a different way. Neither gives a very good sense of the underlying trend because of the dominant influence of very special factors that were rapidly reversed. These irregular forces were large enough, however, to bias strongly analysis of the two adjacent quarters in which they occurred and for many purposes even the annual data for the two years.

Data calculated at the time operations end are the significant data for operational purposes, but theoretically not for any policy impact. These estimates are subject to revisions as more information becomes available, as full universe data replace samples, and as seasonal forces are re-estimated. Revisions between the money supply as first reported and as currently reported averaged $152 million per week over the past three years. They had a range of from $−1.4 billion to $1.0 billion. Their mean deviation was over $490 million. Clearly, they make a significant amount of noise which must be taken into consideration when one looks at the reported weekly changes. In a somewhat similar manner, we might note that one part of the money supply, namely, non-member bank demand deposits, is not subject to reserve requirements of the Federal Reserve nor is information on these movements readily available. Their variance is rather great. Their share of total demand deposits has been growing. The weekly and monthly data for this component are estimates from other types of data. Specific information on how this component has changed is available only semi-annually with a lag of four to eight months.

## Total Reserves and the Narrowly Defined Money Supply

Finally let me comment briefly on some of the problems of attempting to control in any short period the narrowly defined money supply. Many unsophisticated comments and theories speak as if the Federal Reserve purchases a given quantity of securities, thereby creating a fixed amount of reserves, which through a multiplier determines a particular expansion in the money supply.

Much of modern monetary literature is actually spent trying to dispel this naive elementary textbook view which leads people to talk as if (and perhaps to believe) that the central bank determines the money supply exactly or even closely—in the short run—through its open market operations or reserve ratio. This incorrect view, however, seems hard to dislodge. Almost daily I read that last week or last month the Fed increased the money supply by 5 per cent.

Such statements are simply inaccurate. The growth of the money supply in any period is the result of actions taken by the Federal Reserve, the Treasury, the commercial banks, and the public. Over a long period, the Fed may play a paramount role, but this is definitely not the case in the short run. As I have indicated, to the best of my knowledge, the Fed has not attempted to control within rather wide limits the growth of the narrowly defined money supply in any week or month.

It should be clear from previous statements that the Federal Reserve does attempt to influence—but not to control exactly—the expansion of bank credit and, therefore, of total reserves. However, we must recognize wide differences between movements in total reserves and the money supply.

Over the past 10 years the rate of growth of the money supply has averaged about 80 per cent of the rate of growth in total reserves. On the other hand, the coefficient of determination ($r^2$) between the money supply and total reserves for quarterly changes (in the seasonally adjusted data) in this period is only .27; or, on the average, nearly three-fourths of the quarter-to-quarter movements in the two totals are not statistically related. For year-to-year changes the $r^2$ is .73. These are measures of the way in which the market redistributes its use of total reserves in any period.

If it were determined that the Fed ought to change its operating targets, what type of system might be devised to control the money supply? Let me deal briefly with a few possibilities while examining some of the related orders of magnitude so as to give some indication of the types of factors involved. I obviously have not attempted to analyze each of these methods in detail. I have primarily outlined one extremely simplified procedure to show the type of movements and problems involved. While this procedure, clearly, is not that assumed in sophisticated models, it seems to me to follow the type of naive model many people do appear to have in mind.

One method would be to consider changes in $M_1$ as the dependent variable in the type of model now used to predict and somewhat to control the bank credit proxy. Included among the independent variables in such a model would be the existing instrumental variables controlled by the Fed. These variables could then be altered in such a manner as hopefully to result in the desired levels for $M_1$, the dependent variable. A model could be developed and used for any period such as a week, month, quarter, or year, depending on what was believed to be theoretically relevant and operationally feasible.

If it were found that a high correlation existed between $M_1$ and any one or a group of instrumental variables and this correlation was maintained in actual operations, such a model might be rather simple. A problem would still remain as to whether or not the effects of operating the monetary variables to achieve this particular goal would be as efficient as aiming them at a variety of other goals, but that would be a question in basic decision-making rather than an operating problem.

A second procedure would be one similar to that now used to estimate the operations needed to offset technical and seasonal movements in reserves and reserve requirements. In place of the manager operating so as to obtain certain money market conditions, he could use an estimating system similar to his current one and could conduct open market operations in an attempt to control the amount of reserves available to support those demand deposits counted as part of the money supply by exactly offsetting all other forces furnishing or utilizing reserves.

Finally (and surprisingly to me the most difficult to conceptualize since it seems to be what most imagine occurs), would be some system in which open market operations attempted to furnish by a formula a given volume of reserves for expansion of the money supply. This type of system, I imagine, would note deviations of past movements from a desired level and would attempt to close the gap between actual and desired by some form of distributed lag of the type developed in many inventory theories.

### Controlling Reserves Available for Expansion of the Money Supply

The difficulty with attempting to change the reserve base in order to control directly the money supply arises from the fact that there is no exact relationship between them. The money supply can be altered by non-reserve movements while reserves can be used to support non-money supply expansions.

Changes in the money supply are equal to:

$$\Delta MS = \Delta D + \Delta ND + \Delta FD + \Delta C - \Delta F$$

Where MS = Narrowly defined money supply
D = Demand deposits (private) at member banks (less interbank deposits)
ND = Demand deposits (private) at nonmember banks (less interbank deposits)
FD = Foreign demand deposits at Federal Reserve Banks
C = Currency outside member banks
F = Float

The naive assumption seems to be that the growth in the money supply can be controlled by the Federal Reserve altering the amount of reserves available as a base for member bank demand deposits.

When we look at Federal open market operations, we find that the amount of reserves furnished are divided among many uses, namely:

$$\Delta(S + B) = \Delta TF + \Delta\frac{D}{rd} + \Delta\frac{GD}{rd} + \Delta\frac{NIBD}{rd} + \Delta\frac{TD}{rt} + \Delta ER + \text{seasonal reserves.}$$

Where S = Securities
B = Borrowings
TF = Technical factors
rd = Required reserve ratios for demand deposits
rt = Required reserve ratios for time deposits
GD = Government deposits at member banks
NIBD = Net interbank deposits among member banks
TD = Time deposits at member banks
ER = Excess reserves

We can now see what forces must be estimated if we were to furnish an amount of reserves in any period so as to exactly offset all other uses and to allow the amount needed as a base for a specific growth in the money supply. Namely:

$$\Delta(S + B) = \frac{MS^*}{rd} + AOR$$

(All other reserves)

Where $MS^*$ = the desired change in the money supply.

$$AOR = \frac{(ND + FD + C - F)}{rd} + ER + \frac{GD}{rd} + \frac{NIBD}{rd} + \frac{TD}{rt} + \text{seasonal reserves} + TF$$

We see that in addition to operations to offset the technical factors and seasonal forces which are both now part of operations, estimates and offsetting operations would be required for changes in the money supply not dependent on reserves at the Federal Reserve, on changes in excess reserves, and on movements in government, interbank, and time deposits. Insofar as these operations changed total deposits in a period, they would have to be matched by equivalent alterations in bank assets or credit.

What are the orders of magnitude and some of the problems which appear to be raised by this concept? Tables 1 and 2 give some of the background information needed for this analysis.

Column 1 of the table shows the current estimate of the actual growth in the money supply for the first eight months of 1969 distributed equally over the entire period. This growth was at a 3.6 per cent annual rate for the period (which I imagine was a rate satisfactory to many). The second column shows the changes in the money supply due to forces not under the control of the Federal Reserve, namely, currency, non-member bank demand deposits, float, and foreign deposits. We note that for this period, these other components grew at a 9.9 per cent annual rate so that the member bank demand deposit component decreased at a .45 per cent annual rate. We also note that the growth of these other components was irregular, as broken down in columns 7 to 10. As a result in column 11 we see that if it were desired that the expansion of the money supply be constant, the amount of reserves furnished for the theoretically Fed-controllable component could not be constant, but rather they would have to fluctuate to offset the irregular movements in the remainder.

The size and irregularity of the necessary movements are shown in columns 4 and 7. From these columns, we can calculate that the average decrease in member bank deposits was a little over $20 million per week, or $80 million per four-week period, and $260 million per quarter. The desired weekly increments varied from $1582 million to minus $1425 million. Monthly variations ranged from $439 million to minus $751 million. Expressing the desired change in demand deposits in terms of reserves, we find the amount to be withdrawn in an average week would have been $5.5 million, with a four-week average of $22.0 million, and the amount needed for a quarter $71.5 million. The weekly range, however, would have been from $248 million to minus $224 million, with a monthly one from $69 million to minus $114 million.

These requirements to meet a steady growth in the money supply can be compared to the actual fluctuations which occurred. Such actual movements are a measure of irregular and transitory forces, and errors in the seasonal correction mechanism. When we examine column 6, we find that the actual changes in member bank demand deposits, seasonally adjusted, on a weekly basis averaged minus $9.8 million with a range of $1902 million to minus $1659 million. For a month they averaged minus $78 million with a range of $2322 million to minus $1037 million.

Columns 7 and 8 show the required reserves behind seasonal movements and "all other movements" (pages 242–243). Column 9 is the reserve equivalent of the change in each week's money supply estimate, from the initial estimate to the latest (October 1969) revision. Column 10 is the reserve equivalent of the change in $M_1$ required to achieve a constant increase in $M_1$. Finally, column 11 sums columns 7 to 10 to obtain "total required desk operations." The relative magnitudes of columns 10 and 11 are instructive. For example, average total weekly desk operations during this period would have been $355 million. Operations to support a constant increase in $M_1$ alone would have averaged only $70.5 million. Note that in 14 of the 36 weeks reserve movements designed to assure a constant increase in $M_1$ would have had the opposite sign of total reserve movements.

Operations to support other elements averaged $175 million weekly for seasonal movements and $298 million weekly for "all other movements." Reserve equivalent corrections for changes in estimates of $M_1$ would have averaged $127 million weekly.

Table 1 shows data on a week-by-week basis for a recent period of eight months. Table 2 shows average values for roughly the same reserve data for the past three years. The first column shows actual variations in the reserve equivalent of movements in the money supply. We note that over the three-year period, the average change in the money supply multiplied by .152 to give its reserve equivalent was $23 million per week, $97 million per month, and $330 million per quarter. The remaining data in the column show the range and deviations for this series.

TABLE 1. MOVEMENTS IN THE MONEY SUPPLY AND ITS RESERVE COMPONENTS, December 25, 1968, to September 3, 1969 (Deposits, seasonally adjusted, in million dollars)

| | Desired money supply | Component of money supply not based on member bank reserves | Desired member bank private demand deposits | | Actual member bank private demand deposits | | Reserves Required for: | | | | Total required desk operations |
|---|---|---|---|---|---|---|---|---|---|---|---|
| | | | Level | Change | Level | Change | Seasonal movement in member bank private demand deposits | All other reserve movements | To correct for data errors | To obtain constant increase in $M_1$ (S.A.) | |
| | (1) | (2) | (3) | (4) | (5) | (6) | (7) | (8) | (9) | (10) | (11) |
| Dec. 25, 1968 | 194,760 | 77,146 | 117,614 | | 117,614 | | | | | | |
| Jan. 1, 1969 | 194,891 | 76,459 | 118,432 | + 818 | 118,822 | + 1208 | + 332 | + 776 | − 46 | + 124 | + 1186 |
| 8 | 195,023 | 77,136 | 117,887 | − 545 | 119,676 | + 854 | + 2 | − 387 | + 15 | − 83 | − 453 |
| 15 | 195,154 | 78,033 | 117,121 | − 766 | 118,017 | − 1659 | + 514 | + 98 | + 61 | − 116 | + 557 |
| 22 | 195,286 | 77,903 | 117,383 | + 262 | 118,122 | + 105 | − 174 | − 44 | + 61 | + 40 | − 117 |
| 29 | 195,417 | 77,647 | 117,770 | + 387 | 116,592 | − 1530 | − 114 | − 663 | − 76 | + 59 | − 794 |
| Feb. 5 | 195,549 | 77,694 | 117,855 | + 85 | 117,637 | + 1045 | − 289 | + 154 | + 30 | + 13 | − 92 |
| 12 | 195,680 | 78,266 | 117,414 | − 441 | 117,382 | − 255 | − 307 | + 130 | + 198 | − 67 | − 46 |
| 19 | 195,812 | 78,289 | 117,523 | + 109 | 118,798 | + 1416 | − 96 | + 427 | − 152 | + 17 | + 196 |
| 26 | 195,943 | 77,916 | 118,027 | − 504 | 118,914 | + 116 | − 252 | − 240 | − 91 | − 77 | − 660 |
| March 5 | 196,075 | 78,599 | 117,476 | − 551 | 117,809 | − 1105 | − 240 | + 126 | + 45 | − 84 | − 153 |
| 12 | 196,206 | 78,973 | 117,233 | − 243 | 117,461 | − 348 | − 258 | + 41 | + 167 | − 37 | − 87 |
| 19 | 196,338 | 79,978 | 116,410 | − 823 | 117,849 | + 388 | + 320 | − 378 | − 45 | − 125 | − 228 |
| 26 | 196,469 | 78,672 | 117,797 | + 1387 | 118,181 | + 332 | + 48 | + 73 | + 9 | + 211 | + 341 |
| April 2 | 196,601 | 78,938 | 117,663 | − 134 | 118,670 | + 489 | + 63 | + 58 | + 76 | − 20 | + 177 |
| 9 | 196,732 | 79,036 | 117,696 | + 33 | 119,932 | + 1262 | − 255 | + 111 | + 45 | + 5 | − 94 |
| 16 | 196,864 | 79,591 | 117,273 | − 423 | 119,093 | − 839 | + 144 | − 127 | − 137 | − 64 | − 184 |
| 23 | 196,995 | 80,142 | 116,853 | − 380 | 118,245 | − 848 | + 194 | + 770 | − 130 | − 60 | + 774 |
| 30 | 197,126 | 79,763 | 117,363 | + 510 | 117,144 | − 1101 | + 330 | − 253 | + 126 | + 80 | + 283 |

TABLE 1. *(Continued)*

| | Desired money supply (1) | Component of money supply not based on member bank reserves (2) | Desired member bank private demand deposits: Level (3) | Desired member bank private demand deposits: Change (4) | Actual member bank private demand deposits: Level (5) | Actual member bank private demand deposits: Change (6) | Reserves Required for: Seasonal movement in member bank private demand deposits (7) | All other reserve movements (8) | To correct for data errors (9) | To obtain constant increase in $M_1$ (S. A.) (10) | Total required desk operations (11) |
|---|---|---|---|---|---|---|---|---|---|---|---|
| May 7 | 197,258 | 79,700 | 117,558 | + 195 | 117,462 | + 318 | − 125 | + 678 | + 345 | + 31 | + 929 |
| 14 | 197,389 | 81,256 | 116,133 | − 1425 | 117,809 | + 347 | − 240 | − 164 | − 408 | − 224 | − 1036 |
| 21 | 197,521 | 79,806 | 117,715 | + 1582 | 119,711 | + 1902 | − 270 | + 236 | + 188 | + 248 | + 402 |
| 28 | 197,652 | 79,860 | 117,792 | + 87 | 119,247 | − 464 | − 160 | + 117 | − 31 | + 14 | − 60 |
| June 4 | 197,784 | 80,415 | 117,369 | − 423 | 118,347 | − 900 | + 319 | − 405 | + 63 | − 66 | − 89 |
| 11 | 197,915 | 79,924 | 117,991 | + 622 | 118,860 | + 513 | + 244 | − 443 | + 15 | + 98 | − 86 |
| 18 | 198,047 | 79,915 | 118,132 | + 141 | 118,324 | − 536 | + 157 | − 565 | − 188 | + 22 | − 574 |
| 25 | 198,178 | 80,698 | 117,480 | − 652 | 118,383 | + 59 | − 288 | + 218 | + 330 | − 102 | + 158 |
| July 2 | 198,310 | 80,531 | 117,779 | + 299 | 118,716 | + 333 | − 11 | + 545 | − 126 | + 47 | + 455 |
| 9 | 198,44[illegible] | 80,483 | 117,958 | + 179 | 118,942 | + 226 | + 44 | − 368 | + 173 | + 28 | − 123 |
| 16 | 198,573 | 80,796 | 117,777 | − 181 | 118,458 | − 484 | − 177 | + 276 | − 267 | − 28 | + 196 |
| 23 | 198,704 | 80,511 | 118,193 | + 416 | 118,738 | + 280 | + 29 | − 140 | + 126 | + 65 | + 80 |
| 30 | 198,836 | 81,377 | 117,459 | − 734 | 117,691 | − 1047 | + 22 | − 592 | + 62 | − 115 | − 623 |
| Aug. 6 | 198,967 | 81,618 | 117,349 | − 110 | 117,447 | − 244 | + 19 | + 469 | − 518 | − 17 | − 47 |
| 13 | 199,099 | 81,687 | 117,412 | + 63 | 117,434 | − 13 | − 15 | − 67 | − 63 | + 10 | − 135 |
| 20 | 199,230 | 81,446 | 117,784 | + 372 | 118,013 | + 579 | − 192 | + 391 | − 15 | + 58 | + 242 |
| 27 | 199,361 | 81,918 | 117,443 | − 341 | 116,983 | − 1030 | − 67 | − 183 | + 15 | − 54 | − 289 |
| Sept. 3 | 199,493 | 82,233 | 117,260 | − 183 | 117,260 | + 277 | − 6 | + 24 | + 138 | − 29 | + 127 |

TABLE 2. AVERAGE MOVEMENTS IN THE RESERVE EQUIVALENTS OF VARIOUS SOURCES AND USES OF MEMBER BANK RESERVES AND MONEY SUPPLY COMPONENTS, 1966 – 1968 (In billions of dollars; not seasonally adjusted)

| Period and type of average | Money supply (MS)[1] | All Other Reserves | | | | | | All other reserves (AOR) | Reserves required for seasonal movements in demand deposits |
|---|---|---|---|---|---|---|---|---|---|
| | | MS component not based on MB reserves (F-C-FD-ND)[1] | Technical factors (TF) | Excess reserves (ER) | Government demand deposits (GD)[1] | Net interbank deposits among MB's (NIBD)[1] | Time deposits at MB's (TD)[2] | | |
| 1 Week: | | | | | | | | | |
| Av. Δ per period | .023 | −.012 | .048 | .001 | .001 | .002 | .012 | .052 | - - - |
| Range | −.669 to .790 | −.182 to .144 | −1.043 to .871 | −.553 to .374 | −.505 to .648 | −.193 to .227 | −.034 to .047 | −1.733 to 1.554 | −.576 to .591 |
| Mean deviation | .243 | .090 | .304 | .162 | .171 | .051 | .012 | .405 | .248 |
| Std. deviation | .289 | .077 | .384 | .206 | .212 | .067 | .014 | .506 | .210 |
| 4 Weeks: | | | | | | | | | |
| Av. Δ per period | .097 | −.051 | .207 | −.002 | .002 | .010 | .048 | .212 | - - - |
| Range | −.958 to .699 | −.193 to .191 | −.975 to .998 | −.141 to .105 | −.395 to .382 | −.152 to .143 | −.043 to .130 | −1.008 to 1.051 | −.890 to .526 |
| Mean deviation | .304 | .063 | .358 | .045 | .147 | .048 | .032 | .366 | .299 |
| Std. deviation | .380 | .085 | .442 | .058 | .184 | .062 | .040 | .442 | .364 |
| 13 Weeks: | | | | | | | | | |
| Av. Δ per period | .330 | −.170 | .739 | −.006 | .009 | .037 | .154 | .762 | - - - |
| Range | −.122 to .988 | −.350 to −.016 | .030 to 1.857 | −.052 to .046 | −.255 to .136 | −.034 to .138 | −.044 to .249 | −.232 to 1.612 | −.415 to .596 |
| Mean deviation | .350 | .115 | .397 | .028 | .088 | .041 | .070 | .426 | .316 |
| Std. deviation | .380 | .123 | .502 | .032 | .117 | .051 | .087 | .555 | .374 |

[1]Each of these components has been multiplied by .152 to get its reserve equivalent.
[2]Time deposits have been multiplied by .042 to get their reserve equivalent.

These are the summary average equivalents of column 1 in Table 1.

The last column shows that to furnish reserves for seasonal variations in demand deposits, about \$248 million in reserves (the mean deviation) would have to be added or subtracted per week, \$299 million per month, etc. The range and standard deviations of the seasonal component are also shown. The second last column shows the extent of operations needed if all other reserve sources and uses except the movements in the money supply were accommodated. Again the most significant figures are the \$405 million weekly average, and \$366 million monthly average required operations.

The columns between the first and last two measure the sometimes offsetting factors that are covered by these reserve changes. Column 2 contains the other components of the money supply, column 3 shows the reserve operations now engaged in to offset technical factors, etc.

The two tables can be summarized in two statements: The irregular movements in the money supply compared to its underlying trend are large. When we compare the reserves which would have to be furnished in a period to the average irregular changes for the similar periods over the past three years, the ratios for a week are $\frac{243}{4.4}$ or 55; and $\frac{304}{18}$ or 17 for a month; and $\frac{350}{58}$ or 6 times the desired increase for the quarter.

The movements in other forces supplying or absorbing reserves in addition to those required to expand or contract the money supply are also large compared to any desired changes in the money supply. For this three-year period, the ratios are $\frac{506}{4.4}$ or 115 per week; $\frac{442}{18}$ or 25 per month; and $\frac{555}{58}$ or 10 per quarter.

## Problems

The tables give an indication of some of the problems that would be faced by a system which attempted to control the money supply directly by furnishing on a week-to-week basis a fixed amount of reserves to increase the base behind the money supply while at the same time operating to offset the reserves supplied or used for other purposes.

The first problem concerns the irregular movements. We have noted that over a month the average change in reserves required to allow for irregular movements is 17 times as large as the amount required to expand the money supply while for the quarter the ratio is 6 times. The procedure set out would not allow any reserves for irregular movements, yet it appears that for many purposes increasing reserves to allow the money supply to expand and contract as a result of transitory forces in the economy is desirable. The forces which we have called irregular are real and serve an economic purpose. They arise from errors in estimating the seasonal forces and in estimating special transitory needs of the economy. Insofar as they are offsetting over a longer period, they do not affect the total money supply. If reserves were not provided for these needs, banks would be forced to vary their assets in an amount equivalent to a multiplier of the reserves now furnished. There could be alternating periods of extreme ease or tightness in both lending and interest rates for reasons entirely unrelated to the underlying credit situation or policy goal.

The second problem is a technical one. The system outlined above would require the Desk to estimate six series in addition to the group which is now estimated and, hopefully, offset by technical operations. The amount of these operations would be large. Any errors in these estimates or forecasts carried forward to actual operations would either absorb or furnish reserves which could be used to expand the money supply—a result contrary to that for which the system is proposed. While this problem would be nowhere near as great as for the irregular components, it would still be considerable.

We have no exact estimates of how large errors in the forecasts would be, but we can arrive at some values by extrapolating from current data and practices. I have measured the actual weekly forecast errors in current technical operations. The actual forecast error (mean deviation—partially arising from the various problems in data revisions and inability to operate noted earlier) was \$44 million in reserves in an average week. This compares to a weekly mean deviation of \$304 million for these total operations or the forecast error was about 14 per cent of the total. The variance of the forecast error was 2.4 per cent of the variance of all technical operations.

I have assumed for the want of better data that this same percentage error of variance would apply to the seven items shown in Table II that would have to be forecast. Assuming that the variances would be uncorrelated (probably not a good assumption) we can derive the variance and standard deviation of the forecast of AOR (all other reserves) as the sum of the variances of its components—a set of independent random variables. In this case, we find that the standard deviation of AOR for one week is $77 million. In other words, we would expect that about half the time the error in forecasting the amount of operations required would be more than $52 million. Although some errors are likely to be cumulative, if we assume that the weekly forecast can correct for all previous errors in the month or quarter, we would have approximately the same error for the longer periods.

Under such an assumption about forecast errors, we would find that in at least half the months, the amount of reserves furnished in error would enable the money supply to expand or contract in a month by more than 50 per cent above or below the desired amount.

The final complication is far more difficult and is one about which we have little information. It arises from the manner in which a bank and banks as a whole can meet their reserve requirements and from the fact that depositors can shift the type of their deposits. When the Fed alters the reserves it furnishes through open market operations, banks individually can borrow from the discount window, borrow reserves from other banks, or sell assets. Member banks as a whole can either borrow from the discount window or sell assets.

If the Fed is attempting to control total reserves, it can with a slight lag sell securities to offset any additional reserves it furnishes through the discount window. The changes in the actions of banks which result from their increased dependence on borrowed in place of non-borrowed reserves will influence all types of rates as well as the banks' ability and willingness to hold securities or make loans. How great such reactions would be in response to large-scale weekly shifts in discounting is, of course, not clear.

A similar unknown is how large shifts in bank assets would have to be in response to System action to control the rate of expansion in one type of deposit such as the demand deposit component of the money supply. The procedure outlined in the previous section would mean that the System would furnish or absorb all reserves required so long as they were not changing the desired level of private demand deposits. If banks found they had insufficient reserves because the System wanted to curtail the expansion of demand deposits, they would sell assets. If these were paid for from time, inter-bank, or government deposits, the System would show a miss in its forecast of reserves for these purposes. Operations the following week would be planned to absorb additional reserves freed by these assets' sale. The sale of assets and absorption of reserves could continue until the money supply finally converged on its desired track. It is not easy to forecast particularly over a short term how much credit would have to contract or, in the opposite case, expand to bring about such a convergence.

The resulting situation would appear to be similar to the present. Banks and the public would reach an equilibrium among assets and deposits based on liquidity functions and interest rates. The procedure aimed at controlling $M_1$ would bring about an equilibrium at some point. It appears difficult to me, however, to predict with existing information, derived from an entirely different institutional system, where that equilibrium would be or how stable it would be compared to current procedures.

## An Elastic Currency

It is now possible to restate one logical reason for following the money market strategy. We saw how great are the misses, the random movements, and the influence of other forces on reserves when compared to the changes required for growth in the narrowly defined money supply. If one attempted to increase reserves according to an exact schedule, the market would have to shift rapidly in order to accommodate seasonal forces, errors in operation, Treasury cash operations, and the type of irregular movements which the Federal Reserve now accommodates.

An attempt to control growth in the money supply directly through controlling the amount of reserves created runs into the difficulty that in any quantity-price relationship if one controls the quantity tightly the price must be allowed to move freely and through an extremely wide range. In addition to many other considerations, the problem would have to be faced of what costs and what structural changes the economy would experience if interest rates fluctuated widely as the result of an attempt to control directly a single use of monetary reserves.

Our financial structure and capital markets are extremely well developed and efficient. The amount of funds bought and sold in our money markets averages well over 10 to 12 billion dollars per day. The amount of money raised on a gross basis by the economy totals over $600 billion for maturities of under one year and over $220 billion with maturities of over a year each year. In such a system, major advantages result if the monetary aggregates react flexibly to absorb the daily, weekly, and monthly seasonals, shock, and other irregular forces.

This need for flexible reactions in the monetary aggregates was a major factor in the formation of the Federal Reserve. It has always been a central interest in its operations. The need for such flexibility may be greater today than in the past. Our capital markets operate with an extremely low ratio of equity capital. We have developed highly specialized financing institutions and techniques. The underwriting of our public debt is done at extremely low margins. These are possible because the market does not have to shoulder the risks of widely fluctuating interest rates from irregular short-term movements. The additional reserves created to satisfy the purely seasonal or irregular demands for short-term funds disappear quite rapidly. They influence total demand or the supply and demand equilibrium for financial funds only slightly. It is not evident why one should want rates in the money markets to fluctuate in response to their movements.

Most decision models and loss functions would, I believe, show that beyond certain limits it is highly advantageous for the Government to assume the risks from irregular movements. The position of these limits will depend at any time on the ability of the private sector to assume such risks, on the shape of loss functions, on the variance of movements and similar matters.

I recognize, of course, that if such risk assumption is possible only at the expense of other goals it might not be worthwhile. The gains from one program must be weighed against the loss from another. Still, I believe that allowing flexible reactions to temporary reserve requirements is logical. I would also as readily agree that we need a better understanding of how the present system works as well as of how to improve it.

I must conclude, however, that recognizing the degree of noise and irregularity in the existing data, somewhat less attention should be paid to very short-run movements in either the monetary aggregates or in money market conditions than presently seems to be the case. More attention needs to be given to the logic of different control systems and particularly to the logic of different monetary goals.

Given the intensity of the beliefs of the Fed's critics that these problems are vital to formulation of a sensible monetary policy and that the operational problems are fairly simple to solve, I personally feel that more effort should have been and should be spent on analysis of these problems. I recognize, of course, that there are major theoretical problems as well as others concerned with formulating the best decision-making process which are also vital in the determination of optimum operating procedures. It does appear though that a wider understanding of how operations are determined and of possible alternatives should be useful to all.

# 20 ELEMENTS OF MONEY STOCK DETERMINATION*

JERRY L. JORDAN
*Federal Reserve Bank of St. Louis*

Recent discussion of the role of money in stabilization policy has culminated in two central issues. The first involves the strength and reliability of the relation between changes in money and changes in total spending. If this relation is sufficiently strong and reliable, changes in the money stock can be used as an indicator of the influence of monetary stabilization actions on the economy.[1] The second issue centers on whether or not the monetary authorities can determine the growth of the money stock with sufficient precision, if it is deemed desirable to do so.

This article is concerned primarily with the second issue—determination of the money stock.[2] A framework describing the factors which influence the monetary authorities' ability to determine the money stock is presented, and the behavior of these factors in recent years is illustrated. In addition, examples of ways in which these factors influence the money stock are discussed.

## Factors Influencing the Money Stock

The following sections present essential elements and concepts which are used to construct a "money supply model" for the U.S. economy. First, the necessary information regarding institutional aspects of the U.S. banking system are summarized. Then, the main elements of the model—the monetary base, the member bank reserve-to-deposit ratio, the currency-to-demand deposit ratio, the time deposit-to-demand deposit ratio, and the U.S. Government deposit-to-demand deposit ratio—are discussed.

### *Institutional Aspects of the U.S. Banking System*

Students of money and banking are taught that if commercial bank reserve requirements are less than 100 per cent, the reserves of the banking system can support a "multiple" of deposits. In fact it is often said that under a fractional reserve system the banking system "creates" deposits. The familiar textbook exposition tells us that the amount of deposits (D) in the system is equal to the reciprocal of the reserve requirement ratio (r) times the amount of reserves (R):

$$D = \frac{1}{r} \cdot R$$

Thus if the banking system has \$100 of reserves, and the reserve requirement ratio is 20 per cent (.2), deposits will be \$100/.2 or \$500. If the banks acquire an additional \$1 in reserves (for instance from the Federal Reserve), deposits will increase by \$5.

There are many simplifying assumptions underlying this elementary deposit-expansion relation. First, it is assumed that all bank deposits are subject to the same reserve requirement. Second, all banks are subject to the same regulations; in other words, all

* Reprinted from *Review*, Federal Reserve Bank of St. Louis, vol. 51 (October, 1969) pp. 10–19, by permission of the author and the Federal Reserve Bank of St. Louis.

[1] Leonall C. Andersen and Jerry L. Jordan, "Monetary and Fiscal Actions: A Test of Their Relative Importance in Economic Stabilization," this *Review*, November 1968 [reprinted in this volume].

[2] Private demand deposits plus currency in the hands of the public.

**TABLE 1. MONETARY BASE (July, 1969 – billions of dollars)**

Consolidated Treasury and Federal Reserve Monetary Accounts

| Sources of the base | | Uses of the base | |
|---|---|---|---|
| Federal Reserve credit: | | Member bank deposits at Federal Reserve | $22.3 |
| Holdings of securities[a] | $54.3 | Currency in circulation | 51.3 |
| Discounts and advances | 1.2 | | |
| Float | 2.7 | | |
| Other Federal Reserve assets | 2.7 | | |
| Gold stock | 10.4 | | |
| Treasury currency outstanding | 6.7 | | |
| Treasury cash holdings | – .7 | | |
| Treasury deposits at Federal Reserve | – 1.1 | | |
| Foreign deposits at Federal Reserve | – .1 | | |
| Other liabilities and capital accounts | – 2.0 | | |
| Other Federal Reserve deposits | – .5 | | |
| Sources of the base | $73.6 | Uses of the base | $73.6 |
| Reserve adjustment[b] | 3.9 | Reserve adjustment[b] | 3.9 |
| Monetary base | $77.5 | Monetary base | $77.5 |

NOTE: Data are not seasonally adjusted. Member bank deposits at Federal Reserve plus currency held by member banks equals total reserves (required reserves plus excess reserves).

[a]Includes acceptances not shown separately.

[b]Leonall C. Andersen and Jerry L. Jordan, "The Monetary Base: Explanation and Analytical Use," this *Review*, August 1968.

SOURCE: "Member Bank Reserves, Federal Reserve Bank Credit, and Related Items," the first table appearing in the Financial and Business Statistics section of the Federal Reserve *Bulletin*.

banks are members of the Federal Reserve System, and the Federal Reserve does not differentiate among classes of banks. Third, banks do not hold excess reserves; they are always "loaned up." And finally, there is no "cash drain." The public desires to hold a fixed quantity of currency, and their desires for currency are not influenced by the existence of more or less deposits.

Since the above assumptions are not true, the accuracy with which a monetary analyst can estimate how many deposits will be "created" by an addition of $1 in reserves to the banking system, depends on his ability to determine:

(*1*) how the deposits will be distributed between member and nonmember banks;

(*2*) how the deposits will be distributed between reserve city and country banks, which are subject to different reserve requirements;

(*3*) how the deposits will be distributed among private demand deposits, Government demand deposits, and the sub-classes of time deposits, all of which are subject to different reserve requirements;

(*4*) how the change in deposits will affect banks' desired ratio of excess reserves to total deposits; and

(*5*) how a change in deposits will affect the public's desired ratio of currency to demand deposits.

These questions can be answered best within the context of a "money supply model" which is constructed to include the institutional realities of the U.S. banking system, and which does not require the special assumptions of the simple deposit expansion equation. A thoroughly developed and tested money supply model has been advanced by Professors Brunner and Meltzer.[3] The following sections present the general form and essential features of this model.

### *The Monetary Base*

A useful concept for monetary analysis is provided by the "monetary base" or "high-

[3] Karl Brunner and Allan Meltzer, "Liquidity Traps for Money, Bank Credit, and Interest Rates," *Journal of Political Economy*, Vol. 76, January/February 1968. Also see Albert E. Burger, *An Analysis of the Brunner-Meltzer Non-Linear Money Supply Hypothesis*, Working Paper No. 7, Federal Reserve Bank of St. Louis, May 1969.

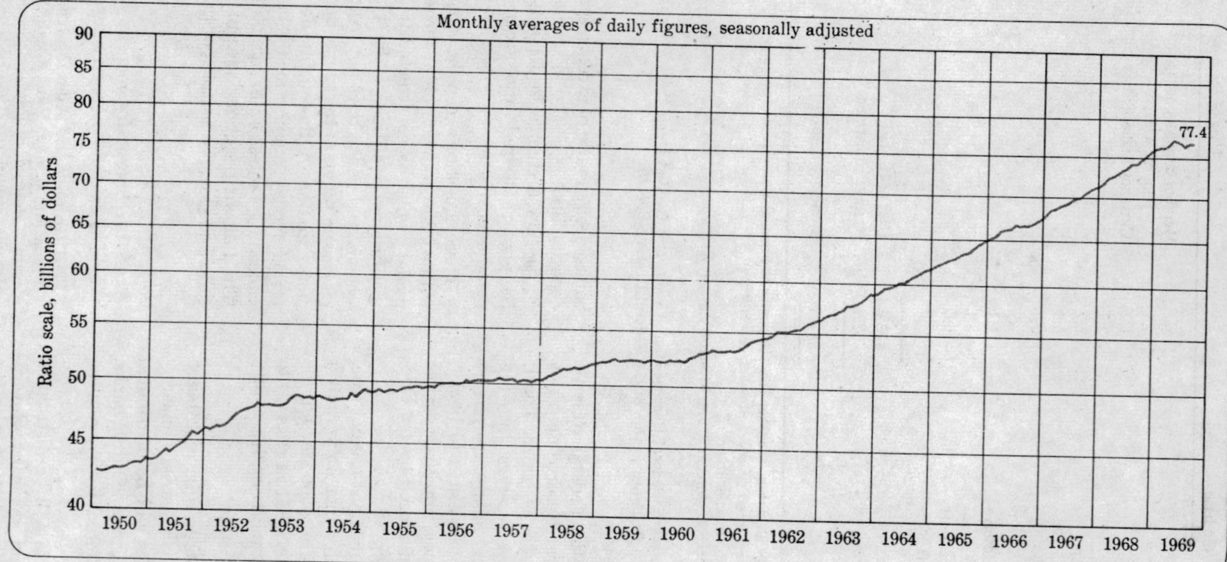


**CHART 1** Monetary base. *Uses of the monetary base are member bank reserves and currency held by the public and nonmember banks. Adjustments are made for reserve requirement changes and shifts in deposits among classes of banks. Data are computed by Federal Reserve Bank of St. Louis. Latest data plotted: September, 1969.*

powered money."[4] The monetary base is defined as the net monetary liabilities of the Government (U.S. Treasury and Federal Reserve System) held by the public (commercial banks and nonbank public). More specifically, the monetary base is derived from a consolidated balance sheet of the Treasury and Federal Reserve "monetary" accounts. This consolidated monetary base balance sheet is illustrated in Table 1, and monthly data for the monetary base (B) are shown in Chart 1.

The growth of the monetary base, that is, "base money," is determined primarily by Federal Reserve holdings of U.S. Government securities, the dominant asset or source component of the base.[5] In recent decades changes in other sources either have been small or have been offset by changes in security holdings. A change in the Treasury's gold holdings is potentially an important source of increase or decrease in the base. However, since March 1968 the size of the gold stock has been changing only by small increments. In the postwar period the influence of changes in the gold stock were generally offset by compensating changes in Federal Reserve holdings of U.S. Government securities.

The liabilities or uses of the monetary base, or net monetary liabilities of the Federal Reserve and Treasury, are shown in Table 1 to be currency in circulation plus member bank deposits at the Federal Reserve. Part of the currency in circulation is held by the public, part is held as legal reserves by member banks, and another part is held as desired contingency reserves by nonmember commercial banks. In order to relate the uses of the base to the money stock, the uses are regrouped from the *uses* side of Table 1 as currency held by the nonbank public plus reserves of all commercial banks, shown in Table 2.

[4] For further discussion of this concept, see Leonall C. Andersen and Jerry L. Jordan, "The Monetary Base: Explanation and Analytical Use," this *Review*, August 1968.

[5] For a discussion of the statistical relation among source components of the base, see Michael W. Keran and Christopher Babb, "An Explanation of Federal Reserve Actions (1933–68)," this *Review*, July 1969.

*Uses of Reserves*

As noted above, analysis of the U.S. monetary system is complicated by the existence of both member and nonmember banks, different classes of member banks, different reserve requirements on different types of deposits (private demand, Government demand, and time), and graduated reserve requirements for different amounts of deposits. It is thus necessary to allocate the uses of bank reserves among the different types of deposits. This is illustrated by an equation showing total bank reserves (R) in terms of their uses:

$$R = RR_m + ER_m + VC_n$$

where $RR_m$ = required reserves of member banks, $ER_m$ = excess reserves of member banks, $VC_n$ = vault cash of nonmember banks.

In turn, required reserves of member banks are decomposed as:

$$RR_m = R^d + R^t$$

where $R^d$ = required reserves behind demand deposits at member banks, $R^t$ = required reserves behind time deposits at member banks.

In turn, required reserves behind demand deposits at member banks are the sum of the amount of reserves required behind demand deposits over and under $5 million at each reserve city and country bank, and similarly

**TABLE 2. USES OF MONETARY BASE (July, 1969 – billions of dollars)**

| | | | |
|---|---|---|---|
| Currency in circulation | $51.3 | Currency held by the nonbank public | $45.1 |
| Member bank deposits at Federal Reserve | 22.3 | Commercial bank reserves* | 28.5 |
| Uses of the base | $73.6 | Uses of the base | $73.6 |

NOTE: Not seasonally adjusted data.
*Includes vault cash of nonmember banks.

TABLE 3. RESERVE REQUIREMENTS OF MEMBER BANKS (In effect September 30, 1969)

| Type of deposit | Percentage requirement |
|---|---|
| Net demand deposits:[a] | |
| Reserve city banks: | |
| Under $5 million | 17.0% |
| Over $5 million | 17.5 |
| Country banks: | |
| Under $5 million | 12.5 |
| Over $5 million | 13.0 |
| Time deposits (all classes of banks): | |
| Savings deposits | 3.0 |
| Other time deposits: | |
| Under $5 million | 3.0 |
| Over $5 million | 6.0 |

[a]Demand deposits subject to reserve requirements are gross demand deposits minus cash items in the process of collection and demand balances due from domestic banks.

SOURCE: Federal Reserve *Bulletin*.

for time and savings deposits.[6] Present required reserve ratios for each deposit category are shown in Table 3.

Alternatively, the total amount of commercial bank reserves can be expressed as a proportion (r) of total bank deposits:

$$R = r(D + T + G),$$

where D = private demand deposits, T = time deposits, G = U.S. Government (Treasury) deposits at commercial banks.

The "r-ratio" is defined to be a weighted-average reserve ratio against all bank deposits, but is computed directly by dividing total reserves by total deposits.[7] The trend of the r-ratio in the postwar period is shown in Chart 2. An important factor contributing to the gradual downward trend of the r-ratio is the relatively more rapid growth of time deposits (which are subject to lower reserve requirements) than demand deposits.

### *Currency Held by the Public*

One of the important factors influencing the amount of money the banking system can create, given an increase in monetary base, is the proportion of currency to demand deposits the public desires to hold. For example, if the public held a fixed total *amount* of currency, all changes in the supply of base money by the Federal Reserve would remain in the banking system as reserves and would be reflected entirely in changes in deposits, the amount depending on the reserve requirement ratios for different classes and types of deposit. On the other hand, if the public

[6] Expanding the equation for total bank reserves,

$$R = R^d + R^t + ER_m + VC_n$$

And since $R^d$, for instance, is the appropriate required reserve ratio times the amount of deposits in each reserve requirement classification, the above expression is rewritten in terms of weighted average reserve ratios and deposits. See footnote 7.

[7] For the interested reader,

$$r = a\,\delta r^d + (1 - a)\,\tau r^t + e + v$$

where a = the proportion of member bank demand deposits to total deposits, $\delta$ = the proportion of net demand deposits of member banks to total demand deposits, $r^d$ = a weighted-average reserve requirement ratio for member bank demand deposits, $\tau$ = the proportion of net time deposits of member banks to total time deposits, $r^t$ = a weighted average requirement ratio for member bank time deposits, e = ratio of excess reserves to total bank deposits, v = ratio of nonmember bank vault cash to total bank deposits.

This definition is altered somewhat by the recently instituted lagged-reserve-requirement provisions of the Federal Reserve. It is worth emphasizing that some of the above ratios are determined by the behavior of commercial banks and the public, and others are determined primarily by the Federal Reserve. The fact that these ratios are not fixed does not impair the usefulness of the analysis.

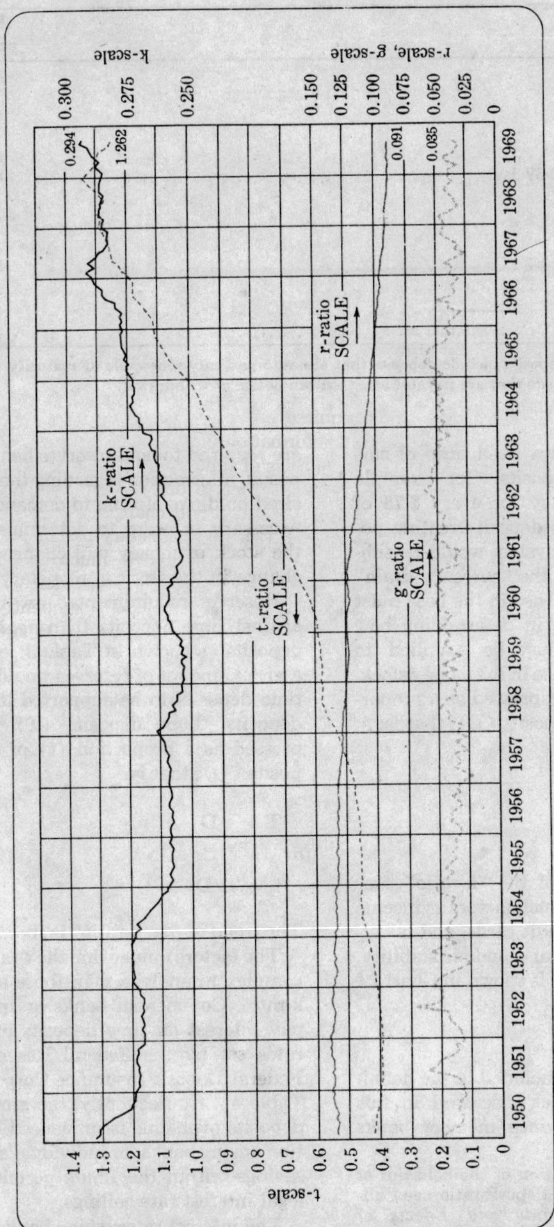


**CHART 2** Monetary multiplier ratios. *Latest data plotted: September, 1969.*

TABLE 4. MAXIMUM INTEREST RATES PAYABLE ON TIME AND SAVINGS DEPOSITS (Effective April 19, 1968)

| Type of deposit | Per cent per annum |
|---|---|
| Savings deposits | 4.00% |
| Other time deposits: | |
| Multiple maturity*: | |
| 90 days or more | 5.00 |
| Less than 90 days (30-89 days) | 4.00 |
| Single maturity· | |
| Less than $100,000 | 5.00 |
| $100,000 or more: | |
| 30-59 days | 5.50 |
| 60-89 days | 5.75 |
| 90-179 days | 6.00 |
| 180 days and over | 6.25 |

*Multiple maturity time deposits include deposits that are automatically renewable at maturity without action by the depositor and deposits that are payable after written notice of withdrawal.

SOURCE: Federal Reserve *Bulletin*.

always desired to hold a fixed *ratio* of currency to demand deposits (for example exactly $.25 in currency for every $.75 of demand deposits), the deposit creating potential of the banking system would be substantially less. Clearly the "currency drain" associated with an increase in the base must be taken into account in determining how much base money must be supplied to achieve a desired increase in the money stock. Currency (C) can be expressed as a proportion (k) of demand deposits (D), that is:

$$C = k D$$

or

$$k = C/D$$

Changes in the level of the "k-ratio" over time are influenced by such factors as income levels, utilization of credit cards, and uncertainties regarding general economic stability. The trend of the k-ratio is shown in Chart 2.[8]

### *Time Deposits*

Time deposits are not included in the definition of the money stock discussed in this article. Nevertheless, since member banks are required to hold reserves behind time deposits, information regarding the public's desired holdings of time to demand deposits is necessary in order to determine how much the stock of money will change following a change in the stock of monetary base.

Reserve requirements are much lower against time deposits than against demand deposits as shown in Table 3; consequently a given amount of reserves would allow more time deposits to be supported than demand deposits. Time deposits (T) can be expressed as a proportion (t) of demand deposits (D), that is:

$$T = t D$$

or

$$t = T/D$$

The trend of the "t-ratio" is shown in Chart 2.

The factors influencing the t-ratio are more complex to analyze than those affecting the k-ratio. Commercial banks are permitted to pay interest on time deposits up to ceiling rates set by the Federal Reserve and the Federal Deposit Insurance Corporation (see Table 4). Consequently, the growth of time deposits over time is influenced by competition among banks for individual and business savings within the limits permitted by the legal interest rate ceilings.

The interest rates which banks are willing to offer on time deposits (below the ceilings) are determined primarily by opportunities

[8] For a detailed examination of the behavior of the currency to demand deposit ratio, see Phillip Cagan, *Determinants and Effects of Changes in the U.S. Money Stock, 1875–1960* (New York: National Bureau of Economic Research, 1965), chapter 4.

that are available for profitable investment of the funds in loans or securities. Similarly, the decisions by individuals and businesses to deposit their funds in banks are influenced by the interest rates available from alternative earning assets such as savings and loan shares, mutual savings bank deposits, bonds, stocks, commercial paper, and direct investments in real assets.[9] If the interest returns from these other assets are sufficiently high that the interest rate ceilings on time deposits prevent banks from effectively competing for the public's savings, then time deposits may not grow (or may even decline) and all increases in commercial bank reserves can be used to support demand deposits. This point will be discussed in more detail below.

### *U.S. Government Deposits*

Commercial banks are required to hold the same proportion of reserves against Federal Government demand deposits as against private demand deposits. Therefore, even though Government deposits are *not* included in the definition of the money stock, changes in the amount of Government deposits influence the amount of private deposits the banking system can support with a given amount of base money or reserves. Government deposits (G) can be expressed as a proportion (g) of private demand deposits (D), that is:

$$G = g\,D$$

or

$$g = G/D$$

The amount of Government deposits in commercial banks is determined by the flow of Treasury receipts (primarily from taxes) relative to Treasury expenditures, and by the Treasury's discretion about what proportion of its balances to keep with commercial banks rather than at the Federal Reserve. Thus, short-run fluctuations in the "g-ratio" are primarily the result of actions by the U.S. Treasury. The Federal Reserve must assess, from past experience and information available from the Treasury, what will happen to Treasury balances in an impending period in order to determine the influence of changes in Treasury balances on the money stock. The monthly pattern of the g-ratio is shown in Chart 2.

[9] Jerry L. Jordan, *The Market for Deposit-Type Financial Assets,* Working Paper No. 8, Federal Reserve Bank of St. Louis, March 1969.

### *The Monetary Multiplier*

All of the essential elements for determination of the money stock have now been discussed. The definitional relations are as follows:

$$M = D + C \tag{1}$$
$$B = R + C \tag{2}$$
$$R = r\,(D + T + G) \tag{3}$$
$$C = k\,D \tag{4}$$
$$T = t\,D \tag{5}$$
$$G = g\,D \tag{6}$$

By substituting (3) and (4) into (2) we get:

$$B = r\,(D + T + G) + kD \tag{7}$$

that is, we express the monetary base solely in terms of the various deposits. Substituting (5) and (6) into (7), we get:

$$B = r\,(D + t\,D + g\,D) + kD \tag{8}$$

that is, we express the base solely in terms of private demand deposits to reduce the number of variables. Simplifying, we write (8) as:

$$B = [r\,(1 + t + g) + k] \cdot D \tag{8$^1$}$$

from which, by simple manipulation, we can express deposits in terms of the base as follows:

$$D = \frac{1}{r\,(1 + t + g) + k} \cdot B \tag{9}$$

Since we want to find D plus C, we use (4) and (9) to redefine C in terms of the base:

$$C = \frac{k}{r\,(1 + t + g) + k} \cdot B \tag{10}$$

Substituting (9) and (10) into (1) gives:

$$M = \frac{1 + k}{r\,(1 + t + g) + k} \cdot B \tag{11}$$

or the money stock defined in terms of the

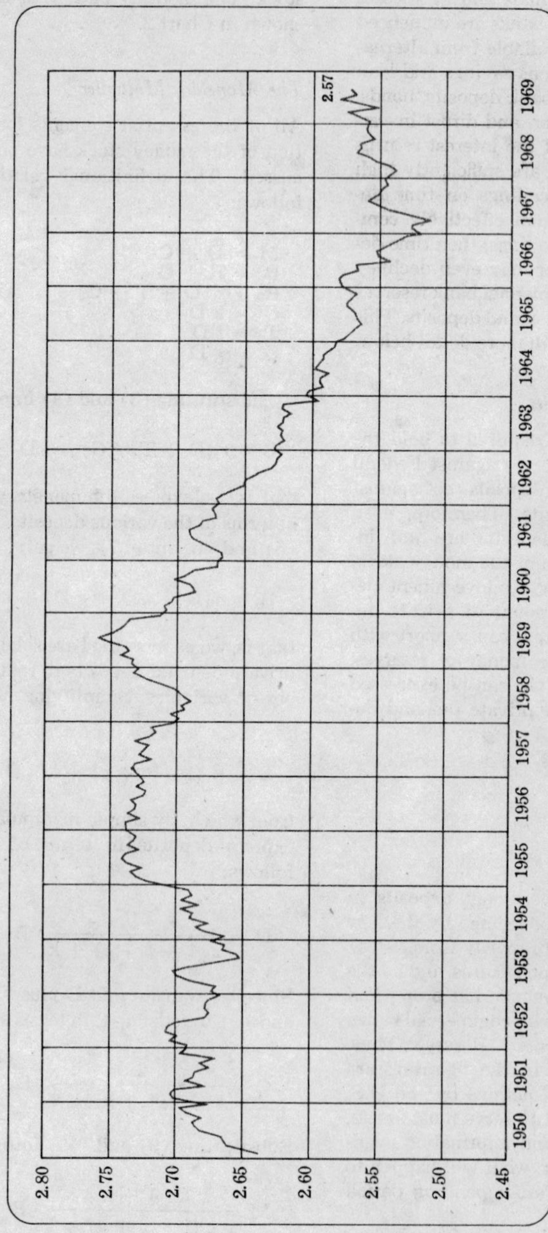


**CHART 3** Monetary multiplier. *Latest data plotted: September, 1969.*

monetary base.[10] We can denote the quotient as:

$$m = \frac{1 + k}{r(1 + t + g) + k}$$

where m is called the "monetary multiplier."[11]

The factors that can cause changes in the monetary multiplier are all of the factors which influence the currency (k), time deposit (t), Government deposit (g), and reserve (r) ratios, that is, the "behavioral parameters." The observed monthly values of these ratios in the past twenty years are shown in Chart 2, and the monthly values for the monetary multiplier (m) are shown in Chart 3. Quite obviously, if the monetary multiplier were perfectly constant, at say 2.5, then every $1 increase in the monetary base would result in a $2.50 increase in the money stock. On the other hand, if the monetary multiplier were subject to substantial unpredictable variation, the Federal Reserve would have difficulty in determining the money stock by controlling the base.

Since the monetary multiplier is not constant, the Federal Reserve must predict the value of the multiplier for the impending month in order to know how much to increase the monetary base to achieve a desired level of the money stock. Techniques for predicting the monetary multiplier go beyond the scope of this paper.[12] However, examples of how changes in time deposits and Government deposits influence the stock of money will be discussed.

## The Influence of Two Factors on the Money Stock

The following sections present examples of the ways changes in the growth of time deposits and U.S. Government deposits influence the money creation process. The effects are illustrated both by changes in the ratios in the monetary multiplier and with the use of commercial bank balance sheet "T-Accounts."

### *Changes in Time Deposits*

The growth of time deposits relative to demand deposits is determined by many factors, including those which influence the interest rates offered by commercial banks on such deposits and those which influence the quantity of time deposits demanded by the public at each interest rate. Both the banks' supply of time deposits and the public's demand for them are a function of relative costs and returns of alternative sources of funds and earning assets. Thus, accuracy of predictions of the t-ratio (time deposits to demand deposits) for a future period is influenced by the ability of the forecasters to anticipate the banks' and public's behavior. Experience has shown that changes in this ratio tend to be dominated by rather long-run trends, with exceptions occurring at those times when interest rate ceilings imposed by the monetary authorities prevent banks from effectively competing for deposits. It is these special cases that will be discussed.

When market interest rates rise above the ceiling rates banks are permitted to offer on time deposits, some individuals and businesses who might otherwise hold time deposits decide to buy bonds or other earning assets instead. This effect has been most pronounced on the banks' class of time deposits called "large negotiable certificates of deposit" (CD's). To depositors, these are highly liquid assets which are considered by the purchasers to be close substitutes for Treasury bills and commercial paper.[13] On at least four occasions since 1965 the yields on these substitute assets have risen above the rates banks were permitted to offer on CD's, causing the growth of CD's to slow sharply or even become negative.

To illustrate the effect on the money stock of a rise in market interest rates above Regulation Q ceilings, assume that the growth of

---

[10] Since the monetary base is adjusted for the effect of changes in reserve requirements, a corresponding adjustment is made to the reserve ratio (r).

[11] The reader should be able to demonstrate that if money is defined to include time deposits $M_2 = D + C + T$), then

$$m_2 = \frac{1 + k + t}{r(1 + t + g) + k}$$

[12] For one straight-forward approach, see Lyle Kalish, *A Study of Money Stock Control,* Working Paper No. 11, Federal Reserve Bank of St. Louis, July 1969.

[13] Jordan, *Deposit-Type Financial Assets,* chapter 4.

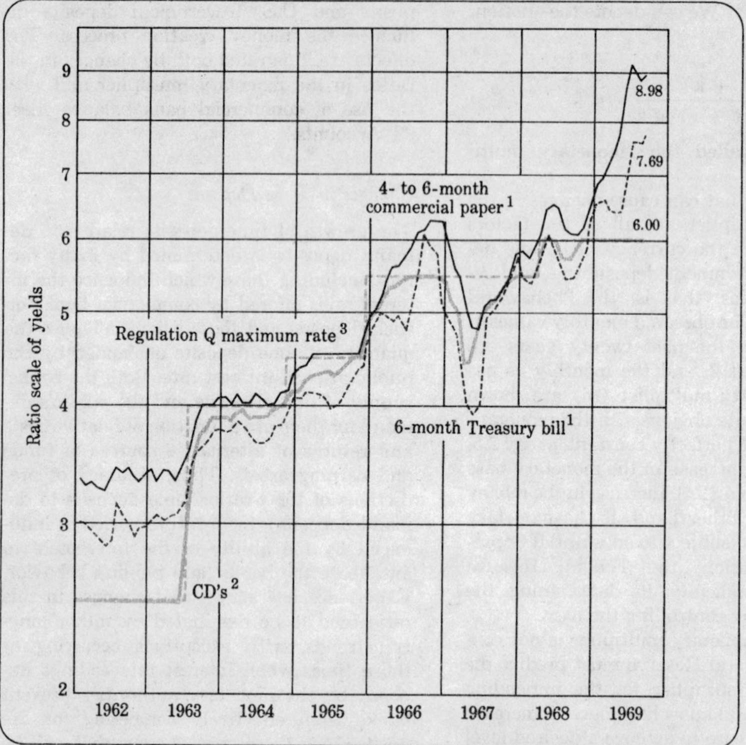


Short-term money market rates. *Latest data plotted: September, 1969.* [1] *Market yields converted from discount to bond equivalent basis.* [2] *Average new issue rates on 6-month certificates of deposit of $100,000 or more. Data are estimated by the Federal Reserve Bank of St. Louis from guide rates published in the Bond Buyer and are monthly averages of Wednesday figures.* [3] *Rate on deposits in amounts of $100,000 or more maturing in 90 to 179 days.*

time deposits ceases, and banks hold the same total amount of time deposits while demand deposits continue to grow. In the money supply model this is reflected in a decline in the t-ratio (time deposits divided by demand deposits), and since the t-ratio appears in the denominator of the multiplier, the multiplier would get larger as the t-ratio gets smaller.

For example, assume the following initial values for the monetary base and the parameters of the multiplier:

$B = \$75$ billion
$t = 1.3$
$g = .04$
$k = .3$
$r = .1$

Since

$$M = \frac{1 + k}{r\,(1 + t + g) + k} \cdot B$$

we can solve to find $M = \$182.6$ billion.

Now suppose that in the course of several months the base increases by $1 billion, but time deposits do not grow at all as a result of the high market rates of interest relative to Regulation Q ceilings. If all of the ratios in the multiplier (including the t-ratio) had remained unchanged in this period, the money stock would have increased by about $2.4 billion to $185 billion. But, since time deposits did not change while demand deposits continued to grow, the t-ratio would fall, to 1.28 for example, which causes the multiplier to increase (still assuming the other behavioral parameters remain the same).[14]

The reader should be careful not to interpret this greater increase in money (especially demand deposits) to mean that the banks can extend more credit than otherwise. Since the reserve requirements on demand deposits are greater than on time deposits, the $1 billion increase in monetary base would have supported a greater amount of *total* deposits (demand plus time) if time deposits grew proportionally to demand deposits, rather than only demand deposits increasing. With the assumed initial values for the parameters of the multiplier and the postulated $1 billion increase in the monetary base, money plus time deposits would have increased by almost $4.8 billion, almost twice as much as money.

To interpret the effects of this increase in money on the economy, it is necessary to analyze the increase in the supply of money compared to the demand for money to hold, and the supplies of and demands for other assets. We postulated above that market interest rates rose above the ceiling rates banks are permitted to pay on time deposits (especially CD's). In such a situation the volume of CD's (quantity *supplied*) is any amount depositors wish at the ceiling rates. Since the yields on good substitutes become more attractive than CD's, the *demand* for CD's declines, resulting in a decline in the outstanding volume of CD's or a slowing in the growth rate. In other words, a change in the relative yields on substitute assets causes a shift in the demand for CD's (negative), which causes a decline in the volume.

### *Disintermediation*

We noted above that *total* deposits of banks may decline as a result of this "disintermediation" of time deposits. This means that banks must contract their assets, either loans or security holdings, as deposits decline. An understanding of the actions of banks in the face of a deposit drain and actions of those who withdraw their deposits is important information in assessing the effects of the disintermediation caused by the interest rate ceilings.

To illustrate two possible effects of disintermediation, we will use highly simplified examples and T-accounts (commercial bank balance sheets). Account I shows the banking system in its initial condition having total reserves (TR) = $25, required reserves (RR) = $25 and excess reserves (ER) = 0, security holds (S) = $100 and loans outstanding (L) = $175. Bank liabilities are demand deposits (DD) = $100 and time deposits (TD) = $200. We have assumed that reserve requirements against demand deposits are 15 per cent and reserve requirements against time deposits are 5 per cent.

Account II shows the effect of a corporation reducing its holdings of time deposits by $20 and buying $20 in securities from the banks, because of the higher return available on the latter. The immediate effect is that the ownership of the securities is changed—the corporation directly holds the securities instead of having a deposit in a bank which

ACCOUNT I
Banking System

| Assets | | | Liabilities | |
|---|---|---|---|---|
| TR | | $ 25 | DD | $100 |
| | {RR $25, ER 0} | | TD | 200 |
| S | | 100 | | |
| L | | 175 | | |
| Total | | $300 | Total | $300 |

ACCOUNT II
Banking System

| Assets | | | Liabilities | |
|---|---|---|---|---|
| TR | | $ 25 | DD | $100 |
| | {RR $24, ER 1} | | TD | 180 |
| S | | 80 | | |
| L | | 175 | | |
| Total | | $280 | Total | $280 |

[14] In practice, as the t-ratio falls from 1.3 to 1.28, demand deposits grow and time deposits do not, and the average reserve requirement ratio (r) will rise. This will slightly attenuate the increase in the multiplier and the money stock.

owns the securities, hence the term "disintermediation"—and the banks are left with $1 of excess reserves. The banking system can create loans (or buy some securities), based on the dollar of excess reserves, and increase demand deposits by a multiple of $1. In this simplified example, the effect of disintermediation resulting from relatively low interest rate ceilings is potentially expansionary on total loans, even though total deposits decrease.

For the second example, a bank, in its usual role as an intermediary, sells CD's to a corporation which wishes to invest short-term funds. With the proceeds of the sale of the CD's, the bank lends to another corporation (less the amount the bank must hold as required reserves, of course). Another simplified example of the potential effects of disintermediation on the banking system and total credit is illustrated in Account III. For exposition, assume that the one-bank holding companies of commercial banks establish subsidiaries for the purpose of buying and selling commercial paper.

For our example, assume the first corporation does not wish to renew $20 of its CD holdings when they reach maturity, but rather, because of generally rising short-term market interest rates, seeks a yield greater than the bank is permitted to pay. Our hypothetical subsidiary of the one-bank holding company can offer to sell its own commercial paper (I.O.U.) to the first corporation at competitive market interest rates (Account IV).

We assume the corporation buys the subsidiary's commercial paper. As a result of their reduced deposits the banks are forced to contract assets proportionately (as a first step in a partial analysis). Instead of selling securities, as in our previous example, the banks can contract loans outstanding by $20, as shown in Account III (as compared to Account I). The subsidiary can in turn use the proceeds of its sale of commercial paper to purchase the paper of another corporation which seeks to borrow short-term money, possibly a corporation which was having difficulty getting a bank loan since bank assets and liabilities were contracting.

We find that the initial effect of the disintermediation is that the total of bank loans plus commercial paper debts of borrowing corporations is the same as the initial amount of bank loans outstanding, and that the total of time deposits plus commercial paper assets of lending corporations is the same as the initial amount of time deposits at banks. However, we also find that banks have acquired an additional $1 of excess reserves which they can lend and thereby increase demand deposits.

In summary, both of the examples of the disintermediation of time deposits caused by the interest rate ceilings show that the same initial amount of reserves in the banking system can, under certain circumstances, support a larger amount of demand deposits (and therefore money stock). In other words, if the disintermediation means only that some funds flow through channels which are not subject to reserve requirements and interest rate ceilings, the effects of the relatively low interest rate ceilings on commercial bank time deposits are potentially expansionary on total loans.

**ACCOUNT III**
**Banking System**

| Assets | | | Liabilities | |
|---|---|---|---|---|
| TR | | $ 25 | DD | $100 |
| | | | TD | 180 |
| RR | $24 | | | |
| ER | 1 | | | |
| S | | 100 | | |
| L1 | | 155 | | |
| Total | | $280 | Total | $280 |

**ACCOUNT IV**
**Subsidiary of One-Bank Holding Company**

| Assets | | Liabilities | |
|---|---|---|---|
| Commercial Paper held | $ 20 | Commercial Paper outstanding | $ 20 |

## *U.S. Government Deposits and Money*

As previously discussed, the monetary base summarizes all of the actions of the Federal Reserve which influence the money stock. However, the Treasury cannot be overlooked as an agency which can influence the money stock over at least short periods. In the money supply model, the influence of changes in the amount of Government deposits is reflected in movements in the g-ratio (Government deposits divided by private demand deposits) in the monetary multiplier.

In recent years the Government's balances at commercial banks have fluctuated from $3 billion to $9 billion within a few months time. Private demand deposits averaged about $150 billion in mid-1969. The g-ratio is therefore quite small, ranging from about .02 to about .06, but frequently doubles or falls by half over the course of a month or two.

Similar to the effect of changes in the t-ratio, increases in the g-ratio result in a fall in the multiplier since the ratio appears in the denominator. Using again the initial values we assumed for the base and multiplier, we have:

$$M = \frac{1 + .3}{.1\ (1 + 1.3 + .04) + .3} \cdot \$75 \text{ billion} = \$182.6 \text{ billion}$$

where .04 is the value of the g-ratio. These values imply that demand deposits (D) are about $140.5 billion and Government deposits (G) are $5.6 billion. Now suppose that individuals and businesses pay taxes of $1 billion by writing checks which draw down (D) to $139.5 billion, and Government balances rise to $6.6 billion. Assuming no change in time deposits or currency held by the public and no change in the base, we would find that the g-ratio rises to .047 (and the k- and t-ratios rise slightly) to give us:

$$M = \frac{1 + .302}{.1\ (1 + 1.309 + .047) + .302} \cdot \$75 \text{ billion} = \$181.6 \text{ billion}$$

A similar example of the effects on the money stock of an increase in Government deposits at commercial banks which is associated with a change in time deposits (people pay taxes by reducing their savings or holdings of CD's) would be somewhat more complicated. In the above example, taxes were paid out of demand deposits, and the reserve ratio (r) was not changed, which implies that the distribution of the increment in Government deposits among reserve city, country and nonmember banks was the same as the distribution of the $1 billion reduction in private demand deposits.

When taxes are paid out of time deposits, the r-ratio rises, since reserve requirements against Government deposits are approximately three times the reserve requirements against time deposits. These movements are very small, and any accompanying reduction in the excess reserve ratio would attenuate the effect. Nonetheless, the effect on money is a combination of small changes in the k-, r-, t-, and g-ratios.

## Summary

The behavioral parameters of the money supply framework presented here are the currency (k), reserve (r), time deposit (t), and Government deposit (g) ratios. The changes in these ratios reflect the actions of the Treasury, banks, and nonbank public which influence the money stock. The k-ratio is determined by the public's preferences for currency versus demand deposits; the t-ratio reflects the interaction of the banks' supply of and the public's demand for time deposits as compared to the supply of and demand for demand deposits; and the g-ratio is dominated by changes in Government balances at commercial banks. The r-ratio is the least volatile of the behavioral parameters, although it is influenced by the banks' desired holdings of excess reserves and the distribution of total deposits among all the subclasses of deposits in the various classes of banks, which are subject to a large array of reserve requirements.

The main policy actions of the monetary authorities—open market operations, changes in reserve requirements, and administration of the discount window—are summarized by the monetary base. The growth of the base summarizes the *influence* of the monetary authorities' defensive and dynamic *actions* on the growth of the money stock, regardless of the *intent* of these actions. The degree of accuracy that can be achieved by the monetary authorities in controlling the money stock is a function of their ability to determine the monetary base, and to predict the net influence of the public's and banks' behavior as summarized by changes in the money supply multiplier.

# 21 TIME DEPOSITS IN MONETARY ANALYSIS*

LYLE E. GRAMLEY
*Board of Governors of the Federal Reserve System*

SAMUEL B. CHASE, JR.
*University of Montana*

Developments in banking over the past decade have heightened the importance of time deposits in discussions of central bank policy. The decade has seen time deposits at commercial banks grow by more than 170 per cent, 10 times as fast as demand deposits held by the public. Since 1961, time deposit growth has averaged $15 billion a year, compared with an average of less than $3 billion per year for private demand balances. Late in 1964, private holdings of time deposits exceeded demand deposits for the first time in history.

Three recent developments are particularly noteworthy. First, investors seem to have become increasingly willing to substitute time deposits for other financial assets, especially for open market securities, in response to changes in yields.

Second, competitive pressures in financial markets have led to departures from established traditions of commercial banking. A decade ago, most time deposits at commercial banks were modest savings accounts held by individuals. Banks adjusted the rates of interest paid on these accounts infrequently; competition with other depositary institutions consisted mainly of advertising appeals. Commercial banks did little to attract time deposits in large denominations—in fact, major banks refused to accept time deposits from nonfinancial corporations.

Then in February 1961, for the first time since before World War II, major commercial banks in New York and Chicago announced that they would issue large-denomination time certificates of deposit (CD's) that would be negotiable in the open market and could be held by any investor. Investors apparently regarded this new instrument as an alternative to both demand balances and market securities in their liquid asset portfolios, and the volume of CD's outstanding grew rapidly. But the increased willingness of investors to substitute deposits for market instruments and of banks to compete aggressively for these funds had their origins at least as early as the mid-1950's.

The third important development relates to regulation. Banking legislation of the early 1930's gave the Federal Reserve and the Federal Deposit Insurance Corporation power to regulate interest payments on time deposits, which the Federal Reserve exercises under Regulation Q. The use of this authority over the past decade has permitted banks to increase the rates paid on time deposits relative to rates on most other financial assets. Four times—in 1957, 1962, 1963, and 1964—interest ceilings have been relaxed, and rates paid by banks subsequently have risen. Policy decisions under Regulation Q

* Reprinted from *Federal Reserve Bulletin*, vol. 51 (October, 1965) pp. 1380–1406, by permission of the authors and the Board of Governors of the Federal Reserve System.

were one of the necessary conditions for recent time deposit expansion.

These developments have reaffirmed the banker's point of view that deposits are attracted, not created, as textbooks suggest. Attracting time deposits in the negotiable certificate market is one of several forms of open market borrowing. With the aid of permissive regulatory rulings, other new methods of borrowing, through unsecured notes and debentures, have also been employed in recent years. In principle, these latter methods are the same as "borrowing" through issuing deposits—the differences are government-made in Washington and the State capitals and relate to reserve requirements, insurance, interest payment limitations, and other creations of the State.

In this new environment, growth rates of deposits have become more suspect than ever as indicators of the conduct of monetary policy. Thus, each increase in Regulation Q ceilings has been followed by an acceleration in time deposit growth, and some observers have warned that the increase in bank credit and deposits has been excessive. Others have been concerned that the diversion of funds from market securities and claims against nonbank intermediaries into time deposits has not been fully compensated by accelerated growth of bank credit.

Systematic consideration of such questions requires a framework of analysis from which the significance of time deposits and of changing time deposit rates can be deduced. Traditional methods of monetary analysis, which postulate that the money stock is an exogenous variable fixed by central bank policies through the "money multiplier," are not well suited to this task. In such analyses time deposits, if discussed at all, are typically assigned a subordinate role among bank liabilities—treated, perhaps, as a "leakage" in the process of money creation or destruction.[1] It would be equally justifiable analytically to regard the money stock as a leakage in the process of time deposit creation or destruction.

The "new view" in monetary economics provides a more useful analytic framework.[2] In the new view, banks—like other financial institutions—are considered as suppliers of financial claims for the public to hold, and the public is given a significant role in determining both the total amount of bank liabilities and their distribution among classes. The special characteristics of the various classes of claims result in behavioral principles that can be incorporated explicitly into monetary analysis.

The next section of this paper presents a model of financial behavior that facilitates treatment of policy questions that arise when the banking system supplies multiple classes of liabilities for the public to hold. Subsequent sections deal with policy implications of recent developments in banking and include some empirical evidence on the implications of increased substitutability between time deposits and securities, and of varying time deposit rates.

The model is simple and permits treatment of only a limited number of questions. It is not a general equilibrium model but a partial equilibrium model of the financial markets. It postulates a single class of open market security and does not consider the effect of changes in time deposit rates, and in the distribution of bank liabilities, on the structure of interest rates. These are severe limitations, but light can be thrown on policy questions even within these constraints, and such an approach is a necessary first step in the development of a more complete analytical framework.

## A Model of Financial Markets

The model assumes there are four financial assets—claims against a central bank in the form of currency and bank reserves, demand deposits, time deposits, and private securities. The three sectors in the model include

[1] A notable recent exception is found in Milton Friedman and Anna J. Schwartz, *A Monetary History of the United States, 1867–1960* (Princeton: Princeton University Press for the National Bureau of Economic Research, 1964), where total bank deposits (demand and time) are viewed as the multiplicand. This approach is no more useful than the traditional one for the questions considered here.

[2] See James Tobin, "Commercial Banks as Creators of 'Money,'" *Banking and Monetary Studies,* edited by Deane Carson (Chicago: Richard D. Irwin, 1963). An application of the "new view" to central bank policy is contained in James Tobin and William C. Brainard, "Financial Intermediaries and the Effectiveness of Monetary Controls," *American Economic Review,* May 1963.

The analytic approach used in this paper parallels that of Tobin and Brainard, although our model is designed to deal with different policy questions.

a central bank, commercial banks, and the nonbank public—or simply the public.

Currency and balances at the central bank are non-interest-bearing claims held either by the public as currency or by the banking system as excess or required reserves. Demand and time deposits are liabilities of the banking system and are held only by the public. Private securities are issued by the public and are held by both the public and the banks. The central bank also buys and sells these securities when it conducts open market operations. Private securities are assumed to be all alike in terms of maturity, risk, and other features and therefore sell at the same price and yield.

At any point in time, the dollar volume of private securities held by the commercial banks and the central bank measures the indebtedness of the public to the monetary system. The model assumes that public holdings of claims against the monetary system in the form of currency and bank deposits

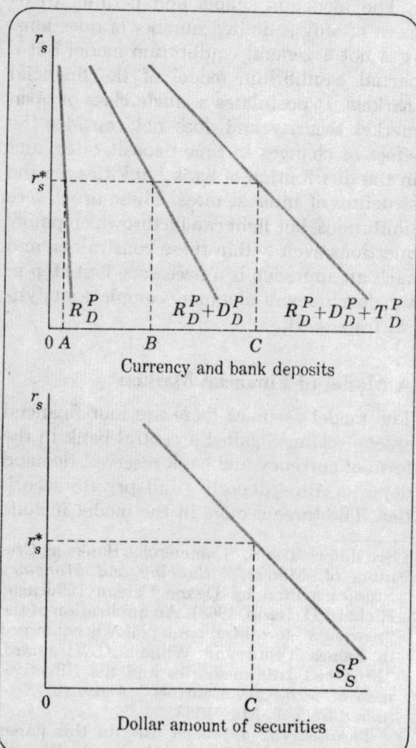


**FIGURE 1**

equal the volume of private securities held by the monetary system—in effect, that the public holds zero net financial claims against the government and commercial bank sectors.[3]

LINKAGES BETWEEN FINANCIAL AND NONFINANCIAL MARKETS. The model deals with the determination of equilibrium prices and quantities in financial markets and, in particular, with immediate financial responses to central bank policy actions. To focus attention sharply on these matters, we define a period short enough that changes in financial market variables do not influence commodity expenditures during this period. The financial markets are therefore a closed system, with nonfinancial variables assumed to be exogenous.

The links between financial markets and markets for goods and services are not investigated here, although these linkages are the heart of the process of monetary control. In drawing out the implications of the analysis for nonfinancial responses to policy actions, it is assumed that the interest rate on private securities is the link between financial and nonfinancial markets. In fact, a vast array of interest rates and other credit terms are involved in the linkage.

FINANCIAL BEHAVIOR OF THE PUBLIC. Much attention has been devoted elsewhere to financial asset demand and supply functions of the public. The controversy that remains pertains chiefly to the role exercised by factors taken here as exogenous—such as current income, wealth, and the yields on real assets. Since these exogenous factors are taken as given, the public's desired allocation of financial asset portfolios among currency, demand deposits, time deposits, and securities depends only upon relative yields of these assets.

Figure 1 shows the influence of the rate on private securities, $r_s$, on financial assets demanded and supplied by the public, for given rates on bank deposits. In the top panel, $R_D^P$

[3] Throughout the model, the wealth implications of fluctuating market prices of securities are ignored for reasons of simplicity. The assumption that the public holds no net claims against the government also is made to simplify the model and would need to be dropped if the model were to be extended to cover a broader range of questions.

represents public demand for currency; $R^P_D + D^P_D$ represents public demand for currency and demand deposits; $R^P_D + D^P_D + T^P_D$ represents public demand for currency, demand deposits, and time deposits. All three are assumed to be substitutes for securities. Since the public wishes to hold more of each at lower rates of interest on securities, the demand functions slope down to the right.[4]

The net supply of securities the public wishes to sell to the monetary system, $S^P_S$, is shown in the bottom panel of Figure 1. The lower the rate of interest, $r_s$, the more securities the public chooses to offer for the monetary system to hold—including both securities outstanding at the beginning of the period that were held by the public and new securities issued during the period. This net supply of securities is not independent of public demands for currency and deposits. On the contrary, the net security supply must, by assumption, equal public demand for currency and bank deposits. Accordingly, the slope and position of $S^P_S$ in the lower panel of Figure 1 is identical to the slope and position of $R^P_D + D^P_D + T^P_D$ in the upper panel.

Public demands for bank deposits also depend on rates paid on bank deposits. The lower right panel of Figure 3, for example, shows the demand for time deposits, $T^P_D$, as an increasing function of the time deposit rate, $r_t$, given the rate on securities and the rate on demand balances. Similarly, the lower left panel shows the demand for demand deposits, $D^P_D$, as an increasing function of the demand deposit rate, $r_d$, holding $r_t$ and $r_s$ constant.

It may seem peculiar to speak of an interest rate on demand deposits, since banks are forbidden by law to pay interest on demand accounts. The legal prohibition, however, relates to explicit interest payments. Banks do, in fact, pay implicit interest on checking accounts—by relating service charges for check handling and other services to the size of customers' balances—and that is the interest rate measured by $r_d$. There is little evidence, however, that implicit rates on demand deposits vary appreciably in the short run, and we assume in the argument to follow that $r_d$ is fixed. (It is also assumed that service charges per check are invariant.)

BEHAVIOR OF THE BANKING SYSTEM. In this model, the banking system issues only two classes of liabilities for the public to hold as assets—demand deposits and time accounts. With funds raised in supplying deposits, banks acquire reserves or private securities. Banks are required to hold reserves equal to specified percentages of demand and time deposits. The percentage requirement for time deposits is lower than that for demand deposits. In addition to required reserves, banks may hold excess reserves.

Banks are assumed to set rates on deposits and to stand ready to supply all the public wishes to hold at these rates. Supply functions for demand and time deposits are thus perfectly elastic at quoted deposit rates, $r^*_d$ on demand balances and $r^*_t$ on time accounts, as shown in Figure 3.

Delving into the forces that determine deposit rates would take us far afield from our main line of inquiry. Initially, therefore, it is supposed that deposit rates quoted by banks are fixed by forces not explained in the model. Subsequently, this assumption is relaxed to explore the implications of variations in time deposit rates.

The deposit supply functions of Figure 3 are at variance with the traditional view found in much of the literature on money and banking. At this point in the argument, it seems desirable merely to indicate the approach to be used here reserving until later a comparison with accepted traditional views.

In this model, banks are not constrained in their ability to supply deposits by the existence of legal reserve requirements or by the level of bank reserves. The required reserve ratio may influence the rates at which an individual bank is willing to supply deposits, but at the rates quoted, the quantity of deposits a bank sells depends on the willingness of the public to purchase its deposits. Since this is true for each and every bank in the system, the constraint on bank deposits —and hence on bank asset holdings—is derived from the public's desire to hold bank deposits.

This constraint on bank assets is shown in Figure 2 by $D^P_D + T^P_D$ the total quantity of

[4] For simplicity, all demand and supply functions of the model are assumed to be linear. The slopes shown in Figure 1 and elsewhere are hypothetical, except to the extent that the logic of the model imposes such requirements as that the demand functions of Figure 1 slope down to the right.

deposits the public is willing to hold at varying rates on securities, given rates on demand and time deposits. $D^P_D + T^P_D$ defines the total quantity of funds available for bank investment in cash reserves and earning assets. Bank demand for required reserves, $R^B_{DR}$, is derived directly from the public's willingness to hold deposits, the mix of deposits it chooses, and the legal reserve requirements on demand and time deposits. Banks may wish to hold reserves in addition to legal requirements, however. The demand for excess reserves, $R^B_{DE}$, is taken to be a decreasing function of the rate on securities, reflecting substitution between cash and earning assets in bank portfolios. The sum of $R^B_{DE}$ and $R^B_{DR}$ measures total band demand for reserves, shown in Figure 2 as $R^B_D$.

At the security rate $r^*_s$ in Figure 2, the public is willing to hold $OD$ in bank deposits. Bank demand for required reserves at this rate is $OB$, while demand for excess reserves is $OA$ $(=BC)$. Dollar demand for securities by banks, at this interest rate, is $CD$, the difference between total demand by banks for reserves and their total assets.

EQUILIBRIUM IN THE FINANCIAL MARKETS. These postulates regarding the financial behavior of banks and the public make it possible to solve for the equilibrium rate on securities, given the rates quoted by banks on deposits and the quantity of currency and bank reserves supplied by the central bank. The solution is shown in the top two panels of Figure 3.

The upper left panel shows aggregate

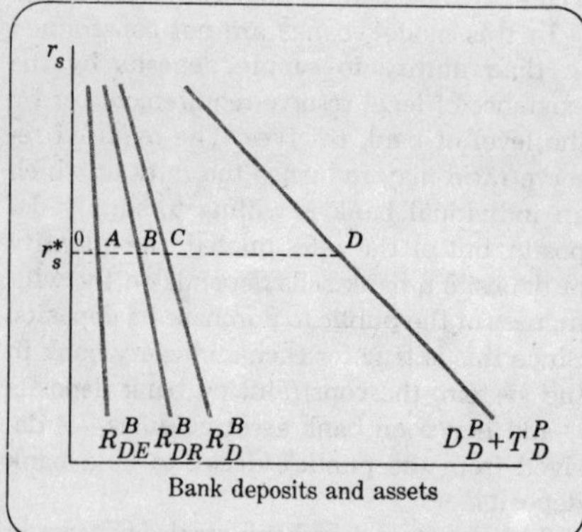


FIGURE 2

demand for currency and bank reserves, $R^{P+B}_D$, derived by summing its two separate components, currency demanded by the public, $R^P_D$ (Figure 1), and total reserves demanded by banks, $R^B_D$ (Figure 2). $R_0$ represents the total quantity of currency and bank reserves supplied by the central bank and is taken as exogenously determined. Given $R_0$, the market for currency and bank reserves clears at the rate $r_{s_0}$

The upper right panel shows the aggregate excess dollar demand for securities by the public and the banks, $S^{P+B}_X$, together with the dollar quantity of securities held by the central bank, $F_0$. This latter quantity is measured to the left of the origin at $O$, and is equal to the dollar quantity of claims against the central bank in the form of currency and bank reserves. The aggregate excess demand for securities, $S^{P+B}_X$, is derived by subtracting the public's net supply of securities, $S^P_S$ (shown in Figure 1), from the banks' demand for securities (represented by the horizontal distance between $D^P_D + T^P_D$ and $R^B_D$ in Figure 2).

It is readily shown that the aggregate excess dollar demand for securities must, at each rate of interest $r_s$, be equal in absolute value to the aggregate demand for currency and bank reserves, $R^{P+B}_D$, but of opposite sign.[5] From this fact, it follows that the rate of interest $r_{s_0}$ which clears the market for currency and bank reserves also clears the market for securities.

The bottom two panels of Figure 3 show the determination of equilibrium quantities of demand and time deposits. The demand functions $D^P_D$ and $T^P_D$ are drawn for the equilibrium rate on securities, $r_{s_0}$. At the deposit rates $r^*_d$ and $r^*_t$ quoted by banks, the equilibrium quantities of demand and time deposits are $D_0$ and $T_0$, respectively.

[5] Let $S^B_D$ represent dollar demand of banks for securities. By assumption:

$$S^P_S = D^P_D + T^P_D + R^P_D$$

and

$$S^B_D = D^P_D + T^P_D - R^B_D$$

Accordingly,

$$-S^P_S + S^B_D = S^{P+B}_X = -(R^P_D + R^B_D)$$

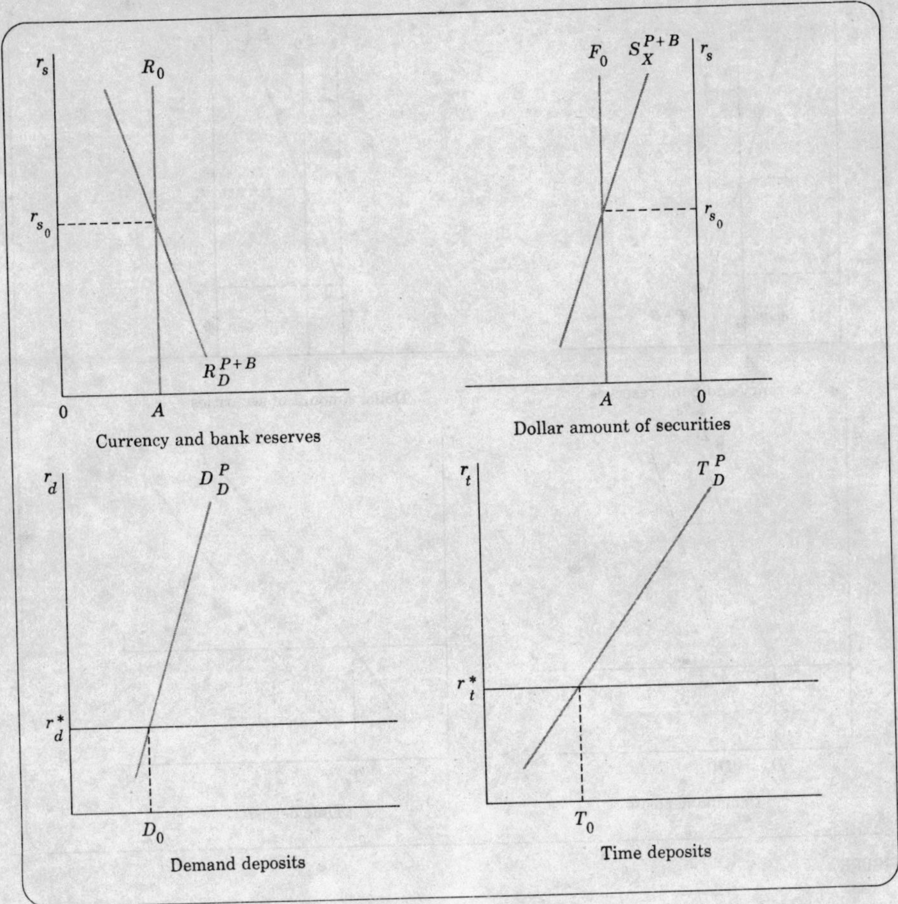


FIGURE 3

## Effects of Open Market Operations

The analysis of financial market responses to exogenous disturbances begins by considering the effect of an open market operation on the money stock, time deposits, and the security rate on the assumption that rates paid by banks on deposits are fixed.

The treatment of an open market operation is shown diagrammatically in Figure 4. Suppose the central bank engages in an open market purchase, shifting $F_0$ to $F_1$, and increasing the quantity of currency and bank reserves outstanding from $R_0$ to $R_1$. Because expenditures for goods and services are assumed to be unaffected by financial market variables in the short run, the aggregate demand functions for securities and for currency and bank reserves are stable. The equilibrium rate on securities must fall from $r_{s_0}$ to $r_{s_1}$ shown by the intersections of $R_1$ with $R_D^{P+B}$ and of $F_1$ with $S_X^{P+B}$.

The model assumes that both time deposits and demand balances substitute for securities. The drop in the security rate, consequently, increases demand for both classes of bank deposits, shifting both $D_D^P$ and $T_D^P$ to the right and increasing equilibrium quantities of time and demand deposits. If currency substitutes for securities in the portfolios of the public, as the slope of $R_D^P$ in Figure 1 implies, public currency holdings also are enlarged.

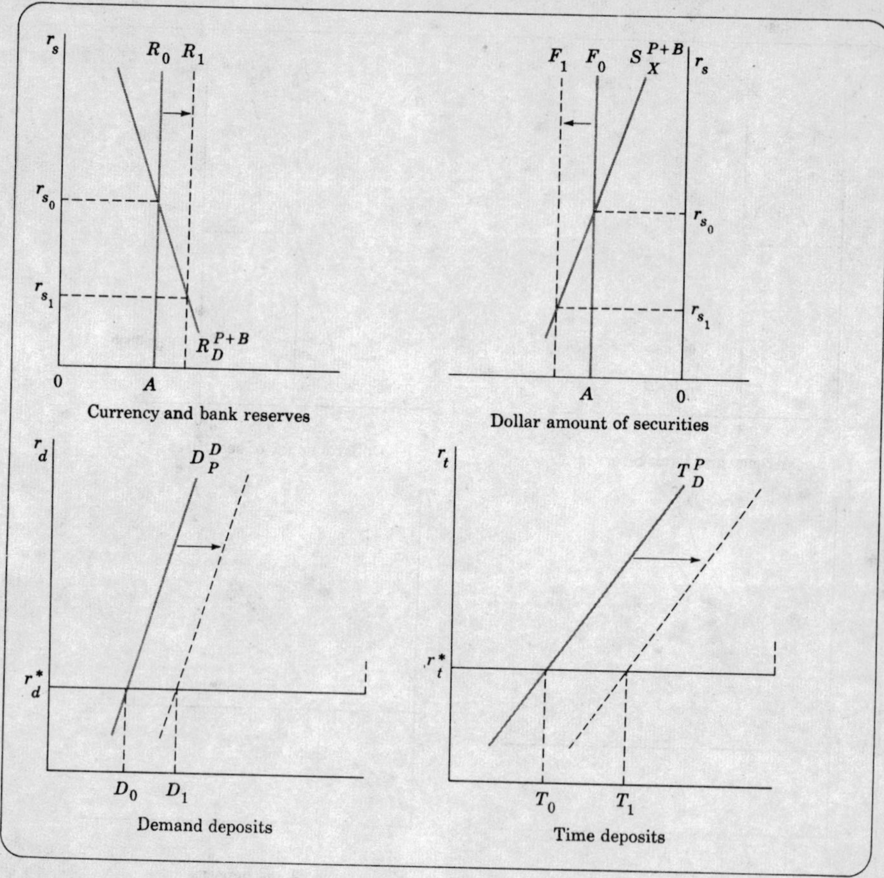


FIGURE 4

Growth in demand and time deposits accompanying an open market purchase is not viewed as the result of an increase in the quantity of deposits that banks are willing to supply, but of an enlarged public demand to hold them that stems from falling security rates. Increased bank willingness to supply deposits would be reflected in higher rates paid by banks to attract time and demand balances; it is hard to imagine such a response to easier bank reserve positions and falling yields on bank earning assets.

It may be objected that the demand-pull interpretation of deposit growth fails to recognize the ultimate limits on the quantity of demand and time deposits that the banking system is capable of supplying, given the total quantity of currency and bank reserves outstanding. These ultimate capacity limits, represented by the dotted vertical segments of the deposit supply functions of Figure 4, are shifted to the right by an open market purchase that increases total claims against the central bank.

These ultimate capacity limits on bank deposits clearly exist, but their existence does not contribute to an understanding of why and how bank deposits change in response to open market operations. The ultimate limit on demand deposits, after all, is encountered when the entire quantity of currency and bank reserves outstanding is absorbed by required reserves against demand balances—and it implies that currency held by the public, excess bank reserves, and public holdings of time deposits are all zero. Similarly, the capacity limit on time deposits reflects zero holdings of currency and demand balances by the public, and zero excess bank reserves. Such extreme conditions are not encountered in the real world.

## Some Contrasts with Traditional Views

The view of the deposit expansion process set forth here may be contrasted with some time-honored doctrines of traditional monetary analysis. The more conventional view focuses on the impact of open market operations on the nominal money stock, taking the stock of money as an exogenous variable set by central bank policy. It has often been implicitly assumed that time deposits are not substitutes for securities sold to the monetary system by the public. At one time, perhaps, this assumption was suitable as a working approximation. As noted earlier, time deposits were once held primarily by small savers, who may have been insensitive to interest rate differentials on alternative financial assets. In such a world, taking the money stock as an exogenous variable might seem justifiable. Yet, the assumption that the money stock is determined by central bank policies has led to substantial confusion, and its usefulness is seriously questionable, no matter what role time deposits play in monetary processes.

THE ELEMENT OF VOLITION IN DEPOSIT EXPANSION. Gurley and Shaw, for example, have argued that commercial banks are like other financial institutions in many respects and that they must compete with such institutions by making their liabilities attractive for the public to hold.[6] This argument was received in some quarters with astonishment and was resisted by defenders of accepted doctrines. Perhaps, Aschheim argued, banks are like other financial institutions in their time deposit business but certainly not in their demand deposit business.[7] When the banking system wishes to create additional demand deposits, said Culbertson, the public has no choice but to acquire them, since the volitional element in the process of deposit expansion lies with the banks, not with the public.[8]

The confusion in this argument perhaps comes from misinterpreting the exogeneity assumption. For example, in the familiar "hot potato" analogy used to explain monetary processes, it is presupposed that the central bank has the capability—through open market purchases—of dictating an increase in the money stock. The public then has no choice but to hold the larger stock of money, and individuals' efforts to part with money balances merely redistribute the stock from one hand to another, raising nominal expenditures and income in the process.

The initial premise is erroneous. Open market purchases increase the aggregate of currency and bank reserves outstanding; reestablishment of equilibrium requires an increase in the amount of currency and bank reserves demanded to match the enlarged supply. This increased demand does not necessarily require expansion of the nominal money stock. Increased demand for currency and bank reserves could, for example, result solely from a rise in public demand for time deposits and the induced increase in bank demand for required reserves. Indeed, public demands for currency, demand deposits, and time deposits might all be unaffected by an open market purchase; the equilibrating adjustment could come entirely from increased bank demand for excess reserves. In short, open market operations alter the stock of money balances if, and only if, they alter the quantity of money *demanded* by the public.

MONEY SUPPLY HYPOTHESES. It is possible to express the quantity of money, and its relation to other variables of the model, in a way that effectively conceals this fact. Thus, the equation:

$$M = \frac{R_0}{k} - \frac{mT_D^P + (1-k)\,R_D^P + R_{DE}^B}{k}$$

where $M$ is the quantity of currency and demand balances, $m$ is the reserve requirement against time deposits, and $k$ is the reserve re-

[6] See John G. Gurley and Edward S. Shaw, *Money in a Theory of Finance* (Washington: The Brookings Institution, 1960), pp. 198–99.

[7] Joseph Aschheim, "Commercial Banks and Financial Intermediaries, Fallacies and Policy Implications," *Journal of Political Economy*, Feb. 1959, pp. 61–62.

[8] J. M. Culbertson, "Intermediaries and Monetary Theory: A Criticism of the Gurley-Shaw Theory," *American Economic Review*, Mar. 1958, p. 122. A similar view is put forth by J. A. Galbraith, *The Economics of Banking Operations* (Montreal: McGill University Press, 1963), p. 9.

quirement for demand deposits, relates the money stock of the model to total claims against the central bank, reserve ratios against time and demand deposits, public holdings of currency and time deposits, and bank ownership of excess reserves. Viewed in this way, changes in the money stock are functions of changes in the monetary base, $R_0$, and a series of "leakages" into time deposits, currency, and excess bank reserves.

Once the nature of these leakages has been specified, the equation is properly viewed as exhibiting a relation between the equilibrium money stock and the reserve base. Constructs of this nature are sometimes identified as "money supply hypotheses."[9] But they are devoid of postulates regarding the willingness of any economic unit to supply either of the two components of the money stock—currency and demand deposits. The construct is, in fact, simply an equilibrium condition specifying that total demand for currency and bank reserves equals the total quantity outstanding.

While the equilibrium quantity of money can be determined in this way, it must—in a consistent model—be identical to that found by summing the equilibrium quantities of currency and demand deposits obtained from the public's demand functions for these two financial assets. Determining the impact of open market operations on the money stock, consequently, requires knowledge of the effect of these operations on the endogenous variables of the system, no matter which procedure is used.

THE ROLE OF INTEREST RATE ADJUSTMENTS. In taking the money stock as an exogenous variable controlled by the central bank, traditional monetary analysis often regards a decline in market rates of interest accompanying an open market purchase as the result of the increase in actual money stocks relative to desired stocks. In fact, changes in the money stock and interest rates are determined simultaneously. But if logical priority is to be assigned to the correlative movements of the two variables, changes in the money stock are properly viewed as the result, not the cause, of declining yields on market securities.

Given the rates on deposits, the security yield bears the entire burden of the adjustment in the current period of the model, since expenditures for goods are assumed to respond to financial market variables with a lag. An open market purchase requires the yield on securities to fall until expanded public demand for currency, together with bank demand for reserves, absorbs the enlarged stock of outstanding claims against the central bank.

The role of the adjustment in the security rate in the short run is displaced subsequently by increases in nominal expenditures and income that result from the initial changes in financial variables. But when central bank actions influence spending decisions with a significant lag, the initial adjustment required to bring the demand for currency and bank reserves into balance with a changed supply is a decline in the security rate. The extent of decline depends on the interest elasticity of aggregate demand for currency and bank reserves. This elasticity depends, in part, on the interest sensitivity of bank demand for excess reserves and public demands for currency and, in part, on the interest elasticity of public demands for bank deposits.

It is interesting to note the implications of a theory that specifies long lags between monetary actions and their effects on spending, but also postulates that public demands for money and time deposits are highly interest inelastic. Friedman, for example, contends that the lag between monetary actions and their effects on money income may be as long as 16 months.[10] Yet he also argues that the interest elasticity of demand for money, which he defines to include time deposits, is unimportant.[11]

These postulates are difficult to reconcile with the way financial markets behave. In the limiting case of complete interest inelasticity of demand for money and time deposits, the effect of central bank operations on the rate of interest would not alter public demands for money and time deposits. The money stock and time deposits would change, there-

[9] Karl Brunner and Allan H. Meltzer, "Some Further Implications of Demand and Supply Functions for Money," *Journal of Finance*, May 1964, especially pp. 242–56.

[10] See Milton Friedman, "The Lag in Effect of Monetary Policy," *Journal of Political Economy*, Oct. 1961, pp. 457–64.

[11] See Milton Friedman, "The Demand for Money: Some Theoretical and Empirical Results," *Journal of Political Economy*, Aug. 1959, especially p. 349.

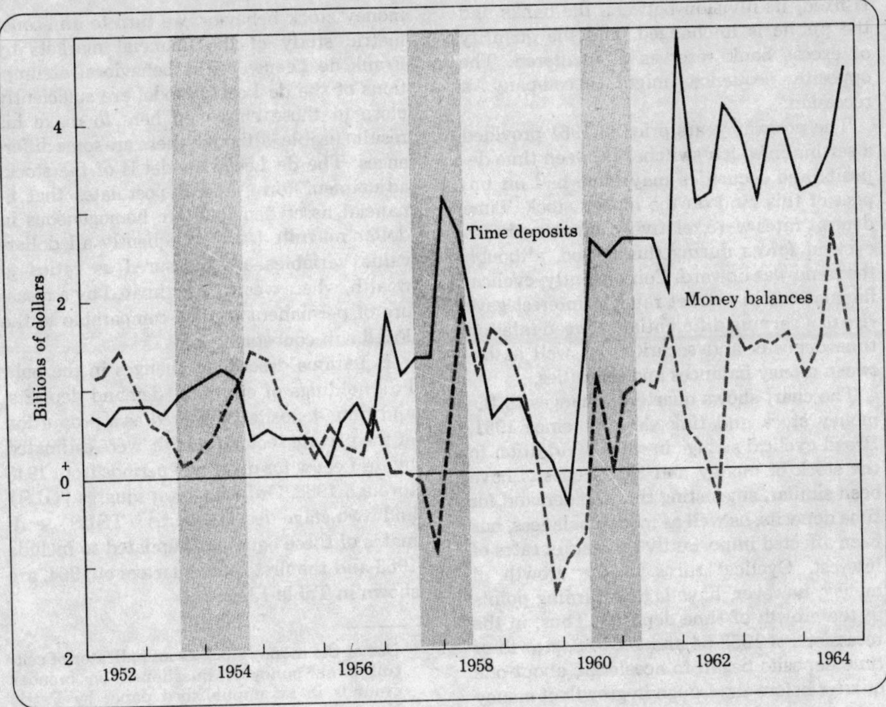


Quarterly changes in money and time deposits, 1952–1964.

fore, only to the extent that expenditures for goods and services responded to a varying rate of interest, thereby changing the demand for these financial assets. Long lags between central bank policy actions and their effects on spending decisions would, in this case, imply the absence of any short-run effect of open market operations on the level of bank deposits and public currency holdings. Changes in the supply of currency and bank reserves, in the short run, would be reflected entirely in variations in bank demand for excess reserves.

## Cyclical Variations in Money and Time Deposits

When the public regards time deposits and securities as substitutes, open market operations of the central bank—by influencing market rates on securities—influence the level of time accounts, as well as money balances, if time deposit rates adjust slowly to changes in the rate on securities. The effect of central bank operations is dispersed over a wide range of financial assets than is contemplated in traditional analysis. Such substitution is also likely to weaken the association between money balances and bank reserves by fostering procyclical movements in the money stock.

Suppose, for example, that economic expansion is initiated by an increased rate of investment, financed by an increased supply of securities. The effect on demands for financial assets depends, in part, on the rise in the rate on private securities, but it also depends on the growth of income and wealth—factors taken as exogenous to the model. If income and wealth elasticities of demand for demand deposits are high relative to those for time deposits, or if the interest elasticity of demand for time deposits is high relative to that for demand balances, the quantity of demand deposits held by the public may rise while the quantity of time deposits held may fall. Thus, the money stock may increase—even if the supply of currency and bank reserves is fixed, its division between the banks and the public is unchanged, and the quantity of excess bank reserves is unaltered. The opposite sequence might accompany a recession.

The postwar years prior to 1961 provided a setting in which switches between time deposits and securities may have had an impact of this kind on the money stock. Time deposit rates were relatively unresponsive to cyclical forces during this period, although the trend was upward. Consequently, cyclical fluctuations in market rates of interest gave rise to a varying differential between rates on time deposits and securities as well as between money balances and securities.

The chart shows quarterly changes in the money stock and time deposits since 1951. Broad cyclical swings in rates of addition to the stock of money and time deposits have been similar, suggesting that the demand for time deposits, as well as money balances, has been affected importantly by market rates of interest. Cyclical turns in the growth of money, however, have lagged turning points in the growth of time deposits. Thus, in the recessions of 1953-54 and 1957-58, growth of time deposits began to accelerate about one quarter before the trough in growth of money balances; in the expansion periods that followed, growth of time deposits began to diminish before the peak advance in money balances. But the cyclical timing of the two series almost coincided in the recession of 1960-61.

The money stock has a procyclical component. As a matter of fact, money balances were not enlarged appreciably during any of the last three recessions—even though the growth of total bank deposits and bank credit accelerated. Periods of rapid monetary growth were concentrated in the early quarters of expansion, when gross national product was rising sharply. Because it takes the stock of money as a policy-determined variable, traditional analysis assigns poor marks to the central bank for its conduct of policy in these cicumstances. It fails to recognize that substitution between time deposits and securities may be an important source of procyclical variations in the stock of money even in the face of countercyclical central bank policy.[12]

To assess the role of substitution between time deposits and securities as a factor in money stock behavior, we turn to an econometric study of the financial markets by Frank de Leeuw.[13] The behavioral assumptions of the de Leeuw model are sufficiently close to those employed here to make his results usable, although there are some differences. The de Leeuw model is of the stock-adjustment form, and it postulates that financial asset demands are homogeneous in dollar magnitudes. Consequently all dollar-value variables are measured as ratios to wealth, where wealth is estimated by a measure of permanent income comparable to the Friedman concept.

Equations describing changes in the public's holdings of currency, demand deposits, and time deposits, measured as a proportion of the private sector's wealth, were estimated by de Leeuw for quarterly periods from 1948 through 1962. Ordinary least squares (OLS) and two-stage least squares (TSLS) estimates of these equations, updated to include 1963 and the first three quarters of 1964, are shown in Table 1.[14]

---

[12] Use of the money stock as an indicator of central bank policy is questioned on broader grounds in an unpublished paper by Patric Hendershott, "Monetary Policy, 1952–62," given at the 1964 meetings of the Econometric Society. Hendershott observes that procyclical movements in the money stock are also engendered by the effects of the business cycle on member bank borrowings and other technical factors affecting bank reserves.

[13] Frank de Leeuw, "A Model of Financial Behavior," in *The Brookings Quarterly Econometric Model of the United States,* edited by James S. Duesenberry, Gary Fromm, Lawrence R. Klein, and Edwin Kuh (Rand McNally and North Holland, 1965). We are deeply indebted to de Leeuw for permitting us to use the results of his work in this paper; he is, of course, free of responsibility for any misuse that we have made of it. Details on definitions of the variables and the sources of data used in the de Leeuw model are contained in a data appendix to his paper. (Requests for this appendix should be addressed to Mr. de Leeuw, Division of Research and Statistics, Board of Governors of the Federal Reserve System, Washington, D.C., 20551).

[14] The de Leeuw model is a 19-equation representation of the financial markets; the three equations extracted for inclusion in Table 1 are the most relevant for our problem. The forms of the equations were not altered in the re-estimation that includes data for 1963 and 1964.

TABLE 1. CHANGES IN PUBLIC HOLDINGS OF CURRENCY, DEMAND DEPOSITS. AND TIME DEPOSITS, 1948 – 1964

| | | | Interest Rates | | | Household Disposable Income | | Business Income | | Capital Spending | | | | | |
|---|---|---|---|---|---|---|---|---|---|---|---|---|---|---|---|
| Item | Constant | Stock, lagged[1] | Treasury bills[2] | Private securities[3] | Time deposits | Current | Lagged[1] | Current | Lagged[1] | Household | Business | Household + business | $R^2$ | s. e. | D. W. |
| Currency: | | | | | | | | | | | | | | | |
| TSLS | –.541 | –.078 | ... | –.071 | –.018 | .004 | .018 | ... | ... | ... | ... | –.007 | .57 | .036 | .84 |
| | ... | (.010) | ... | (.018) | (.014) | (.006) | (.003) | | | | | (.006) | ... | ... | ... |
| OLS | –.648 | –.085 | ... | –.080 | –.019 | .011 | .014 | ... | ... | ... | ... | –.010 | .66 | .032 | .90 |
| | | (.009) | ... | (.014) | (.012) | (.005) | (.004) | ... | ... | ... | ... | (.003) | ... | ... | ... |
| Demand deposits: | | | | | | | | | | | | | | | |
| TSLS | .083 | –.178 | ... | –.333 | –.634 | .069 | .052 | .141 | –.128 | ... | –.163 | .... | .49 | .151 | 1.31 |
| | ... | (.029) | ... | (.076) | (.152) | (.035) | (.018) | (.069) | (.057) | ... | (.051) | ... | ... | ... | ... |
| OLS | –.526 | –.175 | ... | –.346 | –.463 | .076 | .055 | .105 | –.144 | ... | –.115 | ... | .67 | .121 | 1.36 |
| | ... | (.020) | ... | (.052) | (.083) | (.020) | (.018) | (.031) | (.035) | ... | (.030) | ... | ... | ... | ... |
| Time deposits: | | | | | | | | | | | | | | | |
| TSLS | –.589 | –.015 | –.177 | ... | .409 | ... | .021 | ... | ... | –.062 | ... | ... | .72 | .127 | .77 |
| | ... | (.017) | (.039) | ... | (.075) | ... | (.010) | ... | ... | (.028) | ... | ... | ... | ... | ... |
| OLS | .062 | –.019 | –.167 | ... | .392 | ... | .009 | ... | ... | –.037 | ... | ... | .79 | .111 | .92 |
| | ... | (.014) | (.029) | ... | (.056) | ... | (.008) | .... | ... | (.013) | ... | ... | ... | ... | ... |

TSLS = two-stage least squares; OLS = ordinary least squares; s.e. = standard error of estimate; D.W. = Durbin-Watson ratio.

[1]One-quarter lag.

[2]The market yield on 3-month Treasury bills.

[3]A weighted average of rates on corporate and municipal bonds, mortgages, and bank loans to business.

NOTE: Based on the de Leeuw model cited in footnote 13. Figures in parentheses are standard errors of the regression coefficients.

All variables other than interest rates are measured as a percentage of permanent dollar gross national product in the previous quarter. The coefficients may therefore be interpreted as though all dollar variables were measured in the same units. For the dollar-valued independent variables, the numerator of the ratio is the level of the variable. For the dependent variable, the numerator is the change in the level. It may be helpful to express one of the equations in symbols. Let $C$ = currency, $W$ = permanent GNP, $r_s$ = the private security rate, $r_d$ = the rate on time deposits, $Y^h$ = household disposable income, $A^h$ = household capital spending, $A^b$ = business capital spending. The two-stage currency equation is then:

$$\frac{\Delta C_t}{W_{t-1}} = -.541 - .078\frac{C_{t-1}}{W_{t-1}} - .071\, r_{s_t} - .018 r_{d_t} + .004\frac{Y^h_t}{W_{t-1}} - .007\frac{A^h_t + A^b_t}{W_{t-1}}$$

TABLE 2. CYCLICAL TROUGHS AND PEAKS IN INTEREST RATES, 1948 – 1964 (In per cent per annum)

| Trough or peak | Private Security Rate[1] | | | Treasury Bill Rate[2] | | |
|---|---|---|---|---|---|---|
| | Year | Quarter | Level | Year | Quarter | Level |
| Trough | 1950 | III | 3.56 | 1948 | II | 1.00 |
| Peak | 1953 | III | 4.50 | 1953 | II | 2.15 |
| Trough | 1954 | IV | 4.07 | 1954 | II | .79 |
| Peak | 1957 | III | 5.45 | 1957 | III | 3.35 |
| Trough | 1958 | II | 4.87 | 1958 | II | .96 |
| Peak | 1959 | IV | 5.98 | 1959 | IV | 4.23 |
| Trough | 1962 | IV | 5.29 | 1961 | II | 2.30 |
| Latest quarter | 1964 | III | 5.37 | 1964 | III | 3.50 |

[1]A weighted average of rates on corporate and municipal bonds, mortgages, and bank loans to business used by de Leeuw (see footnote 13 for citation).

[2]The market yield on 3-month Treasury bills.

The data there indicate that demands for currency and demand deposits, particularly the latter, are much more strongly influenced by changes in current income than is the demand for time deposits. Holdings of demand deposits are positively related to current household income, lagged household income, and current business income. Time deposit ownership is significantly related only to the second of these three variables, and the coefficient of that income variable is quite small.

In each of the demand functions shown in the table, de Leeuw employed either an average rate on private securities or the Treasury bill rate, but not both. The regression coefficient of the private security rate in the demand deposit equation is higher than the Treasury bill rate coefficient in the demand function for time deposits. As shown in Table 2, however, the bill rate moves through cyclical swings much larger than those in the average rate on private securities.[15]

[15] The de Leeuw model visualizes the adjustment of actual to desired asset stocks as taking place over more than a single quarter and interprets the coefficient of the lagged stock variable as a speed-of-adjustment coefficient. Using this interpretation, it is possible to compute equilibrium stock elasticities of demand for each of the three financial assets. Evaluated at 1948–64 means, using the two-stage regression coefficients, the equilibrium stock elasticity of demand for time deposits with respect to the bill rate is −1.7; the elasticity of demand for demand deposits with respect to the private security rate is −0.3.

These results confirm the view that monetary policy, through its impact on market rates of interest, has an important bearing on the level of commercial bank time deposits. They also indicate why the money stock may vary procyclically around turning points in economic activity despite countercyclical changes in bank reserves.

## Changes in Substitutionary Relations

The chart on page 271 indicates that a marked increase in the cyclical component of time deposits developed in the mid-1950's—judged, for example, by the extent of the cyclical upswing during the recessions of 1957-58 and 1960-61 compared with the upswing during the recession of 1953-54. One possible explanation for this development is an increase in the degree of substitution between time deposits and securities. Developments of a national market for negotiable CD's in 1961 may have been partly responsible, but cyclical swings in time deposits suggest that a growing degree of substitution apparently developed prior to 1961.

Two results of increased substitution between time deposits and securities are immediately evident. First, short-run changes in the money stock, per dollar of open market operations, are reduced, because more of the change in the supply of currency and bank reserves is absorbed in bank demand for required reserves to support time deposits. Substitution between time deposits and securities lowers the "money multiplier." Sec-

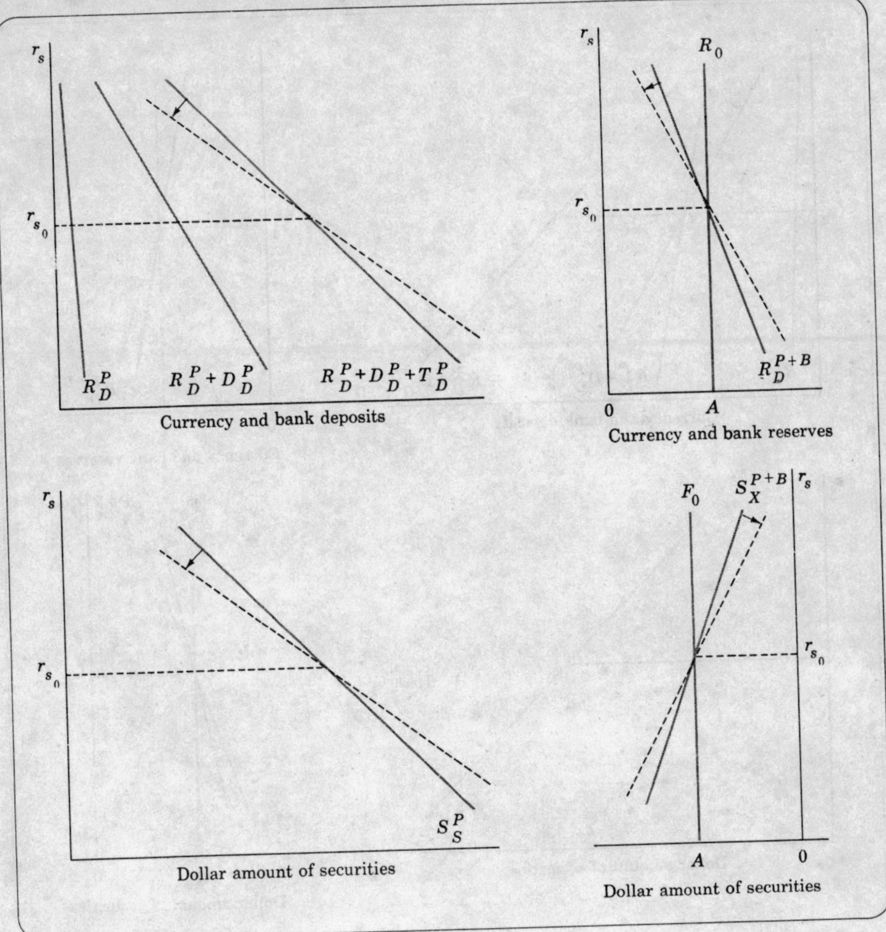


FIGURE 5

ond, because reserve requirements for time deposits are lower than those for demand deposits, changes in total deposits and in bank earning assets, per dollar of open market operations, are increased. Substitution between time deposits and securities raises the "bank credit multiplier."

These two results, however, do not carry any necessary implications for the impact of open market operations on market interest rates, which provide the link between open market operations and nominal expenditures for goods and services. Whether reserve dollars have become more or less "high powered" in a meaningful economic sense cannot be deduced by reference to changes in the money and bank credit multipliers. In the context of the model, the significant question concerns the effect of the increased substitution on the response of aggregate excess demand for securities, and of aggregate demand for currency and bank reserves, to changes in the security rate.

One possible source of greater substitution between time deposits and market securities is an increased response of public security supply to changes in the private security rate, shown by the twist of $S_s^P$ in the lower left panel of Figure 5. As the net supply of securities the public wishes to sell to the

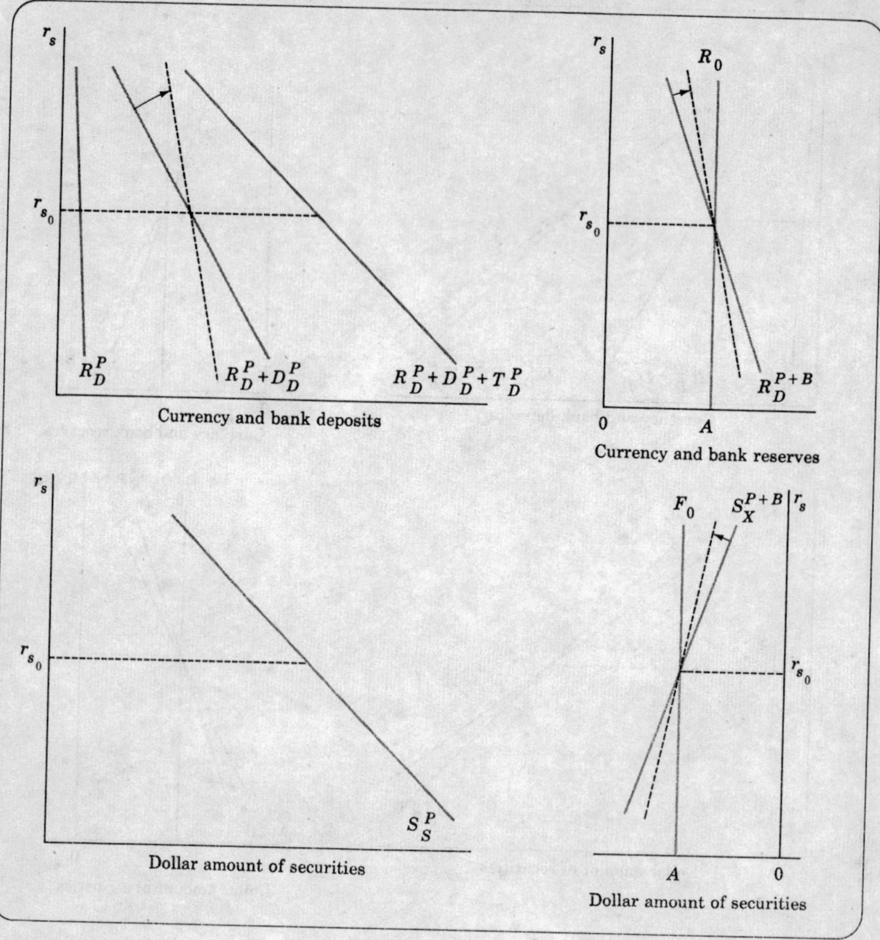


FIGURE 6

monetary system becomes more responsive to $r_s$, public demand for time deposits (and hence for the total of currency and bank deposits) does also, as indicated by the twist of $R_D^P + D_D^P + T_D^P$ to the dotted line in the upper left panel. Since a given decline in $r_s$ increases public demand for time deposits more than before, it raises bank demand for required reserves by a larger amount. Total demand for currency and bank reserves, $R_D^{P+B}$, also becomes more responsive to changes in $r_s$, as shown in the upper right panel. The offset in the market for securities is an increase in the slope of $S_X^{P+B}$. Shifts in $R_0$ and $F_0$ which result from a given dollar amount of open market operations then have a smaller effect on the security rate and ultimately on spending decisions. Consequently, a stabilizing monetary policy calls for wider cyclical swings in bank reserves.[16]

On the other hand, increased substitution between securities and time deposits may reflect a displacement of currency and demand deposits as substitutes for market securities. This possibility is illustrated in Figure 6, where it is assumed that the increased re-

[16] This conclusion depends on the assumption that time deposit rates are fixed.

TABLE 3. CHANGES IN PUBLIC HOLDINGS OF CURRENCY, DEMAND DEPOSITS, AND TIME DEPOSITS, 1948–1957 AND 1958–1964

| | | | Interest Rates | | | Household Disposable Income | | Business Income | | Capital Spending | | | | | |
|---|---|---|---|---|---|---|---|---|---|---|---|---|---|---|---|
| Item | Constant | Stock, lagged | Treasury bills | Private securities | Time deposits | Current | Lagged | Current | Lagged | Household | Business | Household + business | $R^2$ | s. e. | D.W. |
| Currency: | | | | | | | | | | | | | | | |
| TSLS | | | | | | | | | | | | | | | |
| 1948-57 | –.746 | –.096 | ... | –.046 | –.072 | .021 | .011 | ... | ... | ... | ... | –.024 | .70 | .034 | ... |
| | ... | (.012) | ... | (.094) | (.148) | (.008) | (.004) | ... | ... | ... | ... | (.010) | ... | ... | ... |
| 1958-64 | –.932 | –.079 | ... | –.077 | –.004 | .027 | –.005 | ... | ... | ... | ... | .010 | .74 | .019 | 1.67 |
| | ... | (.046) | ... | (.030) | (.042) | (.010) | (.014) | ... | ... | ... | ... | (.013) | ... | ... | ... |
| OLS | | | | | | | | | | | | | | | |
| 1948-57 | –.726 | –.091 | ... | .012 | –.161 | .018 | .009 | ... | ... | ... | ... | –.018 | .76 | .030 | ... |
| | ... | (.009) | ... | (.044) | (.067) | (.005) | (.004) | ... | ... | ... | ... | (.005) | ... | ... | ... |
| 1958-64 | –.654 | –.082 | ... | –.082 | –.009 | .019 | –.001 | ... | ... | ... | ... | .013 | .81 | .016 | 1.68 |
| | ... | (.033) | ... | (.020) | (.027) | (.007) | (.008) | ... | ... | ... | ... | (.007) | ... | ... | ... |
| Demand deposits: | | | | | | | | | | | | | | | |
| TSLS | | | | | | | | | | | | | | | |
| 1948-57 | 1.054 | –.223 | ... | –1.561 | 1.366 | .119 | .070 | –.027 | –.125 | ... | –.076 | ... | .52 | .159 | ... |
| | ... | (.041) | | (.595) | (.839) | (.049) | (.026) | (.085) | (.079) | ... | (.143) | ... | ... | ... | ... |
| 1958-64 | –12.379 | –.279 | ... | –.086 | –.452 | .411 | –.006 | –.343 | .139 | ... | –.528 | ... | .61 | .111 | 2.19 |
| | ... | (.010) | ... | (.378) | (.438) | (.227) | (.081) | (.348) | (.135) | ... | (.249) | ... | ... | ... | ... |
| OLS | | | | | | | | | | | | | | | |
| 1948-57 | .594 | –.186 | ... | –.781 | .189 | .089 | .050 | .080 | –.169 | ... | –.052 | ... | .71 | .124 | ... |
| | ... | (.023) | ... | (.202) | (.300) | (.022) | (.022) | (.037) | (.041) | ... | (.067) | ... | ... | ... | ... |
| 1958-64 | –1.082 | –.186 | ... | –.487 | –.641 | .027 | .128 | –.126 | –.096 | ... | –.238 | ... | .62 | .109 | 1.89 |
| | ... | (.067) | ... | (.147) | (.252) | (.074) | (.073) | (.092) | (.090) | ... | (.104) | ... | ... | ... | ... |
| Time deposits: | | | | | | | | | | | | | | | |
| TSLS | | | | | | | | | | | | | | | |
| 1948-57 | .556 | –.055 | –.106 | ... | .329 | ... | .010 | ... | ... | –.045 | ... | ... | .70 | .065 | ... |
| | ... | (.017) | (.055) | ... | (.139) | ... | (.008) | ... | ... | (.010) | ... | ... | ... | ... | ... |
| 1958-64 | 3.982 | .010 | –.318 | ... | .445 | ... | –.069 | ... | ... | .084 | ... | ... | .82 | .108 | 1.97 |
| | ... | (.030) | (.074) | ... | (.155) | ... | (.077) | ... | ... | (.117) | ... | ... | ... | ... | ... |
| OLS | | | | | | | | | | | | | | | |
| 1948-57 | .847 | –.067 | –.097 | ... | .291 | ... | .007 | ... | ... | –.034 | ... | ... | .75 | .060 | ... |
| | ... | (.014) | (.032) | ... | (.077) | ... | (.005) | ... | ... | (.007) | ... | ... | ... | ... | ... |
| 1958-64 | –.286 | .022 | –.229 | ... | .435 | ... | .012 | ... | ... | –.075 | ... | ... | .83 | .104 | 1.99 |
| | ... | (.030) | (.051) | ... | (.146) | ... | (.049) | ... | ... | (.051) | ... | ... | ... | ... | ... |

For explanation of abbreviations and description of data see footnotes to Table 1.

sponse of time deposit demand to changes in $r_s$ is offset entirely by a decreased response of demand for demand balances to changes in $r_s$. As a consequence, the slope of public demand for the total of currency and bank deposits is not altered. A given decline in $r_s$ enlarges public demand for demand deposits less, while raising demand for time deposits more. Therefore bank demand for required reserves is increased less, because time deposits carry lower reserve requirements. Aggregate demand for currency and bank reserves thus becomes less responsive to changes in $r_s$, as does $S_X^{P+B}$. Open market operations shifting $R_0$ and $F_0$ by given amounts now have a greater effect on the market rate of interest and subsequently on spending decisions.

The increased substitutability of time deposits for market securities since 1957 should not be expected to reflect either of these two cases exclusively, but rather some combination of them. Thus it is possible that increased substitution prior to 1961 reflected primarily a displacement of demand deposits as the "idle balances" of liquidity preference analysis. But it is quite likely that the growth of a national market for negotiable CD's since 1961 has increased the response of private security demands to changes in market interest rates, especially on short-term issues such as Treasury bills, because the marketability feature of CD's made time deposits a closer substitute for market securities.

Evidence on this score can be obtained by re-estimating the three de Leeuw equations of Table 1 for subperiods of the years 1948-64. The subperiods chosen for this purpose were 1948-57 and 1958-64. This breaks the full period at about the time when an increased degree of substitution between time deposits and market securities apparently began to develop.

As Table 3 shows, the regression coefficients of the interest rate variables in the equations for time deposits and demand balances changed appreciably from the first to the second subperiod. The coefficient of the bill rate in the time deposit equation increased (absolutely) nearly three-fold. The coefficient of the private security rate in the demand deposit equation declined absolutely, but the two-stage and ordinary least squares estimates give substantially different impressions of the decline. Demand for time deposits also seems to have become responsive to changes in time deposit rates—very likely reflecting the closer substitutability between time deposits and short-term securities.

The de Leeuw model does not contain equations relating to total public demands for, or supplies of, marketable private securities comparable with the supply function of our model. However, it does contain equations explaining household and business holdings of U.S. Government securities, and it is to be expected that changes in the interest sensitivity of security demand resulting from the increased substitution between time deposits and market instruments would be evident in these equations. Table 4 shows these two de Leeuw equations re-estimated for the subperiods 1952-57 and 1958-64.[17]

The results of the re-estimation for subperiods are mixed. As expected, demands for U.S. Government securities prove to be more responsive to changes in the Treasury bill rate during the latter subperiod, with the increased interest sensitivity confined principally to the business sector. But the data shown in Table 3, together with general reasoning about the effects of increased substitutability between securities and time deposits, lead to the expectation that security demands should also have become more responsive to changes in time deposit rates. The regression coefficients of the time deposit rate in the security demand functions of Table 4 are generally lower in 1958-64 than in the 1952-57 subperiod, however.

The empirical evidence is not conclusive regarding the meaning of increased substitution between time deposits and securities for the impact of open market operations on market rates of interest. The evidence suggests that the interest sensitivity of public demand for both securities and demand balances has been altered significantly, but it does not yield fully satisfactory estimates of these changes. Whether reserve dollars have become more high powered as a consequence of this increased substitution must remain an open question.

### Variations in Deposit Rates

The implications of changes in time deposit rates have not yet been considered. The significance of such changes has been treated

[17] The initial year of 1952, in this instance, was dictated by the availability of quarterly flow of funds data.

TABLE 4. CHANGES IN HOUSEHOLD AND BUSINESS HOLDINGS OF U.S. GOVERNMENT SECURITIES, 1952 – 1957 AND 1958 – 1964

| | | | Interest Rates | | | Business | | | | |
|---|---|---|---|---|---|---|---|---|---|---|
| Item | Constant | Stock, lagged | Treasury bills | Time deposits | Time deposit stock, lagged | Capital spending | Tax liabilities–Payments | $R^2$ | s. e. | D. W. |
| Households: | | | | | | | | | | |
| TSLS | | | | | | | | | | |
| 1952-57 | 1.352 | –.092 | .267 | –.960 | .099 | . . . | . . . | .43 | .121 | 1.27 |
| | . . . | (.050) | (.071) | (.255) | (.182) | . . . | . . . | . . . | . . . | . . . |
| 1958-64 | 4.268 | –.228 | .309 | –.676 | .007 | . . . | . . . | .68 | .144 | 1.16 |
| | . . . | (.074) | (.047) | (.215) | (.039) | . . . | . . . | . . . | . . . | . . . |
| OLS | | | | | | | | | | |
| 1952-57 | –.208 | –.071 | .282 | –.920 | .180 | . . . | . . . | .53 | .109 | 1.46 |
| | . . . | (.038) | (.064) | (.194) | (.157) | . . . | . . . | . . . | . . . | . . . |
| 1958-64 | 3.924 | –.210 | .320 | –.562 | –.010 | . . . | . . . | .74 | .130 | 1.08 |
| | | (.066) | (.042) | (.190) | (.036) | . . . | . . . | . . . | . . . | . . . |
| Businesses: | | | | | | | | | | |
| TSLS | | | | | | | | | | |
| 1952-57 | 4.456 | –.334 | .055 | –.840 | . . . | .021 | .115 | .56 | .147 | .92 |
| | . . . | (.165) | (.165) | (.332) | . . . | (.138) | (.044) | . . . | . . . | . . . |
| 1958-64 | 1.250 | –.288 | .182 | –.396 | . . . | .197 | .133 | .84 | .080 | 1.99 |
| | . . . | (.058) | (.039) | (.068) | . . . | (.086) | (.035) | . . . | . . . | . . . |
| OLS | | | | | | | | | | |
| 1952-57 | 1.835 | –.125 | –.011 | –.346 | . . . | .011 | .147 | .40 | .171 | .88 |
| | . . . | (.195) | (.146) | (.377) | . . . | (.116) | (.048) | . . . | . . . | . . . |
| 1958-64 | 1.565 | –.266 | .185 | –.372 | . . . | .138 | .130 | .81 | .088 | 1.95 |
| | . . . | (.065) | (.038) | (.075) | . . . | (.078) | (.038) | . . . | . . . | . . . |

For explanation of abbreviations and description of data see footnotes to Table 1.

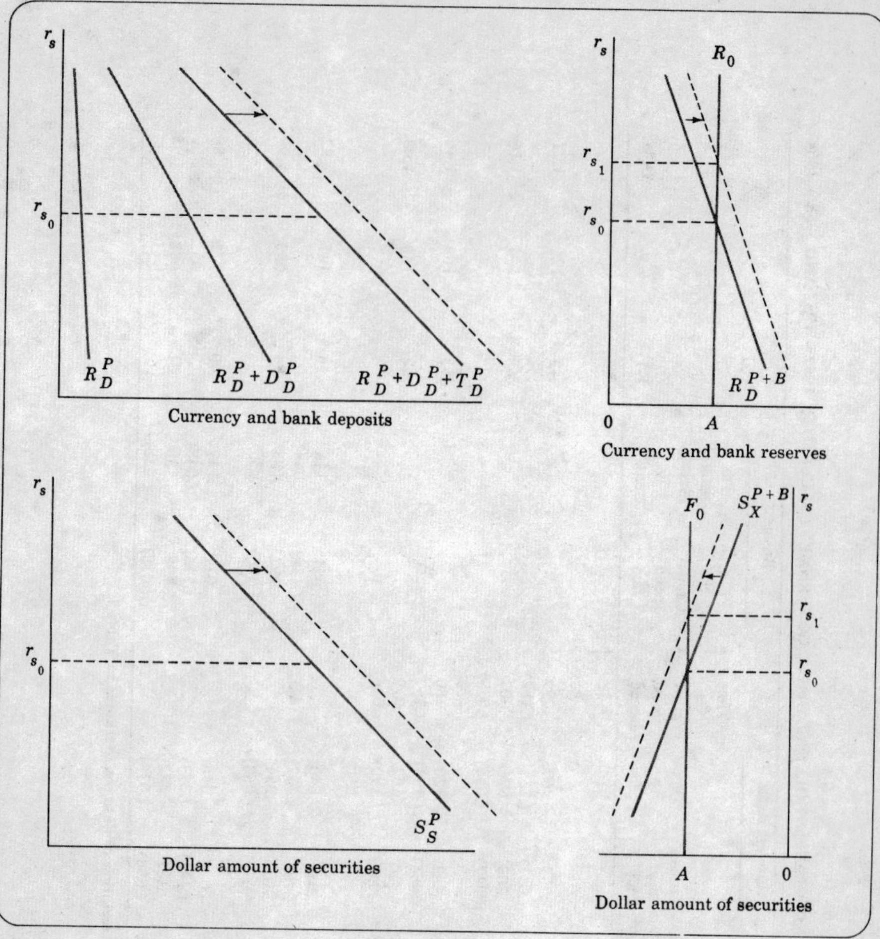


FIGURE 7

sparingly in monetary analysis, probably because there was no clear evidence, until quite recently, that rates paid by banks on time deposits changed much in the short run.[18] Sharp adjustments in time deposit rates have followed each of the four increases in ceiling rates under Regulation Q since 1956, however, and rates quoted by banks on CD's appear to be highly sensitive to changes in market yields on Treasury bills.

[18] Though treated sparingly, the significance of varying deposit rates has not been overlooked completely. See, for example, John G. Gurley and Edward S. Shaw, *op. cit.*, Chapter 5.

Movements in time deposit rates immediately following Regulation Q changes and adjustments in CD rates in response to variations in bill yields illustrate two different categories of deposit rate variation. Those following a change in Regulation Q reflect an exogenous disturbance introduced by policy actions. But the adjustment of CD rates by banks in response to variations in the yields on bank earning assets is a response to market forces. These deposit rate changes are properly characterized as endogenous. The implications of these two categories of deposit rate changes are very different.

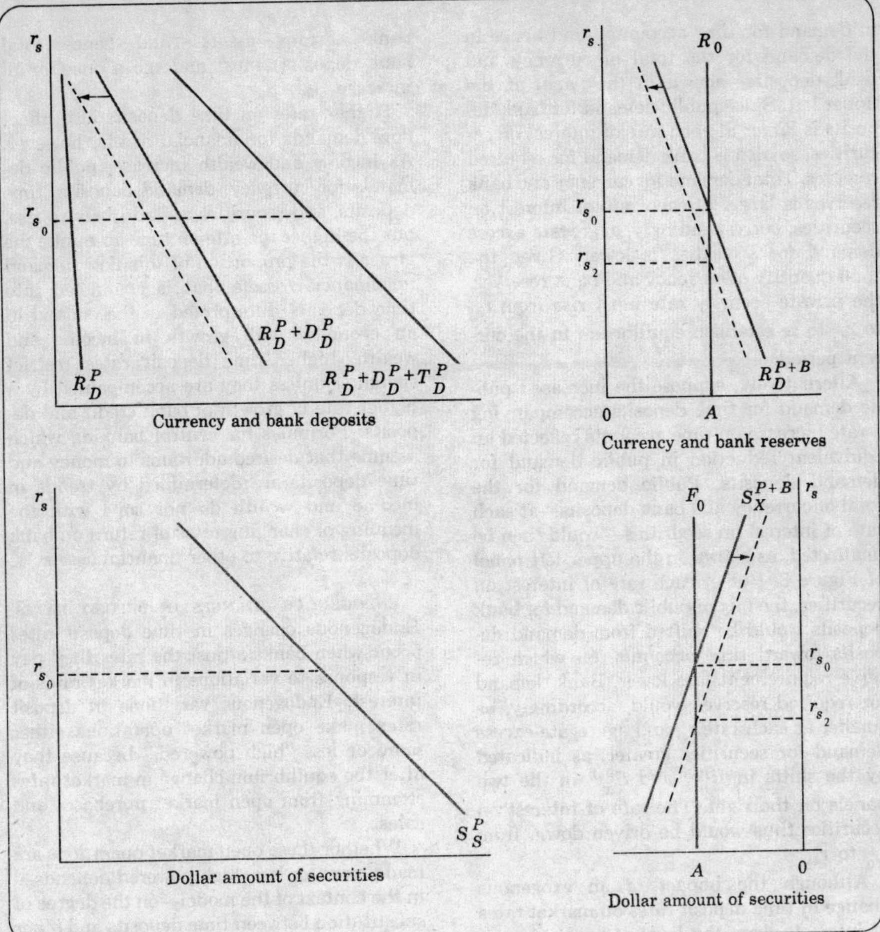


FIGURE 8

EXOGENOUS CHANGES IN DEPOSIT RATES. Exogenous changes in time deposit rates disturb an existing equilibrium in the financial markets, raising or lowering the rate on private securities and thereby influencing expenditures for goods and services in subsequent periods. Unless the resulting impact in commodity markets is in keeping with policy objectives, offsetting open market operations are required to keep interest rates on securities stable.

The effect of an exogenous rise in time deposit rates on the private security rate of the model depends on the shifts it induces in the public's desired holdings of financial assets.[19] Suppose, at one extreme, that the increase in public demand for time deposits that accompanies a rise in time deposit rates is matched by an equal increase in the public's net supply of securities. This case is illustrated in Figure 7, where the increase in net public security supply shown in the lower left panel is counterbalanced by an equal rise

[19] In the discussion that follows, the possibility that currency and time deposits may be substitutes is ignored. The extremely small, and statistically insignificant, coefficient of the time deposit rate in the currency equation for the 1958–64 subperiod, shown in Table 3, seems to justify this.

in demand for time accounts—and hence in the demand for the total of currency and bank deposits—shown in the panel at the upper left. Since public demand for bank deposits is larger at each rate of interest on securities, so also is bank demand for required reserves. Total demand for currency and bank reserves is larger at each rate of interest on securities; correspondingly, aggregate excess demand for securities is lower. Given the total quantity of currency and bank reserves, the private security rate must rise from $r_{s_0}$ to $r_{s_1}$ to re-establish equilibrium in the current period.

Alternatively, suppose the increased public demand for time deposits accompanying a rate increase on time accounts reflected an equivalent reduction in public demand for demand deposits. Public demand for the total of currency and bank deposits—at each rate of interest on securities—would then be unaffected, as shown in the upper left panel of Figure 8. But at each rate of interest on securities, the mix of public demand for bank deposits would be shifted from demand deposits toward time accounts, on which reserve requirements are lower. Bank demand for required reserves would, accordingly, be smaller at each rate $r_s$, and aggregate excess demand for securities greater, as indicated by the shifts in $R_D^{P+B}$ and $S_X^{P+B}$ in the two panels on the right. The rate of interest on securities thus would be driven down, from $r_{s_0}$ to $r_{s_2}$.

Although the impact of an exogenous change in time deposit rates on market rates of interest, given the level of bank reserves and currency, is ambiguous, there is one principle that remains invariant. If time deposits and securities are substitutes, and the empirical evidence clearly indicates they are, an exogenous rise in time deposit rates always increases market rates of interest unless bank earning assets increase. Banks must absorb the securities the public wishes to part with, at existing rates on securities, if security rates are not to rise.

The effect of an exogenous rise in time deposit rates works initially on existing stocks of financial assets, shifting demand from demand deposits and securities to time accounts. To prevent this shift in demand among existing stocks of assets from raising interest rates on market securities, total bank earning assets (and hence total bank deposits) must undergo a once-for-all increase.

Higher rates on time deposits also affect flow demands for financial assets, however. As income and wealth increase, public demands for currency, demand deposits, time deposits, and securities are all likely to rise, but the higher the rate on time accounts, the larger is the proportion of this flow demand for financial assets that is channeled into time deposits. Interpreted in the context of an economy with growth in income and wealth, higher time deposit rates restrict spending unless they are accompanied by a higher rate of growth of bank credit and deposits. Formulas for central banking which assume that desired additions to money and time deposits are determined by trends in income and wealth do not cope with the meaning of changing rates of return on bank deposits relative to other financial assets.

ENDOGENOUS CHANGES IN DEPOSIT RATES. Endogenous changes in time deposit rates occur when banks adjust the rates they pay in response to variations in market rates of interest. Endogenous variations in deposit rates make open market operations either more or less "high powered," because they alter the equilibrium change in market rates stemming from open market purchases and sales.

Whether these open market operations are made more, or less, high powered depends—in the context of the model—on the degree of substitution between time deposits and other financial assets. If time deposits substitute principally for demand balances, a change in time deposit rates generates an opposite movement in the private security rate, as noted earlier. In this case, open market operations are made less powerful. Purchases by the central bank that drive down the security rate induce banks to lower offering rates on time deposits. Falling rates on time deposits, however, reduce aggregate excess demand for securities and moderate the decline in the security rate.

Contrariwise, when time deposits substitute principally for securities, open market operations become more high powered. For when open market purchases drive down the market rate on securities, an induced reduction of time deposit rates increases aggregate excess demand for securities, and this accelerates the decline in the security rate.

EMPIRICAL EVIDENCE. The degree to which time deposits substitute for other financial assets is clearly an important empirical question. Results obtained from the de Leeuw model—reported earlier—shed some light on the question, but they do not provide fully satisfactory answers.

The de Leeuw model is of the stock-adjustment form—it postulates that adjustments to changes in desired asset stocks do not occur within a single quarter but are spread over longer periods. The full equilibrium-stock adjustments in financial asset holdings, following a change in yield relationships, differ materially from the responses in the initial quarter.

Table 5 shows both the initial quarter and the equilibrium-stock response of public demands for currency, demand deposits, time deposits, and household and business security holdings to changes in time deposit rates —based on the two-stage least squares estimates for 1948-64.[20] Changes in desired financial asset holdings are expressed in billions of dollars per 1 percentage point change in the rate on time deposits.

The evidence is not easy to interpret. For initial-quarter responses, the figures shown imply that public demands for money and U.S. Government securities decline more, in response to an increase in time deposit rates, than the demand for time accounts increases —an implausible result. The equilibrium-stock responses do not suffer from this ambiguity, but they suggest shifts among stocks of financial assets, in response to relative yield changes, that seem extraordinarily large.[21]

It seems appropriate to interpret these results with considerable caution. The equilibrium-stock responses suggest that only a small portion of the increased demand for time deposits accompanying a time deposit rate increase represents demand diverted from currency and demand deposits. The largest portion represents funds diverted from household and business holdings of U.S. Government securities, and from other financial assets not encompassed by the five equations—including private securities and claims against nonbank intermediaries. It thus appears that when time is allotted for full equilibrium-stock adjustments to occur, a time deposit rate increase exerts upward pressure on market rates of interest unless compensating open market operations expand the supply of currency and bank reserves. The short-run impact of an increase in time deposit rates, on the other hand, apparently reduces demand for demand deposits significantly. It is thus possible that the short-run effect lowers average reserve requirements enough to generate a temporary fall in market rates of interest, given the supply of currency and bank reserves.

## Some Policy Implications

The principal focus throughout this paper has been on the policy implications of viewing banks as sellers of claims against themselves for the public to hold, rather than as "creators of money." It may be helpful to

**TABLE 5. CHANGE IN DESIRED FINANCIAL ASSET HOLDINGS PER PERCENTAGE POINT INCREASE IN TIME DEPOSIT RATE, 1948 – 1964 (In billions of dollars)**

| Asset | Initial quarter | Equilibrium stocks |
|---|---|---|
| Currency .............. | –.1 | –.9 |
| Deposits: | | |
| Demand .............. | –2.4 | –13.5 |
| Time .............. | 1.6 | 104.1 |
| Holdings of U. S. Government securities: | | |
| Household ............ | –3.2 | –32.8 |
| Business .............. | –1.1 | –12.5 |

NOTE: Based on Table 1 and equations for household and business holdings of securities comparable to those in Table 4 but covering the period 1952–64. Equilibrium stock figures are derived by dividing initial quarter responses shown above by the coefficients of the relevant lagged stock variables.

[20] For securities, the period is 1952–64.

[21] The magnitude of the equilibrium-stock responses depends importantly on the size of the coefficient of the lagged-stock variable. As de Leeuw noted in his study, coefficients of lagged-stock variables are especially sensitive to specification error; it thus seems wise to interpret the results that depend on them cautiously. Additionally, the quarterly interest rate for time deposits used in the de Leeuw model is generated from annual data, because quarterly figures are not available. Because it is not possible to evaluate the accuracy of the resulting quarterly data, estimates of demand elasticities with respect to the time deposit rate may be biased to an unknown degree.

summarize the main thread of the argument.

A traditional way of viewing monetary processes that has recently gained in popularity takes as its initial premise that central bank actions affect spending decisions by altering the actual stock of money balances relative to the desired stock. The public, it is argued, has only negligible power to alter the actual stock of money; that power lies in the hands of the central bank. Consequently, when policy actions raise actual money stocks relative to desired stocks, the public's efforts to exchange money for other assets alter asset prices and the real value of money balances.[22]

One could not object seriously to this view of monetary processes if increases in the money stock took the form of gifts of money distributed to the public by the central bank. But in a world in which expansive policy measures take such forms as open market purchases and lowered reserve requirements, central bank actions do not affect the actual money stock except as they lead to a change in desired money balances. The effect of these actions on money income occurs not because the money stock has been altered, but because financial variables through which the central bank alters the desired stock of money also affect the public's decisions to puchase goods and services.

There are conditions under which changes in the money stock can be rationalized as an appropriate indicator of monetary policy conducted through conventional means. What is required is that movements in the money stock reflect the influence of central bank actions on the prices and yields of financial assets and on the nonprice terms governing the availability of credit to private borrowers. Changes in the money stock may then serve as a proxy for the more complex set of financial variables that enter expenditure functions. Whether financial markets ever behaved in such a way as to permit this interpretation of changes in the money stock is debatable, but there is little doubt that such a simple rule for appraisal of central bank operations is no longer appropriate.

The existence of time deposits and other classes of bank liabilities that substitute for securities loosens the link between central bank actions and money, making the money stock an untrustworthy indicator of the effects of policy actions on financial asset prices and yields. The attractive simplicity of the money-stock guide to central bank policy cannot be salvaged by redefining the money stock to include other classes of bank liabilities, however. Variable rates of return on bank deposits make simple rules of growth in money, regardless of how money is defined, unsuitable guidelines for the conduct of monetary policy.

There remains no alternative but to search for indicators among the relevant financial variables that enter expenditure functions—prices, yields, and nonprice terms on financial assets. It is not pleasant to face the complexities of this task. Unfortunately, there is no single financial variable in which the essence of monetary ease and restraint is distilled, and the influence of financial variables on expenditures is not so conveniently timed as to make possible an easy separation of the financial market effects of policy actions from those produced by shifts in the private sector's demand and supply functions for securities. Financial market behavior is too complex for simple monetary rules to work.

[22] Karl Brunner and Allan H. Meltzer, "Predicting Velocity: Implications for Theory and Policy," *Journal of Finance*, May 1963, p. 322.

# 22 SOME IMPLICATIONS OF MONEY SUPPLY ANALYSIS*

DAVID I. FAND
*Wayne State University*

In money and banking textbooks there is a simple link between bank reserves, deposits, and money. In a world where banks use all their reserves, where there are no free reserves, and where both the banks and the public do not undertake any portfolio changes, there is no need to concern ourselves with the money supply since it is basically a matter of arithmetic. Once we get away from the simple, mechanical link between reserves, deposits, and money, the supply of money has an independent existence as an economic variable determined by behavior and subject to analysis.

A money supply function relates the nominal money supply to a number of policy controlled variables and instruments, to other financial variables (e.g., the bill rate or the rate on time deposits), to nonfinancial variables, and to exogenous variables. This function is derived for a given set of behavior assumptions for the banks and the public and relates changes in monetary base, in reserve requirements, in the discount rate, in other instruments (such as regulation Q) to changes in the nominal supply of money and it may also relate changes in the money supply to changes in other interest rates. More generally, a money supply function may enable us to predict the effects of changes in demand (for money) as well as changes in Federal Reserve actions on the money supply and on interest rates (14).

But while it is desirable to have such a function, there are two kinds of difficulties that need to be considered. One difficulty is statistical in nature. We may not be able to estimate a supply function if the parameters affecting supply also affect demand. In this case the observed data points reflect the joint influence of both and it may not be possible to estimate a supply function. We shall abstract from this problem by assuming that the demand for money is a demand for real balances but that the dependent variable in the supply function is the supply of nominal money balances.[1]

The second kind of difficulty arises from conceptual differences among monetary theorists. Is there any point in estimating an M.S. function if money is a passive variable reflecting primarily movements in the real economy?[2] Is there any point in estimating a function relating $M_1$ or $M_2$ to Federal Reserve instruments if other intermediary claims are relatively perfect substitutes for money? Is there any point in estimating the variables determining the money supply if

* Reprinted from *The American Economic Review,* vol. 57 (May, 1967) pp. 380–400, by permission of the author and the American Economic Association.

[1] This view of the demand function is supported in an empirical study by G. Morrison. In a paper presented at the 1966 Econometric Society meetings he finds that the demand function for nominal balances is homogeneous of degree one in money income and prices.

[2] To save space we shall use symbols for the concepts and the variables that come up repeatedly; see the Glossary in Appendix III.

the private spending responds to changes in interest rates and not necessarily to changes in liquidity?

We shall attempt to show that the issues in dispute between those who take a monetary view—that money may be a causal, active, and independent factor in changing the level of output, employment, and the price level (1) (2) (15)—and those who take a real (nonmonetary) view and argue that money is passive changing primarily in response to changes in the real economy, between those who argue that $M_1$ or $M_2$ is a well-defined and a reasonably well-behaved quantity (2) (5) (15) and those who would apply the money supply concept to a broader liquidity aggregate (29), between those who argue that policy should focus on a liquidity aggregate (2) (12) (15) and those who argue for focusing on interest rates (6) (23), may be clarified and even partially resolved by defining several money supply concepts with alternative behavior specifications. These concepts suggest a number of M.S. functions both to discriminate between opposing views and to reconcile some of the differences.

In this paper we carry out part of this task. Accordingly, in Section I we define several money supply concepts and spell out the behavior assumptions in each; in Sections II and III we compare these concepts with the M.S. functions that have been estimated in several models, construct additional M.S. functions with alternative specifications, and derive elasticities or multipliers for each concept. We then analyze these elasticities. These elasticities and multipliers are calculated from the structural equations and any defects in these equations will affect our estimates.[3] But, in spite of such limitations, we do believe that the M.S. concepts, the behavior specifications, and the M.S. functions defined and constructed in this paper provide a useful framework for analyzing and interpreting the monetary studies that have been made and also for resolving some of the differences among monetary economists.

[3] To avoid misunderstanding we distinguish between the calculated elasticities and multipliers and the estimated structural equations on which they are based. These structural equations are taken from the econometric models analyzed in this paper.

## I. The Four Money Supply Concepts

To define the concept of a money supply function, we need to spell out the *ceteris paribus* conditions and, in particular, the specific adjustments that we permit the banks and the public. There are, however, alternative ways in which to incorporate portfolio behavior for the banks and the public in a financial model and different investigators adopt different assumptions. Consequently, in order to relate the money supply functions that have been estimated by Brunner-Meltzer (linear theory) (1) (2), DeLeeuw-S.S.R.C. (9), DeLeeuw-condensed (10), DeLeeuw and Turek (27), Goldfeld (16) and Teigen (24) (25) as well as the Brunner-Meltzer nonlinear theory (1) (3) and the reduced form framework used by Cagan (5) and Friedman (15), it is useful to distinguish four money supply concepts. For a given definition of money, say $M_1 = C + D$, these four concepts imply a particular set of assumptions concerning the real economy, the commercial banks, and the public; and they also provide a framework to organize, compare, and interpret the available estimates.

In Table 1 we sketch the behavior assumptions of the four money supply concepts.

M.S. I is a short-run supply concept in that it restricts the public's holdings of currency and time deposits but since it does permit free reserves to vary, it gives the supply response under conditions slightly more general than those in the textbook case. M.S. II is a short-run supply concept that brings in additional adjustments; the banks (in some models) can vary the supply of time deposits and the public can adjust their holdings of currency and time deposits. M.S. III is a reduced form equation for the entire financial sector. It may be viewed as a first approximation to a long-run concept which, while constraining the real sector, does bring in bank behavior with respect to their assets as well as their liabilities and portfolio behavior for the public with respect to all financial assets. M.S. IV is a reduced form equation for the entire economy (financial and real). If it is interpreted as a long-run supply concept it should be understood that it indicates the equilibrium stocks of money that will be held for particular sets of policy variables

**TABLE 1. FOUR MONEY SUPPLY CONCEPTS***

| M. S. concept | Bank behavior defined by | Public behavior defined by |
|---|---|---|
| I. $f(X, r_b; T, C: Y)$†, ‡ | Free reserve adjustment<br>Supply of demand deposits | Holdings of currency, time deposits and other financial assets are restricted |
| II. $f(X, r_b, T, C: Y)$<br>$= g(X, r_b: Y)$<br>since $T = T(r_b)$<br>$C = C(r_b)$ | Free reserve adjustment<br>Supply of time and demand deposits | Currency and time deposits adjusted in accord with demand functions |
| III. $f(X, r_b, T, C: Y)$<br>$= g(X: Y)$<br>since $r_b = r_b(X)$<br>$T(r_b) = T(X)$<br>$C(r_b) = C(X)$ | Free reserve adjustment<br>Supply of time and demand deposits<br>Demand for financial assets | Demand deposits and all financial assets are adjusted in accord with demand functions |
| IV. $f(X, r_b, T, C: Y)$<br>$= g(X)$<br>since $Y = Y(X)$ | Free reserve adjustment<br>Supply of time and demand deposits<br>Demand for financial assets | All financial assets, nonfinancial assets, all flow may be adjusted in accord with demand functions; supply of assets to banks |

*The symbols used in this table are defined in the Glossary in Appendix III.

†This is M. S. I for the (P) specification which requires that T and C are held constant. Other M. S. I specifications are defined in Appendix I.

‡We could also show explicitly a vector of variables, Z, which are exogenous to both the financial and the real sectors but we assume these variables are incorporated in the functional form.

and variables exogenous to both the financial and real sectors.[4]

M.S. I $= f(X, r_b; T, C: Y)$ provides an estimate of the supply response assuming that the banks undertake portfolio adjustments while the public's demand for currency and time deposits is suppressed. While M.S. II $= g(X, r_b: Y)$ is defined as a short-run concept, we do allow some substitution between demand deposits, time deposits, and currency; accordingly, M.S. II provides us with an estimate of the substitution possibilities discussed in (6) (23). M.S. III $= g(X: Y)$ is a reduced form for the entire financial sector and therefore allows for substitution among the entire range of financial assets while holding the variables in the real economy constant. It provides an estimate of the Gurley-Shaw effect (29). M.S. IV $= g(X)$ is a reduced form equation for both the financial and real sector and allows for leakages into the real economy.

Those who argue that money is passive, responding primarily to the real economy, would have very little interest in M.S. I, II, and III. On the other hand, those who view money as a causal factor in its own right are obviously concerned with M.S. I, II, and III. Among this group there would nevertheless be considerable disagreement as to the significance of the leakage as we move from M.S. I to M.S. IV. Thus, an analysis of these four concepts has implications bearing on the appropriateness of the active versus passive views of money; and it also has implications for the issues that divide the activists.

These four money supply concepts enable us to structure the money supply functions that have been estimated; but if we were to construct a framework to take account of all the M.S. constructs that may be calculated from the available econometric models, it

[4] It is also possible to go one step further and define M.S. V with some of the policy controlled variables or instruments as endogenous variables. Thus Teigen (25) attempts to predict unborrowed high-powered money while Smith (23) relates the discount rate to other interest rates. For a more general approach, see Wood (28).

TABLE 2. ELASTICITIES AND MULTIPLIERS FOR M.S. I*

| Model | Specification | Elasticities of $M_1$ with Respect to | | | | | Multiplier of $M_1$ with Respect to | | | | |
|---|---|---|---|---|---|---|---|---|---|---|---|
| | | $H_u$ | $r_d$ | $d$ | $t$ | $r_b$ | $H_u$ | $r_d$ | $d$ | $t$ | $r_b$ |
| DeLeeuw (S.S.R.C.) | (W) | 1.00 | −.144† | −.314 | −.074† | .112 | 2.98 | −7.00 | −3.08 | −2.26 | 5.93 |
| DeLeeuw (condensed) | (W) | 1.00 | −.078 | −.317 | −.075 | .066 | 3.00 | −3.82 | −3.11 | −2.28 | 3.52 |
| DeLeeuw-Turek | (W) | 1.00 | −.086 | −.313 | −.073 | .079 | 2.99 | −4.20 | −3.07 | −2.24 | 4.18 |
| Goldfeld | (P) | 2.28 | −.052‡ | −.80 | −.17 | .061‡ | 7.30 | −2.70 | −8.31 | −5.39 | 3.25 |
| Teigen 1966 | (A*) | 1.10 | −.015§ | −.347 | −.080 | .037§ | 3.25 | −0.71 | −3.41 | −2.42 | 1.99 |
| Teigen 1964 | (A) | 1.16 | −.230# | −.353 | −.084 | .250# | 3.41 | −11.21 | −3.46 | −2.54 | 11.21 |
| Brunner-Meltzer | (CO)** | .76 | .043 | | | .046 | 2.23 | −2.09 | | | 2.42 |
| | | .84 | .004 | | | .012 | 2.49 | −2.19 | | | .656 |

*The M.S. formulas used to derive these estimates are given in Appendix. All elasticities evaluated at 1962 means

†The elasticities given in the S.S.R.C. volume of −.348 for $r_d$ and .245 for $r_b$ are incorrect.

‡Goldfield reports −.076 for $r_d$ and .222 for $r_b$. The differences are in part due to his using quarterly data for 1962 (2), and his calculating the elasticity for M.S. II.

§Teigen 1966 develops a function for D based on $R_u$. We have developed this into a formula for M based on $H_u$. He reports −.045 for $r_d$ and .114 for $r_b$.

#Teigen 1964 reports −.170 for $r_d$ and .195 for $r_b$ but he uses means for the period 1946–59. Teigen also uses the commercial paper rate for the bill rate.

**These estimates are based on (1, p. 271) and (2, p. 49).

would necessitate many more categories.[5] To reduce the number of possibilities to a manageable amount but still emphasize the more important differences concerning the M.S. concepts, the behavior specifications, and the relevant variables in the M.S. functions, we restrict our discussion to $M_1 = C + D$. In Section II we analyze the two short-run money supply functions and in Section III M.S. III and M.S. IV.

## II. Short-Run Money Supply Concepts: M.S. I and M.S. II

M.S. I is a short-run supply concept. It gives the supply response on the assumption that the public's demand for C and T and other financial assets is restricted. There are several ways to impose *ceteris paribus* conditions on the public's holdings of financial assets and different investigators often define these conditions in a manner most compatible with their model. In addition to these behavior assumptions (for the banks and the public), M.S. I also assumes that all variables in the real sector of the economy, including stocks of real assets and flows such as consumption and investment, are held constant.[6] Elasticities or multipliers calculated for M.S. I sometimes differ because the authors have, either explicitly or implicitly, imposed different *ceteris paribus* conditions which we label the (W), (P), (A), and (CO) specifications. (See Appendix I.)

If M.S. I, which is a function of financial variables, is fairly stable, it would provide some support for the monetary view. For this reason it seems desirable, first, to examine the results of different investigators and, second, to see whether the differences may be reconciled if we make allowance for the alternative behavior specifications.

THE MULTIPLIERS AND ELASTICITIES FOR M.S. I. In Table 2 we compare the elasticities

[5] To illustrate, M.S. I has been estimated with alternative restrictions on currency and time deposits. Also, we may estimate these four money supply concepts with the steady-state stock functions or with the short-run stock adjustment functions. In addition, these four M.S. concepts can be defined for $M_1 = C + D$, for $M_2 = M_1 + T$, or for an even broader liquidity total; and for any one definition of money and for any one M.S. concept there are anywhere from 2 to 10 or more elasticities or multipliers that we can calculate. And since we have 8 to 10 investigations to analyze, there are obviously too many permutations to cover in this paper.

[6] It is also possible to estimate an M.S. I function using the stock adjustment equation for free reserves.

TABLE 3. ELASTICITIES FOR $r_d$ AND $r_d$ FOR M.S. I: CONSTANT SPECIFICATION*

| | $\epsilon(M_1, r_d)$ | | | | $\epsilon(M_1, r_b)$ | | | |
|---|---|---|---|---|---|---|---|---|
| Model | W | A | P | CO | W | A | P | CO |
| DeLeeuw† | −.144 | | −.383 | | .112 | | .297 | |
| DeLeeuw condensed | −.078 | | −.206 | | .066 | | .174 | |
| DeLeeuw-Turek | −.086 | | −.250 | | .079 | | .211 | |
| Teigen 1964† | −.190 | −.230 | −.468 | | .202 | .250 | .509 | |
| Teigen 1966† | −.013 | −.015 | −.033 | | .035 | .038 | .089 | |
| Goldfeld† | −.030 | | −.056 | | .025 | | .061 | |
| Brunner-Meltzer | | | | −.043 | | | | .046 |
| | | | | −.004 | | | | .656 |

*All elasticities evaluated at 1962 means.
†See footnotes for Table 2.

and multipliers for M.S. I. The four behavior specifications are defined in Appendix I and considering the leakages they permit, DeLeeuw's elasticities or multipliers should be the lowest, Goldfeld's the highest, and Teigen's elasticities or multipliers should be intermediate.[7] For $H_u$ the results conform to our expectations, and the same holds for $d$ and $t$. We also note that the multipliers for $r_d$ are all negative and for $r_b$ all positive. The difference between the largest and smallest elasticity for $r_d$ is approximately .21 but the high estimates are fifteen times as large as the low estimates.

The results for $H_u$ are encouraging since they suggest that the multipliers and elasticities calculated from different models, for different periods from different data (see Appendix II) are in fairly close agreement if we make some allowance for different behavior specifications. The observed differences for the interest rates $r_d$ and $r_b$, while small absolutely, are nevertheless large relatively and this reflects both differences due to the structural equations in the model as well as the differences due to the (W), (P), (A), and (CO) behavior specifications.

M.S. I ELASTICITIES: COMPARABLE BEHAVIOR SPECIFICATIONS. To separate out model differences from specification differences and to see whether the estimates for $r_d$ and $r_b$ are particularly sensitive to specification, we have constructed Table 3 which shows elasticities on a comparable (W) or (P) specification. We note that (W) elasticities are lowest, that the (P) elasticities are highest and that the (A) elasticities are intermediate. In this sense the order of magnitude observed for $H_u$, $d$ and $t$ in Table 2 is preserved. Table 3 indicates that the difference between Teigen 1966 and Goldfeld for $r_d$ is reduced considerably when they are constructed in a comparable manner while the difference between Goldfeld and DeLeeuw (corrected) with respect to $r_d$ is not narrowed but increased whether done on a (W) or on a (P) basis.

The comparisons in Table 3 do not succeed in showing that all the differences in interest rate elasticities are due to behavior specification differences. Some of the differences are due to the structural equations in the model which in turn reflect conceptual differences. Thus Teigen's 1966 elasticities calculated from a D function derived from $R_u$ with an (A) specification are not strictly comparable to DeLeeuw's elasticities calculated from an M function based on $H_u$ with a (W) specification. Similarly, Goldfeld's elasticities calculated from an M function derived from $H_u$ with a (P) specification for an M.S. II concept are not comparable to either DeLeeuw's or Teigen's. To compare Goldfeld with DeLeeuw is to compare (W) elasticities with (P) elasticities and to interchange M.S. I and M.S. II.[8] To compare Goldfeld with

[7] The Brunner-Meltzer linear theory has greater leakages in that they assume a more complete adjustment for the banks and permit C and T to vary. This may account for the fact that they have lower estimates, since M.S. I under the (CO) specification approximates M.S. II.

[8] In these models the demand for C and T is not functionally related to $H_u$, $d$, $t$, or $r_d$, and the use of M.S. II elasticities will primarily affect the Treasury bill comparison.

TABLE 4. ELASTICITIES FOR M.S. II*

| | | Elasticities of $M_1$ with Respect to | | | | | |
|---|---|---|---|---|---|---|---|
| Model | Specification | $H_u$ | $r_d$ | $d$ | $t$ | $r_t$ or $r_t$ max | $r_b$ |
| DeLeeuw (S.S.R.C.) | (P) | 2.71 | −.383 | −.833 | −.196 | .288 | .298 |
| DeLeeuw-Turek | (P) | 2.75 | −.252 | −.84 | −.20 | −.42# | .22 |
| Goldfeld† | (P) | 2.28 | −.052 | −.80 | −.17 | +.16 | .20 |
| Teigen 1966†§ | (A*) | 1.10 | −.015 | −.35 | −.080 | −.46 | −.013 |
| Teigen 1964†‡ | (A) | 1.16 | −.230 | −.353 | −.084 | | .250 |
| Brunner-Meltzer** | (CO) | .76 | −.043 | | | | .046 |
| | | .84 | −.004 | | | | .012 |

*All elasticities evaluated at 1962 means.
†See footnotes Table 2.
‡Teigen 1964 M.S. I elasticities are equal to those in M.S. II since T and C/M are held constant.
§Teigen 1966 elasticities derived from an A* specification assuming that T is fixed while C/D varies.
#In DeLeeuw-Turek model we use $r_t$ max.
**The elasticities are identical with those in Table 2, the (CO) specification being intermediate between the two M.S. concepts.

Teigen is to compare (P) elasticities with (A) elasticities and to interchange an M function based on $H_u$ with a D function based on $R_u$.[9]

These conceptual differences seem to affect the interest rate elasticities. They do not, however, seem to distort the elasticities for $H_u$, $d$ and $t$. With respect to these Federal Reserve instruments, the results are fairly consistent. Since M.S. I is defined so as to permit only short-run leakages, these results would seem to support the monetary view that money is an independent and causal factor.

THE M.S. II ELASTICITIES. Suppose we modify the restrictions implied by the behavior specifications (W), (P), (A), or (CO) and we permit the public to adjust their holdings of currency and time deposits and we also permit the banks to determine supply conditions for time deposits. To calculate the money stock response under these conditions we assume: (1) that the banks will adjust their free reserves and, in some models, we introduce the rates paid on time deposits;[10] (2) that the public's actual holdings of currency and time deposits are no longer held constant but can adjust according to their demand functions; and (3) that we may substitute the demand function for T and C to obtain M.S. II.[11] M.S. II is of the form $M = g(X, r_b : Y)$ and, as in the case with M.S. I, we assume that all variables in the real sector and all other financial assets are held constant.

In Table 4 we compare the elasticities for M.S. II. The demand functions for currency and time deposits in these models are not functions of either $H_u$, $r_d$, $d$ or $t$; and the calculated elasticities for these instruments in M.S. II (for a given specification) do not differ from those for M.S. I. The elasticities with respect to $r_b$ will be changed and we may also calculate elasticities with respect to $r_t$,

[9] Such comparisons are made in (16) (25).

[10] In some models the quantity of time deposits is determined by an exogenously given $r_t$; in others by a behavior function for $r_t$ and in Teigen 1964 the quantity of time deposits is not determined.

[11] This is therefore a generalization of M.S. I with specification (P). In principle, one could similarly generalize the (W), (A), and (CO) specifications by substituting the functions for the ratios or derivatives held constant in M.S. I; in practice this can only be done for Teigen who gives an explicit function for the C/D ratio. We view M.S. II as a short-run function. Consequently, since we use the stock equation for free reserves, C and T, we are, in effect, assuming rapid adjustment. It may be inconsistent to suppose that the public will do nothing about their holdings of financial assets but will adjust their C and T holdings rapidly (which carries the suggestion that financial adjustment is a dichotomous process rather than a continuous one). If so, we should use the short-run stock adjustment equations in M.S. I and M.S. II.

the rate on time deposits, and other exogenous variables.[12]

The difference between these elasticities and those for M.S. I, for the variables other than $r_b$, reflects the fact that the M.S. II calculations in Table 4 are given for the (P) specification. Teigen 1966 does not provide an estimate of the stock demand for T or for C and we calculate the elasticities for M.S. II by using his equation for C/D. Since the M.S. II results for DeLeeuw, Turek, and Goldfeld are on a (P) basis, we compare these with M.S. I calculations on a (P) basis. The changes for the elasticities with respect to $r_b$ are very small. For DeLeeuw it rises from .297 to .298, for Turek from .21 to .22, and for Goldfeld from .061 to .204. For Teigen 1966 it falls from .89 to −.013. (See discussion of Teigen's results in Table 5.)

These results suggest that substitution among demand deposits, time deposits, and currency does not cause significant changes in the elasticities. It may therefore be tempting to conclude that those (6) (13) (23) who concern themselves with the substitution between demand and time deposits are concerned with a minor issue. But since the structural equations for C and T do not contain any of our policy variables or monetary wealth as parameters, this is not entirely surprising. In addition, we note that Brunner-Meltzer, whose (CO) specification permits greater latitude for substitution, do, in fact, have lower elasticities. For these reasons we are inclined to conclude that our results do not reflect so much on the quantitative significance of substitution but rather suggest some needed improvement in the structural equations for currency and time deposits.

## III. Reduced Form M.S. Concepts III and IV

We also define a money supply concept which measures the movements in the stock of money in response to adjustments in the entire financial sector. To derive this money supply we solve all the equations in the financial sector simultaneously. Variables such as the Treasury bill rate and the rate on time deposits which are endogenous to the financial sector will therefore be determined and can no longer enter as arguments in the money supply function. M.S. III is of the form $M = g(X:Y)$ and measures the supply response due to a change in any of the policy controlled variables including their effect on other endogenous variables in the financial sector.[13]

One major difference between M.S. II and M.S. III in all models is that we now bring in explicitly the demand for demand deposits to determine the equilibrium level of deposits. In addition, in the Turek model, in the DeLeeuw-condensed model, and in the Teigen 1966 model we bring in a term structure equation while in the DeLeeuw-S.S.R.C. model we introduce all seven financial markets.

The M.S. III elasticities are calculated on the assumption that both the banks and the public will make any portfolio adjustment they may choose. These multipliers thus take account of the Gurley-Shaw effect (29) since they allow for substitution among the entire range of financial assets. And by comparing the estimated responses for M.S. III with those in M.S. I or M.S. II we obtain a quantitative estimate of the Gurley-Shaw effect.

In Table 5 we compare elasticities for M.S. III. A change in $H_u$ can affect the money supply directly and through its effect on interest rates such as $r_b$ which is no longer an exogenous variable. Thus if an increase in $H_u$ lowers $r_b$ and raises the demand for C and T, it will reduce the $H_u$ multiplier; and similarly for $d$, $t$ and $r_d$. Comparing these elasticities with those for M.S. I and M.S. II, we find that for Goldfeld and Turek but not for Teigen 1966 they tend to decline—sometimes drastically. In Teigen 1966 the C/D behavior is somewhat perverse in that a lowering of say, $r_b$, lowers the C/D ratio. This accounts in part for the rise in the multiplier.[14]

---

[12] Since we are not solving the complete financial model, $r_b$ is still viewed as an exogenous variable and it is not affected by changes in the policy controlled variables.

[13] More specifically we solve the structural equations to obtain the reduced form and calculate the elasticities or multipliers from the coefficients of the reduced form equations.

[14] Teigen 1966 also assumes that C is a relatively inferior good in that the C/D ratio declines with a rise in income. Brunner and Meltzer [1] point out another perverse feature in Teigen's 1964 model is that a rise in the C/M ratio will raise the money supply. This can be corrected by reformulating his M function in terms of $H_u$, and we have derived the estimates for his 1964 model on this basis.

**TABLE 5. ELASTICITIES FOR M.S. III***

| | Elasticities of $M_1$ with Respect to | | | | | |
|---|---|---|---|---|---|---|
| **Model** | $H_u$ | $r_d$ | $d$ | $t$ | $r_i$ or $r_t$ max | $r_b$ |
| Teigen 1966 | 2.22 | −.028 | − .67 | −.15 | −.42 | |
| Teigen 1964 | .33 | −.066 | − .101 | −.024 | | |
| DeLeeuw-Turek | .33 | −.004 | − .102 | −.024 | −.073 | |
| Goldfeld | 1.11 | −.025 | − .386 | −.081 | −.066 | |
| | | **Elasticity Comparisons for Several M. S. Concepts** | | | | |
| DeLeeuw-Turek | | | | | | |
| M.S. I | 2.75 | −.252 | − .84 | −.20 | | .21 |
| M.S. II | 2.75 | −.252 | − .84 | −.20 | −.42 | .22 |
| M.S. III | .33 | −.004 | − .10 | −.02 | −.07 | |
| Teigen 1966 | | | | | | |
| M.S. I | 1.10 | −.015 | − .35 | −.08 | | +.037 |
| M.S. II | 1.10 | −.015 | − .35 | −.08 | −.46 | −.013 |
| M.S. III | 2.22 | −.028 | − .67 | −.15 | −.42 | |
| M.S. IV | 3.85 | −.051 | −1.22 | −.28 | −.60 | |
| Goldfeld | | | | | | |
| M.S. I | 2.28 | −.052 | − .80 | −.17 | | .06 |
| M.S. II | 2.28 | −.052 | − .80 | −.17 | .16 | .20 |
| M.S. III | 1.11 | −.025 | − .39 | −.08 | −.07 | |
| M.S. IV | .88 | −.020 | − .31 | −.06 | −.18 | |

*All elasticities evaluated at 1962 means. See footnotes for Table 2.

Finally we define M.S. IV in the form of $M = g(X)$ which measures the movements in the money stock in response to adjustments in both the real and the financial sector. To derive this money supply we must solve all the structural equations in the financial and real sectors simultaneously to obtain the reduced form; and, in consequence, many of the real variables which are exogenous in M.S. III are now determined by the model. This reduced form M.S. gives the equilibrium stocks of money as a function of policy controlled variables and variables which are exogenous to both the financial and real sectors (e.g., family formation).[15] It is, perhaps, the natural if not the only M.S. function to measure for those who view money as a passive variable responding primarily to developments in the real economy.[16]

In Table 6 we present elasticities for M.S. IV, taking account of the interaction between the real and the financial sector. For Teigen 1966 they rise, but this is due to his C/D equation which is inversely related to Y. For Teigen 1964 the M.S. IV results are identical with those for M.S. III because the real sector is not affected by the monetary variables.

For Goldfeld the M.S. IV elasticities are all lower than for M.S. III which is in accord with our expectations since we are permitting greater leakages here. We also include Goldfeld's short-run elasticities in Table 6 and these are consistently below the elasticities derived from his stock equations. (The short-

[15] A variable exogenous to the real sector of one model may be an endogenous variable in another model.

[16] If we think of an M.S. function defined for different kinds of leakages, M.S. IV introduces leakages into the real economy. In this sense it is a natural step from M.S. II and M.S. III. On the other hand, if we think of the M.S. function as reflecting, or incorporating, a behavior response, M.S. IV is, like M.S. III, a hybrid concept and it is perhaps best to think of it as a reduced form function giving equilibrium stocks of M that are associated with different values of the argument. For lack of better terms we may call both the M.S. III and M.S. IV estimates reduced form elasticities.

**TABLE 6. ELASTICITIES FOR M.S. IV***

| | Elasticities of $M_1$ with Respect to | | | | | | | | |
|---|---|---|---|---|---|---|---|---|---|
| **Model** | $H_u$ | $r_d$ | $d$ | $t$ | $r_t$ | $r_1$ | $r_s$ | $c$ | $r$ |
| Teigen 1966 | 3.85 | −.051 | −1.22 | −.28 | −.60 | | | | |
| Teigen 1964† | .33 | −.066 | − .101 | −.024 | | | | | |
| Goldfeld (Stock) | .88 | −.020 | − .308 | −.065 | −.177 | | | | |
| Goldfeld (Short run)‡ | .43 | −.008 | − .094 | .038 | | | | | |
| Cagan§ | 91% | | | | | | | 9% | 2% |
| | 27% | | | | | | | 46% | 26% |
| Brunner-Meltzer# | .647 | −.195 | | | | .14 | −.034 | | |
| | .347 | −.145 | | | | .46 | | | |

*All elasticities evaluated at 1962 means.
†Teigen's 1964 estimates for M.S. IV are identical with those for M.S. III.
‡Goldfeld's short-run elasticities derived from his impact multipliers.
§Cagan gives the relative contribution of each determinant to the rate of changes of $M_2$ for the period 1875–1955 The second set of estimates give the relative contribution to specific cycles in the trend-adjusted rate of change in $M_2$. See (5, pp. 19, 26) and Appendix II.
#These estimates are based on (1, p. 280) and (3, p. 59) Brunner and Meltzer use K instead of $H_u$. See Appendix II.

run elasticities are derived from his impact multipliers and provide an estimate of the first period response.) Brunner and Meltzer's elasticities, derived from their nonlinear theory, are not directly comparable to Goldfeld's since they use K instead of $H_u$ and they introduce several interest rates.[17]

Cagan's results are derived from a different framework in which the *ex post* rate of change of the money supply is allocated to three determinants, the rate of change of H, of R/D and of C/M. Cagan estimates the percentage contribution of a particular determinant in a given period of time and these are not comparable to the elasticity estimates; and he confines his analysis to $M_2$.

There are at present two few studies available to calculate reliable M.S. IV elasticities. But the available evidence, meager though it may be, does not point to any superiority of M.S. IV over M.S. I, and does not appear to favor a real view over a monetary view. Those who take the view that money is passive, responding primarily to the real economy, have to recognize that this is an assumption rather than a proposition derived from empirical evidence.

## Conclusions

In this paper we have defined four money supply concepts with alternative behavior specifications and developed a framework to compare M.S. elasticities calculated from different econometric models. Analysis of Tables 2 to 6 suggests that while we are far from any consensus there has been a considerable amount of progress. For any one M.S. concept the estimates for $H_u$, $d$ and $t$ derived from the different models are consistent, while the interest rate elasticities exhibit greater variability, and some instability, as we change either the concept, the model, or the specification. Similarly, as we take one model and compare the estimates for different M.S. concepts, they too behave in a reasonably satisfactory way. With one exception, the estimates decline as well as allow greater leakages. These findings suggest that while there are some obvious defects in some of the structural equations, they may nevertheless be used to construct M.S. functions; and the elasticities calculated from these functions are plausible.

Our analysis points up several areas where additional research effort would be rewarding. The first problem is the estimation of a

[17] In their nonlinear theory they use

$$K = \log B^a + \sum_{i=1}^{3} \epsilon(m_1, X_i)dX_i/X_i$$

where $B^a = H_u$, $X_1 = d$, $X_2 = t$, $X_3 = C/D$ and $m_1$ is the monetary multiplier for $M_1$ and $\epsilon\ (m_1 X_1)$ is the elasticity of $m_1$ with respect to $X_i$.

free-reserve equation for the banks. Following the pioneering work of Meigs (20) and Tobin (26) almost all the models use a free-reserve type equation in constructing their M.S. function. But the free-reserve model that they use is based, implicitly, on the secondary equilibrium analysis developed by Meigs in Chapter 4 of (20) to point up the inadequacies of a free-reserve target as a proximate objective of monetary policy (11). This model, while adequate for Meigs's purpose, is not the appropriate model for estimating a structural equation, a deposit function, or a money supply function. And indeed when Meigs attempts to estimate an M.S. function he brings in unborrowed reserves explicitly.[18]

In some of the models the free-reserve equation is one of the structural equations estimated, but the form of the equation follows very closely that given by Meigs in Chapter 4. This is appropriate only when the actual change in the free-reserve ratio is zero (7) (8); otherwise we need to bring in unborrowed reserves. It would also seem desirable to reformulate the free-reserve model so as to develop a deposit supply function directly.[19]

A second problem concerns the specifications of the demand function for currency and time deposits (4) (19). If we could introduce some of the policy controlled variables or monetary wealth in these two demand functions, we may obtain better estimates of the substitution effects in M.S. II. Also, most of the models estimate these demand functions in nominal terms and do not bring in the price level or changes in the price level. These two functions are of crucial importance in constructing the various M.S. concepts. Any improvements in these functions and especially of the currency equation would obviously improve our M.S. functions and the substitution estimates in M.S. II.[20]

Finally, to test our assumption of rapid adjustment (implicit in our use of stock equations) it would be desirable to estimate stock equations directly. In some of the models the stock equations are derived by solving for the steady-state solution. In doing this we are crucially depending on the coefficient of the lag term which affects all the coefficients in the stock equation. For these reasons it would seem appropriate to undertake a direct estimate of the lags.

There are some other models which could provide the basis for an M.S. function. These include Tobin's work on the theory of assets and portfolio selection (26), related work on bank portfolio behavior by Hester (17) and Pierce (22), Horwich's study of effective reserves (18) and Morrison's study on the liquidity preference of banks (21).

In closing we note that those who deny the usefulness of an M.S. concept presumably rest their case either on the hypothesis that no statistically significant money supply function can be estimated or, if such a function is obtained, it would be related to the M.S. IV concept. Although we do not perform any significance tests, the elasticities and multipliers analyzed here suggest that the M.S. functions based primarily on financial variables appear to be stable enough to justify further effort toward their refinement and improvement.[21] In particular, we would suggest (1) a testing of the alternative M.S. I specifications, (2) construction of M.S. II functions based on demand functions for C and T which would attempt to bring in policy

[18] Professor Milton Friedman has pointed out to me that Meigs presents two models in his book: the secondary equilibrium model of Chapter 4 which he uses to analyze the appropriateness of a free-reserve target for open market operations; and the model in Chapter 5 which (although somewhat implicitly) he uses to estimate a supply function.

[19] I am attempting this in a paper which is not yet completed on "The Supply of Deposits in a Free-Reserve Model."

[20] An alternative way to estimate the money supply is to couple a deposit supply function from a more fully articulated free-reserve model with a currency equation—an approach that extends the model in Teigen 1966. The appeal of this method is that it deals explicitly with the two slippages between Federal Reserve action and the money supply. The free-reserve equation deals with the slippage due to bank portfolio behavior while the currency equation deals with the slippage due to the public's portfolio adjustments. The currency equation may also provide a convenient way to pick up the effects that changes in the real economy impart to the money supply in the short run.

[21] The evidence presented by Brunner and Meltzer for their linear M.S. theory in (2) bears directly on our M.S. I and M.S. II concepts.

controlled variables, (3) construction of M.S. III functions to estimate the quantitative effect of substitution and, most importantly, (4) a comparison of these functions with improved estimates of M.S. IV.

## Appendix I
## The Behavior Specifications for M.S. I.

The multiplier or elasticity estimates that have been calculated for M.S. I are based on four alternative *ceteris paribus* conditions which we label the $W$, $P$, $A$, and $CO$ specifications. Thus DeLeeuw's elasticity estimates are defined by specification ($W$) and $C/M$ and $T/M$ are constant.[22] Teigen's estimates are defined by specification ($A$), that the stock of time deposits and the $C/M$ or $C/D$ ratios are constant. Goldfeld's estimates are defined by specification ($P$) that the stock of time deposits and currency are constant.[23] The Brunner-Meltzer linear M.S. estimates are defined by specification ($CO$) that the marginal propensities to hold currency and time deposits are constant. (The marginal propensity relates the change in currency or time deposits to changes in monetary wealth.) In functional form these four specifications may be written as follows:

$$(W) \quad M = f(X, r_b; C/M, T/M; Y)$$
$$(P) \quad M = f(X, r_b; C, T: Y)$$
$$(A) \quad M = f(X, r_b; C/M, T: Y), \text{ or}$$
$$(A^*) \quad M = f(X, r_b; C/D, T: Y)$$
$$(CO) \quad M = f(X, r_b, \partial C/\partial M, \partial T/\partial M: Y)$$

where $X$ is a vector of policy controlled variables and instruments such as ($H_u$, $r_d$, $d$, $t, \ldots$) and $Y$ is a vector of variables from the real sector of the economy. (See Appendix II for the M.S. formulas.)

These specifications on portfolio behavior are related to the structural equations of the model and often help simplify the construction of the M.S. function. DeLeeuw's free-reserve equation is homogeneous in ($D+T$), and the behavior specifications in ($W$) simplify DeLeeuw's M.S. function.[24] Goldfeld's free-reserve equation is not homogeneous in $D$ or $T$, and it is natural in his model to calculate a money supply function with the specification ($P$) that the leakages into currency and time deposits are zero as in M.S. I, or to generalize the ($P$) specification and to take account of these leakages as in M.S. II. In Teigen's 1964 model the money supply is derived from potential money, $M^*$, and is therefore a function of $T$ and the $C/M$ ratio. In Teigen's 1966 model the money supply is derived from potential deposits, $D^*$, and is therefore a function of $T$ and the $C/D$ ratio.[25] Teigen's (A) specification is somewhat intermediate between specifications ($P$) and ($W$). Finally, Brunner and Meltzer's ($CO$) specification enables them to estimate the autonomous changes in $C$ and $T$—two of the variables in their linear M.S. function.[26]

But while the specifications ($W$), ($P$), ($A$), and ($CO$) may reflect nothing more than the quest for algebraic simplicity, they may also be derived from substantive considerations. Specification ($P$) extends the standard textbook treatment by bringing in

[22] DeLeeuw also assumes that $Dg/M$ is constant.

[23] Although Goldfeld seems to describe the concept in the text (16, pp. 190–92), his calculations are based on the behavior assumptions appropriate to M.S. II. Since specification $P$ is most prevalent in standard money and banking texts, we should perhaps label this the standard specification.

[24] Although DeLeeuw's $W$ specification implies that the demand for $C$ and $T$ are proportional to $D$, he does not appear to use these conditions when he estimates the demand functions for $C$, $T$, and $D$.

[25] Teigen defines both $M^*$ and $D^*$ in terms of $R_u$. To compare Teigen's estimates with the others we have expressed his M.S. function in terms of $H_u$. (See Appendix II.)

[26] Brunner-Meltzer need to estimate the portfolio shifts with respect to currency and time deposits that generate or absorb reserves (independently of monetary expansion or contraction) in order to complete their linear theory. These changes in the monetary base are identified with the autonomous changes in $C$ and $T$. The ($CO$) assumptions enable them to estimate the induced changes in $C$ and $T$ and the autonomous changes are obtained as residuals. In their *J.O.F.* article (1) they specify that $c_o$ and $t_o$, the autonomous changes in $C$ and $T$, are functions of interest rates. Since they include two of these interest rates in their M.S. functions to estimate the autonomous movements in vault cash, $v_o$, the regression coefficient for $c_o$ and $t_o$ should be approximately zero. Both Brunner and Meltzer have informed me that they intended to have $c_o$ and $t_o$ as functions of wealth or permanent income.

APPENDIX II *(Continued)* DATA USED IN MONEY SUPPLY FORMULAS

| Model | Based on the data for period | Number of observations | Financial sector | Data | Real sector |
|---|---|---|---|---|---|
| S.S.R.C. | 1948 I*–1962 IV | 60 | Quarterly average of daily or end of month figures | | |
| Condensed | 1948 I*–1966 IV | 60 | Quarterly average of daily or end of month figures | | |
| Turek | 1948 I–1964 IV | 68 | Quarterly average of daily or end of month figures | S.A. | Annual rates S.A. |
| Goldfeld | 1950 III–1962 II | 48 | Call date (or approximation to it) | S.A. | Annual rates S.A. |
| Teigen 1966 | 1953 I–1964 IV | 48 | Call date (or approximation to it) | N.S.A. | Quarterly rates N.S.A. |
| Teigen 1964 | 1946 IV–1959 IV | 49 | Call date (or approximation to it) | N.S.A. | Annual rates N.S.A. |
| B–M (1) | 1949 I–1962 IV | 56 | Quarterly data | N.S.A. | Annual rates N.S.A. |
| (2) | 1949 I–1964 IV | 64 | Quarterly data | | Annual rates |
| (3) | 1919-41, 1952-58 | 30 | Annual data | | Annual rates |
| Cagan | 1875–1955 | | Annual and monthly | N.S.A. | Annual rates N.S.A.<br>Annual rates |

*Some equations start in 1952 and some start in 1954.

free reserve behavior. Specification (*W*) goes one step further in bringing in portfolio behavior but limits this behavior by the assumption that $C/M$, $T/M$ are held constant. Specification (*A*) holds $C/D$ or $C/M$ and $T$ constant and, while a compromise between the (*W*) and (*P*) specifications, may nevertheless be a useful way to deal with the short-run leakages. Finally specification (*CO*) goes a step further in introducing additional adjustments by permitting the autonomous components of currency and time deposits to vary. These four specifications are the natural ways in which to widen the scope of the short-run supply function. It is an empirical question to determine which of these four specifications incorporates the most relevant leakages for short-run analysis.

## Appendix II
## Money Supply Formulas

1. DeLeeuw (SSRC)

$$M_1 = \frac{H_u}{1 - D/M_1 + .84d(D/M_1 + D_g/M_1) + .82(T/M_1) + (a_0 + a_1r_b + a_2r_d)(D/M_1 + T/M_1)}$$

2. DeLeeuw (condensed model)
   Same formula with different coefficients in the free reserve equation
3. DeLeeuw-Turek
   Same formula with different coefficients in the free-reserve equation
4. Goldfeld

$$M_1 = \frac{H_u - T(t_{\gamma5} + a_{1\gamma7}r_b)}{d + a_{1\gamma6}r_b - C(1 - d - a_{1\gamma6}r_b) - (a_0 + a_2r_b + a_3r_d)}$$

5. Teigen 1964

$$M_1 = \frac{(H_u - t_{\gamma5}T)(a_0 + a_1r_b + a_2r_d)}{d(1 - h - C/M) + C/M}$$

6. Teigen 1966

$$M_1 = \frac{(1+C/D)(a_0+a_1r_b+a_2r_d)(H_u - t_{\gamma5}T)}{d + C/D}$$

7. Brunner and Meltzer
   Linear Theory:

$$M_1 = b_0 + b_1(B + L) + b_2c_0 + b_3t_0 + b_4v_0(i)$$

$$\Delta M_1 = b_0 + b_1\Delta(B^a + L + \pi) + b_2\Delta c_0 + b_3\Delta t_0 + b_4\Delta r_b + b_5\Delta r_d$$

   Nonlinear Theory:

$$\log M_1 = a_0 + a_1K + a_2 \log r_d + a_3 \log W/P_a + a_4 \log r_1 + a_5 \log p + a_6 \log Y/\overline{Y}$$

$$\log M_1 = a_0 + a_1K + a_2 \log r_1 + a_3 \log r_s + a_4 \log r_d + a_5 \log W$$

8. Cagan—Friedman

$$M_2 = \frac{H}{C/M + R/D - C/M\ R/D}$$

$$d \log M_2/dt = d \log H/dt + M/H(1 - R/D)d(-C/M)/dt + M/H(1 - C/M)d(-R/D)/dt$$

Using average values for the 2nd and 3rd terms on the right side, we get $m = h+r+c+e$, where $e$ is the error introduced by the approximation.

## Appendix III
## Glossary

M.S. = money supply
$M_1 = C+D$
$M_2 = M_1+T$
$C$ = currency in circulation outside the Treasury, the Federal Reserve, and the vaults of all commercial banks
$D$ = demand deposits as defined in the "Money Supply" series of the *Federal Reserve Bulletin* or "adjusted" demand deposits for call date data
$T$ = "adjusted" time deposits at all commercial banks
M.S. I = $f(X, r_b, T, C: Y)$

M.S. II $= g(X, r_b{:}Y)$
M.S. III $= g(X{:}\bar{Y})$
M.S. IV $= g(X)$

$X =$ vector of monetary policy instruments variables; e.g., $H_u, d, t, r_d, r_{t\,\max}$
$H_u =$ unborrowed high-powered money=adjusted monetary base $= B_a = R_u + C$
$R_u =$ unborrowed member bank reserves
$d =$ weighted average reserve requirement for demand deposits at member banks subject to reserve requirements
$t =$ weighted average reserve requirement for time deposits subject to reserve requirements
$r_d =$ discount rate
$r_{t\,\max} =$ maximum allowable rate on time deposits at commercial banks (regulation $Q$)
$r_b =$ Treasury bill rate (3 month)
$r_c =$ commercial paper rate
$Y =$ vector of real sector variables (GNP, disposable income, durable consumption, fixed business investment, etc.)
$W =$ DeLeeuw specification: M.S. I$=f(X, r_b, C/M, T/M{:}Y)$
$P =$ Goldfeld specification: M.S. I$=f(X, r_b, C, T{:}Y)$
$A =$ Teigen specification: M.S. I$=f(X, r_b, C/D$ or $C/M, T{:}Y)$
$CO =$ Brunner-Meltzer specification: M.S. I$=f(X, r_b, \partial C/\partial M, \partial T/\partial M{:}Y)$
$D_g =$ Treasury deposits at commercial banks

$$M^* = \frac{H_u - t_{\gamma 5}T}{d(1 - h - C/M) + C/M}$$

$$D^* = \frac{H_u - t_{\gamma 5}T}{d + C/M}$$

$\gamma_5 =$ ratio of member bank "adjusted" time deposits to $T$
$c_o = C - \partial C/\partial M$=autonomous component of $C$
$t_o = T - \partial T/\partial M$=autonomous component of $T$
$r_t =$ some measure of the interest rate on time deposits in commercial banks (the average rate as estimated by the FDIC in the S.S.R.C., Condensed, and Goldfeld models; a combination of this average up to 1961 and the rate on new $CD$'s after 1961 in the Teigen 1966 model; $r_{t\,\max}$ in Turek)
$h =$ ratio of nonmember commercial bank "adjusted" demand deposits to $D$
$H =$ high-powered money$=R_T + C$
$R_T =$ total member bank reserves
$B + L =$ "extended base"=monetary base plus "liberated reserves"
$v_o =$ autonomous component of vault cash holdings resulting from changes in interest rates
$K =$ defined in text
$W =$ public's nonhuman wealth at current prices
$P_a =$ deflator for $W$
$r_e =$ interest rate on long-term government bonds
$Y/\bar{Y} =$ index of transitory income
$P =$ income deflator
$\gamma_6 =$ ratio of "adjusted" demand deposits in reserve city banks to $D$
$\gamma_7 =$ ratio of "adjusted" time deposits in reserve city banks to $T$
$r_s =$ short-term interest rate
$\pi =$ cumulated sum of vault cash released for absorption in legal reserves

## References

1. BRUNNER, K., AND MELTZER, A. "Some Further Investigations of the Demand and Supply Functions of Money," *J.O.F.*, May, 1964.

2. ———. *An Alternative Approach to the Monetary Mechanism* (G.P.O., 1964).

3. ———. "Liquidity Traps For Money, Bank Credit, and Interest Rates," *J.P.E.*, Jan./Feb., 1968.

4. CAGAN, P. "The Demand for Currency Relative to the Total Money Supply," *J.P.E.*, Aug., 1958.

5. ———. *Determinants and Effects of Changes in the Stock of Money, 1875–1960* (N.B.E.R., 1965).

6. CHASE, S., AND GRAMLEY, L. "Time Deposits in Monetary Analysis," *F.R.B.*, Oct., 1965 [reprinted in this volume].

7. DAVIS, R. G. "Open Market Operations, Interest Rates, and Deposit Growth," *Q.J.E.*, Aug., 1965.

8. ———. "Testing Some Variants of the Free Reserve Hypothesis" (unpublished paper).

9. DE LEEUW, F. *A Model of Financial Behavior. The Brookings—Quarterly Econometric Model of the U. S.* (Rand-McNally, 1965).

10. ———. "A Condensed Model of Financial Behavior" (unpublished paper).

11. DEWALD, W. "Free Reserves, Total Reserves, and Monetary Control," *J.P.E.*, Apr., 1963.

12. ———. "Money Supply vs. Interest Rates as Proximate Objectives of Monetary Policy," *N.B.R.*, June, 1966.

13. FAND, D. I. "Intermediary Claims and the Adequacy of our Monetary Controls," in *Banking and Monetary Studies* (Irwin, 1963).

14. ———. "A Time Series Analysis of the 'Bills-Only' Theory of Interest Rates," *Rev. of Econ. and Statis.*, Nov., 1966.

15. FRIEDMAN, M., AND SCHWARTZ, A. *A Monetary History of the U. S. 1867–1960* (Princeton, 1963); Appendix B: Proximate Determinants of the Nominal Stock of Money.

16. GOLDFELD, S. *Commercial Bank Behavior* (North Holland, 1966).

17. HESTER, D. "An Empirical Examination of a Commercial Bank Loan Offer Function," *Yale Econ. Essays,* Spring, 1962.

18. HORWICH, G. "Effective Reserves, Credit and Causality in the Banking System of the Thirties," in *Banking and Monetary Studies* (Irwin, 1963).

19. KAUFMAN, G. *The Demand for Currency, Federal Reserve Staff Economic Studies.*

20. MEIGS, A. A. *Free Reserves and the Money Supply* (Chicago, 1962).

21. MORRISON, G. R. *Liquidity Preferences of Commercial Banks* (Chicago, 1966).

22. PIERCE, J. L. "Commercial Bank Liquidity," *F.R.B.,* Aug., 1966.

23. SMITH, W. L. "Time Deposits, Free Reserves, and Monetary Policy" (unpublished manuscript).

24. TEIGEN, R. "Demand and Supply Functions for Money in the United States: Some Structural Estimates," *Econometrica,* Oct., 1964.

25. ———. "An Aggregated Quarterly Model of the U. S. Monetary Sector" (unpublished paper, 1966).

26. TOBIN, J. "Monetary Theory" (unpublished manuscript).

27. TUREK, J. "Prediction of Interest Rates Levels, and Financial Stocks with Simulation Techniques" (unpublished paper).

28. WOOD, J. *A Model of Federal Reserve Behavior, Federal Reserve Staff Economic Studies.*

29. GURLEY, J. G., AND SHAW, E. S. *Money in a Theory of Finance* (Brookings, 1960).

# IV | MONEY, PRICE EXPECTATIONS, and INTEREST RATES

Interest rates have a strategic role in economic theory: they provide a link between the financial and real sectors. Theories explaining interest rates are among the oldest in economics. The earliest investigators tended to analyze interest rates in a nonmonetary framework, examining the determination of interest rates by the interaction of the supply of real saving and the demand for real investment. The supply of real capital reflected time preference between current and future consumption on the part of decision-making units, while the demand reflected both the marginal productivity of producing for future consumption rather than for current consumption and time preferences in consumption.

Later economists expanded this framework. Wicksell introduced financial variables, and Fisher, in addition to refining the theory underlying the determination of the real rate of interest, delineated the effects of expectations of changes in the price level on the nominal rate of interest.[1] The market rate of interest was determined by the demand and supply of credit, including the effects of the price expectations of borrowers and lenders. Thus the market rate of interest could differ from that rate which would exist in the absence of expectations of price changes.

While contemporary economists by and large agree on the identity of the forces affecting interest rates, they tend to disagree as to the relative importance of these forces and, thus, on both the ability of the monetary authorities to influence rates and the interpretation of rate movements. For many years after the Keynesian Revolution, economists emphasized the inverse relationship between money and interest rates. By increasing the stock of money, the Federal Reserve could, within limits, lower market rates of interest. More recently, in part as a result of extended periods of rising interest rates accompanied by increases in the money stock and prices, economists have turned their attention to the effects of income and price expectations on interest rates, both of which tend to reverse the initial negative effects of monetary changes. If the latter influences are empirically significant, the Federal Reserve's ability to control interest is diminished. Likewise, policy interpretations of interest-rate movements based solely on an assumed negative influence from money are likely to be misleading.

The theoretical operation of price-expectations effects was set forth clearly at the turn of the century by Fisher, but apart from his own evidence (which many found unconvincing by itself) little work had been

[1] Knut Wicksell, *Interest and Prices (1936)*, New York, Augustus Kelley, 1965; Irving Fisher, *Appreciation and Interest*, Cambridge, Mass., American Economic Association, 1896, and *The Theory of Interest*, New York, Macmillan, 1930.

undertaken in this area for the United States until recently. However, effects of price expectations had been well identified for other countries experiencing substantial inflation. Recent studies have documented the operation of these effects in this country and have attributed an important role to them in explaining observed interest rate movements in the late 1960s.

In part IV the influences of changes in the stock of money on interest rates are examined by Eisner and Gibson. Both authors argue that interest rates are only moderately affected by the money stock, but for different reasons. Eisner believes that interest rates are sensitive to changes in the money stock only within a limited range of interest rates. At low rate levels, the liquidity trap checks further reductions in rates resulting from increases in money. At high levels, a "liquidity leak" encourages shifts to money substitutes and mitigates further increases in rates resulting from decreases in money. In addition, Eisner discounts the strength of price expectations as an important factor influencing nominal rates of interest. Gibson finds that the inverse influence of money on interest rates is rather quickly reversed at all interest rate levels by offsetting influences originating from changes in income brought about by the initial monetary change. The remaining three articles attempt to quantify the effect of price expectations on market rates of interest. Both Sargent and Gibson estimate very long lags before current interest rates fully reflect price expectations. These findings are consistent with Fisher's original estimates. Sargent also constructs and estimates a model for delineating the differential impact of real, financial, and price-expectation influences on interest rates. By using somewhat different statistical techniques and estimating the model over more recent years, Yohe and Karnosky report evidence of considerably shorter lags in the response of interest rates to price expectations.

# 23 | FACTORS AFFECTING THE LEVEL OF INTEREST RATES*

ROBERT EISNER
*Northwestern University*

Some years ago I was engaged in the probably dubious task of interviewing executives of generally very large manufacturing corporations in an effort to discover the determinants of business investment. Fortunately, I was theory-oriented and had some good notions of what I was looking for and the stubbornness to persist until I found what I was after.

One of the key questions was the role of the supply of money capital, whether measured by price or availability, in determining the rate of investment. What do you think I learned, every time I spoke to a comptroller, treasurer or financial vice president? That money was very important. Everything depended on the terms on which money could be raised and, of course, on the ability of the officer to whom I was speaking to obtain the money on favorable terms. To epitomize it all, in one substantial company in the Midwest a financial vice president said, "Of course money is important. If I can't get the money at reasonable terms we can't invest." As this remark was completed, the company's executive vice president entered. I politely briefed him on what I had just asked: "Do shortages of money or the difficulty of securing favorable terms influence your rate of capital expenditures or prevent you from undertaking or carrying through on investment?" Without waiting to hear what his financial vice president had answered, the executive vice president quickly replied, "Not at all! We make capital expenditures if they appear profitable or if we need the plant or equipment. It's his job to get the money," indicating the hapless financial vice president.

The moral of my story, aside from what you may think it implies about the determinants of investment, is that everyone likes to think he is important. Particularly, people who deal in money—in the creation of money and in monetary policy—including those who invest a good bit of time teaching, writing, theorizing and doing research about money, like to think it is important. But that does not make it so. And more particularly, people concerned with money may well think it important in ways that it is not, and ignore some of the more important ramifications of their doings with money, which go beyond them.

## Money Only Small Element

The first thing to acquire is humility, the humility which comes from recognition that no matter what particular definition of money we use, "money" is only a small element or set of elements in the vast spectrum of assets (and debts) which serve or may serve the various pecuniary functions. If an individual, or the economy, is short of one instrument of money or near money, it will turn to another.

As a general proposition this notion that pecuniary assets are substitutes for each other is hardly startling. I should like to carry it to something of an analytical extreme, and

* Reprinted from *Savings and Residential Financing, 1968 Conference Proceedings,* pp. 29–40, by permission of the author and the United States Savings and Loan Association.

perhaps we shall find that extremism in the pursuit of knowledge has some virtue. After noting the limits of what we can expect any monetary authority, qua monetary authority, to be able to do in the way of affecting interest rates, we may be able to sense more clearly what is affecting the rates we observe in the market place.

I start with one extreme, the Keynesian liquidity trap. What we have in mind here is the right-hand end of the well-known liquidity preference curve, which indicates that no matter how great the (real) quantity of money, there is some positive lower bound below which the long term rate of interest cannot be made to fall. This relates, of course, to the idea, built on a combination of historical experience and perhaps even the analytical insight that financial transaction costs at the least necessitate some non-zero price to borrowing, that future rates of interest may be higher than current rates. The lower the current rate, the greater the number of actual and potential lenders who feel that future rates will be higher and, more directly significant, the greater the demand for money rather than the bonds expected by these bears to go down in price.

That there need be no analytical difficulty in the notion of "absolute" liquidity preference because of a violation of budget constraints—Patinkin has postulated one[1]—may be seen by recognizing that, in principle, if the monetary authority were to continue to try to buy bonds beyond the point at which all existing bonds had been sold by the private sector of the economy, rational speculators would then issue new bonds or promises to repay and sell them to the monetary authority. For, expecting the rate of interest to rise, they could later make their gain by buying back their bonds from the monetary authority. (It would of course not matter if the monetary authority stubbornly refused to sell at the new lower prices; the lenders could make the same gain by buying just enough other bonds at the new lower prices to receive an interest return equal to the interest they were paying the monetary authority.)

## Where Is the Liquidity Trap?

The issue of where the lower bound to the rate of interest might be located and how actions of the monetary authority itself may affect it has been neglected by latter-day Keynesians. This may be related to a curious confusion in some econometric work, where historical data are used in an effort to find—or even determine the existence of—the liquidity trap.[2] As Keynes himself argued, we have never been in the trap; the monetary authority has never acted sufficiently "boldly" to get us there.[3]

Corollary to the view that the monetary authority may be limited in its control over the rate of interest—and in the limiting case, may lose "effective control over" it—is the view that the more the monetary authority seeks to effect changes in the rate of interest the less it will be able to do so. "The market" will hardly expect a current counter-cyclical easy money policy to persist if the monetary authority has shown by its actions that it will engage regularly in a counter-cyclical monetary policy. Unless the market has concluded that cycles are a thing of the past, it will reason that easy money today will be followed by tight money at some future date and vice versa. Hence, any attempt to lower long-term interest rates now will be at least somewhat thwarted by the very rational conviction, on the part of all those who understand monetary policy, that the gears will be reversed so that rates will be higher in the future. A counter-cylical monetary policy thus militates against reduction of the long-term rate of interest to the lowest rate possible and, *pari passu*, militates against reduc-

[1] (5), pp. 216, 225. [Complete references at the end of this reading.]

[2] See, for example, Bronfenbrenner and Mayer (1).

[3] "There is the possibility . . . after the rate of interest has fallen to a certain level, liquidity-preference may become virtually absolute in the sense that almost everyone prefers cash to holding a debt which yields so low a rate of interest. In this event the monetary authority would have lost effective control over the rate of interest. But whilst this limiting case might become practically important in future, I know of no example of it hitherto. Indeed, owing to the unwillingness of most monetary authorities to deal boldly in debts of long term, there has not been much opportunity for a test." [Keynes, (4), p. 207.] Cf. Milton Friedman, who states, "Keynes and most other economists of the time believed that the Great Contraction in the U.S. occurred despite aggressive expansionary policies by the monetary authorities—they did their best but their best was not good enough." [(2), p. 3.] A correct rendition of Keynes and, I believe, of reality would be, "They did *not* do their best, but their best would not have been good enough."

tion of the "required rate of return on capital" which Tobin and Brainard (6) aptly characterize as "the basic criterion of the effectiveness of a monetary action" (p. 387).[4]

It is old hat that monetary policy may prove relatively impotent in combating a substantial depression. It is clearly not so widely recognized that use of monetary policy as a first resort against minor fluctuations of economic activity can be self-defeating and can militate against keeping the long-term rate of interest as low as possible. Indeed, the prevailing view seems to be that monetary policy should be used frequently for counter-cyclical purposes, with fiscal policy, presumably for institutional, political reasons, reserved for the combat of major fluctuations in demand. Yet to the extent that we thus keep interest rates over time on the average higher than they need to be, we risk a welfare loss, provocatively discussed by Friedman in an unpublished paper on "The Optimum Quantity of Money," as we permit a price for a good—money—to rise substantially above its marginal cost of production, which is essentially zero.[5]

What may strike us as truly novel—I hope I can convince you not bizarre—is the view I should like to develop that the traditional asymmetry associated with Keynesian monetary theory is wrong. I suppose I am a bit suspicious of asymmetries in economics. Perhaps this is merely an aesthetic prejudice, but somehow I find the frequent invocation of asymmetrics troublesome in suggesting that the economy is forever being determined by special cases. Maybe so, but this would make the world infinite in its complexity and hopeless to untangle. So, out of faith in our professional capacities, would it not be more appealing to look for consistency and symmetry? By way of consistency, therefore, I am ready to argue, as should now be apparent, that the influence of monetary policy on both the rate of interest and the aggregative level of economic activity is quite generally limited. By way of symmetry, I would suggest that monetary policy is especially limited not only by the liquidity trap in depression, where the elasticity of demand for money is viewed as approaching infinity. It is quite similarly especially limited in analogous efforts to combat inflation by making the quantity of money very low. For again one finds oneself approaching an infinite elasticity of demand for money—another kind of liquidity trap or, better, a "liquidity leak."

The geometry of all this, in terms of conventional liquidity preference figures, is disarmingly simple. All we have to do, as shown in Figure 1, is draw a liquidity preference curve which not only flattens out to the right (on the money axis) but which at the left intersects the vertical (interest rate) axis. What this, of course, implies is that not only is there some rate of interest below which the monetary authority cannot get us by increasing the quantity of money. There is also some rate above which the monetary authority cannot get us by decreasing the quantity of money.

With the liquidity trap, we may recall, there were certain underlying real factors relating to transactions costs and, perhaps, borrowers' and lenders' risks which, along with historical considerations, set an expectation of a floor to the long-term rate of interest. The expected minimum rate then becomes such a floor, since at this rate demand for money on the part of those expecting rates to go up becomes completely dominant or "absolute."

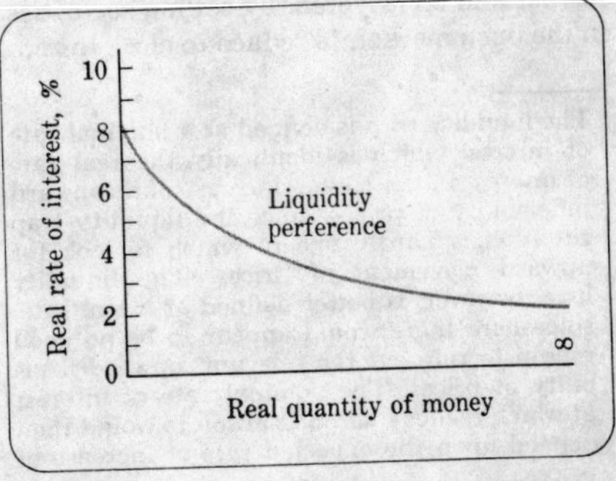


FIGURE 1

[4] Again citing Keynes, "Thus a monetary policy which strikes public opinion as being experimental in character or easily liable to change may fail in its objective of greatly reducing the long-term rate of interest. . . ." (4, p. 203.) Short-term rates may indeed be moved considerably by action of the monetary authority but, for a complex of reasons which I shall not develop here, I do not see in short-term rates a major determinant of investment or of the general level of economic activity.

[5] We lay aside Friedman's suggestion of a steadily falling quantity of money and steadily falling price level as the instruments for reducing the marginal yield of money and the nominal rate of interest to zero.

But now, analogously, there are certain real considerations which will limit what, in equilibrium, will be paid for whatever the monetary authority is offering in the way of "money." As we argued earlier in this paper, "money," whether coin, currency, demand deposits or time deposits, is only a small subset of the elements in the total spectrum of pecuniary assets, actual and, certainly, potential. True, this "money" is particularly convenient. One may well pay a premium to have it. It has its substitutes, however, and there is a limit to the premium which will be paid.[6]

We may ask ourselves, in quest of explication, what would happen if the monetary authority began to cut down on the supply of nickels. Suppose the supply were cut virtually to zero. Would much of a premium be paid in dimes or pennies by those desperately anxious to have nickels to make change conveniently, or to use chewing gum machines? Suppose the monetary authority were to cut the supply of all coins to virtually zero? Would much of a premium be paid for coins? Or would there be a general switch to substitutes, which would include transportation tokens sold by the dollar, checks for payment or change of less than a dollar, and perhaps extensive use of ledger books and IOU slips? There might even be fewer items selling for 98 cents. This is not to say that the all but complete shortage of coins—even a complete shortage—would not inflict some cost on economic activity and have some effect. And the effect would be differential—little on the real estate agent and not much more on the new car salesman, significant for the corner grocer and perhaps quite substantial for the corner newspaper dealer.

Suppose the monetary authority went further and endeavored, by selling securities in the open market, to reduce to close to zero the total amount of "money," including coin, currency and demand deposits. Money would become very scarce. Because of the reserve requirements for time deposits, they too would be drastically curtailed as banks lost reserves and depositors "withdrew" their deposits to buy securities. Rates of interest would rise—6.5%, 7%, 7.5%, 8%—but how high? Would they rise indefinitely, or would there be some point, admittedly more distant than in the case of nickels, all coin, or all coin and currency, where those who normally use "money" would say, in effect, "At that price, who needs it?"

## Economy Would Adjust to Money Substitute

At such a point, General Motors might pay United States Steel and United States Rubber with its IOUs, instead of those of some bank. And U.S. Steel could pay its suppliers of coal and iron ore with the GM IOUs or its own. What would back these up if necessary? Actually, something much more tangible than "full faith and credit": the plant, equipment, inventories and product of the issuing companies. It is true that there would be some inconvenience in all of this but, perhaps sooner than one might expect, the economy would get used to "trade money," or whatever one might call it. It might not even prove so infinitely varied. Economies of scale would show themselves and good trade money would probably drive bad trade money out of circulation. If the antitrust division of the Department of Justice did not intervene we might quickly find a concentration in the issue of trade money, perhaps by Sears, A & P and large air lines as well as GM, which would make present day banking look perfectly competitive by comparison. Credit card companies would have a booming business.

For our purposes the question would be what premium would have to be paid to delay payment by one year. To get $100 of equipment, inventories or services now, how much would General Motors or Sears have to offer in the way of claims on its product one year from now? Would it really be much more than, say, $108? If it would not, could the liquidity preference function for "money," that peculiar instrument issued or controlled by the monetary authority, intersect the ver-

[6] The liquidity trap is defined at a nominal rate of interest which is identically the real rate of interest in the Keynesian case of downward inflexibility of prices, since the liquidity trap situation is hardly one in which to look for upward movement of prices. The liquidity leak, however, is better defined at a real rate, since here there would appear to be no good reason to rule out the relevant, upward flexibility of prices. The nominal rate of interest at which the leak becomes absolute would then depend upon the expected rate of increase of prices.

tical axis much above 8%? We suggest not. As the quantity of money is reduced so that we approach that point of intersection, we may add, the elasticity of demand for money with respect to the rate of interest, in this case of the liquidity leak as in the liquidity trap, would approach infinity.[7]

Once we have established some upper bound beyond which it is not reasonable to expect individuals or businesses to go in paying for that special financial instrument usually known as "money," we should again look to become dominant all the expectational, "speculative" factors which were dominant at the other extreme of the liquidity preference function. Perhaps in a moment of temporary stress the monetary authority can push the short-term rate above, say, 8%. If a large number of people reason that General Motors and Sears and the like will not long continue to pay more than 8% when they have the alternative of issuing their own debt instruments, there will be a dominant demand for any bonds paying more than 8%. Investors expecting the rate of interest to fall below a current rate of more than 8% of course anticipate a capital gain on any bonds they can obtain. Their "speculative motive" would dictate the holding of bonds just as their brothers in the liquidity trap would speculate on cash. The speculative motive might thus, as in Figure 2, make the liquidity preference curve flatten out as it approached the vertical axis; with whatever slope it intersected, however, as noted, the elasticity would be infinite at the point of intersection.

## Issue: Exchange of Money for Nonmonetary Assets

One might suggest that the trouble with this analysis is that we are claiming to reduce the quantity of money but actually we are letting money leak back in through the back door or, should we say, the front door of Sears or General Motors. If we are talking about reducing the supply of money we should really reduce the supply of all money, not just "money." We should perhaps think in terms of prohibiting the issue or use of the trade money we have been postulating. Is this not the nub of the matter? The monetary authority deals in "money." There is no doubt that

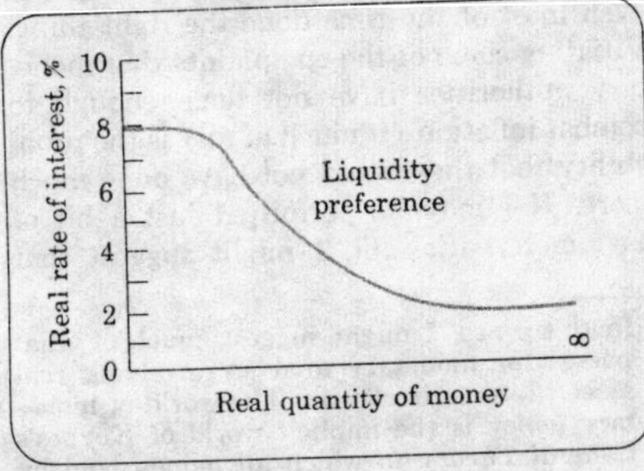


FIGURE 2

[7] The assumption of an intersection with the vertical axis is, of course, the assumption that

$$\frac{dQ}{dP} < \epsilon,\ \epsilon < 0, \text{ as } Q \rightarrow 0$$

whence

$$\frac{dQ}{dP} \cdot \frac{P}{Q} \rightarrow -\infty \text{ as } Q \rightarrow 0$$

By running a sufficient budget surplus and insisting that taxes must be paid in "money," not trade money, the Treasury can presumably drive the rate on "money" above what we have defined as the rate of the absolute liquidity leak. Individuals and businesses could be forced to pay more than this, on pain of imprisonment, to meet their tax obligations. But then surely "money" would be used only to pay taxes and would have ceased to be the medium of exchange relevant to economic activity. Money might be borrowed for taxes but but not to invest. And, as noted below, we would be dealing with certain implications of fiscal policy, not monetary policy.

Similarly, it might be made a criminal offense to issue or use the kind of trade money which I suggest, and the literal-minded among us may insist that this is already largely true. One has to have a charter to create bank money, and General Motors would not get one. But, I would argue, there would be and are an infinite number of ways of economizing on "money," of which conventional trade credit is already recognized as one of the most widespread. My argument is essentially that the ready availability of money substitutes in a developed economy such as our own sets clear and relatively narrow limits on the real power of the monetary authority. One can, of course, change the structure of our system and insist that one *has* to use "money," and spell out myriad rules to stop the "leak." None would deny, as I suggest below, that various forms of compulsion can stop the economy from doing many things, including, ultimately, functioning at all, but surely this takes us far beyond the realm of what is usefully thought of as monetary policy.

the authority, some authority, can have very great effects upon the economy. The Department of Defense could conceivably bring economic activity to a virtual halt by threatening destruction to all who would produce and, if necessary, carrying out the threat. Monetary analysis, however, relates to the instruments which a monetary authority, properly speaking, can control. By a monetary authority we should make clear—clearer than I believe it is always made—that we mean an authority with the power to exchange its obligations for others and to control the power of certain specialized institutions to do likewise, where their instruments of superior liquidity are *defined* as money. This must involve an exchange of obligations, not the giving away of obligations (or money) for nothing. The latter involves fiscal policy, and a different set of considerations, just as authority in the form of the Department of Defense, as suggested above, involves a different set of considerations. The issues which confront us under the rubric of monetary policy, at least in the United States, involve not the creation of net additions to the assets of the private sector of the economy, but merely the exchange of money for nonmonetary assets.[8]

What does this extreme vision of an economy in which the monetary authority cuts the quantity of "money" to the ultimate have to do with the United States of 1967 and 1968? I would argue, "A good deal." Monetary authorities were nowhere bold enough to get us into the liquidity trap during the great depression and monetary authorities can hardly be expected to be bold enough to get us to the liquidity leak in a time of pressing inflation. I am not prepared to argue that monetary authorities have always or even most of the time done the right thing. Vitiating some of the complaints that monetary authorities have not done enough to combat inflation (if much at all) is the probability that they could not have done much more. If I may be permitted just a bit of asymmetry after all, I might suggest that while the effectiveness of the monetary authority in combating serious deflation is largely one of impotence, the difficulty in combating inflation is that long before the final manifestation of impotence in the liquidity leak, a great deal of damage can be done by monetary attempts to combat inflation.

## Tight Money Has Selective Effect

The fact is that different units in the economy have different capacities to obtain money, to economize in its use and to create or obtain money substitutes. If 1967 showed anything it was that tight money, at least as measured by high nominal rates of interest, has a very selective effect on the economy. Residential housing construction, as we all know, felt the pinch badly, and took a severe beating. Business capital expenditures, particularly those of the largest firms which account for most of them, showed no discernible impact of monetary stringency, and indeed reached new record highs (however its precipitate rate of growth slackened). Had money been made more difficult to borrow, the pinch on residential housing construction and some other sectors of the economy would have been even tighter. Yet paradoxically, some of the rest of the economy might have boomed all the more, as resources flowed from the victims of tight money to those with readier access to money or its myriad substitutes.

It may well be argued that, during part of 1967, bank reserves and the money supply were rising so rapidly that by no stretch of the imagination could the Fed be viewed as playing a restraining hand. (One retort might be that you do not know the stretch of my imagination.) I may concede that monetary policy was, like fiscal policy, victim of the same political machinations relating to a lack of candor in anticipating and admitting the inflationary impact of the partly surreptitious continued escalation of war expenditures. I would insist, however, that the inflation has been fiscally induced by the escalating war expenditures and the failure, for political reasons, to impose a tax increase early in the escalatory process; the increasing quantity of money at most kept uneven pace with rising rates of output, demand and expectations which it did not induce. One

[8] In this sense, I might suggest, much of what passes for monetary analysis involving real asset effects is irrelevant. The world of monetary policy is the implicit world of Keynes's *General Theory* in which all money held by the private sector is balanced by private debt; there can be no "Pigou effect."

may well argue, in view of what happened to both nominal rates of interest and residential construction, that the money supply did not really keep pace.

I should pause to meet at least one potential cry of outrage, that we should be talking about not the nominal rate of interest but the "real" rate of interest. The real rate of interest, it might then be claimed, did not really rise. Rather, inflation amounted to at least as much as, possibly more than, the increased nominal interest rates, so that the real rate actually declined. Hence the monetary authority *was* acting in an inflationary fashion.[9] I do not believe it, and I can at least offer some casual empirical evidence to sustain my disbelief.

### Lack Reliable Data on Expectations

For one thing there is frequently in economics a confusion between past trends and expectations as to the future. It is true that we usually do not have much in the way of reliable data on expectations, so that in our empirical work we frequently use past variables as proxies (pretty poor ones) for expectations of the future. But it remains expectations of the future which are relevant. He who acts on the future on the basis of simple extrapolations of past rates of change is not the one on whom I would bet my money, whether in the stock market or anywhere else. The "real" rate of interest relevant to economic activity would be the nominal rate adjusted for the *expected* rate of change in prices. Who is very sure that a 3% increase over the past year makes likely a 3% increase over the next year, and the year after that, and many years still further in the future?

By way of that casual empiricism, I note that, from January 1965 to December 1967, Moody's Aaa corporate bond rates rose from 4.43% to 6.19%. The rate of price inflation may well depend on the measure we use, but on the chance that prices for fixed investment goods may be those most relevant to corporate borrowing, we may note that their index rose over this same period from 107.0 to 114.6, which comes to about 2.5% per year rate of increase. At first glance, we might say that we have more than accounted for the increase in the nominal bond rate of some 1.76% points. But have we? First we might note that price increases in investment goods had not begun in this period of rising interest rates. For the three-year period from 1962 to 1965, the investment goods price index rose from 104.1 to 107.7, roughly 1.2% per year. Hence, the rate of increase of the rise in prices was only in the order of about 1.3%, from 1.2% to 2.5%. Since corporate bond rates had been fairly stable before, we apparently had an increase of some 1.76% in nominal interest rates accompanied by an increase in the rate of increase of prices of only 1.2%. More to the point, is it likely that such an increase in the rate of rise of prices generated an expectation of a corresponding rise in prices over all the long years for which corporate bonds might be borrowed? If the long-run elasticity of expectations for *rates of increases* of prices is substantially less than unity, and I can hardly believe in the present situation that it has not been substantially less than unity (I suspect it is close to zero), then the real rate of interest has indeed risen substantially since 1965 and, probably, in every month in 1967 since April. If you are still doubtful, look at residential housing. Clearly somewhere expected price increases were not sufficient to outweigh the rise in nominal rates of interest (although, again, in some cases they certainly were).

### Limits to What Monetary Authority Can Do

Where does all this leave us with regard to factors affecting interest rates? Essentially, it argues that interest rates are largely determined by some fairly pervasive forces in the economy, relating to productivity and thrift and risk, the shape of production functions and parameters of intertemporal utility functions. Expected future price movements will play a part, but this part can readily be exaggerated, particularly by a confusion between past and current rates of change of prices and these future expectations which alone are relevant. The monetary authority assuredly

---

9 Attention should be called to the striking analysis of my colleague, Patric Hendershott (3), who finds that it is quite generally the endogenous elements of the money supply, stimulated by economic activity itself, which have given the mistaken impression of pro-cyclical action by the monetary authority. The exogenous contributions of the Fed have actually been counter-cyclical.

does play a substantial role, since money substitutes are not without additional cost. In the short run, no doubt, the monetary authority can raise interest rates significantly—or allow them to rise. This is not without effect on the economy, although much more at the non-aggregative level, involving transfer of resources from those with poorer access to credit to those with better access. Curbed by liquidity traps and liquidity leaks and, generally, by the expectational links of past, current and future, there are decided limits to what the monetary authority can do to counteract real forces in the economy. When depression destroys investment demand, interest rates will fall. When an expanding war calls for resources at a faster rate than a growing economy will freely grant them, interest rates rise. Purely monetary measures to cope with such developments are limited in effectiveness and sometimes so selective in their impact as to offend seriously our sense of equity and, in some instances, the efficient working of the economy.

## Money Close to Free Good

So I come around, by what may seem a somewhat devious route, to a conclusion familiar to most of you from the work of my distinguished colleague, Milton Friedman. Money, bless it, is really as close to a free good as we are ever likely to run into. With modern banking systems its marginal cost of production is virtually zero. There is every reason to keep its price as close as possible to its marginal cost. Both contrived scarcity and repeated swings in monetary policy will prevent attainment of that low price.

I cannot fathom the applicability, whatever their elegance, of models which suggest that the way to achieve this virtually zero cost of money (and nominal rate of interest) is to bring about somehow a steadily declining money supply and corresponding declining price level. Among other things, for better or for worse, prices (and not just wages) are fairly rigid in a downward direction in the economy we know, and not so fully flexible upwards either, for that matter. I find myself drawn to the suggestion that the best policy to follow is one which will make the money supply increase at some substantial steady rate and let interest rates then adjust to real forces but hopefully, thus, keep them as low as possible. This may strike many of you as an humble objective—but perhaps, after all this, it is on a note of humility that I should close.

## References

1. BRONFENBRENNER, M., and MAYER, T. "Liquidity Functions in the American Economy," *Econometrica,* Vol. 28 (1960), pp. 810–834.

2. FRIEDMAN, M. "The Role of Monetary Policy," *American Economic Review,* Vol. 58 (1958), pp. 1–17 [reprinted in this volume].

3. HENDERSHOTT, P. A. *The Neutralized Money Stock: An Unbiased Measure of Federal Reserve Actions,* Homewood, Ill.: Irwin, 1968.

4. KEYNES, J. M. *The General Theory of Employment, Interest and Money,* New York: Harcourt, Brace and Company, 1936.

5. PATINKIN, D. *Money, Interest and Prices,* second edition, Evanston: Harper and Row, 1965.

6. TOBIN, J., and BRAINARD, W. C. "Financial Intermediaries and the Effectiveness of Monetary Controls," *American Economic Review,* Vol. 53 (1963), pp. 383–400

# 24 INTEREST RATES AND MONETARY POLICY*

WILLIAM E. GIBSON
*University of California, Los Angeles*

## I. Introduction

This paper investigates the empirical operation of some recognized theoretical effects of the money stock on market rates of interest. The analysis covers the period since World War II, the period for which extensive quarterly and monthly data are available.

There is a widespread belief among economists that an increase in the money stock lowers interest rates.[1] This conclusion seems to follow from the liquidity-preference relation between the level of interest rates and the quantity of money demanded. As stated by Tobin (1947, p. 126):

> If the demand for cash balances is not completely inelastic with respect to the rate of interest, part of an addition to $M$ will end up in idle balances. The added money will be used to bid down the rate of interest, and the lowering of the rate of interest will make the community willing to hold larger idle balances. So long as either investment or the propensity to consume is favorably affected by a lowering of the interest rate, there will also be an increase in money income. But since there is some increase in idle balances, the increase in money national income cannot be proportional to the increase in $M$; $V$ cannot be considered a constant.

In Tobin's view interest rates will not return to their original levels as a result of money stock effects alone, but will end up higher than immediately after the money stock increase because of shift in the liquidity-preference curve in response to an increase in income.

Similarly, monetary authorities tend to take it for granted that an increase in money stock lowers interest rates. From their vantage point, an increase in the money stock by open market purchases tends to lower market rates quickly, since purchasing securities raises their prices and lowers yields. Indeed, they rely on this relation in order to control rates. Accordingly, interest rate movements are frequently viewed as indicators of current monetary policy.

Since the money-interest rate relation is used in implementing monetary policy, it is particularly important that the monetary authorities know how the relation works. If the monetary authorities believed that they lowered interest rates by increasing the money stock, whereas this at first lowered and then later raised rates, the authorities' actions would work first toward and then away from an interest rate goal. Further, if interest rates are viewed as indicators of

* Reprinted from *The Journal of Political Economy,* vol. 78, no. 3 (May/June, 1970), pp. 431–455, by permission of the author and The University of Chicago Press. 

[1] See Ackley (1961); Gramley and Chase (1965, esp. p. 1391); Trieber (1966). See also Federal Open Market Committee, Minutes, 1955 (Allan Sproul, May 10, May 24, and October 25, 1955, pp. 242, 275, 586; W. W. Riefler, August 23, 1955, p. 470; C. E. Earhart, March 2, 1955, pp. 103); 1957 (J. L. Robertson, September 10, 1957, p. 553); 1958 (J. L. Robertson, February 11, 1958, p. 119); 1959 (J. L. Robertson, January 6, 1959, p. 16); and 1960 (A. L. Mills, Jr., December 13, 1960, p. 913).

monetary policy, incorrect conclusions can easily follow if total effects are disregarded in favor of initial effects. The trouble with using interest rates as indicators of monetary policy emerges: If income increases faster than money, interest rates will tend to rise; but if the income increase itself results from increases in the money stock, should monetary policy be called restrictive?

## II. Liquidity, Income, and Price Expectations Effects

In order to maintain equality the quantity of money supplied and the quantity demanded, variables in the demand function (and perhaps in the supply function) must change as the stock of money is altered. To trace the effects of changes in the quantity of money on interest rates, we must therefore specify some of the variables in these functions. For the purpose of this section—to present a general and simplified summary of the effects to be expected on theoretical grounds—it will be sufficient to assume that the quantity of money demanded varies inversely with the level of interest rates and the expected rate of price change, and varies directly with the level of nominal income, that is, the demand for money function is of the following form:

$$M^d = M^d\left[i, \left(\frac{1}{P}\frac{dP}{dt}\right)^*, Y\right] \tag{1}$$

where $M^d$ is the quantity of nominal cash balances demanded, $i$ is the nominal rate of interest or a vector or average of nominal interest rates, $(1/P)(dP/dt)^*$ is the expected rate of price change, and $Y$ is nominal income.

This is a highly simplified demand function. The literature suggests other variables which might also be included, such as wealth, additional interest rates, or the ratio of current to permanent income, and one or more variables measuring the cost of managing a cash balance, since adjusting a stock of cash balances to changes in other variables is not a costless operation.[2]

The effects of money on interest rates can be examined by tracing the movements of the variables in the demand function following change in the money stock.[3] We distinguish three effects: the Fisher (price expectations) effect, the liquidity effect, and the income effect.

### *A. The Fisher Effect*

The Fisher or price expectations effect refers to the relationship between nominal interest rates and the expected rate of change of prices formulated by Fisher:[4]

$$i = r + \left(\frac{1}{P}\frac{dP}{dt}\right)^* + r\left(\frac{1}{P}\frac{dP}{dt}\right)^* \tag{2}$$

where $r$ is the rate of interest net of compensation for expected price changes and is here

---

[2] The managers of cash balances of businesses, for instance, are often regarded as being adept at minimizing the costs of holding cash. They are reputed to be very sophisticated operators in the market for government securities, moving in and out of Treasury bills for short periods and for increasingly smaller amounts. The market transactions costs of such operations have been recognized and taken into account in some studies (see Tobin 1956, and Baumol 1952) but there are also internal costs to a firm engaging in such practices. These include the cost to the firm of managing its cash position. For example, the officer of the firm watching the cash position might be doing something else or, if not, is dispensable. The more of its resources a firm allocates to the management of its money stock, the greater its costs. Similar considerations apply to the costs to households of managing cash positions, although the cost in the form of time consumed might be less obvious. But it takes more time and energy for an individual to handle receipts and payments on a very small working balance than when he has a substantial cushion in his checking account (assuming the same total wealth in each case). Although he may not move frequently in and out of Treasury bills, he may still respond to large enough incentives—costs and returns—in altering his portfolio. The costs of managing cash are therefore measured in wages or the price of leisure, so for the economy as a whole, we can approximate this cost by the level of real wage rates. This also means that, as the cost of managing balances rises, people will be less responsive to changes in transitory income, so that the quantity of money demanded will tend to depend more closely on permanent rather than measured income.

[3] It is assumed that the effects on interest rates are the same no matter how the money stock is increased. Some evidence supporting this assumption may be found in Cagan (1966).

[4] Fisher (1896, 1907, 1930). In what follows the interaction term, $r(1/P)(dP/dt)^*$ which gives the expected rate of depreciation of the interest payments, will be ignored, as it is dwarfed by the other terms.

called the "real" rate of interest, and $(1/P)(dP/dt)^*$ is the expected rate of change of prices. As Fisher noted, price inflation during the period of a loan imposes a capital loss on the lender by lowering the real value of his principal and interest. Lenders who expect that prices will rise during the loan term will try to protect themselves. By exchanging money for real capital goods, they could avoid the capital loss, since the nominal value of real capital goods would rise along with prices in general. If such alternatives are open to lenders (and the presence of willing borrowers suggests that they are), they will be willing to exchange money for nominal assets only at a rate sufficiently high to yield the same return after the expected capital loss. Borrowers who use the funds to acquire real assets, on the other hand, will benefit from a price inflation for any given rate of interest, since the nominal values of the real assets they purchase will rise. Hence they will be willing to pay a higher rate when they expect prices to rise. If lenders and borrowers have identical expectations, the market rate of interest will exceed the real rate by the expected rate of price increase times the sum of the principal plus interest, or, in continuous time, times the principal alone. Expected price declines cause similar but opposite effects on real capital values, driving nominal interest rates below real rates by the expected rate of price decline.

The Fisher effect says nothing about the relation between the stock of money and interest rates, only something about the relation between expected price changes and interest rates. But, if all or part of an increase in the money stock is reflected in an increase in prices, then an increase in the quantity of money will set a Fisher effect in motion.

If there is a once-and-for-all increase in the money stock, prices will settle at some new level. A Fisher effect may be generated in the process, but it is unlikely to last, for prices will stop changing once there is full adjustment to the new quantity of money. If there is a price rise and it generates expectations of further rises, interest rates may rise, but they would fall again when prices stop rising and people readjust their expectations. In order for the Fisher effect to raise interest rates more than temporarily, people must expect prices to continue to increase. Empirically, this requires continued price increases, which require continued increases in the quantity of money (see Section II*E*, below).

### *B. The Liquidity Effect*

One way in which the quantity of money demanded can adjust to equal a change in the amount supplied is through changes in interest rates, via a liquidity-preference relation: At higher interest rates, *ceteris paribus*, less money will be demanded than at lower rates. The rate of interest is an index of the benefits attainable by shifting one's asset holdings from money to assets yielding monetary returns, and, as such, is the opportunity cost of holding cash balances. When this cost rises, *ceteris paribus*, the quantity of money demanded should fall. Alternatively, the relation implies that a larger quantity of cash balances will be held only at a lower interest rate, *ceteris paribus*. An increase in the money stock can therefore bring about a fall in interest rates. This liquidity effect is so widely recognized, especially by formulators of monetary policy, that it might be called the reigning view on the relation between money and interest rates.[5] As mentioned earlier, there is a basis for this view, particularly from the standpoint of the monetary authorities. When the money stock is increased, the addition must be held by someone. If, before the increase, individuals were holding the amount of money they desired at prevailing interest rates and income, there is no reason to assume that they would wish to hold more money after the increase unless income or interest rates change. The very act of increasing the money stock may tend to lower some interest rates: an open market purchase by the monetary authorities tends to raise security prices and lower their yields; banks seeking to expand their loans to absorb excess reserves can then do so only by offering to lend at lower interest rates. However, an increase produced by purchasing goods and services, or by grants to individuals or others need have no such initial effect.[6] The initial effects on lending and security rates will not spread immediately over the entire term structure of rates. But *some* rates can

[5] See, for instance, references in footnote 1.

[6] Actually the yields on the stocks of such goods would fall, insofar as they are calculable, but these yields are not normally regarded as market interest rates.

fall, and further adjustments in other rates will follow in time.

There will also be effects on interest rates beyond those connected with the act of monetary increase. Assume for a moment that the money supply is increased by dropping money from an airplane, and consider the effects in a period not sufficiently long for an income change to take place.[7] Must interest rates fall? On the basis of equation (1) they must, or else $M^s \neq M^d$. If we stop the period an hour after the plane has passed over, however, it may well be that no interest rate has fallen, and in fact $M^s \neq M^d$. But if people are given time to come in from the fields, they should shortly begin to try to draw down their excess balances. Two apparent ways for individuals to do so are to increase spending and to purchase other assets. If nominal income does not increase in the period, people will try to shift into other assets, raising their prices and lowering their yields. Yields will fall until $M^s = M^d$, for otherwise people would be left holding money they did not want. It may be that for very short periods people can be off their demand-for-money schedules, since it may take some time to adjust. In the present context, such excursions off demand schedules will be ignored, and the quantity demanded will be assumed to equal the quantity supplied. This is done, not because people are assumed never to be off demand schedules, but because these departures are assumed to be empirically negligible.

### C. *The Income Effect*

Changes in nominal income can also bring about equilibrium between actual and desired money balances. If income immediately increased following a money stock increase, the quantity of money demanded would increase, perhaps with little change in interest rates. In general, the change in the quantity of money demanded may depend on how the change in nominal income is divided between a change in output and in prices. However, the demand function specified in equation (2) assumes that $M^d$ is a function of *nominal* income only, so that a given increase in nominal income has the same effect on the quantity of money demanded, regardless of how it is divided between prices and output. If, in addition, the demand function for money has a unit income elasticity, it would be necessary, in order for interest rates to be unchanged, that nominal income rise in the same proportion as the money stock.

In this case, if income instantly rises in the same proportion as money, interest rates will remain unchanged, for rates need not move to equate $M^d$ and $M^s$. The income and liquidity effects will have exactly balanced. But if income does not instantly rise in the same proportion as the money stock, the income change alone will not make desired and actual balances equal, and their equality will require a fall in interest rates. If interest rates fall for this reason and if the money stock is not further increased, income will subsequently increase and raise interest rates toward their former levels. As money holders bid up prices of other assets in response to decreases in interest rates, internal rates of return on these assets will fall. Accordingly, investment and income will increase. Interest rates rise because, at a now-constant $M^s$, an increase in income would raise desired balances above actual balances unless interest rates rose. Rates will rise when individuals attempt to increase their cash balances by trying to sell assets, lowering their prices and raising their yields. The income effect thus results when an income rise shifts the demand schedule for money outward so that a given stock of money will only be held at higher interest rates.

### D. *Income and Liquidity Effects Together*

Money holders are assumed always to be in short-term equilibrium, although they need not be always in long-run equilibrium. If the money stock changes, interest rates, income, or both are assumed to change to maintain short-run equilibrium. If interest rates fall, the short-run equilibrium position achieved very likely will not be one of long-run equilibrium. After interest rates fall to make $M^s = M^d$, the public will be on a demand curve, but further changes can occur for several reasons. The public may have planned to lower balances by additional spending which could not be completed. Spending and income would then increase in following

[7] It is possible, on theoretical grounds, that such a period does not exist.

periods. Alternatively, if investment or consumption spending is negatively responsive to interest rates, income will increase, perhaps with a lag. In both cases interest rates will tend to rise, if the stock of money is not further changed, as the demand schedule for money moves outward.

In the absence of additional changes in the money stock there will be no further liquidity effects, and we can ask how far the income effect will raise interest rates. If we assume there is full employment and abstract from price expectations effects, all income increases therefore take the form of price increases, which increase the demand for normal balances. If ex ante savings and investment were equal before the increase in the money stock, then at lower interest rates ex ante investment would tend to exceed saving. Increases in the price level will raise interest rates by raising nominal income and hence the quantity of money demanded. Upward pressure on income and prices will continue until the former level of interest rates is restored, the level which equated ex ante saving and investment. This point is reached when prices and income have increased in the same proportion as the money stock.

If, however, the economy is initially below full employment, interest rates may not return to previous levels. A return to old levels requires that the increase in nominal income be the same as with full employment. In terms of *IS-LM* curve analysis, we need to know the slope of the *IS* curve. If the *IS* curve relating interest rates to nominal income is horizontal (as under full employment), interest rates will return to original levels after the money stock is increased. If, perhaps because investment does not depend on income, the *IS* curve is negatively sloped, interest rates will settle below their original levels. Conversely, if the *IS* curve slopes positively, rates will settle above old levels.

Although equation (1) includes measured income, our conclusions require little if any modification if equation (1) instead includes permanent income. In this case, a given increase in measured income will raise permanent income by a smaller amount, raising interest rates by less than if $M^d$ depended on measured income. But the rate of change of measured income need not be the same in both cases; measured income may rise faster when permanent rather than measured income is the variable in the demand function. A given lag in the income effect is consistent with including either income variable in equation (1), but the permanent income formulation allows a cyclical effect which the measured income counterpart does not. If when the income effect just balances the liquidity effect measured income is above permanent income (and it could be far above if permanent income must adjust rapidly), the latter will continue to rise, raising interest rates with it. Later measured income will fall, leading to cyclical approaches of measured and permanent income and interest rates to their new equilibrium levels.

Finally, most of the above discussion has dealt, explicitly or implicitly, with increase in the money stock. Except for the full-employment constraint, a decrease in the money stock produces similar but opposite effects on interest rates. Money holders must be induced to desire a smaller stock of cash, and interest rates will rise if income does not fall immediately. If permanent income is the appropriate demand variable, there may again be cyclical adjustments.

## *E. The Price Expectations Effect Added*

Figure 1 shows the final effect on interest rates of an increase in the money stock. The economy is initially at point $E_1$, where money stock is $M^s_1$ and real (and nominal) interest rates are $r_1$. If income does not rise immedi-

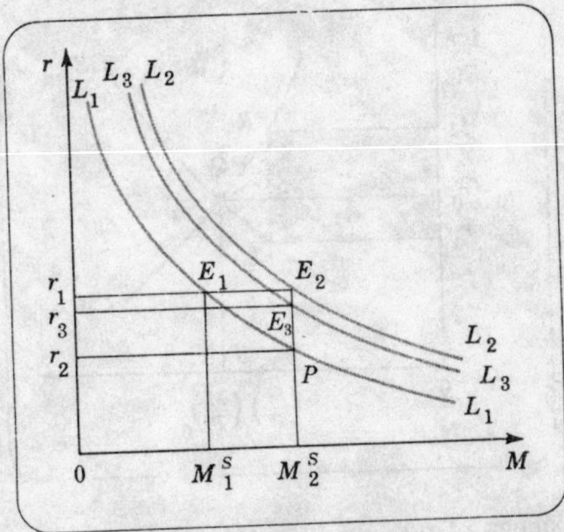


FIGURE 1 Interest rate adjustments to an increase in the money stock.

ately following an increase in the money stock to $M_2^s$, the economy will move immediately to point $P$, along the curve $L_1$, drawn for a given level of income and expected rate of price change. This fall of interest rates from $r_1$ to $r_2$ is the liquidity effect. As income increases, the $L$ curve will shift rightward until it reaches the position $L_2$, which intersects $M_2^s$ at $E_2$, where interest rates are again at $r_1$. We may call the movement from $P$ to $E_2$ the income effect, and it obviously just balances the liquidity effect.

If now the expected rate of price change increases, $L_2$ will shift to the left to $L_3$, lowering real interest rates to $r_3$. Nominal rates will exceed real rates by the expected rate of price increase. The $L$ curve shifts downward when $(1/P)(dP/dt)^*$ increases, so that at a given $r$ less money is demanded. At the new equilibrium $E_3$, real rates are $r_3$, lower than before the shift in price expectations, because at higher expected rates of price change real assets will be more attractive at the old price ratio than both money and bonds. Asset holders will then try to shift from fixed-price assets to real assets, bidding up the prices and down the yields of the latter.

If the new expected rate of price change is to be maintained, there must be continuing increases in money and prices. Sustained price expectations will then keep nominal rates above real rates and real rates below their original levels.

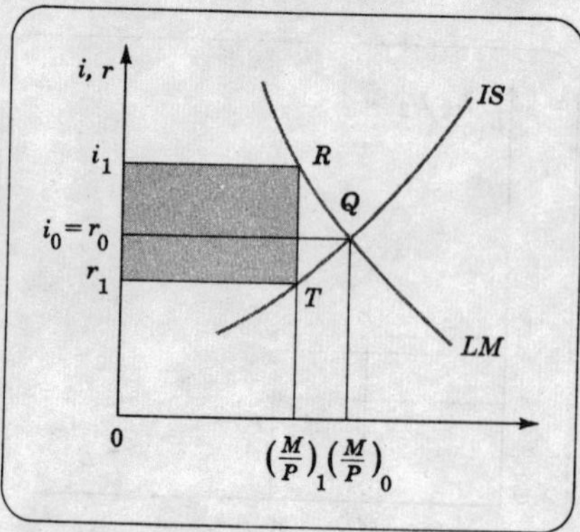


FIGURE 2 Interest rate adjustments to altered price expectations.

The effects of expected inflation on nominal and real interest rates can also be seen from a diagram presented by Mundell (1963).[8] He assumes that real investment depends on the real interest rate[9] and real saving depends on real money balances, and that the desired ratio of money to securities depends on the nominal interest rate. Figure 2 shows the two curves, which Mundell calls *IS* and *LM*, which give pairs of interest rates and real cash balances consistent with equilibrium in the goods and money markets, respectively. Equilibrium is at $Q$ when stable prices are expected. Real balances are $(M/P)_0$ and real and nominal interest rates are equal at level $i_0$. An expected rate of inflation of $RT$ percent per year causes the $LM$ curve expressed in terms of the real rate to shift down by $RT$, and the $IS$ curve expressed in terms of the nominal rate rises by $RT$. When the ordinate is read as the nominal rate, therefore, equilibrium is at $R$, and the nominal rate is $i_1$. In terms of the real rate, however, equilibrium is at $T$, with the real rate at $r_1$. The vertical distance between the two equilibria is the expected rate of inflation ($= RT$), and the shaded area represents the depreciation of real cash balances.

When *IS* and *LM* have the slopes shown in figure 2, therefore, expected inflation raises the nominal interest rate, but not by the full expected rate of inflation. The real rate falls because the inflation reduces real cash balances and the resultant decline in wealth stimulates increased saving. Real investment and real savings are higher than in the absence of inflation.

The amount of the fall in the real rate depends on the slopes of *IS* and *LM* (as defined here) and on the expected rate of inflation. Figure 2 shows that if the *IS* curve is horizontal the real rate will not fall, no matter how much inflation is expected. The

[8] Mundell's result is derived from Lloyd Metzler's model, which assumes flexible wages and prices and full employment, but Mundell later extended it to the Keynesian unemployment case (Mundell 1965).

[9] Mundell implicitly assumes that the effect of the inflationary tax on the cash balances of businesses is not sufficient to offset the negative relation between the real rate and the level of investment.

*IS* curve will be horizontal if either of two conditions holds. First, if investment is perfectly elastic with respect to the real rate, only one real rate will be possible, and the *IS* curve, drawn on the $r$, $(M/P)$ plane, will be horizontal. If an increase in the real rate lowers investment, saving must decrease when real balances are increased if larger real balances are to be associated with higher interest rates. Money therefore cannot be neutral if the real rate is to fall; there must be some outside money in the economy. Therefore, in order for anticipated inflation to alter real conditions in the economy, investment must be imperfectly elastic with respect to the real rate, and there must be some outside money in the economy.

The *LM* curve will normally be negatively sloped if the interest elasticity of demand for real balances is neither zero nor infinite. If the demand were perfectly interest elastic, anticipated inflation would not change nominal rates, and real rates would fall by the anticipated rate of inflation. If the elasticity of demand were zero, real rates would be unchanged, and nominal rates would rise by the anticipated rate of inflation. If (as shown in fig. 2) neither *IS* nor *LM* is horizontal or vertical, both real and nominal rates will change when the expected rate of price change increases, but neither will change by the full expected rate.

## III. Some Existing Evidence of Money's Effects on Interest Rates

Earlier studies have produced some evidence on each of the three effects on interest rates, although the operation of all three does not appear to have been fully documented. Cagan examined the relationship between changes in the rate of change of money ($M_2$) and changes in the commercial paper rate, using reference cycle-stage data (Cagan 1966). He found that an increase in the monetary growth rate in stage $t$ has a negative effect on interest rates in stage $t$, zero net effect in stage $t + 1$, and positive effects thereafter. The initial negative effect is offset by the end of stage $t + 3$, and positive effects were estimated to continue through stage $t + 6$ (Cagan 1966, table 9, p. 389). Since there are nine stages in a cycle, the average duration of a stage is between four and five months. On average, then, positive effects offset negative effects within about a year after the stage in which the monetary growth rate is increased.

Cagan measured the total effects on interest rate changes of an increase in the rate of monetary acceleration for the 1904-61 period (he excluded stages within the 1929-33 contractions and within the World War II years), but he did not consider the relation between the stock of money and the level of interest rates. Other studies have generally not dealt with the total effects of money on interest rates, but some provide evidence on the separate effects.

Tobin's statement, noted earlier, is one of the more straightforward statements of the liquidity effect, for it says that an increase in the money stock lowers interest rates by causing the economy to move down along a liquidity-preference schedule. His evidence for the effect consists of plotting the commercial paper rate against "idle balances," the quantity of money adjusted for transactions needs. He concluded that the resulting negatively sloped curve supports his hypothesis of a liquidity-preference relation. Demand for money studies (Latané 1954; Friedman, 1959; Meltzer 1963) now use more complex techniques but give similar evidence on this point: Holding income constant, increased money balances will be held only at lower interest rates. These studies do not, however, chart the effects on interest rates when both money and income are allowed to change.

The income effect has been documented in two parts. First, the positive effect on interest rates of increases in income has been documented, both overall and holding money and the rate of price change constant (Gibson and Kaufman 1968). Second, the relation between money and income has been under consideration in the literature for generations, beginning in a well-organized fashion with the Bullion debates in England at the beginning of the nineteenth century. More recently the Friedman-Meiselman study for the Commission on Money and Credit provides evidence of a close relation between money and income in the United States over a long period, as well as for subperiods (Friedman and Meiselman 1963). The authors found the stock of money more closely related to consumption six months

TABLE 1. RELATION BETWEEN THE MONEY STOCK AND CURRENT AND PAST INTEREST RATES, MONTHLY OBSERVATIONS, 1947–1966

| | | | | | | | | | |
|---|---|---|---|---|---|---|---|---|---|
| $\ln M_1 =$ | 4.6610* | $+9.5957^*i_t$ | $-2.1764i_{t-1}$ | $-1.8626i_{t-2}$ | $-1.6054i_{t-3}$ | $+0.0356i_{t-4}$ | $+0.7994i_{t-5}$ | $+2.5518i_{t-6}$ | $+0.6586i_{t-7}$ |
| | (0.0081) | (2.2581) | (3.7972) | (3.8213) | (3.8022) | (3.8434) | (3.8561) | (3.8705) | (3.8535) |
| | $+0.0899i_{t-8}$ | $-1.5523i_{t-9}$ | $-2.0591i_{t-10}$ | $-1.2420i_{t-11}$ | $+7.6332^*i_{t-12}$ | SE $Y \cdot X = 0.04775$ | $R^2 = 0.844$ | D-W = 0.130 | |
| | (3.8338) | (3.8141) | (3.8171) | (3.8368) | (2.3413) | | | | $i = i_b$ |
| $\ln M_1 =$ | 4.4142* | $+15{:}351^*i_t$ | $-4.8391i_{t-1}$ | $+2.4377i_{t-2}$ | $-0.5487i_{t-3}$ | $-0.8836i_{t-4}$ | $-1.8809i_{t-5}$ | $+3.0281i_{t-6}$ | $-1.8247i_{t-7}$ |
| | (0.0133) | (4.8582) | (8.3707) | (8.8956) | (8.9833) | (8.9473) | (8.8854) | (8.8327) | (8.8582) |
| | $+0.5720i_{t-8}$ | $-1.2725i_{t-9}$ | $+2.1387i_{t-10}$ | $-4.0239i_{t-11}$ | $+6.7392i_{t-12}$ | SE $Y \cdot X = 0.04082$ | $R^2 = 0.874$ | D-W = 0.049 | |
| | (8.9113) | (9.0095) | (9.0237) | (8.6185) | (5.0389) | | | | $i = i_{bd}$ |
| $\ln M_1 =$ | 4.3934* | $+22.653^*i_t$ | $-11.757i_{t-1}$ | $+3.9689i_{t-2}$ | $-1.3306i_{t-3}$ | $-2.5276i_{t-4}$ | $-0.9245i_{t-5}$ | $+1.2881i_{t-6}$ | $-0.9076i_{t-7}$ |
| | (0.0160) | (6.8401) | (12.813) | (13.975) | (14.219) | (14.586) | (14.649) | (14.624) | (14.657) |
| | $-1.5905i_{t-8}$ | $+0.1232i_{t-9}$ | $+1.3677i_{t-10}$ | $-2.9057i_{t-11}$ | $+6.7228i_{t-12}$ | SE $Y \cdot X = 0.4752$ | $R^2 = 0.845$ | D-W = 0.053 | |
| | (14.686) | (14.691) | (14.732) | (13.666) | (7.2912) | | | | $i = i_{aaa}$ |
| $\frac{1}{M}\frac{dM_1}{dt} =$ | 0.02331* | $+1.1578Di_t$ | $+0.3567Di_{t-1}$ | $-0.2804Di_{t-2}$ | $-0.6297Di_{t-3}$ | $-1.2144Di_{t-4}$ | $-0.5111Di_{t-5}$ | $-1.3891Di_{t-8}$ | $-1.1039Di_{t-7}$ |
| | (0.00241) | (1.6448) | (1.7693) | (1.7630) | (1.7551) | (1.7787) | (1.7760) | (1.7952) | (1.7658) |
| | $-0.6892Di_{t-8}$ | $-0.9224Di_{t-9}$ | $-1.0009Di_{t-10}$ | $-1.6115Di_{t-11}$ | $-2.0497Di_{t-12}$ | SE $Y \cdot X = 0.03481$ | $R^2 = 0.067$ | D-W = 1.451 | |
| | (1.7670) | (1.7674) | (1.7591) | (1.7718) | (1.7037) | | | | $i = i_b$ |
| $\frac{1}{M}\frac{dM_1}{dt} =$ | (0.02360* | $+4.0792Di_t$ | $+6.3755Di_{t-1}$ | $-1.2714Di_{t-2}$ | $+1.9092Di_{t-3}$ | $-1.2361Di_{t-4}$ | $-6.0238Di_{t-5}$ | $-1.1766Di_{t-6}$ | $-2.2423Di_{t-7}$ |
| | (0.00253) | (4.0085) | (4.2417) | (4.3079) | (4.3062) | (4.3047) | (4.2962) | (4.3416) | (4.2845) |
| | $-1.8517Di_{t-8}$ | $-2.5457Di_{t-9}$ | $-7.0717Di_{t-10}$ | $-5.1044Di_{t-11}$ | $-3.7604Di_{t-12}$ | SE $Y \cdot X = 0.03424$ | $R^2 = 0.097$ | D-W = 1.478 | |
| | (4.3083) | (4.3323) | (4.3643) | (4.3572) | (4.1519) | | | | $i = i_{bd}$ |
| $\frac{1}{M}\frac{dM_1}{dt} =$ | 0.02453* | $+10.490^*Di_t$ | $+3.3061Di_{t-1}$ | $-5.1707Di_{t-2}$ | $+6.8284Di_{t-3}$ | $-10.765Di_{t-4}$ | $-6.9056Di_{t-5}$ | $+4.0632Di_{t-6}$ | $-13.967^*Di_{t-7}$ |
| | (0.00244) | (4.7696) | (5.4917) | (5.5944) | (5.7071) | (5.8296) | (5.8315) | (5.8255) | (5.8453) |
| | $+4.0887Di_{t-8}$ | $-2.7537Di_{t-9}$ | $-7.3692Di_{t-10}$ | $-0.1337Di_{t-11}$ | $-11.783^*Di_{t-12}$ | SE $Y \cdot X = 0.03298$ | $R^2 = 0.162$ | D-W = 1.515 | |
| | (5.8544) | (5.8572) | (5.9592) | (5.8664) | (5.0853) | | | | $i = i_{aaa}$ |

NOTE: For sources and more complete notes see Appendix. $Di = i_t - i_{t-1}$.
*Significant at .05 level.

TABLE 2. RELATION BETWEEN THE MONEY STOCK AND CURRENT AND PAST INTEREST RATES, MONTHLY OBSERVATIONS, 1947–1966

| | | | | | | |
|---|---|---|---|---|---|---|
| $\ln M_2 =$ | $+4.8025^*$ | $+18.421^* i_t$ | $-3.7775 i_{t-1}$ | $-3.8638 i_{t-2}$ | $-3.0063 i_{t-3}$ | $-3.3061 i_{t-4}$ |
| | (0.0158) | (4.4020) | (7.4025) | (7.4494) | (7.4123) | (4.40926) |
| | $+1.5323 i_{t-5}$ | $+4.7483 i_{t-6}$ | $+1.9568 i_{t-7}$ | $+0.1463 i_{t-8}$ | $-2.8540 i_{t-9}$ | $-3.9731 i_{t-10}$ |
| | (7.5172) | (7.5454) | (7.5123) | (7.4739) | (7.4354) | (7.4412) |
| | $-2.5842 i_{t-11}$ | $+15.164^* i_{t-12}$ | SE $Y \cdot X$ = 0.09308 | $R^2 = 0.848$ | D-W = 0.126 | $i = i_b$ |
| | (7.4795) | (4.5642) | | | | |
| $\ln M_2 =$ | $4.3068^*$ | $+23.928^* i_t$ | $-6.7184 i_{t-1}$ | $+3.0817 i_{t-2}$ | $-0.2571 i_{t-3}$ | $-0.9505 i_{t-4}$ |
| | (0.0256) | (9.3338) | (16.082) | (17.091) | (17.259) | (17.190) |
| | $-3.8074 i_{t-5}$ | $+5.3238 i_{t-6}$ | $-2.7682 i_{t-7}$ | $-0.5368 i_{t-8}$ | $-1.1694 i_{t-9}$ | $+5.1826 i_{t-10}$ |
| | (17.071) | (16.970) | (17.019) | (17.121) | (17.310) | (17.337) |
| | $-10.375 i_{t-11}$ | $+19.185 i_{t-12}$ | SE $Y \cdot X$ = 0.08228 | $R^2 = 0.881$ | D-W = 0.040 | $i = i_{bd}$ |
| | (16.558) | (9.6811) | | | | |
| $\ln M_2 =$ | $4.2543^*$ | $+36.420 i_t$ | $-19.535 i_{t-1}$ | $+7.4452 i_{t-2}$ | $-0.7068 i_{t-3}$ | $-5.6655 i_{t-4}$ |
| | (0.0302) | (12.953) | (24.265) | (26.464) | (26.927) | (27.621) |
| | $-2.6166 i_{t-5}$ | $+2.9964 i_{t-6}$ | $-1.7820 i_{t-7}$ | $-2.9446 i_{t-8}$ | $+0.6803 i_{t-9}$ | $+2.8499 i_{t-10}$ |
| | (27.742) | (27.695) | (27.755) | (27.811) | (27.821) | (27.897) |
| | $-10.983 i_{t-11}$ | $+22.650 i_{t-12}$ | SE $Y \cdot X$ = 0.08998 | $R^2 = 0.858$ | D-W = 0.047 | $i = i_{aaa}$ |
| | (25.880) | (13.807) | | | | |
| $\frac{1}{M_2}\frac{dM_2}{dt} =$ | $0.04490^*$ | $+0.7048\, Di_t$ | $-1.5985\, Di_{t-1}$ | $-2.0314\, Di_{t-2}$ | $-1.0069\, Di_{t-3}$ | $-1.9834\, Di_{t-4}$ |
| | (0.00248) | (1.6911) | (1.8190) | (1.8126) | (1.8045) | (1.8287) |
| | $-0.7501\, Di_{t-5}$ | $-2.3066\, Di_{t-6}$ | $-1.3599\, Di_{t-7}$ | $-0.8786\, Di_{t-8}$ | $-0.1554\, Di_{t-9}$ | $-1.5484\, Di_{t-10}$ |
| | (1.8260) | (1.8457) | (1.8155) | (1.8168) | (1.8171) | (1.8086) |
| | $-2.1884\, Di_{t-11}$ | $-1.6057\, Di_{t-12}$ | SE $Y \cdot X$ = 0.03579 | $R^2 = 0.106$ | D-W = 0.794 | $i = i_b$ |
| | (1.8216) | (1.7517) | | | | |
| $\frac{1}{M_2}\frac{dM_2}{dt} =$ | $0.04586^*$ | $+1.2121\, Di_t$ | $+3.6758\, Di_{t-1}$ | $-4.6851\, Di_{t-2}$ | $-2.5582\, Di_{t-3}$ | $-4.9604\, Di_{t-4}$ |
| | (0.00267) | (4.2323) | (4.4785) | (4.5485) | (4.5466) | (4.5451) |
| | $-4.9357\, Di_{t-5}$ | $-4.6381\, Di_{t-6}$ | $-2.6509\, Di_{t-7}$ | $-1.2921\, Di_{t-8}$ | $-2.7139\, Di_{t-9}$ | $-4.6411\, Di_{t-10}$ |
| | (4.5361) | (4.5840) | (4.5237) | (4.5488) | (4.5742) | (4.6080) |
| | $-3.2424\, Di_{t-11}$ | $-7.0661\, Di_{t-12}$ | SE $Y \cdot X$ = 0.03615 | $R^2 = 0.088$ | D-W = 0.805 | $i = i_{bd}$ |
| | (4.6004) | (4.3837) | | | | |
| $\frac{1}{M_2}\frac{dM_2}{dt} =$ | $0.04631^*$ | $+7.3984\, Di_t$ | $+0.7765\, Di_{t-1}$ | $-8.4808\, Di_{t-2}$ | $+0.1483\, Di_{t-3}$ | $-7.1197\, Di_{t-4}$ |
| | (0.00259) | (5.0643) | (5.8310) | (5.9401) | (6.0598) | (6.1899) |
| | $-9.9830\, Di_{t-5}$ | $+1.9900\, Di_{t-6}$ | $-12.818^*\, Di_{t-7}$ | $+2.9883\, Di_{t-8}$ | $-0.2164\, Di_{t-9}$ | $-5.4622\, Di_{t-10}$ |
| | (6.1919) | (6.1855) | (6.2065) | (6.2162) | (6.2191) | (6.3274) |
| | $+1.0029\, Di_{t-11}$ | $-12.604^*\, Di_{t-12}$ | SE $Y \cdot X$ = 0.03501 | $R^2 = 0.144$ | D-W = 0.786 | $i = i_{aaa}$ |
| | (6.2289) | (5.3995) | | | | |

NOTE: For sources and more complete notes, see Appendix. $Di = i_t - i_{t-1}$, $M$, $i$ seasonally adjusted.
*Significant at .05 level.

later than at any other date (Friedman and Meiselman 1963, p. 214).

## IV. Evidence of the Three Effects

Even for monthly data, the quantity of money and interest rates are positively correlated,[10] indicating that the liquidity-preference relation is an inadequate description of the overall empirical money-interest rate relation. This positive relation could arise from a positive effect of interest rates on the supply of money or from the operation of income and price expectations effects. Both possibilities are investigated here.

### *A. Interest Rate Levels and Money Stock Levels*

We can use

$$i = f(\ln M_t, \ln M_{t-1}, \ln M_{t-2}, \ldots, \ln M_{t-n}) \quad (3)$$

to measure the total effects of the money stock on interest rates and the distribution of these effects over time.[11] This equation can be interpreted as one of the reduced forms in a system of simultaneous equations, except that it assumes that money is the only exogenous variable. Equation (3) assumes that the primary direction of influence runs from the money stock to interest rates. There are however, reasons for expecting interest rates to influence the money stock: When interest rates rise, banks will be more anxious to acquire earning assets since yields on the latter rise. This will make them willing to operate on a lower reserve-deposit ratio than before, which, given the total amount of reserves available to the banking system, implies a lower excess reserve ratio.[12] For a given rediscount rate, the higher the level of market interest rates, the larger the amount that banks will wish to borrow. If the Federal Reserve does not offset these two effects by open market operations, the money stock will increase. Whether these effects will be as large as the effects of money on interest rates is an empirical question.

The validity of this assumption can be checked by changing the variables in equation (3) to produce

$$\ln M_t = f(i_t, i_{t-1}, i_{t-2}, \ldots i_{t-n}) \quad (4)$$

Estimates of (4) and its first-difference form,

$$\frac{1}{M}\frac{dM}{dt} = f\left[\left(\frac{di}{dt}\right)_t, \left(\frac{di}{dt}\right)_{t-1}, \left(\frac{di}{dt}\right)_{t-2}, \ldots \left(\frac{di}{dt}\right)_{t-n}\right] \quad (5)$$

are presented for monthly data in Tables 1 and 2. There is a strong positive relation between current interest rates and the current money stock, even when past interest rates

---

[10] The simple correlation between the ninety-day Treasury bill rate and $M_2$ monthly is 0.72 for the period 1952–66.

[11] Seasonal variation in interest rates was apparent from the coefficients of three sets of preliminary regressions using monthly and quarterly interest rates: interest rates on seasonal dummy variables, interest rates on past values of the seasonally adjusted money stock, and seasonally adjusted money on past interest rates. Seasonal coefficients showed a generally rising pattern from March through January; interest rates tend to be below February levels in the months following February, and above February levels in the months preceding February.

In addition, there are seasonal variations in the money stock which do not produce the three effects outlined earlier. These are the changes in the money stock made to accommodate seasonal changes in the demand for money and credit. An aim of the Federal Reserve System is to accommodate seasonal swings in the financial needs of trade, and the System tries to do this by removing seasonal fluctuations from interest rates. The seasonal variation remaining in interest rates suggests that the System is not wholly successful in these efforts, but the fact that it attempts to offset these seasonal flucuations means that some changes in the money stock (for example, in response to exogenous seasonal movements in income) do not show liquidity effects. While these distortions appear in unadjusted money data, they should be absent from seasonally adjusted money stock data, from which the influence of the System's seasonal actions should be removed.

In order to avoid the seasonal distortions present in the two sets of data, therefore, the analysis which follows uses seasonally adjusted interest rates and money supply series. The data used are described in detail in the Appendix, where sources are listed.

[12] Cagan treated this problem in some detail, using annual data, and concluded that these interest rate effects on money are not sufficient to produce a positive relation (see Cagan 1965).

TABLE 3. RELATION BETWEEN INTEREST RATES AND CURRENT AND PAST MONEY STOCKS, MONTHLY OBSERVATIONS, 1947–1966

| | | | | | | |
|---|---|---|---|---|---|---|
| $i_b$ = $-0.3737$* | $-0.3873$*$M1_t$ | $+0.0754M1_{t-1}$ | $+0.1483M1_{t-2}$ | $+0.2103M1_{t-3}$ | $-0.0209M1_{t-4}$ | $+0.0550M1_{t-5}$ |
| (0.0145) | (0.1393) | (0.2141) | (0.2137) | (0.2093) | (0.2179) | (0.2166) |
| $+0.1603M1_{t-6}$ | $+0.0161M1_{t-7}$ | $+0.0588M1_{t-8}$ | $-0.0223M1_{t-9}$ | $-0.0382M1_{t-10}$ | $-0.0848M1_{t-11}$ | $-0.0897M1_{t-12}$ |
| (0.2242) | (0.2298) | (0.2324) | (0.2387) | (0.2453) | (0.2461) | (0.1549) |
| | | SE $Y \cdot X$ = 0.00494 | $R^2$ = 0.815 | D-W = 0.121 | | |
| $i_{bd}$ = $-0.2687$* | $-0.1378_t$ | $+0.0355M1_{t-1}$ | $+0.0960M1_{t-2}$ | $+0.0613M1_{t-3}$ | $-0.0138M1_{t-4}$ | $-0.0154M1_{t-5}$ |
| (0.0076) | (0.0729) | (0.1121) | (0.1119) | (0.1096) | (0.1141) | (0.1134) |
| $+0.0317M1_{t-6}$ | $-0.0060M1_{t-7}$ | $+0.0022M1_{t-8}$ | $-0.0021M1_{t-9}$ | $-0.0342M1_{t-10}$ | $+0.0016M1_{t-11}$ | $+0.0429M1_{t-12}$ |
| (0.1174) | (0.1204) | (0.1217) | (0.1250) | (0.1285) | (0.1289) | (0.0811) |
| | | SE $Y \cdot X$ = 0.00259 | $R^2$ = 0.887 | D-W = 0.076 | | |
| $i_{aaa}$ = $-0.2756$* | $-0.1419M1_t$ | $+0.0135M1_{t-1}$ | $+0.0674M1_{t-2}$ | $+0.0721M1_{t-3}$ | $+0.0033M1_{t-4}$ | $-0.0212M1_{t-5}$ |
| (0.0083) | (0.0794) | (0.1221) | (0.1218) | (0.1193) | (0.1242) | (0.1235) |
| $+0.0431M1_{t-6}$ | $-0.00273M1_{t-7}$ | $+0.0374M1_{t-8}$ | $-0.0118M1_{t-9}$ | $-0.0623M1_{t-10}$ | $-0.0126M1_{t-11}$ | $+0.0798M1_{t-12}$ |
| (0.1279) | (0.1311) | (0.1325) | (0.1361) | (0.1399) | (0.1403) | (0.0883) |
| | | SE $Y \cdot X$ = 0.00281 | $R^2$ = 0.874 | D-W = 0.058 | | |
| $\frac{di_b}{dt}$ = $-0.00027$ | $-0.00389DM1_t$ | $+0.00140DM1_{t-1}$ | $+0.00541DM1_{t-2}$ | $+0.00737DM1_{t-3}$ | $+0.00048DM1_{t-4}$ | $+0.00729DM1_{t-5}$ |
| (0.00016) | (0.00352) | (0.00356) | (0.00369) | (0.00379) | (0.00383) | (0.00382) |
| $+0.00804$*$DM1_{t-6}$ | $+0.00633DM1_{t-7}$ | $-0.00157DM1_{t-8}$ | $-0.00426DM1_{t-9}$ | $+0.00196DM1_{t-10}$ | $-0.00569DM1_{t-11}$ | $-0.00266DM1_{t-12}$ |
| (0.00403) | (0.00404) | (0.00404) | (0.00424) | (0.00422) | (0.00401) | (0.00391) |
| | | SE $Y \cdot X$ = 0.00149 | $R^2$ = 0.199 | D-W = 1.435 | | |
| $\frac{di_{bd}}{dt}$ = $-0.00005$ | $-0.00102DM1_t$ | $+0.00091DM1_{t-1}$ | $+0.00394$*$DM1_{t-2}$ | $+0.00368$*$DM1_{t-3}$ | $-0.00127DM1_{t-4}$ | $-0.00049DM1_{t-5}$ |
| (0.00006) | (0.00144) | (0.00146) | (0.00151) | (0.00156) | (0.00157) | (0.00157) |
| $+0.00325DM1_{t-6}$ | $-0.00006DM1_{t-7}$ | $-0.00034DM1_{t-8}$ | $-0.00149DM1_{t-9}$ | $+0.00095DM1_{t-10}$ | $+0.00189DM1_{t-11}$ | $-0.00322$*$DM1_{t-12}$ |
| (0.00165) | (0.00166) | (0.00166) | (0.00174) | (0.00173) | (0.00165) | (0.00160) |
| | | SE $Y \cdot X$ = 0.00061 | $R^2$ = 0.149 | D-W = 1.442 | | |
| $\frac{di_{aaa}}{dt}$ = $-0.00005$ | $+0.00096DM1_t$ | $-0.00051DM1_{t-1}$ | $+0.00002DM1_{t-2}$ | $+0.00314$*$DM1_{t-3}$ | $+0.00152DM1_{t-4}$ | $+0.00007DM1_{t-5}$ |
| (0.00006) | (0.00124) | (0.00126) | (0.00130) | (0.00134) | (0.00135) | (0.00135) |
| $+0.00098DM1_{t-6}$ | $+0.00034DM1_{t-7}$ | $+0.00165DM1_{t-8}$ | $+0.00028DM1_{t-9}$ | $-0.00024DM1_{t-10}$ | $-0.00007DM1_{t-11}$ | $-0.00079DM1_{t-12}$ |
| (0.00142) | (0.00142) | (0.00143) | (0.00150) | (0.00149) | (0.00141) | (0.00138) |
| | | SE $Y \cdot X$ = 0.00053 | $R^2$ = 0.121 | D-W = 1.117 | | |

NOTE: For sources and more complete notes, see Appendix. $M1 = \ln M_1$; $DM1 = \frac{1}{M_1}\frac{dM_1}{dt}$; $M$, $i$ seasonally adjusted.

*Significant at .05 level.

TABLE 4. RELATION BETWEEN INTEREST RATES AND CURRENT AND PAST MONEY STOCKS, MONTHLY OBSERVATIONS, 1947–1966

| | | | | | | |
|---|---|---|---|---|---|---|
| $i_b$ = | $-0.2366^*$ | $-0.6237^*M2_t$ | $+0.2417M2_{t-1}$ | $+0.1475M2_{t-2}$ | $+0.1239M2_{t-3}$ | $+0.0284M2_{t-4}$ |
| | (0.0100) | (0.1456) | (0.2456) | (0.2478) | (0.2445) | (0.2498) |
| | $+0.1336M2_{t-5}$ | $+0.0915M2_{t-6}$ | $-0.0908M2_{t-7}$ | $+0.0580M2_{t-8}$ | $+0.0631M2_{t-9}$ | $+0.0444M2_{t-10}$ |
| | (0.2485) | (0.2496) | (0.2502) | (0.2517) | (0.2555) | (0.2611) |
| | $-0.0505M2_{t-11}$ | $-0.0284M2_{t-12}$ | | SE $Y \cdot X$ = 0.00457 | $R^2$ = 0.841 | D-W = 0.161 |
| | (0.2623) | (0.1575) | | | | |
| $i_{bd}$ = | $-0.1469^*$ | $-0.1503M2_t$ | $+0.0608M2_{t-1}$ | $+0.0381M2_{t-2}$ | $+0.0208M2_{t-3}$ | $+0.0323M2_{t-4}$ |
| | (0.0058) | (0.0836) | (0.1411) | (0.1423) | (0.1405) | (0.1435) |
| | $+0.0238M2_{t-5}$ | $+0.0126M2_{t-6}$ | $-0.0419M2_{t-7}$ | $-0.0048M2_{t-8}$ | $+0.0348M2_{t-9}$ | $-0.0186M2_{t-10}$ |
| | (0.1427) | (0.1434) | (0.1437) | (0.1446) | (0.1468) | (0.1500) |
| | $-0.0150M2_{t-11}$ | $+0.0419M2_{t-12}$ | | SE $Y \cdot X$ = 0.00263 | $R^2$ = 0.883 | D-W = 0.074 |
| | (0.1507) | (0.0905) | | | | |
| $i_{aaa}$ = | $-0.1565^*$ | $-0.1457M2_t$ | $+0.0459M2_{t-1}$ | $+0.0270M2_{t-2}$ | $+0.0113M2_{t-3}$ | $+0.0330M2_{t-4}$ |
| | (0.0062) | (0.0897) | (0.1512) | (0.1526) | (0.1506) | (0.1539) |
| | $+0.0270M2_{t-5}$ | $+0.0150M2_{t-6}$ | $-0.0241M2_{t-7}$ | $+0.0029M2_{t-8}$ | $+0.0243M2_{t-9}$ | $-0.0465M2_{t-10}$ |
| | (0.1530) | (0.1537) | (0.1541) | (0.1550) | (0.1573) | (0.1608) |
| | $-0.0271M2_{t-11}$ | $+0.0942M2_{t-12}$ | | SE $Y \cdot X$ = 0.00281 | $R^2$ = 0.874 | D-W = 0.056 |
| | (0.1615) | (0.0970) | | | | |
| $\frac{di_b}{dt}$ = | $-0.00027$ | $-0.01222^*DM2_t$ | $+0.00352DM2_{t-1}$ | $+0.00285DM2_{t-2}$ | $+0.00540DM2_{t-3}$ | $+0.00095DM2_{t-4}$ |
| | (0.00019) | (0.00400) | (0.00428) | (0.00441) | (0.00455) | (0.00451) |
| | $+0.01172^*DM2_{t-5}$ | $+0.00916^*DM2_{t-6}$ | $-0.00141DM2_{t-7}$ | $-0.00276DM2_{t-8}$ | $-0.00418DM2_{t-9}$ | $+0.00408DM2_{t-10}$ |
| | (0.00453) | (0.00454) | (0.00455) | (0.00456) | (0.00475) | (0.00474) |
| | $-0.00086DM2_{t-11}$ | $-0.00579DM2_{t-12}$ | | SE $Y \cdot X$ = 0.00151 | $R^2$ = 0.181 | D-W = 1.450 |
| | (0.00454) | (0.00427) | | | | |

TABLE 4. *(Continued)*

| | | | | | | |
|---|---|---|---|---|---|---|
| $\frac{di_{bd}}{dt} =$ | $-0.000057$ | $-0.00217DM2_t$ | $-0.00077DM2_{t-1}$ | $+0.00107DM2_{t-2}$ | $+0.00418^{*}DM2_{t-3}$ | $+0.00128DM2_{t=4}$ |
| | (0.000080) | (0.00167) | (0.00178) | (0.00184) | (0.00190) | (0.00188) |
| | $+0.00084DM2_{t-5}$ | $+0.00306DM2_{t-6}$ | $-0.00239DM2_{t-7}$ | $-0.00129DM2_{t-8}$ | $-0.00175DM2_{t-9}$ | $+0.00188DM2_{t-10}$ |
| | (0.00189) | (0.00189) | (0.00190) | (0.00190) | (0.00198) | (0.00198) |
| | $+0.00206DM2_{t-11}$ | $-0.00235DM2_{t-12}$ | | SE $Y \cdot X$ = 0.00063 | $R^2$ = 0.103 | D-W = 1.429 |
| | (0.00189) | (0.00178) | | | | |
| $\frac{di_{aaa}}{dt} =$ | $-0.000055$ | $+0.00028DM2_t$ | $-0.00112DM2_{t-1}$ | $-0.00179DM2_{t-2}$ | $+0.00174DM2_{t-3}$ | $+0.00205DM2_{t-4}$ |
| | (0.000068) | (0.00142) | (0.00152) | (0.00157) | (0.00162) | (0.00161) |
| | $+0.00240DM2_{t-5}$ | $+0.00181DM2_{t-6}$ | $-0.00141DM2_{t-7}$ | $-0.00090DM2_{t-8}$ | $-0.00026DM2_{t-9}$ | $+0.00075DM2_{t-10}$ |
| | (0.00161) | (0.00162) | (0.00162) | (0.00162) | (0.00169) | (0.00169) |
| | $+0.00071DM2_{t-11}$ | $-0.00032DM2_{t-12}$ | | SE $Y \cdot X$ = 0.00054 | $R^2$ = 0.085 | D-W = 1.087 |
| | (0.00162) | (0.00152) | | | | |

NOTE: For sources and more complete notes, see Appendix. $M2 = \ln M_2$; $DM2 = \frac{1}{M_2}\frac{dM_2}{dt}$; $M$, $i$ seasonally adjusted.
*Significant at .05 level.

are included in the regression. Except for this positive relation between current variables, however, there seems to be little systematic relation between the current money stock and past interest rates. Nearly all the coefficients of past rates are statistically insignificant. A fairly high fraction of the variation in the money stock is explained by equation (4), but most of this is due to the current interest rate, not to past rates. Although both money and interest rates are seasonally adjusted, there appears to be a slight seasonal pattern present in the coefficients of past interest rates in equations (4) and (5). These coefficients are predominantly negative for lagged levels and changes of interest rates, but coefficients of variables lagged six and twelve months are positive at least as often as they are negative. The seasonal pattern is less pronounced than when equations (4) and (5) were estimated for unadjusted interest rates, but it is puzzling that any seasonal pattern remains, since seasonal variation should be absent from both series. It is not clear why the pattern appears, but it may reflect an imperfection in the adjustment of published money supply series.

If income adjusted instantaneously to make the quantity of money demanded equal to an increased money supply with no other changes, liquidity and income effects would balance, and only price expectations effects would remain. If it takes time for income to adjust to a new level of the money supply, then it should be possible to measure the adjustment path. The assumption that it takes several months for income to adjust therefore implies that either monthly or quarterly data should be useful for this purpose. If liquidity effects can be observed at all, the coefficient of $M_t$ in equation (3) should be negative. A positive coefficient would imply that income effects have balanced liquidity effects and that only positive effects should follow. Since the liquidity effect reflects immediate interest rate movements to equate $M^d$ and $M^s$, most, if not all, of the negative influence should come in the current period. Following this negative effect, an increase in the money stock should have a positive influence on future interest rates as the income effect operates. In terms of the coefficients of equation (3), this means that coefficients of past values of $M$ should not be significantly negative and there should be some sufficiently distant values of the money stock for which the coefficients are positive. Nothing in Section II tells how far the liquidity effect must push rates, for this depends on the parameters in equation (1), the time required for income adjustments, the length of the period of observations (weekly vs. monthly, and so on), so that we do not know precisely the values to expect for the coefficient of $M_t$. However, for a once-and-for-all increase in $M$ with full employment, the cumulative liquidity and income effects should eventually be equal, so that the initial negative coefficient should be matched by a sum of positive coefficients for past $M$s, raising interest rates to their initial levels. If the economy initially had unemployed resources, the positive coefficients from the income effect may sum to less or more than the absolute value of the negative coefficient, depending on the shape and shifts of the investment schedule. If permanent income is the appropriate variable in equation (1), cyclical adjustments are possible. Income effects could then cause the positive coefficients to sum to more than the initial negative coefficient even at full employment, but we should then find later negative effects as cyclical adjustment continued.

A once-and-for-all increase in the money stock ought not to produce a sustained change in the expected rate of price change since it will not produce a sustained change in the actual rate. Any price expectations effect produced ought therefore to be offset by opposite effects when the price level settles at a new level. There may, however, be short-run price expectations effects which, although later offset, influence interest rates. In the absence of unemployment and cyclical adjustments, these effects would cause the algebraic sum of the coefficients to exceed zero and then fall back to zero as more past $M$s are added. A cyclical effect from permanent income could complicate this sequence, but it ought not to change the final (zero) sum. The entire sequence should change, however, if unemployment exists and real income increases, in which case the sum of the coefficients can be equal to, greater than, or less than zero.

Estimates of equation (3) for monthly and quarterly data on $M_1$ and $M_2$ for 1947-66 appear in Tables 3-6.

The coefficients in Tables 3 and 4 confirm that the negative liquidity effect operates in

**TABLE 5. RELATION BETWEEN INTEREST RATES AND CURRENT AND PAST MONEY STOCKS, QUARTERLY OBSERVATIONS, 1947–1966**

| | | | | | | | | |
|---|---|---|---|---|---|---|---|---|
| $i_b$ = | $-0.4000$* | $-0.3254{*}M1_t$ | $+0.4502M1_{t-1}$ | $+0.1591M1_{t-2}$ | $-0.0257M1_{t-3}$ | $-0.1528M1_{t-4}$ | $+0.0061M1_{t-5}$ | $+0.0878M1_{t-6}$ |
| | (0.0306) | (0.1484) | (0.3035) | (0.3378) | (0.3507) | (0.3518) | (0.3556) | (0.3495) |
| | $-0.0989M1_{t-7}$ | $-0.1789M1_{t-8}$ | $+0.0741M1_{t-9}$ | $+0.0908M1_{t-10}$ | SE $Y \cdot X$ = 0.00498 | | $R^2$ = 0.821 | D-W = 0.340 |
| | (0.3296) | (0.3260) | (0.3132) | (0.1543) | | | | |
| $i_{bd}$ = | $-0.2914$* | $-0.0897M1_t$ | $+0.1457M1_{t-1}$ | $+0.0091M1_{t-2}$ | $-0.0056M1_{t-3}$ | $-0.0285M1_{t-4}$ | $-0.0093M1_{t-5}$ | $+0.0456M1_{t-6}$ |
| | (0.0151) | (0.0731) | (0.1495) | (0.1664) | (0.1727) | (0.1732) | (0.1751) | (0.1721) |
| | $-0.0382M1_{t-7}$ | $-0.0212M1_{t-8}$ | $-0.0741M1_{t-9}$ | $+0.1328M1_{t-10}$ | SE $Y \cdot X$ = 0.00245 | | $R^2$ = 0.900 | D-W = 0.245 |
| | (0.1623) | (0.1605) | (0.1542) | (0.0760) | | | | |
| $i_{aaa}$ = | $-0.2992$* | $-0.1088M1_t$ | $+0.1030M1_{t-1}$ | $+0.0896M1_{t-2}$ | $-0.0389M1_{t-3}$ | $-0.0084M1_{t-4}$ | $-0.0439M1_{t-5}$ | $+0.0577M1_{t-6}$ |
| | (0.0166) | (0.0807) | (0.1651) | (0.1837) | (0.1907) | (0.1913) | (0.1934) | (0.1901) |
| | $-0.0239M1_{t-7}$ | $-0.0015M1_{t-8}$ | $-0.0832M1_{t-9}$ | $+0.1274M1_{t-10}$ | SE $Y \cdot X$ = 0.00271 | | $R^2$ = 0.889 | D-W = 0.196 |
| | (0.1793) | (0.1773) | (0.1704) | (0.0839) | | | | |
| $\frac{di_b}{dt}$ = | $-0.00090$ | $-0.03373DM1_t$ | $+0.8177{*}DM1_{t-1}$ | $+0.03689DM1_{t-2}$ | $+0.00105DM1_{t-3}$ | $-0.02977DM1_{t-4}$ | $+0.01475DM1_{t-5}$ | $+0.00278DM1_{t-6}$ |
| | (0.00073) | (0.02018) | (0.02642) | (0.02762) | (0.0274) | (0.0271) | (0.0273) | (0.0266) |
| | $-0.00697DM1_{t-7}$ | $-0.04179DM1_{t-8}$ | $+0.02105DM1_{t-9}$ | $+0.01138DM1_{t-10}$ | SE $Y \cdot X$ = 0.00272 | | $R^2$ = 0.443 | D-W = 1.116 |
| | (0.0249) | (0.0261) | (0.0272) | (0.02100) | | | | |
| $\frac{di_{bd}}{dt}$ = | $-0.000059$ | $-0.00771DM1_t$ | $+0.03109{*}DM1_{t-1}$ | $-0.00271DM1_{t-2}$ | $+0.00279DM1_{t-3}$ | $-0.00676DM1_{t-4}$ | $-0.00002DM1_{t-5}$ | $+0.00393DM1_{t-6}$ |
| | (0.000293) | (0.00816) | (0.01068) | (0.01116) | (0.01109) | (0.01093) | (0.01105) | (0.01074) |
| | $-0.00550DM1_{t-7}$ | $-0.00424DM1_{t-8}$ | $-0.00348DM1_{t-9}$ | $+0.00929DM1_{t-10}$ | SE $Y \cdot X$ = 0.00110 | | $R^2$ = 0.301 | D-W = 1.562 |
| | (0.01005) | (0.01056) | (0.01100) | (0.00849) | | | | |
| $\frac{di_{aaa}}{dt}$ = | $-0.00012$ | $-0.00829DM1_t$ | $+0.01946DM1_{t-1}$ | $+0.00777DM1_{t-2}$ | $+0.00321DM1_{t-3}$ | $-0.00396DM1_{t-4}$ | $-0.00408DM1_{t-5}$ | $+0.00613DM1_{t-6}$ |
| | (0.00028) | (0.00779) | (0.01019) | (0.01065) | (0.01058) | (0.01044) | (0.01054) | (0.01025) |
| | $-0.00236DM1_{t-7}$ | $-0.00186DM1_{t-8}$ | $-0.00313DM1_{t-9}$ | $+0.00915DM1_{t-10}$ | SE $Y \cdot X$ = 0.00105 | | $R^2$ = 0.244 | D-W = 1.241 |
| | (0.00959) | (0.01008) | (0.01050) | (0.00810) | | | | |

NOTE: For sources and more complete notes, see Appendix. $M1 = \ln M_1$; $DM1 = \frac{1}{M_1}\frac{dM_1}{dt}$; $M$, $i$ seasonally adjusted.

*Significant at .05 level.

the same month in which the money stock is changed. While the relation between current money and interest was positive when past interest rates were included in equation (4), the relation is negative when past values of $M$ are included in equation (3). The most striking result in the estimates is the speed with which the income effects operate. The coefficients show that positive effects offset negative effects by the end of the third month after the month in which $M_1$ is increased and by the end of the fifth month after $M_2$ is increased. For quarterly data, the coefficient of the past quarter's money stock is positive and of the same order of magnitude as the current period's negative coefficient. More often than not the first positive coefficient exceeds the negative coefficient in absolute value.

Estimates of coefficients of earlier monetary variables are generally not statistically significant (see also Table 7).[13] However, they show a slight cyclical pattern. The positive coefficients sum to more than the initial negative coefficient and are followed by small coefficients of varying signs. The algebraic sums of the coefficients show no marked tendency to exceed zero. The negative coefficients for distant $M$s could result from short-lived price expectations effects or from cyclical movements in measured income involved in the adjustments of permanent income.

Since the residuals from equation (3) showed high serial correlation, the first-difference form

$$\frac{di}{dt} = f\left[\left(\frac{1}{M}\frac{dM}{dt}\right)_t, \left(\frac{1}{M}\frac{dM}{dt}\right)_{t-1}, \ldots, \left(\frac{1}{M}\frac{dM}{dt}\right)_{t-n}\right] \qquad (6)$$

was estimated, and the coefficients appear in Tables 3–6. The coefficients show the same general patterns found in the level equations. Liquidity effects are quickly overcome by income effects, and cyclical patterns follow. In some cases, however, the algebraic sum of the coefficients tends to remain greater than zero, particularly for the bill rate. If the positive sum resulted from shifts in the investment schedule, the coefficients in equation (3) should also have summed to more than zero. The positive sums for equation (6) may instead reflect price expectations effects, since (6) includes the rate of change of money. But the price expectations effect relates the level of interest rates to the rate of change of money and prices, while equation (6) contains rates of change of both. If, however, the expected rate of price change adjusts slowly to changes in actual rate, we might find money, prices, and interest rates moving together over some ranges. This is essentially the sequence Fisher envisioned to explain the Gibson Paradox, although he did not emphasize the relation between changes in money and changes in prices. If true, the sequence provides an explanation for the positive sum of the coefficients, a result difficult to explain on other grounds. The price expectations explanation is made more plausible by the fact that the positive sum is most noticeable for the coefficients for shorter-term interest rates, whose shorter-term expectations should be more sensitive to monthly and quarterly changes in money and prices.[14]

### B. *Income and Price Expectations Effects*

These estimates do not permit us to distinguish between income and price expectations effects, since both should be reflected in positive coefficients.[15] Independent evidence on

[13] Although many of the coefficients in equation (3) and following equations are not statistically significant, it should not be concluded that the positive effects of money on interest rates are not significant. As Table 7 shows, for monthly data the combined explanatory influence of $M_{t-1}$ through $M_{t-6}$ is highly significant. Similar significance levels also appear when variables are grouped in other equations below.

[14] The low levels of Durbin-Watson statistics for estimates of equation (6) (and for other equations below as well) should not be cause for alarm. For levels and changes in interest rates are surely also determined by nonmonetary factors not included in these equations.

[15] It is similarly not possible to identify the coefficient of $M_t$ in equation (3) with the total liquidity effect, for the latter may be partially offset by income effects within the current month or quarter. If this were the case, both liquidity and income (and perhaps price expectations) effects would be larger than the coefficients reveal. This possibility has received little attention here for two reasons. First, there is some doubt that income can increase fast enough to raise interest rates within the current month or quarter. Second, emphasis here has been on how rapidly the negative effects are offset by positive effects, and for this purpose the composition of current period effects is less important.

**TABLE 6. RELATION BETWEEN INTEREST RATES AND CURRENT AND PAST MONEY STOCKS, QUARTERLY OBSERVATIONS, 1947–1966**

| | | | | | | | |
|---|---|---|---|---|---|---|---|
| $i_b$ = | −0.2381* | $-0.6142^*M2_t$ | $+0.7129M2_{t-1}$ | $-0.0934M2_{t-2}$ | $+0.1967M2_{t-3}$ | $-0.2502M2_{t-4}$ | $+0.2072M2_{t-5}$ |
| | (0.0239) | (0.1385) | (0.3053) | (0.3520) | (0.3669) | (0.3845) | (0.4005) |
| | $-0.1203M2_{t-6}$ | $+0.1286M2_{t-7}$ | $-0.3506M2_{t-8}$ | $+0.2446M2_{t-9}$ | $-0.0105M2_{t-10}$ | SE $Y \cdot X$ = 0.00453 | $R^2 = 0.852$ |
| | (0.3999) | (0.3801) | (0.3601) | (0.3131) | (0.1468) | D-W = 0.383 | |
| $i_{bd}$ = | −0.1772* | $-0.1597^*M2_t$ | $+0.1638M2_{t-1}$ | $-0.0224M2_{t-2}$ | $+0.0389M2_{t-3}$ | $-0.0193M2_{t-4}$ | $+0.0312M2_{t-5}$ |
| | (0.0130) | (0.0754) | (0.1662) | (0.1915) | (0.1997) | (0.2093) | (0.2179) |
| | $-0.0232M2_{t-6}$ | $-0.00001M2_{t-7}$ | $-0.0181M2_{t-8}$ | $-0.0885M2_{t-9}$ | $+0.1383M2_{t-10}$ | SE $Y \cdot X$ = 0.00246 | $R^2 = 0.899$ |
| | (0.2176) | (0.2069) | (0.1960) | (0.1704) | (0.0799) | D-W = 0.262 | |
| $i_{aaa}$ = | −0.1972* | $-0.1677^*M2_t$ | $+0.1280M2_{t-1}$ | $+0.0257M2_{t-2}$ | $+0.0100M2_{t-3}$ | $+0.0022M2_{t-4}$ | $+0.0092M2_{t-5}$ |
| | (0.0135) | (0.0780) | (0.1719) | (0.1982) | (0.2066) | (0.2165) | (0.2255) |
| | $-0.0171M2_{t-6}$ | $+0.0113M2_{t-7}$ | $-0.0120M2_{t-8}$ | $-0.0974M2_{t-9}$ | $+0.1535M2_{t-10}$ | SE $Y \cdot X$ = 0.00255 | $R^2 = 0.902$ |
| | (0.2252) | (0.2141) | (0.2028) | (0.1763) | (0.0827) | D-W = 0.232 | |
| $\frac{di_b}{dt}$ = | −0.00045 | $-0.0905^*DM2_t$ | $+0.1148^*DM2_{t-1}$ | $+0.0078DM2_{t-2}$ | $+0.0218DM2_{t-3}$ | $-0.0391DM2_{t-4}$ | $+0.0264DM2_{t-5}$ |
| | (0.00077) | (0.0203) | (0.0295) | (0.0294) | (0.0301) | (0.0310) | (0.0318) |
| | $-0.0042DM2_{t-6}$ | $+0.0072DM2_{t-7}$ | $-0.0601^*DM2_{t-8}$ | $+0.0333DM2_{t-9}$ | $+0.0032DM2_{t-10}$ | SE $Y \cdot X$ = 0.00262 | $R^2 = 0.480$ |
| | (0.0314) | (0.0301) | (0.0299) | (0.0299) | (0.0210) | D-W = 1.144 | |
| $\frac{di_{bd}}{dt}$ = | 0.00023 | $-0.0269^*DM2_t$ | $+0.0407^*DM2_{t-1}$ | $-0.0052DM2_{t-2}$ | $+0.0014DM2_{t-3}$ | $+0.0040DM2_{t-4}$ | $-0.0089DM2_{t-5}$ |
| | (0.00032) | (0.0084) | (0.0122) | (0.0121) | (0.0124) | (0.0128) | (0.0131) |
| | $+0.0011DM2_{t-6}$ | $-0.0005DM2_{t-7}$ | $-0.0099DM2_{t-8}$ | $+0.0007DM2_{t-9}$ | $+0.0053DM2_{t-10}$ | SE $Y \cdot X$ = 0.00108 | $R^2 = 0.322$ |
| | (0.0130) | (0.0125) | (0.0123) | (0.0123) | (0.0086) | D-W = 1.516 | |
| $\frac{di_{aaa}}{dt}$ = | 0.00018 | $-0.0249^*DM2_t$ | $+0.0259^*DM2_{t-1}$ | $+0.0034DM2_{t-2}$ | $+0.0020DM2_{t-3}$ | $+0.0015DM2_{t-4}$ | $-0.0055DM2_{t-5}$ |
| | (0.00030) | (0.0080) | (0.0117) | (0.0116) | (0.0119) | (0.0123) | (0.0126) |
| | $+0.0011DM2_{t-6}$ | $+0.0010DM2_{t-7}$ | $-0.0071DM2_{t-8}$ | $-0.0001DM2_{t-9}$ | $+0.0082DM_{t-10}$ | SE = 0.00104 | $R^2 = 0.260$ |
| | (0.0124) | (0.0119) | (0.0118) | (0.0118) | (0.0083) | D-W = 1.369 | |

NOTE: For sources and more complete notes, see Appendix. $M_2 = \ln M_2$; $DM2 = \frac{1}{M_2}\frac{dM_2}{dt}$; $M$, $i$ seasonally adjusted.
*Significant at .05 level.

TABLE 7. F-RATIOS OF ANALYSIS OF COVARIANCES OF REGRESSION COEFFICIENTS OF MONETARY VARIABLES, MONTHLY REGRESSIONS, 1947 – 1966

| | $i$ = Treasury bill rate | | $i$ = Treasury bond rate | | $i$ = Moody's *Aaa* bond rate | |
|---|---|---|---|---|---|---|
| $i = f(M1_t, \ldots, M1_{t-n})$ | 7.080* | 4.394* | 6.309* | 0.272 | 9.968* | 0.604 |
| $di = f(DM1_t, \ldots, DM1_{t-n})$ | 6.793* | 1.494 | 4.437* | 0.983 | 3.033** | 0.321 |
| $i = f(M2_t, \ldots, M2_{t-n})$ | 19.803* | 0.689 | 6.374* | 0.358 | 8.729* | 1.087 |
| $di = f(DM2_t, \ldots, DM2_{t-n})$ | 6.692* | 1.098 | 2.804*** | 1.044 | 2.569*** | 0.261 |

*Significant at 99.9 percent level.
**Significant at 99.0 percent level.
***Significant at 95 percent level.

either positive effect does, however, allow us to determine that the liquidity effects are offset by income effects alone. A one percentage point increase in the rate of change of prices increases short-term interest rates by only 0.03 percentage points within six months, and there is no increase in long rates within this time.[16] This result seems plausible, for we should expect price expectations to be based on a large range of past price experience so that month-to-month variations would have relatively small effects on predicted price behavior. The dependence of price expectations effects on the lag between money and income makes the absence of such effects even more credible.

Ruling out price expectations effects during the first six months allows us to specify that the initial negative and offsetting positive effects are liquidity and income effects alone. The implicit estimates of the lags between money and income are somewhat shorter than often mentioned in the literature on the lag in the effect of monetary policy (Culbertson 1960, 1961; Friedman 1961). Since the coefficients imply that interest rates return to their former levels three to five months after once-and-for-all change in the money stock, they imply that income changes in about the same proportion as money in three to five months.

## V. Summary and Conclusions

The estimates obtained here show that a change in the money stock produces an immediate negative liquidity effect on market interest rates, but also produces (only a little later) positive effects which tend to offset the initial negative influence. Liquidity effects are fully offset by the end of the third month following the month in which $M_1$ is changed and by the end of the fifth month after $M_2$ is changed. These positive effects cannot be directly separated into income and price expectations effects, but evidence on total price expectations effects implies that the latter have very little importance over a period as short as three to five months. The longer period required for offsetting the initial negative effects of $M_2$ suggests that income reacts more slowly to a given percentage change in $M_2$ than in $M_1$.

The short periods required for interest rates to return to their previous levels also imply a short lag in the effect of money on income. On the assumption of a unitary income elasticity of demand for money, income increases in roughly the same proportion as money within five months.

Some implications of these findings are clear. Interest rates can be lowered by increasing the money stock, but this act also produces forces which will offset the lowering within several months. This process will produce increases in nominal income (and perhaps in prices), which may be a goal of monetary policy. But the sequence clearly makes it hazardous to view the levels or changes of interest rates as indicators of monetary policy. Since income increases due to money stock increases will be accompanied by higher interest rates, interest rates can as well be regarded as reflecting an easier as a tighter monetary policy. Moreover, to maintain lower interest rates it is necessary to increase money stocks continuously. But this act itself generates expectations of rising prices that tend to raise interest rates.

[16] See Gibson (1970). For earlier estimates, see references there.

## Appendix: Notes to Tables and Data Sources

All interest rates and rates of change of money are expressed as annual rates. D-W denotes Durbin-Watson statistic. Standard errors are in parentheses.

### *A. Money*

Monthly data, 1947–66 (from which quarterly data were generated) for $M_1$ and $M_2$ seasonally adjusted and unadjusted were obtained from the *Federal Reserve Bulletin*, including all revisions through 1966. All money stock data are in billions of dollars.

### *B. Interest Rates*

$i_b$ = the Treasury bill rate. Data was obtained from the *Federal Reserve Bulletin* and *Banking and Monetary Statistics*. Quarterly data were generated from monthly data, which are averages of daily figures for 1947–66.

$i_{bd}$ = Treasury bond rate. Source same as for $i_b$. Monthly data are averages of daily figures for bonds maturing or callable in ten years or more for 1947–66.

$i_{aaa}$ = Moody's *Aaa* corporate bond yield. Source and years same as for $i_{bd}$. Monthly data are averages of daily figures.

Interest rates are expressed in percentage terms, that is, a yield of $4.00 per year per $100.00 is expressed as 0.04. Monthly and quarterly interest rates were seasonally adjusted by the ratio-to-moving-average technique at the Federal Reserve Bank of Chicago.

## References

ACKLEY, GARDNER. *Macroeconomic Theory*. New York: Macmillan, 1961.

BAUMOL, WILLIAM J. "The Transactions Demand for Cash: An Inventory Theoretic Approach." *Q.J.E.* 66 (November 1952): 545–56.

CAGAN, PHILLIP. *Determinants and Effects of Changes in the Money Stock in the U.S., 1857–1960*. New York: Columbia Univ. Press, 1965.

———. "The Channels of Monetary Effects on Interest Rates." Mimeographed. Nat. Bur. Econ. Res., 1966.

CULBERTSON, J. M. "Friedman on the Lag in Effect of Monetary Policy." *J.P.E.* 68 (December 1960):617–21.

———. "Reply." *Ibid.* 69 (October 1961): 467–77.

FISHER, IRVING. *Appreciation and Interest*. Cambridge, Mass.: American Econ. Assoc., 1896.

———. *The Rate of Interest*. New York: Macmillan, 1907.

———. *The Theory of Interest*. New York: Macmillan, 1930.

FRIEDMAN, MILTON. "The Demand for Money: Some Theoretical and Empirical Results." *J.P.E.* 68 (August 1959):327–51.

———. "The Lag in Effect of Monetary Policy." *Ibid.* 69 (October 1961):447–66.

FRIEDMAN, MILTON, AND MEISELMAN, DAVID. "The Relative Stability of Monetary Velocity and the Investment Multiplier in the United States, 1897–1958." In *Stabilization Policies*, Commission on Money and Credit. Englewood Cliffs, N.J.: Prentice-Hall, 1963.

GIBSON, WILLIAM E. "Price-Expectations Effects on Interest Rates." *J. Finance*, XXV (March 1970): 19–34. (Reprinted in this volume.)

GIBSON, WILLIAM E., AND KAUFMAN, GEORGE G. "The Sensitivity of Interest Rates to Changes in Money and Income." *J.P.E.* 76 (June 1968):472–78.

GRAMLEY, LYLE E., AND CHASE, SAMUEL B., JR. "Time Deposits in Monetary Analysis." *Federal Res. Bull.* 51 (October 1965): 1380–1406.

LATANÉ, HENRY A. "Cash Balances and the Interest Rate: A Pragmatic Approach." *Rev. Econ. and Statis.* 36 (November 1954): 456–60.

MELTZER, ALLAN H. "The Demand for Money: The Evidence from the Time Series." *J.P.E.* 71 (June 1963):231–34.

MUNDELL, ROBERT. "Inflation and Real Interest." *J.P.E.* 71 (June 1963): 280–83.

———. "A Fallacy in the Interpretation of Macroeconomic Equilibrium." *Ibid.* 73 (February 1965): 61–66.

TOBIN, JAMES. "Liquidity Preference and Monetary Policy." *Rev. Econ. and Statis.* 29 (May 1947):124–31.

———. "The Interest Elasticity of Transactions Demand for Cash." *Ibid.* 38 (August 1956):241–47.

TRIEBER, WILLIAM F. "The Challenge of the Boom." *Federal Res. Bank N.Y. Monthly Review* (June 1966), pp. 123–26.

# 25 | COMMODITY PRICE EXPECTATIONS AND THE INTEREST RATE*

THOMAS J. SARGENT
*University of Pennsylvania*

## I. Introduction

Over a long period of time and in a variety of countries, nominal interest rates and the aggregate level of commodity prices have been highly and positively correlated. Keynes named this empirical regularity the "Gibson paradox" since classical economic theory seemed to imply that a correlation of opposite sign would emerge.[1] This expectation was based on the notion that the natural or full stock equilibrium rate of interest is fairly stable over time. If this is true, then upward movements of the market rate generally produce a gap between the market and natural rates, and this generates a deflationary gap between desired saving and investment. Similarly, downward movements in market interest rates produce inflationary pressure. The fact that the data do not correspond to the pattern implied by these considerations is the Gibson paradox.

Several possible explanations of the paradox can be found in the literature of economics, two of which are especially prominent. The first was set forth by Keynes[2] himself who interpreted the empirical association between prices and interest as coming from the workings of the market for loans which behaved according to the Thornton-Wicksell[3] model in disequilibrium. He held that prices tend to rise when the market rate at time $t$, $r_m(t)$, is below the natural rate, $r_e(t)$, and conversely prices tend to fall when $r_e(t)$ is below $r_m(t)$. Thus there is some relation

$$p^*(t) - f(r_e(t) - r_m(t)),\ f' > 0 \tag{1.1}$$

where $p(t)$ is the price level at time $t$ and $p^*(t)$ is the time derivative of the price level. It was also specified that the market rate tends to move toward the natural rate, and so there is a relationship

$$r_m{}^*(t) = g(r_e(t) - r_m(t)) + \epsilon(t),\ g' > 0 \tag{1.2}$$

where $r_m{}^*(t)$ is the time derivative of $r_m(t)$ and $\epsilon(t)$ is a random variable. In this case, $\epsilon(t)$ in part represents the impacts of money supply changes on the interest rate. Integrating both (1.1) and (1.2) over time shows that the level of prices and the level of interest rates both depend on weighted sums of past differences between $r_e(t)$ and $r_m(t)$. If the two sets of weights are sufficiently similar, the levels of interest and prices will be highly correlated.

* Reprinted from *Quarterly Journal of Economics,* vol. 83 (February, 1969) pp. 127–140, by permission of the author and the President and Fellows of Harvard College. [Sections III and V have been revised by the author.]

[1] John M. Keynes, *A Treatise on Money,* II (London: Macmillan, 1930), 198–210. A. H. Gibson had written several articles on the subject, prompting Keynes to name it the Gibson paradox.

[2] *Ibid.*

[3] Henry Thornton, *The Paper Credit of Great Britain, 1802* (New York: Kelley, 1965). Knut Wicksell, *Interest and Prices* (New York: Kelley, 1965).

A second possible explanation was provided by Irving Fisher[4] who noted that in equilibrium the nominal rate of interest must equal the sum of the marginal rate of return from holding real capital and the expected proportionate rate of change of prices. This condition follows from the fact that in a riskless world, holding period yields must be equal for all assets. This can be written

$$r_n(t) = r_e(t) + (\Delta p^e(t)/p(t))$$

where $\Delta p^e(t)$ is the rate of change in the price level expected as of time $t$, and $r_n(t)$ is the nominal rate of interest at time $t$. Fisher further assumed that the expected rate of change of prices was a distributed lag of current and past realized price changes,

$$\Delta p^e(t) = \sum_{i=0}^{m} w(i)\, \Delta p(t-i) + u(t), \qquad w(i) \geqslant 0$$

for all $i$, where $u(t)$ is a random term, and he estimated relations of the form

$$r_n(t) = a + \beta \sum_{i=0}^{m} w(i)\, \Delta p(t-i) + u(t) \tag{1.3}$$

using the distributed lag estimation procedures he had invented.[5] The data which Fisher examined indicated that $m$ was large and that the lag weights dropped off slowly. For Fisher, this finding offered an explanation of the Gibson paradox. A cumulative rise in prices after some lag generates an expectation of further commodity price rises which makes investors willing to hold bonds with their streams of returns fixed in dollars only at lower bond prices. It follows that after a cumulative commodity price rise, both commodity prices and interest rates are high.[6]

Several questions have recently been raised concerning the character of Fisher's empirical results.[7] First, Meiselman[8] has used ordinary least squares to apply Koyck's[9] lag scheme to the data, and he finds that the results do not unambiguously support Fisher's hypothesis. However, apart from the statistical difficulties in Meiselman's procedure, his results may be incomplete since he did not report estimates for sufficiently flexible forms of equation (1.3), which is Fisher's equation.[10] A perhaps more compelling criticism

---

4 Irving Fisher, *The Theory of Interest* (New York: Macmillan, 1930), pp. 399–451.

5 Irving Fisher, "Our Unstable Dollar and the So-Called Business Cycle," *Journal of the American Statistical Association*, vol. 20 (June 1925).

6 While these two explanations have received the most attention, alternative ones are, of course, available. For example, Keynes's model in *The General Theory of Employment, Interest, and Money* (New York: Harcourt Brace, 1936) implies a positive association between interest rates and prices. This follows when it is recalled that Keynes emphasized the position of the rather volatile marginal efficiency of capital curve as the crucial determinant of the volume of income and employment. Provided that the system was not in the liquidity trap initially, an outward shift in the marginal efficiency of capital schedule induced a rise in both prices and interest rates. Alternatively, the modern theories of money demand and supply functions which emphasize the role of interest as an argument in both functions produce an expectation of a positive association between interest and prices.

7 In the *Treatise*, Keynes advanced his reason for rejecting Fisher's explanation of the positive association between interest and prices. He argued that if a rise in the anticipated rate of inflation reduced bond prices in the manner Fisher's argument implies, investors who hold bonds would be worse off both because their money would be worth less in the future and because they had suffered a capital loss. The capital loss would give rise to a fall in nominal holding period yields rather than a rise as Fisher's argument requires. Clearly, Keynes's content rests on a confusion between *ex ante* and *ex post* holding period yields. In an extensive review of the *Treatise*, Hayek properly took Keynes to task on this point. (See "Reflections on the Pure Theory of Money of Mr. J. M. Keynes (continued)," *Economica*, No. 35, Feb. 1932, pp. 38–39.) I am grateful to Professor Gottfried Haberler for drawing my attention to the article by Hayek.

8 David Meiselman, "Bond Yields and the Price Level: The Gibson Paradox Regained," in Deane Carson (ed.), *Banking and Monetary Studies* (Homewood, Ill.; Irwin, 1963), pp. 112–33.

9 L. M. Koyck, *Distributed Lags and Investment Analysis* (Amsterdam: North Holland Publishing Co., 1954).

10 That is, the assumption that the distributed lag weights decline geometrically from zero lag on may be too restrictive.

has been expressed by Cagan[11] who questions the plausibility of the very long lag in expectations formation which is implied by Fisher's estimates. Cagan expresses doubts that investors' commodity price expectations adjust so slowly. Moreover, Fisher's approach was to use simple regression techniques to explore the relationship between nominal rates and the expected price change variable. A more compelling body of evidence could be assembled using partial regression methods which allow the investigator to examine the relationship between the expected price change variable and the nominal rate while in some way holding constant the other monetary and real variables which affect the level of the nominal rate.

In this paper, the impact of price changes on nominal interest rates is studied within the framework of a simple loanable funds model of interest rate determination. This model is discussed in Section II. In Section III the model is set against some data, while in Section IV we take up an objection to Fisher's work raised by Frederick Macaulay. Our conclusions are stated in Section V.

## II. A Loanable Funds Model

A number of interest rate concepts is used in the work which follows. In particular, the following three are employed:

*1.* The nominal rate of interest ($r_n(t)$) is the yield to maturity associated with an instrument and it is calculated in the standard manner. This is the rate generally reported in compilations of economic data.

*2.* The market rate of interest ($r_m(t)$) is the nominal rate adjusted for the expected proportionate rate of price inflation. It thus represents the real expected internal rate of yield associated with holding bonds. The market rate is the single period equilibrium rate which equates one period's desired demand for and supply of funds.

*3.* The full stock equilibrium rate ($r_e(t)$) is the real rate which equates the flows of desired saving and investment. It is the natural rate of Wicksell.

[11] Phillip Cagan, *Determinants and Effects of Changes in the Stock of Money, 1875–1960* (New York: Columbia University Press, 1965), pp. 252–59.

The nominal rate is related to the equilibrium rate by the following identity:

$$r_n(t) = r_e(t) + (r_m(t) - r_e(t)) + (r_n(t) - r_m(t)) \quad (2.1)$$

Our model of nominal interest rate determination is based on hypotheses meant to explain each of the three terms on the right side of this equation. First, recall that $r_e(t)$ is the (real) rate which equates *ex ante* saving and investment in period $t$. The following investment and saving schedules are posited:

$$I(t) = I(r_m(t), \Delta X(t)) \quad \frac{\partial I}{\partial r_m} < 0, \frac{\partial I}{\partial \Delta X} > 0 \quad (2.2)$$

$$S(t) = S(r_m(t), X(t)) \quad \frac{\partial S}{\partial r_m} > 0, \frac{\partial S}{\partial X} > 0 \quad (2.3)$$

where $I(t)$, $S(t)$, and $X(t)$ are desired real investment, desired real saving, and aggregate output at time $t$. Equation (2.2) is a simple accelerator hypothesis modified to allow for interest rate effects. Equation (2.3) is a simple Keynesian saving function. Notice that in both equations we assume an absence of money illusion since both functions have the real rather than the nominal rate as an argument. The condition for full equilibrium is the equality of *ex ante* saving and investment. The rate $r_e(t)$ is thus the rate which solves the equation

$$E(t) = I(t) - S(t) = 0$$

where $E(t)$ is an excess demand function for loanable funds. This can be written

$$E(r_m(t), \Delta X(t), X(t)) = 0$$

Solving for the equilibrium rate produces the equation

$$r_e(t) = f(\Delta X(t), X(t)) \quad \frac{\partial f}{\partial \Delta X} > 0, \frac{\partial f}{\partial X} < 0 \quad (2.4)$$

where the restrictions on the partial derivatives of the function $f$ are implied by the signs of the partial derivatives posited for the saving and investment schedules. In this model, a rise in the rate of increase of output stimulates the demand for funds for investment and drives up the equilibrium interest rate. On the other hand, a once and for all increase in the level of output generates a larger volume of saving and hence diminishes the equilibrium rate of interest.

The second term on the right of (2.1) is the deviation of the market rate from the equilibrium rate. Following Wicksell, we assume that this gap arises in part from the banking system's increasing and decreasing the supply of money. Changes in the supply of money are effected through the banking system's operations in the loan market. In this market the banks generate supplies and demands for funds which augment those summarized in the saving and investment functions. We posit that it is relative changes in the real stock of money which affects the spread between $r_m(t)$ and $r_e(t)$, and so we write

$$r_m(t) - r_e(t) = g((M^*(t) - M^*(t-1))/M^*(t-1)), \quad g' < 0 \quad (2.5)$$

where $M^*(t)$ is the real money supply in period $t$. A rise in the real money supply drives the market rate downward with respect to the equilibrium rate.[12] Notice that a rising level of commodity prices drives up the market rate by reducing the value of real money balances. This is essentially the mechanism Keynes emphasized to link the level of interest rates to commodity price levels through the transactions demand for money in the model in the *General Theory*.

The third term on the right of equation (2.1) is the gap between the nominal and real market rates of interest. Such a gap arises as a result of anticipated commodity price inflation. More precisely, we can write

$$r_n(t) - r_m(t) = (\log p^e(t+j) - \log p(t))/j \quad (2.6)$$

where $j$ is the maturity of the loan and where $p^e(t+j)$ is the expected price level $j$ periods forward. Following Fisher, we assume that the expected average proportionate rate of price inflation over the term of the loan is a distributed lag function of actual current and past rates of inflation. Thus we have the relationship

$$r_n(t) - r_m(t) = \frac{\sum_{i=0}^{\infty} w(i)\, p(t-i) - p(t-i-1)}{p(t-i-1)} \quad (2.7)$$

where $w(i) \geqslant 0$ for all $i$.

Substituting (2.4), (2.5), and (2.7) into (2.1) produces the equation

$$r_n(t) = f(\Delta X(t), X(t)) + g((M^*(t) - M^*(t-1))/M^*(t-1)) + \frac{\sum_{i=0}^{\infty} w(i)\, p(t-i) - p(t-i-1)}{p(t-i-1)} \quad (2.8)$$

which summarizes the impact of monetary and real factors on the level of the nominal interest rates recorded in our statistical data. In the next section we use econometric techniques to implement this model empirically.

## III. Empirical Results

For the purpose of empirical implementation it is convenient to assume that $r_n(t)$ is a linear function of the arguments listed in equation (2.8). Furthermore, we posit that the lag weights $w(i)$ are geometrically declining in $i$. Using a geometric scheme, it was found that empirically the results were much better where the lag coefficients are geometrically declining after lag one. Since no significant loss of goodness of fit was suffered by setting $w(0)$ equal to zero, the lag scheme

$$w(0) = 0$$
$$w(i) = d\lambda^{i-1}\ i > 0$$

was employed. Thus equation (2.8) was written in the special form

$$r_n(t) = a\Delta X(t) + bX(t) + c((M^*(t) - M^*(t-1))/M^*(t-1)) + d\sum_{i=1}^{\infty} \lambda^{i-1}(\Delta p(t-i)/p(t-i-1)) + h + \epsilon(t) \quad (3.1)$$

where $\epsilon(t)$ is assumed to be a stochastic term

[12] See Phillip Cagan, "Changes in the Cyclical Behavior of Interest Rates," *Review of Economics and Statistics*, XLVIII (Aug. 1966), for a discussion which emphasizes the impact of changes in the money supply on the level of interest rates.

with mean zero. The following coefficient signs are implied by the considerations discussed in Section II:

$$a > 0 \quad c < 0$$
$$b < 0 \quad d > 0$$

Equation (3.1) was estimated using annual data for the United States for the period 1902 through 1940.[13] A pair of reasons restricted us to this time period. First, during the eleven years after 1940 the process of interest rate formation was heavily influenced by the pegging operations of the federal government. An additional difficulty is caused by the imposition of price controls over the first half of this period. Second, for the years before 1900, reliable annual series for several of our variables are not available.

The following series were used as the variables in equation (3.1):[14]

$r_n(t)$: Durand's ten year basic yield

$X(t)$: gross national product in billions of 1929 dollars

$M^*(t)$: real money supply in 1929 dollars

$p(t)$: commodity price index, 1929 = 100.

Money is defined as the sum of currency and demand deposits.

In order to estimate the parameters of equation (3.1), two econometric problems had to be faced. First, the price change expectations variable is an infinite sum while we have only a finite amount of data. Second, the equation is nonlinear in the parameters $d$ and $\lambda$. The first problem was solved by following a procedure which was apparently first suggested by Klein.[15] The distributed lag variable can be written

$$d \sum_{i=1}^{t-1} \lambda^{i-1}(\Delta p(t-i)/p(t-i-1)) + d \sum_{i=t}^{\infty} \lambda^{i-1}(\Delta p(t-i)/p(t-i-1)) \qquad (3.2)$$

Notice that the second term equals

$$\lambda^t d \sum_{i=0}^{\infty} \lambda^{i-1}(\Delta p(0-i)/p(0-i-1))$$

or

$$\lambda^t \eta_o$$

where $\eta_o$ equals $d \sum_{i=0}^{\infty} \lambda^{i-1} (\Delta p(0-i)/p(0-i-1))$; this is the systematic part of the initial condition of the difference equation. The strategy is to estimate the param-

---

[13] A referee finds our reasons for so restricting the time period inadequate and he suggests that we present results for data which include the forties. Accordingly, we have estimated (3.1) for both Durand's one year and ten year rates for the period 1902–54. The results follow:

One year rate:

$$\begin{aligned} r'_n(t) = {} & \underset{(.0139)}{.0064}\Delta X(t) - \underset{(.0041)}{.0137}X(t) - \underset{(1.5793)}{2.8566}\,(\Delta M^*(t)/M^*(t-1)) \\ & + \underset{(.5312)}{6.0056}\sum_{i=1}^{t-1} .99^{i-1}\,(\Delta p(t-i)/p(t-i-1)) + \underset{(1.8381)}{15.7202}\,(.99)^t - \underset{(1.8152)}{10.5162} \end{aligned}$$

Durbin-Watson = .8175
Adjusted $R^2$ = .8606

Ten year rate:

$$\begin{aligned} r'_n(t) = {} & \underset{(.0080)}{.0054}\Delta X(t) - \underset{(.0022)}{.0213}X(t) - \underset{(.9116)}{.8438}\,(\Delta M^*(t)/M^*(t-1)) \\ & + \underset{(.3056)}{3.7086}\sum_{i=1}^{t-1} .985^{i-1}\,(\Delta p(t-i)/p(t-i-1)) + \underset{(.7482)}{2.1591}\,(.985)^t + \underset{(.7273)}{2.4615} \end{aligned}$$

Durbin-Watson = .6376
Adjusted $R^2$ = .8711
Standard errors are in parentheses.

While the results confirm that our conclusions about the importance of the distributed lag price change expectations variable remain unaltered when the longer period is used, they also suggest that the model's specification is less adequate for the longer period. In particular, notice that the Durbin-Watson statistics are a good deal lower than those associated with the estimated equations reported in the text.

[14] The data for $X(t)$, $M(t)$, and $p(t)$ are in Tabel A–1 of Appendix A of Gregory C. Chow, "On the Long-Run and Short-Run Demand for Money," IBM Research Paper (1964).

[15] L. R. Klein, "The Estimation of Distributed Lags," *Econometrica*, vol. 26 (Oct. 1958).

eter $\eta_0$ simultaneously with the other parameters of the equation. Clearly the variable in the first term of (3.2) can be formed for all $t$ in our sample, so that by estimating the initial condition in this fashion the problems associated with the infinite tail of the lag are avoided.[16]

The second problem can be handled most easily by employing the type of search procedure suggested by Hildreth and Lu.[17] Notice that for selected values of $\lambda$ the parameters $a$, $b$, $c$, $d$, $h$, and $\eta_0$ can be calculated using standard least squares regression. The Hildreth-Lu scheme involves searching over $\lambda$ for that value which minimizes the calculated sum of squared residuals. The resulting estimates are consistent provided that the $\epsilon(t)$ of (3.1) follow a distribution for which the central limit theorem holds and that they are distributed independently of the independent variables. The estimator is maximum likelihood if, in addition, the $\epsilon(t)$ are serially independent.

In this case, Hildreth and Lu's search procedure was used, and the search was pursued at intervals of .005 in the neighborhood of the optimum.[18] Where $r_n'(t)$ is the value of the nominal rate calculated from the regression, the following regression was obtained:

$$\begin{aligned} r_n'(t) = \underset{(.0084)}{.0099}\Delta X(t) - \underset{(.0053)}{.0456}X(t) \\ - \underset{(.7862)}{2.0151}\,(\Delta M^*(t)/M^*(t-1)) \\ + \underset{(.1963)}{3.8764}\sum_{i=1}^{t-1} .97^{i-1}(\Delta p(t-i)/p(t-i-1)) \\ - \underset{(.5088)}{1.9849}\,(.97)^t + \underset{(.6296)}{7.1338} \end{aligned}$$

Durbin-Watson = 1.6538.
Adjusted $R^2 = .9298$.
Standard errors are in parentheses.

The signs of the estimated coefficients are consistent with the hypotheses outlined in the previous section, although the coefficient on $\Delta X(t)$ has little statistical significance. The parameter estimates suggest that, other things equal, a 10 per cent increase in the real money supply drives the nominal yield down about twenty basis points. A once and for all increase in the level of GNP of ten billion (1929) dollars drives the rate down about forty-five basis points. The results are similar to Fisher's in a couple of ways. Not only do they confirm the importance of the distributed lag price expectations variable, but they imply a very long lag in the process of expectations formation.

To explore the possibility of differential impacts of the arguments in equation (3.1) on yields of long and short bonds, we also estimated the parameters of (3.1) using Durand's one year basic yield as the dependent variable. This seems useful since the horizon appropriate to the expected price change variable depends on the maturity of the instrument whose yield is being studied. The following equation was obtained:

---

[16] For some encouraging evidence on the performance of this estimator see Thomas Sargent, "Some Evidence on the Small Sample Properties of Distributed Lag Estimators in the Presence of Autocorrelated Disturbances," *Review of Economics and Statistics*, XLX (Feb. 1968).

[17] C. Hildreth and J. Y. Lu, *Demand Relations with Autocorrelated Disturbances*, Technical Bulletin 276, Michigan State University, Agricultural Station (East Lansing, Mich., 1960).

[18] The asymptotic variance-covariance matrix associated with the maximum likelihood estimates is given by $[-A_{ij}]^{-1}$ where

$$A_{ij} = \left(\frac{\partial^2 L}{\partial\theta_i \partial\theta_j}\right)_{\theta'}$$

$[A_{ij}]$ is the matrix of second partial derivatives of the likelihood function with respect to the parameters evaluated at $\theta'$, the vector of maximum likelihood estimates of the parameters. An estimate of this matrix emerges as a by-product of applying Newton's method to solve the nonlinear estimation problem. However, there is no guarantee that the variances so estimated will be nonnegative. Moreover, the values of the estimated asymptotic standard errors are frequently very unstable in the region of the optimum $\theta'$. This suggests that in practice these estimated standard errors may be of questionable value, since they may depend sensitively on the tolerance level at which the search for the maximum of the likelihood function is terminated. For this reason, the asymptotic standard errors are not reported here. Instead, we have reported the standard errors associated with the linear part of the equation for the regression which minimized the sum of squared residuals.

$$r_n'(t) = \underset{(.0217)}{.0182}\Delta X(t) - \underset{(.0141)}{.0405}X(t) - \underset{(1.9961)}{6.0260}\,(\Delta M^*(t)/M^*(t-1)) + \underset{(.5247)}{6.4716}\sum_{i=1}^{t-1} .98^{i-1}\,(\Delta p(t-i)/p(t-i-1)) + \underset{(1.6694)}{4.4933}\,(.98)^t + \underset{(2.0183)}{1.4396}$$

Durbin-Watson = 1.2630.
Adjusted $R^2$ = .8718.
Standard errors are in parentheses.

The deterioration in the Durbin-Watson statistic may suggest that our specification of the model is less adequate for rates from the short end of the yield curve than from the long end. The coefficient on the rate of change of output is of even lower significance than in the equation for the ten year rate, although it is almost twice as large. On the other hand, the level of output, change in money supply, and price expectations variables all show up strongly with the expected signs. In addition, the estimate of the expectations decay parameter is close to that obtained from the ten year rate. While the magnitude of the effect of the output level on interest rates is estimated to be about the same for both one and ten year rates, the estimates suggest differential effects for the money supply change and the expected inflation variable: they suggest a larger impact of each variable on the shorter rate than on the longer. The larger magnitude of the price change expectations variable on the shorter maturity yield is consistent with the notion that, on balance, capital market participants anticipated a diminishing rate of inflation or deflation.[19]

An important limitation of equation (3.1) is the restriction that the lag weights decline geometrically. However, the more flexible class of second order rational lags can easily be introduced into our model while continuing to use Klein's nonlinear estimation scheme. This involves estimating the parameters of the equation

$$r_n(t) = a\Delta X(t) + bX(t) + c(\Delta M^*(t)/M^*(t-1)) + d\sum_{i=1}^{t-1}\lambda^{i-1}(\Delta p(t-i)/p(t-i-1)) + \eta_o\lambda^t + g\sum_{i=1}^{t-1}\delta^{i-1}(\Delta p(t-i)/p(t-i-1)) + \eta_1\delta^t + h + u(t) \quad (3.3)$$

where $a$, $b$, $c$, $d$, $g$, $h$, $\eta_o$, $\eta_1$, $\lambda$, and $\delta$ are the parameters to be estimated and $u(t)$ is a random disturbance. Equation (3.3) was estimated using both Durand's one year and ten year basic yields as the dependent variable. Hildreth and Lu's search procedure was employed, and the search was pursued at intervals of .01 for both $\lambda$ and $\delta$ in the region of the optimum. For the ten year rate, the estimates of $\lambda$ and $\delta$ converge to the same value, suggesting that little is gained by adding the second distributed lag variable. For the one year rate, the following equation was obtained:

$$r_n'(t) = \underset{(.0207)}{.0095}\Delta X(t) - \underset{(.0135)}{.0232}X(t) - \underset{(1.8267)}{4.7469}\,(\Delta M^*(t)/M^*(t-1)) + \underset{(.5890)}{6.2774}\sum_{i=1}^{t-1} .99^{i-1}(\Delta p(t-i)/p(t-i-1)) + \underset{(3.3121)}{17.8816}\,(.99)^t - \underset{(1.0691)}{1.8305}\sum_{i=1}^{t-1} .73^{i-1}(\Delta p(t-i)/p(t-i-1)) - \underset{(.8336)}{2.9470}\,(.73)^t - \underset{(1.0691)}{11.3711}$$

Durbin-Watson = 1.5923.
Adjusted $R^2$ = .9028.
Standard errors are in parentheses.

[19] This is seen when it is recognized that the long nominal rate at any moment can be thought of as some kind of average of current and anticipated real short rates together with the proportionate rates of expected commodity price inflation over the period of the long loan. (See D. Meiselman, *The Term Structure of Interest Rates* (Englewood-Cliffs, N.J.: Prentice Hall, 1962) and I. Fisher, *Appreciation and Interest* (New York: Macmillan, 1896) for discussions of this fact.) In our equation for the long rate, the impact of the price change expectations variable can be thought to represent an average of rates of inflation expected to occur 1, 2, . . . , 10 years hence, while in the one year rate equation, the prospective rate of inflation applies to a horizon extending only one year into the future. This is apparent from an inspection of equation (2.6). Thus, the smaller impact of the variable on the long rate suggests that a smaller absolute rate of price change is expected on the average over the period 2, . . . , 10 years hence than over the next year.

While the significance levels of the original variables, particularly the money supply change and change in output, have worsened compared with the estimates for (3.1), each coefficient retains the correct sign. In addition, there is a sizable improvement in the Durbin-Watson statistic over the estimated equation (3.1). The following distributed lag weights are implied by these estimates:

| | | |
|---|---|---|
| $w(1) = 4.45$ | $w(8) = 5.65$ | $w(15) = 5.43$ |
| $w(2) = 4.88$ | $w(9) = 5.64$ | $w(16) = 5.38$ |
| $w(3) = 5.18$ | $w(10) = 5.63$ | $w(17) = 5.33$ |
| $w(4) = 5.38$ | $w(11) = 5.60$ | $w(18) = 5.28$ |
| $w(5) = 5.51$ | $w(12) = 5.56$ | $w(19) = 5.23$ |
| $w(6) = 5.59$ | $w(13) = 5.52$ | . . |
| $w(7) = 5.63$ | $w(14) = 5.48$ | . . |
| | | . . |
| | | . . |

The weights trace out a long humped distributed lag which peaks at a lag of about eight years.

The negative estimate of $g$ and the fairly low estimate of $\delta$ in equation (3.3) are consistent with the notion that regressive elements were present in the process of expectations formation. Thus, for example, rising prices apparently had two effects on expectations. First, they generated expectations of further rises, which is confirmed by Fisher's estimates and our own estimates of $d$ in equations (3.1) and (3.3). But in addition to this extrapolative effect, they may also have generated a shorter-term expectation of a fall in prices.[20] This tended to diminish nominal rates of interest at the short end of the yield curve, as the negative estimate of $g$ suggests. The presence of such a component of expectations was rational given the cyclical properties of price movements over the period we are considering. The proposition that this regressive component of price expectations was a shorter-term phenomenon is consistent with the fact that our estimate of $\delta$ is materially lower than our estimate of $\lambda$. This suggests that the regressive effect of price changes persisted for a much shorter period than the extrapolative effect. In addition, the fact that this component does not appear to be present in the equation for the ten year rate indicates that it affects only near-term price change expectations.[21]

## IV. Macaulay's Criticism Reconsidered

While the estimates presented in the previous section appear to confirm Fisher's explanation of the Gibson paradox, there is a need to examine the results in the light of Frederick Macaulay's criticism of Fisher's work.[22] Macaulay argued that while interest rates are highly correlated with a distributed lag in past price changes, they are generally more highly correlated with the level of prices, and he cited the same data Fisher used to prove his contention. Consequently he thought that Fisher's use of the distributed lag price change variable to explain the high correlation between the levels of interest and prices was weak since in most cases "... the application of the theory lowers the coefficient [of correlation]."[23]

Macaulay's proposition can be put to test by adding the current price level as an explanatory variable in (3.1). On Macaulay's argument, the price level should have a positive coefficient and its presence should eliminate the explanatory power of the distributed lag price change variable. For the period 1902-40, the following estimates were obtained:

One year rate:

$$\begin{aligned} r_n'(t) = {} & \underset{(.0231)}{.0339}\Delta X(t) - \underset{(.0145)}{.0324}X(t) \\ & - \underset{(2.1053)}{7.3852}\,(\Delta M^*(t)/M^*(t-1)) \\ & + \underset{(1.8456)}{9.4527}\sum_{i=1}^{t-1} .98^{i-1}(\Delta p(t-i)/p(t-i-1)) \\ & + \underset{(1.6272)}{4.6254}\,(.98)^t - \underset{(2.4668)}{4.1400}\,p(t) + \underset{(2.1877)}{3.0537} \end{aligned}$$

Durbin-Watson = 1.3781.
Adjusted $R^2 = .8781$.

[20] F. DeLeeuw, "A Model of Financial Behavior," in *The Brookings Quarterly Econometric Model of the United States*, ed. Duesenberry *et al.*, and F. Modigliani and R. Sutch in "Innovations in Interest Rate Policy," *American Economic Review, Papers and Proceedings*, LVI (May 1966), have produced evidence for the simultaneous existence of two such components of expectations in the context of models of the term structure of interest rates.

[21] Reference to equation (2.6) helps make this claim clear.

[22] F. Macaulay, *The Movements of Interest Rates, Bond Yields, and Stock Prices in the United States since 1856* (New York: National Bureau of Economic Research, 1938), Chap. VI.

[23] *Ibid.*, p. 174.

Ten year rate:

$$r_n'(t) = \underset{(.0096)}{.0147}\Delta X(t) - \underset{(.0060)}{.0464}X(t)$$

$$- \underset{(.8733)}{2.3303}\,(\Delta M^*(t)/M^*(t-1))$$

$$+ \underset{(.7656)}{4.2095}\sum_{i=1}^{t-1} .98^{i-1}(\Delta p(t-i)/p(t-i-1))$$

$$- \underset{(.6750)}{1.6814}\,(.98)^t - \underset{(1.0233)}{.2406}\,p(t) + \underset{(.9075)}{7.1095}$$

Durbin-Watson = 1.6564.
Adjusted $R^2$ = .9260.
Standard errors are in parentheses.

The results indicate that even in the presence of $p(t)$, the distributed lag price change variable is an important determinant of nominal interest rates. In fact, $p(t)$ picks up a negative coefficient, an effect opposite to the one Macaulay's argument implies.[24] On the basis of these data, then, Fisher's explanation stands up quite well against Macaulay's attack.

## V. Conclusions

The estimates presented in the previous sections indicate that on the basis of conventional statistical criteria Fisher's explanation of the Gibson paradox holds up even when it is implemented in the context of a multivariate model that also allows for the impacts of several monetary and real variables which influence nominal rates of interest. Perhaps the most surprising aspect of the results is the extent of the contribution which the distributed lag in inflation makes to the explanation of variations in nominal yields after the other monetary and real variables have been taken into account. The estimated lag is of surprisingly long duration, many years being required to elapse before a substantial portion of the adjustment has occurred. The length of that lag is what makes Fisher's explanation of the Gibson paradox "work," since it implies that the perceived rate of inflation that belongs in equation (2.6) looks more like the level of prices than the current rate of inflation. On the other hand, the very length of that lag has been the chief reason that economists have by and large been reluctant to accept Fisher's doctrine of appreciation and interest. As Cagan has pointed out, it is very hard to believe that the market's expectations of inflation adjust as slowly as the estimates in this paper indicate. This suggests that the maintained hypotheses used to obtain those estimates bear re-examination. The critical hypotheses maintained in this paper are classical in nature: namely that the nominal interest rate, not some other variable such as income, clears the loanable funds market and that it is proper to study the loanable funds market in isolation from the goods markets. The incredibly long lags estimated in this study suggest that it may prove fruitful to study the impacts of inflation on bonds yields within a broader theoretical framework that does not require maintaining those hypotheses.

[24] If real wealth enters as an argument in the saving function in the usual way, an increase in the price level would induce an increased volume of saving and hence, *ceteris paribus*, diminish both the real and nominal rates of interest. This effect may provide an explanation of the negative coefficient on $p(t)$. See Robert Mundell, "Inflation and Real Interest," *Journal of Political Economy*, LXXI (June 1963).

# 26 | PRICE-EXPECTATIONS EFFECTS ON INTEREST RATES*

WILLIAM E. GIBSON
*University of California, Los Angeles*

Those of us who have worked in this field know that the thing that really makes high interest rates is inflation getting out of control.

William Mc C. Martin, before the Ways and Means Committee of the House of Representatives, September 14, 1967

## I. Introduction

The relationship between the expected rate of change of prices and the level of interest rates enjoys special status in economic theory. The positive relationship hypothesized long ago by Irving Fisher is widely accepted by students of economic theory, while its existence for United States experiences has, it appears, yet to be conclusively demonstrated. The absence of measurement of the relationship seems, however, not to have detracted greatly from its theoretical acceptability.

Empirical verification of price-expectations effects warrants more attention, not only to substantiate the theory but also as a guide in formulating and evaluating national economic policy. A combination of monetary and fiscal policies which brings about prolonged inflation should by doing so tend also to increase market interest rates. These interest rate increases have important implications for saving and investment behavior and for the demand for money. If we are to assess the importance of these effects, we need some idea of their magnitude and timing, and this paper attempts such an estimation.

In the next section the theoretical formulation of the price-expectations effect will be reviewed, while section III presents new evidence on the effects for U.S. data, and section IV concludes the paper.

## II. Price-Expectations Effects

The price-expectations, or Fisher, effect is well summarized by Irving Fisher's original equation[1]

$$i = r + \left(\frac{1}{P}\frac{dP}{dt}\right)^* + r\left(\frac{1}{P}\frac{dP}{dt}\right)^* \qquad (1)$$

i is the nominal or market rate of interest, $\left(\frac{1}{P}\frac{dP}{dt}\right)^*$ is the expected rate of change of prices, and r is the "real" rate of interest. It is tempting to think of r as the rate which would prevail in the absence of expected price change, but it is simply the rate of return on loans net of depreciation (appreciation) due to inflation (deflation).[2] The

* Reprinted from *The Journal of Finance*, vol. 25 (March, 1970) pp. 19–34, by permission of the author and the American Finance Association.

[1] See Irving Fisher, *The Theory of Interest*, New York: Macmillan, 1930.

[2] In what follows, the interaction term, $r\left(\frac{1}{P}\frac{dP}{dt}\right)^*$, which gives the expected rate of depreciation or appreciation of interest payments, will be neglected, as it is dwarfed by the other terms.

Fisher effect says that nominal interest rates exceed (fall short of) real rates by the expected rate of price increase (decrease). When price inflation lowers the value of nominal assets and liabilities in terms of real goods, loans denominated in money are depreciated as the real value of principal and interest fall. The fall in the real value of borrowers' liabilities provides them with capital gains equal to lenders' capital losses. Lenders who expect inflation during the term of a loan will attempt to protect themselves. If they exchanged money for goods, they could avoid the capital loss, for the nominal value of goods would rise with the price level. With this alternative available, lenders will be willing to exchange money for other nominal assets (loans) only if they receive a yield sufficient to compensate them for capital losses as well as for going without the use of their funds. Since borrowers benefit from the depreciation of their liabilities, they will be able to pay a higher nominal rate than before for a given volume of funds. If lenders and borrowers have similar expectations, the rate of interest on a loan in nominal terms will exceed the real rate by expected rate of inflation. Since similar but opposite effects occur when deflation is expected, nominal rates fall below real rates by the expected rate of deflation.

## III. Testing for Expectations Effects

### *A. Past Price Changes and Expected Price Changes*

The variables in Equation (1) must be well specified if we are to measure price-expectations effects. Quantifying the expected rate of price change is a central problem here. The above discussion has assumed that expected rates are somehow related to actual rates. Undoubtedly there are other determinants of price expectations, but there is reason to believe that people in large measure use past experience to predict future events. For instance, if prices have been rising by twenty per cent per year for the past hundred years, there is likely a presumption that prices will continue rising at this rate—at least if there is no dramatic change in the monetary behavior to act against the record of the past. A number of studies have documented the empirical fruitfulness of relating expected price changes to past price changes.[3]

The variables in Equation (1) should all refer to the same time period; that is, three-month interest rates should be affected by the rate of price change expected for the following three months, and similarly for other loan terms. Price changes occurring after the loan term have no effect on the real value of the principal during the loan term. If it is expected that after a year prices will begin changing at a different rate, rates on loans for less than a year will not be affected, while rates on longer loans will tend to rise. If the public expected deflation followed by inflation, then longer term rates would rise while shorter term rates would fall.[4]

While effects of expectations on interest rates for different terms can be specified theoretically, much less can be said about how expectations are formed. People will try to forecast well, for this will be in their economic interest. We cannot observe the forecasts they make. We can only infer them from the actual behavior of prices and from the behavior of people which is presumed to be a response to expectations. As in other studies, we shall assume that expected price changes have the effect on interest rates

[3] See Phillip Cagan, "The Monetary Dynamics of Hyperinflation," *Studies in the Quantity Theory of Money,* ed. Milton Friedman (Chicago: University of Chicago Press, 1956), pp. 23–117.

[4] The effects of price expectations also depend on the timing of interest payments. For a three-month loan on which the entire principal and all interest are paid at the end of three months, only the total net change in prices over the following three months will matter to lenders, and interest rates will be higher than otherwise by the average rate of price change expected over the three months. Similarly, on a ten-year loan if principal and all interest are paid at the end of ten years, only the net change in prices expected over the ten-year period would matter to lenders, and only the change expected at the beginning of the loan term.

If interest payments are made during the loan term, the distribution of expected price changes over the loan term will also influence interest rates. If, for instance, prices double in the first year of a ten-year loan, all the interest payments will be depreciated along with the principal, whereas if prices double in the tenth year after nine years of stable prices only the final annual interest payment and the principal will be affected.

suggested by Fisher's analysis and shall relate empirical approximations of expected rates of price change to interest rates.

Using past rates of price change to approximate future rates requires some model of how expectations are formed. Cagan's formulation made expected rates a geometrically declining weighted average of past rates but did not cover expectations for varying terms. If longer rates are affected more by more distant past rates of price change than are shorter rates, there will be lower estimates of the coefficient of expectations for longer rates in Cagan's model. If interest rates are instead related to past rates of price change over a finite number of past periods, it is difficult to know how many past periods to consider. Three-month expectations may be based on experience for the past three months or perhaps a longer period. This is an empirical question, but it does seem reasonable to assume that the number of past periods of price change used in forming expectations for one loan term should not be larger than the number used for a longer loan term. For example, if people consider the past five years in forming expectations about the next five years, we should not expect them to look at the past six years in forming expectations about the next four years. We will therefore order past spans; they will increase as the term of the loan lengthens. Alternatively, given the number of past periods considered, we should expect more distant past price changes to receive larger weights as the loan term increases.

The nominal interest rate, i, can be measured with little difficulty; we can use yields on Treasury and high-grade private securities. But the real rate, r, is impossible to observe directly in the United States. If we could obtain a direct measure of r, we would have an equally good measure of the expected rate of price change, and we could examine the relationship between the expected rate and past actual rates of price change. But as long as the market rates we observe are for payments in the form of money—a depreciating asset during inflation—all these rates must include compensation for expected inflation. Any rate which does not include this compensation will not be competitive and will be readjusted by the market. This also holds for yields on common stocks, when the yields are correctly calculated. The returns to a stockholder from dividends plus capital gains must (abstracting from unrelated expectations) be competitive with bond yields and other nominal rates. So while it is tempting to think of common stock as a "real" asset with a "real" yield, as long as the yield is in terms of money (or any other depreciating asset), the yield is a nominal rate. We could only measure the real rate directly if we had observations on an asset whose yields were in the form of a commodity whose real value is unaffected by inflation. Using dividend payments on common stock as a measure of the real rate (the assumption being that price expectations effects are reflected in capital gains) is an inaccurate solution, because cash dividends depend on firms' individual dividend policies, and indeed the firm need pay no dividend at all, leaving its only yield in the form of capital gains.

Because we cannot measure r directly, we cannot measure Equation (1) directly. But we do have measures of i, and we can use them to gain evidence on price-expectations effects on nominal interest rates. Since it is nominal rates that we observe and are concerned with in policy deliberations, this is a highly important relationship. If we hypothesize that expected rates of price change are determined by past rates of price change and that nominal interest rates are affected by expected rates of price change, we can test this double hypothesis by estimating the following equations:

$$i = f\left[\left(\frac{1}{P}\frac{dP}{dt}\right)_t, \left(\frac{1}{P}\frac{dP}{dt}\right)_{t-1}, \ldots, \left(\frac{1}{P}\frac{dP}{dt}\right)_{t-n}\right] \quad (2)$$

$$\frac{di}{dt} = f\left[\left(\frac{d\left(\frac{1}{P}\frac{dP}{dt}\right)}{dt}\right)_t, \left(\frac{d\left(\frac{1}{P}\frac{dP}{dt}\right)}{dt}\right)_{t-1}, \ldots, \left(\frac{d\left(\frac{1}{P}\frac{dP}{dt}\right)}{dt}\right)_{t-n}\right] \quad (3)$$

where P is an index of the general level of prices, and i is the market rate of interest. Equation (2) is in no sense a complete model of interest rate determination: it seeks only to discover the relationship between nominal rates of price change. Nominal interest rates

TABLE 1. RELATION BETWEEN INTEREST RATE CHANGES AND PRICE ACCELERATIONS, ANNUAL OBSERVATIONS, 1869-1963

| | | | | | | | |
|---|---|---|---|---|---|---|---|
| $\frac{di_c}{dt}$ = | −0.0001 | +0.075*$DDP_t$ | +0.048$DDP_{t-1}$ | +0.039$DDP_{t-2}$ | +0.079*$DDP_{t-3}$ | +0.030$DDP_{t-4}$ | +0.007$DDP_{t-5}$ |
| | (0.0015) | (0.032) | (0.035) | (0.037) | (0.038) | (0.040) | (0.041) |
| | +0.026$DDP_{t-6}$ | +0.004$DDP_{t-7}$ | −0.036$DDP_{t-8}$ | +0.031$DDP_{t-9}$ | +0.025$DDP_{t-10}$ | SE $Y \cdot X$ = 0.01398 | |
| | (0.040) | (0.038) | (0.036) | (0.034) | (0.029) | $R^2$ = 0.091 | DW = 2.289 |
| $\frac{di_{cp}}{dt}$ = | −0.0003 | +0.068*$DDP_t$ | +0.052*$DDP_{t-1}$ | +0.025$DDP_{t-2}$ | +0.073*$DDP_{t-3}$ | +0.048$DDP_{t-4}$ | +0.028$DDP_{t-5}$ |
| | (0.0010) | (0.021) | (0.023) | (0.025) | (0.026) | (0.027) | (0.028) |
| | +0.015$DDP_{t-6}$ | +0.010$DDP_{t-7}$ | −0.003$DDP_{t-8}$ | +0.021$DDP_{t-9}$ | +0.005$DDP_{t-10}$ | SE $Y \cdot X$ = 0.00914 | |
| | (0.027) | (0.026) | (0.025) | (0.023) | (0.020) | $R^2$ = 0.212 | DW = 2.517 |
| $\frac{di_{L1}}{dt}$ = | −0.0001 | −0.0001$DDP_t$ | +0.007$DDP_{t-1}$ | +0.006$DDP_{t-2}$ | +0.008$DDP_{t-3}$ | +0.011$DDP_{t-4}$ | +0.008 $DDP_{t-5}$ |
| | (0.0002) | (0.0052) | (0.006) | (0.006) | (0.006) | (0.007) | (0.007) |
| | +0.008$DDP_{t-6}$ | +0.008$DDP_{t-7}$ | −0.0004$DDP_{t-8}$ | +0.007$DDP_{t-9}$ | +0.002$DDP_{t-10}$ | SE $Y \cdot X$ = 0.00232 | |
| | (0.007) | (0.006) | (0.0060) | (0.006) | (0.005) | $R^2$ = 0.104 | DW = 1.989 |
| $\frac{di_{L2}}{dt}$ = | −0.0003 | +0.002$DDP_t$ | +0.005$DDP_{t-1}$ | −0.001$DDP_{t-2}$ | +0.011$DDP_{t-3}$ | +0.012$DDP_{t-4}$ | +0.009$DDP_{t-5}$ |
| | (0.0003) | (0.006) | (0.007) | (0.007) | (0.007) | (0.008) | (0.008) |
| | +0.004$DDP_{t-6}$ | +0.003$DDP_{t-7}$ | +0.003$DDP_{t-8}$ | +0.007$DDP_{t-9}$ | +0.002$DDP_{t-10}$ | SE $Y \cdot X$ = 0.00263 | |
| | (0.008) | (0.007) | (0.007) | (0.006) | (0.006) | $R^2$ = 0.088 | DW = 1.716 |

P = Implicit price deflator for net national product, 1929 = 100

$$DDP = \frac{d\left(\frac{1}{P}\frac{dP}{dt}\right)}{dt}$$

*Indicates significant of .05 level (standard errors in parentheses)

DW: Durbin-Watson statistic

**TABLE 2. RELATION BETWEEN INTEREST RATES AND RATES OF CHANGE OF PRICES AND INCOME, ANNUAL OBSERVATIONS, 1869-1963**

| | | | | | | | |
|---|---|---|---|---|---|---|---|
| $i_c$ = | 0.03289* | $-0.01882DP_t$ | $+0.00199DP_{t-1}$ | $+0.00315DP_{t-2}$ | $+0.05155DP_{t-3}$ | $-0.00167DP_{t-4}$ | SE $Y \cdot X$ = 0.01744 |
| | (0.00194) | (0.03804) | (0.04089) | (0.04101) | (0.03998) | (0.03698) | $R^2$ = 0.030 DW = 0.685 |
| $i_{cp}$ = | 0.03804* | $-0.04640DP_t$ | $-0.00741DP_{t-1}$ | $-0.01729DP_{t-2}$ | $+0.02720DP_{t-3}$ | $-0.00555DP_{t-4}$ | SE $Y \cdot X$ = 0.01772 |
| | (0.00197) | (0.03865) | (0.04154) | (0.04166) | (0.04062) | (0.03757) | $R^2$ = 0.031 DW = 0.352 |
| $i_{L1}$ = | 0.03886* | $-0.03928^{*}DP_t$ | $-0.01154DP_{t-1}$ | $-0.00688DP_{t-2}$ | $-0.00959DP_{t-3}$ | $-0.00179DP_{t-4}$ | SE $Y \cdot X$ = 0.00708 |
| | (0.00079) | (0.01544) | (0.01660) | (0.01665) | (0.01623) | (0.01501) | $R^2$ = 0.147 DW = 0.182 |
| $i_{L2}$ = | 0.04713* | $-0.05822^{*}DP_t$ | $-0.02450DP_{t-1}$ | $-0.02187DP_{t-2}$ | $-0.01850DP_{t-3}$ | $-0.02263DP_{t-4}$ | SE $Y \cdot X$ = 0.01084 |
| | (0.00120) | (0.02364) | (0.02540) | (0.02548) | (0.02484) | (0.02298) | $R^2$ = 0.206 DW = 0.144 |

$$DP = \frac{1}{P}\frac{dP}{dt}$$

P = NNP deflator, 1929 = 100

**TABLE 3. RELATION BETWEEN NOMINAL INTEREST RATES AND RATES OF PRICE CHANGE, QUARTERLY OBSERVATIONS, 1948-1963**

| | | | | | | | | |
|---|---|---|---|---|---|---|---|---|
| $i_b$ = | 0.025* | $+0.004DP_t$ | $+0.007DP_{t-1}$ | $-0.031DP_{t-2}$ | $-0.004DP_{t-3}$ | $-0.014DP_{t-4}$ | $-0.021DP_{t-5}$ | $-0.018DP_{t-6}$ |
| | (0.003) | (0.077) | (0.076) | (0.074) | (0.070) | (0.070) | (0.068) | (0.067) |
| | $-0.007DP_{t-7}$ | $-0.004DP_{t-8}$ | $+0.028DP_{t-9}$ | $-0.006DP_{t-10}$ | $-0.035DP_{t-11}$ | SE $Y \cdot X$ = 0.00920 | $R^2$ = 0.033 | |
| | (0.066) | (0.065) | (0.065) | (0.062) | (0.059) | DW = 0.286 | | |
| $i_{bd}$ = | 0.038* | $-0.042DP_t$ | $-0.029DP_{t-1}$ | $-0.041DP_{t-2}$ | $-0.013DP_{t-3}$ | $-0.011DP_{t-4}$ | $-0.022DP_{t-5}$ | $-0.015DP_{t-6}$ |
| | (0.002) | (0.052) | (0.051) | (0.050) | (0.047) | (0.047) | (0.046) | (0.045) |
| | $-0.020DP_{t-7}$ | $-0.009DP_{t-8}$ | $+0.004DP_{t-9}$ | $-0.001DP_{t-10}$ | $-0.014DP_{t-11}$ | SE $Y \cdot X$ = 0.00617 | $R^2$ = 0.166 | |
| | (0.045) | (0.046) | (0.044) | (0.042) | (0.039) | DW = 0.080 | | |
| $\frac{di_b}{dt}$ = | 0.0005 | $+0.007DDP_t$ | $+0.028DDP_{t-1}$ | $+0.024DDP_{t-2}$ | $+0.023DDP_{t-3}$ | $+0.014DDP_{t-4}$ | $+0.016DDP_{t-5}$ | $+0.010DDP_{t-6}$ |
| | (0.0006) | (0.034) | (0.040) | (0.034) | (0.034) | (0.033) | (0.031) | (0.030) |
| | $+0.004DDP_{t-7}$ | $-0.004DDP_{t-8}$ | $+0.032DDP_{t-9}$ | $+0.025DDP_{t-10}$ | | SE $Y \cdot X$ = 0.00444 | $R^2$ = 0.054 | |
| | (0.029) | (0.030) | (0.030) | (0.026) | | DW = 1.166 | | |
| $\frac{di_{bd}}{dt}$ = | 0.0004 | $+0.0001DDP_t$ | $+0.009DDP_{t-1}$ | $+0.002DDP_{t-2}$ | $+0.011DDP_{t-3}$ | $+0.014DDP_{t-4}$ | $+0.005DDP_{t-5}$ | $+0.007DDP_{t-6}$ |
| | (0.0002) | (0.043) | (0.013) | (0.011) | (0.011) | (0.010) | (0.010) | (0.009) |
| | $-0.008DDP_{t-7}$ | $-0.003DDP_{t-8}$ | $+0.010DDP_{t-9}$ | $+0.014DDP_{t-10}$ | | SE $Y \cdot X$ = 0.00139 | $R^2$ = 0.161 | |
| | (0.009) | (0.009) | (0.009) | (0.008) | | DW = 1.573 | | |

$$DP = \frac{1}{P}\frac{dP}{dt}$$

$$DDP = \frac{d\left(\frac{1}{P}\frac{dP}{dt}\right)}{dt}$$

P = Gross national product deflator, 1959 = 100

will also be influenced by the other determinants of r, and Equation (2) assumes that these other determinants are not systematically related to rates of price change. Because (2) and (3) exclude other determinants of the real rate, we should not expect them to explain anything like all the variation in interest rates whether or not the hypothesis holds. If, however, price expectations are affected by past rates of price change and in turn affect nominal rates, the coefficients in (2) and (3) should be significantly positive.

Estimates of (2) and (3) for annual data appear in tables 1 and 2. Estimates of (2) in table 2 include only five rates of price change to indicate that these offered little evidence on price-expectations effects. When this initial test proved inconclusive, (2) was not estimated using more terms, as the strongest relations should have appeared for the most recent rates of price change. Equation (3) was estimated using current price acceleration plus the past ten years accelerations. "n" was put at ten years to give estimates of initial positive effects and to see whether delayed effects appeared. Coefficients of (3) were generally positive, as shown by table 1. Changes in short-term rates are significantly affected by current, one and three-year lagged price accelerations. The Durbin-Watson statistics for estimates of (3) also suggest that the residuals are free of the autocorrelation which was apparently present in the estimates of (2). The coefficients in table 1 show that a one percentage point increase in the rate of price increase raises short-term interest rates by about .07 percentage points in the current year, and by .22 to .24 points by the time three more years have passed. In ten years short rates rise by about a third of one percentage point. There is virtually no current effect on long rates, and in ten years they rise by only .06 percentage points. The coefficients generally decline as the lag increases, suggesting that expectations are based on past values with declining weights. The exceptions to the pattern—at $DDP_{t-3}$ (where $DDP_{t-3}$ is the change in the rate of price change three years past)—are discussed further in section C. These estimates may underestimate actual expectations effects because price indexes may not measure total effects; the effects of changes in actual prices could be greater. Since a quarter of the total adjustment in short rates occurs in the three following years, we should also examine quarterly data.

Quarterly estimates of (2) and (3) appear in table 3. Again, while the coefficients of (2) give little evidence of price-expectations effects, those of (3) are positive as hypothesized, frequently significantly so. The coefficients show roughly the same patterns that appear for annual data. In the year following a one percentage point increase in the rate of change of prices, the bill rate rises by .08 percentage points. After two and a half years the rise is .18 points for the bill rate and about .06 points for the Treasury bond rate. For both rates, the maximum one-quarter effect (of the eleven estimated) comes in the ninth quarter following that in which prices began rising faster.

### *B. Differential Effects by Term to Maturity*

Nearly all the estimates presented so far imply that relevant price expectations are constructed differently for interest rates on loans of different maturities.[5] If expectations covering a longer future period are based more heavily on less recent experience, coefficients of more recent price change variables should be higher for shorter term rates. These patterns do in fact appear in the coefficients for both approximations of price ex-

[5] The terms of the published rates used are as follows: The bill rate is of three-month term, and $i_{cp}$ covers prime commercial paper of four- to six-month term. The call rate is a one-day rate; although loans are frequently outstanding for more than one day, they may be terminated by either borrower or lender at any time. Furthermore, changes in the rate apply to outstanding call loans as well as to new loans. $i_{bd}$ includes all Treasury bonds maturing or callable in ten years or more. For this and for railroad and corporate bond yields it is difficult to assign a term, for yields are averaged for bonds of different maturities, and the maturity composition changes over time. In the case of $i_{bd}$ the terms vary from ten to about thirty years. We might call the term twenty years, but this is but a rough approximation of the true (varying) average term. The averages of terms to maturity of corporate bonds seems similarly unavailable, but the February 1964 average term of the Standard and Poor's bond sample was twenty-six years, and the July 1964 average for Moody's sample was twenty-four years.

TABLE 4. DIFFERENTIAL PRICE-EXPECTATIONS EFFECTS BY TERM TO MATURITY

| | Quarterly Observations | | | | |
|---|---|---|---|---|---|
| | Effect after 10 quarters | Effect after 3 quarters | Percentage of 10-quarter effect | Effect after 8 quarters | Percentage of 10-quarter effect |
| $Di_b$ on *DDP* | 0.124 | 0.063 | 51.05 | 0.069 | 55.52 |
| $Di_{bd}$ on *DDP* | 0.050 | 0.019 | 39.04 | 0.035 | 69.67 |
| $Di_{aaa}$ on *DDP* | 0.069 | 0.032 | 47.05 | 0.053 | 76.96 |
| *P = CPI* | | | | | |
| | Annual Observations | | | | |
| | Effect after 10 years | Effect after 3 years | Percentage of 10-year effect | Effect after 8 years | Percentage of 10-year effect |
| $Di_c$ on *DDP* | 0.328 | 0.241 | 73.47 | 0.272 | 82.92 |
| $Di_{cp}$ on *DDP* | 0.333 | 0.218 | 65.46 | 0.316 | 94.89 |
| $Di_{L1}$ on *DDP* | 0.065 | 0.021 | 32.30 | 0.056 | 87.15 |
| $Di_{L2}$ on *DDP* | 0.057 | 0.017 | 29.82 | 0.048 | 84.21 |
| | Effect after 6 years | Effect after 3 years | Percentage of 6-year effect | | |
| $Di_b$ on *DDP* | 0.211 | 0.134 | 63.55 | | |
| $Di_{bd}$ on *DDP* | 0.067 | 0.041 | 60.90 | | |
| $Di_{aaa}$ on *DDP* | 0.038 | 0.019 | 49.13 | | |
| *P = NNP* deflator | | | | | |

$$\mathrm{Di} = \frac{di}{dt}$$

$$\mathrm{DDP} = \frac{d\left(\frac{1}{P}\frac{dP}{dt}\right)}{dt}$$

pectations. The estimates suggest that "more recent" covers at least the past five years.

As table 4 shows, quarterly estimates of (3) imply much faster adjustments of short rates to changes in the rate of price change than of long rates. In twelve quarters the bill rate rises by about .17 percentage points, while Treasury and corporate bonds rates rise by .05 and .07 percentage points, respectively. In addition, a larger percentage of the total twelve-quarter effect is completed at the end of three quarters for short rates than for long rates. Over 51 per cent of the twelve-quarter effect on the bill rate is completed at the end of three quarters compared with 39 and 47 per cent for bond rates. The relationships also hold for annual estimates of (3) which include price accelerations over the past ten years. Estimates of (3) show that short rates rise by a third of a percentage point in ten years, while long rates rise by a sixteenth. Further, the fraction of the total ten-year effect which is completed at the end of three years is 73 and 65 per cent for short rates, versus 32 and 30 percent for long rates.

## C. *The Generation of Price Expectations*

Coefficients of Equation (3) display a common tendency to decline in value as the independent variables are further in time from the dependent variable. This suggests that people give greater weight to more recent experience when forming expectations. But there are exceptions to this tendency, many of which are small, insignificant coefficients for price accelerations lagged several years, but some of which are significantly positive coefficients and are thus difficult to ignore.

Rather than declining smoothly, figure 1 shows that the coefficients of (3) for short rates decline, then rise, and then decline again. In addition the coefficient at the second peak ($DDP_{t-3}$) is larger than any other.

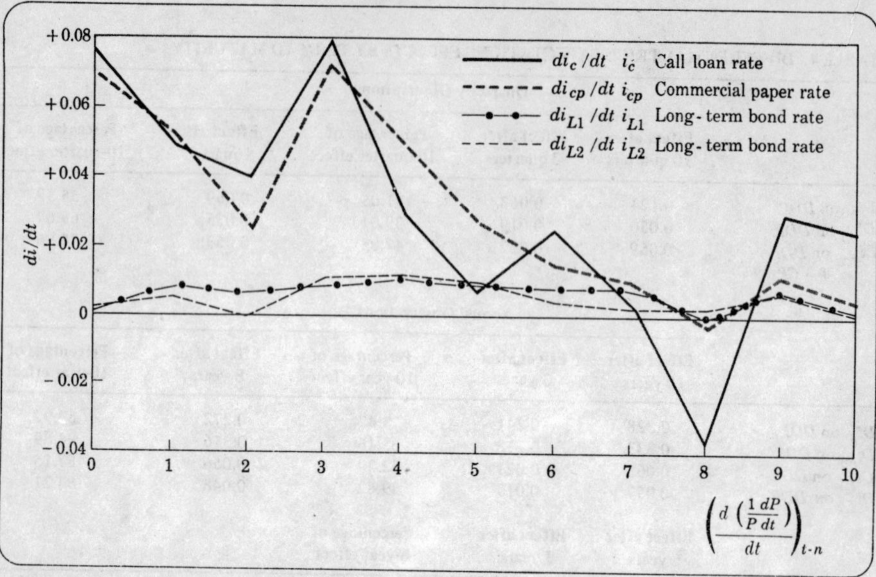


**FIGURE 1** Time response of interest rate changes to price accelerations. *P = NNP deflator, 1929 = 100.*

Expected price accelerations are therefore apparently related to past accelerations not by a first-order weighting scheme but rather by a higher-order scheme that generates a cyclical pattern in the coefficients. It is often assumed that people assign declining weights to observations in the more distant past in predicting future values, but it is less obvious why the three years past value should receive greater weight than the two years past value. However, the peak at the three-year lag marks an interval which corresponds roughly to the average duration of a reference cycle, so that the peak in the coefficients may reflect responses to business cycles. The coefficients suggest that the weights do decline as the lag increases but that the decline shows a cyclical pattern. This suggests that people use knowledge about the current stage of the cycle in forming expectations. For example, if the economy is in the midst of an expansion phase, people remember what happened to prices in the last expansion and use this information in forming their price expectations. This seems reasonable, since at the same stage of different cycles we might expect roughly similar ratios of used to unused productive capacity and other determinants of the fraction of nominal income changes which take the form of price changes. In these similar stages, increases in the money stock should have similar effects on prices.

Since the lengths of business cycles vary, however, such a cyclical effect would not always come at three years. But since the regression measures the average lag, and the average length of a business cycle is approximately three years, we should expect this cyclical effect to appear in a higher coefficient of price acceleration lagged three years. The variability of the length of the cycle would be reflected by a lower fraction of the variation of the dependent variable explained than if the effect always occurred after three years. We should not expect the levels of the $R^2$'s for estimates of (3) to be anywhere near unity, and in fact they are not. The cyclical effect does appear in higher coefficients for $DDP_{t-3}$, and in addition, coefficients of price accelerations lagged more than three again decline as the lag increases, as expected.

The theory that explains why the coefficients might show a cyclical pattern for short-term rates implies why these should be absent from long-term rates. For the rate on a loan for, say, twenty years, cyclical price movements should have a smaller effect, since the loan term is far longer than a business cycle. The average anticipated intracycle deviations from the average should have less effect on long rates. For loans maturing within a cycle, the relevant price behavior refers to the cycle phases during the duration of the loan. The effect could work on longer rates as well since the net rate of price change for the loan term would probably be different according as the loan ended during a peak or a trough. This effect should be more difficult to estimate for long rates, however, since price movements in the final half cycle are more distant and difficult to predict than in the first cycle, and price movements during the early years of the loan might well swamp this effect. Probably more important, the effect's appearance depends on people's predicting what stage of a cycle the economy will be in twenty or thirty years hence. The coefficients for long-term rates are thus also consistent with the theory, for they do not show the cyclical pattern.

The coefficients of (3) are smaller for long-term rates than for short-term rates, although there is nothing inherent in long-term rates to cause this relationship. It seems rather to reflect differing price expectations. There may be a lag in the effect of longer-term price expectations on longer-term interest rates, but the nature of longer expectations suggests that there is a lag in the response of longer-term price expectations to changes in current price behavior. Current and recent rates of price changes have less effect on longer rates presumably because longer-term expectations depend less on recent experience and more on less recent experience than do shorter expectations.

The unavailability of a measure of the real interest rate precludes the measurement of total price-expectations effects, although we can still estimate price-expectations effects on nominal rates. If we assume that the real rate is unaffected by changes in price expectations, Equation (3) gives total price-expectations effects. Although the coefficients are positive, they imply that for the fastest-adjusting interest rate, the call rate, only a third of the total adjustment occurs in ten years. That more of the hypothesized effect does not occur in ten years is almost certainly due in part to errors in measuring changes in actual and expected prices. Besides the great difficulties with price indexes, expectations are difficult to measure for years of price control during World War II and for the period of pegged interest rates (1942-53). World War II data are difficult to interpret since prices were rising, prices indexes were rising at slower rates, but people are said to have anticipated price declines after the War. (3) should therefore predict interest rate changes poorly after the War, and it does. Interest rates should also have been less responsive to price-expectations effects during the post-War peg period, since any tendency for yields on Treasury securities to rise would have been offset by Federal Reserve support operations. If other rates rose, funds would tend to move out of Treasury securities and into other securities, lowering yields again. Expectations effects might not have been entirely offset, but their strength should have decreased.

Equation (3) was estimated for the period 1869-1941, and the estimates, presented in table 5, were used to predict interest rate change for 1942-65. The equation estimated for changes in the call rate was

$$
\begin{aligned}
\frac{di_c}{dt} = {} & \underset{(0.00211)}{-0.00067} \; \underset{(0.04065)}{+0.09208^{*}DDP_t} \\
& \underset{(0.04731)}{+0.07174DDP_{t-1}} \; \underset{(0.04916)}{+0.05900DDP_{t-2}} \\
& \underset{(0.04965)}{+0.09978^{*}DDP_{t-3}} \; \underset{(0.05428)}{+0.05702DDP_{t-4}} \\
& \underset{(0.05765)}{+0.03562DDP_{t-5}} \; \underset{(0.05563)}{+0.04975DDP_{t-6}} \\
& \underset{(0.04985)}{+0.02087DDP_{t-7}} \; \underset{(0.05032)}{-0.01861DDP_{t-8}} \\
& \underset{(0.05122)}{+0.05714DDP_{t-9}} \; \underset{(0.04205)}{+0.04437DDP_{t-10}} \\
& SE\ Y.X = 0.01639 \\
& R^2 = 0.214 \qquad DW = 2.334
\end{aligned}
$$

The coefficients show price-expectations effects more clearly than those for the longer period. For every interest rate except $i_{L2}$, more coefficients rise than fall. The ten-year adjustment is increased for every rate: to .57 and .45 percentage points from .33 each for short rates and to .12 and .09 from .06 each for long rates. In addition, significant coefficients are estimated for long rates. The equations predict reasonably well for the 1942-65 period; they generally underestimate interest rate changes during the 1942-46 period and overestimate for the 1947-1953 period. The

TABLE 5. RELATION BETWEEN CHANGES IN NOMINAL INTEREST RATES AND RATES OF PRICE ACCELERATION, ANNUAL OBSERVATIONS; PREDICTION EQUATIONS 1869–1941

| | | | | | | |
|---|---|---|---|---|---|---|
| $\frac{di_c}{dt}$ = | −0.00067 (0.00211) | +0.09208*$DDP_t$ (0.04065) | +0.07174$DDP_{t-1}$ (0.04731) | +0.05900$DDP_{t-2}$ (0.04916) | +0.09978*$DDP_{t-3}$ (0.04965) | +0.05702$DDP_{t-4}$ (0.05428) |
| | +0.03562$DDP_{t-5}$ (0.05765) | +0.04975$DDP_{t-6}$ (0.05563) | +0.02087$DDP_{t-7}$ (0.04985) | −0.01861$DDP_{t-8}$ (0.05032) | +0.05714$DDP_{t-9}$ (0.05122) | +0.04437$DDP_{t-10}$ (0.04205) |
| | | SE $Y \cdot X$ = 0.01639 | $R^2$ = 0.214 | DW = 2.334 | | |
| $\frac{di_{cp}}{dt}$ = | −0.00097 (0.00133) | +0.07887*$DDP_t$ (0.02555) | +0.05934*$DDP_{t-1}$ (0.02974) | +0.03007$DDP_{t-2}$ (0.03090) | +0.08954*$DDP_{t-3}$ (0.03120) | +0.07076*$DDP_{t-4}$ (0.03412) |
| | +0.03859$DDP_{t-5}$ (0.03624) | +0.01993$DDP_{t-6}$ (0.03497) | +0.02443$DDP_{t-7}$ (0.03133) | +0.01090$DDP_{t-8}$ (0.03163) | +0.01909$DDP_{t-9}$ (0.03220) | +0.00788$DDP_{t-10}$ (0.02643) |
| | | SE $Y \cdot X$ = 0.01030 | $R^2$ = 0.274 | DW = 2.577 | | |
| $\frac{di_{L1}}{dt}$ = | −0.00036 (0.00028) | +0.00319$DDP_t$ (0.00531) | +0.00898$DDP_{t-1}$ (0.00618) | +0.00808$DDP_{t-2}$ (0.00642) | +0.01405*$DDP_{t-3}$ (0.00649) | +0.02115*$DDP_{t-4}$ (0.00709) |
| | +0.01539*$DDP_{t-5}$ (0.00753) | +0.01100$DDP_{t-6}$ (0.00727) | +0.01304*$DDP_{t-7}$ (0.00651) | +0.00855$DDP_{t-8}$ (0.00657) | +0.01519*$DDP_{t-9}$ (0.00669) | +0.00591$DDP_{t-10}$ (0.00549) |
| | | SE $Y \cdot X$ = 0.00214 | $R^2$ = 0.222 | DW = 2.087 | | |
| $\frac{di_{L2}}{dt}$ = | −0.00062 (0.00033) | +0.00340$DDP_t$ (0.00630) | +0.00327$DDP_{t-1}$ (0.00733) | −0.00121$DDP_{t-2}$ (0.00762) | +0.01816*$DDP_{t-3}$ (0.00769) | +0.02176*$DDP_{t-4}$ (0.00841) |
| | +0.01111$DDP_{t-5}$ (0.00893) | +0.00356$DDP_{t-6}$ (0.00862) | + .00963$DDP_{t-7}$ (0.00772) | +0.01221$DDP_{t-8}$ (0.00780) | +0.01166$DDP_{t-9}$ (0.00794) | +0.00126$DDP_{t-10}$ (0.00652) |
| | | SE $Y \cdot X$ = 0.00254 | $R^2$ = 0.227 | DW = 1.744 | | |

$$\mathrm{DDP} = \frac{\mathrm{d}\left(\frac{1}{\mathrm{P}}\frac{\mathrm{dP}}{\mathrm{dt}}\right)}{\mathrm{dt}}$$

P = NNP deflator, 1929 = 100

1942-46 underestimates are consistent with underestimation of price indexes, and the 1947-53 overestimates are consistent with shifts in price expectations and lowered responsiveness in rates as a result of pegging. We should expect the prediction equation to work better when the effects of the War and pegging were over, and in fact the equation seems to predict at least as well at the end of the 1942-65 period as at the beginning.

The lags in price-expectations effects also reflect delays in the effects of actual rates of price change on expected rates and of expected rates of interest rates. Long delays between changes in actual and expected rates of price change may well be due to the history of price changes in the United States. Rates of price acceleration have tended to be neither high nor stable, so that predictions based on one or two years' experience could easily be wide of the mark. Better predictions would likely come from minimizing the effects of year-to-year aberrations by averaging over many years.

The long lags may also be due to stability of the factors determining interest rates, even short rates, as Friedman and Schwartz note:

> The rate of interest is a forward-looking price connected with economic transactions involving the most far-sighted and long-lived considerations—the savings and investment process or the accumulation and maintenance of wealth. This is true even for short-term interest rates, in the sense that the funds being made available for lending at short-term are generally part of a total stock of wealth accumulated for long-term purposes; it just happens to be prudent or profitable to make this part of wealth available to others for short periods at a time; and corresponding statements apply to the funds borrowed at short-term. Hence, it is reasonable that participants in this market should be taking a fairly long view, forming fairly firm opinions and altering them only gradually rather than permitting their anticipations to alter substantially with every momentary change of circumstances.[6]

The delay in the expectations effect may also result from slowness of interest rate reponses to changes in expectations. Even if expectations adjusted rapidly, the effect on interest rates could be slow if savings and investment adjusted slowly to price expectations. The investment schedule may shift slowly due to difficulties in recognizing increased profitability of investments and because of the costs of changing investment. A firm's cost of increasing its investment ought to decrease as the increase is spread over a longer period.[7] Each of these delays would slow the price-expectations effects and lower the weights attached to recent price accelerations in (3).

Plausible as delays in price-expectations effects are, the lags implied by the estimates of (3) seem too long to make the assumption of a constant real rate believable. Intuitively, 50- or 100-year lags for the effect on interest rates seem too long. The relatively low sums of the price coefficients for eleven years may alternatively be due to opposite changes in the real rate of interest in response to variations in price expectations. The connection between price expectations and the real rate is still not precisely clear,[8] but Robert Mundell has presented an analysis suggestion that the real rate falls when the expected rate of price increase rises.[9] Mundell's result depends importantly upon a wealth-saving relationship, but if it holds it would help to explain those patterns which appear in our coefficients.

If an increase in the expected rate of price change of one percentage point lowered the real rate, the coefficients of (3) would never sum to unity. If, however, we arbitrarily assume that after ten years the entire price-expectations effects has occurred, the coefficients of (3) tell by how much the real rate must have fallen. If we take the estimates of (3) for the 1869-1941 period (the highest coefficients obtained), at the end of ten years the call rate has increased by .57 percentage

[6] Milton Friedman and Anna J. Schwartz, "Trends in Money, Income, and Prices, 1867–1966," unpublished study for National Bureau of Economic Research, 1967, ch. 4, p. 2–141.

[7] For a discussion of the costs of changing investment in inventories, see Charles C. Holt and Franco Modigliani, "Firm Cost Structures and the Dynamic Responses of Inventories, Production, Work Force, and Orders to Sales Fluctuations," in *Inventory Fluctuation and Economic Stabilization,* materials prepared for the Joint Economic Committee, Congress of the United States, Washington: Government Printing Office, 1961, pp. 1–55.

[8] See Reuben A. Kessel and Armen A. Alchian, "Effects of Inflation," *Journal of Political Economy* (December, 1962), p. 535.

[9] Robert Mundell, "Inflation and Real Interest," *Journal of Political Economy,* LXXI (June, 1963), 280–83.

points. If the full price-expectations effect has operated on short-term rates, real rates will have fallen by .43 percentage points. If estimates of (3) for the 1869-1965 period are used, real rates must fall by .67 percentage points in response to a one percentage point increase in the rate of price change. Such declines in the real rate may seem large, but they are the maxima estimated, because actual price-expecations effects may well be understated by changes in price indexes.

## IV. Summary and Conclusion

The evidence presented documents the effects hypothesized long ago by Irving Fisher. There is indeed a positive relationship between nominal interest rates and expected rates of price change detectable in U.S. data. Nominal rates rise in response to positive price expectations but apparently not by the full amount of the percentage point increase in the expected rate of price change. Since the difference between the new levels of nominal and real rates equals the rate of price change expected, real rates appear to fall.

The expectations effects of a change in current prices are spread over lengthy periods, and a given effect is spread over a longer period the longer the term of the rate. This suggests that longer-term price expectations are based more heavily on less recent past price behavior than are short rates. A one percentage point increase in the rate of price change raises short rates a third of a percentage point in the following ten years and raises long rates a sixteenth of a point. If the measurement error is lessened by deleting the years during and after World War II from the estimation period, short rates are estimated to rise by .57 and .45 percentage points and long rates by .12 and .09 points. Although each price index has drawbacks, the implicit price deflator for net national product proved best at measuring expectations. It tended to produce more statistically significant coefficients and coefficients closer to those expected theoretically than any of the other indexes considered.

Finally, there appears to be a cyclical factor in the formation of price expectations in the United States, implying a higher-order weighting pattern for past price changes. The second peak comes after three years, the average duration of a reference cycle, suggesting that price expectations also depend on the stage of a business cycle the economy is in. With this exception, however, expected price changes do appear to be related to past changes by a weighting scheme which gives lower weights to less recent past values.

There results have some very clear policy implications, for any policy which gives attention to interest rates must reckon with price-expectations effects. These effects may require more time to operate than do other factors influencing interest rates, but their influence will be felt in time. In particular, monetary policies designed to maintain interest rates below their equilibrium levels will generate inflation and consequent price-expectations effects which put direct pressure on interest rates in the direction opposite to that desired by the authorities.

## Notes to Tables

* Denotes statistically significant at 0.05 level.

DW denotes Durbin-Watson statistic.

All interest rates are expressed as annual rates, and all rates of change of prices are also expressed as annual rates.

### *A. Interest Rates*

$i_b$—the Treasury bill rate—was obtained from the *Federal Reserve Bulletin* and *Banking and Monetary Statistics.* Quarterly data were generated from monthly data, which are averages of daily figures for 1947-1966. Annual data begin in 1929.

$i_c$—call money note—annual average data for 1869-1965 for New York City were obtained from the National Bureau of Economic Research, Inc.

$i_{cp}$—commercial paper rate—annual average of "Commercial Paper Rates in New York City," 1869—January 1937, from F. R. Macaulay, *Some Theoretical Problems Suggested by the Movements of Interest Rates, Bond Yields and Stock Prices in the United States Since 1856* (New York: National Bureau of Economic Research, Inc., 1938), pp. A145-A161; thereafter (through 1965) from monthly averages of weekly figures from Bulletin and Quotation Record of *Commercial and Financial Chronicle.*

$i_{bd}$—Treasury bond rate—source same as for $i_b$. Monthly data are averages of daily figures for bonds maturing or callable in 10 years or more for 1947-1966. Annual data begin in 1919.

$i_{L1}$—long-term interest rate — obtained from National Bureau of Economic Research. 1869-1899: annual average of yields on American railroad bonds adjusted for economic drift, computed from Macaulay, . . . *Interest Rates, Bond Yields, and Stock Prices* . . . , pp. A141-A152, plus 0.114 per cent (from 1900-1902 overlap with following segment). 1900-1963: basic yield on corporate bonds to 30 years' maturity, *Banking and Monetary Statistics* and *Supplements.*

$i_{L2}$—index of yields of high-grade industrial bonds, Standard and Poor's Corporation, 1869-1965 — obtained from National Bureau of Economic Research. 1869-1899 derived from American railroad bond yields, adjusted. Annual averages, each raised by 1.578.

Interest rates are expressed in per cent terms. That is, a yield of $4.00 per year per $100.00 is expressed as 0.04.

### *B. Prices*

Implicit price deflator for net national product (1929 = 100), 1869-1965: annual data obtained from Milton Friedman and Anna J. Schwartz. Implicit price deflator for gross national product (1958 = 100): obtained from *The National Income and Product Accounts of the United States, 1929-1965.*

# 27 INTEREST RATES AND PRICE LEVEL CHANGES *

WILLIAM P. YOHE
AND
DENIS S. KARNOSKY
*Duke University*

In summarizing his many years of work on the subject, Irving Fisher cited four empirical relationships between interest rates and price levels:[1]

(*1*) Interest rates tend to be "high" when prices are rising and "low" when prices are falling.

(*2*) Interest rate movements lag behind price level changes, which obscures the relationship between them.

(*3*) There is a marked correlation between interest rates and a weighted average of past price level changes, reflecting effects that are distributed over time.

(*4*) "High" interest rates accompany "high" prices, and "low" interest rates accompany "low" prices.

The first of these relationships derives from the fact that, if lenders and borrowers could perfectly foresee future price level movements, the former would hedge against changes in the real value of their loan principal by adding the percentage change in prices over the life of the loan to the interest charge; the latter, expecting money income to change in proportion to prices, would readily accept the higher rate.

Fisher attributed the second and third relationships to imperfect foresight about future prices and the resulting inclination to extrapolate past price changes into the future in order to adjust interest rates for expected changes in prices. He devised the concept of the "distributed lag" to explain the way information about the past affects expectations of the future.

Fisher thought the fourth relationship, frequently called the "Gibson paradox," was an accidental consequence of the other three.[2] What is paradoxical is that the theory prevalent in that period presumably led to the conclusion that interest rates must be low in order to stimulate sufficient investment

* Reprinted from *Review*, Federal Reserve Bank of St. Louis, vol. 51 (December, 1969) pp. 19–36, by permission of the authors and the Federal Reserve Bank of St. Louis.

[1] Irving Fisher, *The Theory of Interest* (New York: Macmillan, 1930), p. 438. Fisher first discussed these relationships in *Appreciation and Interest* (New York: Macmillan, 1896), pp. 75 and 76.

[2] The term "Gibson paradox" was coined by J. M. Keynes in *A Treatise on Money*, Vol. II (London: Macmillan, 1930), pp. 198–208. A. H. Gibson had studied the high correlation between levels of interest rates and prices in England throughout the 19th and early 20th centuries. The phenomenon was earlier called the "Ricardo-Tooke conundrum," after the leading antagonists in the Currency School-Banking School controversy in England in the first half of the nineteenth century. For a concise exposition of the *controversy*, see Knut Wicksell, *Lectures on Political Economy*, Vol. II (London: Routledge and Kegan Paul, 1935), pp. 168–190.

spending for the price level to be high, while empirically this has not been observed.

The present study is an examination of the second and third of Fisher's propositions, making use of modern data sources and statistical techniques. There is, at present, a major controversy over (1) the advantages and disadvantages of using monetary aggregates as opposed to using interest rates as indicators of the effect of monetary policy actions on the economy, and (2) the adjustments, if any, which must be made to an indicator to "neutralize" it with respect to changes that are not directly the result of policy actions.[3] Previous studies of the effect of price level changes on interest rates, some of which will be reviewed below, have found the lags to be so long that recent price behavior could be ignored in evaluating changes in observed interest rates. In contrast, results will be presented here based on the 1952-69 period which indicate that the lags are very short, with most of the effect of price level changes on both long- and short-term interest rates occurring within two years. Interest rates adjusted to remove the apparent influence of price changes have sometimes moved contrary to movements in observed rates. Furthermore, price changes have had a greater effect on interest rates in the 1960's than in the 1950's, and indeed, price changes in the latter period account for nearly all of the movement in interest rates.

## Previous Studies of Price Expectations (Fisher) Effects

Tests for Fisher effects have generally been based on two hypothesized relationships:

$$rn_t = \dot{P}^e_t + rr_t \qquad (1)$$

$$\dot{P}^e_t = \sum_{i=o}^{n} w_i \dot{P}_{t-i} \qquad (2)$$

The first equation states that the nominal interest rate ($rn$) prevailing at time $t$ for a particular debt instrument is equal to the annual rate of change in prices ($\dot{P}^e$) expected at time $t$ to occur over the life of the instrument plus its "real" rate of interest ($rr$).[4]

Equation (2) is an application of the theory of "adaptive expectations," "error-learning," or, alternatively, "extrapolative forecasting." Faced with uncertainty about the future, an economic decision-making unit is presumed to base its predictions about future price movements on a weighted average of current and past changes in prices. Thus, in equation (2) the rate of price change expected at time ($\dot{P}^e_t$) for some future period is the weighted sum of actual past price changes ($\dot{P}_{t-i}$), where the importance of each past change is reflected in the weight $W_i$, and where $n$ indicates how many periods in the past are relevant in forming expectations.[5] The approach is "adaptive" in the sense that in each period expectations are adjusted (or forecasting errors are corrected) for actual price changes. The approach is "extrapolative" in that past changes are extended (extrapolated) into the future.

[3] See, for example, Leonall Andersen, Michael Keran, and Emanuel Melichar, "The Influence of Economic Activity on the Money Stock," this *Review*, August 1969, and Patric H. Hendershott, *The Neutralized Money Stock* (Homewood, Illinois: R. D. Irwin, 1968).

[4] Fisher used "real" rate in the sense of "virtual" or "true" rate. Technically, he also included a third term, $rr_t\dot{P}^e_t$, on the right side of equation (1). This is the interest that would be earned on the price adjustment to the nominal rate. The term is ordinarily so small that it is customarily omitted. For the complete derivation of equation (1), see *Appreciation and Interest*, pp. 8–11, 66 and 67.

Some studies have also been concerned with the effect of changes in the rate of price change (i.e., price level accelerations) on changes (rather than levels) in interest rates. To see how this may be done, it is necessary to expand $\dot{P}^e_t$:

$$\dot{P}^e_t = \frac{dP^e_t}{P_t}$$

Substituting this term in equation (1), differentiating, and manipulating the result yields:

$$d(rn_t) = \left(\frac{d^2P^e_t}{dP_t} - \frac{dP^e_t}{P_t}\right)\frac{dP_t}{P_t} + d\,(rr_t)$$

The term within the large parentheses represents price acceleration. See, *inter alia*, Allan H. Meltzer, "The Appropriate Indicators of Monetary Policy, Part I," *Savings and Residential Financing: 1969 Conference Proceedings* (Chicago: U.S. Savings and Loan League, 1969), p. 14.

[5] For a concise survey of the theoretical literature on adaptive expectations, see Zvi Griliches, "Distributed Lags: A Survey," *Econometrica*, January 1967, pp. 42–45.

Substituting equation (2) into equation (1) yields the form of the equation that is usually estimated:

$$rn_t = \sum_{i=0}^{n} w_i \dot{P}_{t-i} + rr_t \qquad (3)$$

The unmeasurable price expectations are not explicitly considered, but instead it is assumed they can be approximated by the observable pattern of past changes in actual prices (or in some other variable that may be critical to the formation of expectations about prices).

Fisher assumed that the weights in equation (3) declined arithmetically as one goes backward in time. His procedure was first to posit a time interval over which the entire effect of price level changes would be reflected in a nominal interest rate series, for example, ten years. Ignoring the current period price change, he then computed for each year the weighted average of past price level changes, using a weight of nine for one year earlier, a weight of eight for two years back, and so forth. The weighted price changes divided by the sum of the weights (9 + 8 + . . . . + 0) yielded the weighted average of past rates of price change. Fisher then observed which of these weighted averages best correlated with the nominal interest rate.[6] The "best fit" would be obtained where the correlation was highest or where further lengthening of the interval would not add appreciably to the correlation.[7]

A useful statistic for comparing the results of many distributed lag studies is the mean (or average) lag, that is, the time that elapses until half of the effect of a change in the independent variable is reflected in the dependent variable.[8] Using annual and quarterly data for the United States, Fisher found very long mean lags for the effect of price changes on long- and short-term interest rates. For example, the highest correlation between commercial paper rates and rates of change in the wholesale price index from 1915-27 was obtained when the latter was lagged over 120 quarters (30 years), implying a mean lag of about 40 quarters (10 years).

In recent years there has been a considerable revival of interest in the study of Fisher effects, ostensibly the result of the reappearance of substantial variability in interest rates and price levels and methodological developments in the estimation of distributed lags. Two studies have attempted to measure "real" rates directly and then to relate the spread between various nominal rates and the estimated "real" rates to historical time series for price level changes, with inconclusive results.[9]

---

[6] Within the framework of equation (3), Fisher calculated the correlation coefficient corresponding to the following regression equation:

$$rn_t = \sum_{i=1}^{n} \frac{(n-i)}{n(n-1)/2} \dot{P}_{t-i} + rr_t + u_t$$

where $n(n-1)/2$ is the sum of $n$ terms ranging from zero to $(n-1)$.

[7] His procedure was directly related to the present-day practice of choosing an estimated equation with the highest $R^2$ (coefficient of determination or square of the correlation ratio).

[8] The mean lag is simply the weighted-average lag, where the coefficients [$w_i$'s in equations (2) and (3)] are used for the weights. When all of the weights are positive, the formula for the mean lag is as follows (Griliches, p. 31):

$$\frac{\sum_{i=0}^{n} i \cdot w_i}{\sum_{i=0}^{n} w_i}$$

that is, a weighted sum divided by the sum of the weights. In Fisher's calculations, the denominator is unity (his weights necessarily sum to one), so the formula for his mean lags is

$$\sum_{i=1}^{n} \left( i \cdot \frac{n-i}{n(n-1)/2} \right)$$

which simplies to $(n-1)/3$. Fisher estimated his mean lags as $n/3$.

[9] Suraj B. Gupta, "Expected Rate of Change in Prices and Rates of Interest" (unpublished dissertation, University of Chicago, 1964), and Phillip Cagan, *Determinants and Effects of Changes in the Stock of Money, 1875–1960* (New York: National Bureau of Economic Research, 1965), pp. 305–309. Gupta's work is summarized and his empirical work extended in William E. Gibson, "Effects of Money on Interest Rates," *Staff Economic Studies*, No. 43, Board of Governors of the Federal Reserve System, March 1968, pp. 45–48 and 88–89. Preliminary work along similar lines was reported in David Meiselman, "Bond Yields and the Price Level: The Gibson Paradox Regained," in Deane Carson (ed.), *Banking and Monetary Studies* (Homewood, Illinois: R. D. Irwin, 1963), pp. 119–122.

Most of the published studies have regressed nominal rates directly on current and past rates of price changes (or changes in nominal rates on price accelerations).[10] Data intervals have ranged from quarters (Gibson) to business cycle phases (Friedman and Schwartz). The time span has ranged from as early as 1873 to as late as 1966. Lagged rates of change in various price level indexes and even nominal income (Gibson) have been tried as indicators of price expectations. The forms of the distributed lags estimated have generally been either "unconstrained" lags or "geometrically decaying" lags.[11] Without exception, the mean lags of interest rates behind price changes were found to be very long. For example, Friedman and Schwartz found mean lags for short-term rates of about ten years and for long-term rates of 25 to 30 years, which they attributed to the "slow and gradual adjustment of anticipations of price changes to the actual behavior of prices."[12]

## A Search for Fisher Effects

This study is based upon earlier work but departs from previous studies in ways that appear to have significant effects on the results, in particular:

(*1*) Monthly, instead of exclusively quarterly or annual, data are used for short-term and long-term interest rates (dependent variables) and for price level changes and other independent variables. Further, the interest rate series have been seasonally adjusted.

(*2*) A variety of kinds of distributed lags are estimated, in order to investigate the effect of lag form on the length of the lags.

(*3*) The monthly data are aggregated into quarterly and annual series to determine the effect of aggregation over time on the lag estimates.

(*4*) The study is purposely confined to the period following the Treasury-Federal Reserve Accord of 1951 in order to avoid having to contend with the constraint on interest rate movements imposed by the Federal Reserve's "par pegging" of Government securities prices. Further, the 1952-69 period is divided into two sub-periods to see whether there has been any apparent change in the mechanism relating past price changes to the formation of price expectations and any clues to the reasons for earlier findings of very long lags.

(*5*) A model will also be tested to see what happens to the explanatory power of past price level changes when variables assumed to affect "real" rates of interest are added to the regressions.

(*6*) Experimental "real" rate series will be generated and their movements compared with nominal rates to see whether there have been times when nominal rate movements might have been misleading indicators of changes in "real" interest costs.

### *Seasonal Movements in Interest Rates*

A number of economists have observed not only seasonal movements in monthly and quarterly interest rate series, but also the influence on the seasonal of changes in Federal Reserve operating strategy for open market

[10] Meiselman, pp. 112–133; Milton Friedman and Anna Jacobson Schwartz, "Trends in Money, Income, and Prices, 1867–1966" (unpublished manuscript, National Bureau of Economic Research, November 1966), chapter 2, pp. 110–143; and Gibson, pp. 44–66 and supplementary tables. In their multiple regression study, Michael J. Hamburger and William L. Silber ("An Empirical Study of Interest Rate Determination," *Review of Economics and Statistics,* August 1969, pp. 369–373) rejected the rate of change in prices as insignificant.

[11] Both forms will be discussed later. To estimate unconstrained lags, one merely regresses the current value of the dependent variable on the current and a predetermined number of lagged values of the independent variable—there is thus no *a priori* constraint on the time shape of the coefficients. Geometrically decaying lags impose a geometrical decay on the coefficients, that is, part of each coefficient is a constant decay term less than one which, when raised to higher powers as the lag recedes into the past, decays (asymptotically approaches zero). See Griliches, pp. 16–49, and Lawrence R. Klein, "The Estimation of Distributed Lags," *Econometrica,* October 1958, pp. 553–565.

[12] Friedman and Schwartz, chapter 2, p. 139. Gupta, estimating, geometrically distributed lags for the nominal rate—"real" rate spread behind price changes, found a mean lag of 16 years for long-term rates. Gibson estimated unconstrained lags for relatively short lag intervals (ten quarters and four years), so it is not possible to calculate mean lags for the total effect of price changes on interest rates. In Meiselman's study, the geometric decay coefficients came out very close to one, implying a long mean lag (nearly twenty years, for example, with a decay coefficient of 0.967, which he found in regressing bond yields on price changes over the 1873–1960 period).

purchases and sales.[13] Since some of the data used for independent variables in the regressions were seasonally adjusted, it was advisable to seasonally adjust the short-term and long-term interest rate series, so that the results could be compared with those generated using unadjusted series.[14] As expected, stronger seasonals were detected in the short-term than in the long-term interest rates. The finding of pronounced seasonals in both for the 1952-60 period and the virtual elimination of seasonal movements for the 1961-65 period, probably the consequence of the Federal Reserve strategy to assist the balance of payments, confirms the conclusions of earlier studies. The resumption of pronounced seasonals is apparent in the calculations for the 1966 to mid-1969 period. The explanation may lie in the insertion of "proviso clauses" in the Federal Open Market Committee directives over the later period and the implementation of such directives by the Trading Desk at the Federal Reserve Bank of New York.[15]

### *Empirical Results—Interest Rates Regressed on Rates of Price Change*

Data for the period 1952-69 were used to test the hypotheses about the effect of price expectations on the level of nominal interest rates. Several measures of both prices and interest rates were used in the estimation, and various lengths for the total lags were tested. In addition, several estimation techniques were employed. The results were very similar across the many combinations of data, length of the lag distribution, and estimation procedures, all suggesting a much shorter time horizon in formation of price expectations than had previously been found.

The interest rates used in this study are yields on securities issued by the private sector.[16] Short-term interest rates ($rn^s$) were approximately by the yield on four- to six-month commercial paper. The yield to maturity on Aaa-rated corporate bonds was used as the measure of long-term interest rates ($rn^L$). Price expectations were approximated by the rate of change of the consumer price index for all items, $\dot{P}^c$.[17]

Using monthly data for the period January 1952 to September 1969, the function

$$rn_t = a_0 + a_1\dot{P}^c_t + a_2\dot{P}^c_{t-1} + a_3\dot{P}^c_{t-2} + \cdots + a_{n+1}\dot{P}^c_{t-n}$$

was estimated first by least squares regression of $rn_t$ on current and lagged values of price changes for $n = 24$, 36 and 48 months. The coefficients of the regressions are presented in Chart 1.

[13] Leonall C. Andersen, "Seasonal Movements in Financial Variables—Impact of Federal Reserve and Treasury," *Business and Government Review,* University of Missouri, July-August 1965, pp. 19–26; "A Closer Look at Interest-Rate Relationships," *The Morgan Guaranty Survey,* April 1961, pp. 3–5; Gibson, pp. 30–32 and Tables 3 and 4; and Hamburger and Silber, pp. 370–371.

[14] Data have been seasonally adjusted using the X-11 Variant of the Census Method II Seasonal Adjustment Program, U. S. Department of Commerce, Bureau of the Census. *Source:* Board of Governors of the Federal Reserve System, Federal Reserve *Bulletin.*

[15] Jan Warren Duggar, "The Proviso Clause and the Bank Credit Proxy" (unpublished manuscript, Federal Reserve Bank of New York, 1969).

[16] Since there are many factors in addition to price expectations that affect the level of interest rates, the dependent variable used in the regressions should be the one least influenced by those other factors. Yields on private securities were selected, instead of rates on Government debt, because they are more free of the direct influences of debt-management and monetary actions. However, Fukasawa obtained similar results using yields on Government securities. Greene found that price expectations were somewhat easier to identify using interest rates on private debt.

[17] Mortgage costs are included in the consumer price index and might contribute to some degree of spurious correlation between interest rates and price movements. Since mortgage interest rates tend to move with other nominal rates, using the consumer price index as the measure of price movements would tend to result in a positive bias in the observed relationship between interest rates and price movements. To test for this effect the consumer price index was purged of mortgage rate effects. Data on the mortgage component of the CPI were available from the Bureau of Labor Statistics only for the period 1954–64. Thus, nominal interest rates were regressed on the rate of change of the CPI and the adjusted CPI for this period only. The regressions using this adjusted $\dot{P}^c$ series were still quite close to those using the index inclusive of mortgage costs. Gibson's procedure of using changes in national income as a proxy for price expectations was also treated, using however, personal income, which is available on a monthly basis. The results, summarized in the appendix, were quite similar to those using the consumer price index.

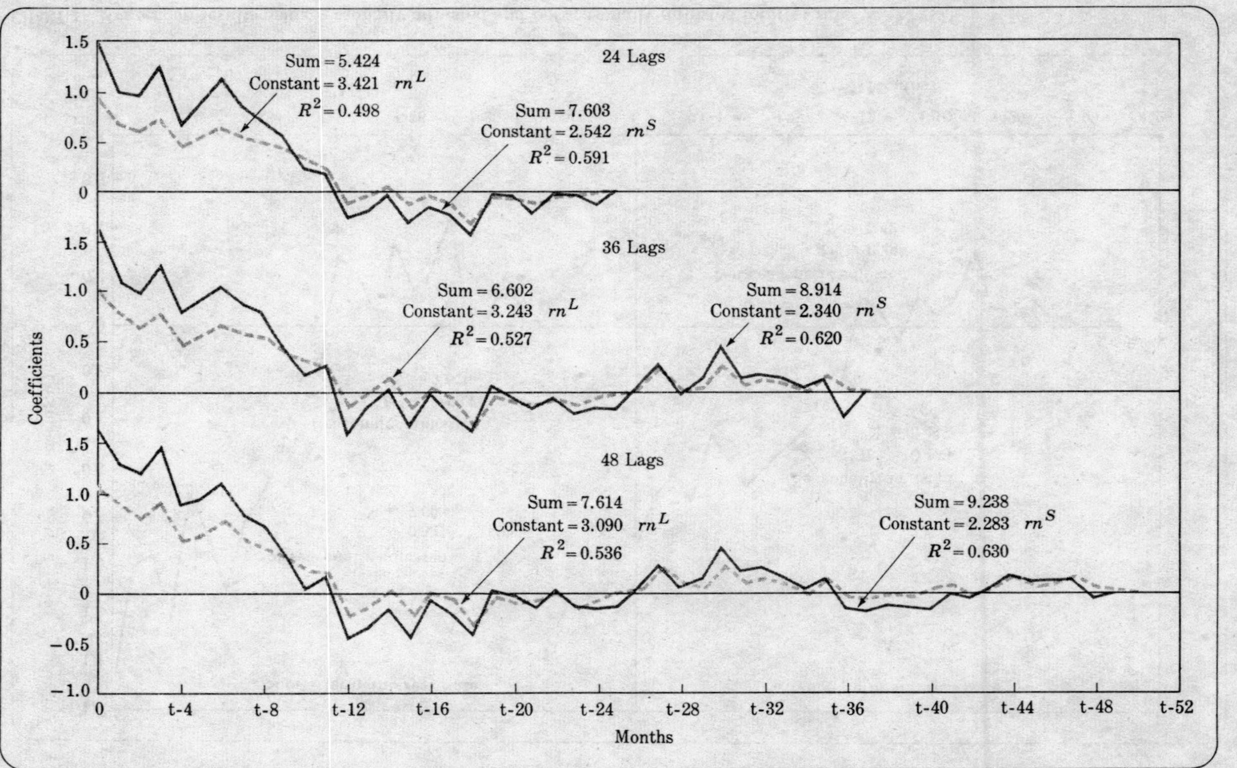


**CHART 1** Summary of regression results. Ordinary least squares (1952–1969).

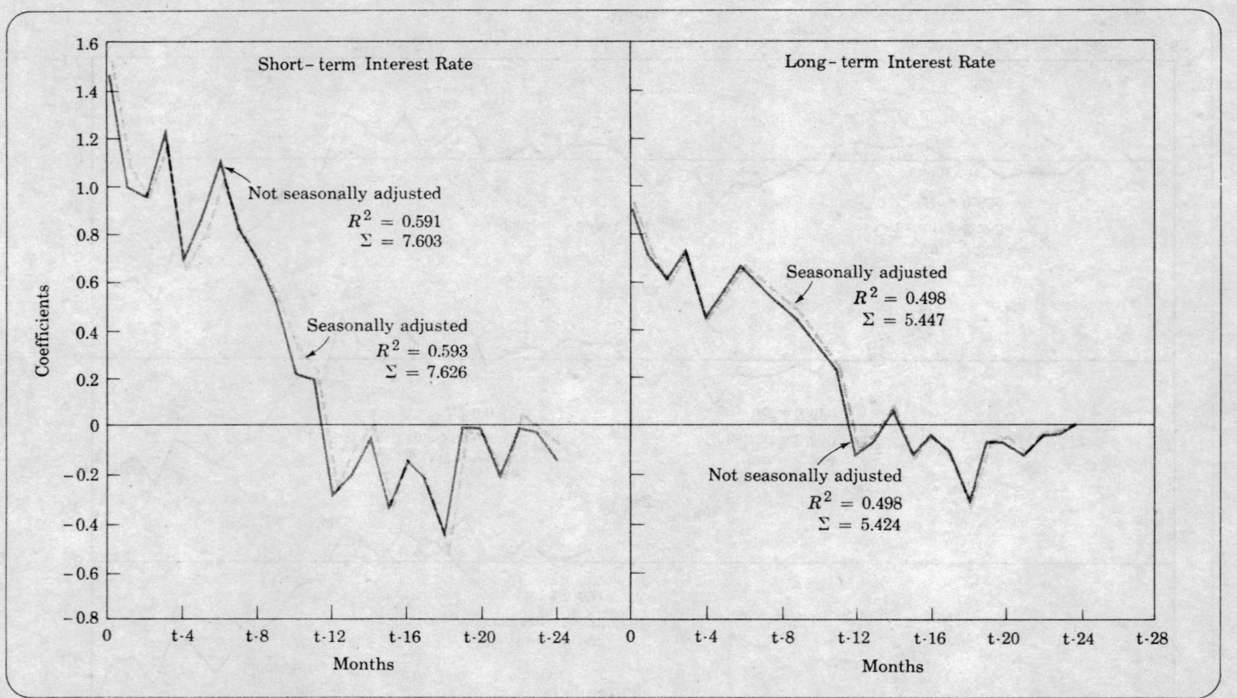


**CHART 2** Regression results using seasonally adjusted and not seasonally adjusted interest rates.

These regressions were run with both seasonally adjusted and nonseasonally adjusted interest rate series, and in each case the results using seasonally adjusted data traced quite closely those using unadjusted data. The introduction of the seasonal factor decreased the unexplained variance (increased the adjusted coefficient of determination, $R^2$) only slightly. Chart 2 presents the coefficients of the regressions:

$$\overset{S}{rn_t} = a_0 + a_1\dot{P}^c{}_t + a_2\dot{P}^c{}_{t-1} + \cdots + a_{25}\dot{P}^c{}_{t-24}$$

$$\overset{L}{rn_t} = a_0 + a_1\dot{P}^c{}_t + a_2\dot{P}^c{}_{t-1} + \cdots + a_{25}\dot{P}^c{}_{t-24}$$

The coefficients using seasonally adjusted interest rates are quite similar to those using unadjusted data. Since this close relationship was observed in all of the tests, only the results using unadjusted data will be explicitly considered.

The regressions show that price movements accounted for about 50 per cent of the variance in interest rates between 1952 and late 1969. The pattern of coefficients is consistent with the adaptive expectations hypothesis, that is, they are generally declining. The presence of small negative coefficients in the "tails" of the distributions could be explained theoretically by the eventual domination of positive "extrapolative effects" by negative "regressive effects." Although the t-test is suspect in dealing with a distributed lag regression,[18] the coefficients tend to be small beyond t-24 months and generally insignificant. Increasing the length of the lag from 24 to 48 months had little effect on the distribution of coefficients. The sum of the coefficients increased as the lag was extended, however, suggesting that, although great weight in the formation of price expectations comes from quite recent experience, the total adjustment procedure is probably somewhat longer, with only relatively small weight given to price movements in the distant past. In other words, the "true" distribution probably has a "tail" of small declining coefficients. These results suggest a much shorter information time horizon of price expectations than had been found in the investigations cited earlier.

Due to multicollinearity, direct estimation of an unconstrained distributed-lag function tends to result in wildly fluctuating coefficients. In order to reduce this fluctuation, the relationships were estimated using the Almon lag technique.[19] This procedure results in a much smoother distribution, which is more consistent with the adaptive-expectations hypothesis, that is, expectations are a continuous function of past price movements.

The Almon lag estimates are presented in Chart 3.[20] The distribution of the Almon coefficients follows the least squares estimate quite closely. For lags from 24 to 48 months, most of the effect on interest rates come from price movements over the previous year. The tails of coefficients beyond these points sum to nearly zero.

The regression using 48 lags suggests that, if the annual rate of change of the consumer price index increased by one per cent in a given month (for example, from a 3 per cent annual rate of increase to a 4 per cent annual rate) and prices continued to rise at that rate, the yields on four- to six-month commercial paper would rise 72 basis points (for example, from 4 per cent to 4.72 per cent) during the first year, if all other factors affecting interest rates were unchanged. After

[18] Multicollinearity (correlation between independent variables) is a possible source of difficulty in estimation of this type of distributed-lag relationship. In the presence of multicollinearity, the ordinary least squares regression technique is unable to identify the exact parameter associated with each independent variable. See J. Johnston, *Econometric Methods* (New York: McGraw-Hill, 1963), pp. 201–207.

[19] Shirley Almon, "The Distributed Lag Between Capital Appropriations and Expenditures," *Econometrica*, January 1965, pp. 178–196.

[20] The regressions presented here were generated using a sixth-degree polynomial. Other degree polynomials were tested and gave similar distributions. The sixth-degree was chosen because it best approximated the unconstrained estimates, in that it minimized the sum of the squares of the difference between the unconstrained and Almon estimates. The only constraint on the selection of the degree of the polynomial is that it must be less than or equal to the number of lagged coefficients. The sixth-degree polynomial was the maximum which could be used in the program available to the authors.

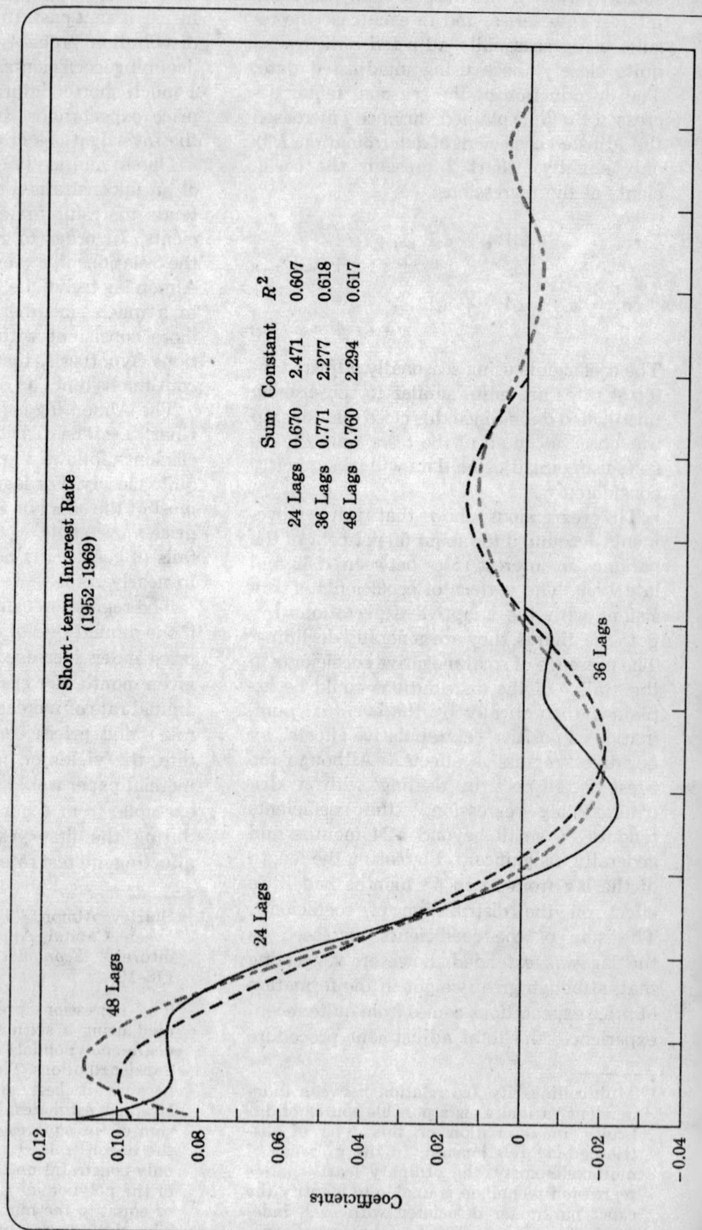

Short-term Interest Rate
(1952-1969)
Sum Constant $R^2$
24 Lags 0.670 2.471 0.607
36 Lags 0.771 2.277 0.618
48 Lags 0.760 2.294 0.617
48 Lags
24 Lags
36 Lags
Coefficients
0.12
0.10
0.08
0.06
0.04
0.02
0
−0.02
−0.04

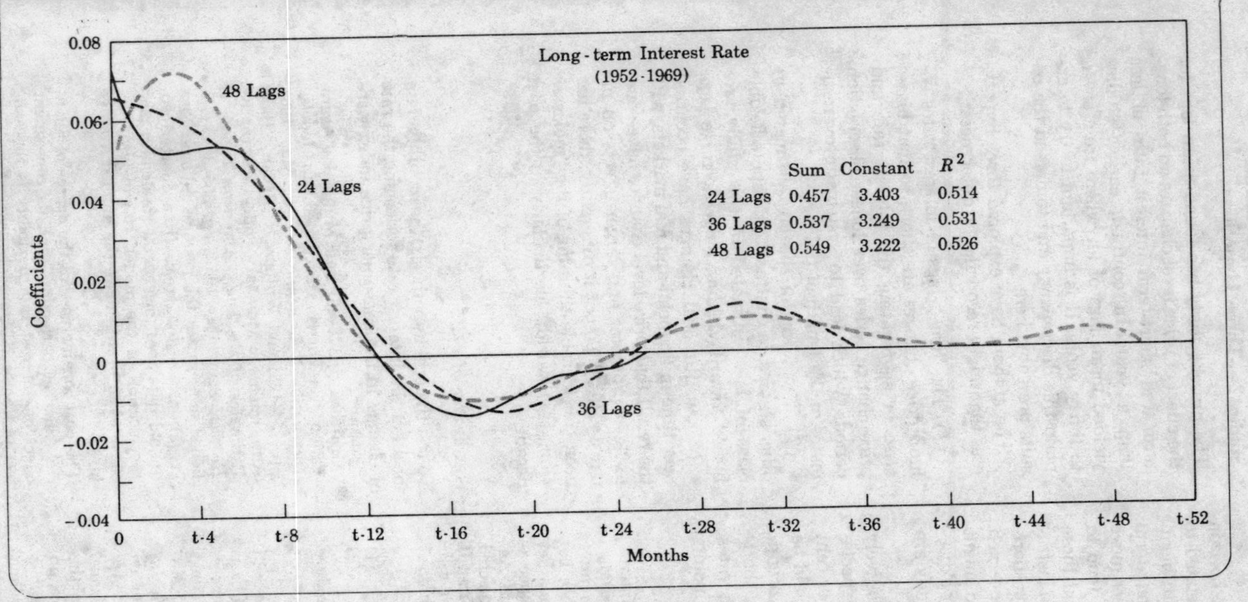


**CHART 3** Summary of regression results (Almon lag).

48 months, short-term interest rates would have risen by 69 basis points.[21]

Fisher hypothesized that the time horizon in forming price expectations was related to the term to maturity of the instrument. Potential buyers and sellers of long-term debt would be interested in how prices move over an extended period and would tend to look further into the past than would those people who were dealing in short-term instruments. Participants in the market for short-term securities are less likely to be concerned with long-term price movements and might need less information in forming their expectations. The results in the present study are consistent with this idea.

The long-term interest rate is relatively less responsive to changes in price expectations. Twelve months after the one per cent increase in prices, long-term rates would be 59 basis points higher than they were originally, as opposed to 72 basis points for short-term rates. The effect on long-term rates would be a total increase of 56 basis points after 48 months.

[21] In the long run, the nominal rate of interest does not rise by the full amount of the change in price expectations. An increase in price expectations will increase the difference between the nominal and Wicksellian market rates. However, the change in price expectations will tend to lower the market rate. Assuming an equilibrium position with expected price changes equal to zero, then $rn_t = rm_t$. If price expectations increase by one per cent per year, after 4 years the nominal interest rate will rise by 69 basis points, thus

$$rn_{t+48} - rm_{t+48} = 1.00 \quad (1)$$
$$rn_{t+48} - rn_t = 0.69 \quad (2)$$

Since $rn_t = rm_t$, equations (1) and (2) reduce to

$$rm_{t+48} - rm_t = -0.31 \quad (3)$$

Thus the market interest rate falls by 31 basis points following the increase in price expectations. This result is consistent with findings of other investigators; for example, see Keith M. Carlson and Denis S. Karnosky, *The Influence of Fiscal and Monetary Actions on Aggregate Demand: A Quantitative Appraisal*, Federal Reserve Bank of St. Louis, Working Paper No. 4, March 1969. In the aggregate demand model developed there, an increase in expected prices *ceteris paribus* generates a Government budget surplus which results in a decrease in the stock of wealth and reduces the "real" interest rate. The net result is an increase in nominal rates less than the increase in expected prices.

## Why Such Long Lags in Earlier Studies?—Three Hypotheses

The present study has found mean lags for the effect of price level changes on both long-term and short-term interest rates of less than a year. In contrast, earlier studies yielded mean lags of anywhere from seven to thirty years. It is important to try to explain this discrepancy and to defend the results presented here.

The authors have explored three hypotheses that might reconcile the differences:

(*1*) The "true" lags of interest rates behind price changes are short, so that biases arise in aggregating the interest rate and price change series over longer observation periods, which lead to systematic overestimates of the length of the lags.[22]

(*2*) The forms of the lags estimated in other studies, in contrast to the more flexible class of lags estimated in this study, are biased toward yielding longer average lags.

(*3*) Institutional changes have occurred over time in financial and real markets, with the result that price level changes have come to have prompter and larger effects on interest rates.[23] To put it differently, there has been considerable thinning of the "molasses (long-lag) world," particularly in the past decade.

### *Aggregation of Data*

To test the first hypothesis, the monthly data for all of the interest rate series and the rate of change in the consumer price index were

[22] Griliches, pp. 45–46; Yair Mundlak, "Aggregation Over Time in Distributed Lag Models," *International Economic Review*, May 1961, pp. 154–163; and William R. Bryan, "Bank Adjustments to Monetary Policy: Alternative Estimates of the Lag," *American Economic Review*, September 1967, pp. 855–864. Griliches summarizes the issue as follows: "aggregation over time (e.g., from quarterly to annual data) will in general result in a misspecification of the model. It will also . . . cause us to overestimate the implied average lags."

[23] The post-war increase in the degree of financial "market perfection" and its consequent effect on interest rate flexibility is the subject of James S. Duesenberry's essay, "The Effect of Policy Instruments on Thrift Institutions," in *Savings and Residential Financing: 1969 Conference Proceedings*, pp. 135–143.

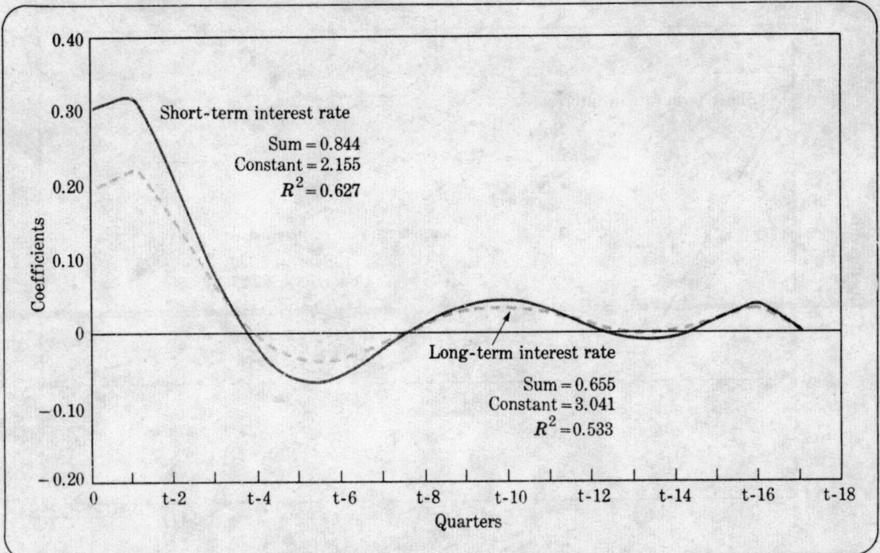


**CHART 4** Summary of regression coefficients. Quarterly data (1952–1969).

aggregated to quarterly and annual averages of monthly data for the 1952-69 period. Almon distributed lags over 16 quarters with sixth-degree polynominals were estimated for the quarterly series. The results (see Chart 4) were virtually identical to the original monthly regressions with 48 month lags and the same degree polynomials.[24]

The quarterly regressions suggest that if the annual rate of change of prices increases by one per cent in any quarter and remains at the higher level the short-term rate would rise by 84 basis points after 4 years. The long-term rate would rise by 66 basis points over the same period. Using the results of the monthly estimates, an increase by one per cent in the annual rate of change in prices, would yield an increase of 69 basis points in short-term rates and 56 basis points in long-term rates after four years.

There were too few observations, given the length of the lags and the degree of the polynomials, to fit Almon lags to the annual observations, so only unconstrained lags were estimated, ranging from one to five years (see Chart 5). For the unadjusted commercial paper rate, the $R^2$ was highest (0.709) with only the current rate of change in prices in the regression; in all cases, only the coefficient for the current price changes was significant. As might be expected, the $R^2$ for the unadjusted corporate Aaa yield was highest (0.552) when the current and one year lagged price change term were included, although in every case only the coefficient on the current term was significant. The regressions using annual data gave somewhat larger total effects. If the rate of change of prices rises by one per cent per year, short-term rates would be 137 basis points higher after four years. Long-term rates would rise by 134 basis points.

The discrepancy between this and earlier studies apparently cannot be explained on grounds of an aggregation bias in the latter, and the first hypothesis cannot be accepted. The reason probably lies in the fact that the adjustment of interest rates to price level changes is not so rapid that aggregation of monthly into quarterly and annual data leads to systematic overestimates of the underlying lags.

[24] Fukasawa has run unconstrained lags extending back six quarters with quarterly data from IV/1951-IV/1968 for Treasury bill and bond rates regressed on the rate of change in the GNP deflator. His results are similar to those reported here.

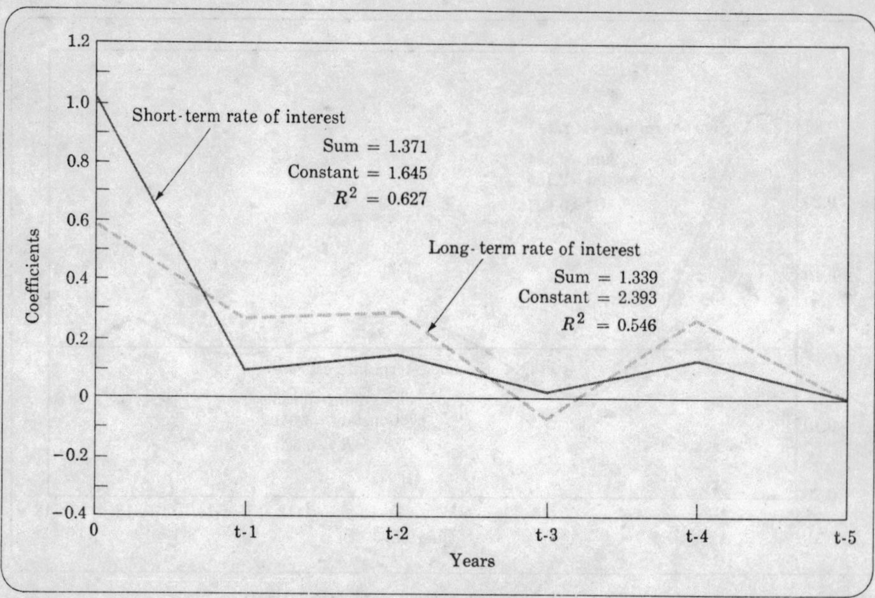


**CHART 5** Summary of regression coefficients. Annual data (1952–1968).

*Estimation Procedure*

The second hypothesis pertains to the nature of the lag distributions estimated in other studies. Since several of the studies have estimated geometrically decaying (Koyck) lags, the monthly data used in the earlier part of the present study were used to estimate such lags. The following regression was run for each of the yield series, using for $\dot{P}_t$ both the simple monthly rate of change and compounded annual rates of change:[25]

$$rn_t = \lambda rn_{t-1} + \beta\dot{P}_t + \text{constant}$$

The decay coefficient λ, presumably somewhere between zero and one, indicates the rate at which the weight of the past rates of price change declines backward in time (that is, $\lambda = 1$ means that the lagged terms never decay at all, while $\lambda = 0$ means that only the current price change term has any effect).

All of the initial regressions yielded decay coefficients slightly greater than one, which, taken at face value, suggests that the lagged terms do not decay.

$$rn^s_t = 1.012\ rn^s_{t-1} + .057\ \dot{P}^c_t - .024 \qquad R^2 = .980$$

$$rn^L_t = 1.007\ rn^L_{t-1} + .053\ \dot{P}^c_t - .020 \qquad R^2 = .994$$

A danger in such estimates of the decay coefficients and the β parameter is that they are inconsistent, and the estimate of λ is probably biased upward.[26] Following procedures outlined by Griliches and by Goldberger, the decay coefficients were re-estimated, which reduced them by only a very small amount:

[25] This is the convenient form in which such lags are usually estimated. This equation may be expanded into the following:

$$rn_t = \lambda^0\beta\dot{P}_t + \lambda^1\beta\dot{P}_{t-1} + \lambda^2\beta\dot{P}_{t-2} + \ldots + \lambda^\infty\beta\dot{P}_{t-\infty} + \text{constant}$$

or, more simply,

$$rn_t = \beta\sum_{i=0}^{\infty} \lambda^i\dot{P}_{t-i} + \text{constant}$$

[26] See Griliches, p. 41, and Arthur S. Goldberger, *Econometric Theory* (New York: John Wiley and Sons, 1964), pp. 276–278, and Kenneth F. Wallis, "Some Recent Developments in Applied Econometrics: Dynamic Models and Simultaneous Equation Systems," *Journal of Economic Literature,* September 1969, pp. 774–775.

$$rn^s_t = 1.005\, rn^s_{t-1} + .071\, \dot{P}^e_t - .024$$
$$rn^L_t = 1.003\, rn^L_{t-1} + .054\, \dot{P}^e_t - .020$$

Decay coefficients greater than one are clearly inconsistent with the adaptive expectations hypothesis. It would not be unreasonable to expect decay coefficients only slightly less than one to result from tests using different sample periods or data definitions than were used here.

The monthly data were divided into two subperiods, 1952-60 and 1961-69, and separate estimates of the decay coefficients obtained. For the earlier period, the coefficients dropped below one, ranging (unadjusted for consistency) from 0.977 for commercial paper rates to 0.996 for corporate Aaa yields. These results imply long mean lags for both interest rates, with longer lags for the long-term rates. The coefficients on the current rate of price change in the commercial paper rate regressions strangely became negative for the 1952-60 period.[27] For 1961-69, the decay coefficients were nearly the same as for the entire 1952-69 period, that is, slightly greater than one, for which it is difficult to find any theoretical rationalization.

To see what would happen to the decay coefficients, the monthly data were aggregated into quarterly data and the decay coefficients re-estimated for the 1952-69 period and for the subperiods mentioned above. All of the decay coefficients for the entire period declined, which would be expected if a monthly decay process were to be converted into an equivalent quarterly process, but the decay coefficients for short-term rates fell to below one (0.968 for commercial paper rates, with a mean lag of 20 quarters or five years). For 1952-60 alone, all the coefficients were less than one, but the decay process was again negative for short-term rates. For 1961-69 the results were all plausible, and the decay coefficients were all lower than corresponding coefficients for 1952-60. The effect of price level changes on commercial paper rates for the latter period decayed with a $\lambda$ of 0.834 (mean lag of about three quarters), while the decay factor was 0.919 (mean lag of seven quarters) for corporate Aaa yields.[28]

The preceding experiments with simple geometrically declining lag structures suggest that such lags, requiring an exponential decay, may not be the most appropriate ones to impose on the interest rate and price level data for the period of this study in the attempt to capture the "true" underlying lag distribution. In every case the average lags obtained with this procedure were considerably longer than with either unconstrained or Almon lags, which provides some explanation for the differences between this and previous studies.[29]

### *Institutional Changes*

The third hypothesis asserts that price level changes have come to have larger and prompter effects on interest rates because of institutional changes in the economy. As a preliminary test of this hypothesis, the 1952-69 period was again divided into two subperiods, 1952-60 and 1961-69, and various Almon lag structures estimated separately for each.[30] Table 1 contains the sum of the lag coefficients for 12 to 48 lags and second- to sixth-degree polynomials.

As was the case with the entire period, there was little difference in the total price expec-

[27] This implies that the lagged price change effects are opposite in sign from those hypothesized; they could be interpreted as evidence for Sargent's "regressive effects" of price changes on short-term rates.

[28] James B. Greene, using quarterly data for 1961–68, obtained a decay coefficient of 0.824 for the commercial paper rate regressed on the rate of change in the consumer price index, which implies a mean lag of about 2½ quarters; for the corporate Aaa yield his decay coefficient was 0.919 implying a mean lag of about seven quarters.

[29] Experiments were also conducted for the whole period and the subperiods with simple second-order lags (in the regressions the dependent variable was lagged one and two periods). The results were not appreciably different from those for the first-order lags.

[30] The "Chow test" was conducted to see whether there was a fundamental shift in behavior patterns within the 1952–1969 period. For both commercial paper rates and corporate Aaa yields the "F" statistics were significant at the one per cent level, which indicates a substantial difference in the anticipations-forming mechanism in the two subperiods. For an explanation of the test, see Gregory C. Chow, "Tests of Equality between Sets of Coefficients in Two Linear Regressions," *Econometrica*, July 1960, pp. 591–605.

TABLE 1. SUM OF THE REGRESSION COEFFICIENTS (monthly data)*

Short-term Interest Rates

| Degree of polynomial | 1952–1960: 12 | 24 | 36 | 48 | 1961–1969: 12 | 24 | 36 | 48 |
|---|---|---|---|---|---|---|---|---|
| 2 | .2825 | .2265 | .0899 | −0.482 | .9211 | .9518 | .8039 | .5726 |
| 3 | .2760 | .2254 | .3055 | .1856 | .9105 | .9035 | .7235 | .5344 |
| 4 | .2837 | .2402 | .3418 | .1349 | .9118 | .9231 | .7373 | .4750 |
| 5 | .2836 | .2406 | .3378 | .0539 | .9134 | .9210 | .7124 | .4668 |
| 6 | .2834 | .2439 | .3340 | .0960 | .9131 | .9172 | .7180 | .4759 |

Long-term Interest Rates

| Degree of polynomial | 1952–1960: 12 | 24 | 36 | 48 | 1961–1969: 12 | 24 | 36 | 48 |
|---|---|---|---|---|---|---|---|---|
| 2 | .1432 | .1154 | .0537 | .0081 | .5854 | .7086 | .8406 | .8321 |
| 3 | .1417 | .1122 | .1639 | .1580 | .5881 | .7405 | .8618 | .7945 |
| 4 | .1445 | .1140 | .2078 | .1374 | .5886 | .7531 | .8540 | .8210 |
| 5 | .1445 | .1193 | .2062 | .0798 | .5889 | .7533 | .8474 | .8227 |
| 6 | .1444 | .1200 | .2023 | .0756 | .5886 | .7524 | .8526 | .8303 |

Length of lag in months (12, 24, 36, 48).

*All coefficients in the table for the 1961–69 period are significant at the one per cent level. Those for the 1952–60 period were insignificant for 48 lags.

tations effect between different degree polynomials. The length of the lag distribution was crucial, however. The total effect on short-term interest rates tended to decline as the lag was extended beyond 24 months, and this was quite pronounced in the 1961-69 period. The effect on long-term rates, however, increased as the lag was extended up to 36 months. Beyond 36 months, the sum of the coefficients remained almost constant. None of the coefficients beyond 48 months were significant. These results suggest that the time horizon in forming price expectations increases as the term to maturity of the security increases.

The total price expectations effect is much larger in the 1961-69 period than in the earlier period. In the latter period the total effect on short-term rates is about 90 per cent of the annual rate of change in prices. The effect on long-term rates is about 80 per cent of the rate of price change. In the 1952-60 period the sum of the coefficients range between 5 and 35 per cent of the price change for a lag of 36 months. Chart 6 contains the lag coefficients for short-term rates (second-degree polynomial and 24 lags for 1961-69, and sixth-degree with 36 lags for 1952-60) for the relationship between the commercial paper rate and the rate of change in the consumer price index. The sum of the coefficients for the earlier period was .344 and the mean lag, 1 to 2 months. For the latter period, the sum was .952, and the mean lag 4 to 5 months. While it is true that the smaller effect in the earlier period was exhausted more quickly (the mean lag was shorter), the peak in total effect for the earlier period was reached after eleven months, while the same level of effect was attained in the latter period in only 2 to 3 months. Further, the $R^2$ jumps from 0.255 to 0.901, so for the latter period the rate of change in prices accounts for over 90 per cent of the variation in commercial paper rates.[31] These results are thus consistent with the hypothesis of the effect of institutional changes.[32]

Similar results were obtained for the corporate Aaa yield (Chart 6), and the jump in

[31] The highest $R^2$ (0.938) for the commercial paper rate was obtained for 1961–69 using sixth-degree polynomials and 48 month lags.

[32] Fukasawa has estimated unconstrained lags with quarterly data for five subperiods from 1951–68 and has obtained similar results.

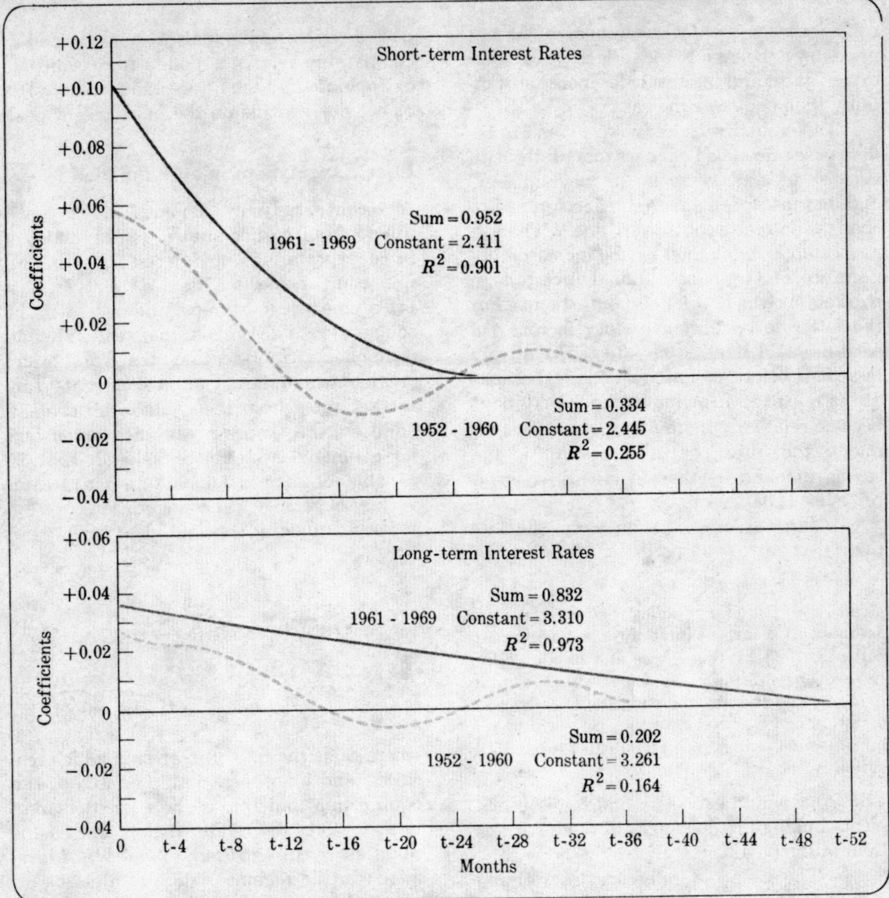


**CHART 6** Summary of regression results.

$R^2$ for the latter period is even more pronounced, from 0.164 to 0.973. The coefficients of the long-term rate were generated using a second-degree polynomial and 48 lags for 1961-69 and sixth-degree with 36 lags for 1952-60. All of the coefficients estimated for the 1961-69 period are significant at the one per cent level. A mean lag of 16 months is implied by this result, meaning more than half of the adjustments in interest rates to price changes in the period were attained in less than a year and a half. A summary of the 1961-69 regressions appears in the appendix.

What factors might cause a shift in the framework for transmitting past price level changes, via price expectations, to nominal interest rates? A listing of plausible explanations might include the following:

(*1*) According to Friedman and Schwartz, "the period used in forming anticipations should depend on the characteristics of price behavior," particularly the "variability in the behavior of the general level of prices."[33] Thus, one could argue that prices have been more variable, at least in an upward direction, in the 1950's and 1960's than over long, earlier historical periods. Further, the greater publicity given to price level movements, as well as the more rapid processing of data,

[33] Friedman and Schwartz, p. 143.

could convey greater awareness of recent price level behavior and affect price level expectations and interest rates more substantially than once was the case.

(*2*) Nominal rates may have come to reflect past price level changes more fully both because of a decrease in "money illusion" and because of decreased effects of price changes on real wealth over time.[34] The former could be explained by the increased importance of large institutional investors in markets such as that for corporate bonds. For the latter to be a contributory factor, real wealth would have to be affected relatively less than before by price changes (because assets not fixed in nominal terms may have become relatively more important), thus reducing the "drag" on upward shifts in the saving function by the amount of expected price level changes.

(*3*) Interest rates are more flexible than in many past periods. According to Duesenberry,

> Restrictive monetary policy has in the past operated to a large extent through [nonprice] rationing. . . . Market forces and public policy have been working toward perfecting capital markets, and thereby reducing the effectiveness of rationing . . . [and resulting in] a world requiring wide swings in interest rates for stabilization purposes . . .[35]

Thus, one would expect to find larger coefficients linking price changes to interest rates than in the past.

(*4*) The frame of reference for forming expectations may well have changed, particularly in the 1960's. The relative absence of cycles in prices except for the very distant past deprives individuals of a succession of comparable reference points from which to extrapolate into the future and forces the use of heavier weights on the more recent past.

## Price Expectations in an Expanded Model

A recent study by Thomas J. Sargent[36] differs from earlier studies of the effect of price expectations on interest rates in two important respects. Besides relating past price changes to nominal interest rates, he sought also to decompose the "real" rate into components representing the equilibrium "real" rate and the deviation of current "real" market rates from the equilibrium rate. In addition, the shapes of the distributed lags he estimated were more general, that is, capable of fitting the data into a greater variety of geometrical configurations.

Sargent devised a useful identity:[37]

$$\mathrm{rn}_t = \underbrace{\overset{(a)}{\mathrm{re}_t} + \overset{(b)}{(\mathrm{rm}_t - \mathrm{re}_t)}}_{\text{``Real'' rate } (\mathrm{rm}_t = \mathrm{rr}_t)} + \underbrace{\overset{(c)}{(\mathrm{rn}_t - \mathrm{rm}_t)}}_{\text{Fisher effect } (\dot{P}^e_t)}$$

where $re_t$ is the rate of interest at which real saving and investment would be in long-run equilibrium and $rm_t$ is the current market level of the "real" rate, that is, $rm_t$ is the same as $rr_t$ in equation (1) above. Movements in the nominal rate may then be attributed to changes in the equilibrium rate (a), to a deviation between the equilibrium rate and the "real" market rate (b), and to a Fisher effect (c).

Earlier studies (including that which we have reported above) regarded either (b) or (a+b) as a residual and regressed nominal interest rates on past price changes only, but Sargent attempted to estimate each of the components of the level of nominal rates. The relationships among the components of the nominal rate and how he sought to identify

[34] "Money illusion" means that behavior is based on and directed toward nominal magnitudes rather than "real" magnitudes, for example, investment outlay in money terms would be related to money income and nominal interest rates.

If real wealth influences the decisions of savers, the saving function would not shift upward by the expected rate of increase in prices because of expected decreases in the real value of assets fixed in nominal terms (for example, money), which dampen the effect of price expectations on nominal rates (see Robert Mundell, "Inflation and Real Interest," *Journal of Political Economy*, June 1963, pp. 280–283).

[35] Duesenberry, pp. 136 and 140.

[36] Thomas J. Sargent, "Commodity Price Expectations and the Interest Rate," *Quarterly Journal of Economics*, February 1969, pp. 127–140 [reprinted in this volume].

[37] Sargent, p. 130. It is an identity, since it simplifies to $rn_t = rn_t$.

them statistically are shown in Figure 1. Assume that real investment $(I/P)$ and real saving $(S/P)$ are functions of real income and "real" market rates of interest and that real income is given (so shifts in the saving and investment schedules do not have to be accounted for). The equilibrium "real" interest rate $(re)$ is the rate at which real saving and investment would be in equilibrium. The market rate $(rm)$ below the equilibrium rate indicates that some portion $(AB)$ of current investment is being financed from sources other than intended saving, for example, by newly created money from the banking system or through the drawing down of previously accumulated money balances. This is sometimes called the "Wicksell effect" on interest rates.[38]

Assuming savers and investors form the same price expectations and that neither are subject to "money illusion" (an important Fisherian concept[39]), both functions would be shifted upward by the expected rate of change in prices, $\dot{P}^e_t = rn_t - rm_t$.

Since the equilibrium rate cannot be directly observed, Sargent used a reduced form proxy for it. He solved his real saving and investment functions simultaneously, so that the one market rate consistent with equilibrium (equality of intended savings and investment) is a function of the other determinants of real saving and investment, namely real income and (from an investment accelerator) the change in real income. This solution was then used to measure component (a) in the equations he estimated. Similarly, having no independent observations for the market rate, he used another proxy, the current rate of change in the "real" (deflated) money stock, for the deviation of the market rate from equilibrium.[40]

Finally, Sargent estimated geometrically distributed lags on past price changes as a proxy for price expectations. Using annual data for 1902-40 (two of the regressions were also run for 1902-54) and taking for nominal rates Durand's one-year and ten-year basic yields, he obtained estimates implying very

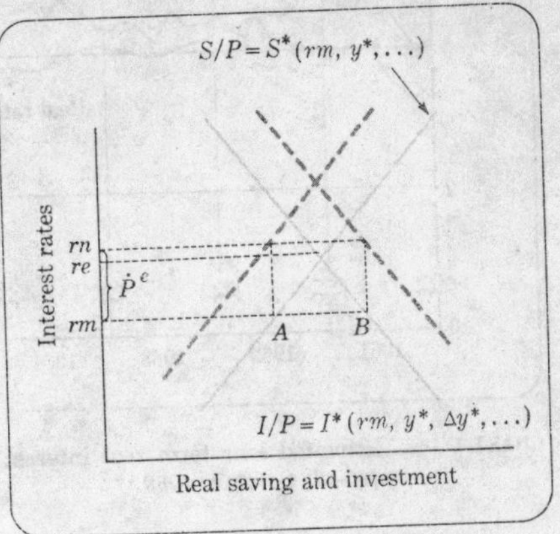


**FIGURE 1** Illustration of Sargent's identity.

[38] Knut Wicksell, *Lectures on Political Economy*, pp. 190–198, and *Interest and Prices* (London: Macmillan, 1936). Wicksell assumed that savers and investors expected current prices to continue into the future, so he did not need to account for price expectations effects on interest rates. As Sargent points out, views similar to Wicksell's were also held by Henry Thornton in 1802 and by Keynes in *A Treatise on Money*. Emphasis on the equilibrium rate-market rate relationship as the proper one in using interest rates as monetary policy indicators and rejection of price expectations effects on empirical grounds characterizes recent work of Patric H. Hendershott and George Horwich (see, for example, "The Appropriate Indicators of Monetary Policy, Part II," in *Savings and Residential Financing: 1969 Conference Proceedings*, pp. 42–44) [reprinted in this volume under the title "Money, Interest, and Policy"].

What is here called the "Wicksell effect" may also be interpreted as the "liquidity effect" or "impact effect" of changes in the money stock; similarly, the real GNP variables reflect the "income effect" or "feedback effect" on interest rates associated with changes in the money stock (see references to works by Friedman and Schwartz, Gibson, and Meltzer cited above).

[39] See footnote 34 above.

[40] In Figure 1 the gap between the equilibrium and market interest rates will widen as the portion of real investment not financed by current real savings $(AB)$ increases. The rate of change in the real money stock, on the other hand, should be positively correlated with the magnitude of $AB$. As a proxy for $(rm\text{-}re)$ the rate of money change should have a negative coefficient (that is, be positively related to an $(re\text{-}rm)$ gap).

The entire reduced form for "real" rates should also capture the effects of other capital market disturbances, for example, Government surpluses or deficits and the ways they are financed (banking system versus nonbank public).

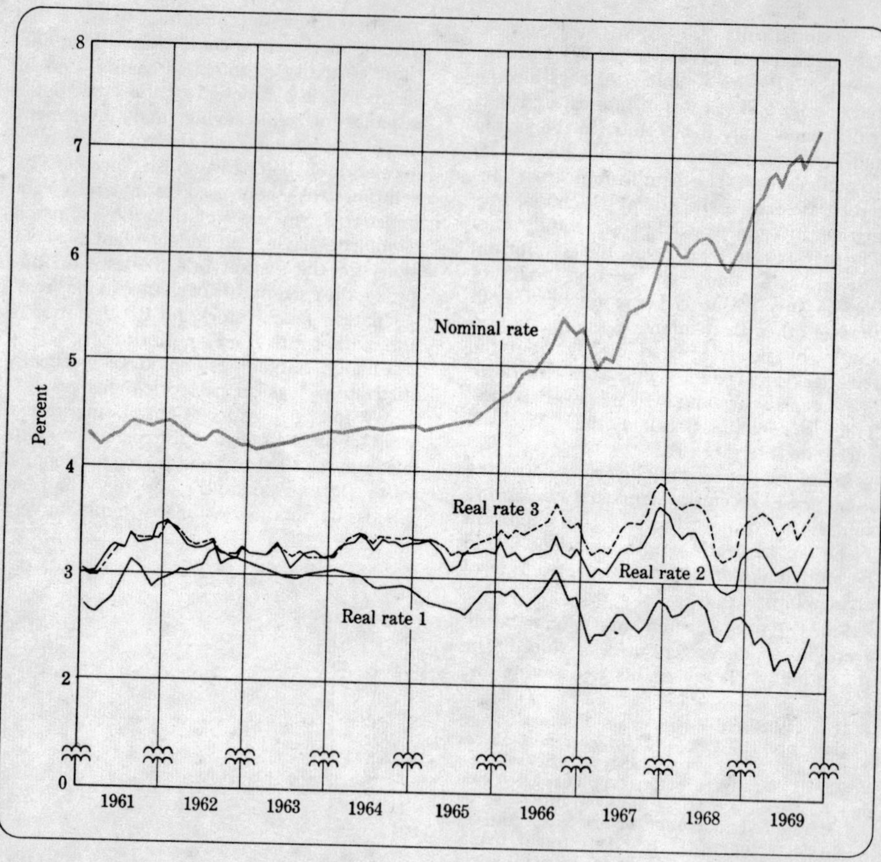


**CHART 7** Estimated long-term real interest rates (yields on corporate Aaa bonds). *Latest data plotted: October, 1969.*

long mean lags (twenty years or more for short- and long-term rates).

In several of his regressions he estimated two sets of decay coefficients. Both were positive for the long-term rate; for the short-term rate one was negative and more quickly decaying, which Sargent rationalized as indicative of a "regressive effect" of price changes on short-term rates (as opposed to the positive "extrapolative effect"), that is, price changes temporarily generate expectations of changes in the opposite direction (that is, that they will move back to a "normal" level). The sum of the regressive and extrapolative weights did not reach a peak until eight years and declined even more slowly thereafter (since the negative component decayed more rapidly), so the mean lag would not be much different from his other results.

The authors have subjected Sargent's basic approach to a further test, with the following modifications:

(*1*) Both real saving and investment are assumed to depend on both real GNP and "real" market rates of interest. Thus, there is no *a priori* expectation as to the sign of the coefficient for the real GNP term in the regressions. A negative coefficient would presumably indicate that shifts in the saving function in response to a change in real GNP outweighed shifts in investment, so that nominal and "real" rates would tend to fall as real GNP rose.[41] A positive coefficient would suggest just the opposite, while a coefficient near zero might indicate roughly offsetting effects of saving and investment shifts.

(2) Quarterly and monthly instead of annual data are used, and as before, the emphasis is completely on the entire post-accord period and the 1961-1969 subperiod. The regressions with monthly data necessarily use proxies for real GNP (personal income deflated by the consumer price index and, alternatively, the index of industrial production) and the GNP price deflator (consumer price index).

(3) The interest rate series and distributed lag forms are different; further, regressions were run with and without a constant term (Sargent did not suppress the constant term in any of his regressions).

The equations estimated are of the following form:

$$rn_t = a_0 + \sum_{i=o}^{n} a_{i+1}\dot{P}_{t-i} + \beta_1 Y^*_t + \beta_2 \Delta Y^*_t + \beta_3 \Delta M^*_t$$

where $\dot{P}$ is the annual rate of change in the GNP deflator (or a monthly proxy), $Y^*$ and $\Delta Y^*$ are the level and rate of change in real GNP (or a monthly proxy), and $\Delta M^*$ is the average change in the real money stock (nominal money stock deflated by the GNP deflator or its monthly proxy). Nominal rates ($rn$) are again the four- to six-month commercial paper rate ($rn^s$) and the corporate Aaa yield ($rn^L$), using quarterly averages of monthly data in the quarterly regressions. Only results for the 1961-69 subperiod will be reported here, in Chart 7.

The explanatory power of price level changes was changed little when the equations were more fully specified, and the adjusted $R^2$'s rose by small amounts. For example in the equations for the long-term rate with second-degree Almon polynomials, total lags of 16 quarters (best statistical fit), and a constant term, the sum of the coefficients on current and lagged rates of price change actually rose from 0.80 to 0.86, and the $R^2$ was unchanged at 0.977 when the current real GNP and real change in the money supply were added to the regression; further, the mean lag for the effect of price changes on nominal rates increased from 3.2 quarters to 5.5 quarters. In other words, recent price changes alone tend to overstate the necessary adjustment of nominal rates to account for the Fisher effect. As would be expected, the coefficients on current and lagged rates of price change were redistributed toward the past in the expanded equations, since the current and last quarters' price levels implicitly enter into the other independent variables.[42]

Suppressing the constant term in the equation (that is, forcing $a_o$ to zero) forces a redistribution of its effects over the other coefficients. In the case of the long-term rate, the constant was not significant, and suppressing it enhanced slightly the explanatory power of real GNP and the change in the real money supply, lowered the sum of the price change coefficients (to 0.80) and the acceleration coefficient ($\beta_2$), left the $R^2$ virtually unchanged, and lengthened the mean lag (by three quarters with total lags of 16 quarters). In the case of the short-term rate, the mean lag rose from zero to nearly one quarter. Otherwise, the effects on the coefficients were exactly opposite to what happened when the constant was suppressed in the equation for the long-term rate.

Since the expanded equations contain variables not all measured in the same units, "beta" coefficients were computed in order to assess the relative contribution of each independent variable to the determination of nominal interest rates. In the equation for the long-term rate with various lag lengths the "beta" coefficient for price level changes is nearly three times as large as for real GNP, which ranks second in importance.

Sargent's expanded model was also tested with monthly data, using, alternatively, per-

[41] Sargent obtained negative coefficients in all of his regressions. In his theoretical model he assumed that only saving was functionally related to the level of real GNP.

[42] The equation was also estimated for various lengths of total lags without the current rate of price level change (all of Sargent's regressions were of this form) to try to reduce multicollinearity. With total lags of 16 quarters, the sum of the coefficients on the lagged price changes

$$\left(\sum_{i=o}^{n} a_{i+1}\right)$$

rose slightly, $\beta_1$ and $\beta_2$ remained about the same, $\beta_3$ declined in absolute value by about 10 per cent, and the $R^2$ and Durbin-Watson statistics rose slightly.

sonal income deflated by the consumer price index and the index of industrial production as proxies for the real GNP (a series derived from the regression using the latter appears in Chart 7 as "real" rate 3). The results closely paralleled those for the equations using quarterly data. For example, in the equation for the long-term rate with a total lag of 48 months, the index of industrial production as the real GNP proxy, and a constant term (which was significant in the monthly regressions), the sum of the price change coefficients fell from 0.87 to 0.82, the mean lag rose slightly from 15.6 to 16.4 months, and the $R^2$ went from 0.968 to 0.971.[43] The change in industrial production and the change in the real money supply had the correct signs but were not significant; one month is probably too short a period to capture the full "Wicksell (liquidity) effect." The level of industrial production turned out to be quite significant, but the coefficients were smaller than in the quarterly regressions, suggesting that the response of the equilibrium "real" rate of interest to real income growth may occur over a substantially longer period than the current month.[44]

Thus, the findings reported in this section appear to support the specification of variables in Sargent's model. The use of quarterly and monthly data over post-accord period and the estimation of Almon lags provide better statistical results than in his study. The importance of price level changes in explaining nominal interest rates is diluted very little by the expanded equations, and the mean lags are not sufficiently lengthened to alter the conclusions of the earlier sections of the present study.

### Experimental Time Series for the "Real" Rate of Interest

The Federal Reserve Bank of St. Louis began calculating and publishing an experimental monthly series for the expected "real" rate of return on Corporate Aaa bonds in 1966.[45] The procedure employed was to subtract from the actual Aaa yield a simple average of rates of change in the implicit GNP price deflator for the previous twelve months (quarterly price deflator data were interpolated to obtain an estimated monthly index). Such a procedure necessarily implies that the mean lag is half as long (six months) as the total lag and that the coefficients are constrained to sum to one.[46] Shortly afterward the lag for averaging price changes was extended to 24 months (mean lag of 12 months), and the resulting proxy for the "real" rate has been reported periodically ever since. As a testimonial to the intuition of the series' creator, the distributed lag results in the present study yield estimates of the magnitude of effect and the mean lag which are remarkably close to the original "real" rate series.

Chart 7 contains the nominal corporate Aaa yield from 1960 to October 1969 and various estimated monthly "real" rate series. "Real" rate 1 is the original series, that is, the nominal rate minus the average of rates of price change over the preceding two years. "Real" rate 2 is obtained from the regression using monthly data for 1961-69, total lags of 48 months, and second-degree polynomials. "Real" rate 3 is derived from the regression reported in the preceding section,

[43] Results using personal income deflated by the consumer price index were virtually identical to those using the index of industrial production as the proxy for real GNP.

[44] It should also be noted that there is another possible source of mis-specification in all of the expanded equations, namely, the interrelationship between changes in the nominal money stock and both price levels and rates of change. In other words, the monetary authorities would be expected to respond to departures from stable prices. One way around this problem is to make the policy variable endogenous in a simultaneously estimated model containing a "reaction function" for the Federal Reserve (see Michael W. Keran and Christopher T. Babb, "An Explanation of Federal Reserve Actions (1933–68)," this *Review,* July 1969, pp. 7–20; and Raymond G. Torto, "An Endogenous Treatment of the Federal Reserve System in a Macro-Econometric Model," unpublished dissertation, Boston College, 1969.

[45] "Strong Total Demand, Rising Interest Rates, and Continued Availability of Credit," this *Review,* August 1966, pp. 3 and 4.

[46] Mathematically,

$$\dot{P}_t^e = \sum_{i=1}^{n} \frac{1}{n} \dot{P}_{t-i}$$

where $n$ is the length of the total lag, and there are exactly $n$ coefficients, each of which equals $1/n$ (hence, the sum is $n \cdot 1/n = 1$). Moving averages with equal weights are discussed by Griliches, p. 25.

which seeks to explain the contribution of "real" rates, as well as price expectations to nominal rates of interest; "real" rates here are assumed to be related to the level of and changes in the index of industrial production and changes in the deflated money stock.

Detailed analysis of the movements in these series will require a separate study.[47] Only a few observations will be made here. The pattern of movement in all three "real" rate series is remarkably similar. The old "real" rate 1, however, appears to have overstated the price expectations component of the nominal rate over most of the period. What is of particular interest are the occasions when changes in nominal rates gave apparently false signals about the nature of changes in "real" rates and the extent of agreement about directions of movement among the three "real" rate series.

All three "real" rates indicated that credit conditions were progressively tighter during the first half of 1961, when the nominal rate was virtually unchanged. The nominal rate was a reasonably good proxy for "real" rates 2 and 3 during 1962 but not for "real" rate 1, which rose for most of the year (the consequence of heavier implicit weights than the other two series on price changes two years earlier and lighter weights on the past year). The gradual upward creep in prices from 1963-65 caused "real" rate 1 to creep smoothly downward, generally opposite in direction to the nominal rate. With the different pattern of weights, movements in the "real" rates 2 and 3 were more pronounced, indicating that underlying price level changes were not entirely smooth over the interval.

"Real" rates 1 and 2 fell and "real" rate 3 oscillated around a constant level during the first half of 1966, while the nominal rate rose. From late 1966 until early 1967, all rates moved down in step. From 1967-69, the original "real" rate 1 tended to drift downward and oscillate somewhat ambiguously, although the three "real" rate series fell before nominal rates declined in the summer of 1968.

"Real" rates 2 and 3 moved upward with the nominal rate from late 1968 until early 1969. For several months thereafter, nominal rates did not rise by enough to offset the effects of rapid inflation, with the consequence that the monthly "real" rates actually fell from about February until late in the summer. Such movement in "real" rates could be used to explain, in part, the strength of the 1969 surge in investment spending.

## Conclusions

Citing the findings by Gibson and Sargent of long lags in the forming of price expectations, Hendershott and Horwich recently argued:

> . . . Their experience contradicts the monetary voices in government, industry and the academy that proclaim, but do not demonstrate, that price level expectations, rather than real forces, are largely responsible for interest rate movements in this decade.[48]

In contrast, the present study has shown that, unlike the earlier historical periods on which most of the previous studies have been based, price level changes since 1952 have evidently come to have a prompt and substantial effect on price expectations and nominal interest rates. In addition, the total effect of price expectations on interest rates and the speed at which they are formed appear to have increased greatly since 1960. This conclusion is invariant to the form on the term of the flexible classes of distributed lags estimated. Most significant is the finding that price level changes, rather than "real" rates, account for nearly all the variation in nominal interest rates since 1961. Furthermore, the addition of variables to the regressions to account explicitly for the "real" rate components of nominal rates does not appreciably alter these findings.

The causes of price level changes over the period of the study have not been investigated. The primary concern has been to determine the extent to which nominal rate movements may be attributed to expectations about future rates of change in prices, so that nominal rates may consequently be adjusted to yield information about move-

[47] A variety of other monthly and quarterly "real" rate series have been computed, including short-term "real" rates.

[48] Hendershott and Horwich, "Appropriate Indicator," p. 44. Criticizing the earlier "St. Louis 'real' rate," they continue, "The Fisherian zeal of that institution would shock no one more than Irving Fisher, who himself stressed the fantastically long lags in the formation of price level expectations and their impact on interest rates in this country."

ments in underlying "real" rates.[49] The failure to make such an adjustment and the sole use of changes in nominal rates as indicators of monetary ease or tightness may on occasion give misleading information about the direction and the extent of movements in "real" rates. The importance of the Fisher effect to the controversy over appropriate monetary policy indicators has been succinctly stated by David Fand:

> . . . As we get closer to a world of high employment, and especially if interest rates and prices are both rising, the money stock may be a better (less misleading) indicator or target variable than [nominal] interest rates. Paradoxically, the current tendency to emphasize interest rates and to ignore changes in the money stock would seem more relevant to a society where interest rates and prices are falling while the money stock is constant, or rising at a lower rate than output.[50]

According to economic theory, changes in "real" rates should then reflect both shifts in the equilibrium relationship between real saving and investment and current capital market disequilibrium. Further, it is such "real" rate series that should be employed in studies of the term structure of interest rates and of the effects of international interest rate differentials on short- and long-term capital flows.

---

[49] An interesting attempt to "neutralize" interest rates with respect to the impact of movements toward or away from full employment was reported in Dennis R. Starleaf and James A. Stephenson, "A Suggested Solution to the Monetary Policy Indicator Problem: The Monetary Full Employment Interest Rate," *Journal of Finance,* September 1969, pp. 623–641. Unfortunately, the authors did not incorporate price level changes into their analysis, which is a serious deficiency in their work.

[50] David Fand, "Keynesian Monetary Theories, Stabilization Policy, and the Recent Inflation," *Journal of Money, Credit and Banking,* August 1969, p. 576.

# V | INDICATORS OF MONETARY POLICY

Evaluation of monetary policy first requires a description of policy, but, unfortunately, there is little agreement on how to describe or measure policy. While most economists may use the same words—e.g., expansionary, easy, restrictive, and tight—they assign different meanings to these terms. For the most part, the terms summarize changes in one or more economic variables. But all economists do not examine the same variables, and even if they did, they might interpret these changes differently. A particular change in interest rates, for example, may be considered to reflect either an expansionary or a restrictive monetary policy depending on the frame of reference used.

Disagreements in describing policy arise because of insufficient knowledge of the structure of the economy. In a world of perfect knowledge where all the interrelationships among economic variables are known with precision, identification of the nature of a policy would not be a serious problem. All variables would indicate the same policy to all observers. Moreover, one could assess current policy simply by asking the policy maker his intent.

In the absence of perfect knowledge, however, different variables can project different signals, and different interpretations can be given the same signal. Because the structure of the economy is not perfectly known, the intended objective of the policy maker may not be attained. In such a scenario, identification of one or more variables that indicate the posture of monetary policy with minimum likelihood of error is crucial.[1] Most economists restrict their choice of indicator variables to either one or more financial yields—the Treasury bill rate, the Treasury bond rate, the corporate bond rate, the equity yield, and market rates adjusted for price expectations (see part IV)—or to one or more monetary aggregates—various measures of the money stock, bank credit, liquid assets, and bank reserves. Part V contains evidence on the usefulness of various suggested indicators of monetary policy.

The initial article by Guttentag describes and evaluates the recent strategy of Federal Reserve open-market operations. He discusses in particular the implications of uncertainty about the structure of the

[1] Use of variables as indicators should be differentiated from their use as intermediate targets for open-market operations. Intermediate targets are necessary because the chain of causation from policy action to the ultimate targets of policy is long and the speed of transmission of a policy action along this chain is slow. Thus policy makers find it useful to direct their operations at one or more variables closer to their control. The problem of selecting an appropriate intermediate target is discussed in part III.

economy for the behavior of policy makers. Mitchell, member of the Board of Governors of the Federal Reserve System, discusses the difficulties in conducting and evaluating monetary policy in an environment of uncertainty and cautions against accepting any single economic variable as the Rosetta stone for interpreting Federal Reserve actions. Brunner and Meltzer and Saving develop criteria for the optimal policy indicator under conditions of uncertainty and conduct preliminary conceptual tests to evaluate the appropriateness of variables frequently used as indicators. They find that monetary aggregates satisfy the criteria better than either interest rates or bank reserve positions.[2] Horwich and Hendershott disagree with the criteria and tests applied by the preceding authors. Instead, they propose a measure of money supply that reflects only noncyclically induced monetary actions, not all monetary actions. They also hesitate to discard interest rates as an appropriate indicator.

---

[2] The results of simple empirical tests of alternative indicator variables within the same framework are reported in George G. Kaufman, "Indicators of Monetary Policy: Theory and Evidence," *National Banking Review* (June, 1967), pp. 481–491.

# 28 | THE STRATEGY OF OPEN MARKET OPERATIONS*

JACK M. GUTTENTAG
*University of Pennsylvania*

The view is gaining ground that there is something wrong with the procedures used in open market operations. These procedures have recently come under academic attack, largely on the grounds that they do not provide firm control over the money supply, and they have also been subjected to soul-searching within the Federal Reserve (some minor modifications have been introduced since 1960). I do not believe, however, that the crux of the difficulty, as opposed to its myriad symptoms, is well understood.

Confusion regarding procedures has stemmed partly from lack of a conceptual framework for examining open market operations, and partly from a lack of explicit and detailed knowledge regarding the procedures actually employed. The concept of an "open market strategy" is introduced in Section I and used in Section II to describe and assess the "money market strategy," which was used exclusively during 1953–60 and in modified form thereafter. The main weakness of the strategy, and this is the main argument of the paper, is its incompleteness, i.e., the fact that the Federal Open Market Committee (FOMC) does not set specific quantitative target values, for which it would hold itself accountable, for the money supply, long-term interest rates, or any other "strategic variable" that could serve as connecting link between open market operations and system objectives; rather it tends to rationalize the behavior of these variables after the fact. This results in innumerable problems including inadvertent changes in long-term interest rates and in the money supply. Section III compares my proposal for a complete strategy with some alternative proposals, while Section IV considers modifications in strategy that have actually occurred since 1960.

## I. The Concept of Open Market Strategy[1]

The deliberations of the Federal Open Market Committee culminate in an instruction given either to itself or to the manager of the System Open Market Account at the Federal Reserve Bank of New York. An instruction includes open market *targets* and *constraints.* A target is something the FOMC aims at, while a constraint is a limiting value of something else the Committee is concerned with. The time period to which the target value applies is the control period. For example, if the Committee instructs the manager to hit weekly average free reserves of $100 million subject to the proviso that 90-day bill rates at daily closings are not to fall below 3 per cent, then free reserves are a target, 90-day bill rates are a constraint, and the control periods are a week and day,

* Reprinted from the *Quarterly Journal of Economics,* vol. 80 (February, 1966), pp. 1–30, by permission of the author and the President and Fellows of Harvard College.

[1] The concept of an open market strategy, which is the author's and not the Federal Reserve's, is used both to describe and to evaluate open market procedures. The purpose will be evident from the context.

respectively. An *open market strategy* can be considered the set of open market targets, constraints, and control periods that is being employed at any one time.[2]

Open market strategy should be distinguished from *policy formulation*. The latter is the process of setting specific values ("dial-settings") for open market targets and constraints. The factors consulted by the FOMC in setting open market target dials can be considered *policy determinants*. Whereas only a small number of targets can figure in an open market strategy, the number of possible policy determinants is almost limitless.

An open market strategy may include several targets having control periods of different length. For example, one possible strategy would include a nonborrowed reserve target on a weekly basis (total reserves less borrowing from the Reserve Banks), total reserves on a monthly basis, and total commercial bank credit on a quarterly basis. The ordering is in terms of the extent to which the targets are under open market control.

Several characteristics of a good strategy may be noted (others will emerge as we proceed).[3] First, a strategy should have no more than one target for a given control period. The function of the target is to facilitate control over the next target in the sequence, and the one target that is best for this purpose should be used. Second, targets and constraints should be precise and quantifiable. Third, it should be possible to relate the final target in the strategy—the one with the longest control period—empirically to the system's objective(s) (say GNP). If this is not possible, the strategy is "incomplete."

There are no doubt a number of strategies that would meet these specifications including liquid asset strategies (the final target is some measure of the public's liquidity position), and long-term interest rate strategies. No attempt is made here to appraise the various alternatives, despite the obvious importance of this question. A rational choice would be heavily influenced (though not exclusively determined) by one's views on the mechanism through which monetary policy affects the economy—a subject on which there is no consensus within the profession.

The Federal Reserve cannot, on the other hand, avoid using *some* open market strategy. For various reasons that will be developed later the Federal Reserve prefers not to face up to this. As a result, the strategy employed has been obscure and difficult to unravel. Still, it must be unraveled if it is to be fairly appraised.

## II. The Money Market Strategy

The open market strategy described below is a hypothetical construct. In addition to published sources, it is based on a study of the official minutes of the Federal Open Market Committee and its Executive Committee during the period 1951–60, which were recently made available to the public;[4] and on the author's own observations and experience inside the Federal Reserve.[5] The conceptions offered are consistent with a wide range of public statements in official and quasi-official publications, some of which will be cited.[6] In good part, however, the real test of the conception is its usefulness in making order

[2] Under some conditions a strategy would also specify *routes*, namely, the maturity range within which purchases or sales are to be made. Until 1961, however, this element of strategy was frozen by the "bills only" policy. This policy has been thoroughly raked over in the literature and will not be examined in this paper.

[3] A good strategy, it may be noted, is no guarantee of good policy any more than a bad strategy precludes it. An appropriate analogy is to formal organizational structure in a large institution. A sound organization encourages and facilitates effective decision-making while a poor structure creates unnecessary roadblocks and distractions.

[4] Federal Open Market Committee, *Minutes of the Committee 1936–1960, and its Executive Committee, 1936–1955* (hereafter cited as *Minutes*), The National Archives, Washington: 1964 (microfilm).

[5] The writer was an economist at the Federal Reserve Bank of New York during the period 1954–1962.

[6] Among the more revealing of the official or quasi-official sources are: Joint Economic Committee, *Review of Annual Report of the Federal Reserve System for the Year 1960*, Replies of the Board of Governors to Questions of Chairman Patman, pp. 147–161; Frederick L. Deming, "Monetary Policy Objectives and Guides," paper delivered at the Commercial and Central Banking Seminar, Chapel Hill, North Carolina, August 28, 1963 (mimeo); Peter M. Keir (and others), "The Open Market Policy Process," *Federal Reserve Bulletin*, Oct. 1963, pp. 1359–1370; Albert R. Koch, "An Approach to Monetary Policy Formulation," *Business Review*, Federal Reserve Bank of Philadelphia, Feb. 1965; Guy E.

out of seeming chaos. The construct differs from a recent attempt in the same direction by Brunner and Meltzer[7] in its focus on operational aspects, i.e., on what the system does rather than on the views of system spokesmen regarding monetary theory and the causal processes through which open market operations affect the economy. These views sometimes have little relationship to open market strategy.[8]

### A. Open Market Targets

Under the money market strategy the principal open market target is the condition of the money market. This is evident from the published record of Committee meetings,[9] from the comments (as reported in Committee minutes) of the Board Chairman, whose "consensus"—customarily given at the close of a meeting—is a sort of instruction; and from the reports to the Committee of the manager of the System Open Market Account on operations transacted during the period between meetings.[10] The last is, indeed, the crucial evidence, since targets are in the final analysis what the manager understands them to be.[11]

By market condition is meant the complex of interest rates on short-term claims—usually ranging from overnight credit (federal funds) to three-month Treasury bills—and the availability of credit in the different segments of the market at quoted rates. It must be emphasized that it is the condition of the *entire market* that is the target. Since the market as a whole is something of an abstraction, it is usually defined qualitatively in terms of various degrees of "ease" or "tightness." The control period is variable, ranging from one day to several weeks.

Actual assessment of market condition is based on a wide range of quantitative and other information: by the complex of quoted rates; by member bank free reserves (excess reserves less borrowing from the Reserve Banks), which are correlated with short-term interest rates; by statistical data on the financial position of market participants; and by direct communication with such participants (or with sources who themselves have contact with them), sometimes called the "feel of the market." One very important element in the feel of the market is the report of nonbank government securities dealers to the trading desk at the New York Reserve Bank regarding the availability to them of overnight financing for carrying their portfolios.

Noyes, "Short-Run Objectives of Monetary Policy," *Review of Economics and Statistics,* XLV (Supplement: Feb. 1963), 147–149; Robert V. Roosa, *Federal Reserve Operations in the Money and Government Securities Markets,* Federal Reserve Bank of New York, 1956; Robert G. Rouse, "Implementation of the Policies of the Federal Open Market Committee," *Monthly Review,* Federal Reserve Bank of New York, Vol. 43 (July 1961); Frank W. Schiff, "Statistical Guides to Monetary Policy," paper delivered at the Seventh Meeting of the Central Bank Technicians of the American Continent, Oct. 1963 (mimeo); Peter D. Sternlight and Robert Lindsay, "The Significance and Limitations of Free Reserves," *Monthly Review,* Federal Reserve Bank of New York, Vol. 40 (Nov. 1958); Robert W. Stone, "Federal Reserve Open Market Operations in 1962," *Federal Reserve Bulletin,* April 1963; Robert W. Stone, "Review of Open Market Operations in Domestic Securities (1963)," in Board of Governors of the Federal Reserve System, *Fiftieth Annual Report,* 1963; and R. A. Young, "Tools and Processes of Monetary Policy," in *United States Monetary Policy,* American Assembly (Durham, N.C., 1958). Many of these are recent and reflect a growing concern within the Federal Reserve regarding some of the issues dealt with in this paper. Other aspects of this concern are noted in Section IV.

7 Karl Brunner and Allan H. Meltzer, *Some General Features of the Federal Reserve's Approach to Policy,* a Staff Analysis for the Subcommittee on Domestic Finance of the House Committee on Banking and Currency, Feb. 10, 1964; in the same series, *The Federal Reserve's Attachment to the Free Reserve Concept,* May 7, 1964; and *An Alternative Approach to the Monetary Mechanism,* August 17, 1964.

8 The expressed view that open market operations affect GNP by influencing, say, variable $x$, may or may not mean that the FOMC issues instructions to achieve specific values of variable $x$.

9 For example the record of the June 17, 1958 meeting notes ". . . that for the next three weeks no action should be taken to cause the tone of the market to get materially easier or tighter" (1958 *Annual Report of the Board of Governors,* p. 52).

10 An explicit published statement on targets by the account manager during 1953–1961 will be found in Rouse, *op. cit.*

11 This is not inevitable, since the Committee could issue instructions to itself that included targets with longer control periods than those included in its instructions to the manager. But under the money market strategy it does not do this.

Free reserves have a dual function in the strategy.[12] First, the measure is a quantitative proxy for money market conditions. It is, in fact, the only gauge of market condition that is both quantifiable and considered generally indicative of the condition of the money market as a whole. Despite the fact that it is imperfectly correlated with overall market condition, therefore, it plays a key proxy role in the money market strategy. Second, free reserves are employed as an independent target; discussion of this function will be deferred until later.[13]

### *B. Money Market Condition and Free Reserves*

The proxy role of free reserves in the money market strategy can be illustrated with a model that assumes that there is an interest rate relevant to the abstract money market. The banks' demand for free reserves $(F)$ and the public's demand for deposits $(D)$ are assumed to be functions of this rate $(r)$; the volume of nonborrowed reserves $(N)$ and the reserve ratio $(k)$ are controlled by the Federal Reserve, the first by open market operations and the second by fiat; and the supply of deposits $(S)$ is derived from $k$, $N$ and $F$.

$$F = f(r)$$

$$D = g(r)$$

$$S = \frac{1}{k}(N-F)$$

A geometrical representation of the model is shown in Figure 1. Note that since each supply curve is drawn with reference to a fixed amount of nonborrowed reserves, movements along a supply curve imply changes in free reserves. Each supply curve implies a unique schedule of desired free reserves, shown in the right-hand panel, but the reverse is the case only for specified levels of nonborrowed reserves.

Suppose, now, that no direct information is available on the actual money market rate (which is the case) but the Committee has some desired rate in mind (say, $R_1$ in Figure 1), and also knows the function $F$. It will then instruct the manager to achieve free reserves of $F_1$ which is the level associated with the desired rate. In this way free reserves serve as proxy for the condition of the abstract money market.

The Committee's judgment regarding the function $F$ is based on the relationship between free reserves and the degree of market ease or tightness (as indicated by other measures) in the recent past—perhaps over the three weeks prior to the Committee's regular meeting.

Ordinarily the Committee would not set a single free reserve value $(F_1)$ as a hard and fast target but as the midpoint of a range within which the manager may exercise discretion. Discussion at the Committee meeting may indicate, with varying degrees of explicitness, the magnitude of the target range.[14] One important determinant of the range is the Committee members' judgments regarding impending shifts in the level of free reserves associated with the desired condition of the money market. The range needed to maintain a steady market tone of $R_1$ in Figure 1 would be $F_2 - F_3$, for example, implying that desired free reserves are expected to fluctuate within the limits $F' - F''$.

Sometimes the account manager can employ the repurchase agreement as a sort of quasi-automatic mechanism for maintaining the desired condition of the money market in the face of shifts in desired free reserves. As indicated above, the availability of dealer financing is an important clue to market condition. If free reserves appear to be on target,

[12] Free reserves are referred to as "net borrowed reserves" when borrowing exceeds excess reserves. The earliest reference to free reserves in the Committee minutes is in the meeting of Oct. 6, 1953. During the prior two years or so borrowing from the Reserve Banks was used in a similar way.

[13] The control period for free reserves, whether viewed as proxy or independent target, is usually a statement week (Wednesday to Wednesday). Free reserves are much more loosely related to market condition and also much more difficult to control on a daily than on a weekly basis. With the exception of Wednesday figures, moreover, weekly average rather than daily figures are published and are widely used by the public to gauge the direction and intent of monetary policy. Hobert C. Carr, "Why and How to Read the Federal Reserve Statement," *The Journal of Finance,* XIV (Dec. 1959), 504–519.

[14] Actual ranges mentioned at Committee meetings during 1953–1960 run for the most part from \$50 million to \$380 million with a tendency to decline over the period probably due to the development of better reserve projections.

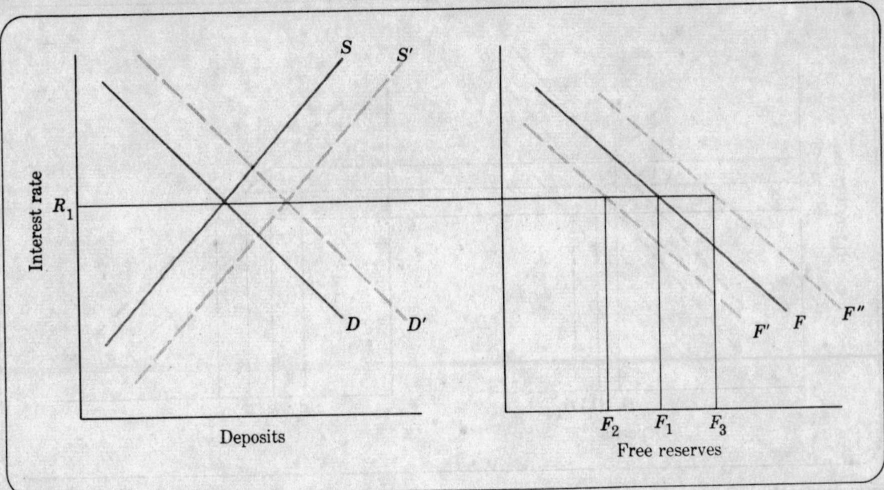


FIGURE 1

for example, but dealer financing is available under conditions that are more restrictive than is consistent with the desired money market tone, the desk may provide such financing under repurchase agreements, thus easing the pressure and raising free reserves above the target level. In the opposite case, dealers may exercise their option to repay outstanding repurchase agreements and free reserves will fall.

A second determinant of the free reserve target range is the magnitude of probable errors in reserve projections.[15] From the manager's vantage point, errors in the data are (*ex ante*) indistinguishable from shifts in desired free reserves, and he responds to them in the same way. Suppose, for example, that the target range is set $F_2 - F_3$ in Figure 1; that the reserve projections indicate that free reserves will be $F_1$ in the absence of open market operations; but that the manager discerns greater tightness than is normally associated with that free reserve level. He accordingly allows free reserves to rise to what is then projected as $F_3$. It is later revealed, when final data become available, that free reserves initially had been overestimated, that they would have amounted only to $F_2$ in the absence of operations, and actual free reserves turn out to be $F_1$ after all. This means that the open market purchases designed *ex ante* to raise free reserves served *ex post* to correct an error in the reserve projection.

A third determinant of the free reserve target range, which has the effect both of narrowing and blurring its limits, is the amount of discretion the Committee is prepared to delegate to the manager to "feel the market";[16] the wider the range the greater the discretion. The reluctance of some Committee members to delegate wide discretion

[15] Reserve data for the day on which operations are undertaken are projections that are subject to sizable errors. Toward the end of a statement week the manager has estimated actuals for earlier days in the week but even these sometimes undergo substantial revisions later.

[16] During 1953–1960 some Committee members opposed such delegation as a matter of principle. For example, ". . . he [Malcolm Bryan] would like to express the judgment that a directive to feel the market is not the sort of directive that a principal can appropriately give to his agent or that an agent can wisely accept from his principal." (*Minutes,* Dec. 7, 1954) And "Mr. Robertson said that he also believed that too much reliance on 'feel of the market' as seen in New York could be disastrous in the conduct of operations to carry out Committee policy. . . ." (*Minutes,* Oct. 22, 1957) The President of the Federal Reserve Bank of New York, on the other hand, tended to emphasize the need for granting the manager wide latitude.

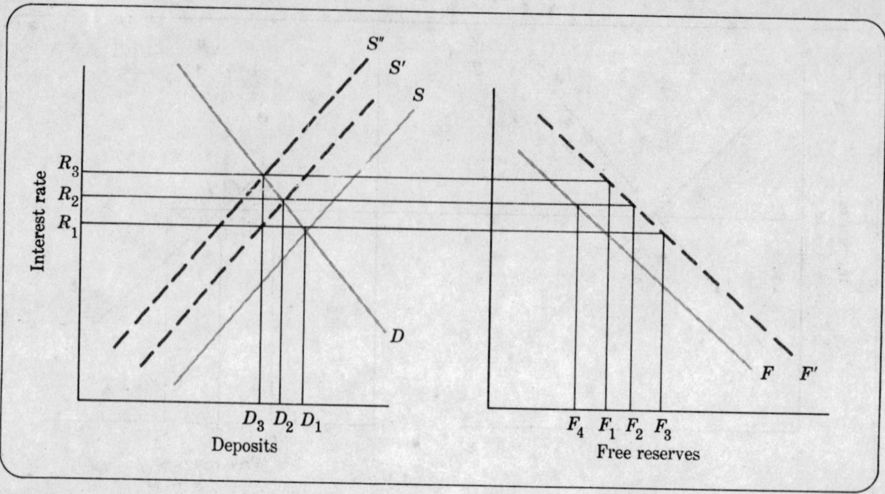


FIGURE 2

may result in a *de facto* free reserve target range narrower than the range required to maintain a constant market tone in the face of shifts in desired free reserves. Where this is the case free reserves become an independent target as well as a proxy for market condition.

### C. Treatment of Operating Transactions

The money market strategy implies that the account manager will offset changes in nonborrowed reserves from so-called "operating transactions" such as changes in currency in circulation, Federal Reserve float, Treasury gold transactions, and the like.[17] Use of a free reserve target implies such offsetting. If the target is $F_1$ in Figure 2, for example, and a drain of reserves from gold outflows would shift the supply curve from $S$ to $S'$, free reserves would fall from $F_1$ to $F_4$ unless the manager supplies enough reserves to hold the supply curve where it is. The largest part of system transactions reflects offsetting of this type. During the period 1954–1963 the Federal Reserve purchased $68 of securities for every $100 drained by net operating transactions on a weekly average basis (see Table 1); in 1962 and 1963 the figure was over $90.[18]

The treatment of operating transactions implied by the money market strategy marks a significant advance over the more primitive practice, signs of which were still evident in 1953, of issuing instructions in terms of purchases and sales.[19] The latter procedure requires the Committee to involve itself in the purely technical problem of projecting changes in reserves.

Open market operations for the purpose of offsetting operating transactions, which are often called "defensive," tend to stabilize the money market and also the flow of money and credit, since they moderate changes that would otherwise occur in total member bank reserves. The use of any reserve target, it may be noted, implies similar treatment of operating transactions, though the offset period could be different. Under the money market strategy the offset period is a week, comparable to the control period for free reserves.

### D. Treatment of Changes in Required Reserves

Under the money market strategy changes in required reserves are accommodated by the Federal Reserve.[20] Such accommodation

[17] See R. A. Young, *op. cit.*, p. 17.

[18] I am indebted to the Research Department of the Federal Reserve Bank of Philadelphia for these computations.

[19] By 1954 this practice had largely died out, due in good part to the efforts of Allan Sproul of the New York Reserve Bank.

[20] See Keir, *op. cit.*, p. 1365, and Koch, *op. cit.*, p. 6.

**TABLE 1. MULTIPLE REGRESSION, WEEKLY CHANGES IN FEDERAL RESERVE SECURITY HOLDINGS ON CHANGES IN REQUIRED RESERVES AND IN OPERATING TRANSACTIONS**

| | b – Coefficient | | Partial correlation coefficient | | |
|---|---|---|---|---|---|
| Year | RR | OT | RR | OT | $R^2$ |
| 1963 | .86 | –.95 | .90 | .98 | .96 |
| | (.07) | (.03) | | | |
| 1962 | .83 | –.92 | .86 | .97 | .94 |
| | (.07) | (.03) | | | |
| 1961 | .65 | –.75 | .67 | .91 | .82 |
| | (.10) | (.05) | | | |
| 1960 | .67 | –.71 | .58 | .82 | .66 |
| | (.13) | (.07) | | | |
| 1959 | .76 | –.63 | .75 | .84 | .71 |
| | (.10) | –(.06) | | | |
| 1958 | .84 | –.76 | .83 | .88 | .81 |
| | (.08) | –(.06) | | | |
| 1957 | .95 | –.41 | .71 | .68 | .58 |
| | (.13) | (.06) | | | |
| 1956 | .96 | –.55 | .66 | .70 | .50 |
| | (.16) | (.08) | | | |
| 1955 | .99 | –.52 | .58 | .70 | .47 |
| | (.20) | (.08) | | | |
| 1954 | .40 | –.24 | .34 | .35 | .12 |
| | (.16) | (.09) | | | |
| 1954–63 | .78 | –.68 | .64 | .81 | .67 |
| | (.04) | (.02) | | | |

SOURCE: Federal Reserve Bank of Philadelphia.
NOTE: Standard errors are in parentheses.

is implied by use of a free reserve target.[21]

[21] The open market purchases needed to hit a specified free reserve target are calculated as follows:

$$O = F_t - [F_a + \Delta OT - \Delta RR]$$

where $O$ = open market purchases
$F_t$ = target level of free reserves
$F_a$ = actual free reserves in the preceding period
$\Delta OT$ = the projected increase in nonborrowed reserves from operating transactions
$\Delta RR$ = the projected increase in required reserves (including those stemming from $\Delta OT$)

This aspect of the money market strategy is unique and has important implications.

1. MONEY MARKET STABILITY AND MONEY SUPPLY INSTABILITY. First, it implies short-run stabilization of free reserves and the money market but destabilization of the flow of money and credit. This is because accommodation of changes in required reserves is tantamount to accommodation of changes in the demand for deposits. If the free reserve target is $F_1$ in Figure 1, for example, and the demand for deposits increases from $D$ to $D'$, enough nonborrowed reserves would be pro-

vided to shift the supply curve from $S$ to $S'$. In effect the Federal Reserve allows nonborrowed reserves to increase by the amount of the rise in required reserves generated by the increase in deposits. Interest rates and free reserves remain unchanged, as the bulge in demand is accommodated by open market purchases.[22]

Changes in required reserves are a rough measure of the pressures that would impinge on banks to alter their free reserves in the absence of accommodation by the Federal Reserve. These changes are often substantially larger than even the largest policy-induced changes in free reserves. For example, during the period of sharp transition in policy from "ease" to "tightness" between mid-1958 and mid-1959, the average weekly change in free reserves between the beginning and end of the period was less than \$20 million per week. In contrast, the weekly changes in required reserves exceeded \$100 million in twenty-nine separate weeks and ranged up to \$440 million.

System accommodation of changes in required reserves moderates seasonal and erratic swings in short-term interest rates. Such stabilization has positive social value but its importance is hard to assess. Perhaps the most important beneficiary is the federal government, which would otherwise incur rate penalties when it sold large blocks of securities. The other side of the coin is that short-run instability in the money supply is given free play. The implications of this will be discussed in Section III *C* below.

2. BIASED RELATIONSHIP BETWEEN MONEY SUPPLY AND RESERVE BASE. Since under the money market strategy the Federal Reserve more or less automatically accommodates changes in the demand for deposits—in effect the system "feeds in" reserves as the banks demonstrate they are prepared to use them—an association is generated between actual changes in deposits and in nonborrowed reserves (or related reserve base measures). The result is a high statistical correlation found by Brunner and Meltzer and by Meigs between money supply and various reserve base measures. These high correlations are deceptive insofar as they are taken to imply the possibility of close short-run control over the money supply.

3. NEUTRALIZATION OF SHIFTS IN DEPOSIT MIX. Accommodation of changes in required reserves under the money market strategy implies that shifts in the demand deposit-time deposit mix have no effect on total deposits. A shift from demand deposits to time deposits, for example, tends, other things being equal, to release reserves because of the lower reserve requirement against time deposits, and in the absence of open market operations this would lead to additional bank credit expansion. Under the money market strategy, however, the system automatically absorbs these reserves.

The same result would be obtained, of course, through an equalization of reserve ratios against demand and time deposits, but so long as the reserve ratios differ this function of the strategy is desirable. I am inclined to believe that it has been of real, if unappreciated, value to the Federal Reserve in recent years when shifts in deposit mix have been quite pronounced. Time deposits grew very sharply during 1961, for example, following the decision by New York City banks to issue certificates of deposit, and also in early 1962 following the rise in the maximum allowable interest rate on time deposits under Regulation Q. There is no reason why shifts of this sort should influence the rate of growth of total deposits.[23]

### *E. Treatment of Changes in Desired Free Reserves*

As noted earlier, free reserves not only serve as a proxy for the condition of the money market but to some extent are an independent target. In part the independent role of free reserves reflects the preference of Committee members for a quantitative target, as well as a disinclination by some to delegate

---

[22] Complete stabilization of interest rates is an implication of the stock model used in this paper but Davis' flow model implies only partial stabilization. See Richard G. Davis, "Open Market Operations, Interest Rates and Deposit Growth," this *Journal*, LXXIX (Aug. 1965), 431–454.

[23] Shifts in deposit mix that reflect changes in the public's demand for real assets show up in other economic indicators (unemployment rate, GNP, etc.) and are taken into account in setting the dials on open market targets. This will be discussed further below.

authority to the manager to "feel the market." In part it reflects a presumed relationship of free reserves to the "degree of credit restraint."[24]

The independent and proxy roles involve the same open market operations in the face of changes in operating transactions and shifts in the demand for deposits, but divergent operations in the face of shifts in the demand for free reserves. Suppose, for example, desired free reserves in Figure 2 rise from $F$ to $F'$. The proxy role (wherein the initial free reserve target $F_1$ stood for rate $R_1$) implies open market purchases to raise free reserves to $F_3$ while the independent role implies open market sales to restore free reserves to $F_1$. The independent role implies a change in interest rates and deposits (to $R_3$ and $D_3$ in the example) while the proxy role does not.

It is not clear, either from my own observations, from the minutes or from the statistical data I have looked at, that either the proxy or independent role of free reserves has priority when desired free reserves shift. The money market strategy includes no operational criteria for determining the proper course of action, and the most likely result is *ad hoc* compromise. Compromise occurs automatically if the system does nothing. Passivity in face of the shift to $F'$ in Figure 2, for example, would involve a rise in free reserves and in interest rates to ($F_2$ and $R_2$), and a decline in deposits to $D_2$. An actual case is given further below.

### F. Policy Determinants

A policy determinant is anything that affects open market dial-settings. Three broad types of policy determinants may be distinguished. The most important, as is well known, is current data on business conditions—GNP, industrial production, price indices, unemployment and the like (including in recent years the balance of payments). This requires no elaboration here.

A second policy determinant, relevant only to marginal changes in policy, is the "market." The Committee minutes contain many references to "allowing" the market to ease or tighten from "natural" forces.[25] The Committee generally specifies the direction in which the change is to be tolerated. If an imminent recession is suspected, for example, the market will be allowed to ease but not to tighten.[26]

Under the money market strategy, strategic variables such as money supply, bank credit, long-term interest rates, etc., constitute a third set of policy determinants. The Committee may change the dial-settings toward greater ease, for example, if it feels the money supply is growing too slowly, or long-term rates are too high. The behavior of these variables is always reported and often discussed at Committee meetings. Yet the overwhelming impression gained from the Committee minutes is that these variables carry an effective weight close to zero. The basic reason is that typically the Committee does not hold firm views as to what constitutes appropriate behavior of these variables; within rather wide limits it is prepared to rationalize whatever behavior materializes.

Thus, under the money market strategy, the value of strategic variables is, within wide limits, indeterminate. Indeterminancy

---

24 It has never been clear whether this has meant the elasticity of the supply of bank credit function, or the rate of bank credit expansion. A tendency to confuse the two is pervasive in the published record of policy actions by the FOMC. On the other hand, a clear recognition of the distinction is found in some official sources (the articles by Keir, and by Sternlight and Lindsay for example). The minutes suggest that most Committee members have thought in terms of elasticity.

25 "Chairman Martin expressed the view that any overt action on the part of the System in either direction would be unfortunate at this time. However, he felt that the Account Management might look toward a lower level of net borrowed reserves when that level was coming about from natural sources and could be avoided only by sales from the System Account portfolio." (*Minutes,* April 20, 1960)

26 Assuming the dynamic factor at work in the market is a change in the demand for deposits, this procedure might be rationalized on the grounds that current data on business conditions provide insufficient basis for, say, easing policy but a movement toward ease by the market, if it occurred, would provide sufficient additional evidence that business conditions had weakened, as to warrant the policy shift. If the dynamic factor at work in the market is a shift in desired free reserves, however, the procedure is indefensible, although it is better than following free reserves. References to "natural" forces in the minutes do not distinguish changes in the demand for deposits from changes in desired free reserves.

| 1959 | Average rate on three-month Treasury bills (percent) | Average level of free reserves (millions of dollars) | Seasonally adjusted change in money supply (billions of dollars) |
|---|---|---|---|
| July | 3.24 | −556 | .8 |
| August | 3.36 | −536 | −.5 |
| September | 4.00 | −493 | −.3 |
| October | 4.12 | −459 | −.4 |
| November | 4.21 | −433 | −.1 |
| December | 4.57 | −424 | −.7 |

SOURCE: *Federal Reserve Bulletins*

implies the possibility of inadvertent (unplanned) changes in these variables in response to irrelevant causes, i.e., developments that are unrelated to the appropriate values of these variables. A shift in the banks' desired level of free reserves is such a development.[27]

Monetary policy during the second half of 1959, which was widely criticized for being too tight, is probably a good example. There is reason to believe that the sharp rise in interest rates and contraction in money supply during this period was at least partly inadvertent, the result of a change in desired free reserves.[28] Each of three regression equations used by A. James Meigs to explain free reserves shows a drop in the "predicted" ratio during this period,[29] while actual free reserves were rising, indicating that the desired free reserve function was drifting to the right.[30] In the face of this shift, the system "compromised" by allowing free reserves to rise and the money market to tighten (see table).[31]

[27] The problem is analogous to that of a fractional reserve banking system with *no* central bank, where the total money supply is influenced by developments affecting the public's desired composition of money as between deposits and currency.

[28] The problem of indeterminancy may be distinguished from loss of control, where the limits of the Committee's indifference are exceeded. The 1959 decline in money supply was tolerated by the Committee with misgivings. By February 1960, however, a majority of the Committee had swung to the view that the money supply decline should be arrested, yet for a number of reasons it was unable to accomplish this objective (see IV below). For a short period the money supply was out of control.

[29] Free reserve levels calculated from Meigs's equations T35 and T36 are charted in his *Free Reserves and the Money Supply* (Chicago: University of Chicago Press, 1962), p. 75, and the levels calculated from his T34 are in Giorgio Basevi, "Vault Cash and the Shift in the Desired Level of Free Reserves," *Journal of Political Economy,* LXXI (Aug. 1963), 411.

[30] Cyclical changes in desired free reserves may reflect persistent changes in the opposite direction in bank portfolio liquidity. The liquidation of government securities and expansion of loans during 1959 pushed loan-deposit ratios progressively higher during the year to levels banks had not experienced since the 1920's.

[31] I am not suggesting that the rise in desired free reserves was the sole factor working toward higher interest rates during this period; credit demands also were rising. The point is that if the Federal Reserve is maintaining a "steady policy" (under the money market strategy), as it claimed to be doing during the latter part of 1959, a rise in credit demands will be largely accommodated and a sharp rise in interest rates avoided by keeping free reserves steady, as explained earlier. To the extent that the dynamic influence on rates is a rise in desired free reserves, however, the system can prevent rates from rising only by allowing free reserves to rise. My argument is that the rise in free reserves needed to prevent a run-up in rates in late 1959 far exceeded the increase that the FOMC would have considered consistent with its "steady policy." It thus allowed rate increases much larger than those it would have tolerated if the upward pressure on rates had originated elsewhere than with the banks.

There is no evidence in the published record or in the Committee minutes of an explicit rationale for this compromise, the system describing its posture during this period as one of "steady pressure."[32] Similarly, there is no indication in the official minutes that the Federal Reserve intended the money supply to decline. On the contrary, toward the end of the year some Committee members became concerned about the decline in money supply, but policy was not changed.[33]

### G. *Communications and Internal Controls*

A Federal Reserve "insider" has noted, with regard to certain parts of my description of the mechanics of the money market strategy, that it is "my interpretation," implying that there is room for other interpretations. This is correct and it is also revealing. It bespeaks a looseness of the strategy as one of its hallmarks. A good strategy is not subject to different interpretations.

Ambiguity in the strategy arises from the following sources:

*1.* Free reserves have an ambiguous role, as noted above.

*2.* The words used in the first instance to define current policy are imprecise.

Chairman Martin referred to Mr. Rouse's comment that the market had been "tight but not too tight," and he enquired whether it would also be correct to say that it had been "easy but not too easy."

Mr. Rouse responded that this statement also would apply.[34]

*3.* Even if a given set of words always meant some well-understood condition of the money market, they could not have the divisibility and precise ordering that is characteristic of numbers.[35]

*4.* The underlying reality to which the words refer is not completely clear. "The" money market is a series of individual submarkets which, although closely interrelated, are also partially segmented. On a weekly average basis rates on federal funds and on 90-day Treasury bills, for example, often diverge sharply.[36] Free reserves would be only partially satisfactory as a proxy for the overall condition of the money market, even if it were used solely and explicity for this purpose.

*5.* "Market developments" or "natural forces" are sometimes allowed to effect open market dial-settings without specification as to the source of such developments.

Ambiguity inherent in the money market strategy generates a problem of communicating policy to the public. Analysts interested in something more precise than words—which are not regularly available on a current basis in any case—have naturally seized upon free reserves. It has been the only quantitative expression of the FOMC's objectives and it is available to the public in a weekly press release. System spokesmen complain intermittently that free reserves are unduly

---

[32] The uneasy nature of the compromise is suggested by the following explanation in the *1959 Annual Report of the Federal Reserve Bank of New York* (p. 28): "In the face of divergence between statistical indications of somewhat reduced pressures on reserves and the fact of continued tightness in the money markets, the System sought, through its open market operations, to keep the tone of these markets from changing significantly in either direction."

[33] In late November "Chairman Martin said he shared some of the apprehension that had been expressed about the money supply and the relationship of credit to growth, but he did not believe this was the time to correct it." (*Minutes,* Nov. 24, 1959) And in the following month the Chairman noted that ". . . the System is doing well . . . This was not in any sense to say that the Committee should disregard Mr. Mills' basic point regarding the quantity of the money supply. Personally, he did not know just how to measure the money supply . . . he was unable to make heads or tails of the money supply on either a quantitative or a qualitative basis." (*Minutes,* Dec. 15, 1959)

[34] *Minutes,* Jan. 25, 1955.

[35] Very ingenious semantic devices have been employed to denote the fine gradations called for by a flexible policy. For example, a favorite terminological tactic to indicate finer gradations of policy within broad categories of ease or restraint is to leave the basic nomenclature unchanged but to add that "doubts are to be resolved on the side of ease (or restraint)." The task is essentially hopeless, however, since there are more policies than words to describe them.

[36] Robert W. Stone, "Federal Reserve Open Market Operations in 1962," *op. cit.*, p. 431; and Board of Governors of the Federal Reserve System, *The Federal Funds Market* (Washington, 1959), p. 103.

emphasized by the public but the complaints are futile so long as they offer the public nothing else.[37]

Ambiguity also generates a problem of accountability within the Federal Reserve. Since the instruction to the manager of the System Open Market Account is loose, it is difficult for the FOMC to hold him to account for carrying it out. Brunner and Meltzer have argued that the result of this has been that the manager has himself often introduced policy changes which have subsequently been ratified by the Committee.[38] My own impression is that this does not happen. It is prevented by periodic detailed reports required of the manager, and by close over-the-shoulder surveillance of the manager's actions by the Committee and by senior Board staff.

This method of control, however, is extremely clumsy, requiring that the Committee or its staff involve itself to some extent in day-to-day developments, and that the manager spend a great deal of time on reports to the Committee. These reports, moreover, do not provide as valuable a flowback of information as they might because of their generally defensive tone and their ambiguities. They are defensive to the extent that the manager, not being sure exactly what the Committee wants him to do, finds it necessary to convince the Committee that what he did was what they wanted. The reports are ambiguous to the extent that the original instruction to the manager is ambiguous.[39]

### *H. The Organization of Knowledge for Use in Policy Formulation*

Since the money market strategy does not include any targets that can be related empirically to Federal Reserve objectives, the FOMC has no analytical framework for translating the complex of factors consulted in policy formulation into an open market directive. The translation is a matter of "art."

The scope and volume of information employed in this process, including special research projects on problems of current concern, is truly impressive. Difficulty arises in using this material not because it is short-run (as Brunner and Meltzer allege),[40] but because there is no explicit procedure for tying it all together. In effect each of the myriad pieces of data and research reports is sorted into one of three piles: a pile that argues for more ease, a pile that argues for more restraint and a pile that argues for no change (or does not argue at all; as I noted above, this is almost always true of information on strategic variables). The weights attached to the items in the piles exist in the minds of the Committee members and it is no exaggeration to say that there are as many systems of weights as there are members.

### *I. Foundations of the Money Market Strategy*

Meigs and Brunner and Meltzer attribute the system's operational procedures to a particular intellectual conception of the monetary process; practice follows theory. They term this conception the "free reserve (or

[37] Chairman Martin has stated publicly that he rues the day that data on free reserves were first published. Joint Economic Committee, *January 1963 Economic Report to the President. Hearings,* January 28 to February 6, 1963, Part I, p. 357.

[38] See (*The Federal Reserve's Attachment to the Free Reserve Concept, op. cit.*, pp. 31–50). Brunner and Meltzer base their view on the supposed finding that ". . . movements of free reserves quite frequently precede rather than follow decision of the FOMC." Their interpretation of this evidence is, however, largely impressionistic. No criteria are presented for distinguishing turning points in free reserves from random variations, and no justification is provided for comparing turning points in free reserves with the date of "major" policy changes rather than with the earliest date of a policy change. The finding that free reserves change "in advance of the decision by the FOMC" at five of six cyclical turning points, for example, is reduced to two of six if the earliest date of a policy change is used. Nor is account taken of the proxy role of free reserves, whereby the manager may allow free reserves to change in order to maintain a given tone of the money market.

[39] It is natural and a type of poetic justice that the words used by the Committee in giving instructions to the manager are thrown back to the Committee. If the Committee instructs him to follow an "even keel tipped on the side of ease," for example, he can report back that he "maintained an even keel. . . ." and the Committee is not in a position to complain that it does not understand what these words mean.

[40] See *Some General Features of the Federal Reserve's Approach to Policy, op. cit.*, p. 10.

reserve position) doctrine" and trace its origins back to the 1920's.[41]

System experience during this early period indicated that borrowed and nonborrowed reserves were inversely correlated—when the system sold securities the banks repaid borrowings—while the volume of borrowed reserves was directly related to short-term interest rates. The Federal Reserve thus found it could influence short-term rates by controlling the volume of borrowed reserves through open market operations, and Riefler, Burgess and others articulated this into a theory of open market control.

A more detailed historical study than has yet been made would be necessary to determine whether the money market strategy as it developed in the 1950's owes very much to the monetary doctrines of the 1920's, or whether the strategy is largely a "rediscovery" under roughly similar conditions. In either case, the money market strategy has certain "advantages" to the central bank relative to alternative strategies that are not often appreciated by outsiders, and which the system is loath to relinquish.

*1.* The money market strategy stabilizes the money market, and the Federal Reserve values such stability.[42] In part this reflects the system's heritage (underlying one of its stated purposes, the provision of an "elastic currency," was the strongly felt need to moderate seasonal swings in interest rates). In part, concern with stability reflects a tendency to be solicitous of the market's welfare, perhaps because the system depends upon the market so heavily.[43]

*2.* The money market strategy provides targets that can be employed over very short periods, which is the first priority for an institution that lives in the short run. The system's front line exposure to sizable short-run fluctuations in the demand for deposits suggests that such measures as money supply, bank credit and even total reserves are unsuitable as short control-period targets.[44] The system is convinced, and no evidence has ever been presented to the contrary, that the attempt to control such variables in the short run would accomplish nothing (except to destabilize the market). This does not explain why the system does not set target values for money or any other strategic variable over longer control periods.

*3.* The main reason is that a more complete strategy would widen the range of system commitments, potential "failures" and exposure to external attack. The money market strategy minimizes the system's commitments, and maximizes its apparent wisdom. By not setting explicit longer-run targets for anything, the Federal Reserve can appear to "take account of everything." Maximum opportunity is afforded (in *Annual Reports,* for example) to shift emphasis from one strategic variable (say money stock) to another (say bank credit) after the fact, depending on hindsight assessment of their behavior during the period.[45]

The system's propensity to minimize commitments while appearing retrospectively all-wise gives it a sort of vested interest in obscuring its strategy. As one small but revealing piece of evidence, the word "tar-

[41] See Brunner and Meltzer, *The Federal Reserve's Attachment to the Free Reserve Concept,* pp. 2–10; and Meigs, *op. cit.*, pp. 7–14.

[42] See Koch, *op. cit.*, p. 5.

[43] This solicitude was, of course, much in evidence in the controversy over "bills only." Dr. Grinzberg of the Institute for the Study of Institutional Psychopathology suggests that the system's attitude toward the government securities market has striking parallels to that of a "certain type of Jewish mother who is not averse to finding her boy a little sick because it means she can feed him chicken soup."

[44] Prior to 1960 money supply data pertained to one day a month (the last Wednesday) and the time series of such data were extremely erratic and difficult to use. Because of large intra-monthly fluctuations, the one-day series sometimes sent out false signals for three or four months running. Revisions were sometimes quite sizable, moreover, and on at least one occasion—in 1957—revisions altered the direction of movement of the series for a period of seven months. In 1960 the one-day series was replaced by the much-improved daily average series. Bank credit data, however, have always been on a one-day basis.

[45] The Federal Reserve has often been criticized for being more concerned with "credit" than with "money." It is true that in *Annual Reports* and other *ex post* analyses of Federal Reserve policy credit usually takes up more pages. I suspect, however, that this merely reflects the fact that credit lends itself to sectoral disaggregation (there is more to write about). From an operational point of view, neither credit nor money is used as a target, and neither carries any significant weight as a policy determinant.

get" is anathema to the Federal Reserve; I have never seen it in an official published document. My proposal for a complete strategy necessarily overrides this unsavory feature of the money market strategy.

## III. Recommendations for Procedural Change

### *A. Toward a Complete Strategy*

The central weakness of the money market strategy is that it is incomplete; the basic targets of the strategy cannot be related to system objectives. As a matter of emphasis my recommendation for a complete strategy stops short of specifying its form. There appears to be much support in academic circles for a money supply strategy, but other plausible possibilities exist and in the last analysis it may not make much difference which is chosen. Only one complete strategy is needed.

A complete strategy would not replace the money market strategy; rather it would enlarge upon it by adding additional target variables with longer control periods. A money supply strategy, for example, might look something like the following:

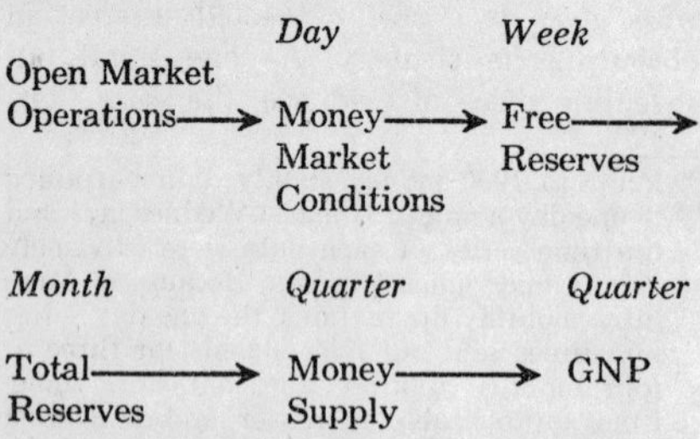


A complete strategy would accomplish the following:

*1.* It would force the FOMC to formulate views regarding appropriate behavior of the strategic variable included in the strategy and to ask why deviations had risen, when they did arise, between target and realized levels. The strategic variable in the strategy would no longer be indeterminate, and changes in desired free reserves could no longer influence policy.

*2.* It would resolve the problem of communications and internal accountability. Policy would be defined quantitatively in terms of the longest-run target included in the strategy. Over-the-shoulder surveillance by the FOMC of day-to-day operations could be relaxed since these operations would be constrained by the necessity of hitting the longer-run target.

*3.* It would provide an analytical framework for bringing directly to bear on policy formulation the immense flow of information available to the Federal Reserve. Though it is doubtful that the element of art can ever be eliminated from policy formulation, an effort should be made gradually to reduce its scope in favor of analytical procedures. The adoption of a complete strategy would focus the powerful intellectual and informational resources of the Federal Reserve on *the* relevant question: What value of the longer-run target variable included in the strategy should be sought in order to accomplish system objectives?

This proposal may be compared with some other recent suggestions for the reform of open market procedures.

### *B. Scrap Free Reserves*

The reform that appears to command almost universal assent is that free reserves (as a guide, target, theory, or whatever) should be scrapped in favor of some reserve base measure.[46] This is based largely on the finding that free reserves have a much lower degree of correlation with the money supply than do various reserve base measures.

Accepting for argument's sake the assumption that a money supply strategy is desirable, this recommendation is nevertheless based on a series of misconceptions.

46 See the studies by Brunner and Meltzer, cited above, and William G. Dewald, "Free Reserves, Total Reserves and Monetary Control, *Journal of Political Economy,* LXXI (April 1963), 141–153. By a peculiar quirk of fate academic economists discovered free reserves about the time the Federal Reserve abandoned "bills only," and the former bids fair to replace the latter as a focal point of academic criticism. Some good samples are found in the 1964 Patman Hearings, for example, the comments by O. H. Brownlee and Dudley Johnson (House Committee on Banking and Currency, *The Federal Reserve System after Fifty Years, Hearings,* Feb. 11–Mar. 25, 1964, Vol. 2, pp. 1062 and 1439).

TABLE 2. $R^2$, MONEY SUPPLY AND RELATED MONETARY FLOWS ON FREE RESERVES AND OTHER MONEY MARKET MEASURES JANUARY, 1953 – AUGUST, 1963

| | Independent variables | | |
|---|---|---|---|
| | Free reserves | | Distributed free reserves and bill rate-discount rate differential |
| Dependent variables | 3 Month | 12 Month | 12 Month |
| Money Supply | .30 | .19 | .51 |
| Money Supply plus Time Deposits | .38 | .50 | .70 |
| Required Reserves | .30 | .58 | .63 |
| Bank Credit | .44 | .62 | .77 |

SOURCE: Richard G. Davis.

NOTE: Dependent variables in three-month and twelve-month equations are three-month averages of monthly per cent changes (seasonally adjusted data), and per cent changes over corresponding months in previous year (unadjusted data) respectively. Independent variables are monthly levels and twelve-month average levels respectively. Distributed free reserves involve three separate variables for central reserve city, reserve city and country banks. All $R^2$'s are significant at the 99 per cent level.

*1.* It is implicitly assumed that free reserves and reserve base targets are exclusive alternatives. For a given control period this is the case—only by coincidence would targets for each be mutually consistent. There is nothing inconsistent, however, about using them both as targets for control periods of different length. Using free reserves as a short-run target retains the stabilizing feature of the money market strategy.[47]

[47] It may be wondered why the use of a seasonally adjusted total reserve target would not also stabilize the market and obviate the need for free reserves. First, the seasonal in desired free reserves is not fully or even correctly registered in total reserve series that cover the period when the Federal Reserve was using a money market strategy. Second, although seasonal changes in the demand for deposits are registered in the series, weekly seasonal factors (which are needed to stabilize the market) are inherently crude because of the shifting dates of Treasury financings, corporate tax payments, and the like. Third, erratic changes in the demand for deposits are not registered in the seasonals. The seasonally-adjusted total reserve target could, of course, be adjusted on a current *ad hoc* basis to take account of erratic changes and shifting seasonals, but this would in effect convert it into a free reserve target. For example, if a total reserve target is adjusted to accommodate an erratic rise in the demand for deposits, the impact of this demand on required reserves must be estimated, and this additional amount provided to the banks, which is exactly what is done in maintaining a free reserve target.

*2.* It is not clear that free reserves would be less effective than a reserve base measure in controlling money (the latter could turn out to be a fifth wheel in a money supply strategy). Studies by Meigs and Brunner and Meltzer show that the relationship of free reserves to money supply is very low on a monthly basis, but they do not show that such short-run control of the money supply is necessary. If the appropriate control period for money is three months or longer, the available evidence regarding the best method of control is inconclusive. When money supply is regressed on free reserves and other money market measures using three-month and twelve-month data, quite respectable coefficients are generated (see Table 2).[48] Coefficients obtained from regres-

[48] I am indebted to Richard G. Davis for these data. Davis' data indicate that it is possible to generate negligible coefficients of multiple determination between free reserves and money *only* by using monthly unadjusted data, or by including the pre-accord period in the computations. All the tests used by Brunner and Meltzer in examining the "modified free reserve doctrine" did one or the other (*The Federal Reserve's Attachment to the Free Reserve Concept, op. cit.*, pp. 56–62). In testing their alternative hypothesis, however, (the "modified base conception" advanced in *An Alternative Approach to the Monetary Mechanism*) they employ annual changes between corresponding quarters of adjacent years, a procedure that would have generated much higher coefficients for the "modified free reserve doctrine" if they had used it.

sions in which money is related to reserve base measures are usually higher but because of the accommodation aspect of the money market strategy (see Section II D above), they are subject to an upward bias of unknown extent.

This is not to extol free reserves but simply to indicate that existing research provides little real basis for choosing between free reserves or some reserve base measure as the best intermediate target for controlling money. Additional research is needed on the relevant control period for money supply; on possible disaggregation of money into more easily predictable components;[49] on the degree of system control over the independent variables included in existing regressions; and on the pattern of errors generated by the relationships. Emphasis on statistical regressions tends to obscure the fact that the system may be able to "improve on the fit" operationally by progressively adjusting its short-run targets to take account of errors as they unfold.[50]

### C. Reduce the Volume of "Defensive" Operations[51]

Some observers feel that system policy would be more effective if the volume of reversible open market operations was sharply reduced. In most cases this view is based on the suspicion that these operations simply do not accomplish anything, and may be distracting. Robertson refers to "... a great deal of monkeying around in the marketplace for very little net effect."[52] But Brunner and Meltzer make the more serious charge "that the so-called defensive operations ... impart substantial variation to the changes in money supply."[53] If they are right, a cessation of defensive operations would free the system from short-run distractions, and stabilize money and credit. My view, in contrast, is that the Federal Reserve accommodates variability in the demand for deposits and in the money stock but does not cause it.

The regressions of weekly changes in system securities holdings on changes in required reserves and in operating transactions, shown in Table 1, shed some light on this. If changes in required reserves originate mainly on the demand side, the coefficient for required reserves, assuming system accommodation is incomplete,[54] should be less than 1.0. If system operations are the main cause of short-run instability in required reserves, on the other hand, the coefficient for required reserves should be greater than 1.0. This is because a rise in required reserves resulting from open market operations cannot exceed, and on a weekly basis would almost certainly fall short of, the reserves provided through open market operations. The coefficient for the period 1954–63 was .78 and the

---

[49] The currency component of money, for example, is not related to free reserves but can be predicted quite closely using other approaches. (See Irving Aurbach, "Forecasting Currency in Circulation," Federal Reserve Bank of New York, *Monthly Review*, Feb. 1964). Similarly, some work I have done relating free reserves to various components of bank credit growth indicates that the relationship with investments is substantially higher than the relationship with loans.

[50] Autocorrelated errors provide scope for such adjustments. If errors are random and unpredictable, of course, the system cannot improve on the fit but the degree of its control will increase as the time period lengthens.

[51] The term "defensive" in this context can be taken to mean both offsets to operating transactions and accommodation of changes in required reserves. It is not clear whether or not Roosa, who coined the term, meant it to embrace accommodation operations (see *Federal Reserve Operations in the Money and Government Securities Markets, op. cit.*, p. 76).

[52] *The Federal Reserve System after Fifty Years,* p. 1358. Similar objections are found in Joseph Asehheim, "Financial Intermediaries and the Goals of Monetary Policy," *American Economic Review*, Papers and Proceedings LIII (May 1963), 360–371; and Albert H. Cox, Jr., and Ralph F. Leach, "Defensive Open Market Operations and the Reserve Settlement Periods of Member Banks," *The Journal of Finance,* XIX (Mar. 1964), 76–93.

[53] *An Alternative Approach to the Monetary Mechanism, op. cit.*, p. 44. See also *ibid.*, p. 82, and *The Federal Reserve's Attachment to the Free Reserve Concept, op. cit.*, p. 55.

[54] This assumption cannot be proved but its intuitive plausibility is supported by the fact that the coefficient for operating transactions is less than 1.0. Since the system only partially offsets changes in reserves from operating transactions, it is highly unlikely that it would fully accommodate changes in required reserves.

standard error .04.[55] The coefficients were less than 1.0 in every one of the ten years calculated separately.[56]

If short-run variability in money stems from the demand side of the market, a cessation of accommodation operations would accomplish little or nothing. The "noise" generated by transient fluctuations in demand is no less distracting when the system sits on the sidelines than when it engages in accommodation operations. The system cannot eliminate the noise; what it can and should do is set itself a clear signal to listen for through the noise, in the form of longer-run targets.

By the same token, a policy of nonaccommodation would not lead to any significantly greater stability in money and credit, since the pressures now eased through open market operations would impinge on the discount window. Recognizing this, Brunner and Meltzer would impose stability on money and the reserve base by using the discount window for accommodation purposes (at a penalty rate), while *offsetting* the resulting defensive changes in borrowed reserves using open market operations.[57] Paradoxically enough, the volume of reversible open market operations required to smooth out the reserve base and money supply could be many times larger than that now required for accommodation purposes, while marked short-run fluctuations in interest rates and credit availability would be reintroduced by the agency created to eliminate them. There is no evidence that such constant whipsawing of the market is necessary to assure Federal Reserve control of the money supply.

### D. Research on the Monetary Mechanism

Brunner and Meltzer attribute much of the shortcomings of monetary policy to the Federal Reserve System's failure to understand how the money supply is determined and to provide a meaningful theoretical conception of the process. This allegation has some truth, but it is much too indiscriminate.

*1.* The system *has* shamefully neglected research on problems central to its concern, including the mechanism of money supply determination. Indications are that this is now being rectified.

*2.* Nevertheless, research on the best method of controlling money clearly is subordinate to the question of whether money should be controlled. I suspect that the system knows enough now to control the money supply over periods of reasonable length if it were prepared to set money supply targets. The customary assumption of monetary theory, that the central bank controls the money supply, has been incorrect more because the system has not had the intention to do so, than because it has not had the technical know-how.

*3.* The system is properly subject to criticism for not having an explicit and complete open market strategy, but the precise nature of that strategy remains an open question. Brunner and Meltzer provide no evidence for their insistence that the money supply is the only strategic variable worth considering.

*4.* Ambiguity in the system's monetary theory reflects conflicting views on the channels of monetary influence within the economics profession, and should not be taken too seriously. So long as there are alternative theories of respectable lineage, we should expect a public agency in its own theoretical statements to cultivate the black art of double meanings. But this is no defense of an ambiguous open market strategy. We should be lenient of ambiguity in the system's monetary theory but intolerant of ambiguity in its open market strategy.

---

55 The results are not conclusive, however, since I cannot rule out possible bias in the coefficient. One possible source of bias is changes in desired free reserves, which can affect both required reserves and open market operations. If the Federal Reserve was passive in the face of a shift in the banks' demand for free reserves, the coefficient for required reserves would not be affected. System operations either to stabilize the market or to stabilize free reserves, however, would affect the coefficient.

56 Brunner and Meltzer cite a negative correlation between changes in the money supply in one month with changes in the preceding month as evidence supporting their view that the Federal Reserve causes instability (*The Federal Reserve's Attachment to the Free Reserve Concept, op. cit.*, p. 55). In my view this merely reflects the general reversibility of short-run changes in demand, which is part of the justification for a policy of short-run accommodation.

57 *An Alternative Approach to the Monetary Mechanism, op. cit.*, pp. 89–91.

## IV. Recent Tendencies in Open Market Strategy

The minutes of the FOMC reveal that in 1960 the Committee was in ferment over procedures. The precipitating factor was the Committee's growing belief that the decline in the money supply that had begun in mid-1959 should be brought to a halt and its seeming inability to accomplish this objective.[58] Malcolm Bryan, President of the Atlanta Reserve Bank, who had long pressed for the use of a total reserve target, argued that

> By inadvertence we have not done what we intended. It does not seem to me in the slightest accurate to say that a single one of us, in the last two and one-half months, has wanted to enforce an actual diminution of the money supply or to effect an actual diminution of the seasonally adjusted reserves of the banking system.[59]

Long an isolated voice, Bryan now found strong support from, among others, Delos Johns of the St. Louis Bank. The time had come, in his opinion, for the Committee to subordinate its consideration of net borrowed reserves and other money market pressures to objectives expressed in terms of total reserves or the money supply. He did not mean to say that the Committee thereby would have adopted a system that would assure the avoidance of mistakes, but the use of such a technique would help to avoid doing things to total reserves and money that the Committee did not intend.[60]

### A. The "Discovery" of Reserve Flows

The 1960 episode resulted in considerable soul-searching within the Federal Reserve and to re-examination of long-held preconceptions.[61] The most important tangible consequence was a heightened interest in reserve flows and their incorporation into open market strategy. In May 1960 the manager of the System Open Market Account

[58] The reason the money supply continued to decline in the face of an easing in policy is the subject of another paper. In brief, upper turning points in general (and the 1960 one in particular) are associated with a decline in the demand for demand deposits. (The effect of this decline on money supply swamps an expansionary tendency from a shift to the left in the desired free reserve function.) Whether very substantial countermeasures by the Federal Reserve could avert the decline is not clear but it *is* clear that very rigorous action is not in fact taken. This lack of action reflects the FOMC's propensity for gradualism. Conflicting views on policy by individual Committee members, which are especially likely around turning points, must be compromised. (In 1960 particularly, a tendency for caution was natural in view of the fact that the first steps toward ease were taken well before the cyclical peak in May.) Gradualism means small changes in policy, which implies small changes in the targets included in open market strategy. Since money supply is not included, the FOMC finds it difficult to make the large changes in free reserves needed to prevent the money supply decline without appearing to contradict the prior decision to change policy only slightly. It is doubtful that the Committee's expressed concern over the money supply in 1960 had any impact at all on open market dial-settings. Realization of this by the Committee was, indeed, the main stimulus for changing procedures.

[59] *Minutes,* Mar. 22, 1960.

[60] *Ibid.* In addition to the *Minutes* valuable information on the 1960 episode is contained in *Review of Annual Report of the Federal Reserve System for the Year 1960,* cited above. It was fortuitous that the Joint Economic Committee investigation of a number of issues connected with the Board of Governors' *Annual Report* happened to focus on the 1960 *Report.* In a critical memorandum on the Report to Chairman Patman, John Gurley noted reference in the record of FOMC policy actions to the "disappointing" behavior of the money supply during 1960 (*ibid.,* pp. 116–117). This led Gurley to raise a number of relevant questions regarding implementation procedures, the replies to which (*ibid.,* pp. 147–161) are revealing as to the thinking of the Board Staff at that time.

[61] Brunner and Meltzer, in discussing answers given by the Presidents of the Reserve Banks and the Board of Governors to a questionnaire on open market policy and procedures submitted by them in August 1963, noted that "These statements when read in detail, seem to suggest that some earlier criticisms of Federal Reserve pronouncements made in this report are not applicable to the present FOMC. . . . The replies suggest that the Federal Reserve has abandoned, perhaps recently, much of the previous analysis of the monetary process that has been criticized here." (*The Federal Reserve's Attachment to the Free Reserve Concept, op. cit.,* p. 25) These replies present Federal Reserve thinking in 1963 as if it had been held since time immemorial. This is perhaps an appropriate counterploy to Brunner and Meltzer's technique of using 1963 insights to criticize Federal Reserve statements enunciated ten years and even earlier.

began for the first time to report current data on total reserves and nonborrowed reserves to the FOMC.[62] A great deal of technical statistical work began on these series and a new synthetic series termed "available reserves" was developed.[63] This series began to appear in FOMC policy directives beginning December 19, 1961.[64]

Instructions to the account manager continue to run in terms of free reserves and the condition of the money market (including bill rates), but the Committee sets rough growth objectives for available reserves which have appeared in its formal policy directives.[65] The desk keeps these measures under surveillance on a weekly basis and deviations from the desired growth rate are brought to the Committee's attention for possible adjustment of the short-run targets. The Committee, however, continues to view the condition of the money market as the primary target.

[62] *Minutes,* May 24, 1960.

[63] Available reserves consist of seasonally-adjusted required reserves held against private deposits plus total excess reserves unadjusted. In the July 1963 *Federal Reserve Bulletin* a number of other reserve flow series were published in seasonally-adjusted form for the first time.

[64] Noyes, *op. cit.*, p. 148.

[65] This paper must pass quickly over a second development in open market strategy which is much better known and which affects my main thesis only marginally. This is the emergence in 1960 of the balance-of-payments problem as a matter of policy concern, and the abandonment of "bills-only" in early 1961. While these developments were widely interpreted to mean that the system would aim at reducing long-term rates while holding up short-term rates ("operation twist"), neither long rates nor short rates have become an open market target. Rather short-term rates, specifically the three-month Treasury bill rate, have become a *constraint* while purchases of long-term securities have been made for the purpose of meeting reserve targets without forcing short-term rates below constraint levels (see Stone, "Federal Reserve Open Market Operations in 1962," *op. cit.*, p. 432; and Deming, *op. cit.*, p. 11). One might expect that the increasing importance of a specific segment of the money market (along with increasing emphasis on reserve flows) would result in a corresponding de-emphasis of the abstract money market; but the 1962 and 1963 records of FOMC policy actions indicate quite clearly that this is not the case.

The "discovery" of reserve flows has been associated with an extraordinary concern over possible overemphasis of free reserves. System spokesmen have joined academicians in criticizing the measure and they have gone to great pains to emphasize that the Federal Reserve does not rely on free reserves exclusively or even primarily.[66]

The adoption of a reserve flow target is a reform of questionable value. Available reserves cannot be related to GNP, and therefore open market strategy remains incomplete. True, the use of available reserves (or any of several related measures) reduces the probability that the FOMC will lose control of the money supply. The problem of money supply control, however, arises only when the Committee knows what it wants the money supply to do, and, judging from the 1953–60 record, this is the exception rather than the rule. If the Committee does not have an explicit objective for money supply (or related measures), available reserves are of no help. The development of a reserve flow strategy might, of course, be viewed as a stepping stone toward a money supply or related strategy but the Federal Reserve has placed the cart before the horse.

### B. Why Not All the Way?

The system is manifestly reluctant to go all the way. It has three objections that should be squarely faced:[67]

[66] For example, see Harry Brandt, "Controlling Reserves," *Monthly Review,* Federal Reserve Bank of Atlanta, Sept. 1963. This concern over free reserves was nothing new. The FOMC minutes reveal that the Committee began to worry about free reserves as they came to rely on them, and by 1957 its general attitude had become strongly ambivalent. The Committee did not like the measure but it didn't know how to do without it. "Chairman Martin stated that he still considered the limitations of the net borrowed reserve figures to be too great to make them of use as more than a target. . . .!" (*Minutes,* Oct. 10, 1957, my exclamation point.) It was not until 1960 that the system's concern over free reserves came to focus on its relationship to money supply growth. In earlier years the Committee's concern was largely that free reserves were not a reliable indicator of money market condition.

[67] Several of these are strongly hinted at by Koch, *op. cit.*

First, it is argued that the Federal Reserve should not restrict itself to consideration of one or a few strategic variables; rather it should be eclectic and take account of many. The tendency to make a virtue of eclecticism, however, is based on confusion between policy formulation and open market strategy. (The money market strategy breeds this confusion as noted earlier.) Some amount of eclecticism might be a virtue in formulating policy; the amount of information that the FOMC can fruitfully consider is limited only by its ability to sift, analyze and weigh. But ultimately an instruction must be issued and it cannot be eclectic (it can, of course, be ambiguous).[68]

Second, it is argued that even if the system wanted to restrict itself to one final target, it would not know which specific one to choose (a public agency should not play favorites). This reluctance to declare for one specific final target among the competing alternatives rests on the illusion that the system can choose *not* to have such a target. This alas is not the case. If open market strategy does not include any long-control period targets, then the short-run targets become the long-run targets as well. Nor is there point in being immobilized in choosing between, say, money supply including and excluding time deposits, since the empirical relationships employed to implement the strategy would be based on the specific concept used. When two bridge sites appear equally plausible, one is nevertheless chosen.

[68] One good indication of this confusion is the system's firmly held view that it is essential that the manager attend meetings of the FOMC. "To assist him in carrying out the necessary operations, the manager has the benefit of the full discussion at the meeting at which a policy decision is reached" (*Review of Annual Report of the Federal Reserve System for the Year 1960,* p. 149). In my view the manager should be barred from meetings except to report on operations. In this way the Committee would force itself to issue a clear instruction.

Third, it is argued that even if the system made a choice it would have little or no basis for setting quantitative target values. Would it not be prudent to hold off until better empirical bridges are built? No. Open market strategy is based on *some* presumption regarding the relationship of final targets to GNP. If we know all too little about the relationship of GNP to, say, money supply, we know much less about its relationship to free reserves, money market condition or available reserves. The choice of a strategy, furthermore, is a vital stepping stone toward the development of the empirical relationships needed to implement it; it provides both the focus and the incentive for research effort. The history of the money market strategy suggests that so long as the system is not committed it will build no empirical bridges.

## V. Concluding Comment

The real barrier to the adoption of a complete strategy is largely psychological. The Federal Reserve would have to relinquish the illusion that it "takes account of everything," while exposing its real objectives nakedly to public scrutiny. This could be risky. There is much unreasonable hostility to monetary policy to begin with, and it is likely that in some cases further exposure would merely invite more vigorous attack. My own view, however, is that this would be more than offset by heightened support and help from other (and particularly academic) quarters. The Federal Reserve inadvertently encourages a great deal of hostility by failing to provide constructive outlets to monetary economists on the outside—most of whom view the Federal Reserve as "their" institution and would like to identify with it if they could. Let the system shout "5 per cent in the second quarter," and I suspect that much hostile and irrelevant carping would be rechanneled into pertinent econometric and other analytical exercises.

# 29 | MONITORING MONETARY POLICY*

GEORGE W. MITCHELL
*Board of Governors of the Federal Reserve System*

Monetary policy deals most directly with banks, financial markets, credit flows and interest rates. To monitor its course, its ebbs and flows, one should, therefore, observe the state of banking and the tone of the money and capital markets, noting the flows and yields on funds that the economy is using.

J. P. Morgan once voiced the best forecast ever made for a financial market. "It will fluctuate!" was his prediction. No doubt many of you, drawing on recent experience-hardened judgment, would be willing to add some impressive dimensions to that cautious platitude. For recent experience has driven home anew to all financial officials two expensive lessons: not only can prices and yields in our money and financial markets fluctuate, they have fluctuated, and very widely on occasion. Further, these fluctuations, whether within the day, the month, or the year, are extraordinarily difficult to predict and, thereby, to anticipate when portfolio decisions are made.

Security prices necessarily mirror the changing flows in the demand for, or supply of, credit funds. But as a practical matter, these changing demand and supply influences are only inadequately and tardily apprehended by present-day public economic intelligence systems.

As a consequence, every shred of additional public and private evidence about money flows is sought by professional market participants and reporters of the financial press at the earliest possible moment. Their purpose is to evaluate such evidence in the least possible time and to inform their principals, clients or the financial community at large, and thus to aid portfolio managers in establishing market positions from which profits are most likely to be maximized or losses to be minimized.

These analysts must also have a feel for the general course or trend of the "real" economy—whether it is expanding, stagnant or receding, whether it has under-utilized manpower and capital resources or is fully employed, whether it suffers from inadequate demand and hence is subject to deflationary tendencies, or whether from exececssive demand and so is experiencing inflationary pressures.

In attaining their ends, financial managers rely on a wide range of financial instruments and maturities and the arbitraging mechanism of money and capital markets. In doing so, they try to anticipate security price and yield changes and trends as closely as possible.

One of the elements in understanding the operation of this very complicated financial system is the role of the Federal Reserve. That role is to serve as a marginal source of supply of market funds—to a small extent directly in the Government securities market,

---

* Speech presented to the New Hampshire Bankers Association, Whitefield, New Hampshire, October 14, 1966. Reprinted by permission of the author.

but to a much larger extent indirectly, as commercial banks pyramid their loans and investments and deposits on the basis of the reserve credit which the System has furnished. Accordingly, what the Federal Reserve is doing by way of supplying funds or what it will do, under some assumption of market conditions, is a common query among professional traders and speculators. Even a few small, innocent-appearing clues can give the knowledgeable market participant a "leg up" on his less well-posted counterpart.

Over the years the System has developed a method of communicating with the market which is as straightforward, accurate and objective as quantitative relationships can make it. It is a "you see it as we do it" policy. A weekly financial statement is released to the public every Thursday afternoon, showing a detailed breakdown of System assets and liabilities as of the close of business the preceding Wednesday. These statements are supplemented by weekly and monthly releases, reporting changes in aggregate commercial bank assets and liabilities. From these data one can ascertain if the System is replacing gold with bills or bonds; if it is expanding or contracting Reserve Bank credit and commercial bank reserves; to what degree the discount window is being used; how the banking system is responding to available investing opportunities, and so forth.

Now it is true there are no adjectives, no judgments and no explanations of present actions or inaction in these financial statements and reports; nor are there tips, predictions, threats or promises of future action. Nor, given our present state of knowledge, does it seem desirable or appropriate that there should be.

The time may come when analytic capacity built into a commodious computer will enable market analysts to identify, quantify and date the demands for and supplies of goods and services and flows of funds, and to work out the effect of arbitraging time and market alternatives. Such a program might also assimilate the feedback from alterations in future business and financial expectations and indicate an appropriate course for monetary policy. When, and perhaps if, operations research practically achieves this control over the data and accompanying business and financial decisions, I have no doubt it can also reveal the current shade of tightness, ease, or neutrality in monetary posture to market participants and further suggest what the Federal Reserve ought to be doing next. This is probably as close to functional obsolescence as either monetary or portfolio managers would ever care to get.

Regardless of what the future may make possible by way of communication between the Federal Reserve and market participants it seems clear to me that the present flow of quantitative data on current banking operations, and the economy generally, provides enough information, supplemented by occasional interpretive comments, for professionals to function effectively within tolerable limits of financial risk. And most of these quantitative facts can be made available without prejudicing to a significant degree future monetary policy decisions.

Two additional types of information are frequently sought from the participants in money management: one has to do with the rationale of current policy—what are the economic factors and assumptions with respect to financial behavior that underlie current policy? The other has to do with the likely course of future policy. Not only the Federal Reserve System but central bankers everywhere have continuing difficulty with these informational requests.

Historically, the solution to both types of questions at most central banks has been "no comment" and the prevalence of this policy gave rise to the tradition of "tight-lippedness" which has long been associated with central bankers. The Federal Reserve, in its annual reports to Congress, in hearings before Congressional Committees, and in the official records maintained on meetings of the Board and Federal Open Market Committee has endeavored to provide as complete a record of policy decisions and considerations leading up to them as is practicable.

The policy record in the Annual Report, for example, carefully summarizes the economic and financial background of each action taken. No written document, however, can accurately record why each of seven Governors on the Board or each of twelve members of the Open Market Committee voted for a given course of action. The reasons enumerated are relevant but unweighted. The assumptions with respect to linkage among monetary variables are often vaguely stated because the state of our economic, financial and monetary knowledge does not, at times, permit greater precision. Semantic compromise unavoidably runs all through the record, not only because the same words have different meanings to different people in the unexact business of monetary management but also because decisions have to be made and semantic compromises are of less consequence than substantive concessions.

Reasons are important and it is reassuring to be able, in retrospect, to know that the monetary managers were often right for the right reason. But it must always be borne in mind that our facts are sometimes limited or our theoretical framework for certain situations deficient and, under these circumstances, rather than be wrong it is better to be right for the wrong reason and admit that intuition, "market sense" or luck saved the day.

The informant who alleges he has an inside look at a central bank's prospective monetary posture is convicted by his own ignorance. However he comes by his information it can hardly include all the caveats, the qualifications, and amendments needed to raise gossip to the level of speculation. As monetary policy is made today, no one knows how soon or how much economic events, financial conditions, or expectations will modify the current thrust of policy. Monetary management works through markets and decisions that are exceptionally sensitive to changing environment. As a consequence, monetary management itself is exceptionally flexible and responsive to market conditions and pschology; it could hardly be otherwise.

My remarks have been directed at communications with the business and financial community. The related problem of communication with the general public, not covered here, is certainly no less important. However, that problem does not seem to me to involve the same measure of technical difficulty. The public's concern is mainly for a timely and certain understanding of the broad and evident thrust of System policy. This is readily met by the System's official announcements and press releases and from the wide coverage of monetary developments in the nation's news media.

Some monetary analysts say that the best view of the changing monetary scene does not come from observing the tone and feel of the money and capital markets, or from following the trend and churning of interest rates. Nor, they say, can it be found by sifting through the masses of daily, weekly or monthly banking data, however carefully and selectively. Among these observers are a few who contend that it does little good to listen to what the Federal Reserve says or thinks it is doing because its methods of communication are too often too obscure. And coming to the end of the line, there are those who believe that the System itself is unaware of its monetary moves and, hence, can hardly describe them adequately to others.

To what monetary monitoring measures do these analysts (and others) look for an indication of the direction and force of monetary policy? Among the measures used none is more widely observed, if not deified, than changes in the active money supply—(currency and demand deposits)—and which for convenience I will call M-1.

As a measure of monetary action, M-1 has a long tradition in theory and academic respectability. It is simple to understand, to compute, to graph. It is verifiable and has the ring of authenticity. And even for those who do not accept the quantity theory of money, it can be a good first or second approximation to variables they regard as more significant. It is theoretically plausible if not overexposed to a close examination of its quantitative and generative relationship to goals sought by the monetary authority. Moreover, it has variants devised by disciples who probably have actually improved the original gospel, or at least better adapted it to our present financial structure and system.

One of these variants, which I will call M-2, adds time deposits at commercial banks to the currency and demand deposits included in M-1. Impressed with the fact that there is little to distinguish time deposits at commercial banks from shares at savings and loan associations, deposits at mutual savings banks or short-term money market instruments, other students have suggested that the relevant definition of money should cover a whole family of near-money aggregates. Thus, they would extend the definition to include some or all of deposits in savings and loan associations, mutual savings banks, credit unions, policy loans at insurance companies, short-term marketable securities of the U.S. Government and its agencies, short-term municipal securities, short-term corporate securities, Euro-dollars, and so on. We can refer to the broadest of such definitions as M-x.

These expanding definitions of money share, to decreasing extent, a characteristic that only money, narrowly defined, has to the nth degree, that quality so essential for transactions use—namely, instant liquidity. And near-monies which more and more have taken over the store of value function of money can usually be converted into M-1 without delay or significant loss. It is the ability of our intermediaries and security markets to effect such conversions that imparts monetary significance to M-x.

Without any doubt, recent years in the United States have seen an enormous shift from the use of money narrowly defined (M-1) toward the use of money broadly defined (M-x), i.e., including income-yielding financial assets or time deposits. This conceptual shift is evident in the financial management of individuals, corporations, and governments. At least in the United States, money in the narrow sense of the word is being reduced closer and closer to the simple role of a transactor or medium of exchange. And this trend is about to be greatly accelerated by the computerization of the entire money settlement process.

The over-all statistics of money stock and money use have long revealed an economizing trend. Today, turnover of private demand deposits in New York City metropolitan area is twice weekly, more than double the levels prevailing in a period of high economic activity a decade ago. In six other large financial centers, current turnover rates are once a week and up 80 per cent over the past decade. In 200-odd other reporting metropolitan areas, turnover is roughly 34 times per year and up 50 per cent over the mid-fifties. The very high levels of turnover in New York and other major centers are a reflection of a large volume of financial transactions. But the increases in rates of turnover in all centers are a manifestation of closer money management by banks' customers, including increasing readiness to invest idle balances in interest-earning instruments.

On the other hand, liquidity, the non-transaction characteristic of money, is becoming an increasingly important feature of the stock-in-trade of financial intermediaries and a broadly-based resilient money market. Inevitably these markets and institutions will increasingly become the evident target of monetary action.

Turning now to the 1966 experience with money supply as an indicator of monetary action, let me illustrate some of the practical difficulties of using M-1 or M-2 as a chief monitor of monetary trends.

Changes in M-1 most directly mirror the combined effects of changes in the economy's demand for money—especially in recent years for transaction purposes—and the Federal Reserve's policy with respect to supplying the reserves for bank credit and monetary expansion. But the mixture of significant and insignificant influences at work on M-1 do not trace out any simple pattern. Distracting movements in M-1 of the order that produce large annual rates of change derived from weekly or monthly data often arise from unexpected seasonal fluctuations, erratic changes in velocity, and shifts between the private money supply and the Federal Government's demand deposits in commercial banks. In the background of economic and financial developments in 1966 affecting changes in M-1 are changes in the timing of personal and corporate tax payments, wide fluctuations in the Government's balance for reasons having a non-symmetrical effect, and, in addition, a sustained tightening in monetary policy. All of these recent shifts, I might add, make it increasingly difficult to discern seasonal from non-seasonal movements.

It is of some help in explaining the behavior of M-1 in 1966 to ignore the changes in currency and coin in circulation, which have been rising about $2 billion annually for the past four years and whose seasonal fluctuations are stable enough to be reliably adjusted. The remainder—the seasonally adjusted demand deposit component of M-1—was stable in the first 10 weeks of 1966 at about $131.5 billion. Around the March 15 tax date it rose about $1 billion and around the April date another $1.5 billion, hitting a peak of $134.0 billion in a week when the U.S. Government deposits were at their lowest point of the year (thus far). Early in May, demand deposits settled back to $133 billion, rose briefly but sharply after the June 15 tax date and have been in the range of $132-$133 billion ever since (early October).

This record, as it developed during the year, was, by some observers, first assailed as highly inflationary when the temporary bulges around March, April and June tax dates appeared. It was later assailed as dangerously deflationary when August levels were compared to the last-half June peak. Since August, demand deposits have risen somewhat in addition to the September tax period bulge; they are now above the June level.

In retrospect, and considering the transitory factors at work (i.e., the frictional effects of changes in the Government balance and tax payment schedule changes), it appears M-1 has increased very modestly during the year and that such variations as were thought to indicate sharp changes in policy direction were simply manifestations of temporary aberrations that took some time for the market to adjust out. It should be obvious that the very slow growth in M-1 has been one of the signals of a steadily tightening monetary policy throughout the year.

If one shifts the spotlight to M-2—the money supply plus time deposits—the combined effects of varying economic demands and monetary restraint are still clear, but the timing and magnitude of the changes are quite different from those shown by M-1. This is not in the least surprising, since M-2 incorporates the results of the banking system's competitive efforts to attract time funds from other intermediaries and from the money and securities markets, as well as the modest incidental effect of such competition in pulling down the aggregate of its own demand deposits.

During the 1960s and until recently, the banking system has been spectacularly successful in the game of intermediation. The growth in its time aggregates averaged about 15 per cent per year. The time deposit component of M-2, therefore, has been a robust element indexing the competitive success of the banking industry—but hardly a dependable indicator of change in the monetary climate.

In recent months time deposits have been rising much more slowly, as the differential between deposit rates and market rates has turned against depository institutions. Up to September, the rate of time deposit growth has been at only two-thirds of the growth rate in 1965, and, in recent weeks, time deposit growth has ceased altogether in the face of attrition in CD and passbook totals, as rate ceiling barriers serve to shunt funds into market instruments and other intermediaries' offerings.

Thus, it is impossible to interpret recent M-2 movements in the light of monetary factors alone and it is hard to see the rationale for isolating this one component of near monies for inclusion with demand deposits and currency in a measure of monetary action. As we are indeed increasingly using demand deposits and currency for transaction uses only, M-1 has to be interpreted accordingly. M-2 is a hybrid of very limited use in today's environment. As intermediaries and market instruments take on more and more of the task of providing liquidity for the economy, we need to sharpen up the definitional and the data requirements necessary to develop the more comprehensive money concept, M-x, a significant monitor of monetary change.

One final monetary monitor merits our attention—not because of outstanding quality but because of its widespread use and ease of misuse. I refer to total bank credit at all commercial banks.

This indicator has some technical disadvantages; it is available but once a month and then only on the basis of bank balance sheets as of a single day. Thus it tends to be erratic and even misleading in its signals as well as late in its availability. However, another set of numbers with greater stability and availability can be used as a proxy for total bank credit—namely, total net member bank time and demand deposits. These data are available weekly on a daily average basis which proofs them against single day irregularities, such as window dressing.

In performance, total bank credit, or its proxy, closely resembles M-2 but avoids net, some of the erratic movements in that series being due to the exclusion of Government deposits. Its major shortcoming is the same one which disqualifies M-2 as a measure of monetary action—its sensitivity to intermediation trends in the banking system.

If public preferences are turning away from cash and demand deposits and toward near-monies generally, this is an important fact for the central bank to recognize and, if possible, accommodate. It is the kind of change that some variant of M-x would usefully portray. But any indicator such as M-2 or aggregate bank credit which merely registers the shifting competitive positions among intermediaries is more likely to be misread than correctly interpreted.

Consider the accelerated intermediation in the banking system beginning in 1962 and the disintermediation of recent weeks; these appear to have symmetrical effects so far as monetary policy implications are concerned. When banks in 1962-64 were gaining time deposits at the expense of other intermediaries and of market instruments, bank credit and bank deposits rose at an accelerated rate, giving an exaggerated impression of the degree of stimulation from monetary policy.

Under present conditions, holders of negotiable CDs and other time contracts with banks which they do not wish to renew are probably purchasing short-term agency issues, municipals, commercial and finance company paper, and bankers' acceptances. To the extent banks hold these types of paper, we can simply imagine that banks redeem maturing time instruments by handing over such short-term assets, thus reducing both their assets and liabilities.

Although bank credit and bank deposits would thus appear to contract, total credit available to the economy would not necessarily be affected nor need there be any further impact on interest rates. All that is happening is a reshuffling of assets between the banks and the public with attendant effects on the *distribution* of total credit availability and the *shape* of the yield curve. In short, there is a trend away from intermediation by the banks.

Now to return to our indicator—total bank credit. In the current environment it is signaling great tightness just as it signaled excessive ease from 1962 until the summer of 1966. But if the monetary managers had choked off the economy's credit resources earlier we would not have had the expansion and prosperity of the 60s. Similarly, we should not exaggerate the degree of monetary tightness being signaled by the slower growth of bank credit today.

This speech has dealt with a problem of communication—communication between the Federal Reserve and the financial and business public. It covers much the same issues I am often called upon to discuss with student and study groups who will ask: How does monetary action affect the economy; What are the evidences that it is having its intended effect; How can I tell what is taking place? Often, after I have finished my work I realize the still attentive audience before me is still unenlightened. And so, with reverence, if not confidence that my mission has been accomplished, I conclude then as I do now. One must always bear in mind that monetary policy works in mysterious ways its wonders to perform.

# 30 | THE MEANING OF MONETARY INDICATORS*

KARL BRUNNER
*Ohio State University*

ALLAN H. MELTZER
*Carnegie-Mellon University*

Among the topics that monetary economists discuss, few have been debated as much or as long as the meaning of a given change or rate of change in the stock of money or the interest rate. Some have stressed the importance of monetary or of interest rate changes as a guide to the future pace of economic activity. Yet it seems reasonable to conclude that the partisans have not succeeded in convincing others that one or the other of these variables is the most reliable measure of the effect of monetary policy. There is not even agreement that the choice is restricted to these two measures. Bank credit, free reserves, liquid assets, and other variables are mentioned frequently. Since it is not unusual to find that quite different—even opposite—conclusions are suggested by the various measures, a comparison of the information provided by some of the variables proposed as indicators is called for.

The problem may be restated as a series of questions. What information about monetary policy is conveyed by the position of, or change in, a particular variable? How do we choose from among the many available time series those that are to be watched more carefully than others? By what criteria do we decide that a particular variable is a good or better indicator of current or recent monetary policy?

Many discussions of monetary policy take a rather different starting point from the one taken here. A particular hypothesis relating monetary policy to prices and output is assumed—usually implicitly—to be well established. Policy implications are obtained from the hypothesis. Attention is then directed toward the problem of forecasting the future, selecting a policy goal, and/or measuring lags of various kinds.[1] Without disputing the importance of these problems, an obvious point should be noted, that is, that the policy conclusions depend on the hypothesis selected. Equally important, the measurement of lags depends on two types of hypotheses: (1) relatively crude approximations to an underlying dynamic theory of

* Reprinted from George Horwich (ed.), *Monetary Process and Policy: A Symposium* (Homewood, Ill.: Richard D. Irwin, Inc., 1967.) By permission of the authors and Purdue University.

[1] L. A. Metzler, "Three Lags in the Circular Flow of Income," *Employment and Public Policy: Essays in Honor of Alvin Hansen* (New York: W. W. Norton, Inc., 1948), pp. 11–32; J. M. Culbertson, "Friedman on the Lag in Effect of Monetary Policy," *Journal of Political Economy,* December, 1960, pp. 617–621; M. Friedman, "The Lag in Effect of Monetary Policy," *Journal of Political Economy,* October, 1961, pp. 447–467; A. Ando, E. C. Brown, R. M. Solow, and J. Kareken, "Lags in Fiscal and Monetary Policy," in *Stabilization Policies* (Commission on Money and Credit) (Englewood Cliffs, N.J.: Prentice-Hall, Inc., 1963), pp. 1–163.

economic activity or policy-making behavior and (2) hypotheses about the remaining structure of the economy.

In this paper, we acknowledge our ignorance—or relatively incomplete information—about the structure of the economy. Given this state of knowledge, particularly the absence of quantitative estimates of many of the parameters of a general-equilibrium macromodel, of the speeds of adjustment of many of the variables, and of the distribution of the effect of monetary policy through time, a number of questions arise. What information does the policy maker have available to decide on a future course of action, or to judge the present or recent position of the economy? How does he assess the results achieved by past policy or likely to be achieved in the near future? How does he decide whether his policy has resulted in relative restraint or relative ease?

One solution is to decide that additional knowledge is so difficult to obtain, so subject to error, or so hard to interpret that reliance must be placed on simple solutions, for example, monetary rules, very simple qualitative hypotheses,[2] or perhaps on "color, tone, and feel." An alternative is to use the available quantitative and qualitative information, while recognizing the incomplete and uncertain character of the knowledge possessed.

A strategy for combining incomplete information about the structure of the economy with an assumption about the goal of policy is discussed here. The problem is referred to as the "indicator problem," since we are concerned with the relative merits of a number of variables often used to indicate the current direction of monetary policy or the future effect of recent policies. Our tentative results are not presented as a resolution of the problem, only as a means of opening for analysis a topic that is more frequently debated than analyzed. At the outset we acknowledge that many of the questions raised here can be answered more fully if (and only if) more useful knowledge about the structure of the economy is assumed or obtained. Put otherwise, the theorist may choose to ignore this problem by assuming the possession of reliable information currently outside the scope of quantitative economics. The policy maker is not as fortunate.

## The General Problem

By way of contrast with our present state of knowledge, consider a situation in which there is a fully identified, highly confirmed theory of macroeconomic processes. There is then quantitative information about the structural parameters, or useful knowledge, to use Marschak's apt phrase.[3] Since the policy maker can infer, from the comprehensive model, the expected effect of policy action on any or all variables that are of interest to him, he can determine the amount that policy must contribute to achieve a particular set of social goals. If the structure is known and the goal or social utility function is specified, knowledge of the change in monetary policy permits the policy maker to evaluate the effects of his past actions. The indicator of monetary policy summarizes in an index the relative degree of monetary ease or restraint. Let $I$ be the indicator of monetary policy. Then

$$I = \frac{du}{dy_1}\frac{dy_1}{dx_1}dx_1 + \frac{du}{dy_2}\frac{dy_2}{dx_1}dx_1$$

where $u$ represents the social utility function, $y_1$ and $y_2$ are endogenous variables of the system—for example, prices and real output—and $dx_1$ is the change in variables expressing monetary policy operations.[4]

The derivatives of the endogenous $y$ variables with respect to $x_1$ describe the responses of the goal variables to policy operations. These derivatives are, of course, total derivatives obtained by differentiating over the whole system of relations, and depend on the derivatives of the structural equations. Since

[2] See the recommendations of P. A. Samuelson, "Reflections on Central Banking," *National Banking Review*, September, 1963, pp. 15–28.

[3] J. Marschak, "Economic Measurements for Policy and Prediction," in Hood and Koopmans (eds.), *Studies in Econometric Methods* (New York: John Wiley & Sons, Inc., 1953), pp. 1–26.

[4] The nature of the index depends, of course, on the goal or utility function. If the latter is unique only up to order-preserving transformations, $I$ must be treated as an ordering. For most practical purposes this would be sufficient. Note that since $y_1$, $y_2$, and $x_1$ are vectors, $\frac{du}{dy_i}$, $dx$ are vectors and the $\frac{dx}{dy_i}$ are matrices.

the derivatives of each of the structural equations and of the utility function are assumed to be known, all that is required to measure changes in the degree of ease or restraint is a measure of the change in one or more of the monetary policy variables that has been altered.

Some of the elements in the more general problem have been introduced in the example just considered. First, there is a choice to be made about the nature of the utility function. Second, hypotheses must be selected. Economics has not advanced far enough as an empirical science to make the choice obvious. Moreover, very little is known about the values of the parameters of any set of hypotheses that might be used. The example suggests that any change in the structural relations is capable of altering the indicator. Hence, the index value of any particular policy depends on the hypotheses. Third, changes in institutional arrangements alter the channels and effects of monetary policy. With relatively complete knowledge, institutional rearrangements do not create serious problems for the construction of an indicator. However, we will note below that there is a trade-off between complex institutional arrangements and the amount of knowledge about the system that is required. Finally, the example suggests that there is only one relevant strategy, namely, to construct the appropriate indicator for the evaluation of policy. This simple strategy is no longer meaningful when we revert to the position of relatively incomplete knowledge. A choice of strategy must then be made. For example, it may be desirable to choose policies or indicators that minimize the extent to which knowledge is required about the structure of the system; or, the strategy may be one of choosing an indicator that minimizes the chance of serious misinterpretation of the result of policy actions.

The indicators of monetary policy usually mentioned by economists are not even approximately related to the indicator function introduced above. Most of them are endogenous variables. As such, their position or rate of change at any time is the result of the joint interaction of the whole system and reflects more than the effect of current monetary policy. Fiscal policies and noncontrolled exogenous variables also influence the endogenous indicators. Moreover, their current position or rate of change is the result of partial or incomplete adjustment to the long-run position implied by the expected response to changes in policy and other exogenous forces. Information is rarely available on the proportion of the adjustment which has already occurred.[5]

The danger of misinterpreting the current direction of monetary policy exists in principle when any endogenous variable is used as an indicator. Suppose interest rates on financial assets are accepted as the indicator. Relatively high rates are interpreted as a "tighter" policy, and rising rates are taken as an indication of "tightening." Further, assume that interest rates are accepted as the principal financial variable that transmits monetary impulses to the real variables and hence to the pace of economic activity. The bond yield is endogenous. Its behavior is determined by the interaction of the whole system under the impact of changes in the monetary and nonmonetary policy variables and in the noncontrolled variables. If there is sufficient information available to construct the indicator function $I$, there is no danger of misinterpretation. A rise in interest rates that results from nonmonetary forces, say an increase in the expected yield on real capital, can be separated from the effect on interest rates of expansive monetary policy. Without the information required for construction of the indicator function, the rise in interest rates will be interpreted as an indication that monetary policy has become tighter and more restrictive when the indicator, if it were available, would reveal the error in this interpretation.

The fact that interest rates are taken as the central element transmitting monetary policy from the financial to the real sector does not establish that they are a better (or worse) indicator of current monetary policy than some other endogenous variable. But the central role assigned to interest rates would suggest that they are influenced greatly by feedbacks from the real to the financial sector, so that their position or direction of change at any time is a result of opposing influences. Similar statements apply to the money supply and other endogenous variables, although the relative size of

[5] Even if the length of the lags is assumed to be well established, the time distribution of the adjustment may be known less precisely.

policy and nonpolicy influences will differ with the endogenous variable selected as an indicator.

It is possible to rank many of the endogenous variables by their quality as indicators, if we are not completely ignorant about the goals of policy and the operation of the economic system. To do so, a class of hypotheses must be selected. In principle, this choice should be made by systematically comparing alternative classes. In practice, we have selected one with which we are familiar, on the grounds that it includes among the endogenous variables many of the indicators that are frequently suggested or used to appraise the direction of monetary policy and is sufficiently rich in detail to bring out clearly the problem of choosing an indicator.[6]

## An Outline of the Hypothesis

The indicator function introduced above expressed the connection between monetary policy ($x_1$) and the indicator $I$. In the model, changes in policy affect the level of output, prices, and other real variables by changing financial variables and relative prices. Absence of useful knowledge about many structural relations of the transmission process does not alter the need for a framework like the one underlying the indicator function. To appraise the effect of policy operations, we require both a theory and a utility function. Relations summarizing behavior on the financial and output markets must be presented before several of the variables proposed as indicators can be compared. The hypotheses used for this purpose are described briefly in this section. The appendix provides a condensed, formal statement.

The set of relations that determine the partial equilibrium solutions for the money supply, the banks' portfolio of earning assets, and interest rates have been presented in some earlier work.[7] The equations of the monetary system underlying the equilibrium conditions summarize the allocation decisions of the banks and the public and their responses to the decisions of the monetary authority.

The public's behavior is expressed through three relations: (1) the allocation of money between currency and demand deposits, (2) the allocation of bank deposits between demand and time accounts, and (3) the supply function of earning assets to banks. Banks are assumed to allocate assets in response to changes in a number of cost, yield, stock and flow variables. Of particular importance, at present, is the dependence of the money supply and the banks' demand for earning assets on interest rates and real income. This dependence is a consequence of the effect of interest rates on the banks' demand for excess and borrowed reserves, of real income on the currency ratio, and of both interest rates and real income on the ratio of time to demand deposits.[8] Interest rates, real income, and the expected yield on real capital also affect the equilibrium solution for interest rates and bank credit through the public's supply of earning assets to banks.

Six policy variables record the decisions of the monetary authorities. The open market portfolio is one of the sources of the adjusted base—an exogenous variable of the system. The adjusted base is equal to reserves plus currency minus member bank borrowing. The remaining policy variables affect the monetary system by changing the monetary and asset multipliers. The rediscount rate and the ceiling rate on time deposits affect the multipliers through the desired free reserve and time deposit ratios, respectively. Changes in the reserve requirement ratios and in the proportion of vault cash included in required reserves change the weighted average of reserve requirement ratios, denoted by $r$.

The solutions for the money supply and interest rates from the financial sector are

[6] The statement in the text should not suggest that no effort has been made to compare alternative theories. The velocity relation plays a key role in the analysis below. It has been compared to a variety of alternatives in our "Predicting Velocity: Implications for Theory and Policy," *Journal of Finance*, May, 1963, pp. 319–354, and in "The Demand for Money: The Evidence from the Time Series," *Journal of Political Economy*, June, 1963, pp. 219–246. See also the references cited in the next footnote.

[7] "Some Further Investigations of Demand and Supply Functions for Money," *Journal of Finance*, May, 1964; and "A Credit Market Theory of Money Supply," to be published in the *Essays in Honor of Marco Fanno*.

[8] In the appendix this is expressed by the dependence of the free reserves and time deposit ratios on interest rates. [A complete model is presented in the appendix which has been omitted in this volume.]

connected to the real sector by a quantity equation. A demand function for money, akin to the one emphasized in much of our recent work, is expressed as a velocity relation. The aggregate demand for output, $MV + G$, is the sum of government expenditure ($G$) plus private expenditure ($MV$). The quantity equation relates aggregate government and private demand with nominal supply. A price-setting function expresses the adjustment of supply prices to variations in current and past output and in capital stock.

Fiscal policy operations affect both financial and real variables. As noted above, the government's income-generating expenditure has been introduced as a component of total spending. In addition, the government's cash deficit is related to the volume of government expenditures and to the means by which the deficit is financed. A surplus or deficit in the cash budget raises or lowers the sum of interest- and noninterest-bearing government debt. Changes in both types of debt affect real output and the equilibrium position of the financial sector. If the deficit is financed by noninterest-bearing debt, the adjusted base is increased.

The relations just described do not constitute a specific hypothesis of the type required for construction of the indicator function introduced above, since little is known about the speeds of adjustment or other parameter values in the equations. Rather, the system remains quite general and is representative of a large class of hypotheses. This is particularly true of the relations describing the real sector.

Nevertheless, preliminary investigations suggest that sufficient information is available about the class of hypotheses to reach tentative conclusions about some of the indicators frequently used by economists. The reason is that the comparative merit of various indicators is not greatly affected by the particular relations used to describe the real system. The analysis presented in a later section furnishes a firmer foundation for this conclusion.

This is not the place to discuss the implications of the model in detail. However, a few of the implications bear directly on the indicator problem since they describe some of the effects of monetary policy on output and prices, the requirements of an effective monetary policy, and some determinants of the length of the lag between policy action and its effect.

First, the elasticity of real output with respect to the coordinates of the monetary policy vector, $x_1$, is taken as the measure of the effectiveness of monetary policy operations of given size. The necessary and sufficient conditions for an effective monetary policy depend on the interest elasticities of velocity, of the public's supply of assets to banks, and of the monetary and asset multipliers.

Second, the larger the interest elasticity of velocity and/or of the monetary multiplier, the smaller the response of output to monetary policy (and the larger the response to fiscal policy). A large interest elasticity of the public's asset supply and of the banks' earning asset multiplier raises the size of the response to monetary policy.

Third, constant growth of monetary magnitudes affects the *level* of output and the rate of change of prices. Constant growth generates no fluctuations, although fluctuations may occur for other reasons—for example, through the delayed adjustment of supply prices. The variability of monetary magnitudes is more important than their level in explaining their contribution to large fluctuations in output. (Similar statements apply to fiscal policies.)

Fourth, a "Friedman lag" emerges whenever acceleration or deceleration of monetary magnitudes (that is, second differences in the stocks) becomes pronounced and persistent. The length of the lag is dependent on the length and magnitude of the acceleration or deceleration of the monetary variables.

Fifth, the delayed adjustment of output prices in response to past output and capital stock means that the short-term effects of monetary policy are on real output. Over the longer term, the price level absorbs the effects of policy.

## The True or Ideal Indicator

The relations in the previous section do not provide all the information required for the derivation of the true indicator. A social utility function must be introduced and a policy goal must be selected. Since this paper is concerned primarily with the comparison of several suggested indicators and with the general problem, a rather simple utility function is used. Utility is treated as a monotonic, increasing function of real income which has the form $u(\log\frac{y}{c})$, where $y$ is real income and $c$ is the capacity level of output. The only goal of monetary policy is to increase real income.[9]

Once the goal is selected, the theory outlined in the appendix can be combined with the goal in an index that permits monetary policy to be ordered and compared. If there is enough information to compute the index, vague terms such as "easing" and "tightening," often used to characterize policy, can be replaced by statements about the movement of the indicator. A rising index denotes an easier policy; reductions in the index show that policy is tighter.

The movements of the "true" indicator are given by $I$, where

$$I = \epsilon(y, B^a)\frac{dQ}{Q}$$

A multiplicative factor consisting of the marginal utility with respect to log $y$ has been omitted. The first component, $\epsilon(y,B^a)$, is the elasticity of real income (the goal) with respect to open market operations and other changes in the adjusted base $B^a$. Since this component enters the indicator function as a scalar, it can be neglected in the subsequent discussion. The second component, $\frac{dQ}{Q}$, provides all of the information required to order monetary policy under the given hypothesis and a simple goal. It contains three terms:

$$\frac{dQ}{Q} = \frac{dB^a}{B^a} + \frac{dq}{q}\left[\frac{h_1 - h_2\alpha}{h_1 - h_2}\right] \qquad (1)$$

The first two ratios contain all of the monetary policy variables—the monetary base, the reserve requirement ratios, the rediscount rate, and so forth. Policy variables other than $B^a$ operate through the monetary multiplier and are expressed in $\frac{dq}{q}$ as weighted relative rates of change.[10] The third (bracketed) term in equation (1) is a combination of interest elasticities on the credit market ($h_1$) and on the output market ($h_2$) and a parameter ($\alpha$) equal to the ratio of the money supply plus time deposits to bank earning assets. These expressions are more fully defined in section C of the appendix, where it is noted that $\alpha$ is greater than unity and that the bracketed expression on the right is positive, but less than unity, under the hypothesis.

Reliable information is available about some, but not all, of the components. The percentage rate of change of the base and of other policy variables can be measured exactly. Some of the weights used to combine the policy variables in $\frac{dq}{q}$ have been computed; others can be placed within a narrow range. Much less is known about several of the elasticities in $h_1$ and $h_2$. Without such information, the indicator cannot be computed reliably.

The problem of inadequate information vanishes if policy action is restricted to open market operations. The base and the true indicator then coincide. Construction of the indicator is reduced to measurement of changes in an exogenous variable, and the policy position is completely and accurately described by the growth rate of the base.[11]

[9] The choice of per capita real income as the argument of the utility function would not alter the discussion in the text, if population is introduced as an exogenous variable. More complex utility functions containing the rate of change of prices and of real income could be used also. The method used to derive the results would not be affected by the increased complexity of the utility function. But judgments about the trade-off between policy goals—for example, inflation and employment—would be required.

[10]
$$\frac{dq}{q} = \epsilon(m, r^d)\frac{dr^d}{r^d} + \epsilon(m, r^t)\frac{dr^t}{r^t} + \cdots$$

plus similar terms for the rediscount rate, the vault cash counted as required reserves, and the ceiling rate on time deposits. The expressions $\varepsilon(m,x)$ are elasticities of the monetary multiplier ($m$) with respect to a particular policy variable. For a description of the variables see the symbol dictionary in the appendix.

[11] The effect on the indicator of redistributions of deposits between classes of banks with different requirement ratios is ignored. Otherwise, the statement in the text must be changed to eliminate the minor effect on the indicator caused by the slight difference in the average reserve requirement ratio resulting from deposit redistribution.

The conclusion that the relative change in the base is equivalent to the ideal indicator when $q$ is unchanged does not hold for every utility function. It holds in the present case because increased real income is chosen as the only goal of policy.

It is apparent from the above that prevailing monetary arrangements increase the amount of information required by the policy maker. In short, there is a trade-off between knowledge and the complexity of policy arrangements. The unknown benefits of having a variety of policy instruments seem a high price to pay for the substantial increase in the amount of information required to measure the quantitative impact of policy. Until the requisite knowledge becomes available, it would be useful to restrict policy operations to changes in the adjusted base.

Much of the time, policy operations are dominated by open market operations, so that the true indicator and the percentage rate of change in the base coincide. Unfortunately, this happy coincidence occurs least frequently when the desire for correct information is most pressing. At or near the peak of an expansion, bill rates generally rise above the prevailing discount rate, and the discount rate is raised while the growth rate of the base is compressed. Our estimate of the response in $q$ to a 1 percent change in the discount rate is relatively small, but percentage changes in the discount rate are generally quite large and therefore capable of dominating the movement of the indicator at or near the upper turning point in real income.

## A Comparison of Some Proposed Endogenous Indicators

Since construction of the true indicator requires information that is not available, it is useful to consider the merits of variables often accepted as indicators. Movements of interest rates, free reserves, the money supply, and other entities have been used to measure the effect of monetary policy. All of these variables have the advantage of being observable. But each is an endogenous variable in the hypothesis introduced earlier, so that current movements are in part the result of feedback from the financial or output markets. The fact that the endogenous indicators can be measured need not, therefore, be an advantage. Separation of the influence of monetary policy from other influences often requires more information than the construction of the true indicator.

In this section, several endogenous indicators are discussed. Solutions for the rates of change are derived from the hypothesis, and the problems caused by the presence of structural parameters of unknown value are considered. Several of the indicators are expressed in terms of the true indicator, so that differences between them can be compared. The discussion of alternative strategies for choosing an appropriate, observable indicator is deferred, however, to a later section.

### *The Money Supply*

A small but vociferous group of economists takes the rate of change of the money supply as a simple and straightforward indicator of monetary policy. Increases in the money supply are interpreted as expansive and decreases as contractive. Leaving aside, momentarily, differences of opinion about the suitable definition of the money supply, we will define the money supply as currency and demand deposits. The percentage rate of change of the money supply so defined is given by equation (2), where $\epsilon(m,i)$ and $\epsilon(m,y)$ are the interest and real income elasticities of the monetary multiplier, $m$:

$$\frac{dM}{M} = \frac{dB^a}{B^a} + \frac{dq}{q} + \epsilon(m, i)\frac{di}{i} + \epsilon(m, y)\frac{dy}{y} \qquad (2)$$

The money supply is by no means an ideal indicator. It misstates the magnitude of changes in the policy variables and records the effects of changes in other exogenous variables. The solution for $\frac{dM}{M}$ incorporates the influence of monetary policy variables, feedback effects, and the influences of fiscal and noncontrolled exogenous variables. The latter are merged with the feedback effects and summarized by the variations in two endogenous variables, interest rates ($i$) and real income ($y$).

Changes in the adjusted base appear to have the same effect on the money supply as on the ideal indicator. But policies that expand the money supply lower interest rates on financial assets, so that a given percentage change in the base induces a smaller percentage change in the money supply. The size of the difference depends on the size of the interest elasticity of the monetary multiplier, $\epsilon(m,i)$. Our estimates suggest that this elasticity is in the neighborhood of .1 or .2.[12] If these estimates are correct, the effect of changes in interest rates on the money supply is attenuated. Nevertheless, the money supply slightly understates the effect of changes in $B^a$ relative to the true indicator.

On the other hand, a money supply indicator overstates the direct effect of changes in the reserve requirement ratios, the rediscount rate, and other policy variables in $q$. The reason is that $dq/q$ appears in the solution for the ideal indicator, weighted by a ratio of elasticities with a value less than 1. Changes in interest rates (induced by the changes in $q$) lower the amount by which $dM/M$ overstates the effect on the ideal indicator of policies operating through $q$. But it is unlikely that the induced change in interest rates offsets the error caused by the absence of the ratio $(h_1 - h_2\alpha)/(h_1 - h_2)$ in equation (2).

Finally, $dM/M$ is affected by the exogenous, noncontrolled, and fiscal policy variables which affect $i$ and $y$ but which do not appear in the solution for the ideal indicator. Since $\epsilon(m,i)$ is quite small, variations in interest rates induced by changes in interest-bearing government debt, capital stock, and so forth do not greatly reduce the usefulness of $dM/M$ as an indicator. However, the combined effects of the many changes summarized by $dy/y$ have not been carefully estimated. Although the evidence which has been collected strongly suggests that monetary policy operations and changes in the currency ratio are the dominant influences on the money supply, the problem of separating the effects of monetary policy from other influences remains if the money supply is used as an indicator.

[12] See "Some Further Investigations . . ." *op. cit.* Additional estimates have since been computed using both quarterly and annual data. While such estimates are tentative, $\varepsilon(m,i)$ is generally small and positive. It is, of course, possible that

$$\epsilon(m, i)\,\frac{di}{i} = \epsilon(m, y)\,\frac{dy}{y},$$

so that the error in using $\frac{dM}{M}$ in place of the true indicator would be quite small. Our analysis gives no reason to believe that this fortunate result should be expected. Nor can the similar terms appearing below in the equations for free reserves and interest rates be expected to cancel.

### *Other Monetary Variables*

The rates of change of commercial bank credit ($E$) and the money supply plus time deposits ($M + T$) are also used as indicators of monetary policy. The solutions for these variables contain terms very similar to the solution for the money supply. Relative to the true indicator, they, too, overstate the effect of policy variables combined in $q$, and understate the effects of policies operating through the adjusted base. Moreover, $M + T$ and $E$ are more responsive than the money supply to relative changes in interest rates and in the variables operating through the relative change in real income. The reason is that the elasticities of the multipliers of $M + T$ and $E$ with respect to interest rates and real income are larger than the similar elasticities for the money supply.

Our analysis suggests that because the elasticities are largest for $E$ and smallest for $M$, the difference, relative to the ideal indicator, is also largest for $E$ and smallest for $M$. This is particularly true for open market operations and other changes in the base. In addition, nonmonetary policy changes are more fully reflected in $E$ and $M + T$ than in $M$. The money supply is likely to be a better indicator of current or recent monetary policy than the other monetary variables. However, it bears repeating that the money supply is not equivalent to the ideal indicator.

### *Interest Rates*

Market rates of interest are perhaps the most popular indicators of monetary policy among academic economists. One reason may be that the transmission of monetary policy is generally described as operating through a number of interest rates before reaching the components of aggregate expenditure. The theory underlying the discussion of indicators is not incompatible with general statements about the importance of interest rates in the transmission mechanism. But it does not follow from such statements that interest rates are (or are not) closely related to the ideal indicator. The quality of interest rates as an indicator is given by the comparison of the information they convey with the information conveyed by the ideal indicator.

Equation (3) states the solution for the relative change in $i$ in terms of the ideal indicator, where $z$ is a vector of fiscal and noncontrolled variables including the capital stock, the stock of outstanding government debt, and other variables treated as exogenous under the hypothesis; $g_1$ and $g_2$ are combinations of elasticities with respect to real income on the output and credit markets, defined in section $C$ of the appendix; and $\epsilon(i,B^a)$ and $\epsilon(y,B^a)$ are the elasticities of interest rates and output with respect to the extended base:[13]

$$\frac{di}{i} = \epsilon(i, B^a)\left[\frac{dQ}{Q} + \frac{dq}{q}\frac{(\alpha - 1)}{(g_1 - g_2)\quad \epsilon(y, B^a)}\right] + \epsilon(i, z)\frac{dz}{z} \quad (3)$$

The bracketed expression contains all of the monetary policy variables. Since $\epsilon(i,B^a)$ is negative, and the ratio modifying the effect of $dq/q$ is positive, expansive policies (rising $B^a$ or $q$) lower interest rates on financial assets. Lower interest rates are interpreted, therefore, as an indication of expansive policies.

Two important consequences follow from this interpretation of interest rate movements. First, the bracketed expression containing the monetary policy variables exceeds the true indicator whenever policy operates through $q$. Thus the effects of changes in the reserve requirement ratios, the rediscount rate, vault cash policy, or the ceiling rate on time deposits are subject to misinterpretation. This difficulty can be removed by restricting monetary policy to open market operations. The relative change in interest rates is then proportional to the relative change in the indicator. But there would then be no reason to use interest rates or any other endogenous variable as an indicator. Monetary policy would be measured correctly by the relative change in the adjusted base.

The second consequence is the result of a more fundamental problem. The choice of $i$ as an indicator attributes the effects of changes in the fiscal and noncontrolled variables, represented by $dz$, to monetary policy. Changes in the outstanding stocks of interest-bearing government debt or of real capital are important influences on $di/i$. A large government deficit financed by new debt issues imparts substantial momentum to rising interest rates. Even if an increasing portion of the new issues is absorbed through expansion of the monetary base so that $Q$ rises, $di/i$ may increase. Reliance on interest rates would lead to the conclusion that monetary policy is restrictive, despite the rise in $dQ/Q$ indicative of an acceleration of expansive policy action.

With the exception of the thirties, interest rates generally move procyclically. The influence of $dQ/Q$ is usually overwhelmed by the effects of variables combined in $dz/z$. Interpretations of monetary policy based on interest rate movements neglect the powerful influence on interest rates of new issues of interest-bearing debt or of changes in the capital stock. Policies are judged to be restrictive whenever the effect of $dQ/Q$ is dominated by the effect of $dz/z$, despite the possible large value of $dQ/Q$ and the true effect of monetary policy on output and economic activity. Similarly, monetary policy is judged to be easy early in the downswing because of the delayed effects of a slower growth rate of $Q$. The slower growth rate of $Q$ gradually reduces the growth rate of income and prices and thus lowers $dz/z$. The effect of falling $dz/z$ more than offsets the fall in $dQ/Q$, generating falling interest rates or falling $di/i$. The interpretation of policy as easy when the true indicator decelerates convinces the monetary authority that a policy of expansion has been initiated, when their actual policies are in the opposite direction.[14]

### *Free Reserves*

Few indicators of monetary policy have been used more consistently than the level of free

---

[13] To obtain the solution for $\frac{di}{i}$ in terms of $Q$, we make use of the solution for $\epsilon(y,B^a)$ derived from the hypothesis:

$$\epsilon(y, B^a) = \frac{h_1 - h_2\alpha}{g_1h_1 - g_2h_2}$$

[14] It may appear that the problem just discussed arises if $dM/M$ is used as an indicator, Since $dM/M$ depends on $di/i$ and, in addition, on the components of $dz/z$, the relative change in the money supply can lead to a misinterpretation of monetary policy. However, the data suggest that the behavior of the money supply is generally dominated by the currency ratio and the monetary policy variables, as noted earlier, so that the problem is much less serious for $M$ than for $i$.

reserves. Nearly every week, the financial press describes Federal Reserve policy in terms of the movement of free reserves, and evidence of the Federal Reserve's attachment to free reserves has been presented elsewhere.[15] Increases in free reserves are interpreted as expansive or indicative of easier policy; reductions are presumed to reflect less ease or greater restraint.

The solution for the volume of free reserves, $F^*$, implied by our theory,

$$F^* = \phi B^a$$

makes free reserves depend on all of the monetary policy variables. Open market operations affect free reserves through the base, $B^a$, and other monetary policies affect $F^*$ through $\phi$, where $\phi$ is a rational function of the free reserve ratio and of the time deposit, currency, and weighted average reserve requirement ratios.[16] In short, $\phi$ depends on the monetary policy variables summarized in $q$, on the components of the monetary and asset multipliers, and thus indirectly on output and interest rates as well. The joint determination of these central endogenous variables in terms of the policy and noncontrolled exogenous variables makes $\phi$ dependent on all of the exogenous variables—fiscal, monetary, and noncontrolled. Equation (4) is a compact statement of the result for nonzero $F^*$.[17]

$$\frac{dF^*}{F^*} = \frac{dB^a}{B^a} + \frac{dq}{q} + \epsilon(f, \rho)\frac{d\rho}{\rho} + \epsilon(\phi, i)\frac{di}{i} + \epsilon(\phi, y)\frac{dy}{y} \quad (4)$$

The first three terms contain the monetary policy variables. The direct effect of changes in $B^a$ are recorded correctly by the free reserves indicator. But changes in the base modify interest rates on financial assets so that the full effect of open market operations and other changes in $B^a$ on $dF^*/F^*$ includes the response represented by $\epsilon(\phi,i)\ di/i$. While the effect of $i$ on the money supply is small, its effect on free reserves is quite large. Moreover, the sign of $\epsilon(\phi,i)$ is opposite to the sign of $F^*$. When free reserves are negative, the free reserves indicator exaggerates the magnitude of expansive policy actions and understates the size of contractive policies. Positive free reserves have precisely the opposite effect. They cause the free reserves indicator to overstate the size of reductions in the base and understate the size of increases.

Additional problems arise when monetary policy operates through $q$. Since $dq/q$ is not multiplied by the ratio of interest elasticities that appears in the true indicator, the direct effects of variations in the reserve requirement ratios, the rediscount rate, and other policies are misstated. Moreover, the rediscount rate, $\rho$, appears as a separate term in addition to its effect on $dF^*/F^*$ through $dq$. This term is another source of differences between the free reserves indicator and the true indicator when the discount rate is changed. Furthermore, changes in any of the terms in $q$ induce changes in interest rates and hence lead to either overestimates or underestimates of the magnitude of policy operations, depending on the sign of $F^*$. Those who rely on free reserves as an indicator are likely to be misled by their interpretation of the size of policy actions.

Toward the end of a period of economic expansion, free reserves are generally negative and monetary policy is frequently moving in a deflationary direction. The use of free reserves as an indicator underrates the size of the deflationary impulse. A drastic application of policies designed to "prevent inflation" might seem called for because of the attenuated response in free reserves. During a downswing, free reserves are generally positive. Expansions in the base or in the variables denoted by $q$ are understated by the free reserves indicator. If the $F^*$ indicator is used by policy makers as a guide to desired policy, it is likely to produce abrupt changes in the direction and magnitude of the size of policy action.

---

15 See our *The Federal Reserve's Attachment to the Free Reserves Concept* (Washington, D.C.: House Banking and Currency Committee, 1964).

16
$$\phi = \frac{f(1+t)}{(r+f)(1+t)+k}$$

17 A coefficient of the third term has been assumed to be unity and hence omitted. The coefficient is $1 - \epsilon(m,f)$ where $\epsilon(m,f)$ is the elasticity of the monetary multiplier with respect to the free reserve ratio. The omitted term is almost always between .99 and 1.01.

Variations in interest rates and in free reserves induced by monetary policies cannot be separated from the influence of fiscal and noncontrolled forces without reliable information about the structure of the process. Major changes in free reserves are often a response to changes in real variables. For example, a decline in the expected yield on real capital induces an increase in free reserves. This typically happens toward the end of an expansion phase and is one of the forces contributing to the termination of the expansion. Influenced by the expansion in free reserves, the monetary authority becomes convinced that policy is "aggressively easy." This error in interpretation is superimposed on the underestimation of deflationary policies associated with the sign of $F^*$, discussed above. Attributing the movements in free reserves to monetary policy misconstrues the effect of actual policy operations.

## The Choice of Strategy and Indicator

None of the endogenous variables we have considered indicates the exact effect of monetary policy on real income. Each is potentially or actually misleading. But the imperfections are not the same and vary substantially with the choice of endogenous indicators. In the absence of knowledge about the structure, some choice must be made among imperfect alternatives.

One solution is to confine policy operations to changes in the base, so that relative changes in the base become the ideal indicator. Another is to choose a strategy or criterion under which the performance of the various endogenous indicators can be compared. A third alternative is to search for measurable indicators that bracket the ideal indicator between an overestimate and an underestimate. In this section, some alternative solutions are discussed.

The choice of a strategy depends on the utility function of the policy maker. He may wish to minimize the expected loss of utility or minimize some function of the mean and variance of the deviations between measured and ideal indicators. Most choices of strategy require substantially greater additions to knowledge than is required to compute the ideal indicator.

The strategy we have selected for illustrative purposes is a minimax strategy.[18] Given the hypothesis and the simple goal, we minimize the worst possible outcome (misinterpretation) attributable to incomplete knowledge about the effect of a specific set of policy changes occurring through changes in $B^a$ and $q$. In the particular case, this means that the maximum deviations between the various endogenous indicators and the ideal indicator are computed, using our limited knowledge of the structural parameters. The endogenous variable that has the smallest maximum deviation is then chosen as the optimal indicator.[19]

The material for the solution has been provided. The ideal indicator, $dQ/Q$, is given in equation (1) above. The difference between the value of $dQ/Q$ and the solution for each of the endogenous variables can be computed easily. When the computations are performed, the money supply (currency and demand deposits) emerges as the optimal indicator.

Investigation of five frequently used financial variables thus establishes that, relative to the goal function, hypothesis, and strategy, the money stock is the best approximation to the true indicator. It is not ideal and has been quite misleading on occasion in the postwar period. Nevertheless, it is the least misleading and least dangerous single guide to the position of monetary policy.

A solution of quite a different kind is to combine two indicators, one more responsive and one less responsive than the ideal indicator. Fortunately, a prolonged search for measures with these properties is not required if the particular hypothesis and goal are maintained. Let one approximate indicator be

$$\frac{dQ^*}{Q^*} = \frac{dB^a}{B^a} + \frac{dq}{q}$$

It is clear from inspection of the ideal indicator that $dQ^*/Q^*$ is identical to the ideal

[18] Theories of search provide another means of investigating the problem of choosing an optimal indicator. Optimal search procedures can generally be stated as a minimax problem. See D. J. Wilde, *Optimum Seeking Methods* (Englewood Cliffs, N.J.: Prentice-Hall, Inc., 1964). We are indebted to M. Kamien for this reference.

[19] Appendix D [omitted] presents the formal outline of the procedure.

indicator whenever $q$ is unchanged. Otherwise, this approximation misstates the influence of $q$ on the ideal indicator. When $dq/q$ is positive, $dQ^*/Q^*$ *exceeds* $dQ/Q$ by an amount

$$\left[\frac{h_2(\alpha - 1)}{h_1 - h_2}\right]\frac{dq}{q}$$

reductions in $q$ are understated by the same amount. We will refer to the bracketed expression as the "error of overstatement," since it exaggerates the influence of $q$ relative to the ideal indicator.

For the "error of understatement," a measure is required that always is less than $dQ/Q$ when $dq/q$ is positive and always is greater than the ideal indicator when $dq/q$ is negative. Relative changes in the base have this property. The error of understatement is the bracketed term in

$$\frac{dQ}{Q} - \frac{dB^a}{B^a} = \left[\frac{h_1 - h_2\alpha}{h_1 - h_2}\right]\frac{dq}{q}$$

Since the hypothesis implies that the error of understatement is numerically larger than the error of overstatement, the true indicator is nearer to $dQ^*/Q^*$ than to $dB^a/B^a$ whenever $q$ changes. The sum of the two errors is always unity. Unless the change in $q$ is extremely large, a reasonable approximation to the ideal indicator is given by

$$\frac{1}{2}\left(\frac{dQ^*}{Q^*} + \frac{dB^a}{B^a}\right) = \frac{dB^a}{B^a} + \frac{dq}{2q}$$

The difference between the ideal indicator and this approximation has the same sign as $dq/q$ and hence is known. The approximate indicator is greater than the ideal when $dq/q$ is negative and less than the ideal indicator for positive $dq/q$.

Thus the approximate indicator has three distinct advantages. First, it is easily computed, since $dB^a/B^a$ can be measured exactly and most of the components of $dq/q$ can be approximated quite closely. Second, the direction of error is known—an advantage that is not generally obtained with the use of endogenous indicators. Third, for small changes in $dq/q$, the error is quite small.[20]

[20] Using the hypothesis, goal, and strategy above, the proposed indicator is better than any of the endogenous indicators considered.

## Limitations

Computation of the approximate indicator would not reveal the magnitude of the change in real income induced by monetary policy. At best, the indicator would correctly scale the size of the impulse that policy is directing toward the final goal. Measurement of the magnitude of the change in real income induced by monetary policy requires information about the structure, and particularly about the elasticity of output with respect to the base, $\epsilon(y,B^a)$, as noted earlier.

Successive computations of the indicator would not furnish information useful for the computation of the correct lags or of $\epsilon(y,B^a)$. The length of the lags depends, in part, on the acceleration and deceleration of monetary policy, while the computation of the "true" value of $\epsilon(y,B^a)$ depends on knowledge of the structure. More importantly, changes in income depend on the fiscal and noncontrolled exogenous variables. The indicator, therefore, does not provide a forecast of future output, but only a scale on which the relative magnitudes of the monetary impulse can be measured.

Moreover, the scale is not unique. It depends on the particular class of hypotheses and goal selected. Some of the more complicated goal functions require substantially more information about structural properties than is required in the case discussed here. Although we have not investigated the problem thoroughly, this is likely to be true of alternative hypotheses as well. The analysis underlying our effort has the advantage of reducing, perhaps to a minimum, the required amount of knowledge about structural details.

Random elements have been ignored. The structural equations have been treated as if they held exactly. Errors in these equations will appear in the partially reduced forms used to compare the endogenous indicators and in the equation for the ideal indicator. However, it should be noted that the problem of errors in the equation is likely to be at least as serious for the endogenous indicators that are in common use as for the approximate indicator we have developed.[21]

[21] The introduction of errors in the equations would not alter the comparative merits of the indicators considered here. Under the hypothesis and goal we have discussed, the ordering of indicators would remain identical.

## Conclusion

One means of obtaining information about the direction and effect of monetary policy has been illustrated in this paper. While our solution is neither exact nor ideal, it is likely to be less misleading than many of the variables used to describe the content of monetary policy.

Policy makers must continuously interpret the effects of their past decisions. Their future actions depend on these interpretations. If the indicators they select are misleading, their policy decisions will be inappropriate or misinterpreted and will introduce fluctuations in output, prices, and other goal variables. One need only look at 1962-63 to recognize that when the Federal Reserve described its action as a shift to "slightly less ease," our suggested indicator began growing at the fastest rate in the postaccord period.

Numerous other years reveal the same pattern. When the Federal Reserve describes its action as a move toward restraint, the indicator accelerates. Description of policies as "increased ease" is frequently followed by deceleration of the indicator summarizing the effect of monetary policy on real output. Clearly, the problem is worthy of more attention than it has received from government or academic economists.

## Appendix A—Alphabetical List of Symbols

- $B^a$ the adjusted monetary base: the monetary base minus member bank borrowing
- $E$ commercial banks' earning assets net of Treasury deposits and the banks' net worth
- $E_b$ banks' demand for earning assets
- $E_p$ public's supply of earning assets to banks
- $f$ the ratio of free reserves to total deposits
- $G$ government expenditures (national income accounting definition)
- $I$ the ideal indicator
- $i$ an index of interest rates on financial assets
- $i_e$ expected rate of interest
- $i^t$ interest rate paid on commercial bank time deposits
- $k$ the ratio of currency to demand deposits
- $K$ the stock of real private capital
- $m$ the monetary multiplier
- $M$ the money supply: currency and demand deposits of the public
- $n$ the real yield on real capital
- $p$ the income deflator
- $P_a$ the deflator for wealth
- $q$ the component of the indicator incorporating monetary policy variables not included in $B^a$
- $Q$ the "true" indicator
- $r$ a weighted average of reserve requirement ratios including the vault cash ratio
- $S$ the stock of interest bearing government debt
- $t$ the ratio of time to demand deposits
- $T$ the stock of time deposits
- $V$ circuit velocity of private expenditures
- $W$ the nominal stock of wealth held by the public
- $Y$ nominal income or output
- $y$ real income or output
- $y_p$ expected real income
- $\alpha$ the ratio of money plus time deposits to bank earning assets
- $\beta$ the ratio of money supply to bank earning assets
- $\gamma$ money expenditures of the government sector
- $\epsilon$ an elasticity
- $\theta$ money receipts of the government sector
- $\rho$ the rediscount rate

# 31 MONETARY-POLICY TARGETS AND INDICATORS*

THOMAS R. SAVING
*Texas A. & M. University*

The revival of interest in monetary economics and the return to the idea that "money matters" have rekindled concern on the part of economists over the problems of monetary policy-making. As a result there has been an outpouring of research on the effectiveness of various aspects of monetary policy, including both considerable criticism of and advice to the monetary authorities. However, both the criticism and the advice often have been contradictory. As Allan Meltzer so aptly put it at the close of the UCLA Conference on Targets and Indicators of Monetary Policy, "Moreover, our advice to the Fed most often took the form of nearly unanimous agreement that what they had done was wrong and nearly zero agreement about what they had done."[1]

If agreement cannot be reached on what the past policy has been or on what the current policy is, it is difficult to agree on the course of future policy. A recent example will illustrate the extent of the disagreement. The July, 1966, *Federal Reserve Bulletin* characterized the monetary policy of the first six months of 1966 as one of *monetary restraint,* while the October, 1966, issue of the *Federal Reserve Bank of St. Louis Review* characterized the policy during this same period as one of rapid *monetary expansion.* The recurrence of such contradictory descriptions of past policy has led to discussion by economists of what has come to be known as the "indicator problem" (see Brunner and Meltzer, 1965), that is, the problem of finding a variable or combination of variables that will best describe the effect that current monetary policy is having on economic activity. The importance of the problem arises from the fact that the choice of future policy is influenced by the policymaker's estimate of the effect of his current policy.

To illustrate how such differences in interpretation of past and current policy may arise, consider again the period of the first six months of 1966. For purposes of discussion define a restrictive policy as one that reduces aggregate demand and an expansionary policy as one that increases aggregate demand. Since the effect of current policy on aggregate demand is not directly observable, the monetary authority must gauge the effect of its policy by observing some proxy variable. If the chosen variable is the interest rate or free reserves, then the first six months of 1966 would be characterized as a period of restrictive monetary policy. On the other hand, if the money supply was used as the proxy, then this same period

* Reprinted from *Journal of Political Economy,* vol. 75 (August, 1967) Part II, pp. 446–465, by permission of the author and the University of Chicago Press.

[1] The quotation is taken from a summary of the proceedings of the UCLA Conference on Targets and Indicators of Monetary Policy, held in Los Angeles in April, 1966, prepared by Jerry L. Jordan (1966) of UCLA. This summary will not be published, but a summary of the conference will be. [Karl Brunner (ed.), *Targets and Indicators of Monetary Policy,* San Francisco, Chandler Publishing Company, 1969).]

would be characterized as one of monetary expansion. Of course, how the monetary authority characterizes past policy is irrelevant as long as these policy evaluations do not affect the course of future policy. However, this is an unlikely circumstance in view of the uncertainties surrounding the policy decisions. Thus, a characterization of a given past and current policy as restrictive in a period when the monetary authority desires to reduce aggregate demand will affect the course of future policy differently than if the same policy were characterized as expansionary.

## The Justification for Monetary-Policy Targets and Indicators

The need for monetary-policy targets and indicators is derived from the desire to pursue that particular monetary policy which is optimal in some sense. Thus, the justification for the use of targets and indicators must begin with a discussion of the choice of optimal policy. For this purpose define "monetary policy" as the manipulation of certain aspects of the economy that are under the direct control of the monetary authority, usually called "policy instruments," so as to attain goals that are considered desirable (see Tinbergen, 1956). A policy is then a particular vector of the various policy instruments, for example, a given level of the discount rate, reserve requirements, and rate of change in portfolio.

Since the choice of an optimal path for policy requires that "optimal" be defined, it is assumed that the policymaker has some objective function in mind; this is usually called a "goal function." Such a goal function may be a single-valued function of unemployment, or it may be a complicated function of many arguments, for example, employment, real income, stability of prices, rate of growth in real income, and balance of trade. Denote this function as

$$G = G(y_i) \tag{1}$$

where $y_i$ represents the levels of various endogenous variables in the economic system and will in general be a proper subset of the set of all endogenous variables in the system.

In addition to defining the objective function, the choice of optimal policy requires a specific hypothesis of the structure of the economic system. That is, if the policy-maker is to choose that policy which maximizes his goal function, he must know the effects of various policies on the endogenous variables. Denote the structure as

$$Y_t = F(Y_{t-i}, X_t, X_{t-i}, Z_t, Z_{t-i}) \tag{2}$$

where $Y_t$ is the vector of current values of the endogenous variables; $Y_{t-i}$ is the vector of past values of the endogenous variables; $X_t$ is the vector of the current values of the policy-determined variables, that is, instruments; $X_{t-i}$ is the vector of past policy variables; $Z_t$ is the vector of current values of the non-policy-determined exogenous variables; and $Z_{t-i}$ is the vector of past values of the non-policy-determined exogenous variables.[2]

The problem generally considered in the literature on optimal-policy choice is the maximization of (1), that is, the goal function, subject to (2), that is, the known structure of the economic system, through the manipulation of the policy instruments, that is, the vector $X_t$. The optimal policy is that vector $X_t$ which yields the maximum for $G$ (see Marschak, 1953; Tinbergen, 1956; Theil, 1961). This problem has been considered in two forms: (*a*) when the function $F$ in (2) is assumed non-stochastic and (*b*) when the function $F$ in (2) is considered to be stochastic. The stochastic form of the optimal-policy problem has been shown to be equivalent to the non-stochastic form (that is, these two forms yield the same optimal-policy vector) for the case in which the choice of policy does not affect the variance of the endogenous arguments of the goal function (see Theil, 1961).

Both the stochastic and the non-stochastic forms of the optimal-policy problem usually assume the policy-maker has complete knowledge of the structure and of the current economic situation; that is, it is assumed that

[2] Equation (2) can also be expressed as a system of differential equations that describes the time path of the endogenous variables. When expressed in this way the relevant goal function would be a functional of the time paths of selected endogenous variables.

the function $F$ in (2) is known and that the vectors $Y_{t-i}$, $X_{t-i}$, $Z_t$, $Z_{t-i}$ are all known with certainty.[3] In fact, however, the policy-maker has many different and competing hypotheses of the structure available to him. In addition, many of the important endogenous and exogenous variables are observable only after a considerable lag. Thus, the monetary policymaker does not have complete knowledge of either the function $F$ or the non-policy determined arguments of $F$. It is the union of these two problems that leads to the need for targets and indicators of monetary policy.

THE TARGET PROBLEM. Consider a world in which the policy-maker does not know the correct form of the structural equations or the values of all the parameters of any one form. Assume, however, that he has adequate information to determine the direction of the effect of his policy actions on the various endogenous variables; that is, he has enough information to make qualitative statements about the world. Additionally, assume that those variables that are arguments of the goal function are observable only after considerable lag. Under these conditions it can be shown that it is reasonable for the policy-maker to choose an endogenous variable, which is observable with little or no lag, and aim his policy at making this endogenous variable take on some desired value. Such a value of an endogenous variable is usually called a monetary-policy target, that is, a value that the monetary authority shoots at in determining the policy vector.

There are two reasons for the use of target variables. First, since the structure is unknown, the exact effect of a policy cannot be obtained from the structure (in the stochastic specification of the structure take "exact" to mean "expected effect").[4] However, our lack of knowledge is not uniform throughout the structure. Thus, the policy-maker may be reasonably certain of the relationship between some observable endogenous variable and the goal variables, even if he is very uncertain about the exact effect of his instruments on the goal variables. He may then choose this observable endogenous variable as a target variable and adjust his instruments until this variable reaches its desired (target) level. Presumably this desired level will be the one that is consistent with the goal variables reaching their desired levels. Using this approach, the policy-maker circumvents some of the uncertainties in the effect of policy on the goal variables.[5] Second, since the goal variables are observable only after considerable lag, the effect of policy will only be seen after the policy has been pursued for some time. During this period, exogenous changes may occur, making the effect of the policy chosen larger, or smaller, than it otherwise would have been. If a target variable is used, however, then these exogenous changes may simply affect the magnitude of the operation necessary to make the target variable reach the level desired. Thus, the use of a target variable can remove some of the uncertainty resulting from unobservable goal variables.

For example, consider a situation in which (1) the goal function is an increasing function of real income, (2) the monetary authority lacks complete knowledge of the structure, (3) the level of real income is observable only after a considerable lag, and (4) policy affects the level of real income with a lag. Now the monetary authority chooses as a target variable an endogenous variable that is close to monetary policy, that is, affected rapidly by policy; readily observable; and related to the goal variable, real income. Such a target variable is the interest rate. It is close to monetary policy, readily observable, and in most structural hypotheses related to real income. The advantage of using a target such as interest rates is that many changes in exogenous variables that affect the required magnitude of policy, such

[3] This complete knowledge may or may not include the knowledge of the means, variances, and covariances of the stochastic elements. However, it is generally assumed that the probability distributions of the stochastic terms at time $t$ are independent of the value of these terms at time $t - i$ for all $i$.

[4] If the problem were considered in the Bayesian framework, then we could construct a measure over the class of all structural hypotheses and calculate expected values. In this sense the problem of lack of knowledge is similar to introducing a stochastic element into a known structure.

[5] In other words, part of the variance in the goal variables is due to uncertainty between the target variable and the policy. If the policy can be adjusted instantly to account for any random change between the policy and the target, then this part of the uncertainty can be removed.

as a change in the currency-deposit ratio, will result in an adjustment in policy even though the changes in exogenous variables are unobservable. In addition, if the relationship between interest rates and income is known, the correct magnitude of policy may be achieved by simply pursuing policy until the rate of interest reaches a desired level, even if the relevant monetary parameters are unknown.

For a target variable to perform in the manner suggested above, it must be (1) readily observable with little or no lag, (2) rapidly affected by the policy instruments, and (3) related to the goal variables in the sense that policies resulting in the target variable taking on certain values must in turn result in the goal variables taking on certain values.[6] The choice of an optimal-monetary-policy target variable will require a structural hypothesis and a goal function. However, the choice will not require complete knowledge of the structure, since it is lack of knowledge of the structure that gives rise to the need for a target variable. Thus, if complete knowledge is available, and the goal variables are observable with little or no lag, then the need for a target variable disappears, since the optimal policy may now be uniquely determined. Even with the goal variables unobservable, an optimal policy may be chosen as long as the stochastic element of the structure contains no serial correlation.[7]

THE INDICATOR PROBLEM. Unfortunately, the use of an endogenous variable to adjust policy actions is not without its drawbacks. In particular, changes other than those induced by policy actions may occur in the economy resulting in changes in the target variable. Such non-policy-induced changes in the target variable may result in the attainment of the target being inconsistent with the goal. For example, assume that the policy-maker uses interest rates as a target and that his goal is to reach full employment from an initial position of unemployment. Assuming the structure is such that monetary actions which reduce the rate of interest increase aggregate demand, a target level below the current market level is chosen for the interest rate. The monetary authority then manipulates its instruments until this target level of the interest rate is attained. If, during the period of the policy action, business expectations turn more pessimistic, the investment function will shift leftward, and the equilibrium rate of interest will fall, possibly below the target level set by the monetary authority. Thus, the policy actually undertaken may be one of raising the rate of interest to the target level rather than reducing it, with the result that the policy will have reduced aggregate demand and further reduced employment.

The possibility that changes in the economy will occur during the implementation of policy raises the need for an indicator of the effect of the policy being pursued. That is, if the policy-maker is to adjust his policy to changes in his environment occurring during the implementation of a particular policy, he must have an index of the effect of current policy. Essentially, the policy-maker requires a separation of the change in his target variable into a policy effect and an exogenous effect. Since observation of the changes in the target variable yields only the total effect, some other variable or combination of variables is required to reflect the policy effect. This other variable or combination of variables, usually called a "monetary-policy indicator," must be distinct from the target variable in the sense of being mathematically independent; that is, the indicator must not be a scalar multiple of the target variable. In addition, since the purpose of the indicator is to measure the policy effect, it must be chosen so that either (1) exogenous changes that affect the target variable do not affect the indicator or (2) if these exogenous variables do affect the indicator their effect must be swamped by the policy effect.

Since the task of the indicator is to gauge the effect of monetary policy, the choice of an indicator requires some hypothesis concerning the structure. In addition, if the indicator is used to measure the effect of policy on the goal variables rather than the target variables, knowledge of the goal function will

[6] What is required is that the reduced-form equations for the target variable and the goal variables be such that a policy vector that results in the target variable taking on its desired magnitude will, when substituted into the reduced form for the goal variables, result in their taking on certain values.

[7] If serial correlation exists, then the fact that a stochastic variable took on a certain value at a point in time will change the expected values of this variable in the future and may result in a change in the optimal policy.

also be required. Even in the latter case the choice of the target variable requires the goal function, so that the choice of the indicator indirectly involves the goal function. Just as in the target case, the indicator must be (1) easily observable with little or no lag, (2) close to the policy actions in the sense that it is quickly affected by the policy undertaken, and (3) related to the target and goal variables. Because the indicator of policy gauges the effect of the immediate past policy and because the future course of policy will be influenced by the policy-maker's estimate of the effect of policy, it is crucial that the indicator yield at least qualitatively correct results. Otherwise there is a danger that a policy will continue to be pursued that amplifies rather than moderates the cyclical fluctuations in the goal variables.

To illustrate the use of an indicator, consider the previous example of a policy designed to reduce interest rates that encounters a subsequent leftward shift in the investment function. In that example it was shown that the pursuit of policy until the target is reached may result in a rate of interest that is higher than would have existed in the absence of policy. Suppose that this worst possible case occurs so that the effect of policy actually decreases aggregate demand instead of increases it. How can the policy-maker warn himself of such a contingency? If he had, for example, used the monetary base as an indicator of the effect of his policy on interest rates, the fact that policy had actually resulted in an increase in interest rates would have shown up as a decrease in the monetary base. Thus, the use of an indicator can serve to separate the exogenous effect from the policy effect in those cases where the exogenous changes affect only the target variable. The above discussion can be extended to show why the indicator must be distinct from the target. Consider the case of the interest rate being used as both target and indicator. Then the policy effect will be indistinguishable from the total effect, so that any time the target is hit, the policy will be depicted as being correct.

## The Characterization of Policy

Monetary economists frequently refer to monetary policy as being "expansionary" or "restrictive," "tight" or "loose," "more expansionary" or "more restrictive," "tighter" or "looser." Such terms may be interpreted in two fundamentally different ways: (1) these terms may simply involve a taxonomic scheme for classifying policy, or (2) they may describe the policy's effect on some endogenous variable or combination of endogenous variables. The taxonomic approach is useful as a summary of the policy itself, but it is important to recognize that the terms "expansionary" and "restrictive" or "tight" and "loose" are then determined by the levels of the instruments and not by the net effect of policy. The second interpretation of policy statements involves going a step further than simple taxonomy, since it is based on the net effect of policy on some variables considered to be important, for example, aggregate demand. In this second case, policies are not restrictive or expansionary in and of themselves but are restrictive or expansionary only in terms of a specific structural hypothesis and criterion for characterization. Hence, a given policy might be expansionary under one structural hypothesis and criterion and restrictive under another.

If policy statements are of the first type, that is, purely taxonomic, then the classification of policy will have no effect on subsequent policy actions. The reason is that future policy action, whether this entails a continuation of present policy or some change in policy, depends on the policy-maker's view of the effect of policy and not on the taxonomic classification of current policy. On the other hand, if policy statements are interpreted in the second sense, that is, as descriptive of the *effect* of policy, then a particular description will affect the decision to continue or change policy because this description reflects the policy-maker's view of the effect of current policy.

## Diverse Issues Concerning Indicators

Since the problem of monetary-policy indicators was first raised by Brunner and Meltzer, considerable debate (both written and at various conferences) has ensued. During these discussions many issues were raised that still remain in the air. I shall discuss below several of these issues which I feel are as yet unresolved in the eyes of those who have raised them; I state these issues for brevity in the form of assertions.

SINCE THE PROBLEM IS ESSENTIALLY LACK OF KNOWLEDGE OF THE STRUCTURE, WE SHOULD DEVOTE OUR TIME TO FILLING THIS GAP. Considerable sentiment has been expressed, in various discussions of monetary-policy indicators, that finding an indicator is really a "second best" solution. Since the need for targets and indicators arises because of lack of knowledge about the structure, the optimal procedure is to acquire the missing knowledge. This objection to spending time on the problem of indicator choice misses the point of the discussion entirely. True enough, the problem arises because we desire to pursue policy in spite of lack of knowledge concerning the structure. However, from this fact it does not follow that the problem is best solved by devoting all our energies to getting the missing knowledge. This solution would only be optimal if it were true that the marginal return to additional effort spent on knowledge acquisition exceeds the marginal return to additional effort spent on the choice of indicator, at any level of effort on the indicator problem. Moreover, since this form of solution requires complete knowledge, I would venture to say that even with a total effort this complete knowledge is unobtainable in the foreseeable future. Thus, either we must (1) continue to live with the problem until such time as complete knowledge is available, or (2) discontinue policy entirely, or (3) devote some of our energy to finding ways to live better with the lack of complete knowledge. It seems to me that the third alternative is the only reasonable solution. Note that I am not suggesting that the search for new knowledge be abandoned but only that some (not all) of our efforts be devoted to the problem of optimal-policy decisions under the existing conditions of lack of complete knowledge.

THE WORLD IS SO COMPLEX THAT THE CHOICE OF TARGETS AND INDICATORS IS AN INSURMOUNTABLE PROBLEM. It is often asserted that, even though an indicator would be a useful tool, a reliable indicator cannot be found because of the complexity of the economic system. This statement may be interpreted in two ways. First, the antecedent of the proposition, that is, that the world is complex, may mean that the structural relations are many and that each is complicated, for example, non-linear. From this, however, it does not follow that a reliable indicator cannot be found, since presumably a solution for the system exists; the reduced form may be found. Using the reduced form and the goal function, targets and indicators can be constructed. Hence, in this form the statement is false. Second, the antecedent may be interpreted to mean that there are many stochastic links in the chain of effect so that the variances of the endogenous variables are large relative to the policy effect. Thus, the stochastic effect may easily swamp the policy effect for any given indicator, resulting in unreliability. In this form the argument may be valid but up to this point it merely represents an assertion about the world. Lastly, those economists who profess to hold this view continue to make comparative statements about policy, implying that they have found an indicator that at least they believe to be reliable. As long as indicators are to be used, they should be chosen in some systematic fashion.

THE USE OF AN INDICATOR IS EQUIVALENT TO PUTTING ON BLINDERS. Since an indicator of policy is essentially a proxy for the effect of policy on the target or goal variables, indicators by their nature exclude most of the other information in the economy. Thus the question arises: Instead of looking at an indicator, why not look at all the variables? There are basically two reasons for concentrating on an indicator. First, most of the information available is about endogenous variables that are of little interest, that is, not goal variables and only tenuously connected to the goal variables, so that their use simply clouds the issue. Second, the variables in which we are ultimately interested are observable with a considerable lag, so that by the time we find out what the effect of our policy has been, considerable damage may have been done. Hence, the choice of indicator does not imply that useful information is being discarded but only that all the information is not necessarily useful or available or both. With this view in mind, I believe that the use of an indicator is better characterized as the use of a *spotlight* rather than of blinders.

THE CHARACTERIZATION OF POLICY IS OF SECONDARY IMPORTANCE. As was noted earlier in this paper, the way current policy is characterized is unimportant if agreement can be reached on the future course of policy. As Franco Modigliani put it at the UCLA Conference on Targets and Indicators of Monetary Policy, "That is, it seems to me that the question of the terminology of tight or loose, or easy and expansionary or restrictive, is what I refer to as a matter of semantics, and of secondary importance, in the sense that I don't really care whether you want to call a situation loose or tight as long as we agree in what direction to go."[8] I agree with Modigliani's statement, but this begs the question of the choice of indicator. It is exactly because the characterization of policy affects the future course of policy that we cannot agree on "what direction to go." For example, consider again the first six months of 1966. As pointed out earlier, the Board of Governors of the Federal Reserve System was characterizing policy during this period as tight and was pointing to interest rates and free reserves for verification (see *Federal Reserve Bulletin* 1966). If the Federal Reserve acts on the belief that their past policy was tight in the determination of future policy, then the characterization of policy becomes more than just an issue over semantics. In other words, the decision on how to revise the current policy cannot be made without evaluating the effect of the current policy. Every policy action involves in some way the interpretation of policy, that is, involves the indicator problem.

THE CHOICE OF A "BEST" INDICATOR IS SIMPLY A MATTER OF ONE'S UTILITY FUNCTION. Since the choice of an indicator involves, either directly or indirectly, the assumption of a goal function, it is often asserted that this choice is entirely subjective. However, this does not imply that this choice should not be discussed in a systematic manner. Moreover, it is not at all apparent that the goal functions of various individuals differ in a way that would affect the choice of indicator. It is more likely that these differences will affect the choice of policy rather than the criterion for evaluating the effects of policy.

## The Problem of Indicator Choice

Up to this point I have discussed the justification for monetary-policy targets and indicators and some of the objections that have been raised concerning the relevance of indicators and the existence of a "best" indicator. The problem of a criterion for choosing a "best" indicator still remains. Since any choice of an indicator necessarily involves only a proper subset of all information available, we must have a criterion for judging the numerous candidates for indicators. An example of the use of a criterion to solve such a problem is provided in some recent work done by Brunner and Meltzer (1965).

Brunner and Meltzer proceed by considering a general macroeconomic model with only the signs of the partial derivatives specified. Thus, their results are valid for a wide range of structural hypotheses. They further assume the goal function of the policymakers to be a monotonically increasing function of real income. Various endogenous indicators are then compared to see how well they gauge the effect of policy on real income. A minimax strategy is then used to choose the best indicator. In this case "best" is taken to be the indicator that has the minimum-maximum deviation between the actual effect and the indicated effect, using the limited knowledge that Brunner and Meltzer assume they have of the structural parameters. For the class of hypotheses of the structure and the criterion of choice used, the money stock was judged to be the "best" indicator among those endogenous indicators considered. Brunner and Meltzer emphasize that this indicator is not ideal and does at times yield misleading results but that it is the least misleading of those considered. They also emphasize that consideration of combinations of endogenous variables rather than single variables as indicators may improve the results.

Perhaps some insight into the problem of indicator choice can be obtained by considering the behavior of several alternative indicators during both boom and downswing periods. The indicators to be considered are (1) the rate of interest, (2) the level of free

[8] From Jordan's summary cited in footnote 1.

reserves, (3) the money stock, and (4) the monetary base. For purposes of this discussion, assume that the goal of the policy-maker is the maximization of real income, that is, the attainment and maintenance of full employment. In addition, assume a structural hypothesis in which the level of income is affected ultimately only by the level of aggregate demand. Hence, policy may be characterized by its effect on aggregate demand. In this circumstance a good indicator should reveal the magnitude and direction of the effect that the policy being pursued is having on the level of aggregate demand. Then the relationship between aggregate demand and our goal function reveals whether this is the appropriate policy. Assume that the structural hypothesis is such that (1) the interest rate is negatively related to aggregate demand, (2) free reserves are positively related to aggregate demand, (3) the money stock is positively related to aggregate demand, and (4) the monetary base is positively related to aggregate demand. In addition, assume that inflation and deflation both result in lower real income so that during inflationary periods the aim of policy will be to reduce aggregate demand while during deflationary periods the aim of policy will be to increase aggregate demand. The four indicators of policy can now be evaluated using only the general assumptions of the goal and structure listed above.

THE RATE OF INTEREST. Since the rate of interest follows a pro-cyclical pattern—that is, it rises during upswings and falls during downswings—its use as an indicator will tend to show that current policy is affecting aggregate demand in the desired direction when the actual effect is just the opposite. That is, the exogenous effect has the same sign as the desired policy effect so that the actual policy effect may be in the wrong direction and the total effect still be in the right direction. Since the indicator shows only the total effect, it can be misleading. Moreover, the likelihood of this type of mistake is greater the greater the cyclical effect on the rate of interest. In particular, if the cyclical effect is greater the larger the rate of change in income, then the policy followed is more likely to be ill timed in periods of rapid inflation or deflation than in periods of slower change. For example, assume a rapid downswing so that the cyclical effect on the rate of interest is large and in the downward direction. This downward movement in the rate of interest will indicate that current policy is increasing aggregate demand, that is, current policy is expansionary, when in fact the policy may be reducing aggregate demand. What has happened, of course, is that the cyclical effect has swamped the policy effect. Thus, the difficulty with the interest rate as an indicator is that the cyclical effect cannot be easily separated from the policy effect. Of course, if the policy-maker knows what the rate of interest would have been in the absence of policy, then his problem is solved, since the policy effect may now be isolated.

FREE RESERVES. Because of its relationship to the rate of interest, the level of free reserves moves countercyclically. But, since increases in free reserves increase aggregate demand and decreases reduce aggregate demand, a free-reserve indicator suffers from the same problems as an interest-rate indicator. In particular, a downswing results in increased desired free reserves on the part of banks, both because of the decrease in the rate of interest and because of an increase in the expectation of currency drains. The use of free reserves as an indicator will then show that the policy being pursued is expansionary when in reality it may be restrictive. That is, the cyclical effect on the level of free reserves may swamp the policy effect. Again, if the monetary authority knew the level of free reserves desired by the banks at all times, then it could, of course, separate out the policy effect.

MONEY STOCK. The money stock, like interest rates, moves pro-cyclically, since during the upswing the increase in the cost of holding free reserves causes the banking system to draw down its free reserves, with the result that the money stock increases. But here the similarity ends as far as the indicator problem is concerned. For a downturn, which results in a downward movement in the money stock, a money-stock indicator has a cyclical effect that makes policy appear restrictive even when it may be expansionary. Thus, the money stock when used as an indicator tends to result in policy that is either more restrictive (in time of inflationary boom) or more expansionary (in time of deflation) than the policy desired by the monetary authority. If a minimax criterion were used, this type of error would generally be preferred to an error that resulted in feeding the boom and starving the bust. Thus, the money stock would be preferred to either interest rates or free reserves on this basis.

THE MONETARY BASE. The stock of base money need not move cyclically at all, and thus may be the ideal indicator, since changes in it will completely reflect changes in policy as long as that policy is confined to open-market operations. The proviso that policy actions be confined to open-market operations is necessary since a given stock of base money is consistent, given the structure, with a different level of aggregate demand for each level of the discount rate or required reserves. Thus, in a period when discount rates and required reserves are constant, the monetary base will not deviate from the ideal indicator and hence will reflect the direction of the effect of policy on aggregate demand.

## Monetary-Policy Targets or Indicators?

Much of the controversy over the indicator problem boils down to a failure to distinguish between a target and an indicator. Arguments concerning the relationship between monetary variables and policy are used to support the use of particular variables as indicators. Such arguments fail to realize that, while the indicator must be related to policy, this relationship is not sufficient for a variable to be a good indicator. Moreover, in these discussions there is a general failure to realize the necessity for the indicator to be distinct from the target.

For example, the statement that free reserves should be used as an indicator because the behavior of bankers can be controlled by making free reserves deviate from what the bankers desire them to be is not an argument for the use of free reserves as an indicator but is rather an argument for their use as a target. A free-reserve indicator, by this reasoning, must be the difference between the actual level of free reserves and the level desired by the bankers. Thus, unless a mechanism is included to estimate the desired level of free reserves, the fact that the behavior of the banking system is affected by the level of free reserves, while true, does not imply that free reserves are a good indicator of monetary policy. Similarly the argument that, because the primary effect of monetary policy occurs via changes in the rate of interest, this rate should be looked to for an indication of the effect of policy is also a non-sequitur. All that follows from the assumption that monetary policy affects aggregate demand through the rate of interest is that the rate of interest is a good candidate for a policy target. For the rate of interest to be a reliable indicator of monetary policy, the monetary authority must know what the rate of interest would have been in the absence of policy. Since this information is unavailable, the use of interest rates as an indicator of policy is questionable. Thus it appears that at least a portion of the discussion on targets and indicators has been at cross-purposes simply because of a failure to distinguish clearly between a target and an indicator.

## Conclusion

Considerable progress has been made in the last three decades on the study of the problem of optimal policy under conditions of complete knowledge of the structure of the economic system and no information lags. However, much of this work is not relevant for the implementation of policy when both incomplete knowledge of the structure and information lags exist. In such a world the necessity of short-run targets for policy and indicators of the effect of policy arises. The choice of these targets and indicators requires a hypothesis of the structure and an explicit goal of policy. Because of this it is often asserted that the problem is insoluble. However, some of the work discussed in this paper seems to indicate that the choice of target and indicator may be relatively insensitive to changes in structural hypothesis and goal functions. Thus, targets and indicators may be found that are "robust" in the sense that they are optimal over broad classes of hypotheses of the structure and goals of policy. Work in this important area is only just beginning, and much may be accomplished in the next few years.

## References

1. BRUNNER, KARL, and MELTZER, ALLAN H. "The Meaning of Monetary Indicators," in George Horwich. *Monetary Process and Policy: A Symposium,* Homewood, Ill.: Richard D. Irwin, 1967 [reprinted in this volume].

2. *Federal Reserve Bank of St. Louis Rev.* (October, 1966).

3. *Federal Reserve Bull.* (July, 1966).

4. MARSCHAK, JACOB. "Economic Measurements for Policy and Production," in W. C. Hood and T. C. Koopmans (eds.). *Studies in Econometric Methods.* New York: John Wiley & Sons, 1953.

5. THEIL, H. *Economic Forecasts and Policy.* Rev. ed. Amsterdam: North-Holland Publishing Co., 1961.

6. TINBERGEN, J. *Economic Policy: Principles and Design.* Amsterdam: North-Holland Publishing Co., 1956.

# 32 MONEY, INTEREST, AND POLICY*

PATRIC H. HENDERSHOTT
and
GEORGE HORWICH
*Purdue University*

As late as the early 1950s the prevailing sentiment among monetary and financial economists, inherited from Keynes and the depression, was emphatically that money and monetary policy mattered very little. By the early 1960s the majority view was that money mattered significantly, but so did interest rates and real expenditure functions. Today, in the late 1960s—and doubtless into the 1970s—the overwhelming sentiment among monetary economists is that money is virtually all that matters; changes in interest rates are more apparent than real; and even that Keynesian bulwark, fiscal policy unaccompanied by changes in the stock of money, is on the defensive.

Nothing so polarizes the views of the opposing camps today as the majority belief that the observed stock of money can and should be the indicator of monetary policy actions. For if one can accept this proposition, and we cannot, then all the rest of the supporting doctrine follows quite automatically. This includes the following assertions: Money income is determined directly by observed changes in the stock of money, which are wholly attributable to Federal Reserve actions. All the other behavioral paraphernalia that might affect money and income—the government's propensity to spend and private propensities to save and invest and to hold and supply financial assets—are impotent; either their interest elasticities are equal to zero or infinity (depending on what it takes to deprive them of their punch) or, best of all, they are relatively stable functions that do not shift. While the inevitable wide swings in the government deficit seem inconsistent with this simplistic quantity theory world, monetarists believe that the deficit, if privately financed, will in fact have little impact on the economy. The deficit will not alter money income because of the almost zero interest elasticity of the demand for money; it will not alter interest rates because of the virtual infinite interest elasticity of both private saving and investment. Of course, if the Federal Reserve finances an increase in the government deficit, the quantity theorists readily affirm that the resulting rise in money will raise prices. Then even interest rates will rise, for they respond mainly to inflationary expectations generated by the monetary increase.

By contrast, our framework holds that both the stock and the demand for money are interest sensitive, positive and negative, respectively. Investment, and perhaps saving, respond to interest rates in the expected direction, but rather weakly in the short run owing to long lags of adjustment. Both functions and, of course, government spending undergo frequent shifts. The short-run interest elasticities of the supply and demand

* Reprinted from *Savings and Residential Financing, 1969 Conference Proceedings,* pp. 33–52, by permission of the authors and the United Savings and Loan Association. [The title and sectional headings were changed by the authors.]

for money are not high in absolute value (i.e., not over one-half), but they are high enough to give the economy a firm Keynesian tone. The evidence for the interest sensitivity of investment and the demand for money is well established.[1] We shall describe the interest response of the observed stock of money and argue that this response renders money useless as an indicator of policy. Instead, money is an indicator of all the forces, internal and external, that determine interest rates. Within our generalized framework, we shall derive an adjusted monetary series that can serve as the indicator of monetary policy and we shall define the sense in which interest rates can be the target of policy, in spite of—or, more accurately, because of—the tendency in the economy to recurring shifts in real expenditure functions.

## I. Some Definitions

We begin our analysis by defining the terms and concepts relevant to this discussion. These include financial ease or restraint, monetary ease or restraint, restrictive or easy monetary policy, indicators of monetary policy, and targets of monetary policy.

As the financial adjective suggests, financial restraint and ease refer to conditions in the financial markets, to the cost and availability of credit. If interest rates are rising and/or credit is being rationed, there is an excess demand for funds and financial restraint is said to exist. If interest rates are falling and credit is not being rationed, there is an excess supply of funds and financial ease exists. Similarly, as the monetary adjective suggests, monetary restraint and ease generally refer to what is happening to a monetary aggregate such as the quantity of money. If money is growing slowly or declining, monetary restraint is said to exist; if money is growing rapidly, monetary ease exists. Finally, restrictive and easy monetary policy refer to the direction of monetary policy actions. Defined appropriately, when one's indicator of monetary policy is growing slowly or declining, policy is said to be restrictive; when the indicator is growing rapidly, policy is easy.

Most monetary and financial economists would agree with these definitions. Disagreement arises when one selects a specific indicator of policy actions. Some define the indicator so that restrictive and easy monetary policy are synonymous with financial restraint and ease—i.e., with the rise and fall of interest rates or the presence and absence of credit rationing. Others define the indicator so that restrictive and easy monetary policy are synonymous with monetary restraint and ease. These views are equally incorrect. Since both interest rates and monetary aggregates are endogenous variables that are influenced significantly by forces other than monetary policy actions, neither can be an accurate indicator of monetary policy. By definition, if an indicator of monetary policy actions alone is desired, the indicator must be independent of economic activity and fiscal policy actions. An example of such an indicator is the neutralized money stock.

Another controversial concept that often arises in discussions of monetary policy is the target of policy. Ultimate policy targets are, of course, such things as full employment, stable prices, and so on. In the present context, however, targets refer to intermediate financial targets, which, if achieved, should lead, or at least contribute, to the attainment of the ultimate goals of policy. Examples of intermediate policy targets are a constant growth rate of the quantity of money or a market rate of interest equal to the natural rate of interest.

The determination of interest rates and money is described in the next section. The endogenous nature of these variables, including their simultaneous determination in a general-equilibrium framework, is emphasized. The following section details the general inadequacies of observed interest and money as indicators, describes an appropri-

[1] On the demand for money, see F. Modigliani, R. Rasche, and J. P. Cooper, "Central Bank Policy, the Money Supply, and Short-term Rate of Interest, *The Journal of Money, Credit, and Banking,* II, May, 1969, pp. 166–218; and F. deLeeuw, "The Demand for Money: Speed of Adjustment, Interest Rates, and Wealth," in G. Horwich, ed., *Monetary Process and Policy: A Symposium* (Homewood, Ill.: Richard D. Irwin, Inc., 1967), pp. 167–186. On the investment response, see the investment studies produced by the Federal Reserve—MIT research project (summarized in F. deLeeuw and E. M. Gramlich, "The Channels of Monetary Policy," *Journal of Finance,* XXIV, May 1969) [reprinted in this volume].

TABLE 1. FUNDS RAISED BY AND ADVANCED TO DOMESTIC NONFINANCIAL SECTORS

| | 1965 | 1966 | 1967 | 1968 |
|---|---|---|---|---|
| Funds Raised: | 67.1 | 62.6 | 74.6 | 91.4 |
| Private domestic nonfinance | 66.0 | 62.0 | 66.4 | 79.7 |
| Short-term debt | | | | |
| Households | 11.3 | 8.3 | 7.1 | 15.5 |
| Businesses | 14.6 | 13.6 | 9.0 | 13.0 |
| State & local gov't | 1.3 | 0.4 | 1.3 | 0.3 |
| Long-term obligations | | | | |
| State & local gov't | 6.5 | 6.4 | 9.1 | 10.9 |
| Households | 16.2 | 11.0 | 11.5 | 15.4 |
| Businesses | 15.9 | 22.5 | 28.4 | 24.6 |
| Federal government (net) | 1.1 | 0.6 | 8.2 | 11.8 |
| Funds Advanced: | 67.1 | 62.6 | 74.6 | 91.4 |
| Private domestic nonfinance | 8.6 | 20.1 | 2.0 | 17.0 |
| Households | 1.8 | 10.7 | −6.2 | 1.7 |
| Businesses | 1.0 | 3.2 | 0.4 | 7.7 |
| State & local gov't | 5.8 | 6.2 | 7.8 | 7.7 |
| Financial institutions (net) | 56.0 | 40.7 | 66.1 | 69.2 |
| Banks | 28.3 | 17.3 | 36.1 | 38.6 |
| Nonbank saving institutions | 14.2 | 8.7 | 15.0 | 15.1 |
| Other | 13.5 | 14.6 | 14.9 | 15.5 |
| Rest of the World (net) | − 1.2 | − 1.6 | 1.7 | 1.6 |
| Federal Reserve | 3.8 | 3.5 | 4.8 | 3.7 |
| Memorandum: | | | | |
| Fed. gov't funds raised as % of total | 1.6 | 1.0 | 11.0 | 12.8 |
| Fed. Reserve funds supplied as % of total | 5.7 | 5.6 | 6.4 | 4.0 |
| Long-term business funds raised plus change in profit tax liability | 17.8 | 22.7 | 24.6 | 27.1 |

Data Sources for Table 1: Most of the data are from the financial summary table in the flow-of-funds accounts. However, the component breakdown of private-domestic-nonfinance funds raised differs from that of the flow-of-funds; the Rest-of-the-World funds raised (from sources other than the Federal Government) have been netted against its funds advanced, Federal Government mortgages and loans to private domestic nonfinance have been netted against its funds raised, and Federal Government loans to sectors other than private domestic nonfinance (i.e., Saving and Loan Associations and the Rest of the World) have been excluded from the table.

The component breakdown is the following:

Household short-term debt: consumer credit plus banks loans n.e.c. plus other loans other than those from the Federal Government.

Business short-term debt: banks loans n.e.c. plus other loans other than those from the Federal Government.

State and local short-term debt: same as that given in the flow-of-funds.

Households long-term: 1–4 family mortgages of both household and business sectors.

Business long-term: security issues and other mortgages and Federal Government loans of both the business and household (nonprofit) sectors.

State and local long-term: bond issues and loans from the Federal Government.

ate indicator of monetary policy, and documents the specific errors that would have resulted from using the observed money stock or interest rates as the indicator during the 1950s. Alternative policy targets (or rules) are discussed in the last section.

## II. The Determination of Interest and Money

The essential point of this section is that interest rates and the stock of money are determined simultaneously along with everything else in a general equilibrium system. Unlike the ruling majority in money and finance who pay lip service to the proposition, we believe it and make use of it. Nevertheless, we shall begin by isolating proximate or more immediate determinants of interest and money. After doing so, we shall take the broader view and describe the interaction of money and interest rates as they mesh to form the "money supply process." Finally, we shall consider an alternative to our analysis.

### *A. Interest Rates*

As is customary at this level of aggregation, a single rate of interest is taken to be a representative or average of the rates on all nonmonetary financial claims—both short and long term, government and private, equity and debt. The rate of interest varies inversely with the price of claims—or securities, to use a more precise term—and, like any price, is determined by total supply and demand. The approach to interest rate determination is thus very direct, in glorious contrast to the common obsession with IS and LM curves and other weary devices designed to conceal the underlying forces at work in the securities market. The general framework is more Wicksellian than Keynesian or Fisherian, and the guiding principle is the fact that nothing can affect the rate of interest except as it creates excess security supply or demand.

We—or at least one of us—are currently engaged in a major econometric effort in which the price and quantity of five broad, all-inclusive security categories will be explained by demand and supply schedules of each security. The study uses flow-of-funds data and, if successful, will enable decisive determination of the impact of such factors as preferred habitats, interest rate expectations, and price level expectations on the general level and structure of interest rates. We are not ready to report on the outcome of this research but can indicate something of the scope of the approach to interest rate determination by considering the interaction of specific participants in the securities markets.

The upper half of Table 1 presents the quantities of funds raised by the private domestic nonfinancial sectors and the federal government during the last four years. The lower half of Table 1 contains the quantities of funds advanced by private domestic nonfinancial sectors, financial institutions, the rest of the world, and the Federal Reserve. Funds raised have been divided according to their basic investment use. Households supply short-term debt (largely consumer credit) to finance consumer durables and they supply residential mortgages to finance housing expenditures; nonfinancial businesses supply short-term debt (largely to banks) to finance inventories and they supply long-term issues to finance plant and equipment investment; and state and local governments issue their obligations, at least in part, to finance construction expenditures.

The financial flows say a great deal about the underlying real expenditures, even though there is significant substitutability of funds between uses, including expenditures on consumption and financial assets. For example, the decline in 1967 in short-term debt issued by households and businesses and its rise in 1968 follows the simultaneous slowdown and the acceleration in consumer durable and inventory expenditures.[2] Likewise, the deceleration in the growth of residential mortgages in 1966 and the subsequent acceleration in 1968 is associated with a similar movement in expenditures.[3] At first glance, business long-term issues do not appear to have moved in accord with plant and equip-

[2] Consumer durable expenditures fell from $14.9 billion in 1966 to $12.1 billion in 1967 and rose to $16.9 billion in 1968; inventory expenditures fell from $14.7 billion to $6.1 billion and rose back to $7.6 billion in 1968.

[3] Residential construction expenditures on 1–4 family units fell from $20.0 billion in 1965 to $18.0 billion in 1966, rose slightly to $18.6 billion in 1967, and accelerated to $21.9 billion in 1968.

ment expenditures. The rate of growth of the latter slowed markedly in 1967 and accelerated in 1968, while business issues continued their rapid rise in 1967 and then declined in 1968.[4] However, when account is taken of the permanent acceleration of corporate tax payments in 1967—businesses apparently issued long-term debt to raise the needed funds—the discrepancy between movements in issues and expenditures is eliminated. The sum of long-term business issues and the change in corporate profit tax liabilities grew slightly in 1967 and accelerated in 1968 (see the memorandum at the bottom of the table).

In the advancing of funds, the most obvious phenomenon is the substitutability between direct financing by the nonfinancial sectors, particularly households and businesses, and indirect financing by financial institutions. State and local governments advanced relatively constant amounts during these years, but households and businesses shifted in 1966 toward advancing funds directly, and in 1967, back to the normal indirect channeling of funds through financial intermediaries. Also, there was a substantial decline in funds advanced by commercial banks and nonbank savings institutions in 1966 with an increase in 1967. Other financial institutions were not affected by this relative disintermediation.

Other participants in the securities markets include the federal government (a net demander of funds), the Federal Reserve (a net supplier of funds) and the rest of the world. The latter demanded funds (on net) in 1965-66 and supplied them in 1967-68.

Two interesting phenomena regarding the influence of the fiscal and monetary authorities on interest rates emerge from Table 1. First, in terms of their average contribution (see the memorandum at the bottom of the table), the authorities do not appear to dominate the securities market. Over this four-year period, the federal government accounted for only 6.6% of the total funds raised and the Federal Reserve supplied only 5.4%.[5] Second, while the Federal Reserve has supplied a relatively constant proportion of the total funds[6]—its contribution varied between 4.0% and 6.4%—the federal government's proportion fluctuated widely. After having been largely out of the market in 1965 and 1966, the Treasury raised $8 billion in 1967 and $12 billion in 1968, accounting for over 10% of the funds raised in these two years. This is, of course, just another example of a financial phenomenon reflecting real events—in this case the substantial fiscal deficits in 1967 and 1968.[7]

## B. *Money*

The determination of the quantity of money is at least as involved as the determination of the rate of interest, because the latter plays a role in determining the former. The quantity of money is equal to the amount that the public wishes to hold. This, in turn, depends importantly on the rate of interest and the level of national income. Since one of us has previously investigated the proximate determinants of the stock of money in detail,[8] we can present a simplified description of the movement of money over the course of a typical postwar business cycle. We abstract for the moment from actions of the Federal Reserve.

Consider a business upswing, characterized by an investment schedule shifting to the right. As a consequence, both interest rates and income rise. Since the rise in interest rates generates the bank reserves needed to support an increased demand for

---

[4] Plant and equipment expenditures (including net direct investment abroad) rose from $81.6 billion in 1965 to $91.4 billion in 1966, $92.3 billion in 1967, and $99.0 billion in 1968.

[5] The Federal Reserve percentage is not purported to be an accurate measure of its impact on the securities markets. For one thing, changes in reserve requirements (and the discount rate and Regulation Q) do not show up in this series, but they have significant impacts on the banking system's ability to supply funds. For another, if the Federal Reserve is simply offsetting the impact of an external event on bank reserves, say a gold drain caused by the Vietnam war, one might not wish to view the Federal Reserve as making a positive contribution to the supply of funds.

[6] Annual data conceal some interesting quarterly variations. For example, the Federal Reserve was a substantial seller of securities in the fourth quarter of 1968.

[7] The average surplus for 1965 and 1966 was $1 billion; the average deficit for 1967 and 1968 was $9 billion.

[8] P. H. Hendershott, *The Neutralized Money Stock: An Unbiased Measure of Federal Reserve Policy Actions* (Homewood, Ill.: Richard D. Irwin, Inc., 1968).

money, the money stock rises. The increase in available reserves results from an increase in member bank borrowing, a decrease in member bank excess reserves, a relative decrease in time deposits, and a *ceteris paribus* inflow of gold via the capital account of the balance of payments. Income effects on reserves work in the opposite direction, but the interest rate effects dominate.[9] Since interest and income move together, money tends to rise in the upswing. The reverse occurs in the downswing. Thus the quantity of money moves procyclically.

Of course, the Federal Reserve influences the money stock. By taking expansionary actions it initially lowers interest rates, inducing the public to hold more bank deposits, while simultaneously supplying the reserves to support them. In the longer run the actions tend to be translated into money income increases, rather than interest rate decreases. Early in the upswing the Federal Reserve is generally feeding the rising demand for money, later in the upswing it usually acts to restrain the rising demand by raising interest rates, and in the downswing it is generally attempting to offset the falling demand for money. These responses are documented in the following section.

### C. *The Interaction of Interest and Money*

The formal mechanism by which a rise in the rate of interest raises the quantity of money is not well understood. In order to see precisely how interest and money interact, it is necessary to extend the security market determination of interest rates in a Wicksellian direction. In that noteworthy framework, there are two kinds of interest rates, the natural or equilibrium rate and the market rate. Only the market rate is observable and it is taken to be the average of the prevailing rates on all securities. The natural rate is more abstract but is an essential part of the apparatus by which changing market rates alter the stock of money.

On a first approximation, the natural rate is defined as that market rate of interest at which desired saving and investment *would* be equal. In general, this is not the same as the prevailing market rate, since desired saving and investment are undergoing constant change and cannot be equal, except after a rather prolonged period of adjustment.

From the viewpoint of observable financial phenomena, it is necessary both to narrow and broaden the saving and investment totals relevant to the natural rate. Only those components of saving and investment channeled directly or indirectly through the money and capital—the securities—markets can have any bearing on the rate of interest, which is, as we noted, an inverse function of the price of claims. Moreover, since saving and investment are continuing or flow variables, characteristic of a growing economy, they generate a flow demand and flow supply, respectively, of nonmonetary financial claims. The natural rate is thus the rate of interest at which the flow supply and flow demand for securities would be equal.

Securities are defined in the broadest possible sense to include all nonmonetary claims. The security supply side is thus extended beyond Wicksell to include the very considerable quantity of government debt in this country. Its relevance to the rate of interest as a source of continuing flow supply is substantial, and on at least one occasion in recent years, overwhelming.[10]

There is no unique natural rate. There is only one at any instant of time, but there will be a different one for every combination of all the variables that determine saving, investment, the government deficit, and, thereby, flow security demand and supply. Since saving depends significantly on disposable income, which in turn is a function of government tax receipts, the balanced portion of the government budget is also relevant to the level of the natural rate.

The market rate, once again, is the observed rate and is determined by all security supplies and demands—new flows and preexisting stocks of claims combined. In a brief interval, the flows are negligible and market

---

[9] The resulting increase in income causes a drain of bank reserves into currency, but it also increases Federal Reserve float and member bank borrowing (by increasing the demand for bank loans), and these somewhat more than offset the impact of the currency drain on reserves. In addition, the increase in income raises imports of foreign goods, which contracts the money stock by inducing a gold outflow. On net, the increase of income in the upswing reduces bank reserves.

[10] The federal government accounted for nearly two-thirds of the 20% increase in total funds raised in 1967.

rate is determined solely in the existing-securities market.

When the market rate and the flow equilibrium or natural rate are the same, the market rate is constant over time and, for a given growth rate of the economy, so is the endogenously determined money stock. When, because of rising investment prospects or increasing government borrowing, an increased rate of security supply raises the natural rate, there is at the still unchanged market rate an excess flow supply of securities. The excess securities cause the price of securities to fall and the yield to rise, whereupon they are purchased by bankers, expanding total bank credit and the money stock.[11] This process continues, with the yield on securities (the market rate) gradually rising toward the natural rate, carrying the money stock with it. The increase in expenditures financed by the additional quantity of money will raise the general price level and possibly output as well.

In the opposite case when the natural rate falls below the market rate, there is at the higher market rate an excess flow demand for securities. The excess security demand lowers the market rate and induces bankers to sell off earning assets, contracting bank credit and money. In response, the price level and probably output fall. The greater the gap there is between the market rate and the natural rate, the greater, of course, is the force altering market rates and the stock of money.

### D. A Qualification: Price Level Expectations and Interest Rates

It is important to stress that the movements of the market rate in the Wicksellian system are intended to be "real" in the sense that they do not merely reflect changes in the expected rate of price level movement. Suppose a rise in the nominal (quoted) market rate on fixed money-value claims is in fact caused by widely held inflationary expectations. The rise would apply equally to the nominal natural rate, which is simply that interest rate at which saving and investment happen to be equal. As a consequence, the difference between the market and natural rates, whether in real or nominal units, would be unchanged and could have no impact on the quantity of money.

The use of the Wicksellian framework to explain observed movements in interest rates and the money stock is thus qualified by the requirement that the nominal and real rates shift only gradually relative to each other. What is the empirical evidence that expectations of price level change have in fact influenced the trends and cycles of interest rates in the postwar period?

Recently there have been two serious studies of the influence of price expectations on interest rates. A dissertation using Fisherian methodology by William E. Gibson, formerly of the University of Chicago, concluded that a 1% rise in the price level raises the short-term rate .33% and the long-term rate .06%—both after a lapse of 10 years.[12] Using his price index (the GNP deflator), interest rates, and weighting system, annual real series of the prime commercial paper rate and the Moody Aaa bond yield were computed. Each year's price change was carried forward four years in both nominal interest series, applying the sum of the fourth to tenth-year weights to the fourth year. The patterns of the resulting real series, plotted in Chart 1, are scarcely distinguishable from the nominal ones.

A study by Thomas Sargent reports results that are consistent with Gibson's.[13] Sargent is not explicit about the long-run effect of expected price changes on nominal rates, but arrives at the longest expectational

[11] The bank purchase reflects more than the interest rate sensitivity in the banking system's demand for securities (or equivalently, free reserves) at a given reserve level. Other interest rate responses raise total bank reserves. Foreigners buy some of the securities with funds other than U.S. bank demand deposits and households purchase some of their securities by first converting time deposits into demand deposits. This leads to a direct increase in demand deposits; firm demand deposit balances rise more than household and foreign demand balances fall on net. At the same time, these transactions increase excess bank reserves above desired levels and thus lead to additional purchases of securities by the banks themselves.

[12] William E. Gibson, *Effects of Money on Interest Rates* (University of Chicago doctoral dissertation, 1967).

[13] Thomas J. Sargent, "Commodity Price Expectations and the Interest Rate," *Quarterly Journal of Economics*, LXXXIII, February 1969, pp. 127–140 [reprinted in this volume].

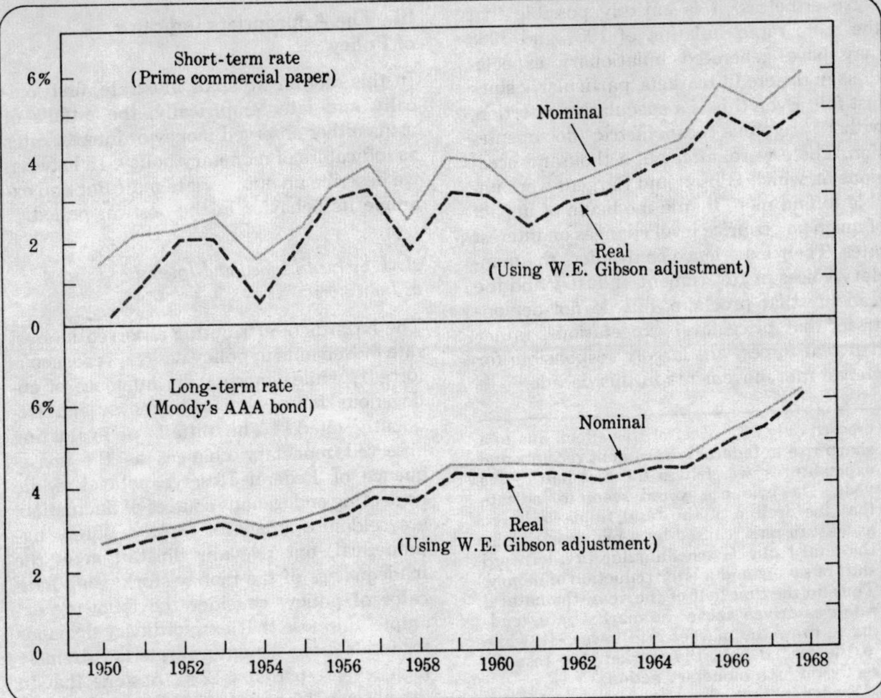


**CHART 1** Selected short- and long-term interest rates (1950–1968).

lag that has yet been claimed; only 2% of the long-run response occurs in the first year and the full response does not occur for 40 years. Unless the long-run effect is unbelievably large, Sargent's results imply an even smaller impact of price expectations on interest rates than do Gibson's.

Thus the evidence supporting the price-expectations hypothesis as a major determinant of postwar interest rates is not yet available. Moreover, in evaluating the 1960s with reference to wholesale prices, the index of which is the most sensitive and least biased by quality changes, 1964 concludes a seven-year period of unbroken price stability. It is not evident how a very strong case can be made for the impact of price expectations on interest rates in the succeeding two or three years. When one considers that the ratio of total funds raised to GNP rose by one-fourth between 1966 and 1968, even with rising interest rates, an alternative explanation involving price expectations is hardly needed.[14]

[14] The causes of the rise in interest rates throughout most of 1966 are somewhat less obvious. The total funds series, relative to 1965, fell from 9.8% to 8.4% of the GNP. One important factor raising interest rates was the actual decline in observed money, reflecting the restrictive action of the Federal Reserve as measured by the decline in effective unborrowed reserves (see footnote 21). This was the "crunch" of that year. However, it occurred in the second half of the year, while market rates rose from the very beginning of 1966.

The cause of the earlier rise in interest rates might be due to fluctuations in desired saving. The only evidence we can provide on the movement in desired saving is indirect, and involves a comparison of total personal income to disposable personal income. If the two income aggregates rise by equal relative amounts, then personal taxes are exercising a constant impact on disposable income, and on that account, desired saving should remain a constant fraction of GNP. In 1966 personal taxes rose 15%, while personal income increased only 9%. Disposable income thus in-

Nevertheless, it is entirely possible that the more rapid inflation of 1967 and 1968 may have generated inflationary expectations in the credit markets, particularly since last fall. Even this is a speculative assertion, without rigorous econometric documentation. There were, after all, a thousand occasions on which Gibson and Sargent were unable to find more than a modicum of impact of much larger price level changes on interest rates. Their experience contradicts the monetary voices in government, industry and the academy that proclaim, but do not demonstrate, that price level expectations, rather than real forces, are largely responsible for interest rate movements in this decade.[15]

creased only 8%. Most of this effect, due to a sharp rise in federal government receipts and expenditures, was felt in the first half of the year. The evidence would seem to indicate that the decline of the total funds series is, at least in part, caused by a movement along the total I plus G schedule due to a leftward shift of saving and a later reduction of money. Thus, in the first half of the year, the natural rate was driven above the market rate, tending to draw the market rate toward it, while in the second half, the market rate rose directly through monetary action.

Evidence that the rise in interest rates might also be due to an outward shift of the private investment schedule, even though total funds raised in 1966 fell, can be gleaned from Table 1. Long-term business issues actually rose in 1966, while mortgages fell. The latter is the most interest-responsive borrowing component. The evidence would seem to indicate that in the face of rising business issues, the other investment components were merely reacting to the rising interest rate (the G component fell marginally during the year).

[15] There is thus, no documented justification for the publication of the "real" rate of interest by the St. Louis Federal Reserve Bank in the 1968–69 winter issues of its *Review* (see the December 1968 issue, p. 5, and January 1969, p. 6). The St. Louis "real" rate is the long-term corporate Aaa yield reduced by the preceding twenty-four months' average annual percentage movement of the implicit GNP deflator. The Fisherian zeal of that institution would shock no one more than Irving Fisher, who himself stressed the fantastically long lags in the formation of price level expectations and their impact on interest rates in this country. In particular, for the long-term rate of interest, he found that price changes influenced interest rates for over a 20-year period; half the total effect of an increase in the price level is not felt until 7.3 years later. See Irving Fisher, *The Theory of Interest* (New York: Kelley and Millman, Inc., 1954), p. 423.

## III. The Appropriate Indicator of Policy

In this section we shall illustrate, first logically and later empirically, the pitfalls of using either observed money or interest rates as indicators of monetary policy. In between we describe an appropriate indicator and examine its behavior in the postwar period.

### *A. Observed Money and Interest as Indicators*

The hazards of attributing observed interest rate movements to policy actions (exogenous forces), while ignoring the influence of endogenous forces, are well known and frequently cited.[16] The pitfalls of evaluating observed monetary changes as the consequence of Federal Reserve policies, while neglecting endogenous sources of fluctuation, are seldom appreciated.[17] As a purely hypothetical, but relevant illustration of the inadequacies of the money stock as an indicator of policy, consider the following example. Suppose that extraordinary demands for funds drive the natural rate to extremely high levels—perhaps 12%. Assume that in the absence of monetary policy actions, the market rate is 5% and rising, and the endogenously-determined money stock is advancing at an annual rate of 9%. The Federal Reserve reduces the growth rate of money from 9% to 6% as it raises market rates from 5% to 7%. The market rate is still below the natural rate, but the discrepancy has been reduced from 7% to 5% and monetary growth cut by 33%. Whether the continued growth rate of the observed money

[16] The first (and perhaps best) discussion of these hazards appeared a full decade ago. See Milton Friedman, *A Program for Monetary Stability* (New York: Fordham University Press, 1959), pp. 39–45.

[17] One of the rare statements in which the pitfalls are appreciated is K. Brunner and A. H. Meltzer, "The Meaning of Monetary Indicators," in G. Horwich, ed., *Monetary Process and Policy: A Symposium* (Richard D. Irwin, Inc., 1967), pp. 187–217 [reprinted in this volume]. Brunner and Meltzer carefully point out the inadequacies of the money stock as the ideal indicator, noting that "It misstates the magnitude of changes in the policy variables . . . and incorporates the influence of . . . feedback effects" (p. 197). Recently Meltzer seems to have lost this appreciation; see "Controlling Money," Federal Reserve Bank of St. Louis *Review*, May 1969, pp. 16–24.

stock is the proper rate depends on the current rate of inflation, the extent of unemployment, the balance of payments, and the allocative and political effects of still higher market rates of interest. The main question here is, whether, in these circumstances, observed monetary behavior can be taken as prima facie evidence of expansionary monetary policy actions. Is it accurate to say, as many would, that in this example the central bank is pursuing an easy money policy, even while it has reduced the growth rate of money by one-third of what it otherwise would have been? We think not.

Just as we have illustrated the inappropriateness of the observed money stock as an indicator of the central bank's influence on money, so we may contrive an example in which interest rate movements are a deceptive measure of policy impact. In the preceding example, suppose that the natural rate of 12% would, in the absence of policy, itself raise the market rate from 5% to 7% within a year's time. The Federal Reserve considers this an unacceptable annual increase and limits the interest rate rise to 1% by raising the growth rate of money from the endogenous 9% to 10%. Obviously, the fact that interest rates continue to rise is no evidence of restrictive policy actions.

Neither example is intended to question the ability of the Federal Reserve to fix the growth rate of money or the interest rate at any desired level. Nor is stability of either the monetary growth rate or interest rates defended as a goal of policy. The purpose is merely to emphasize that endogenous responses should not be confused with Federal Reserve actions.

### B. *The Neutralized Money Stock*

An accurate indicator of Federal Reserve policy actions must distinguish between the endogenous and exogenous components of either interest or money. Which series is analyzed is probably inconsequential, because their exogenous components should have similar cyclical patterns; the only systematic cyclical movement in them would be due to Federal Reserve actions. For example, since a Federal Reserve open-market purchase simultaneously lowers interest rates and increases the money stock, a measure of the impact of current Federal Reserve actions on interest rates is likely to exhibit the same cyclical turning points as would a measure of the impact of such actions on the money stock.

The neutralized money stock represents an empirical effort to derive an exogenous monetary series. It is calculated in the following way.[18] First, a money-stock identity is derived by substituting for the member-bank demand deposit component of the narrowly defined money stock. The money-stock identity includes exogenous components (the Federal Reserve's portfolio of government securities, Treasury cash holdings, and so on) and endogenous components, and the coefficient of most components is the reciprocal of the reserve requirement against demand deposits. The endogenous components are: borrowings from the Federal Reserve, the U. S. gold stock, currency outside banks, Federal Reserve float, member bank time deposits, and excess reserves. Second, regression equations explaining these endogenous components are estimated. The principal regressors are such patently endogenous variables as national income and interest rates. Third, neutralized or "exogenized" components are calculated by applying the computed regression coefficients to cycle-free or trend values of income and interest rates. Finally, the neutralized money stock is calculated by applying the coefficients in the money stock identity to the neutralized components. The resulting series, from which the impact of the business cycle has effectively been removed, reflects the influence of only Federal Reserve policy actions and other exogenous forces.[19] Thus it is a measure of

---

[18] See P. H. Hendershott, *op. cit.*, chap. 9, esp. p. 103.

[19] An important underlying assumption in the neutralization procedure is that the explanatory variables whose cyclical fluctuations are removed a  not themselves influenced by current Federal Reserve actions. This is certainly true of income in any quarter, which may reflect past, but hardly current, monetary policy actions. However, interest rates are, as we have been arguing, jointly determined by internal forces and monetary and fiscal policies. The fact that interest rates are not entirely endogenous causes the neutralized money stock to rise and fall more precipitously than it otherwise would, but failing to take account of the Federal Reserve's influence on interest rates does not alter the turning points of neutralized money. On this, see *The Neutralized Money Stock*, *op. cit.*, p. 105.

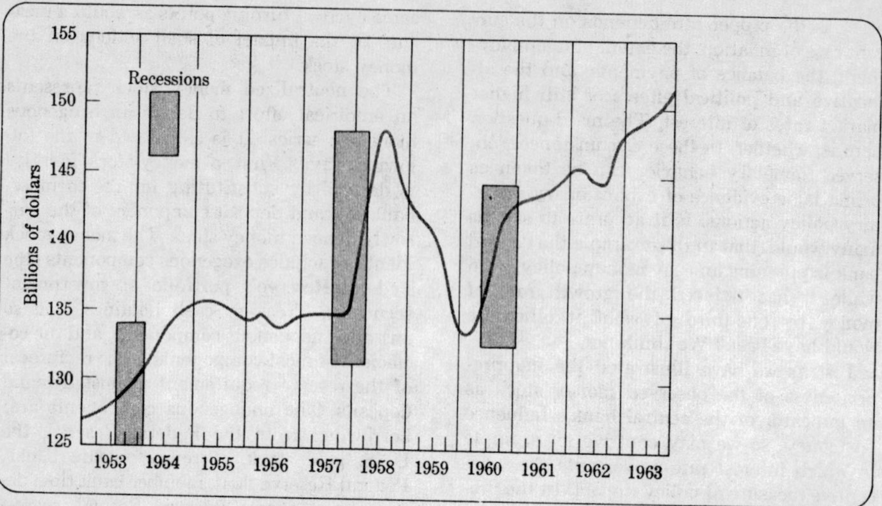


**CHART 2** Neutralized money stock (1952–1963).

monetary policy that is analogous to the full-employment budget surplus measure of fiscal policy. Just as the latter reflects the influence of fiscal policy, not the business cycle, on the budget surplus, the neutralized money stock reflects the influence of monetary policy, not the business cycle, on the money stock.

The neutralized money stock offers an interesting chronicle of Federal Reserve policies during the 1952-64 period (see Chart 2).[20] During those years, there were three recessions: 1953-54, 1957-58, and 1960-61. In the year prior to the 1953 recession, the neutralized money stock was rising, but it accelerated in August 1953, the first month of that recession. It continued to rise strongly past the end of the recession in August 1954 into the subsequent upswing. Monetary restraint, signaled by the turnaround in neutralized money, occurred in April 1955, the eighth month of the boom, and continued, with a brief respite during the second half of 1956, through all the rest of the upswing and beyond, until November 1957, the fourth month of the 1956-58 recession. The sharpest increase in neutralized money over the entire period began at this point and continued through the first half of 1958. A very pronounced decline in neutralized money began in August 1958, the fourth month of the upswing, and ended in March 1960, anticipating the 1960-61 recession by three months. The ensuing monetary expansion continued, with 1962 as an exception, at least through 1964.[21]

A brief summary of the timing of antire-

[20] The original neutralization of the money stock contained a computational error that was kindly pointed out by Michael Hamburger and has been corrected. In equation (6.6) on page 70 of *The Neutralized Money Stock, op. cit.*, the U.S. bill-Eurodollar deposit rate differential should have been expressed as a linear combination of recent changes in, not levels of, the U.S. bill rate. Thus the bill rate terms in equation (6.10) on page 72 should also be increments, not levels. (This error did not affect the "modified" neutralized money stock.)

[21] For the years since 1964, preliminary evidence supports the use of effective unborrowed reserves (unborrowed reserves adjusted for changes in legal reserve requirements) as a proxy for neutralized money. Analysis of this series implies that the monetary expansion continued until mid–1966, the beginning of the "crunch." (Effective unborrowed reserves combines three of the variables generally taken to be exogenous Federal Reserve policy instruments in econometric models: unborrowed reserves, the legal reserve requirement against member bank demand deposits, and that against time deposits. The series is regularly published in the Federal Reserve *Bulletin* in the table "Aggregate Reserves and Member Bank Deposits" on page A17.)

TABLE 2. COMPARISON OF TURNING POINTS OF OBSERVED MONEY (Mo), THE BILL RATE (R) AND NEUTRALIZED MONEY (Mn)

| New policy | Date suggested by analysis of Mn | Months turning point of Mo followed that of Mn | Months turning point of R preceded that of Mn |
|---|---|---|---|
| Ease | August, 1953 | 9 later | 2 earlier |
| Restraint | April, 1955 | 21 later | 10 earlier |
| Ease | November, 1957 | 3 later | 1 earlier |
| Restraint | August, 1958 | 11 later | 2 earlier |
| Ease | March, 1960 | 5 later | 3 earlier |

cession monetary policies is probably of interest, particularly in light of the severe criticisms that have been made of these policies.[22] Analysis of the neutralized money stock suggests that policy switched to ease in the first month of the 1953-54 recession, the fourth month of the 1957-58 recession, and actually anticipated the 1960-61 recession by three months. Thus, on the average, policy switched to ease in the first month of post-accord recessions. This analysis of policy contrasts markedly with the earlier studies of Brunner and Meltzer and Kareken and Solow. The former, for example, contend that policymakers did not switch to ease, on the average, until the ninth month of these recessions. The extreme differences between the conclusions of these studies and those based on the neutralized money stock are due to differences in the indicator of monetary policy actions selected and to errors in the analysis of earlier investigators.[23] Regarding the choice of indicator, both Brunner and Meltzer and Kareken and Solow chose money-stock related indicators, whose turning points, as we show below, tend to lag those of policy. The principal error was Brunner and Meltzer's analysis of annual changes, rather than monthly or quarterly changes, in their indicator. Since turning points in an annual-change series tend to lag those in the observed series, this procedure reinforced the bias toward an unfavorable interpretation of policy already introduced by the selection of a money-stock related variable as the indicator of policy.

### C. *A Measure of the Bias in Observed Indicators*

Popular indicators of monetary policy fall into two general categories: money-market variables and money-stock related variables. The former, which include such variables as free reserves and the three-month Treasury bill rate, are biased toward a favorable assessment of policy; the latter, which include such variables as the money stock, however defined, and the monetary base, however extended or adjusted, are biased toward an unfavorable assessment of policy. That is, turning points in money-market variables tend to precede policy reversals, while those of money-stock related variables tend to follow policy reversals.

Table 2 illustrates the bias in the selection of policy turning points that is introduced by analyzing observed movements in money-market or money-stock related variables. The dates of policy reversals, as denoted by turning points in neutralized money, and the turning points in the observed money stock and the three-month bill rate, relative to these reversals, are recorded. Notice that the

22 See K. Brunner and A. H. Meltzer, "An Alternative Approach to the Monetary Mechanism," Subcommittee on Domestic Finance, Committee on Banking and Currency, 88th Cong., 2nd Sess. (Washington, D.C.: U.S. Government Printing Office, 1964) and J. Kareken and R. M. Solow, "Lags in Monetary Policy," *Stabilization Policies* (Englewood Cliffs, N.J.: Prentice-Hall, Inc., 1963), pp. 1–96.

23 For documentation of these errors, see P. H. Hendershott, "The Inside Lag in Monetary Policy: A Comment," *Journal of Political Economy*, LXXIV, October 1966, pp. 519–523.

turning points in observed money *always* follow those in neutral money and that those in the bill rate *always* precede those of neutral money. For example, a policy switch from ease to restraint, as revealed by the downturn of neutral money, will be preceded by the rise in the bill rate and followed by the fall in the observed stock of money. The average lag in turning points of observed money behind those of neutral money is 9.8 months; the average lead in turning points of the bill rate relative to neutral money is 3.6 months. The average timing discrepancies for policy reversals to ease are a 5.7 month lag for the observed money stock and a 2.0 month lead for the bill rate.[24]

The short lead in peaks in the bill rate relative to policy reversals to ease suggests that during this period policy makers might have been responding to the bill rate or the money market, rather than to economic activity or the goods market. This implication is reinforced by the fact that in the one recession where the bill rate fell after the peak in economic activity—1957-58—the Federal Reserve was very late in taking action, while in the single recession where the bill rate declined substantially before the peak in economic activity—1960-61—the Federal Reserve anticipated the recession.[25]

[24] Given the apparently smaller bias in turning points of the bill rate relative to that of the observed money stock, it is difficult to understand the basis for the frequent assertion that interest rates are a more misleading policy indicator than is the observed money stock (see, e.g., Brunner and Meltzer, "The Meaning of Monetary Indicators," *op. cit.*, p. 204).

[25] This could be interpreted as striking evidence that the Federal Reserve in fact pursues a policy of equating the market rate of interest to the natural rate (see the following section). If the Federal Reserve believes that movements in the market rate are caused primarily by movements in the same direction in the natural rate, then changes in the bill rate (a key market rate) would in the Wicksellian framework call for central-bank-induced opposite changes in the stock of money (as reflected in the neutralized series). For example, a fall in the bill rate due to a fall in the natural rate tends to reduce the stock of money, spending, and ultimately economic activity. The Wicksellian central bank response, aimed at heading off these endogenous consequences, is to lower the market rate immediately by engaging in open-market purchases.

## IV. An Appropriate Monetary Policy

If a vote were taken today among monetary and financial economists, to say nothing of Congressmen, economic advisers to the President, journalists and the general public, there is little doubt that a rule requiring the Federal Reserve each year to raise the stock of money within relatively narrow bounds would win hands down. Viewed as a delayed reaction to the catastrophe of 1929-33 and other major monetary miscalculations, the advocacy of a monetary growth rule is understandable. However, in general, such a rule is a crude policy that does not represent the best the central bank can and should aspire to in the 1970s. It is only a minimum risk policy aimed at preventing severe monetary errors. It provides no offsets against the more frequent real disturbances to the economy and assigns no stabilization role to fiscal policy.

A constant growth rate of money of, say 3% or 4% a year, is designed to counter the deflationary tendency of a growing economy. Under ideal circumstances, rising output would be met by equal demand at more or less constant prices. The economy would achieve the growth equivalent of the stable equilibrium of IS and LM—the schedules we disparaged earlier in this paper. In particular, the growth rule would stabilize the LM schedule by neutralizing the tendency of falling prices to shift it downward.

Of course, the equilibrium will not last. Inventory and fixed investment cycles will continue to occur, and future government deficits to finance wars in Southeast Asia or on urban poverty would not be too surprising. In terms of the IS-LM framework, the IS curve, where I includes the government deficit, will continue to undergo substantial fluctuations. In Wicksellian terms, the natural rate will fluctuate. With monetary policy unable to respond selectively to disturbances, the movement of the natural rate will be translated into an equal movement of the market rate. The LM schedule, once again, will shift gradually to the changing equilibrium defined by the intersection of IS and the supply function of output. This time, however, LM will be moved not by the exogenous money stock, but by the price level, fed by endogenous monetary responses.

If policy were free from the shackles of a

monetary growth rule, it could, if it wished, carry LM immediately to its new equilibrium by altering the growth rate of money. This would equate the market rate to the natural rate instantly, preventing the endogenous stock of money, the demand for money, and thereby the price level from responding to a discrepancy between the rates as part of an internal adjustment process. Or, if the bank were so disposed, it could maintain some degree of difference between the market and natural rates in exchange for some amount of price level or output movement. This might be done at the trough of the business cycle when the natural rate, having risen above the market rate, is allowed to pull money, velocity, prices, employment, and output up along with it. Some inflation might also be tolerated at high employment if, as was considered earlier, an extremely high natural rate might draw the market rate above politically acceptable levels.

### A. *Ideal Monetary Policy: Equation of Market to Natural Rate*

The ideal monetary policy is one in which the central bank, starting at a position of full employment, acts immediately to equate the market rate to the natural rate. At the same time the fiscal authority manipulates the natural rate by tax and expenditure policies so as to keep it within a politically acceptable range. The fiscal authority is also responsible for taking action against disturbances that do not involve changes in market or natural rates —destabilizing direct movements between money and commodities. This leaves both the Treasury and the central bank with a clean and clear understanding of what each must do. The central bank has a mandate to take interest rates as the immediate target of policy. But it is the relation between the market and the natural rate, conditioned by ultimate goals such as full employment and stable prices, that shapes policy, never the observed market rate alone.[26]

This approach has many advantages. It enables the central bank to do what it does naturally—to operate in the financial markets and set a proper interest rate. It defines the proper interest rate.[27] It limits the lags in the effect of policy to the very little time required for a change in market rates to spread from one security to another. For policy tries only to prevent unwanted movements of the price level and output, not to reduce prices or raise GNP through an inevitable time consuming process.

The natural rate has not yet been measured. Its measurement, however, is not far off. As part of the econometric study of financial markets referred to earlier, three natural rates—a residential mortgage, a combined bond-equity, and an aggregate short-term—will be measured. With these rates in hand, the consequences of a policy of equating the market and natural rates will be relatively easy to evaluate. We are confident that these consequences will support such a policy.

---

26 For a detailed discussion of the stabilization program described in this paragraph, see G. Horwich, "A Framework for Monetary Policy" in K. Brunner, ed., *Targets and Indicators of Monetary Policy* (San Francisco: Chandler Publishing Co., 1969). This volume contains the proceedings of a conference held at the University of California, Los Angeles, in April 1966.

27 In a paper presented to the Savings and Residential Financing Conference three years ago, Warren Smith also advanced interest-rate policy as the proper target of central banking stabilization efforts. See Warren L. Smith, "Some Reflections on Interest Rates and Their Economic Implications," *Conference on Savings and Residential Financing* (Chicago: U.S. Savings and Loan League, 1966), pp. 44–57. However, Smith did not provide a criterion for the appropriate interest rate in terms of an immediate target level, as we have suggested here in the form of the natural rate.

# THE INCIDENCE OF MONETARY POLICY

The incidence of monetary policy concerns changes in the distribution of output among industries and of income among segments of the population in consequence of a monetary policy action. This incidence has received far less attention from policy makers and economists than have the overall implications of policy for aggregate levels of income, employment, and prices. Yet, the redistribution effects of policy have important economic implications for the economy. Complaints of discrimination against particular sectors accompany almost every policy decision. To the extent that incidence has been considered by the policy makers, concern has focused primarily on the differential effects of monetary policy on various industry sectors. Thus the Federal Reserve has expressed concern over, and modified policy in light of, the relative impact of its policies on thrift institutions, residential construction, state and local governments, and the U.S. Treasury. High and rising interest rates, for example, are considered to endanger the solvency of thrift institutions, to reduce expenditures on housing and municipal capital projects more than proportionately, and to make the marketing of new Treasury securities at times of large deficits in the Federal budget more difficult and costly.

The studies in part VI attempt to quantify the incidence of monetary policy. By itself, however, such information is insufficient to translate into welfare statements. This requires a comparison of the incidence of monetary policy both with alternative policies and with the incidence associated with the disturbances that the policy is intended to prevent or offset. Thus, the incidence of restrictive monetary policy directed at curbing inflation at full employment must be compared with the effects and incidence of alternative restrictive policies or of the inflation that would result in the absence of policy actions.

The first selection by Brownlee and Conrad summarizes the analysis and findings of a larger investigation of the incidence of restrictive monetary and fiscal policies and of the increase in prices that would have occurred in their absence. The study concludes that higher interest rates, assumed to reflect restrictive monetary policy, would redistribute income from higher to lower income groups. A similar transfer would accompany an increase in Federal income taxes. An increase in the price level, on the other hand, would result in a redistribution of income in favor of the higher income groups.[1]

[1] Space limitations prevent the inclusion of articles analyzing the incidence of inflation. For examples of such studies see Martin Bronfenbrenner and Franklyn D. Holzman, "Survey of Inflation Theory," *American Economic Review*, vol. 53 (September, 1963), pp. 593–661; Armen Alchian and Reuben Kessel, "Effects of Inflation," *Journal of Political Economy*, vol. 70 (December, 1962), pp. 527–537; and Albert E. Burger, "Effects of Inflation, 1960–68," *Review*, Federal Reserve Bank of St. Louis, (November, 1969), pp. 24–36.

The incidence of monetary policy on industry sectors is considered in the next selections. Crocket, Friend, and Shavell discuss the results of a survey among businessmen conducted to determine the reasons underlying cutbacks from planned expenditures on fixed plans and inventories in 1966 and 1967. Although some reductions were attributed to financial reasons, by far the largest proportion was attributed to capacity limitations of suppliers. The lack of emphasis of financial factors by the businessmen is in agreement with the results of previous similar surveys.[2] McGouldrick and Petersen also employed a survey to investigate the incidence of monetary policy on state and local governments in 1966 and 1967. They report that the high interest rates in this period significantly reduced long-term borrowings by these governments but affected capital outlays considerably less. Using primarily econometric methods, Maisel finds evidence that by raising interest rates and reducing inflows into thrift institutions restrictive monetary policy greatly reduces residential construction. Business expenditures on capital investment are also reduced, but somewhat less and only after a considerable time lag.

Investigation of the incidence of monetary policy presupposes correct identification of policy. The selections in part V reveal, however, considerable disagreement on how to describe policy. All the studies cited above use interest rates as the appropriate indicator of policy. Bowsher and Kalish demonstrate that insofar as all indicators do not describe policy similarly, the choice of indicator affects the measurement of incidence. Employing the money stock as the indicator of policy, they find no evidence that housing has been unduly affected by restrictive monetary policy. Rather, they attribute the observed contracyclical movements in residential construction to the phase of the business cycle and price expectations.

[2] James R. Schlesinger, "Monetary Policy and Its Critics," *Journal of Political Economy*, vol. 68 (December, 1960) pp. 601–616. On the other hand, a recent study reinterprets the data obtained in the Friend survey and reports evidence of a stronger and quicker response to monetary policy actions than identified by the original author. See William H. White, "Effects of Tight Money on 1966 Business Investment," *Journal of Money, Credit and Banking*, vol. II (November, 1970) pp. 446–460. While not discussed in the readings included in this volume, the incidence of monetary policy on small business has also been investigated in a large number of studies. For an example of a recent study see William L. Silber and Murray E. Polakoff, "The Differential Effects of Tight Money: An Econometric Study," *Journal of Finance*, vol. 25 (March, 1970) pp. 83–97.

# 33 EFFECTS UPON THE DISTRIBUTION OF INCOME OF A TIGHT MONEY POLICY*

OSWALD BROWNLEE
*University of Minnesota*

ALFRED CONRAD
*City University of New York*

## The Nature of the Analysis

This analysis is designed to estimate the effects upon the distribution of personal income of monetary actions to stabilize the general level of prices for goods and services. In particular, we attempted to estimate how the "average" income receiver in a given personal income size class would fare—with respect to his real income—if there were an increase in the demand for goods and services and (1) no offsetting monetary or fiscal action were taken so that the price level rose, (2) monetary action were taken to keep the price level at its inital value, or (3) no monetary action were taken but (*a*) some tax rates were increased to keep the price level from rising and (*b*) federal expenditures were reduced without any offsetting change in tax rates. It is assumed that anti-inflationary monetary action would result in increased interest rates, whereas anti-inflationary fiscal action could keep both the price level and the interest rate from increasing.

Our estimates are necessarily relatively crude ones. The analytical framework ignores certain impacts upon the economy that will influence the distribution of income. And, of greater importance, we have been able to obtain only crude descriptions regarding many of the important "facts"; e.g., who holds various kinds of assets and liabilities, the amounts borrowed and loaned by various economic units, how interest rates affect purchases, the incidence of various kinds of taxes and the wage and profit structures in various industries.

From among the many different kinds of stabilizing fiscal actions that could be taken, only three different changes in the tax pattern and one change in federal spending have been chosen for consideration in this analysis.

The estimates that are to be presented are for the average income receiver in each income class. Few, if any, income receivers would be affected in exactly the same way as one of these average income receivers and a sizable fraction may experience changes in the direction opposite to that in which the average has moved. Although we have not described quantitatively the variation in income effects within the various income

---

* Reprinted from *The American Economic Review*, vol. 51 (May, 1961), pp. 74–91, by permission of the authors and the American Economic Association. This reading is a summary of the results of a study commissioned and financed by the Commission on Money and Credit. The complete study is published in Commission on Money and Credit, *Stabilization Policies*, Englewood Cliffs, Prentice-Hall, Inc., 1963, pp. 499–588.

classes, available data indicate that this variation is relatively large, due to differences in preferences, age, family status, and the many other characteristics influencing the economic behavior of income-receiving units with a given current income.

Increased interest rates mean increased borrowing costs and increased alternative returns from saving rather than spending. These changes will influence decisions to purchase durables and to save, both directly and via their effects upon the capitalized value of income. Comparisons at given equilibrium values emphasize substitution between durables and nondurables, with no change in total resources employed. In the analysis of employment effects, however, we assume a net reduction in employment, the substitution taking place between present purchasing and saving.

Restrictive fiscal policy may operate by reducing government expenditures or by increasing taxes or, of course, by some combination of these two possibilities. A smaller total of government spending, accompanied by no change in taxation (or, at least, by a smaller reduction in the tax bill), will reduce the flow of incomes throughout the economy, private as well as public. Correspondingly, increased taxes at a given level of income mean lower disposable income and hence reduced spending for goods and services if expenditure depends upon either income or wealth.

By taxing more (or expending less) and purchasing debt, the government could counter an inflationary disturbance and keep the interest rate at a lower level than if it reduced the money supply. The budget action will reduce total spending at given interest rates; the retirement of debt will reduce the interest rate and therefore increase private spending.

The redistribution of income resulting from inflation is a transfer from people with assets whose nominal values increase less rapidly than the price level to people with assets whose nominal values increase faster than the price level. In particular, creditors lose and debtors gain from inflation. Some wages and commodity prices may rise proportionately more than others because of institutional factors. However, such possibilities are not analyzed in this study.

Increased interest rates will result in a revaluation of streams of income from assets yielding fixed flows and, therefore, in the market prices of existing assets. Relative market values may change, since assets have different durabilities or maturities, but unless there are actual sales, there is no necessary change in income flows as a result of the increased rates. New contracts, however, will be made at higher interest rates, thus resulting in a shift of income from interest payers to interest receivers. Among the interest payers should be included taxpayers in their capacities as servicers of certain governmental debt.

If the aggregate level of economic activity were not affected by the interest rate change, this effect would be the only redistributive one—except insofar as the demands for various goods and services are not affected proportionately. In the event that they are not and that wages and profit structures in different industries are not the same, there will be additional alterations in the income distribution. A net decline in activity levels is a special case of this change in proportions, in which activity in certain sectors declines without compensating increases elsewhere: there is a net loss to the economy.

An inflationary disturbance that is countered by reduced government expenditure or increased taxes and purchases of debt to keep the interest rate at its initial level also results in a partially compensating transfer of income from taxpayers to interest payers. Again, there may be structural changes—including a reduced over-all level of economic activity—that will affect the pattern of income.

In order to estimate quantitatively the effects of the various possibilities, we shall first assume that there has been a once-and-for-all autonomous increase in the demands for goods and services sufficient to raise the price level by some arbitrarily given amount—in the absence of any monetary or fiscal action to counter this demand increase. The redistributive effects of this possibility will be estimated according to the estimated distribution of liquid assets.

We are making the simplest assumption about the shape of the autonomous demand increase; namely, that the increase is proportionate to the 1957 composition of goods and services. Another assumption would not

**TABLE 1. ESTIMATED INTEREST ELASTICITIES AND RESPONSES TO A ONE PERCENTAGE POINT INCREASE IN INTEREST RATES, 1957**

| Type of Asset | Per cent borrowed | Borrowing rate (%) | Lending rate (%) | Life of instrument (years) | Life of asset (years) | Depreciation plus maintenance (%) | Weighted average interest rate | One minus marginal tax rate | Elasticity c[f] cost with respect to the interest rate | Price elasticity | Interest elasticity | 1957 Expenditures (billions of dollars) | Proportionate change in interest rate | Change in 1957 expenditure due to a 1 per cent change in interest rate (billions of dollars) |
|---|---|---|---|---|---|---|---|---|---|---|---|---|---|---|
| Construction for maintenance | 0.75 | 6 | 6 | 5 | 30 | 3.33 | 6 | 0.7 | .39 | – 1 | – .39 | 15.3 | .167 | – 1.0 |
| Industrial | 1.00 | 5 | 6 | 5 | 40 | 3.13 | 5 | 0.5 | .29 | – 1 | – .29 | 5.4 | .20 | – 0.3 |
| Commercial | 1.00 | 6 | 6 | 25 | 40 | 3.13 | 6 | 0.5 | .32 | – 1 | – .32 | 24.4 | .167 | – 1.3 |
| Residential | 0.80 | 6 | 6 | 25 | 60 | 2.08 | 6 | 0.9 | .56 | – 1 | – .56 | 11.7 | .17 | – 1.1 |
| Highways | 1.00 | 4 | 6 | 25 | 25 | 5.00 | 4 | 1. – | .286 | – ½ | – .14 | 5.1 | .25 | – 0.2 |
| Institutional | 1. – | 5 | 6 | 30 | 50 | 2.5 | 5 | 1. – | .5 | – ½ | – .25 | 4.5 | .20 | – 0.2 |
| Producers' durables | 1.00 | 6 | 6 | 5 | 15 | 8.33 | 6 | 0.5 | .15 | – 1 | – .15 | 25.0 | .167 | – 0.6 |
| Farm machinery | .80 | 10 | 6 | 4 | 15 | 8.33 | 7.1 | 0.9 | .28 | – 1 | – .28 | 1.1 | .14 | – .04 |
| Autos | .70 | 12 | 6 | 2.75 | 10 | 12.5 | 7.4 | 0.9 | .21 | – 1 | – .21 | 13.2 | .14 | – .39 |
| Durable consumers goods | .90 | 15 | 6 | 2.5 | 10 | 12.5 | 8 | 0.9 | .22 | – 1 | – .22 | 20.0 | .125 | – .55 |
| | | | | | | | | | | | | | Total | – 5.68 |

TABLE 2. ESTIMATED EFFECT OF A 3 PER CENT INCREASE IN THE PRICE LEVEL UPON THE AVERAGE "REAL" NET WORTH IN VARIOUS INCOME-SIZE CLASSES, 1957 (With Alternative Assumptions about the Distribution of Federal Debt*)

| Income class | Assumption I | Assumption II |
|---|---|---|
| $ 1,999 or less | $ – 96 | $ – 86 |
| 2,000– 2,999 | – 77 | – 66 |
| 3,000– 3,999 | – 61 | – 43 |
| 4,000– 4,999 | – 64 | – 41 |
| 5,000– 5,999 | – 53 | – 24 |
| 6,000– 7,499 | – 9 | + 23 |
| 7,500– 9,999 | + 19 | + 58 |
| 10,000–14,999 | + 74 | + 98 |
| 15,000–19,999 | + 98 | + 66 |
| 20,000 and over | + 667 | + 540 |

*Assumption I is that one-third of corporation income tax is distributed proportionately to consumer expenditure and two-thirds proportionately to dividend receipts. Assumption II is that two-thirds of the tax is allocated proportionately to consumer expenditure and one-third proportionately to dividend receipts.

make any difference in the estimation of equilibrium values following from restrictive fiscal or tight money policies. However, some other distribution of the demand increase might result in different structural effects.

We shall assume, second, that whatever monetary action might be taken to counter the inflationary disturbance will exert its direct effect through increased interest rates. The increased interest charges will make expenditures upon certain classes of goods lower than otherwise would be the case, even though money income were unchanged. However, reductions in expenditures for some classes of goods will subsequently cause lower expenditures on other classes that are not sensitive to interest rate changes, because of the general reduction in income.

Few direct estimates of the interest elasticities of expenditures for various classes of goods are available. But we can make use of other knowledge about expenditure behavior and estimate these interest elasticities indirectly. Increased rates of interest increase the total payments made for an asset with a given purchase price when payment is deferred. Furthermore, increased payments due to a higher cash price cannot be distinguished from increased payments due to higher carrying charges (because of higher interest rates). Consequently, we assume that the elasticity of demand for an asset with respect to its total cost is the same as the elasticity of demand with respect to price. If we can determine how changes in interest rates affect total costs, then we can estimate the elasticity of demand with respect to interest rates by multiplying the price elasticity by the elasticity of cost with respect to interest rates. This product is the interest elasticity of demand, if one further condition is fulfilled; namely, that interest rates affect the cost of only this good—say, houses—relative to the costs (prices) of other goods. The estimated interest elasticities are presented in Table 1.

The value assumed for the multiplier is not crucial for this analysis, since it is only a determinant of the magnitude of the change in the rate of interest or the tax change required to obtain a given equilibrium result. The absolute amounts of income transfers will be dependent upon the size of the multiplier, but whether a person gains or loses from a particular policy is not dependent upon the multiplier. We assume a multiplier of 1.4. This is consistent with a marginal propensity to spend with respect to disposable income of .70 and a net marginal leakage rate of 0.6.

## The Estimates

To estimate the effects of an increase in the general level of prices upon the distribution of income, we assume that real wages and real profits are invariant with respect to the changes in prices. Real government purchases of goods and services also are assumed to remain unchanged. The real tax burden, however, is reduced, assuming that tax collections are employed to meet interest payments on government debt. Thus, the change in the distribution of income as a result of inflation will be dependent upon the amount of the increase in the price level and the distribution of federal tax collections and of income-earning assets whose nominal earnings are fixed.

Assets earning no income, namely, cash and demand deposits, as well as assets earning fixed monetary incomes will depreciate in value as a result of a rise in prices. If we assume that the marginal utility of money is the same as that of the income-earning assets, a measure of the change in the value of assets is a better approximation to the change in welfare than is a change in money income. Consequently, the effect of inflation is described according to the manner in which inflation affects the real values of asset holdings. We have assumed that there are no structural effects in the example of unopposed inflation.

A 3 per cent price increase in 1957 would have been detrimental to the average income receivers in the lower income classes and beneficial to those in the upper income classes. The estimates are shown in Table 2.

A change in interest rates will change the flows of interest payments and receipts. The manner in which these flows will be altered was estimated from data relating to the structure of assets and liabilities according to size of income. Our estimates imply that borrowing and lending patterns among the income-size classes are the same after the interest rate change as they were before. The absolute levels of borrowing and lending may be different, but the relative net asset positions are assumed to be unchanged.

A 3 per cent increase in prices—with no change in real output—in 1957 would have meant an increase in gross national product of approximately 13 billion dollars. With a multiplier of 1.4, interest rates would have had to be increased sufficiently to cut spending on account of the interest rate change alone by about 9 billion dollars—the other 4 billion reduction occurring because income would be lower than otherwise would be the case. A 1.7 per cent increase in the interest rate would have brought about approximately this reduction. The estimated increase is the amount required to keep the equilibrium level of spending from rising. No attempt is made to estimate the time period required for the new equilibrium to be achieved nor of the movement of gross national product between the initial position and the new equilibrium. If both long- and short-term Treasury rates were increased by, say, 1 per cent, it is assumed that both rates paid by other borrowers and received by lenders would be increased by 1 per cent.

In Table 3, estimates of the increases in interest payments and receipts flowing from one income class to another are presented. If gross debt were 1 trillion dollars, gross interest payments would be increased by at least 10 billion dollars as a result of an increase of 1 per cent in interest rates. The interest that we would be able to net out would total about 4 billion dollars.

A change in interest rates also will alter the structure of the economy, since the interest elasticities of expenditure for the various classes of goods and services differ and the requirements of labor, capital equipment, and intermediate goods are not the same for each class of final goods. From input-output data for the U.S. economy, we have estimated how the activity levels of each industry would be altered if the income effects of interest rate changes on the demand for final goods were ignored. This provides an estimate of the short-run effects of the interest rate change upon the structure of the economy.

Assuming first that an index of total output were unaffected by increased interest rates, i.e., that resources moved readily from one industry to another, the differences between wage and profit structures among industries whose activity levels are most affected by interest rates and those least affected will determine the effect upon aggregate wage and profit shares due to a tight money policy. Dividing industries into two classes—those declining more than the average (and therefore declining absolutely with no change in over-all activity) and those declining less than the average (therefore increasing absolutely with no change in over-all activity), we find that the average hourly wage in 1957 for the first group was $2.68 and that for the second was $2.20. Since these differences are not statistically significant, one can say that it is unlikely that wage income would be affected by interest rate changes if total employment were unaffected.

Assume, at the other extreme, that there is no movement of resources among industries, so that a decline in activity in one sec-

**TABLE 3. ESTIMATED CHANGE IN AVERAGE (PER INCOME-RECEIVING UNIT) NET INTEREST RECEIPTS, BY INCOME CLASSES, DUE TO A 1 PER CENT INCREASE IN ALL INTEREST RATES, 1957**

| Income class | Increase in mortage and consumer credit payments | Increase in payments on share of government debt* | | Increase in payments on share of business debt† |
|---|---|---|---|---|
| | | Assumption I | Assumption II | |
| $ 1,999 or less | $ 29.50 | $ 9.83 | $ 15.28 | $ 3.84 |
| 2,000– 2,999 | 30.99 | 18.89 | 25.14 | 4.79 |
| 3,000– 3,999 | 35.11 | 27.61 | 37.59 | 4.93 |
| 4,000– 4,999 | 37.52 | 34.71 | 47.80 | 6.19 |
| 5,000– 5,999 | 45.71 | 44.68 | 61.11 | 6.87 |
| 6,000– 7,499 | 53.91 | 57.94 | 76.55 | 8.04 |
| 7,500– 9,999 | 68.90 | 76.47 | 98.26 | 13.04 |
| 10,000–14,999 | 88.93 | 115.92 | 129.44 | 17.68 |
| 15,000–19,999 | 102.73 | 202.81 | 184.38 | 28.24 |
| 20,000 and over | 140.81 | 926.48 | 871.71 | 108.58 |

| Income class | Total increase in interest paid* | | Increase in receipts for bonds, savings, time, and building and loan deposits and pensions and annuities plus insurance | Net change in receipts minus payments*‡ | |
|---|---|---|---|---|---|
| | Assumption I | Assumption II | | Assumption I | Assumption II |
| $ 1,999 or less | $ 43.17 | $ 48.62 | $ 84.56 | $ 41.39 | $ 35.94 |
| 2,000– 2,999 | 54.67 | 60.92 | 85.05 | 30.38 | 24.13 |
| 3,000– 3,999 | 67.65 | 77.63 | 88.38 | 20.73 | 10.75 |
| 4,000– 4,999 | 78.42 | 91.51 | 100.45 | 22.03 | 8.94 |
| 5,000– 5,999 | 97.26 | 113.69 | 111.89 | 14.63 | – 1.80 |
| 6,000– 7,499 | 119.89 | 138.50 | 111.84 | – 8.05 | – 26.66 |
| 7,500– 9,999 | 158.41 | 180.20 | 131.97 | – 26.44 | – 48.23 |
| 10,000–14,999 | 222.53 | 236.05 | 158.88 | – 63.65 | – 77.17 |
| 15,000–19,999 | 333.78 | 315.35 | 245.29 | – 88.49 | – 70.06 |
| 20,000 and over | 1,175.87 | 1,121.00 | 708.46 | –467.41 | –412.64 |

*See Table 2 for a description of the two assumptions.
†Allocated proportionately to consumer expenditure.
‡Average payments will exceed average receipts for the population as a whole since allocated debt exceeds allocated assets by about 19 billion dollars.

tor is not offset to any extent by increases in others. The pattern of the induced reduction in demand due to interest rate increases, compared to the pattern of the autonomous demand change, is the determining factor with regard to both the decrease in output and its structure. In the special case in which all commodities have identical interest elasticities of demand and there is an across-the-board proportionate increase in demand countered by tighter money, there would be no reduction in output in any sector, even though resources were completely immobile. This would also be the outcome in the event that the sectoral increases in demand were proportional to the interest elasticities. The decline in activity in the case in which resources are completely immobile comes about because the autonomous increase in demand does not match the pattern of interest elasticities and, therefore, the pattern of demand reduction brought about by monetary action. One can generalize that, if the pattern of autonomous demand increase is not matched by the induced reduction in demand due to any counter-inflationary policy and resources are immobile, there will be a net decline in activity.

Assuming that the increase in autonomous demand were proportional to the 1957 de-

TABLE 4. ESTIMATED REDUCTIONS IN ANNUAL INCOME ON ACCOUNT OF TAX INCREASES, BY INCOME-SIZE CLASS

| Size of income | All federal taxes are increased proportionately* | Personal income tax increased | Corporation income tax increased* |
|---|---|---|---|
| Less than $2,000 | $ 28.83 | $ 10.18 | $ 44.10 |
| $ 2,000– 2,999 | 60.24 | 45.78 | 69.88 |
| 3,000– 3,999 | 90.10 | 74.08 | 88.09 |
| 4,000– 4,999 | 115.87 | 106.37 | 96.87 |
| 5,000– 5,999 | 151.16 | 153.26 | 107.07 |
| 6,000– 7,499 | 198.67 | 210.76 | 138.21 |
| 7,500– 9,999 | 264.88 | 285.99 | 153.55 |
| 10,000–14,999 | 409.19 | 448.59 | 336.44 |
| 15,000–19,999 | 730.11 | 821.37 | 719.97 |
| 20,000 and over | 3,487.00 | 3,367.14 | 4,816.43 |

*Assumes two-thirds of the tax is borne by dividend receivers and one-third by consumers.

mand levels and the direct, induced declines were distributed according to the interest elasticities presented earlier, the 9 billion dollar reduction in the demand for durables would cause a total (direct-plus-indirect) decline in gross output levels of 2.2 per cent. Since the decline in labor requirements need not be proportional to the decline in the output level in any sector and this relationship may differ from sector to sector, the induced decline in employment may be greater or smaller than the decline in activity. In fact, the amount of unemployment generated by the first-round impacts of a tight money policy, under the assumptions made above, would have been 1.6 per cent of the total man-hours in 1957. Because of the difference we noted earlier between the average wage in industries suffering greater than average declines in output as compared to those with less than average declines, the loss in compensation of employees would have been 1.9 per cent of the 1957 level or 4.4 billion dollars.

We assume that the deflationary impact of an increase in tax collections depends only upon the size of the increase and not upon its composition. The distributional effect, however, does depend upon the nature of the tax change. The effects of three changes in tax patterns are considered: equal proportionate increases in every taxpayer's federal taxes, equal proportionate increases in every taxpayer's federal personal income taxes, and an increased rate of federal corporation income taxation. The amount by which the total tax bill should be raised to counter a particular inflationary disturbance is estimated from the expenditure relation described previously.

Since some of the proceeds of increased tax collections are in effect employed to subsidize interest payers, the tax collections needed to prevent prices and interest rates from rising are offset by the reductions in interest payments. Approximtely 13 billion dollars of additional taxes would need to be raised to prevent prices from rising, and this amount—collected according to the patterns described above—would be distributed among income-size groups according to the incidence patterns shown in Table 4.

Since the higher taxes, even though progressive in their direct impact, are offset by reduced interest payments, the policy of raising taxes and purchasing debt will include a partially compensating redistribution of income, to some extent at the expense of the lower income classes.

As was the case with monetary policy, an increase in the revenue bill at a given income level will have structural effects that are due to the pattern of decline in the purchases of goods and services when disposable incomes fall. These effects, assuming no compensating shifts in the flows of resources, were estimated by the use of the input-output accounts.

An increase of federal revenues of 13 billion dollars would cause a direct decline in consumer expenditures of 9 billion. With no resource mobility, the direct reduction would cause a total (direct-plus-indirect) reduction in gross output of 2.4 per cent of the 1957 level. Under this structure of sectoral declines, the amount of unemployment generated would be 1.3 per cent and the loss of compensation of employees, 1.3 per cent, or 3.2 billion dollars. If resources were perfectly mobile, the average wage rate would rise in contrast to the corresponding tight money case, since the average wage of the industries that would suffer greater-than-average declines in output due to higher taxes is $2.00 per hour, compared to $2.20 in the industries declining less than the average. (Again, these differences are not statistically significant, using Student's *t*.)

An alternative fiscal policy is a surplus brought about by reducing government expenditures without changing revenues correspondingly. Structural effects and net unemployment will occur under the conditions outlined in the previous sections, but with the pattern of decline due to a federal spending cutback replacing the pattern due to interest increases. With no resource mobility, a decline of 9 billion dollars in federal spending would cause a total (direct-plus-indirect) reduction in gross output of 1.9 per cent (1957 levels). The amount of unemployment generated would be 1.5 per cent of the 1957 total man-hours and the loss of wage and salary compensation would be 1.8 per cent or 4.3 billion dollars. The average wage in the industries declining most was $2.73 per hour, contrasted with an average of $2.25 in the industries declining relatively less. (These averages were not significantly different.)

Since the surplus generated by reduced expenditures would also be used to purchase debt, there is an interest payments subsidy in this case, as there was with the tax-induced surplus. In fact, the funds for this subsidy previously were being used to provide government services and we might therefore consider that the reduction in income is distributed in proportion to the enjoyment of services which have been reduced.

## Conclusion

This analysis has estimated the effects upon the distribution of personal income of alternative monetary and fiscal actions to stabilize the general price level.

The long-run estimates, based upon the distribution of asset holdings and liabilities among income classes in 1957, show the following:

*1.* An uncountered price increase would have reduced the average real net worth in the income classes that receive less than $6,000 and increased the net worth in the classes above $7,500. The $6,000-7,499 class experienced a slight loss under the first assumption about the distribution of federal debt and a gain under the other.

*2.* An increase in interest rates to counter inflation would result in a net gain in receipts for classes receiving less than $6,000 of personal income (under Assumption I) with a net increase in payments for incomes above that level. Under the second assumption there is a slight net increase in payments for the $5,000-5,999 class.

*3.* A tax increase would cause progressive reductions in disposable income with maximum progressivity under a corporate income tax increase. There would be a partially compensating decrease in the interest burden upon the upper income classes, since the increased tax receipts and purchase of debt would make interest rates lower than would otherwise be the case.

The short-run, structural effects from the induced reductions in demand would result in the following losses in employment and in wages and salaries, under the assumptions about immobility of resources described earlier:

*1.* An investment reduction caused by an interest increase of 1.7 per cent would have reduced employment by 1.6 per cent of total man-hours in 1957 and caused a loss in compensation of employees of 4.4 billion dollars, or 1.9 per cent.

*2.* A reduction in consumer expenditures of 9 billion dollars due to a tax increase of $13.00 would have reduced both employment and compensation of employees by 1.3 per cent of the 1957 levels.

*3.* A comparable reduction in 1957 federal spending levels without a tax decline would have caused employment to decline by 1.5 per cent of total man-hours and compensation to fall by 1.8 per cent.

# 34 THE IMPACT OF MONETARY STRINGENCY ON BUSINESS INVESTMENT*

JEAN CROCKETT
*University of Pennsylvania*

IRWIN FRIEND
*University of Pennsylvania*

HENRY SHAVELL
*U. S. Department of Commerce*

The year 1966 was characterized by one of the severest credit squeezes of the past half century. In the late summer, interest rates on high quality corporate bonds reached a level that had not been matched since the early 1920's and that was approached only briefly in 1932. The 1966 developments reflected a series of restrictive monetary measures taken by the Federal Reserve Board to offset the inflationary effect of a surging demand for goods and services from virtually all sectors of the economy. While fiscal policy and moral suasion were also used to combat inflationary tendencies, there was an unusually heavy reliance on monetary measures.

These measures were initiated around the end of 1965 and were intensified from the spring of 1966 until the fall, when the Board apparently moderated its restrictive policy because of the waning of inflationary pressures. Net free reserves of member banks (excess reserves less borrowings from Reserve Banks) declined substantially from January to October and then started to increase. The seasonally adjusted money stock (currency plus demand deposits), which had been rising markedly, declined from April to October; it then leveled off and in early 1967 experienced a recovery. Although the money stock plus time deposits (which is considered by some economists to be a more comprehensive measure of money supply) increased moderately from April to October, the rate of growth was much lower than in the preceding or following periods. Most capital market interest yields reached a peak in the late summer, though others—such as those on short-term bank loans and housing—did not ease until close to the end of the year.

As a result of these developments, 1966 provides an unusually favorable basis for studying the economic effects of restrictive monetary measures. Economists have generally assumed that such measures (acting through interest rates, credit availability, and perhaps directly through the money sup-

* Reprinted from *Survey of Current Business*, vol. 67 (August, 1967), pp. 10–27, by permission of the authors and the U.S. Department of Commerce. [Abridged by the editors. Note *** indicates sections omitted in abridgement.]

ply) have their most important impact on the demand for different types of investment and quasi-investment goods, including housing, plant and equipment, inventories, consumer durables, and State and local construction. However, except for housing where the evidence is reasonably clear, there has been no convincing empirical verification of this. One of the basic difficulties, of course, involves separating the effects of tight money from the effects of all the other influences on investment demand, particularly since restrictive monetary policy and booming demand usually coincide. The rapid and substantial decline in housing investment starting in the second quarter of 1966—which was associated with evidence of a tightening in the availability of mortgage money rather than with a weakening in basic demand—points to the dramatic impact of tight money on the housing market in that period. However, it is much more difficult to isolate the impact on other sectors. For business investment in plant and equipment and in inventories, which constitutes by far the largest part of total private investment, there are no obvious indications in the 1966 national accounts or in other available data of any substantial effect of restrictive monetary policy, though there is some evidence of a moderate slackening in nonresidential construction starting in the second quarter of the year.

An examination of earlier experience also points to an indeterminate relationship between tight money policy and business investment, again reflecting, at least in part, the coincidence of such policy and booming demand. Econometric attempts to isolate the effects of monetary policy from other supply and demand considerations affecting business investment have been inconclusive. Depending on the econometric model utilized, it is possible to point to significant interest rate effects on plant and equipment but not on inventories, on inventories but not on plant and equipment, on both, or on neither. Generally the negative results seem more impressive than the positive results. The latter are frequently derived by testing a large number of models that turn out to have insignificant or even incorrect interest rate effects before models with nominally significant effects of correct sign are obtained. Many attempts have also been made to obtain insights into the relationship between financial factors and business investment on the basis of interviews with businessmen or questionnaires filled in by them. However, these have provided qualitative rather than quantitative information and have suffered from the absence of objective data against which the responses could be checked.

### *The Survey Approach*

In an attempt to fill in this striking gap in our basic knowledge about the effects of monetary policy, we decided to use the unique potential provided by the surveys of actual and anticipated investment in plant and equipment and in inventories conducted regularly by OBE and the Securities and Exchange Commission.[1]

In late March, a special questionnaire was sent to all firms cooperating in these surveys (except for certain transportation companies). The questionnaire asked for: (1) the factors causing *appreciable* differences between actual plant and equipment expenditures in 1966 and the expenditures anticipated early in the year (both figures are collected in the regular surveys); (2) detailed information on the timing and magnitude of *any* reductions in plant and equipment or inventory outlays that resulted from financial market factors during 1966, along with the specific factors or conditions primarily responsible; and (3) detailed information on the impact of 1966 financial market factors on 1967 investment anticipations both for plant and equipment and for inventories, again with the factors primarily responsible. The first section of the questionnaire was designed to give essentially qualitative information, along lines collected in two earlier studies,[2] on the relative importance of the different factors (including fi-

[1] The plant and equipment survey normally collects both annual and quarterly data on actual and anticipated outlays for up to a year ahead from a large sample of U.S. nonfarm business firms. Anticipated quarterly inventory investment is collected regularly from manufacturing firms only. For the present study, the reporting panel for the broader plant and equipment survey was used.

[2] See Irwin Friend and Jean Bronfenbrenner, "Business Investment Programs and Their Realization," *Survey*, December 1950, and Murray F. Foss and Vito Natrella, "Investment Plans and Realization," *Survey*, June 1957.

nancial market developments) responsible for revisions in planned plant and equipment expenditures in 1966. The second and third sections were designed to probe, for the first time, much more deeply into the size and timing of, as well as the reasons for, the impact of the financial market developments on business investment, including inventories as well as plant and equipment, and to separate the direct from the indirect effects more explicitly. [The questionnaire used for this study and the technical notes describing the sample are omitted in this volume.]

Before turning to a discussion of the survey results, we might note that 1966 can be regarded as a critical test of the potential impact of monetary policy on business investment. In view of the severe impact on the housing market in the second half of the year and the disruption of the municipal bond market in late August, it is difficult to conceive of the application of even stronger doses of generally restrictive monetary policy, unless more heroic measures are taken to at least partially insulate those sectors most sensitive to credit stringency from its impact.

### Factors Accounting for Appreciable Changes in 1966 Plant and Equipment Expenditures

Of the 4,418 firms (out of 8,876 firms surveyed) whose replies to the special questionnaire were received in time to be included in the tabulations for this article, 1,057 replied that their actual 1966 plant and equipment expenditures had been changed appreciably—either in aggregate dollar amounts or in composition—from the outlays expected early that year.[3] These firms were asked to indicate the most important ("principal") factor and other major factors causing upward and/or downward deviations between actual and anticipated expenditures. The major purpose of this part of the questionnaire was to give perspective on the relative importance of different factors causing revisions in 1966 plant and equipment programs. Since similar information had been collected for 1949 and 1955 in earlier studies, rough comparisons can be made with these earlier periods.

Both for the 1,057 respondents as a group[4] and for the different size categories,[5] increases in anticipated plant and equipment expenditures were more common than decreases in 1966 (Table 1). Moreover, a change in the sales outlook was by far the most important single factor accounting for increased plant and equipment outlays over anticipated levels in 1966. The other factors that on balance tended to increase outlays significantly were changes from expected plant and equipment costs or prices, technological developments, mergers or acquisitions, and routine underestimates.

The most important factor depressing plant and equipment outlays was the delay in equipment deliveries and/or construction progress; this was more dominant than any of the factors accounting for increases. The other factors that on balance tended to significantly depress outlays included financial market conditions, the investment tax credit, working capital requirements, and net earnings. The most important single factor depressing outlays in the "other factors" category was the program of voluntary restraint initiated by the Administration in early 1966. Not surprisingly, in view of the

[3] A comparison was made betwen the qualitative replies ("yes" or "no") to question 1 of the questionnaire ("Were your actual expenditures for plant and equipment changed appreciably, either in terms of aggregate dollar amount or in composition or form, from those expected early that year?") and the dollar amount of difference between anticipated and actual expenditures as reported in the regular OBE-SEC investment surveys. A higher proportion of firms answering "yes" than of those answering "no" to question 1 had deviations greater than plus or minus 20 percent (76 percent as compared with 67 percent). For the largest size manufacturing firms, this difference was more pronounced (69 percent as compared with 53 percent). If allowance were made for the inclusion of compositional as well as aggregative changes in the replies to question 1, the differences indicated above would presumably be larger.

[4] It should be noted that the 1,057 respondents gave 423 principal factors and 798 other major factors as reasons for increases from planned expenditures and 322 principal factors and 692 other major factors as reasons for downward revisions from planned expenditures. Thus, the figure 1,057 cannot be constructed from the data in Table 1.

[5] A more detailed size distribution than the one presented in this article is available and has been used for analytical purposes.

TABLE 1. FACTORS RESPONSIBLE FOR DEVIATIONS BETWEEN ANTICIPATED AND ACTUAL PLANT AND EQUIPMENT EXPENDITURES IN 1966[1]

| Number of firms reporting changes from expectations in | Distribution of Principal Factors | | | | Distribution of Other Major Factors | | | |
|---|---|---|---|---|---|---|---|---|
| | Increasing outlays[2] | Decreasing outlays[2] | Increasing outlays[2] | Decreasing outlays[2] | Increasing outlays[2] | Decreasing outlays[2] | Increasing outlays[2] | Decreasing outlays[2] |
| | Number[3] | | Percent | | Number[4] | | Percent | |
| 1. Sales outlook | 112 | 21 | 26.5 | 6.5 | 163 | 101 | 20.4 | 14.6 |
| Firms with sales above expectations | 98 | 2 | | | 133 | 9 | | |
| Firms with sales below expectations | 6 | 19 | | | 18 | 82 | | |
| Firms not specifying direction | 8 | 0 | | | 12 | 10 | | |
| 2. Current expenses | 9 | 5 | 2.1 | 1.6 | 65 | 66 | 8.1 | 9.5 |
| 3. Net earnings | 18 | 18 | 4.3 | 5.6 | 89 | 119 | 11.2 | 17.2 |
| Firms with earnings above expectations | 15 | 1 | | | 65 | 3 | | |
| Firms with earnings below expectations | 3 | 16 | | | 15 | 108 | | |
| Firms not specifying direction | 0 | 1 | | | 9 | 8 | | |
| 4. Working capital requirements | 11 | 15 | 2.6 | 4.7 | 57 | 93 | 7.1 | 13.4 |
| 5. Timing of deliveries and/or construction progress | 69 | 154 | 16.3 | 47.8 | 98 | 78 | 12.3 | 11.3 |
| 6. Plant and equipment costs (viz, prices paid) | 31 | 8 | 7.3 | 2.5 | 93 | 26 | 11.7 | 3.8 |
| Firms with costs above expectations | 26 | 1 | | | 80 | 17 | | |
| Firms with costs below expectations | 1 | 4 | | | 4 | 6 | | |
| Firms not specifying direction | 4 | 3 | | | 9 | 3 | | |
| 7. Financial market conditions[5] | 4 | 35 | .9 | 10.9 | 44 | 86 | 5.5 | 12.4 |
| Firms mentioning availability and cost of debt financing | 2 | 31 | | | 38 | 73 | | |
| Firms mentioning availability and cost of equity financing | 2 | 4 | | | 22 | 37 | | |
| 8. Technological developments | 27 | 6 | 6.4 | 1.9 | 67 | 25 | 8.4 | 3.6 |
| 9. Investment tax credit[6] | 2 | 16 | .5 | 5.0 | 12 | 44 | 1.5 | 6.4 |
| 10. Mergers or acquisitions[6] | 40 | 8 | 9.5 | 2.5 | 44 | 8 | 5.5 | 1.2 |
| 11. Routine underestimation or overestimation[6] | 31 | 9 | 7.3 | 2.8 | 21 | 1 | 2.6 | .1 |

| Number of firms reporting changes from expectations in | Distribution of Principal Factors | | | | Distribution of Other Major Factors | | | |
|---|---|---|---|---|---|---|---|---|
| | Increasing outlays[2] | Decreasing outlays[2] | Increasing outlays[2] | Decreasing outlays[2] | Increasing outlays[2] | Decreasing outlays[2] | Increasing outlays[2] | Decreasing outlays[2] |
| | Number[3] | | Percent | | Number[4] | | Percent | |
| 12. Accidental damage[6] | 11 | 1 | 2.6 | .3 | 6 | 0 | .8 | .0 |
| 13. All other factors | 58 | 26 | 13.7 | 8.1 | 39 | 45 | 4.9 | 6.5 |
| Totals[7] | 423 | 322 | 100.0 | 100.0 | 798 | 692 | 100.0 | 100.0 |

[1]Based on factors cited by firms answering "yes" to question: "Were your actual 1966 expenditures for plant and equipment changed appreciably, either in terms of aggregate dollar amount or in composition or form, from those expected early that year?"
[2]Increasing (decreasing) outlays refer to 1966 expenditures higher (lower) than anticipated by the firm early in 1966.
[3]Not all firms specified the principal factor. Where only one major factor was indicated, this was taken to be the principal factor.
[4]A number of firms specified several major factors.
[5]The total may be smaller than the sum of the components since some firms mentioned both debt and equity financing.
[6]Specified under "other factors" in the questionnaire.
Percentage components may not add to 100 percent because of rounding.
SOURCES: U.S. Department of Commerce, Office of Business Economics, and Securities and Exchange Commission.

greater importance of debt than of external equity financing, unanticipated changes in the availability and cost of debt financing affected many more firms than corresponding changes in the equity markets.

*Size and Industry Comparisons*

Chart 1 portrays differences in the relative importance of factors responsible for deviations between anticipated and actual plant and equipment expenditures by size of firm. It indicates that unexpected delays in equipment deliveries and in construction progress were much more important in reducing outlays for the larger firms than for the smaller ones. Although the capital goods supply situation was also influential in raising planned outlays—whenever an unexpected easing of equipment deliveries and construction progress occurred—its impact was clearly less on upward capital outlay revisions than on downward revisions, and also varied directly with the size of firm. The net reduction in expenditures (decreases less increases) attributable to the capital goods supply situation was relatively most important for the largest firms.

Among firms spending more than originally planned for plant and equipment, the relative importance of higher-than-expected sales was greatest for those with assets of $10 million to $50 million. Deviations from expected sales were considerably less important among firms with downward revisions in capital spending than among firms with upward revisions. Changes from earlier expectations in net earnings were far less influential than changes in sales outlook for companies reporting increased capital spending, especially among larger firms, but were as important as, or more important than, sales among firms spending less than programed. The relative importance of other frequently cited factors, such as financial market conditions and plant and equipment costs, did not appear to vary significantly among firms of different asset size.

An analysis of the reasons given for deviations in 1966 between planned and actual capital outlays did not reveal appreciably different patterns of motivation for changes in outlays, except for public utilities. Utilities mentioned financial market developments as a factor responsible for reducing

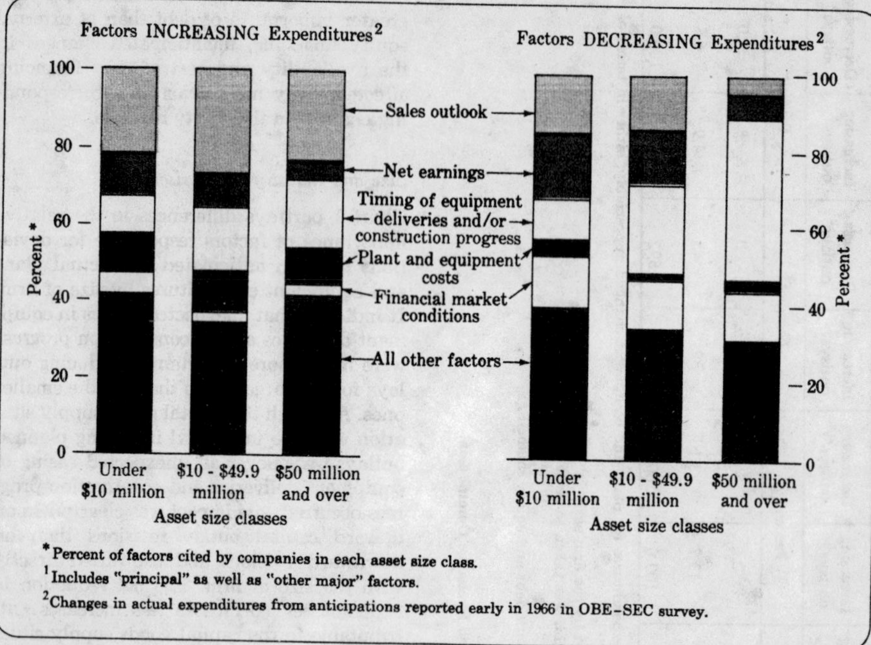


**CHART 1** Factors responsible for deviations between anticipated and actual plant and equipment expenditures, all industries, 1966. *(Source: U.S. Department of Commerce, Office of Business Economics.)*

planned capital outlays relatively much more frequently than did manufacturing and all other industries covered. Financial markets accounted for one-fourth of all cases of decreased outlays among the utilities and for one-tenth and one-eighth of all cases among manufacturing and all other industries respectively. Among companies spending less than planned, public utility firms cited equipment delivery and construction delays as major factors twice as often as manufacturing firms and about three times as often as all other industries.

### *Comparison with Earlier Studies*

The relative influence of factors principally responsible for deviations from planned investment in plant and equipment as reported in the survey for 1966 may be roughly compared with similar information collected for 1949 and 1955 in two earlier studies. This comparison (Chart 2) is limited to manufacturing firms. Perhaps the most striking difference between the 1966 results and those for 1949 and 1955 is the increased influence of both financial market developments and capital goods supply conditions in effective reductions from planned capital outlays. Financial market developments were mentioned as the principal factor inducing downward revisions in plans in 11 percent of the 1966 cases as compared with 1 percent or less in 1949 and 1955. Slower-than-expected equipment deliveries and construction progress were cited as the principal reason for downward changes in spending in about 48 percent of the cases in 1966, as compared with 38 percent and 17 percent, respectively, in 1955 and 1949.

The marked decline in the relative importance of the sales outlook among firms spending less than planned from 1949 (34 percent of all principal factors cited) to 1955 (10 percent) and 1966 (7 percent) is not too surprising in view of the cyclical differences among the years concerned. The year 1949 was essentially a recession year, and down-

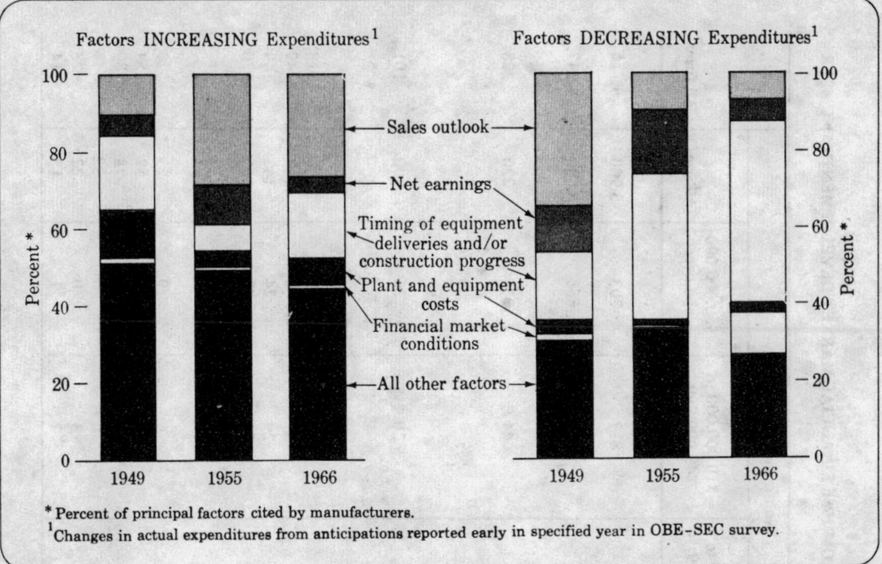


**CHART 2** Principal factors responsible for deviations between anticipated and actual plant and equipment expenditures of manufacturers, 1949, 1955, and 1966. *(Source: U.S. Department of Commerce, Office of Business Economics.)*

ward changes in sales outlook during the year were far more common than in 1955 and 1966, years of relatively high demand.

* * *

## Impact of Financial Market Factors on 1966 Plant and Equipment Expenditures

Tables 2 and 3 provide the basic data needed to appraise the impact of 1966 developments in the money and capital markets on plant and equipment expenditures in that year. The most important differences between the data indicating the proportion of firms with *some* reduction in expenditures because of financial market developments (Table 2 and subsequent tables) and the data indicating the proportion of firms with an *appreciable* reduction in expenditures for the same reasons (Table 1) is, of course, the broader coverage of the data in Table 2.[6] However, there are also several other differences in the scope of the data presented in these two sets of tables. In their replies to the questions presented in Table 2, a number of firms included the voluntary restraint on investment urged by the Administration early in 1966 as a financial development causing a reduction in their outlays, whereas such restraint was treated separately in the questionnaire data presented in Table 1. On the other hand, the coverage of financial market effects in Table 2 may be less inclusive than in Table 1, both because differences in composition as well as magnitude may be reflected in Table 1, and because the indirect impact of credit restraint on the firm's investment operating through its customers may have been treated differently.

### *Direct and Indirect Effects*

In addition to the direct impact that credit restraint has on investment (i.e., through the increased cost of financing), two other mechanisms may be of considerable importance: (1) an indirect, or "accelerator," effect, which occurs when a firm's sales, and there-

[6] It is even possible that a few firms included in Table 2 experienced appreciable reductions in plant and equipment expenditures due to financial market developments but may not be included in Table 1 because of offsetting increases in expenditures due to other reasons.

TABLE 2. REDUCTIONS IN 1966 PLANT AND EQUIPMENT EXPENDITURES RESULTING FROM 1966 FINANCIAL MARKET DEVELOPMENTS: NUMBER OF FIRMS BY ASSET SIZE

| | Nonfinancial Firms Only | | | | | |
|---|---|---|---|---|---|---|
| | Under $1,000,000 | $1,000,000 to $9,999,999 | $10,000,000 to $49,999,999 | $50,000,000 and over | All sizes | All firms[1] |
| 1. All firms answering question on 1966 impact of financial market developments (question 5a)[2] | 847 | 1,533 | 817 | 703 | 3,900 | 4,275 |
| 2. Number indicating no reductions (question 5a)[2] | 802 | 1,439 | 773 | 666 | 3,680 | 4,047 |
| 3. Number indicating reductions in plant and equipment expenditures because of financial market developments (question 5a)[2] | 45 | 94 | 44 | 37 | 220 | 228 |
| 4. Number indicating both reductions in plant and equipment expenditures (question 5a) and financial market conditions as a factor accounting for an appreciable deviation between actual and planned expenditures (question 2g)[2] | 19 | 35 | 20 | 26 | 100 | 101 |
| 5. Number indicating significant reductions occurring in (question 6)[23]: | | | | | | |
| a. First quarter | 3 | 7 | 6 | 2 | 18 | 18 |
| b. Second quarter | 7 | 25 | 7 | 8 | 47 | 49 |
| c. Third quarter | 27 | 63 | 29 | 24 | 143 | 149 |
| d. Fourth quarter | 31 | 69 | 35 | 30 | 165 | 170 |
| 6. Number indicating reductions amounting to (question 7)[2]: | | | | | | |
| a. Less than 5 percent of actual plant and equipment expenditures | 4 | 4 | 6 | 9 | 23 | 23 |
| b. 5 percent to 9.9 percent | 7 | 22 | 11 | 12 | 52 | 54 |
| c. 10 percent to 24.9 percent | 14 | 38 | 16 | 10 | 78 | 80 |
| d. 25 percent to 49.9 percent | 6 | 15 | 6 | 5 | 32 | 34 |
| e. 50 percent or more | 7 | 12 | 3 | 0 | 22 | 23 |
| f. Amount not specified | 7 | 3 | 2 | 1 | 13 | 14 |

| | | | | | | |
|---|---|---|---|---|---|---|
| 7. Number expecting to carry out in 1967 (question)10)[2]: | | | | | | |
| a. None of the eliminated 1966 plant and equipment expenditures | 9 | 28 | 12 | 4 | 53 | 54 |
| b. Some of the eliminated 1966 plant and equipment expenditures | 17 | 45 | 19 | 20 | 101 | 106 |
| c. Most of the eliminated 1966 plant and equipment expenditures | 9 | 9 | 7 | 11 | 36 | 36 |
| d. All of the eliminated 1966 plant and equipment expenditures | 4 | 3 | 1 | 1 | 9 | 9 |
| e. Not specified | 6 | 9 | 5 | 1 | 21 | 22 |
| 8. Number mentioning as cause of reductions (question 9)[2]: | | | | | | |
| a. Rise in interest rates, total[4] | 30 | 71 | 35 | 27 | 163 | 167 |
| Business outlook effect | 24 | 31 | 10 | 7 | 72 | 76 |
| Cost of financing effect | 17 | 59 | 28 | 22 | 126 | 126 |
| b. Decline in the stock market, total[4] | 8 | 15 | 7 | 6 | 36 | 36 |
| Business outlook effect | 8 | 11 | 4 | 3 | 26 | 26 |
| Cost of financing effect | 3 | 4 | 3 | 4 | 14 | 14 |
| c. Difficulties in raising funds from financial institutions, total[4] | 21 | 41 | 18 | 15 | 95 | 95 |
| Unattractiveness of lending conditions (other then interest rates) | 7 | 17 | 5 | 4 | 33 | 33 |
| Unwillingness of institution to supply desired funds | 16 | 29 | 13 | 11 | 69 | 69 |
| d. Difficulties in raising funds from capital markets, total[4] | 2 | 8 | 4 | 5 | 19 | 19 |
| Unattractive terms (other than offering price or yield) | 1 | 4 | 3 | 2 | 10 | 10 |
| Unwillingness of underwriters to handle issue | 1 | 4 | 1 | 1 | 7 | 7 |
| e. Other financial market developments | 11 | 20 | 6 | 6 | 43 | 46 |

[1]Includes financial institutions as well as a small number of nonfinancial firms for which asset-size information was not available.

[2]Question numbers refer to questionnaire.

[3]Some firms indicated more than 1 quarter.

[4]Includes firms which indicated both, or which did not distinguish between, (*a*) business outlook and cost of financing effects and/or (*b*) unattractiveness of lending conditions and unwillingness of institutions to supply desired funds.

SOURCES: U.S. Department of Commerce, Office of Business Economics, and Securities and Exchange Commission.

TABLE 3. REDUCTIONS IN 1966 PLANT AND EQUIPMENT EXPENDITURES RESULTING FROM 1966 FINANCIAL MARKET DEVELOPMENTS: NUMBER OF FIRMS BY MAJOR INDUSTRY

| | Manufacturing | Utilities[1] | Finance | Trade | All other [2] | All industries |
|---|---|---|---|---|---|---|
| 1. All firms answering question on 1966 impact of financial market developments (question 5a)[3] | 2,022 | 205 | 364 | 894 | 790 | 4,275 |
| 2. Number indicating no reduction (question 5a)[3] | 1,917 | 188 | 356 | 836 | 750 | 4,047 |
| 3. Number indicating reduction in plant and equipment expenditures because of financial market developments (question 5a)[3] | 105 | 17 | 8 | 58 | 40 | 228 |
| 4. Number indicating both reduction in plant and equipment expenditures (question 5a) and financial market conditions as a factor accounting for an appreciable deviation between actual and planned expenditures (question 2g)[3] | 40 | 12 | 1 | 29 | 19 | 101 |
| 5. Number indicating significant reductions occurring in (question 6)[34]: | | | | | | |
| a. First quarter | 9 | 1 | 0 | 5 | 3 | 18 |
| b. Second quarter | 23 | 4 | 2 | 12 | 8 | 49 |
| c. Third quarter | 70 | 12 | 6 | 38 | 23 | 149 |
| d. Fourth quarter | 78 | 14 | 5 | 42 | 31 | 170 |
| 6. Number indicating reduction amounting to (question 7)[3]: | | | | | | |
| a. Less than 5 percent of actual plant and equipment expenditures | 9 | 7 | 0 | 3 | 4 | 23 |
| b. 5 percent to 9.9 percent | 28 | 5 | 2 | 8 | 11 | 54 |
| c. 10 percent to 24.9 percent | 39 | 4 | 2 | 22 | 13 | 80 |
| d. 25 percent to 49.9 percent | 17 | 1 | 2 | 9 | 5 | 34 |
| e. 50 percent or more | 9 | 0 | 1 | 9 | 4 | 23 |
| f. Amount not specified | 3 | 0 | 1 | 7 | 3 | 14 |
| 7. Number expecting to carry out in 1967 (question 10)[3]: | | | | | | |
| a. None of the eliminated 1966 plant and equipment expenditures | 24 | 1 | 1 | 15 | 13 | 54 |
| b. Some of the eliminated 1966 plant and equipment expenditures | 54 | 8 | 5 | 20 | 19 | 106 |
| c. Most of the eliminated 1966 plant and equipment expenditures | 16 | 6 | 1 | 10 | 3 | 36 |
| d. All of the eliminated 1966 plant and equipment expenditures | 3 | 0 | 1 | 4 | 2 | 10 |
| e. Not specified | 8 | 2 | 0 | 9 | 3 | 22 |

| | | | | | | |
|---|---|---|---|---|---|---|
| | | | 4 | 43 | 28 | 167 |
| Business outlook effect | .. | | 4 | 22 | 17 | 76 |
| Cost of financing effect | 61 | 13 | 0 | 35 | 17 | 126 |
| b. Decline in the stock market, total[5] | 18 | 2 | 0 | 9 | 7 | 36 |
| Business outlook effect | 10 | 1 | 0 | 9 | 6 | 26 |
| Cost of financing effect | 10 | 1 | 0 | 1 | 2 | 14 |
| c. Difficulties in raising funds from financial institutions, total[5] | 46 | 5 | 0 | 15 | 29 | 95 |
| Unattractiveness of lending conditions (other than interest rates) | 18 | 1 | 0 | 8 | 6 | 33 |
| Unwillingness of institution to supply desired funds | 34 | 3 | 0 | 17 | 15 | 69 |
| d. Difficulties in raising funds from capital markets, total[5] | 10 | 4 | 0 | 3 | 2 | 19 |
| Unattractive terms (other than offering price or yield) | 3 | 3 | 0 | 2 | 2 | 10 |
| Unwillingness of underwriters to handle issue | 6 | 0 | 0 | 1 | 0 | 7 |
| e. Other financial market developments | 22 | 3 | 3 | 9 | 9 | 46 |

[1]Includes communications.
[2]Includes transportation, construction, mining, and services.
[3]Question numbers refer to questionnaire.
[4]Some firms indicated more than one quarter.
[5]Includes firms which indicated both, or which did not distinguish between, (*a*) business outlook and cost of financing effects, and/or (*b*) unattractiveness of lending conditions and unwillingness of institutions to supply desired funds.
SOURCES: U.S. Department of Commerce, Office of Business Economics, and Securities and Exchange Commission.

fore its capital requirements, are reduced because of the impact of financial market conditions on its customers, and (2) an "expectational," or "quasi-accelerator," effect, which arises when the firm anticipates—whether correctly or not—a subsequent reduction in sales below the level that would have occurred in the absence of credit restraint and, on the basis of that expectation, reduces its current investment.

In the replies on which Table 2 is based, firms were asked to exclude indirect effects.[7] The questionnaire further attempted to distinguish cases in which the increased cost of funds was the primary consideration from those in which an unfavorable influence on expectations was most important.

(A reduction in investment resulting directly from the higher cost of funds is considered autonomous, while one resulting from a decline in actual sales is an induced effect. The latter is particularly likely to occur for capital goods producers or for firms supplying the housing industry; however, it may also occur quite generally if the autonomous reduction in investment causes, through a multiplier relationship, a reduction in consumption. The impact of an anticipated decline in sales is autonomous in the period prior to the realization of the anticipation. However, to the extent that the anticipated effects are ultimately realized, such reductions can be regarded as induced in a longer run perspective.)

Table 2 probably includes expectational (or "quasi-accelerator") effects to a significant degree, since many firms indicated that financial market developments, by affecting the general business outlook, caused a reduction in investment and this presumably reflects an attempt by these firms to anticipate the resultant decline in their sales. The relatively high incidence of firms citing the changed business outlook as the basis for the financial market influence perhaps also indi-

[7] In contrast, firms were not specifically requested to exclude such indirect effects in their replies presented in Table 1. (These replies were obtained from the first section of the questionnaire, which followed the format of the two earlier surveys.) However, respondents to the first section of the current survey questionnaire were provided with a checklist that included such factors as the sales outlook, net earnings, and the availability and cost of debt and equity financing.

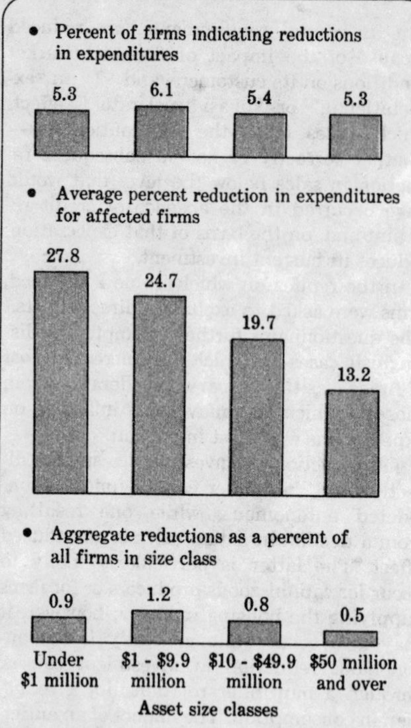


**CHART 3** Reductions in 1966 plant and equipment expenditures resulting from 1966 financial market developments.[1] *(Source: U.S. Department of Commerce, Office of Business Economics.)*

cates that, notwithstanding questionnaire instructions to exclude such cases, some companies attributed to financial market developments those reductions in investment resulting proximately from actual declines in sales and only indirectly from monetary stringency. Thus, even Table 2 may contain some indirect effects, though probably not to the same extent as Table 1.

* * *

*Timing and Magnitude of Impact*

Table 2 indicates that the number of firms stating that they had made some reduction in plant and equipment expenditures as a result of financial market developments increased throughout 1966. A relatively small number of firms were affected in the first quarter of the year. The rate of growth in the number affected picked up in the second and third quarters but moderated in the fourth quarter. Nevertheless, the final quarter of the year showed a peak number of firms affected in all of the four size classes.

The data used to compile this table also make possible a rough estimate of the quantitative impact of monetary restrictions on plant and equipment expenditures in 1966, and constitute perhaps the first plausible evidence on the overall impact of monetary policy on such outlays during any period. Only 5.3 percent of the total number of firms responding indicated that they had made some reduction in expenditures as a result of financial market developments, and there was relatively little variation in this proportion among different size groups. (See Chart 3; for basic data, see Table 2, lines 1 and 3.) However, there was substantial variation in the relative magnitude of the effect for firms curtailing their expenditures, with smaller firms much more strongly influenced on the average than larger firms.

The average percentage effect for firms curtailing outlays may be approximated for nonfinancial firms within each size class from the two-way distribution of these firms by asset size and by size of the reduction due to financial market developments (Table 2, lines 6a-6e) and for financial firms from a one-way distribution by size of reduction (Table 3, lines 6a-6e). Two types of averages were used for this purpose, the estimated median, which probably understates the true mean, and the average obtained by assuming that the mean for each percentage reduction class interval was at its midpoint, which probably overstates the true mean.[8] On the basis of the medians, the average percentage reduction for affected firms ranged from 19.1 percent for the smallest nonfinancial firms to 9.0 percent for the largest nonfinancial firms. On the basis of the second set of averages, the corresponding figures ranged from 27.8 percent to 13.2 percent.

*Estimation of National Impact for 1966*

The overall impact of monetary restrictions on plant and equipment expenditures in

[8] For the 50 percent or more class, the average reduction—which has as its base actual plant and equipment expenditures—was assumed to be 75 percent, and this may be unduly large, again contributing to overstatement of the true mean.

1966 was estimated by first computing the sample ratio of the reduction in expenditures resulting from financial market developments to the aggregate outlays in each size class of nonfinancial business and in all financial business and then multiplying this ratio by the universe distribution of plant and equipment outlays among these categories. The sample ratio for each size class of nonfinancial business is obtained by multiplying the average percentage reduction of affected firms by the plant and equipment expenditures of affected firms and dividing by total plant and equipment expenditures of all sample firms in that size class. The corresponding ratio for financial business is obtained simply as the product of the percentage of all sample financial firms reporting some reductions in expenditures as a result of financial market developments and the average percentage reduction of affected firms in that industry (with both percentages expressed in ratio form).

Reasonably reliable data are available on the universe distribution of plant and equipment outlays in nonfinancial business by asset-size class and in financial business as a whole for the $60.6 billion aggregate of expenditures in 1966 covered by the periodic OBE–SEC surveys—which is essentially the universe sampled in our special survey. However, perhaps a more useful universe for purposes of general economic analysis is the comprehensive total of $75.0 billion for nonfarm nonresidential fixed investment appearing in the national income and product accounts and including outlays of nonprofit institutions, real estate companies and professionals, capital outlays in oil and gas well drilling charged to current account, and a number of smaller items. The estimated size distribution of the difference between the national accounts aggregate and the investment covered by the periodic surveys is subject to considerably more error than the OBE–SEC distribution but not enough to affect our results significantly.

If we use the $75.0 billion total and assume that the survey results are representative of all industries included in the national accounts aggregate, the estimated reduction in 1966 plant and equipment expenditures as a result of financial market developments ranges from $370 million if the sample median percentage reductions are used to $560 million if the sample "means" are used; the average is somewhat under $500 million.[9]

* * *

*Impact by Size of Firm*

As was noted earlier, although there did not appear to be much difference in the proportion of smaller and larger firms affected at least to some extent by monetary tightness in 1966, the relative magnitude of the effect was much greater for the smaller firms. This presumably reflects mainly the readier access of the large firms to the financial markets, particularly in a period of credit rationing, but it may also reflect a greater ability of the larger firms to predict financial market developments.

Only about one-fourth of the firms that reduced their plant and equipment expenditures in 1966 as a result of financial market developments did not plan to carry out some of this postponed investment in 1967. The proportion of expenditures either canceled or postponed beyond 1967 was higher for the smaller asset classes than for the largest. A relatively small proportion of firms in all size classes planned to restore in 1967 all of the cutbacks in their 1966 plant and equipment programs related to financial market developments. The great majority of the firms planned to make up "some" or "most" of these 1966 investment reductions in 1967, with "some" a more common response than "most," particularly for the smaller size classes.

*Interest Rates Most Important*

The firms that indicated a reduction in their 1966 plant and equipment expenditures as a result of financial market developments most commonly attributed the reduction to the rise in interest rates. The rise in interest rates was considered important more often because of its impact on the firm's cost of borrowing than because of its influence on the firm's appraisal of the general business outlook. This was especially true of the firms in the larger size classes, which were much less concerned than the smallest companies with the

[9] Using the less inclusive $60.6 billion total, for which the survey results are more representative, the estimated reduction ranges from $300 million to $450 million.

impact of higher interest rates on the general business outlook. It may be recalled that the impact on the firm's cost of borrowing is more clearly autonomous than the influence on the firm's appraisal of the general business outlook, much of which may be regarded as indirect at least in a longer run perspective.

The second most common reason given for the reduction in 1966 expenditures was difficulty in raising funds from banks or other financial institutions, a type of capital rationing effect; this again is addressed primarily to the cost of borrowed rather than equity funds. Here, the unwillingness of institutions to supply the desired funds seemed more important than the unattractiveness of lending conditions other than interest rates.

The decline in the stock market was cited much less frequently as a financial market development accounting for the reduction in 1966 expenditures, and difficulty in raising funds from the capital markets (either stock or bond) was cited even less often. It is interesting, though perhaps not surprising, that unlike the situation in the bond market, the decline in the stock market was considered important more often because of its effect on the firm's appraisal of the general business outlook than because of its implications for the firm's cost of equity capital. However, this was more true of firms in the smallest size class than of firms generally. Although there were no consistent differences in the proportions of companies in the various size classes that were affected by stock market developments, it should be noted that this finding has no necessary implications for the relative access to stock financing by smaller firms, since such firms may have planned to rely less on stock issues for financing their capital programs than the larger companies.

*Industry Differences*

Table 3 presents a breakdown by industry rather than by assets for firms stating that they had made some reduction in 1966 plant and equipment expenditures as a result of financial market developments. In view of the relatively small number of firms indicating some reduction, only five industry groups are segregated, viz., manufacturing, utilities (including communications), finance, trade, and an all-other category, which includes railroads, airlines, trucking, pipelines, construction, services, and mining. The proportion of firms affected by monetary restrictions in 1966 was greater for the utilities than for any other group. This apparently cannot be attributed to the larger average size of the utilities since, at least for nonfinancial industries combined, there was not much difference in the proportion of smaller and larger firms affected by monetary tightness in 1966. In contrast, the relative magnitude of the reduction in 1966 outlays was smaller for the typical utility firm than for other firms; however, it is not possible to determine the extent to which this simply reflects the larger average size of the utilities.

For the utilities, the rise in interest rates was somewhat more important and the decline in the stock market somewhat less important than for the other firms which stated that they had reduced their 1966 plant and equipment expenditures because of financial market developments. Moreover, to a much greater extent in the utilities than in the other industries, it was the cost of financing rather than the business outlook effect that predominated.

*Other Findings for 1966*

For the firms indicating reduced 1966 plant and equipment expenditures due to financial market developments, some additional breakdowns were carried out: Actual sales and earnings were related to expectations, and manufacturing firms were classified by the percentage of capacity utilized (in June 1966 as indicated in periodic reports to OBE-SEC). The more interesting findings may be summarized briefly. A very much higher proportion of firms with sales or earnings below expectations than of firms with sales or earnings above expectations stated that they had cut their expenditures because of financial developments. Similarly, firms operating at a low percentage of capacity were more prone to reflect the effects of monetary tightness than firms generally, and the magnitude of the impact was also likely to be greater.

## Effects on 1967 Plant and Equipment Programs

The impact of 1966 financial market conditions was somewhat stronger on anticipated plant and equipment expenditures for 1967 than on actual 1966 expenditures. Table 4

TABLE 4. REDUCTIONS IN 1967 PLANT AND EQUIPMENT
NUMBER OF FIRMS BY ASSET SIZE

| | Nonfinancial Firms Only | | | | | |
|---|---|---|---|---|---|---|
| | Under $1,000,000 | $1,000,000 to $9,999,999 | $10,000,000 to $49,999,999 | $50,000,000 and over | All sizes | All firms[1] |
| 1. All firms answering question on impact of 1966 financial market developments on 1967 programs (question 11a)[2] | 684 | 1,365 | 761 | 692 | 3,502 | 3,824 |
| 2. Number indicating no reduction in 1967 programs (question 11a)[2] | 624 | 1,228 | 700 | 632 | 3,184 | 3,498 |
| 3. Number indicating reduction in 1967 programs (question 11a)[2] | 60 | 137 | 61 | 60 | 318 | 326 |
| 4. Number indicating reduction amounting to (question 12)[2]: | | | | | | |
| a. Less than 5 percent of programed plant and equipment expenditures | 10 | 14 | 4 | 4 | 32 | 32 |
| b. 5 percent to 9.9 percent | 9 | 32 | 17 | 19 | 77 | 80 |
| c. 10 percent to 24.9 percent | 16 | 52 | 30 | 24 | 122 | 123 |
| d. 25 percent to 49.9 percent | 6 | 18 | 6 | 8 | 38 | 40 |
| e. 50 percent or more | 7 | 11 | 2 | 0 | 20 | 21 |
| f. Amount not specified | 12 | 10 | 2 | 5 | 29 | 30 |
| 5. Number mentioning as cause of reduction (question 13)[2]: | | | | | | |
| a. Rise in interest rates, total[3] | 36 | 105 | 53 | 54 | 248 | 251 |
| Business outlook effect | 24 | 52 | 26 | 26 | 128 | 130 |
| Cost of financing effect | 16 | 78 | 41 | 39 | 174 | 175 |
| b. Decline in the stock market, total[3] | 7 | 32 | 13 | 7 | 59 | 59 |
| Business outlook effect | 5 | 26 | 11 | 6 | 48 | 48 |
| Cost of financing effect | 3 | 8 | 3 | 3 | 17 | 17 |
| c. Difficulties in raising funds from financial institutions, total[3] | 20 | 53 | 23 | 18 | 114 | 114 |
| Unattractiveness of lending conditions (other than interest rates) | 9 | 20 | 13 | 9 | 51 | 51 |
| Unwillingness of institutions to supply desired funds | 9 | 33 | 12 | 11 | 65 | 65 |
| d. Difficulties in raising funds from capital markets, total[3] | 2 | 8 | 5 | 3 | 18 | 18 |
| Unattractive terms (other than offering price or yield) | 1 | 2 | 5 | 3 | 11 | 11 |
| Unwillingness of underwriters to handle issue | 0 | 6 | 0 | 0 | 6 | 6 |
| e. Other financial market developments | 12 | 31 | 12 | 15 | 70 | 73 |

[1]Includes financial institutions as well as a small number of nonfinancial firms for which asset-size information was not available.
[2]Question numbers refer to questionnaire.
[3]Includes firms which indicated both, or which did not distinguish between, (*a*) business outlook and cost of financing effects, and/or (*b*) unattractiveness of lending conditions and unwillingness of institutions to supply desired funds.

SOURCES: U.S. Department of Commerce, Office of Business Economics, and Securities and Exchange Commission.

TABLE 5. IMPACT OF 1966 FINANCIAL MARKET DEVELOPMENTS ON 1966 PLANT AND EQUIPMENT OUTLAYS AND 1967 PROGRAMS, NONFINANCIAL FIRMS BY ASSET SIZE (by percent)

| | 1966 Outlays–Firms with Assets of | | | | 1967 Programs–Firms with Assets of | | | |
|---|---|---|---|---|---|---|---|---|
| | Under $1,000,000 | $1,000,000 to $9,999,999 | $10,000,000 to $49,999,999 | $50,000,000 and over | Under $1,000,000 | $1,000,000 to $9,999,999 | $10,000,000 to $49,999,999 | $50,000,000 and over |
| 1. Percentage of firms indicating reduction in outlays | 5.3 | 6.1 | 5.4 | 5.3 | 8.8 | 10.0 | 8.0 | 8.7 |
| 2. Average percentage reduction for affected firms[1] | 27.8 | 25.3 | 19.7 | 13.2 | 23.4 | 21.1 | 17.6 | 15.9 |
| 3. Aggregate reduction as a percentage of outlays for all firms in size class[2] | .92 | 1.19 | .82 | .50 | 1.48 | 2.00 | 1.04 | 1.08 |
| 4. Percentage of affected firms mentioning rise in interest rates as cause of reduced outlays | 66.7 | 75.5 | 79.5 | 73.0 | 60.0 | 76.6 | 86.9 | 90.0 |
| 5. Percentage of affected firms mentioning decline in stock market | 17.8 | 16.0 | 15.9 | 16.2 | 11.7 | 23.4 | 21.3 | 11.7 |
| 6. Percentage of affected firms mentioning difficulties in raising funds from financial institutions | 46.7 | 43.6 | 40.9 | 40.5 | 33.3 | 38.7 | 37.7 | 30.0 |
| 7. Percentage of affected firms mentioning difficulties in raising funds from capital markets | 4.4 | 8.5 | 9.1 | 13.5 | 3.3 | 5.8 | 8.2 | 5.0 |

[1]Computed from the frequency distributions in lines 6a–6e of Table 2 and lines 4a–4e of Table 4, using the midpoint of closed-end class intervals and a value of 75 percent for the open-end interval. This procedure probably leads to some overstatement of the average.

[2]Computed by multiplying line 2 by 1966 plant and equipment expenditures of firms reporting reduction and dividing by expenditures of all firms. In the case of 1967 programs there is an implicit assumption that, for firms reporting reduction, these programs on the average were similar in magnitude to 1966 expenditures of the same firms (see text).

SOURCES: U.S. Department of Commerce, Office of Business Economics, and Securities and Exchange Commission.

presents basic data on the number of firms reporting reductions in 1967 investment plans, the magnitude of these reductions, and the particular aspects of financial market conditions that were primarily responsible. Table 5 shows comparative data, derived from Tables 2 and 4, on the effects of credit stringency on 1966 investment and 1967 investment plans. (See also Chart 4.)

For all firms combined, including financial institutions, the percentage of respondents indicating a reduction in plant and equipment expenditures rose from 5.3 percent for 1966 to 8.5 percent for 1967. There was little variation among size groups, except that the $1 million to $10 million asset class showed higher proportions than other classes in both years. The average percentage reduction for affected firms declined steadily with size in both years but less sharply in 1967. The aggregate reduction ranged from one-half of 1 percent of aggregate expenditures to a little over 1 percent in 1966 and from 1 to 2 percent in 1967, doubling for the largest size class but showing smaller increases elsewhere.

### *Estimated National Impact for 1967*

An estimate of the dollar reduction in 1967 investment plans for the Nation as a whole may be obtained by a procedure similar to that described for estimating the overall impact on 1966 plant and equipment outlays. Under the assumption that the 1967 programs of firms reporting reductions were on the average similar in magnitude to the 1966 expenditures of the same firms, the reduction within each size class of nonfinancial business can be estimated for the sample from the 1966 outlays of the affected firms and from the average percentage reduction reported in 1967 programs.[10] The total reduction for financial institutions in the sample may also be obtained in much the same way.

As was indicated previously, nationwide estimates of plant and equipment expenditures derived from the national income and product accounts are available for 1966 by size class for nonfinancial business and for financial business as a whole (though the universe figures represent a somewhat broader coverage of industries and expenditure items than the OBE–SEC series and the sample results are therefore not fully

[10] The average percentage reduction of affected firms, which has as its base programs after the reduction due to credit stringency, was computed from the frequency distribution in lines 4a-4e of Table 4—utilizing the midpoint for each closed-end class interval and a value of 75 percent for the open-end interval. This procedure probably leads to some upward bias in the average, which considerably exceeds the estimated median for the frequency distribution. Further overstatement of the aggregate sample reduction in 1967 programs may arise because the programs of the firms affected, since they are known to have been reduced because of credit restraint, may in fact be expected to fall a little short of the 1966 expenditures of these firms. However, an offsetting consideration is the prospective moderate rise in 1967 investment expenditures over 1966 as reported in the OBE–SEC survey.

**CHART 4** Reductions in 1967 plant and equipment expenditure programs resulting from 1966 financial market developments.[1] *(Source: U.S. Department of Commerce, Office of Business Economics.)*

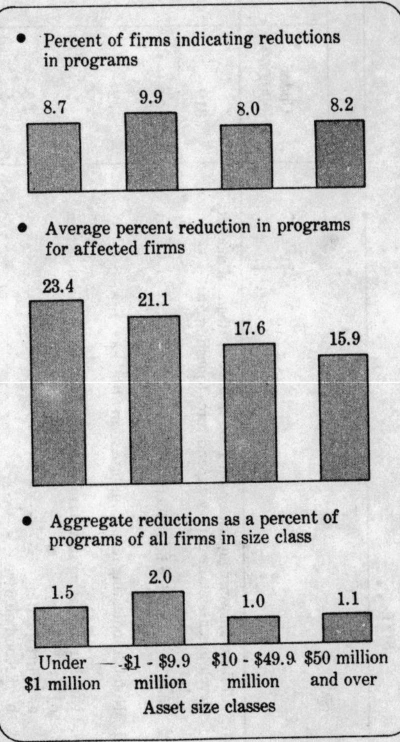

TABLE 6. REDUCTIONS IN 1966 INVENTORY INVESTMENT RESULTING FROM 1966 FINANCIAL MARKET DEVELOPMENTS: NUMBER OF FIRMS BY ASSET SIZE

| | Nonfinancial Firms Only | | | | | |
|---|---|---|---|---|---|---|
| | Under $1,000,000 | $1,000,000 to $9,999,999 | $10,000,000 to $49,999,999 | $50,000,000 and over | All sizes | All firms[1] |
| 1. All firms answering question on 1966 impact of financial market developments on inventory expenditures (question 5b)[2] | 819 | 1,500 | 803 | 687 | 3,809 | 4,047 |
| 2. Number indicating no reduction (question 5b)[2] | 780 | 1,428 | 773 | 680 | 3,661 | 3,899 |
| 3. Number indicating reduction (question 5b)[2] | 39 | 72 | 30 | 7 | 148 | 148 |
| 4. Number indicating significant reductions occurring in (question 6)[23]: | | | | | | |
| a. First quarter | 3 | 6 | 2 | 0 | 11 | 11 |
| b. Second quarter | 5 | 21 | 5 | 1 | 32 | 32 |
| c. Third quarter | 25 | 51 | 19 | 3 | 98 | 98 |
| d. Fourth quarter | 23 | 59 | 28 | 6 | 116 | 116 |
| 5. Number indicating reduction amounting to (question 8)[2]: | | | | | | |
| a. Less than 2 percent of actual 1966 year-end inventories | 4 | 4 | 0 | 0 | 8 | 8 |
| b. 2 percent to 4.9 percent | 8 | 18 | 9 | 4 | 39 | 39 |
| c. 5 percent to 9.9 percent | 8 | 21 | 10 | 2 | 41 | 41 |
| d. 10 percent or more | 13 | 28 | 10 | 1 | 52 | 52 |
| e. Amount not specified | 6 | 1 | 1 | 0 | 8 | 8 |
| 6. Number mentioning as cause of reduction (question 9)[2]: | | | | | | |
| a. Rise in interest rates, total[4] | 29 | 63 | 23 | 7 | 122 | 122 |
| Business outlook effect | 23 | 33 | 12 | 3 | 71 | 71 |
| Cost of financing effect | 19 | 53 | 17 | 6 | 95 | 95 |
| b. Decline in the stock market, total[4] | 11 | 15 | 5 | 1 | 32 | 32 |
| Business outlook effect | 11 | 12 | 4 | 1 | 28 | 28 |
| Cost of financing effect | 4 | 3 | 1 | 0 | 8 | 8 |
| c. Difficulties in raising funds from financial institutions, total[4] | 20 | 32 | 14 | 0 | 66 | 66 |
| Unattractiveness of lending conditions (other than interest rates) | 5 | 15 | 6 | 0 | 26 | 26 |
| Unwillingness of institutions to supply desired funds | 15 | 21 | 11 | 0 | 47 | 47 |

| | | | | | | |
|---|---|---|---|---|---|---|
| d. Difficulties in raising funds from capital markets, total[4] | 2 | 4 | 2 | 0 | 8 | 8 |
| Unattractiveness of terms (other than offering price or yield) | 1 | 3 | 1 | 0 | 5 | 5 |
| Unwillingness of underwriters to handle issues | 1 | 1 | 1 | 0 | 3 | 3 |
| e. Other financial market developments | 4 | 15 | 5 | 0 | 24 | 24 |

[1] Includes financial institutions as well as a small number of nonfinancial firms for which asset-size information was not available.

[2] Question numbers refer to questionnaire.

[3] Some firms indicated more than one quarter.

[4] Includes firms which indicated both, or which did not distinguish between, (*a*) business outlook and cost of financing effects and/or (*b*) unattractiveness of lending conditions and unwillingness of institutions to supply desired funds.

SOURCES: U.S. Department of Commerce, Office of Business Economics, and Securities and Exchange Commission.

representative of the universe). Multiplying the sample reduction in 1967 programs by the 1966 ratio of universe outlays to outlays for all sample firms within each class and summing over classes, we obtain an estimated reduction of $940 million in 1967 programs for nonfarm fixed business investment.

* * *

### *Business Outlook More Important*

The responsibility attributed to particular aspects of 1966 credit conditions is much the same for reductions in 1967 programs as for reductions in 1966 expenditures, but some differences may be noted. (See Table 5, lines 4–7.) For the two largest size groups, the proportion of affected firms mentioning the rise in interest rates is substantially higher in the case of the 1967 programs, rising to between 87 percent and 90 percent. However, the increase is due almost entirely to those mentioning the business outlook rather than the cost of financing and thus probably reflects in large part indirect or expectational effects associated with actual or expected failure of sales to grow as rapidly as in the absence of credit restraints.

Difficulty in raising funds from intermediaries is mentioned less frequently, particularly by the largest and smallest firms, but it is still an important factor for over one-third of the firms reducing 1967 programs. The effect of the stock market decline is higher than in 1966 for the two middle size groups, affecting more than one-fifth of the firms in this range, but lower for the two extreme groups. As in the case of interest rates, the business outlook aspect increases in importance from 1966 to 1967 relative to the cost aspect, particularly for the larger firms.

## Effects on Inventory Investment

The impact of 1966 credit conditions on 1966 inventory investment appears to be about the same in dollar value as on fixed investment, and again there is some suggestion of an increased reaction in 1967. Table 6 presents basic data on the frequency and magnitude of reported reductions in 1966 inventory investment and on the particular financial market conditions to which these were at-

TABLE 7. IMPACT OF 1966 FINANCIAL MARKET DEVELOPMENTS ON 1966 INVENTORY INVESTMENT AND 1967 INVENTORY PLANS, NONFINANCIAL FIRMS BY ASSET SIZE (by percent)

| | 1966 Investment—Firms with Assets of | | | | 1967 Investment Plan—Firms with Assets of | | | |
|---|---|---|---|---|---|---|---|---|
| | Under $1,000,000 | $1,000,000 to $9,999,999 | $10,000,000 to $49,999,999 | $50,000,000 and over | Under $1,000,000 | $1,000,000 to $9,999,999 | $10,000,000 to $49,999,999 | $50,000,000 and over |
| 1. Percentage of firms indicating reduction in investment | 4.8 | 4.8 | 3.7 | 1.0 | 6.4 | 8.7 | 6.2 | 5.0 |
| 2. Average percentage reduction for affected firms[1] | 10.7 | 11.0 | 10.6 | 7.0 | (2) | (2) | (2) | (2) |
| 3. Aggregate reduction as a percentage of inventory holdings of all firms in size class[3] | .64 | .50 | .20 | .11 | (2) | (2) | (2) | (2) |
| 4. Percentage of affected firms mentioning rise in interest rates as cause of reduced investment | 74.4 | 87.5 | 76.7 | 100.0 | 57.1 | 81.0 | 93.5 | 91.2 |
| 5. Percentage of affected firms mentioning decline in stock market | 28.2 | 20.8 | 16.7 | (4) | 21.4 | 25.0 | 23.9 | 14.7 |
| 6. Percentage of affected firms mentioning difficulties in raising funds from financial institutions | 51.3 | 44.4 | 46.7 | (4) | 38.1 | 40.5 | 37.0 | 20.6 |
| 7. Percentage of affected firms mentioning difficulties in raising funds from capital markets | 5.1 | 5.6 | 6.7 | (4) | 9.5 | 6.9 | 4.3 | 5.9 |

[1]Computed from the frequency distribution in lines 5a–5d of Table 7, using the midpoint of closed-end class intervals and a value of 20 percent for the open-end interval. This procedure probably leads to some overstatement of the average.

[2]Not available.

[3]Computed by multiplying line 2 by end-of-year inventory of firms reporting reduction and dividing by end-of-year inventory of all responding firms.

[4]Percentage not meaningful due to size of sample.

SOURCES: U.S. Department of Commerce, Office of Business Economics, and Securities and Exchange Commission.

tributed, while Table 7 compares the effects of credit stringency on actual 1966 and planned 1967 inventory investment.

For all firms combined, including financial institutions, only 3.7 percent of the respondents and only 1.0 percent of firms with assets over $50 million reported reductions in 1966 inventory investment. However, the percentage for all firms rose to 6.6 percent for 1967 investment plans. The largest firms showed the greatest increase though they still reported reductions less frequently than smaller firms, especially those in the $1 million to $10 million asset size class (Chart 5). In both years, the percentage of firms affected was higher for the trade group than for other major industry groups.

When reductions occurred, their average size was surprisingly large. In 1966, they amounted to almost 11 percent of end-of-year inventory levels for the three smallest size classes and 7 percent for the largest, with three-eighths of the firms indicating reductions in excess of 10 percent.[11] Information as to the magnitude of the reduction was not available for 1967 investment plans. Some firms may have reported their 1966 reductions as percentages of their 1966 inventory investment rather than their total yearend holdings; in that case, the estimate derived below of the overall impact on 1966 inventory outlays may represent a considerable overstatement.

The aggregate reduction in 1966 inventory investment within each size class of nonfinancial business may be estimated for the sample from the yearend inventory holdings of affected firms and the average percentage reduction that they reported in these holdings. Expressed as a fraction of yearend stocks of all responding firms, the aggregate reduction decreased sharply with size from 0.6 percent to 0.1 percent.

[11] The average percentage reduction, which has as its base actual yearend inventories at book value, was computed from the frequency distribution shown in lines 5a-5d of Table 6, utilizing the midpoints of the closed-end class intervals. The open-end interval is troublesome in this case because of the apparently high relative frequency (which may be due to misinterpretation of the questionnaire). An estimated mean of 20 percent, which is probably on the high side, was arbitrarily assigned to this class.

*Estimation of National Impact*

Utilizing a distribution by size class of the nationwide estimate of $151 billion for inventories held by nonfarm, nonfinancial business in 1966, we estimated the overall impact of credit restraint on outlays for such inventories in that year by multiplying the aggregate sample reduction in dollar terms, as described above, by the ratio of universe-to-sample inventory levels for each size class and summing over classes. This procedure yields a value in the neighborhood of $500 million, which must, however, be considered subject to an even larger margin of error than are plant and equipment outlays.[12] In view of the greater number of firms reporting reductions in 1967 inventory investment plans than in 1966 investment, the overall impact

[12] The figure is relatively sensitive to the treatment of the rather large open-end interval in the frequency distribution of the percentage reduction for affected firms. It varies from $440 million, if in computing the average percentage reduction we assign a value of 15 percent to all firms in the range over 10 percent, to $530 million, if we assign a value of 20 percent.

CHART 5 Reductions in 1966 inventory investment resulting from 1966 financial market developments.[1] *(Source: U.S. Department of Commerce, Office of Business Economics.)*

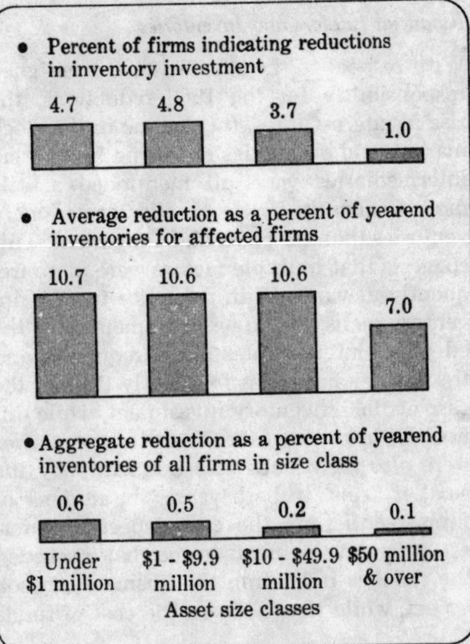

on planned additions to inventory for the current year may be expected to exceed $500 million, but data for a more precise estimate are not available.

*Size Effects*

Even more than in the case of fixed investment outlays, there is evidence of relatively slow reaction by the larger firms, with the number reporting reductions in inventory investment in the fourth quarter of 1966 increasing very substantially over the third quarter for the two larger size groups but not for the smaller firms (Table 6). Furthermore, the largest size group experienced by far the greatest increase in the proportion indicating reductions in 1967 inventory investment plans as compared with those reducing 1966 investment, while the smallest size group experienced the smallest increase (Table 7). The slower reaction of large firms is more difficult to rationalize for inventory than for fixed investment but may perhaps reflect the greater internal resources of the large firms to handle temporary needs for funds. Also, as in the case of plant and equipment expenditures, large firms tend to have more formal and rigid capital budgets than small firms and perhaps more advanced arrangements for financing.

*Financial Factors and Inventories*

With respect to the specific factors assigned responsibility for the 1966 reductions, the rise in interest rates, the decline in the stock market, and difficulties in raising funds from intermediaries were all mentioned a little more frequently by the smaller firms for inventories than for plant and equipment. This suggests that multiple factors were more frequently at work. With reference to 1967 inventory plans, the larger firms mentioned the effects of interest rates more frequently and the smaller firms less frequently than in the case of 1966 inventory investment, while difficulties in raising funds from intermediaries were also mentioned less frequently by the smaller firms. In both years, the number of firms mentioning the cost aspect of interest rate developments somewhat exceeded the number indicating the business outlook aspect, while the effect on the cost of funds of the stock market decline was of negligible importance.

## Summary and Conclusions

While the major objective of our special survey is to provide a reliable an estimate as possible of the quantitative impact of last year's monetary stringency on business investment, the survey also makes available a wealth of other data on factors affecting business investment programs. It may be noted that the most interesting difference between the 1966 results on the relative importance of various factors affecting business investment programs and earlier results for 1949 and 1955 (obtained from similar though considerably less comprehensive surveys) was the increased influence of both financial market developments and of capital goods supply conditions in effecting reductions in planned plant and equipment expenditures.

Since monetary tools have been increasingly relied upon for economic stabilization purposes, it seems imperative that we gain more insight into the effectiveness of these tools and their impacts on different sectors of the economy. Until this survey, no reasonably satisfactory estimates of the effect of monetary policy on business investment have been available, even though business expenditures on plant and equipment and inventories constitute a high proportion of the total investment that credit policy is designed to affect.

On the basis of data collected in the survey, financial market developments in 1966 are estimated to have resulted in a reduction of approximately $500 million, or two-thirds of 1 percent of that year's $75 billion total of nonresidential, nonfarm fixed investment. The aggregate effect on nonfarm inventory investment in 1966 was of the same general order of magnitude, also amounting to an estimated $500 million, as compared with actual investment of $13.7 billion and a stock of nonfarm business inventories of $151 billion at the yearend. These estimates may include some indirect effects, reflecting the failure of sales to grow as rapidly as in the absence of credit restraint.

The restrictive impact of the 1966 credit squeeze on business investment increased significantly from the first to the fourth quarter of the year and was considerably larger on the 1967 investment programs than on 1966 expenditures. As a result of developments associated with the monetary stringency in 1966, business plans (made early in 1967) to invest in plant and equipment during 1967 were reduced by an amount estimated at somewhat under $1 billion, less than 1⅓ percent of anticipated fixed investment. Although the available data do not permit an estimate of the corresponding impact on business inventory investment in 1967, this is believed to be higher than the $500 million figure for 1966. The effects on business investment for 1966—and probably to a greater extent also for 1967—would be increased somewhat if full allowance is made for the indirect effects of the 1966 financial market developments, which would initially be expected to increase as the period of time is extended.

These estimated effects of monetary policy in 1966 on business investment in 1966 and 1967 seem quite small in almost any perspective, particularly when it is recalled that last year witnessed one of the periods of greatest credit stringency in many decades. There is interest not only in the small size of the "ultimate" impact but also in the significant lag between monetary action and any appreciable effect on business investment; this reflects both the time required to intensify monetary restrictions and the relatively slow impact on the large firms, which account for a high proportion of total investment. Apparently, not until the third quarter of 1966—more than six months after the decision to implement significant monetary restrictions—were even the small average 1966 effects on plant and equipment and inventory investment achieved. The somewhat larger 1967 effects, which were indicated even after the restrictive policy was reversed, were of course associated with significantly longer time lags. Lags tended to be shorter and the impact somewhat severe for the smaller firms.

The relatively small and significantly delayed overall impact of monetary policy on business investment is in interesting contrast to the shock effect of such policy on investment in housing. Although we do not have a reliable framework for estimating the effect of the credit stringency on housing, the rough magnitude of the effect seems reasonably clear. Housing investment had been quite stable from 1964 through the first quarter of 1966. It started to decline in the second quarter of 1966, apparently largely in response to developments in the financial markets, and showed major weaknesses in the third and fourth quarters, declining $6.1 billion or 23 percent from a seasonally adjusted annual rate of $27.0 billion in the first quarter to $20.9 billion in the fourth. There were time lags here as well, but even by the third quarter, housing investment had declined $3.3 billion at an annual rate, or 12 percent, from the first quarter. As compared with either the 1965 or first quarter 1966 rate, the reduction in housing investment for the entire year 1966 amounted to $2.6 billion, or close to 10 percent.

Thus, it appears that monetary policy impinges to a much greater extent on the housing market than on business investment and that the former, unlike the latter, bears much of the brunt of economic stabilization through monetary policy. It should be pointed out, however, that as compared with business investment, housing presumably is also more greatly (and favorably) affected by monetary policy designed to stimulate investment during recessionary periods. Therefore, it is not clear whether over the entire business cycle the net effect of monetary policy is significantly greater for housing than for business investment. Moreover, even in 1966 nonmonetary policies may have been somewhat more restrictive on business investment than on housing. Late in the year, the suspension of the investment tax credit and of certain accelerated amortization procedures imposed some fiscal restraint on investment in plant and equipment expenditures (though the suspension was of relatively short duration).[13] Earlier in the year, the Administration had urged voluntary restraint. A consideration of the net effects of credit policy on housing and business investment over the cycle and a comparison with available alternatives from the viewpoint of economic stabilization and development are beyond the scope of this article.

[13] These measures, particularly the suspension of certain accelerated amortization procedures, may also have had a restrictive effect on apartment houses and consequently on residential construction.

# 35 MONETARY RESTRAINT AND BORROWING AND CAPITAL SPENDING BY STATE AND LOCAL GOVERNMENTS IN 1966*

PAUL F. McGOULDRICK
*State University of New York, Binghamton*

JOHN E. PETERSEN
*Investment Bankers Association of America*

In 1967, the Federal Reserve System conducted two surveys on the impacts of changing credit market conditions in 1966 on both large and small State and local governmental units throughout the United States. This article reports and analyzes the results of the first of these surveys, that covering approximately the 1,000 largest State and local governments. A later article will analyze the results of the companion survey of nearly 13,000 small and middle-sized State and local units.

* * *

*The Problem of Interest Rate Impacts*

Higher interest rates might be expected to have a negative impact on State and local borrowing and capital spending for at least two reasons. First, taking the shorter view, an increase in the interest rate raises the current cost of debt service in an area of the economy where revenues are relatively inflexible in the short run. Taking the longer view, an increase in the cost of borrowing to finance long-lived physical assets means that the capital facilities themselves have gone up in price. Potential borrowers, examining the alternatives, might thus desire to postpone or abandon the acquisition of such assets.

However, application of conventional economic theory in an effort to determine the impact of market rates of interest on public investment is not altogether satisfactory. Generally, governments do not compete with other units in selling their goods in free markets. Nor can their behavior be explained by a logical system in which they are expected or compelled to maximize profits or some other readily quantifiable index of activity.

While simple notions of the maximization of profits or preferences do not neatly describe the decisions of governments in determining and meeting social needs, a rise in the interest rates paid by them might be expected to generate one or more of the following reac-

* Reprinted from *Federal Reserve Bulletin*, vol. 54 (July, 1968), pp. 552–581 and (December, 1968) pp. 953–982, by permission of the authors and the Board of Governors of the Federal Reserve System. [Abridged and consolidated by the editors. Note *** indicates sections omitted in abridgement.]

tions, unless government demand schedules for long-term borrowed funds are completely inelastic:[1]

(*1*) Government units could increase tax rates to compensate for reductions in planned borrowing.

(*2*) They could shift from long-term to short-term borrowing in order to postpone their definitive financing plans until borrowing costs are lower.

(*3*) They could reduce current expenditures, reduce capital outlays and new outlay commitments, or draw down their liquid assets.

(*4*) They could seek and obtain intergovernmental grants or loans.

(*5*) Finally, governments that ordinarily borrow well in advance of capital outlay needs could postpone borrowing to a date immediately prior to actual cash disbursements. Borrowing postponements of this kind result in gaps between actual and previously desired liquid asset levels.

The empirical literature on how State and local governments in fact have responded to credit market conditions is sparse.[2] But it does indicate that these governments have cut back on their borrowing when interest rates were above their upward postwar trend and that they borrowed more when rates were below that trend; there has been no measured response to the upward trend itself. Moreover, this literature is inconclusive as to whether or not these governments curtailed their capital outlays following borrowing curtailments in periods of monetary restraint.

Measurement of the impact of interest rates on capital outlays is complicated by the interaction of long, structural lags in public construction projects and of the general shortness of cyclical periods of rising interest rates. Public capital outlays are much more heavily weighted by the structures component than are business investment outlays; and the construction of such long-lived facilities is peculiarly insensitive to short-run changes in underlying demand for capital services because of the long period of time needed for planning, site acquisition, and construction.[3]

In view of the lack of information about the relative importance of the possible various responses to high and rising interest rates, the Federal Reserve survey was designed with the following two objectives: First, to measure the impact of credit conditions on the long-term borrowing of State and local governments and their capital outlays.[4] Second, to determine the degree of dependence between long-term borrowing and spending decisions, and to identify and measure factors which influence that linkage.

* * *

[1] Throughout this article "governmental" and "governments" refer to State and local government units, including special districts and authorities, except when specified otherwise. "Long-term borrowing" refers to borrowing of one year or longer original maturity. "Bond offerings" are bond issues at the date when the lowest bid was accepted (for competitively bid issues) or the underwriting agreement or other borrowing agreement was signed. The survey asked respondents to time all borrowings, by month and year, by the offering date of the bond, not by the date of issue. The date "1966" refers only to calendar 1966.

[2] For a summary of that literature, see Paul McGouldrick, "The Effect of Credit Conditions on State and Local Bond Sales and Capital Outlays Since World War II," *State and Local Public Facility Needs and Financing*, vol. 2, U.S. Congress, Joint Economic Committee, 89th Cong., 2d Sess., Washington: U.S. Government Printing Office, 1966.

[3] In fiscal year 1965–1966, construction expenditures made up over 90 per cent of State and local capital outlays exclusive of outlays for land and existing structures. In contrast, expenditures on new nonresidential structures amounted to only about a third of total private fixed investment in 1966. U.S. Bureau of the Census, *Governmental Finances in 1965–1966*, p. 21; U.S. Department of Commerce, *Survey of Current Business*, vol. 47 (June 1967), p. 21.

[4] The decision to focus on long-term borrowing and capital outlays was made for these reasons: (1) the unique relationship between long-term borrowing (debt of more than 1 year in maturity) and capital outlays, a sizable proportion of which are 100 per cent debt-financed; (2) the greater postponability of these decisions in comparison to those involving current revenues and short-term borrowing; (3) the much greater total financial cost consequences involved in decisions to borrow long-term as compared to those involved in temporary borrowing decisions, and (4) the dollar volume of long-term borrowing is typically nearly twice as great as that involved in short-term borrowing.

TABLE 1. ACTUAL AND PLANNED LONG-TERM BORROWING OF STATE AND LOCAL GOVERNMENTS IN 1966, BY TYPE OF EXPERIENCE AND PURPOSE
(In millions of dollars)

| Experience | Total | Purpose of Borrowing | | | | | |
|---|---|---|---|---|---|---|---|
| | | Utilities | Educational facilities | Transportation | Health and welfare | Administrative facilities | Other |
| (1) Planned borrowing[1] | 7,563 | 1,243 | 2,214 | 2,263 | 412 | 304 | 1,127 |
| (2) Net change in planned borrowing | −1,360 | −237 | −219 | −589 | −108 | −25 | −182 |
| (a) Reduction | −105[2] | −11 | −63 | −29 | −1 | (3) | −1 |
| (b) Increase | 34 | 5 | 10 | 9 | ...... | 6 | 4 |
| (c) Abandonment (includes postponements beyond (1966) | −1,289 | −231 | −166 | −569 | −107 | −31 | −185 |
| (3) Actual borrowing | 6,203 | 1,006 | 1,995 | 1,674 | 304 | 279 | 945 |
| (4) Ratio of actual to planned borrowing (per cent) | 82 | 81 | 90 | 74 | 74 | 92 | 84 |

[1]Line (3) minus line (2).
[2]Amount differs from that shown in Table 2 because of a judgmental reallocation in Table 2.
[3]Less than $500,000.

## Large Government Units

### *General Borrowing Experiences*

Of the 987 State and local governments replying to the survey, somewhat less than half, or 440 units, actually borrowed long-term funds in 1966. Of these, 69 had modified their borrowing plans downward, either by reducing the amount they had originally planned to borrow or by temporarily postponing offerings during the year.[5] An additional 53 units had intended to borrow, but found it necessary or desirable to abandon all plans of doing so. Thus the total of governmental units is almost equally divided between those units having had at least an intention to borrow (493) and those reporting no intention to borrow long-term in 1966 (494).

One quarter of those units that expressed at least an intention to borrow long-term in 1966 found it necessary to alter their plans in one way or another. Among the types of governmental units, State higher educational institutions had the highest frequency of alterations in plans: 27 out of the 90 potential borrowers.

The dollar volume of long-term borrowing actually accomplished in 1966, as compared with that originally planned for that year, is presented in Table 1. Most of the shortfall of borrowing ($1.36 billion) reflected *abandonments* of $1.29 billion, that is, issues cancelled in their entirety during 1966. The sale of these issues could have been suspended indefinitely or delayed until 1967. Another $0.1 billion of issues were *reduced,* that is, the government borrowed less than originally planned. Only an insignificant volume of borrowing represented *increases* in issue size from that originally planned. *Postponements,* that is, issues temporarily delayed but later sold in 1966, are not displayed in this table since they would not affect annual totals.

[5] The different types of changes in plans are taken up in detail below. The term downward is used to denote actions that led either to a reduction in the amount actually borrowed or a failure to borrow at the time originally planned. It should be borne in mind that distinction between changes in amount and in timing is a function of the length of the period of time covered by the survey. That is, had we chosen to look at a longer interval of time, much of the shortfall in borrowing would prove to be postponements.

TABLE 2. REDUCTIONS IN BOND OFFERINGS DURING 1966, BY REASONS FOR REDUCTION AND TIMING OF OFFERING (In millions of dollars)

| Reason | Total for year | QI | QII | QIII | QIV |
|---|---|---|---|---|---|
| Court proceedings | 0.9 | ...... | 0.9 | ...... | ....... |
| Underwriting delays *not* due to interest rates[1] | ..... | ...... | ...... | ...... | ....... |
| Referendum defeat | 3.2 | ...... | 3.2 | ...... | ....... |
| Interest rates exceeded pre-set ceiling | (2) | (2) | ...... | ...... | ....... |
| Interest rates were too high for other reasons than above | 101.5 | 10.0 | 62.4 | 0.2 | 28.9 |
| High construction costs | 0.8 | ...... | ...... | ...... | 0.8 |
| Revenue increases or expenditure decreases[1] | ..... | ...... | ...... | ...... | ....... |
| Other | 8.8 | 0.5 | [3]6.0 | 2.3 | |
| Total | 115.3 | 10.5 | 72.5 | 2.5 | 29.7 |

[1]Zero entries in all columns of this line.
[2]Less than $50,000.
[3]No reasons at all checked for this amount.

Postponements amounted to almost $0.4 billion. *Accelerations,* that is, issues whose time of sale was advanced, amounted to about $0.1 billion.

For all purposes, borrowing planned by large units for 1966 amounted to $7.6 billion, while borrowing realized was $6.2 billion or 82 per cent of the planned level. By contrast, borrowing for all educational purposes—by cities and States as well as by independent school and university authorities—was 90 per cent of the planned level.[6] The largest shortfalls were in borrowing for health and welfare and transportation facilities; only 74 per cent of borrowing planned for these two purposes was actually realized. This tends to confirm earlier findings that borrowing for educational purposes is less sensitive to fluctuations in interest rates than other types.[7]

* * *

*Borrowing Abandonments and Reductions*

During 1966, 24 government units abandoned the imposing sum of $1.29 billion of long-term borrowing. In addition, 1966 bond offerings actually sold were reduced by $0.12 billion. Together, abandonments and reductions led to a total shortfall of $1.41 billion from planned borrowing levels, exclusive of the very small increases in borrowing plans discussed above. (See Tables 2 and 3.) High interest rates were the primary cause of $1.01 billion (78 per cent) of offerings abandonments and $0.10 billion (89 per cent) of reductions in offerings sold. Clearly, stringent credit markets in 1966 had more than a transitory impact on the borrowing plans of State and large local governments, and created a large carry-over of unsatisfied credit demands into the following year.

Abandonments amounted to 16 per cent of the actual total long-term borrowing shown in Table 1. Of all functional categories, transportation was affected the most by borrowing abandonments: the latter amounted to slightly over 34 per cent of actual borrowing for the same purpose. It should be noted that the one very large abandonment of borrowing by a toll road authority accounted for about 23 per cent of total abandonments in 1966. Abandoned educational bond offerings were only 8 per cent of actual borrowing for that purpose during the year. Reductions were concentrated in borrowings for educational purposes but only accounted for 4 per cent

[6] However, colleges and universities may have had unique borrowing problems in 1966 that are obscured in Table 1 by high proportions of actual to planned borrowing achieved for elementary and secondary education facilities. A later study combining data from both the small and large government surveys will investigate this possibility.

[7] Frank Morris, "Impacts of Monetary Policy on State and Local Governments: An Empirical Study," *Journal of Finance,* May 1960.

**TABLE 3. ABANDONMENTS OF BOND OFFERINGS, PURPOSE OF OFFERING RELATED TO REASON FOR ABANDONMENT[1] (In millions of dollars)**

| Primary reason for abandonment | All purposes | Purpose: (a) Utilities | (b) Educational facilities | (c) Transportation | (d) Health and welfare | (e) Administrative facilities | (f) Other |
|---|---|---|---|---|---|---|---|
| Referendum defeat | 92.3 | 3.4 | 28.1 | ...... | 14.8 | ...... | 46.0 |
| High construction costs[1] | ...... | ...... | ...... | ...... | ...... | ...... | ...... |
| High interest rates | 1,006.9 | 115.8 | 117.4 | 558.0 | 86.2 | 15.6 | 113.9 |
| Revenue increases or expenditure decreases | 10.0 | ...... | ...... | 0.7 | (2) | 1.5 | 7.8 |
| Availability of intergovernmental grants | 4.0 | ...... | 4.0 | ...... | ...... | ...... | ...... |
| Other | 175.9 | 112.0 | 16.6 | 10.1 | 6.2 | 14.0 | 17.2 |
| All reasons | 1,289.2 | 231.2 | 166.0 | 568.7 | 107.2 | 31.2 | 184.9 |

[1]Abandonments includes offerings postponed into 1967 or later as well as those suspended indefinitely.
[2]Zero entries in all columns of this line.
[3]Less than $50,000.

**TABLE 4. REDUCTIONS IN BOND OFFERINGS IN 1966, BY PURPOSE AND PER CENT OF OFFERING**

| Purpose of borrowing | Amount[1] (in millions of dollars) | As percentage of bond offerings |
|---|---|---|
| Utilities | 11.0 | 1.1 |
| Education | 72.9 | 3.7 |
| Transportation | 28.6 | 1.8 |
| Health and welfare | 1.4 | 0.5 |
| Administrative facilities | (2) | (3) |
| Other | 1.4 | 0.2 |
| Total | [4]115.3 | 1.9 |

[1]Reductions in multipurpose issues were allocated, arbitrarily, among purposes by amounts finally borrowed.
[2]Less than $50 thousand.
[3]Less than 0.05 per cent.
[4]This is $6.0 million greater than the corresponding total in Table 2 because one government failed to check a reason for a borrowing reduction of this amount.

of actual bond sales for that category, as is shown in Table 4.

* * *

### *Induced Changes in Capital Outlays*

A large proportion of respondents filling out the questionnaire were finance officers or treasurers. These men are intimately acquainted with borrowing postponements and abandonments and their proximate causes. But they may be less well acquainted with the ultimate consequences of such actions in terms of operating as well as capital outlays.

Thus, respondents were asked primarily about contract award cancellations resulting from changes in borrowing plans, rather than about induced changes in total capital spending or spending plans during 1966. Such cancellations are "news" because each usually involves a large amount of projected spending on a single project. It was believed that finance officer respondents would therefore have a reasonably complete knowledge of when cancellations occurred and the approximate dollar magnitude involved.[8] Re-

[8] It was also expected that borrowing would have had a much greater impact on new contract awards than on spending on projects for which contracts had already been awarded. Projects under construction are almost never abandoned due to a borrowing setback, because the outlays have already been legally committed and because funds often are required to be fully in hand before construction begins.

spondents were also questioned about the purpose of such awards. Finally, they were asked to report on, and quantify, any other impacts of borrowing disappointments on 1966 capital spending and on 1967 contract awards.

CONTRACT AWARDS. The reported effects of changes in borrowing plans on contract awards were small. Twenty-two governments canceled $121 million of awards in 1966 because of borrowing difficulties—less than a tenth of the $1.41 billion total shortfall from planned borrowing. Nearly all of the award cancellations were associated with abandonments rather than short-term postponements or reductions of bond offerings, as is shown in Table 5.

* * *

After making allowances for those items not asked about in the survey—such as award cancellations after July 1967 and lagged reductions in outlays on equipment, land, and existing structures during 1967—the total impact of 1966 borrowing changes by large units on combined 1966-67 capital and current outlays was probably $250 million or more. Since spending follows contract awards by moderately long lags in the government sector, the bulk of the impact on spending undoubtedly came after the peak of monetary restraint in the late summer and early fall of 1966. It should also be noted that even reductions of $300 million, spread over both 1966 and 1967, would be small rela-

TABLE 5. CONTRACT AWARD CANCELLATIONS BECAUSE OF BORROWING DIFFICULTY (In millions of dollars)

| Type of borrowing | Contract award cancellations |
|---|---|
| Reduction, or postponement until later in 1966 | 10.0 |
| Abandonment, or postponement into 1967 | 104.0 |
| Combination of both[1] | 6.7 |
| Total | 120.7 |

[1]Units both postponing until later in 1966 and abandoning offerings.

TABLE 6. VOLUME OF CONTRACT AWARDS CANCELLED FOLLOWING BORROWING ABANDONMENTS, PURPOSE OF AWARD RELATED TO PRIMARY REASON FOR ABANDONING BORROWING (In millions of dollars)

| | | Purpose of Intended Award | | | | | |
|---|---|---|---|---|---|---|---|
| Reason for abandonment | Total | Utilities | Education | Transportation | Health and welfare | Administrative facilities | Other |
| Referendum defeat | 12.4 | 3.3 | 9.1 | .... | .... | ... | ... |
| High construction costs | ... | ... | ... | .... | .... | ... | ... |
| High interest rates | 82.1 | 9.7 | 14.9 | 36.4 | 10.8 | 3.2 | 7.2 |
| Revenue increases or expenditure decreases | .... | ... | ... | .... | .... | ... | ... |
| Availability of grants-in-aid | .... | ... | ... | .... | .... | ... | ... |
| Other | 16.3 | 3.0 | 7.9 | .... | .... | 3.0 | 2.3 |
| Total | 110.7 | 16.0 | 31.9 | 36.4 | 10.8 | 6.2 | 9.5 |

NOTE: These cancellations do not include those by units that reduced long-term borrowing or made up postponements within 1966 unless they also abandoned borrowings. However, this portion not included is less than 10 per cent of the total shown here. See Table 5.

TABLE 7. BORROWING ABANDONED BY UNITS GOING AHEAD WITH CAPITAL OUTLAYS, PURPOSE OF INTENDED BORROWING RELATED TO MEANS OF FINANCING OUTLAYS (In million of dollars)

| Primary means of financing outlays | Total | Purpose of Borrowing | | | | | |
|---|---|---|---|---|---|---|---|
| | | Utilities | Education | Transportation | Health and welfare | Administration | Other functions |
| Short-term borrowing for: | | | | | | | |
| Interest–expectational reasons | $225.0 | $16.5 | $81.0 | $39.9 | $65.5 | $6.5 | $15.5 |
| Other reasons | 13.7 | 1.7 | 1.5 | 2.8 | 5.0 | 1.1 | 1.7 |
| Stretch-out of cash disbursements | 17.5 | 6.1 | 8.0 | 1.4 | 1.4 | .... | 0.6 |
| Current expenditures reduced | 18.0 | ..... | ..... | 13.0 | ..... | .... | 5.0 |
| Increase in revenues | 10.0 | ..... | ..... | 0.7 | (1) | 1.5 | 7.8 |
| Liquid assets drawn upon | 245.7 | 63.6 | 23.4 | 151.2 | 6.4 | 0.1 | 1.0 |
| Intergovernmental grants | ...... | ..... | ..... | ..... | ..... | ... | ..... |
| Other means[2] | 582.1 | 122.2 | 12.9 | 320.9 | 17.8 | 6.8 | 101.5 |
| Total | 1,112.0 | 210.1 | 126.9 | 529.9 | 96.1 | 16.0 | 133.1 |

[1]Less than $50,000.
[2]Predominantly funds not needed for 1966 capital spending because borrowing was planned well in advance of actual cash needs.

tive to the total capital outlays of large governments.[9]

## *How Capital Outlays Were Maintained*

The great majority of governments experiencing a reduction or an abandonment of borrowing (93 out of 115 units) went ahead with capital outlays in 1966 despite financing difficulties. Among the specific means for proceeding with capital spending after changes in borrowing plans, two stand out: the substitution of short- for long-term borrowing, and drawing upon liquid assets. Those respondents that reduced or abandoned long-term borrowing in 1966, but maintained their capital outlays, were asked to check various alternative means by which these outlays were financed. The amount of capital spending thus maintained by these alternative means was assumed to be equal to the amount of long-term borrowing abandonments or reductions by the units involved. By this approximation used in Table 7, $239 million of spending was maintained by short-term borrowing[10] and about the same amount, $246 million, was maintained by drawing upon liquid assets. These amounts were far in excess of any flows maintained by other specific means such as stretch-outs of cash disbursements or reductions in current expenditures. The lack of adjustments to current receipts and expenditures confirms that such flows are very resistant to short-run adjustments.[11]

* * *

[9] There are no statistics on the capital outlays or contract awards made by the large-government group in this survey. But they borrowed $6.2 billion during 1966, nearly all of which was for capital outlays. If we add to this a reasonable estimate of outlays financed from other sources, such as tax revenues and government grants, we have an implied large-government capital spending total of at least $10.0 billion, and probably more, in 1966. This, in turn, would imply that $250 to $300 million of outlay reductions due to borrowing difficulties over the 2-year period represents a reduction equivalent to no more than 1.3 or 1.5 per cent per year of capital outlays.

[10] In addition, several governments commented that they had shortened the maturities of long-term borrowing (although still borrowing on maturities of more than 1 year).

[11] These results were not due to the weight of any exceptionally large bond offerings abandoned, as is shown by their general agreement

## Small Government Units

Estimates based on the sample survey of small local governments and State-administered colleges indicate that all units combined experienced delays and decreases in planned long-term borrowing amounting to approximately $2.6 billion in 1966. An estimated $5.8 billion in long-term borrowing was actually accomplished by small units in that year. The largest share of small-unit borrowing setbacks in 1966, about 40 per cent of the dollar volume, resulted from bond referendum defeats. Only about one-third of the total of such borrowing delays and decreases, $0.9 billion, was primarily attributable to the high and rising interest rates of that year. Large units, previously surveyed, had shortfalls and postponements in long-term borrowing due to credit market conditions amounting to $1.4 billion.

Nevertheless, while small governmental units experienced relatively less borrowing difficulty because of restrictive credit conditions than large units, such difficulties did lead them to cancel a higher volume of planned contract awards. During 1966, cutbacks in planned contract awards by small units induced by the high costs of borrowing amounted to about $150 million, as compared with about $90 million for the large units. Allowing for a variety of added expenditure reductions and postponements stretching into 1967 by both large and small State and local governments, it is estimated that stringent credit market conditions in 1966 reduced State and local government spending by somewhat over $400 million. This probably is equal to less than 1 per cent of State and local government capital outlays for 1966 and 1967 combined.

About half of the small governments surveyed that experienced borrowing difficulties were able to proceed as planned with their capital expenditures. While a large percentage did so by short-term borrowing, a significant minority resorted to reductions in current expenditures or postponements of cash disbursements, relying on the flexibility of their current budget to absorb the shortfall in long-term borrowing. Relatively few were able to sustain planned projects because they used liquid asset holdings or because they had planned to borrow well in advance of cash needs, two principal methods used by the larger units to insulate spending plans from borrowing difficulties.

Once small units had obtained permission to borrow, their financing plans appeared to be less sensitive to rapidly changing credit market conditions than those of the large units. The survey indicates that small units were less inclined to speculate on interest-rate fluctuations, in part because changes in long-term borrowing plans were more likely to disrupt planned expenditures than was the case with the large governments.

with underlying data on governmental *units* maintaining capital outlays.

* * *

## Conclusions

By and large, the major finding of the survey of the large State and local governments still stands: the rapid escalation of interest rates in 1966, though greatly affecting the long-term borrowing plans of State and local governments, had only a marginal impact on their spending in that year. But the general observation for the sector needs to be tempered by an appreciation for the significant differences that appeared in the composition of that experience among units of different sizes. First, it is evident that the largest governments were able to abandon offerings and to speculate on the future course of interest rates without spending cuts either because they had a cushion of liquid assets or because they had planned on substantial lags between the time when they borrowed and when cash balances would be needed for disbursement. It is likely, however, that such flexibility would be reduced if interest rates were to remain high for some time. For chipping away at liquid assets without their periodic restoration and pushing borrowing dates back onto project starts provide only temporary insulation, which would be worn thin by prolonged periods of monetary restraint.

Second, small units that had received approval to borrow evidently were less likely to speculate on interest-rate fluctuations and more inclined to see their long-term borrowing plans through. This inclination to persevere in the face of the high costs of borrowing no doubt stemmed from a lack of temporizing alternatives. For small units, unwilling or unable to borrow long-term, a withdrawal from the credit markets greatly increased the probability that their spending plans would be cut back as well. Those small units that did go ahead with capital projects despite 1966 borrowing setbacks for the most part did not have the insulation provided by long borrowing lead times or stores of liquid assets. They turned instead either to their current cash budget or to short-term loans for funds. Short-term borrowing by these units—presumably the bulk of it loans from commercial banks—was the major buffer relied on to protect spending plans from borrowing setbacks. But for a sizable number, capital spending was maintained only by allocating needed cash from the current budget, and with no offsetting increase in revenues this spelled delays and cutbacks in other expenditures.

Third, institutional features of State and local governments did influence how units reacted to the pressures of high interest rates, though they were not of overwhelming importance in 1966. Interest-rate ceilings generated only about one-twelfth of all the borrowing abandonments brought on by high interest rates. Clearly most downward revisions induced by high borrowing costs were made at the discretion of the responsible government official. But there is evidence that, as a structural feature of the State and local sector, the diffusion of governmental responsibility among thousands of smaller local units tends to decrease governments' financial flexibility in the face of restrictive credit conditions and to tighten the linkage between borrowing setbacks and spending reductions.

Lastly, the survey findings have broader implications for a better understanding of the relationships between monetary policy and the real and financial flows in the economy. They suggest that causation runs from changes not only in borrowing plans to changes in liquidity but in the reverse direction as well. Governments—and perhaps other economic units—that are relatively more liquid are probably more apt to postpone long-term borrowing in the hope that interest rates might decline at a later date, because they can do so without disrupting their spending plans. For such units, withdrawal from the capital markets denotes financial strength rather than weakness. And the converse of this also holds: the fact that the borrowing of others might be relatively less affected by tightening credit conditions in the initial phases of restraint might mask a lack of financial flexibility that would mean more severe consequences for the expenditure plans of those ultimately finding it necessary to alter borrowing plans. The extensive use of short-term borrowing as an alternative means of financing projects also has a bearing on the role of State and local governments in transmitting the effects of monetary policy throughout the economy. To the extent that governments—by virtue of the attractiveness of their tax-exempt securities as well as the magnitude of their deposits—have preferred access to commercial bank credit, other borrowers are turned down, and thus the impact of credit stringency is relayed to other sectors of the economy.

In assessing the survey results and in any attempt to extrapolate them into later years, it is important to consider special factors that may have conditioned State and local reactions in 1966. An important one, no doubt, was the tremendous upsurge in Federal assistance during the period.[12] While the approximately $8 billion in capital facilities assistance flowing into State and local units may have been substituted for some long-term borrowing that otherwise would have been done by these units, it most likely had a stimulative impact on borrowing and spending plans at least in the short run. Units were surely of no mind to jeopardize projects partially financed by Federal aid through failure to come up with their share on time and in the full amount.

Moreover, capital market conditions by any measure had been relatively placid for the 5 to 6 years preceding 1966 and this gave many units ample time to build up liquid asset reserves. These, coupled with the generally high levels of revenues and grants and widespread advanced financial planning and borrowing on the part of the largest units, loosened the tether between current-period borrowing and capital outlays. But prolonged periods of capital market restrictiveness might have cumulative effects beyond those implied by the experience of any single period.

---

[12] Federal Government loans and grants to State and local governments were $16.8 billion in fiscal year 1967 and $13.8 billion in fiscal year 1966. It is estimated that approximately 55 per cent of this aid was destined for capital facilities. See "Federal Aid to State and Local Governments," Special Analyses, *Budget of the United States*, 1968. (Washington: U.S. Government Printing Office, undated.)

# 36 THE EFFECT OF MONETARY POLICY ON EXPENDITURES IN SPECIFIC SECTORS OF THE ECONOMY*

SHERMAN J. MAISEL
*Board of Governors of the Federal Reserve System*

Analysis requires theories. A plethora exist in the monetary field. At least four major descriptions of the relationships between changes in monetary policy and specific expenditures compete for attention.

*1.* Monetary policy influences interest rates which affect spending. Interest rates may alter the desire to consume or save. They also determine the cost of borrowing which influences the profitability of investment. Higher rates may limit the ability to borrow.

*2.* Spending is a function of the wealth or the assets of individual units. Monetary policies have an impact on wealth. The measurement of policy movements, for this purpose, can be performed in many ways. Some consider movements of the money supply narrowly defined as a measure or proxy for such changes. Others use broader definitions including other commercial bank deposits, deposits in all financial institutions, all liquid assets, or all wealth.

*3.* Expenditures may be influenced through the creation or intermediation of credit. The availability or rationing of credit to spending units will affect their spending. Monetary authorities through their creation of reserves and their impact on relative interest rates influence the amount and type of credit creation, of lending, and of borrowing.

*4.* Shifts in monetary policy cause changes in attitudes and expectations. These in turn may influence the spending of particular units.

### *Interpreting Data*

Even with a theory in hand, testing the theory against available data is complex. Demand theories in any sector stress many significant variables. Monetary variables are only a few among many which will be shifting simultaneously. Expenditure data reflect the results of all of these separate impacts. Analysis requires that their individual effects be traced.

The variables may influence the levels of expenditures, changes in the levels, or the rate of change. A search for policy effects must, therefore, consider the statistics on the average level of a sector's spending as well as its first and second differences.

Most theories point out that policy changes alter expenditures only with a lag. Effects may occur over periods running from one to twenty or more quarters into the future. Conversely, the movements of the dependent variable in any quarter reflect the influence of each of many past quarters' changes in the monetary variables. A period's data may

* Talk presented at the Fifth Annual Conference of University Professors sponsored by The American Bankers Association, New York, Long Island University, September 7, 1967. (Revised by the author.)

TABLE 1. FINANCIAL AND MONETARY INDICATORS (END OF PERIOD TO END OF PERIOD)

| | 1961–1964 annual average | 1965 1st H. | 1965 July – Nov. | Dec. 65– Mar. 66 | 1966 2d Q. | 1966 3d Q. | 1966 4th Q. | 1967 1st Q. | 1967 2d Q. |
|---|---|---|---|---|---|---|---|---|---|
| | (Annual Rates of Change, Seasonally Adjusted, in Per Cent) | | | | | | | | |
| Total member bank reserves | 3.7 | 7.0 | 1.6 | 4.7 | 4.5 | −0.9 | −3.6 | 17.7 | 3.5 |
| Member bank non-borrowed reserves | 3.5 | 4.5 | 3.3 | 2.8 | 2.9 | −3.0 | 0.4 | 24.8 | 4.9 |
| Private money supply | 2.8 | 2.6 | 4.2 | 5.5 | 2.7 | −1.8 | −1.5 | 6.4 | 7.7 |
| Time and savings deposits: | | | | | | | | | |
| Commercial banks | 14.8 | 15.2 | 16.5 | 7.9 | 11.2 | 8.8 | 3.0 | 18.9 | 15.2 |
| S&L's | 13.2 | 7.4 | 10.6 | 6.3 | −0.3 | 2.9 | 4.3 | 10.2 | 8.9 |
| Mutual savings banks | 7.9 | 7.5 | 7.1 | 4.1 | 3.2 | 4.6 | 6.6 | 8.7 | 10.7 |
| Total time & savings deposits | 12.8 | 10.9 | 12.8 | 6.6 | 6.0 | 6.0 | 4.1 | 14.2 | 12.3 |
| Liquid assets[1] | 7.4 | 7.4 | 9.5 | 8.8 | 3.4 | 2.7 | 5.4 | 9.0 | 3.8 |
| GNP | 6.7 | 8.4 | 8.6*[2] | 10.2*[3] | 6.1 | 6.6 | 7.1 | 2.2 | 4.7 |
| | (In Per Cent) | | | | | | | | |
| Liquid assets/GNP | 80.2 | 80.7 | 80.3[2] | 79.7 | 79.7 | 79.0 | 78.5 | 79.1 | 79.6 |
| Money supply/GNP | 25.6 | 23.3 | 23.0 | 22.7 | 22.5 | 22.2 | 21.9 | 21.9 | 22.1 |
| | (In Basis Points) | | | | | | | | |
| 3-mo. bill rate | +40 | −01 | +30 | +40 | +06 | +76 | −53 | −80 | −01 |
| 3-5 yr. Treasury | +18 | --- | +39 | +37 | +32 | +26 | −58 | −47 | +89 |
| 20-yr. US bonds | +03 | −01 | +19 | +20 | +21 | +07 | −31 | −02 | +52 |
| Corp. Aaa (new issue) | −03 | +11 | +20 | +20 | +23 | +49 | +04 | −30 | +71 |
| Municipal Aaa | −03 | +18 | +20 | +14 | +07 | +30 | −14 | −28 | −39 |
| Prime rate | --- | --- | +50 | +50 | +25 | +25 | --- | −50 | --- |

Includes money supply, time and savings deposits, savings and loan shares, U.S. savings bonds, and U.S. direct and agency issues maturing in less than one year and are data reported as of the last Wednesday of the month. Government bond holdings of banks, S&L's, and U.S. government agency and trust funds have been excluded.
3rd Quarter.
[3]4th Quarter and 1st Quarter.
SOURCE: Federal Reserve Board.

reflect several opposing movements of the independent variables in the past each of which influences the later period but with differing weights.

Finally we recognize that the aggregative data for a sector may hide significant movements in specific parts. Thus monetary impacts on total business investment may differ greatly from their impacts on the investment of small businesses or on those in particular industries. The availability of credit may be extremely significant for small finance companies while comparatively unimportant for large chemical firms. In attempting to evaluate the influence of monetary policy on a sectoral basis through an examination of spending statistics for each of the sectors taken as a whole, this type of impact may be completely hidden.

### *Plan of Paper*

Recognizing all of these difficulties, we propose to examine various types of data in the light of existing theory. Using the period 1961-64 and the first half of 1965 as base measures, we examine the quarterly data for 1965, 1966, and early 1967. We first consider the more direct measures of monetary policy. Then we go on to figures showing changes in the flow of funds during these periods and finally to data on expenditure flows.

We examine the data in relation to existing theories and in particular to that found in the recent empirical literature. Our approach to theory is eclectic rather than monolithic. Experience of over 50 years of business fluctuations analysis indicates, at least to me, that the field was retarded and damaged by misguided attempts to impose single, all-inclusive explanations on the very complex relationships. The ability both to explain and predict expanded rapidly as eclectic theories took over from those stressing single causes. It seems likely that this experience should hold for monetary theories also.

Based on this examination of the data, we select two specific sectors in which to examine the apparent relationships between monetary changes and final expenditures. Whether anyone is convinced of the existence of one rather than another relationship will remain a question of style and choice. Examinations of the data themselves, however, should lead to some better understanding of what occurred by giving each reader a better idea of the timing and magnitudes of movements during this period.

## Measures of Monetary Change

Table 1 shows the rate of change in a group of monetary variables. The general relationships are familiar. In the base period, 1961-64, member bank reserves and the money supply expanded around 3.5 per cent slightly more than half as fast as the gross national product. As a result, during this period, the ratio of money supply to the GNP dropped from 27.6 at the start to 24.1 per cent at the end of the period.

Time and savings deposits expanded rapidly particularly at commercial banks and savings and loan associations. Liquid assets as a whole rose somewhat faster than the GNP so that their ratio rose slightly from 79.2 per cent at the end of 1960 to 81.5 per cent at the end of 1964.

The first 11 months of 1965 show far more diverse movements. The division into six- and five-month periods catches some of the randomness and erratic movements that dominate these specific measures in short periods. Total reserves show a rapid expansion followed by a much slower one. The money supply data picture an opposite movement. Non-borrowed reserves fall between. The rate of expansion of commercial bank time deposits speeded up in this period as banks went more heavily into negotiable certificates of deposit. At the same time, funds in thrift institutions grew more slowly. The opposing movements averaged to a somewhat slower growth for total time and savings deposits compared to the base period. The ratio of the money supply to the GNP continued to fall while the ratio of liquid assets fell in contrast to its previous expansion.

December 1965 marked a well-publicized change in monetary policy. This was followed by a slower expansion rate for non-borrowed reserves. Through the middle of 1966 total reserves and the money supply expanded at close to their rates for the first 11 months of 1965, but they then declined absolutely in the last half of the year.

The impact on time and savings deposits was more immediate and drastic. Flows were affected by the change in reserves, by changes in Regulation Q, and by a sharply altered relationship between the rates offered for deposits and money market rates. Their total rate of growth fell by more than half in the first quarter of 1966. It then continued at reduced levels. The second and third quarters exhibited a dramatic shift in the relationship between commercial banks and savings and loans. Banks raised their rates paid on consumer-type deposits rapidly to offset the increases in market rates. S&L's in particular could not respond, so they lost funds to both the market and banks.

All of these movements are reflected in a much slower expansion of liquid assets and in a continuing fall in the ratios of liquid assets and of the money supply to the GNP.

The related changes in interest rates are only too familiar. Rates rose sharply after the December action. Most continued to move up in the second quarter and reached record levels by September. The initial movements were primarily expectational, but thereafter they mirrored changes in the creation of reserves and deposits as well.

TABLE 2. DEFICITS AND BORROWING (IN BILLIONS OF DOLLARS, SEASONALLY ADJUSTED)

| | Average annual change 1961 – 1964 | 1965 | | | 1966 | | | | 1967 | |
|---|---|---|---|---|---|---|---|---|---|---|
| | | 1st H. | 3d Q. | 4th Q. | 1st Q. | 2d Q. | 3d Q. | 4th Q. | 1st Q. | 2d Q. |
| Businesses: | | | | | | | | | | |
| Internal funds | 42.9 | 54.5 | 56.1 | 57.8 | 58.8 | 59.2 | 59.8 | 63.5 | 58.6 | 57.6 |
| Capital outlays | 45.5 | 61.8 | 64.8 | 67.1 | 70.6 | 74.3 | 76.4 | 81.0 | 73.3 | 68.5 |
| Net deficit | −2.6 | −7.3 | −8.7 | −9.3 | −11.8 | −15.1 | −16.6 | −17.5 | −14.7 | −10.9 |
| Federal | −3.6 | −3.2 | −4.8 | −1.2 | 1.2 | 1.5 | −1.9 | −4.5 | −12.6 | −18.3 |
| State & local | −1.8 | −1.5 | −1.0 | −1.5 | .2 | .3 | .6 | .3 | −1.7 | −3.1 |
| Total | -8.0 | −5.6 | −14.5 | −12.0 | −10.8 | −13.3 | −17.9 | −21.7 | −29.0 | −32.3 |
| | | | | | (Private Funds Raised) | | | | | |
| Business: | | | | | | | | | | |
| Bank loans not elsewhere counted | 3.9 | 12.2 | 9.9 | 14.8 | 10.5 | 16.5 | 7.6 | 9.2 | 6.5 | 8.9 |
| Corp. securities | 5.3 | 5.7 | 7.4 | 2.9 | 11.9 | 15.2 | 11.7 | 6.9 | 14.0 | 14.9 |
| Mortgages | 7.2 | 8.5 | 8.7 | 8.4 | 9.0 | 7.9 | 5.0 | 3.1 | 5.3 | 6.7 |
| Other[1] (inc. tax liabilities) | 3.1 | 4.0 | 4.7 | 8.9 | 7.4 | − 2.2 | 4.1 | 6.8 | 5.8 | −19.7 |
| Total* | 19.5 | 30.4 | 30.7 | 35.0 | 38.8 | 37.4 | 28.4 | 26.0 | 31.6 | 10.8 |
| Households: | | | | | | | | | | |
| Consumer credit | 5.6 | 9.8 | 9.3 | 8.9 | 9.2 | 7.0 | 6.9 | 4.6 | 4.3 | 4.4 |
| Mortgages | 14.6 | 16.4 | 17.3 | 17.6 | 16.3 | 15.7 | 14.7 | 12.4 | 11.0 | 11.7 |
| Other | 1.5 | 1.9 | 2.1 | 2.6 | − .5 | 2.4 | 2.8 | 1.6 | 2.6 | 2.2 |
| Total | 21.7 | 28.1 | 28.7 | 29.1 | 25.0 | 25.1 | 24.4 | 18.6 | 17.9 | 18.3 |
| Rest of world | 3.1 | 3.4 | 1.0 | 2.7 | 2.3 | 2.4 | .1 | .9 | 5.5 | 4.3 |
| Private total | 44.3 | 61.9 | 60.4 | 66.8 | 66.1 | 64.9 | 52.9 | 45.5 | 55.0 | 33.4 |
| Government: | | | | | | | | | | |
| State & local | 6.0 | 7.8 | 7.2 | 8.4 | 5.8 | 7.8 | 6.3 | 6.6 | 10.1 | 12.1 |
| US Govt. direct & savs. bonds | 5.5 | 2.7 | −8.4 | 7.7 | 9.5 | −14.4 | 8.0 | 2.3 | 8.6 | −29.0 |
| Nonguar. & PC's | 1.4 | 2.5 | 3.8 | .5 | 5.4 | 17.2 | −1.0 | −.1 | 2.1 | 7.3 |
| Total | 12.9 | 13.0 | 2.6 | 16.6 | 20.7 | 10.6 | 13.3 | 8.8 | 20.8 | −9.6 |
| Total funds Raised* | 57.2 | 74.9 | 63.0 | 83.4 | 86.8 | 75.5 | 66.2 | 54.3 | 75.8 | 23.8 |

[1]Includes corporate tax liability.
SOURCE: Federal Reserve Board Flow of Funds.

## The Flow of Funds

Table 2 indicates how shifts in the monetary variables were reflected in the availability of credit to the different sectors of the economy.

Businesses expanded their deficits or requirements for external funds fairly steadily until the first quarter of 1967. In this same period, the deficits of both levels of government fluctuated without any trend.

The next section of the table shows business borrowing expanded rapidly through the middle of 1966. The initial and most rapid increase took the form of bank loans. These reached record-breaking heights in the middle of 1966. The additions to loans slowed somewhat matching the similar movement in bank deposits, but they continued to be made in amounts far above the base period. The year 1966 also witnessed a record level of borrowing in the security markets. Here, too, the amount of flotations decreased in the last quarter.

Mortgage funds for income properties fell sharply in the last half of 1966. The availability of other funds shifted rapidly primarily as a result of changed tax liabilities as corporations had to pay more taxes on a current basis. In total, businesses increased their borrowings through the second quarter. Funds raised then decreased quite sharply but remained well above earlier periods.

Households showed a sizable expansion in funds raised in 1965. These sums reflected high and increasing sales of new automobiles. New housing starts were also high and a larger share of expenditures was being financed through mortgages.

Auto sales and the expansion of consumer credit were at record levels in the first quarter of 1966. Consumer credit then slowed its expansion sharply. Mortgage lending by private sources started down immediately in the first quarter of 1966. By the first quarter of 1967, household borrowing on mortgages was nearly 40 per cent below the 1965 high.

Changes in governmental credit flows were erratic reflecting primarily movements in tax collections, Treasury balances, and agency issues.

Given theories that explain monetary impacts in terms of creation and availability of credit and assets as well as the interest rates, what facts stand out in these two tables? We see: the steady fall in the ratio of money to the GNP throughout the period; the fall in the ratio of liquid assets to the GNP after the end of 1964; and the fall in the creation of non-borrowed reserves after the first half of 1965. Compared to the previous periods, total reserves and the money supply grew somewhat faster in the fiscal year 1966, but they then decreased absolutely starting in the summer of 1966. Finally, apparently there were significant shifts in the expansion rates of time and savings deposits in response to new instruments, changes in Regulation Q, and market rates.

The credit demands of businesses and the sharp increase in loans from banks as well as in the sale of securities are reflected in Table 2. This expansion slowed gradually after the middle of 1966. The availability or use of credit by households dropped sharply from the end of 1965.

The interest rate or price of money increased throughout the period until the final quarter of 1966. The movements in rates were particularly sharp between December 1965 and October 1966.

## Sector Expenditures

How do these changes in the monetary variables appear to have carried over to the actual sector expenditures? Let us examine Table 3. If we lacked knowledge of the monetary changes during this period, what movements in spending would stand out as requiring explanation? In levels, only the movement in housing expenditures is clear. These fell rapidly in 1966 to well below the amounts registered in both the 1961-64 and first-half-of-1965 bases. Inventories were also lower in the second quarter of 1967, but this low figure followed extremely high peaks for most of their prior observations.

Considering changes in levels, we note that after the end of 1965 the rate of increase in spending on non-residential investment and on consumers' durables slowed down and then stopped. State and local expenditures semed to increase at a steady or rising rate. The growth of other consumption expenditures fluctuated in a quite random manner. Their average growth rate was higher than in the base period, although the per cent of available income actually spent fell slightly.

Both the discussion in this period of what was happening as well as the demand theory

**TABLE 3. SELECTED INDICATORS, ANNUAL RATES, SEASONALLY ADJUSTED**

| | Annual average 1961 – 1964 | 1965 | | | 1966 | | | | 1967 | |
|---|---|---|---|---|---|---|---|---|---|---|
| | | 1st H. | 3d Q. | 4th Q. | 1st Q. | 2d Q. | 3d Q. | 4th Q. | 1st Q. | 2d Q. |
| | | | | | (In Billions of Dollars) | | | | | |
| GNP total | 575.8 | 669.1 | 690.0 | 708.4 | 725.9 | 736.7 | 748.8 | 762.1 | 766.3 | 775.3 |
| Residential | 25.5 | 27.1 | 26.9 | 26.8 | 27.0 | 25.8 | 23.7 | 20.9 | 21.4 | 22.7 |
| Nonresidential | 53.5 | 68.3 | 71.9 | 75.7 | 78.3 | 78.7 | 81.2 | 82.8 | 81.9 | 81.3 |
| Change in business inventory | 4.9 | 9.7 | 9.4 | 9.9 | 9.9 | 14.0 | 11.4 | 18.5 | 7.1 | 2.1 |
| State and local | 56.4 | 67.8 | 70.4 | 72.5 | 74.3 | 76.2 | 78.1 | 80.2 | 83.3 | 85.6 |
| Consumer durables | 51.7 | 64.7 | 66.1 | 68.6 | 71.6 | 68.2 | 70.9 | 70.6 | 69.4 | 72.1 |
| Other consumption | 314.9 | 359.5 | 370.2 | 379.2 | 386.7 | 393.4 | 399.3 | 403.2 | 410.8 | 416.8 |
| Net export balance | 6.3 | 7.2 | 7.4 | 6.1 | 6.1 | 5.4 | 4.6 | 4.3 | 5.3 | |
| | | | | | (In Per Cent) | | | | | |
| % of DPI after interest | | | | | | | | | | |
| Consumer durables | 13.3 | 14.4 | 14.1 | 14.4 | 14.8 | 13.9 | 14.2 | 13.9 | 13.4 | 13.7 |
| Consumer nondurables & services | 81.0 | 80.2 | 79.2 | 79.5 | 79.7 | 80.2 | 80.0 | 79.3 | 79.2 | 79.3 |
| Personal saving | 5.7 | 5.4 | 6.6 | 6.1 | 5.5 | 5.9 | 5.8 | 6.8 | 7.5 | 7.1 |
| | | | | | (In Millions of Units) | | | | | |
| Sale of new autos | 6.8 | 8.8 | 8.9 | 8.6 | 9.3 | 7.8 | 8.5 | 8.1 | 7.3 | 7.8 |
| Private housing starts | 1.48 | 1.43 | 1.46 | 1.50 | 1.42 | 1.28 | 1.08 | .92 | 1.12 | 1.26 |
| | | | | | (In Billions of Dollars) | | | | | |
| Increase in savings available for mortgages (Index)[1] | 100.0 | 107.4 | 106.2 | 100.0 | 94.0 | 63.8 | 58.4 | 54.3 | 127.0 | N.A. |
| Change in outstanding mortgage commitments | 1.40 | .52 | -.32 | .49 | -.87 | -5.15 | -5.36 | -3.14 | 1.87 | 6.72 |
| Net change in residential mortgage debt | 17.3 | 19.6 | 20.2 | 20.5 | 18.9 | 15.7 | 11.0 | 9.7 | 11.1 | 15.7 |
| Contracts & orders for new plant & equipment | 11.8 | 14.5 | 15.2 | 15.5 | 16.8 | 17.3 | 18.3 | 16.7 | 16.2 | 16.8 |
| Newly approved capital appropriations | 3.3 | 5.3 | 5.6 | 6.1 | 6.3 | 6.7 | 6.0 | 6.0 | 5.7 | N.A. |

[1]See Table 5 for definition.

SOURCES: Economic Indicators; text; Business Cycle Developments.

of these expenditures can furnish rather complete explanations of the course of almost all of the major variations—probably with the exception of housing—found in this table without any necessary reference to monetary events. Inventory cycles, the acceleration principle, etc., give adequate reasons for most movements. Furthermore, while evidence of the impact of monetary variables on many streams was searched for during this period, few signs of a direct relationship were obvious although some special surveys and statistical descriptions of this period do point out probable relationships between the monetary changes and expenditures in specific sectors.

In a way this is surprising, but not too much so. We know that most econometric studies of the past covering State and local expenditures, inventories, outlays for consumer durables, and other consumption have attempted without success to relate changes in monetary variables to expenditures. While at times monetary variables have added some explanatory values, in more cases these variables appear to have lacked statistical significance. Future attempts based on the past two years added observations, better estimating procedures for leads and lags, and use of more comprehensive models may alter this situation.

In the remainder of this paper, we discuss only the relationship of monetary changes to expenditures in housing and other fixed investment. These are the areas where past and current studies give most hope for success. For the remaining sectors, the relationships are probably far more complex, so much so that many would hold that explicit proof of their existence must still be considered as lacking. We would expect, of course, that with a more complete disaggregation of these sectors other examples would be more evident. New techniques may also lead to the discovery of significant relationships not yet explored.

## Expenditures on Residential Structures

The basic theories relating monetary shifts to expenditures tell us that we should, in this period, expect major reactions in the residential construction sphere. The data of Table 3 confirm our expectations. In 1966, the table shows an extremely sharp fall in both residential investment and in housing starts. While the relationship between these two measures is not exact, they are tied sufficiently for us to use variations in starts as a short-cut approach to explaining expenditures.[1]

The reasons for expecting monetary shifts to influence housing starts are clear. By its nature, monetary policy should, in the first instance, affect those units whose spending is highly dependent on either the cost or availability of credit. Among these groups, the degree of impact will vary. The variations will depend on the per cent of purchases made with credit, the amount of credit required per unit of expenditure, the ability or willingness to absorb higher interest rates, the institutional character of the market, and the degree to which traditional lenders are influenced by policy changes.

Housing ranks high on all these counts. About 95 per cent of new single-family housing is sold with the benefit of long-term financing. In any given year, the gross amount of mortgage lending on residential structures may be 160 per cent or more of this sector's GNP expenditures. The net amount lent approximates 70 per cent. Most borrowers allot a high percentage of their annual income to cover the costs of financing a house. They have limited ability or willingness to absorb changes in the cost or availability of credit.

While residential financing is the largest of all capital market operations, its institutional structure is rather unique. Its importance to the separate types of lending institutions varies greatly. Thus in 1963-65, a fairly typical period, each institutional group placed a very different percentage of its net inflow of funds into net residential mortgage expansion. The averages for this period, for example, were 18 per cent for commercial banks, 98 per cent for mutual savings banks, 96 per cent for savings and loan associations, and 28 per cent in the case of life insurance companies.

For commercial banks and life insurance companies, in particular, these percentages have traditionally been subject to rather wide variations. Mortgage lending usually does not arise from customer or other long-

[1] It is expected that the level of housing starts shown in the table will be revised downward shortly. This should not affect the analysis of this paper.

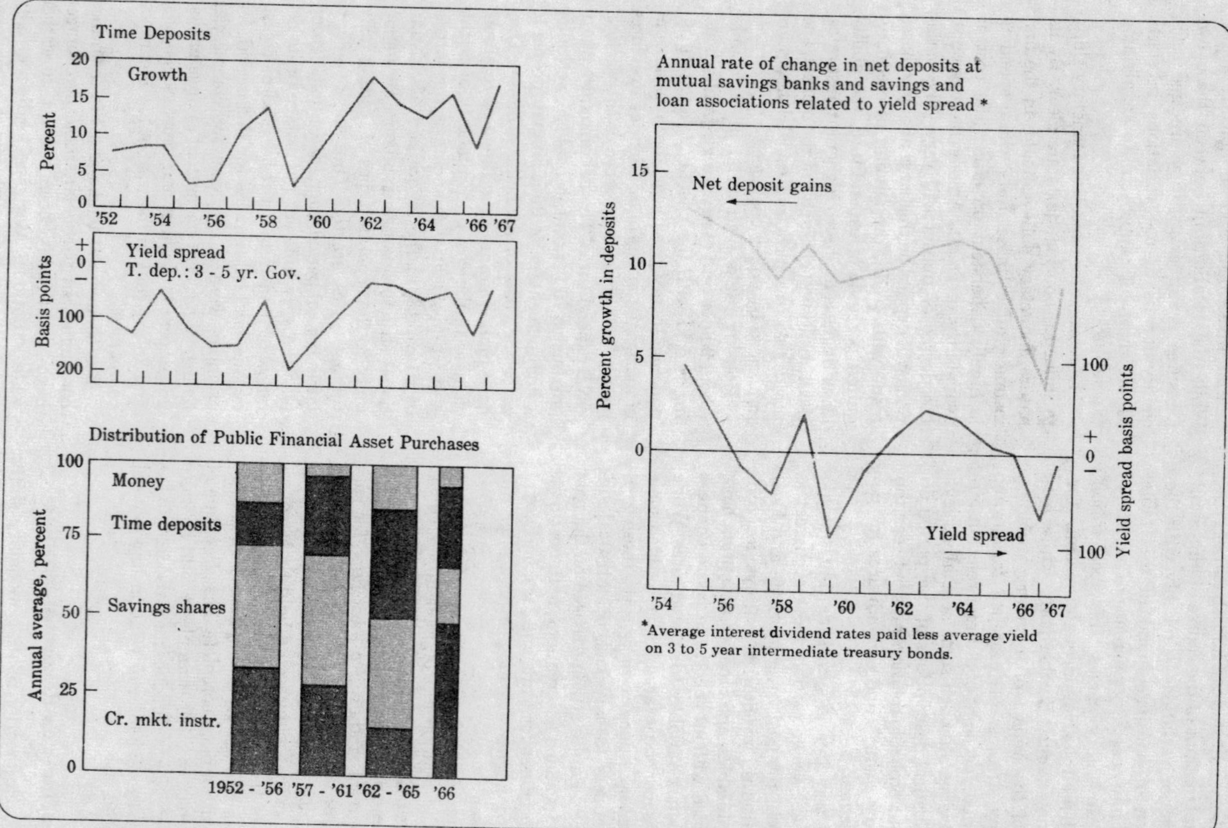


**CHART 1** Shifts in savings.

TABLE 4. SAVINGS FLOWS DURING SELECTED MONTHS (IN MILLIONS OF DOLLARS)

| | Commercial banks[1] | Savings & loan associations | Mutual savings banks | Life insurance companies[2] |
|---|---|---|---|---|
| | | (Not Seasonally Adjusted) | | |
| 1966 | | | | |
| January | 831 | −77 | 227 | 824 |
| April | 1,261 | −773 | −341 | 658 |
| July | 1,751 | −1,508 | 195 | 831 |
| October | 481 | −56 | 131 | 943 |
| 1967 | | | | |
| January | 764 | 184 | 433 | 1,268 |
| April | 1,929 | 497 | 189 | 705 |
| June | 2,046 | 1,935 | 624 | 643 (p) |
| | | (Seasonally Adjusted[3]) | | |
| 1966 | | | | |
| January | 1,632 | 470 | 226 | 824 |
| April | 1,125 | 227 | 27 | 658 |
| July | 2,151 | −170 | 201 | 831 |
| October | 934 | 168 | 293 | 943 |
| 1967 | | | | |
| January | 783 | 862 | 485 | 1,268 |
| April | 1,859 | 1,546 | 580 | 705 |
| June | 1,965 | 864 | 451 | 643 (p) |

[1]Into consumer-type time and savings deposits.
[2]Net increase in assets.
[3]Except for life insurance companies.
(p)Preliminary.
SOURCE: Federal Reserve Board.

term relationships. The willingness over time of institutions to make loans varies greatly in accordance with the current situation in the capital market as a whole. They vary the per cent of their funds put into mortgages widely.

These factors give a clear indication of why construction expenditures should be expected to feel a heavy impact as monetary policy shifts. Two paths seem to lead from an increase in interest rates to a curtailment of starts: (a) Higher interest rates raise the cost of borrowing on mortgages fairly rapidly. This directly lowers the profitability of builders. It also decreases the demand for units by final purchasers. (b) The availability of money to both builders and purchasers is also decreased. (1) Savers react to rate movements by shifting their deposits among financial institutions or increasing their direct market investments. (2) This shift among institutions will alter the availability of mortgage funds in accordance with the weight each type places on this sphere of lending for traditional or other reasons. (3) Many financial institutions will lower the relative share of funds to be placed in mortgages.

The decreased availability of mortgage funds and higher interest rates have no great impact on the needed number of housing units. They decrease construction and turnover. Initially most of the construction shortfall is absorbed in fewer vacancies. Eventually, however, it raises rents and leads to lower housing standards and a higher cost of living. In the meantime production in this sector is reduced.

### *Shifts Among Financial Institutions*

Chart 1 and Table 4 reflect some of the alterations which occurred in both the amount and availability of funds among financial institutions. Sharp movements took place in both the share of savings going to financial institutions and in its distribution among institutions.

A simple explanation for these phenomena arises when one relates them to the yields paid depositors by financial institutions and by the money market. Chart 1 for example shows the growth of time deposits in commercial banks and thrift institutions as the spread of the amounts they paid their depositors varied from market rates.

We see from the chart that the experience of last year was foreshadowed in several previous periods. The year 1966 was dramatic but not unique.

While major fluctuations seem related to the market spread, they also are influenced by government regulations. The chart shows the increasing share of savings put in commercial bank time deposits. Part of this movement reflects banks' greater interest in competing for time deposits. Part, however, reflects the greater leeway available for such competition beginning with the 1957 increase in Regulation Q ceilings. This upward movement was aided by the additional upward adjustments in the ceilings between 1962 and 1965 and by the decision of banks to enter vigorously the market for negotiable certificates of deposit.

The year 1965 witnessed a considerably slower growth rate for S&L's, traditionally the major source of mortgage funds. This downward movement accelerated in the course of 1966. Market rates were moving up, but rates paid by the thrift institutions lagged. They were squeezed because on one hand their earnings depended mainly on long-term, lower-yield assets bought in the past. On the other, S&L's found it difficult to move the marginal rate offered without altering the average for all share accounts. The optimum speed of adjustment of these rates, therefore, depended on the average rather than the marginal elasticity of demand for their accounts. What this elasticity was caused considerable debate particularly among those concerned by the fact that reserves had not caught up to the previous growth in liabilities.

This problem was less acute for commercial banks both because the average maturity of their assets was far shorter and because they differentiated their deposits offering separate rates in each market. As a result, they were able to compete far more effectively.

Table 4 shows the type of movements that occurred among institutions in 1966. It also shows the clear impact on the flow of funds into these institutions of the reduction in Q ceilings in September 1966 and the later movement in market rates.

### *Changes in Housing Finance*

These shifts in the flow of funds into and among the institutions had an immediate impact on the mortgage market. For example, Table 3 shows a weighted index of savings available for mortgage lending. This is simply a weighted aggregate of the net deposit flows into financial institutions with weights based on the percentage of each type's flow placed in mortgages in the first half of the 1960's. We note that funds available began to fall in the third quarter of 1965. By the fourth quarter of 1966, the index had fallen nearly 50 per cent.

The impact of this change in flows was augmented by a not unusual shift by each type of institution away from the mortgage market. By the first half of 1967 for example the net investment in residential mortgages as a share of new inflow of funds had fallen to 6 per cent for commercial banks, 50 per cent for mutual savings banks, 43 per cent for savings and loans, and 16 per cent for life insurance companies. These shifts reflected these institutions' views as to relative returns, desire for liquidity, the availability of mortgages, and differing lags among these forces.

In 1963-65, the financial institutions invested an average $45 billion a year in residential mortgages. The net mortgage investments averaged $19 billion a year or nearly 50 per cent of their net fund inflow. In the first half of 1967, the annual rate of gross investments had fallen by more than 45 per cent to $24 billion a year. Net mortgage investments were at the rate of $11 billion or only 20 per cent of the net inflow into financial institutions. While the use of seasonally unadjusted data somewhat overstates the case, mortgages' share of funds decreased by nearly 60 per cent from their 1963-65 share.

The timing of these shifts and their impact on starts show up clearly in Table 3. The decrease in available savings was fol-

**TABLE 5. HOUSING STARTS REGRESSION EQUATIONS**

1. $$St_o = -269.8 - \underset{(3.6)}{.2582} \sum_{-1}^{-3} FHA - \underset{(4.7)}{.1098} \sum_{-1}^{-3} FNMA - \underset{(4.0)}{.0873} \sum_{-1}^{-3} V_s + \underset{(3.4)}{.6581} \sum_{-1}^{-3} R/C + \underset{(4.0)}{.0420}\ DIH_{-1}$$

$\bar{R}^2 = .73$ SEE = 22.68 D.W. = .8333

2. $$St_o = -118.5 - \underset{(2.2)}{.2570} \sum_{-1}^{-3} Int - \underset{(3.7)}{.0678} \sum_{-1}^{-3} FNMA - \underset{(2.6)}{.0550} \sum_{-1}^{-3} V_s + \underset{(2.4)}{.4501} \sum_{-1}^{-3} R/C + \underset{(2.7)}{.0271}\ DIH_{-1} + \underset{(6.1)}{.6042}\ St_{-1} - \underset{(4.0)}{.3231}\ St_{-3}$$

$\bar{R}^2 = .86$ SEE = 16.76 D.W. = 2.2017

3. $$\Delta St_o = 2.86 - \underset{(2.5)}{.5299}\ \Delta FHA_{-1} - \underset{(2.4)}{.0820}\ \Delta \sum_{-1}^{-3} FNMA_{-1} + \underset{(1.2)}{.5350}\ \Delta \sum_{-1}^{-3} R/C_{-1} - \underset{(2.2)}{.1356}\ [\Delta Vs_{-1} + \Delta (St_{-1} - St_{-3})]$$

$\bar{R}^2 = .31$ SEE = 20.38 D.W. = 2.144

4. $$St_o = -404.7 - \underset{(3.4)}{.3745} \sum_{-1}^{-3} Int + \underset{(3.7)}{.0221} \sum_{-1}^{-3} FIN - \underset{(4.3)}{.1082}\ V_{-2} + \underset{(4.1)}{.9096} \sum_{-1}^{-3} R/C + \underset{(1.9)}{.0347}\ DIH_{-1}$$

$\bar{R}^2 = .68$ SEE = 24.83 D.W. = .7981

5. $$St_o = -345.2 - \underset{(2.6)}{.2969} \sum_{-1}^{-3} Int + \underset{(2.0)}{.0098} \sum_{-1}^{-3} FIN - \underset{(3.4)}{.0775}\ V_{-2} + \underset{(3.4)}{.6955} \sum_{-1}^{-3} R/C + \underset{(2.3)}{.0359}\ DIH_{-1} + \underset{(5.3)}{.6176}\ St_{-1} - \underset{(5.1)}{.4083}\ St_{-3}$$

$\bar{R}^2 = .83$ SEE = 18.34 D.W. = 2.0289

Definitions for Maisel Model. Period for fitting: 2nd quarter 1953–4th quarter 1967. (This table was revised by the author March 20, 1968.)

DIH Disposable personal income, seasonally adjusted, in 1958 dollars per household.

FHA Yields on FHA-insured Section 203, new-home mortgages sold in the secondary market, as reported by the Federal Housing Administration.

FIN Sum of seasonally adjusted *net inflows* to financial institutions available for mortgages on residential properties, derived as follows: 16.3 per cent of Commercial Bank time and savings deposits, including negotiable certificates of deposit; 98.1 per cent of Mutual Savings Bank savings deposits; 86.9 per cent of Savings and Loan Association share accounts and advances from the Federal Home Loan Banks; and 26.3 per cent of Life Insurance Company increases in assets.

FNMA Dollar volume of offerings of mortgages by private holders to FNMA for purchase for its secondary market portfolio less dollar volume of sales by FNMA from that portfolio. Functionally comparable data prior to 1955 estimated.

Int Contract rate on conventional first mortgages on new homes; FHLBB series for period beginning 1963 and FHA estimates for earlier period.

R/C Ratio of rent component of BLS Consumer Price Index to residential cost component of GNP implicit price index.

St Seasonally adjusted quarterly rate of private housing starts, including farm starts, as reported by the Census Bureau.

V Number of housing units available and fit for use, derived by comparing available inventory, including new completions, with number of households at beginning of each quarter.

$V_s$ Vacancies adjusted downward by .04 per cent increase in number of households, cumulated.

$\sum_{-1}^{-3}$ A three-quarter moving average of periods minus one, minus two, and minus three.

lowed within a quarter by a decrease in outstanding mortgage commitments. The lag to decreased housing starts visually appears to be between one and two quarters. The net change in mortgage debt lags the decrease in funds also.

### *Results of Econometric Models*

The impact of monetary changes on housing expenditures can be checked by use of an econometric model. The model has the advantage of giving a specific weight to the monetary impacts while holding all other variables constant. It retains, however, all the well-known disadvantages inherent in its problems of statistical techniques and measurements.

Table 5 shows current versions of the Maisel model first published in the *American Economic Review* in June 1963. The present form includes two monetary variables, one measuring interest rates and one availability of financing. In equations 1 to 3, the availability variable is based on offerings net of purchases of mortgages by private holders to FNMA. This moves inversely to credit availability. In equations 4 and 5, credit availability is measured by the savings available for mortgages discussed in the previous section. Other variables are vacancies, disposable income per household, relative rents to costs, and the inventory under construction.

What do the models suggest as to monetary impacts? Both the interest rate and availability variables are three-quarter moving averages with a further one-quarter lag. On the average, a change in monetary conditions affects the rate of starts six months later. At the means, the average interest elasticity is $-.56$ and the average credit availability elasticity is $+.07$. This means that a 100-basis-point increase in mortgage interest rates is related to a fall in housing starts of about 140,000 at annual rates. A decrease of $1 billion in savings available for mortgages is equivalent to a decrease of 33,000 in starts.

How significant are monetary changes in the total? We have various measures of significance. In calculating these we combine both monetary variables because of their high inter-correlation. On the average using simple relationships (not correcting for the interaction of money and other independent variables), the monetary variables are related to 42 per cent of the shifts in starts. Taking into account the other variables, the addition of the monetary variables accounts for about one-third of the movements not previously explained. Similarly removing the monetary variables decreases the relationships shown in Table 5 by about 20 per cent.

What do these models show for the year 1966? Let us take as a measure of change, the decrease in starts at annual rates between the last halves of 1965 and 1966. Because of the random variances in the data, fairly lengthy measurement periods are required. Over this year, the number of housing starts dropped by 480,000. The average of the models estimated a movement in this period of only 325,000. They failed to account for 32 per cent of the drop in this extremely dynamic period.

Of the decrease estimated by the model, the two monetary variables accounted for some 75 per cent. The remainder was accounted for by an increased number of vacancies and a decrease in relative rents, offset somewhat by an increase in disposable income. The estimated impact of the monetary variables was about one-half of the actual reported change—the difference, of course, being the amount unexplained by the model.

While I do not want to over-estimate the importance of the econometric results, it is clear that they do tend to confirm our previous analysis of the major factors at work in this market.

## Business Fixed Investment

If we examine the tables with respect to business fixed investment, what factors stand out? We note a steady decrease in corporate liquidity and a rise in interest rates from the middle of 1965. The amount of borrowing continued to increase till the end of the first half of 1966—with the sums borrowed from banks and the security markets far above previous rates. In the second half of 1966, borrowing fell quite sharply. Business appropriations for capital followed a similar path. Actual orders placed continued to rise through the third quarter, while GNP expenditures on business fixed investment went up through the fourth quarter of 1966.

When the measures began to fall, the amount of decrease followed an order similar to that of the turning points. The cut in busi-

TABLE 6. RESPONSES OF GROSS INVESTMENT TO CHANGES IN THE RATE OF INTEREST

| | | | Effects of a 100 Basis Point Decrease in R in Period T+8 | | | | |
|---|---|---|---|---|---|---|---|
| | End of period elasticity $E_{I \cdot R}$ | End of period response of gross investment $\frac{\partial I}{\partial R}$ | Decrease in period t+8 as a percentage of investment in '65 4th Q. | Cumulative decrease of investment as defined in col. I to period t+8 '65.dollars | Average quarterly decrease as a percentage of investment '65 4th Q. | I | R |
| Jorgenson[1] | −.17 | −.385 billions/ quarter in 1965 dollars | 15.2% | 10.5 billions | 9.6% | Total plant and equipment | U. S. Govt. long-term bond rates |
| Griliches-Wallace[2] | −.37 | −.271 billions/ quarter in 1965 dollars | 10.8% | 4.4 billions | 9.2% | Manufacturing plant and equipment | Moody's industrial bond yield |
| Bischoff[3] | −.12 | −.618 billions/ quarter in 1965 dollars | 3.2% | 2.1 billions | 1.6% | Producers durable equipment | Moody's industrial bond yield |
| | | | | | | Nonresidential construction | Moody's industrial bond yield |

[1]Jorgenson, D.: "Anticipations and Investment Behavior," *The Brookings Quarterly Econometric Model of the United States*, eds. J. S. Duesenberry, G. Fromm, L. R. Klein, and E. Kuh, Chicago; Rand McNally and Company, 1965, pp. 35–92.
[2]Griliches, I., and Wallace, N.: "The Determinants of Investment Revisited," *International Economic Review*, VI (September 1965), pp. 247–59.
[3]Bischoff, C.: "Elasticities of Substitution, Capital Malleability, and Distributed Lag Investment Functions," unpublished working paper for FRB-MIT model, 1966.
———"A Model Explaining Non-Residential Construction," unpublished working paper for FRB-MIT model, 1967.

ness borrowing was sharpest and that in GNP expenditures the least. All stayed at high levels in comparison with those of 1961-64.

The theory of capital investment has been well specified in many places.[2] It starts with an assumption that there is a basic demand for capital based on its expected profitability. This in turn depends on the amount of output sold, the selling price for the output, and factor costs. The cost of using the capital depends on the interest rate, tax rates, and depreciation. Thus monetary policy is assumed to influence the demand for capital through the cost of using it. These various factors interrelate in a rather complex non-linear form because some variables have a multiplicative effect while interest costs enter through a discounting process.

The shifting desires of a firm to own capital are not, however, immediately reflected in investment expenditures. The demand has to go through a planning and design period. Appropriations will be made. Financing will be arranged. Contracts will be let. Finally expenditures begin and are spread over a fairly lengthy period depending on particular production processes. The change in demand resulting from a movement in any of the independent variables will influence the level of production in each of many future periods.

[2] D. W. Jorgenson, "Anticipations and Investment Behavior," *The Brookings Quarterly Econometric Model of the United States*, J. S. Duesenberry et al., Chicago, Rand-McNally, 1965.

During the planning, appropriating, and contracting process, monetary changes may enter in an additional way. Many believe that the ability of firms to finance desired capital investments constrains their actual purchases. Thus, credit has an impact not only on profitability, but also on the ability of businesses to purchase profitable items.

Several surveys conducted by Donaldson, Lufkin, and Jenrette in 1966 among firms with assets of over $1 million seem to confirm the general theory.[3] In the vicinity of 20 per cent of these firms report cutting back somewhat on their capital investment because of changes in the monetary situation. In the first half of the year, most of these firms were primarily influenced by changes in interest rates. By the end of the year, however, a sizable minority indicated they had reduced spending because of the unavailability of credit. The great majority of those who cut back said that both the rate and availability of credit influenced their decisions. Larger firms seemed to find credit easier to obtain and were less influenced by its availability than by its cost.

### *Results of Econometric Models*

Several econometric models have been developed in recent years which follow the general outline of the theory discussed above. Important characteristics of three of these models are shown in Table 6. A major variance from the theory is that in their present form these models have not measured the impact of availability of credit during the planning and appropriation process. They are designed so they could do so, but they have not yet found this factor statistically significant. This may be either because of the high correlation among monetary variables or because prior to this year availability never became a really significant problem.

The first column of Table 6 shows the interest elasticity of these models. The Bischoff model is evaluated at the investment level of the fourth quarter of 1965. The simple mean of the three elasticities (which have been averaged from sub-parts) is −.22. The following columns show the type of impact which these models estimate from the monetary variable. The magnitude of response in any period depends on the final elasticity, the amount of monetary change, and the time intervening between the change and the period under consideration.

The table shows the impact of an assumed change in investment in manufacturing plant and equipment two years after interest rates rise by 100 basis points. Clearly, while the models have the same general relationships, there are major differences in their measured response. Again averaging these dissimilar results, we note that if interest rates rose by 100 basis points or nearly 25 per cent over their 1965 base then at the end of two years or eight quarters, the average level of investment (*ceteris paribus*) would be about 9.7 per cent less than it otherwise would have been. In the two-year period, the value of investment would have experienced a total cumulative decline of about $9.9 billion. This would have been a decrease of about 6.7 per cent of the investment in this two-year period.

The range of results produced by the three models is rather large and possibly misleading. In terms of total impact, the models are quite similar. Dissimilar results arise from considerable differences in lag patterns of response. In the Jorgenson and Griliches-Wallace models, the peak-period response of investment to a change in interest rates occurs within two years of the change. The Bischoff model in contrast produces responses that do not peak until eleven quarters after the change.

Since we are interested in 1966, we ask what approximately do these models show with respect to the impact of the monetary changes of this period? In this period the changes would be less since the total impacts are spread far into the future because of the lengthy ordering, production, and replacement process. Again we average the models in the table making some rather heroic assumptions about comparability in the process.

Non-residential investment expenditures in the last half of 1965 were at an annual rate of not quite $74 billion. The interest rate on long-term government bonds and on corporates ranged in 1963, 1965, and first half of 1965, the relevant periods influencing expenditures in the last half of 1965, at around

[3] Donaldson, Lufkin & Jenrette, Incorporated, *Timely Review of 1966 Credit Shortage Effects on Business Financing and Spending Decisions,* New York, July, 1967.

4.10 per cent and 4.35 per cent respectively. These rates rose at intervals in 1965 and 1966 reaching peaks up about 70 basis points for government bonds and 115 basis points for corporate bonds by the fall of 1966.

The ultimate effect of the increase in interest rates in 1966, if maintained far into the future, would according to the model decrease annual investment by from 3 to 5 per cent or from 2¼ to 3¾ billions of 1965 dollars. However, because of the lags in the investment process very little of this impact was felt during 1966. In fact, the estimated decrease from interest changes over the prior year would by the fourth quarter of 1966 have been only in the vicinity of $.9 billion at an annual rate or 1.2 per cent of the fourth quarter of 1965 base.

Obviously, these models do not show a very significant impact on monetary policy in 1966. Although they do seem to confirm the importance of long lags in this sector. However, I would guess that because the monetary shift was far larger and more dramatic than in the periods used for estimating their coefficients, these models, just as in the housing model, under-estimated monetary effects. We know from the Donaldson, Lufkin, and Jenrette study that far more companies reported that availability of funds was influencing their expenditures in the second half of the year than in the first half. This lack of financing also appears to account for some of the cuts in appropriations and orders.

## Conclusions

We have noted sizable impacts in both housing and other investment of monetary policy although with considerable lags. The influences appear to work through both the price of credit and its availability. The shifts in the flow of funds among different financial institutions and the differing lags and ability to pay in the sub-sections of the capital market seem to have reinforced the direct influence of policies on reserves and short-term interest rates.

It should be clear that this analysis leaves out several other possible channels of impact. Omitted are the expectational effects, as well as those of the multiplier and the accelerator.

We note, for example, the increased rate of borrowing after the 1965 increase in the discount rate. We see the high rate of car sales and of consumer borrowing in the first quarter of 1966. The rate of inventory investment in 1966 was extremely high. We have no available method of determining whether the expectational forces caused these expenditures to be higher or lower than they otherwise would have been.

The multiplier effect appears clear. The percentage of available disposable income spent in 1966 was slightly below the last half of 1965, but slightly above the average rate for that year. Variations in spending appear to be fairly normal, similar to those of many years in the past. This means that the measured impacts in housing construction and investment were carried through and had equivalent influences on consumption.

Similarly we would expect that normal acceleration for both fixed and inventory investment also occurred. The various econometric models give specific magnitudes for these forces. The Donaldson, Lufkin, and Jenrette survey reported that firms altered their inventories and investments somewhat as their final demand varied. This was particularly true of suppliers to the residential construction industry.

While the results of this analysis of these different sectors are interesting and significant, they do, of course, leave many unanswered questions. They appear to indicate, as we would guess, that the specific impacts were influenced by the amount of co-variance with events and other related variables. We do not know how much of the measured results depended upon the state of demand, the prior lack of liquidity, or the time it takes to learn and to adjust to a new environment. These are the types of additional answers we need if we want to estimate the probability that monetary shifts will have greater or lesser impacts in the future.

# 37 DOES SLOWER MONETARY EXPANSION DISCRIMINATE AGAINST HOUSING?*

NORMAN N. BOWSHER
and
LIONEL KALISH
*Federal Reserve Bank of St. Louis*

The "Declaration of National Housing Policy" in the Housing Act of 1949 establishes as one of the national objectives "the realization as soon as feasible of the goal of a decent home and suitable living environment for every American family"; and it requires programs "to encourage and assist . . . the stabilization of the housing industry at a high volume of residential construction." In view of the importance of housing, there is a natural hesitancy on the part of any policy maker to take actions which he considers to be detrimental to the housing industry.

In our complex society it is difficult to determine which policies are detrimental to the housing situation, and there are few standards for judging to what extent other desirable objectives should be subordinated to achieve this one.[1] This study is an investigation of the extent to which the residential construction industry is affected by a shift from rapid monetary expansion to a more moderate rate of monetary growth. The study presents and examines the evidence frequently cited as bearing on the question of whether the housing sector should act as a constraint in the formulation of monetary policy designed for the general welfare.

## Recent Economic Developments

Total demand for goods and services (gross national product) has been excessive since last summer, adding to inflationary pressures. Since the third quarter of 1967, total demand has gone up at over a 9 per cent annual rate. By comparison, the upward trend growth in spending since 1957 has been about 6 per cent per year, and the increase in productive capacity has been at an estimated 4 per cent rate. Reflecting the strong demands, overall prices have risen at a 4 per cent rate since last summer, about double the trend rate since 1957.

Despite the rapid growth in total demand, the increasing upward pressures on prices, and a resulting deterioration in the nation's balance of payments with the rest of the world, monetary growth continued at a rapid rate. In the ten months ended November 1967, the money supply rose at a 7.7 per cent annual rate, the fastest rate of increase over any ten-month period since 1948. Since November money has risen at about a 5.7 per cent rate, faster than 90 per cent of the six-month periods. By comparison, the trend

---

* Reprinted from *Review*, Federal Reserve Bank of St. Louis, vol. 50 (June, 1968) pp. 5–12, by permission of the authors and the Federal Reserve Bank of St. Louis.

[1] The Employment Act of 1946 requires the Government to initiate policies "to promote maximum employment, production, and purchasing power."

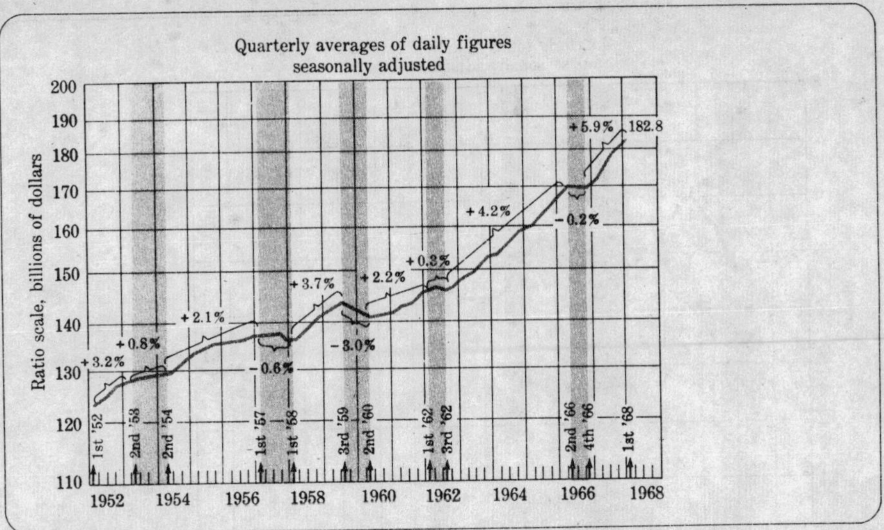


**CHART 1** Money stock. *Percentages indicate rates of change for periods of relatively uniform rates of growth. Shaded areas are periods of slow growth or decline in money stock. Latest data plotted: first quarter 1968.*

growth in money supply was 2.4 per cent per year from 1957 to 1966.

One reason that sharp monetary expansion was not abated last fall and winter was a fear that monetary restraint would bear heavily and inequitably on the housing sector. As early as the July 18, 1967, meeting of the Federal Open Market Committee, a reason cited in the published record of the policy actions for not moving toward monetary restraint was "that any significant further increases in market interest rates might reduce the flows of funds into mortgages and slow the recovery under way in residential construction activity." According to the published record, similar sentiments have been expressed or implied at other meetings.

The economic problem facing the nation since last summer has been one of excessive total demands for goods and services. According to traditional views, monetary actions should be designed with the objective of reducing these demands to the extent necessary to attain price stability while continuing to achieve relatively full utilization of resources. In reducing total demands, the demand for housing also will be affected. The issue is whether the burden of the cutbacks falls particularly heavily or inequitably on this industry.

## Monetary Periods

Some insight into the effect of monetary actions on residential construction can be obtained from a review of periods in our recent history when monetary actions were relatively less expansive. Rates of growth in the money supply (demand deposits plus currency) are used in this phase of the study as a measure of monetary expansion.[2]

Chart 1 plots the money stock since 1951. The shaded areas are periods of relatively slow (or negative) money growth. The fastest rate of growth of the money supply during these slow growth periods was an 0.8 per cent annual rate, whereas the average growth over the entire 1951-1967 period was at a 2.3 per cent rate. Throughout the rest

[2] Constructing periods on the basis of unadjusted market interest rates would give much different results. It is not clear, however, that a more sophisticated interest rate study which includes an analysis of changing inflationary expectations, methods of Government finance, and other forces influencing the demand for credit would give a significantly different picture.

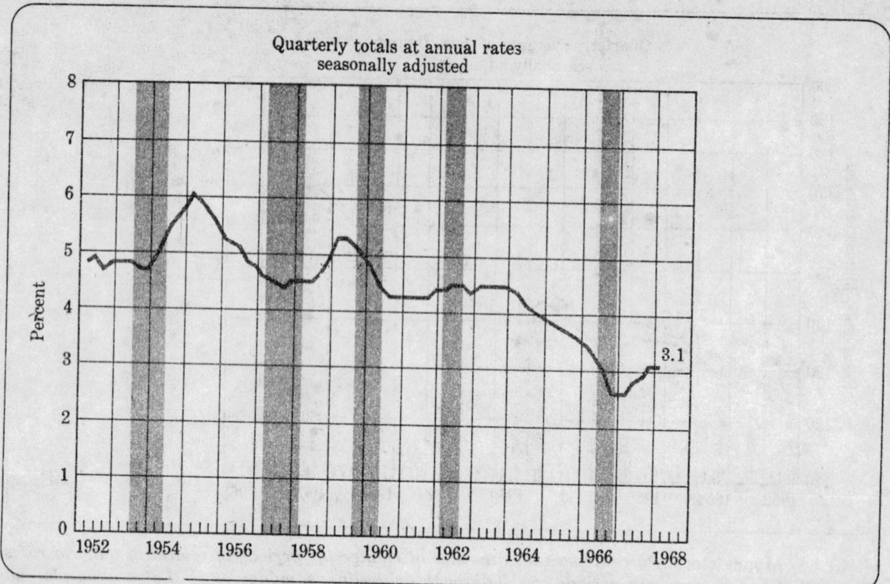


**CHART 2** Outlays on residential structures as a percent of GNP (in real terms—1958 prices). *Shaded areas are periods of slow growth or decline in money stock. Latest data plotted: first quarter 1968.*

of this article these periods are considered to be ones of monetary restraint and are denoted on the charts by shading.

## Slow Monetary Growth and Residential Construction

Comparison of expenditures on housing relative to total spending indicates that relatively slow rates of monetary growth do not cause excessive cutbacks in spending for homes. Chart 2 shows outlays on residential construction as a per cent of gross national product in real terms since 1951. In this period the housing sector has begun a prolonged decline relative to other sectors on three occasions. An interesting aspect of the chart is that each of these three instances was during a period of monetary expansion. During the first three to six months of a period of slow monetary expansion, the housing sector has tended to continue its relative decline begun during a previous period of monetary expansion;[3] but then as monetary restraint continued, housing tended to level off or start rising relative to other activities. The one exception was the 1959-1960 period.

The number of new, private, nonfarm houses started each quarter (Chart 3) has followed a similar pattern. All marked and sustained declines in housing starts began in periods of monetary expansion. In several cases the decline in starts was reversed after three to six months of monetary restraint, and the number of housing starts actually increased.

One reason a traditional view has developed that a relatively slow growth of money damages the housing industry is a belief that high interest rates indicate monetary restraint. However, the facts do not bear out this association, as an article in the November 1967 issue of this *Review* pointed out.

An examination of recent history indicates that rapid expansion in bank credit and money has resulted, after a brief lag, in excessive demands for goods and services, higher prices, and hence, rising interest rates. A slowdown in monetary growth imposed during an inflationary period has temporarily reinforced upward pressures on interest rates as the supply of credit was reduced. After about four months, however, when monetary

[3] The decline was particularly sharp in the early months of the 1966 monetary restraint period, when Government regulations caused a marked reduction in the flow of funds into mortgages. A discussion of these market interferences is presented later.

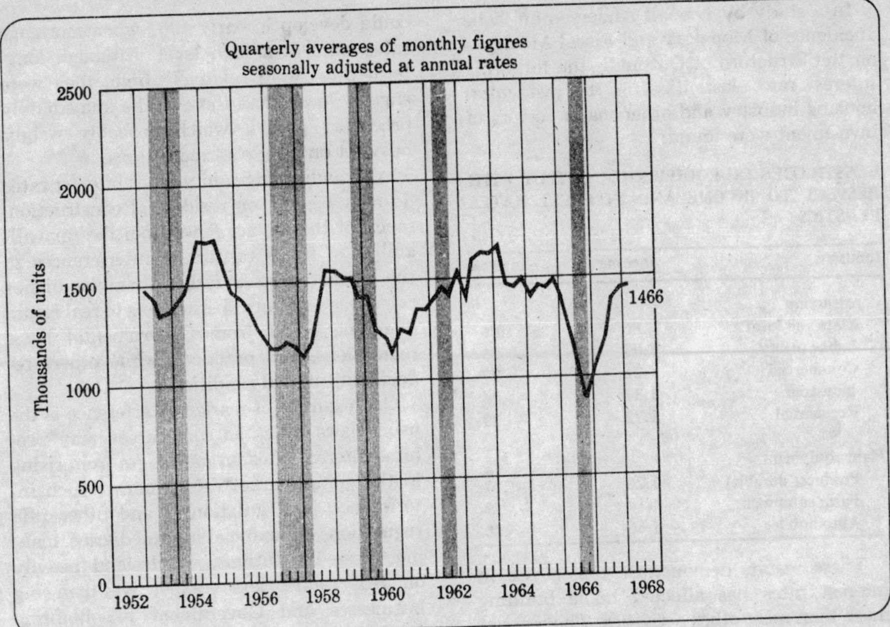


**CHART 3** New housing starts—total private nonfarm. *Shaded areas are periods of slow growth or decline in money stock. Latest data plotted: first quarter 1968 preliminary.*

actions have become effective in reducing aggregate spending and inflationary expectations, the demand for credit also has fallen. Entrepreneurs' demands for investment were lessened not only because of the lower overall demand, but due to reduced pressures to buy goods today to get a cheaper price. Contraction in the demand for credit has caused interest rates to fall. Mortgage interest rates have behaved in roughly the same manner as other interest rates.[4]

[4] The following regression indicates that during the 1960–1967 period conventional mortgage rates have been negatively related to a three-month period of monetary restraint, but positively related during ten-month periods.

Monetary restraint was considered to be an annual growth rate of less than 2.6 per cent (the trend over the 1957–1967 period). At this rate money would grow 0.6 per cent over three months, and 2.4 per cent over ten months. Assuming that this rate of growth is neutral, a negative regression coefficient implies a reverse relationship between money growth and mortgage interest rates, and a positive coefficient suggests that rates move in the same direction as money's movement around the neutral rate of growth. These assumptions are incorporated in the definitions of $M^*_3$ and $M^*_{10}$.

$i_t$ = National average of the average monthly contract interest rates on conventional mortgages on new homes made by savings and loans.

$M_t$ = Monthly average of seasonally adjusted private demand deposits plus currency in the hands of the public.

The equation estimated was:

$$i_t = a_o + a_1 i_{t-1} + a_2 M^*_3 + a_3 M^*_{10},$$

Where:

$$M^*_3 = \frac{M_t - 1.006\ M_{t-3}}{M_{t-3}}$$

$$M^*_{10} = \frac{M_t - 1.024\ M_{t-10}}{M_{t-10}}$$

The results were:

$$i_t = -.0003 + \underset{(.002)}{1.001}\ i_{t-1} - \underset{(.79)}{2.318}\ M^*_3 + \underset{(.38)}{1.54}\ M^*_{10}$$

$$\frac{\text{Standard Error of Estimate}}{\text{Mean of } i_t} = \frac{0.03}{5.30} = .006$$

All variables were significant at the 1 per cent level.

In a study by Leonall Andersen on "The Incidence of Monetary and Fiscal Measures on the Structure of Output,"[5] the following interest rate elasticities for the residential housing industry and other major sectors of investment were found:

**ELASTICITIES OF EQUILIBRIUM OUTPUT WITH RESPECT TO INCOME AND INTEREST RATES ELASTICS**

| Industry | Income | Interest |
|---|---|---|
| Construction | | |
| State and local | .86 | −.06 |
| Public utility | 1.03 | −.25 |
| Commercial | 1.21 | −.27 |
| Industrial | 1.34 | −.24 |
| Residential | 1.72 | −.29 |
| Plant equipment | | |
| Producer durables | 1.20 | −.17 |
| Farm equipment | 1.14 | −.19 |
| Automobiles | 1.66 | −.26 |

These results demonstrate that a rise in interest rates has affected home building more than most other activities. The responsiveness of housing to interest rates results in large part because financing normally represents a large proportion of total costs. Now, Charts 2 and 3 are more understandable. Rising interest rates, which usually accompany prolonged periods of monetary expansion, act as a deterrent to housing. The damaging effect might be continued temporarily by initial upward pressures on interest rates resulting from a more restrictive monetary action, but the falling rates resulting from the over-all effect of a more moderate growth in money are a powerful stimulus to the housing sector.

Interest rates are not the only factor affecting housing demand, and its responsiveness to interest rates probably changes as people's expectations of a "normal" or future interest rate change. If, for example, rates remained at a high level for an extended period, increasing demand might result as the "normal" rate gradually shifted upward. This partially explains how a spurt in housing could develop in early 1967 when mortgage rates were at a high level. Although long-term rates were relatively high, they were slightly lower than those in the immediately preceding period, which probably weighs heaviest on people's expectations.

Although changes in market interest rates do bear heavily on residential construction, much of the impact flows from the unavailability of funds caused by interferences to the market process rather than the higher rates, *per se*. Many obstructions to real estate financing result from Governmental laws, regulations, and practices, while others reflect institutional rigidities.

One example of market interference is the usury laws which in some areas may prohibit interest rates on mortgages from rising to the going market rate. Another such interference is Regulation Q and other rate regulations on financial intermediaries, making these institutions, which lend heavily on real estate, less competitive than big businesses and Government in obtaining funds during periods of relatively high market rates. Another practice discriminating against real estate financing is administrative pressure on Federal Home Loan Banks at times of money market tightness to restrain their borrowing and relending to savings and loan associations. Another is the rigidity of contract rates on FHA and VA loans, with the accompanying discriminating "point" discounting system of mortgage financing.

## Alternatives to Slower Monetary Expansion

Inflation, an alternative to proper monetary restraint, not only hurts the housing industry by increasing the cost of financing, but it raises the costs of building a house.[6] According to data published by the U. S. Department of Housing and Urban Development for twenty major pricing areas of the country, the labor and materials cost of constructing a selected sample of brick and frame houses rose at a 4.2 per cent annual

[5] Andersen, Leonall, *The Review of Economics and Statistics*, August, 1964, Harvard University, Cambridge, pp. 260–268.

[6] The higher construction costs may be offset only partly by a rise in the expected future resale value of the house.

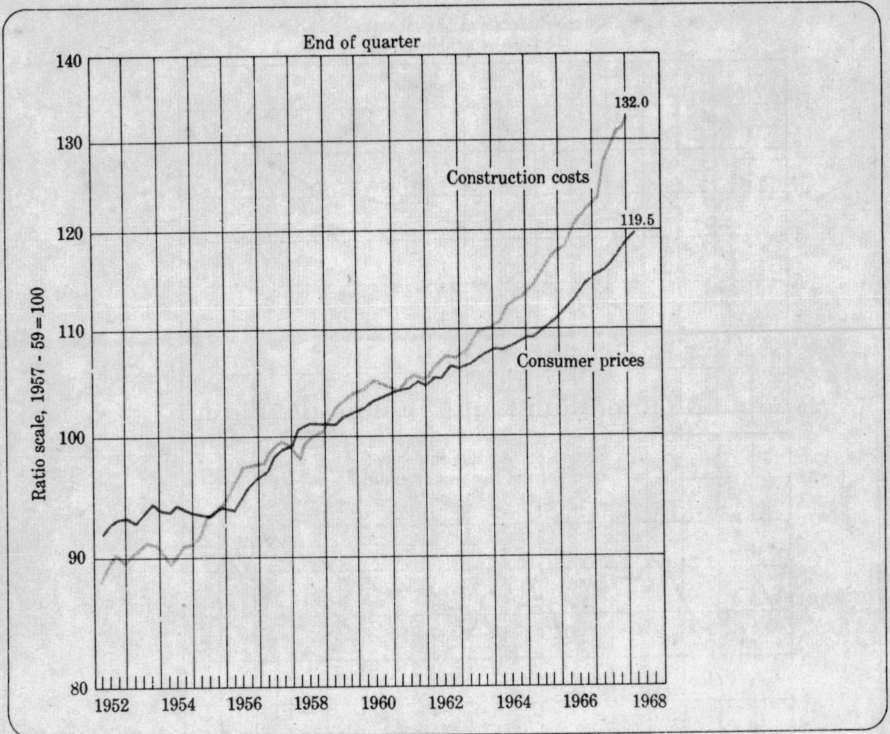


**CHART 4** Comparison of construction costs and consumer prices. *Latest data plotted: construction costs, first quarter 1968 estimated; consumer prices, first quarter 1968.*

rate from 1963 to 1967 (Chart 4). Some of the rise in costs may have reflected a bidding away of men and materials for the war effort, but about two-thirds of this increase can be attributed to a general inflationary price rise. The increase in the price of homes between 1963 and 1967 resulted in 13.5 per cent higher monthly payments on housing. During the same period average interest rates on new mortgages rose about 1¼ percentage points, resulting in about 12.5 per cent higher monthly payments on a 25-year loan. However, this increase in interest rates took place mainly in periods of rapid money expansion and may come back down after excessive demands and inflationary pressures are eliminated. The higher cost of housing as a result of inflation is not likely to be reduced by much.

## Slower Monetary Growth and Other Sectors of the Economy

### *Consumer and Business*

Although monetary restraint may affect the total real dollars spent on housing, the housing sector is not the only one to feel a monetary squeeze. Chart 5 shows two other sectors plotted along with residential construction: (1) outlays on consumer durable goods, such as automobiles, appliances, and furniture, and (2) expenditures on business machines and other producers' durable equipment plus changes in business inventories. Each sector is plotted as a percentage of real GNP to relate the effect on it to the effect on over-all activity.

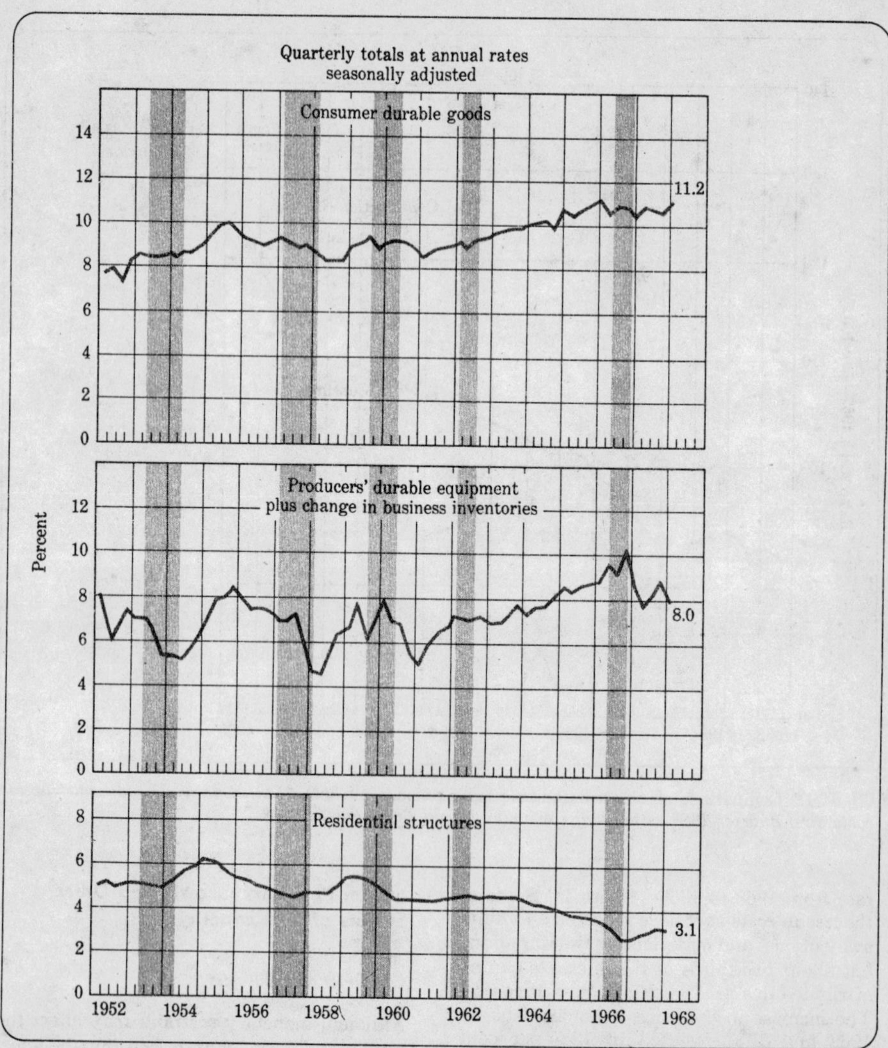


**CHART 5** Outlays of selected sectors as a percent of GNP (in real terms—1958 prices). *Shaded areas are periods of slow growth or decline in money stock. Latest data plotted: first quarter 1968.*

Both consumer durable goods and producers' durable equipment have had a slight upward trend relative to total production since 1951, while residential construction has trended downward; yet the formers' declines or slower rates of increases during periods of slow money growth have been roughly equal to those in the latter. Also, declines in the other two sectors sometimes actually began during the periods of slow monetary expansion. It appears that housing has not been any more adversely affected during periods of relatively slow monetary growth than have these other sectors.

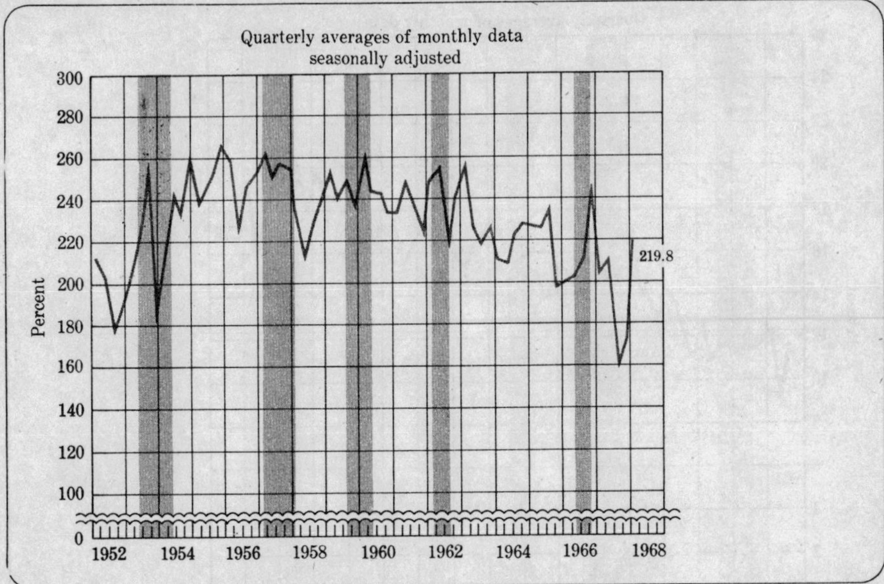


**CHART 6** Unemployment in construction compared with total unemployment (rate of unemployed private wage and salary workers in construction as a percent of the rate of total unemployed civilian workers). *Shaded areas are periods of slow growth or decline in money stock. Latest data plotted: first quarter 1968.*

### *Construction Employment*

Monetary restraint does not appear to bear unduly on construction workers. Although an initial move toward slower monetary growth has temporarily reinforced a decline in the housing sector, the evidence suggests that most workers in residential construction have not been at an increased disadvantage in finding jobs. Unemployment among construction workers typically is higher than unemployment generally, as can be noted in Chart 6. From the chart it is evident that periods of slower monetary growth usually did not affect construction workers much more than they did workers in other activities. Unemployment in this industry rose at times in the first few months of the restrictive period, but, in general, the relative unemployment of construction workers changed little during periods of monetary restraint. Construction workers, being relatively mobile and skilled, may have been better able to find jobs than were others with less skill and mobility.

### *Contractors*

The experience of contractors has been similar. Chart 7 plots failures of construction firms as a per cent of total business failures. Although there has been an upward trend in failures of construction firms relative to other businesses, their relative position improved temporarily in four out of the five cases of monetary restraint since 1951. The one exception was the 1959-1960 period.

The upward trend in construction failures may have reflected the uptrend in interest rates resulting from excessive total demands and inflation. Then, too, it may have been partially a reaction to some overbuilding in the fifties. The relatively small size of most contractors, prepetuated in part by zoning laws and building ordinances, may have

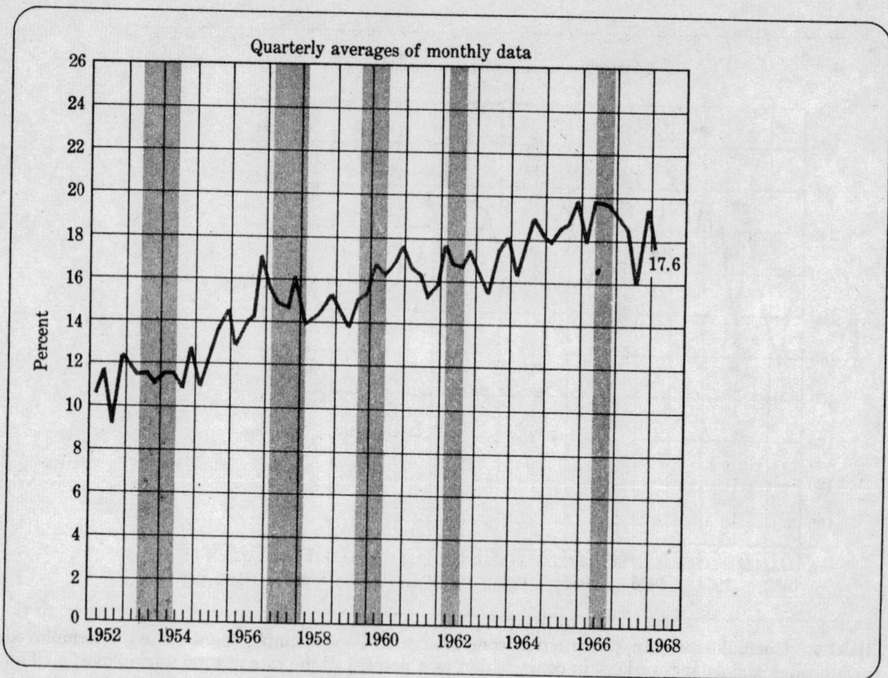


**CHART 7** Business failures in construction as a percent of total business failures. *Shaded areas are periods of slow growth or decline in money stock. Latest data plotted: first quarter 1968.*

made the industry less viable. A bigger enterprise with more capital and reserves more easily could accept temporary losses and changes in the economy. A part of the hardships suffered by contractors, as well as a factor tending to discourage large amounts of capital from coming into the industry, may be associated with those regulations which the same concerns use to gain temporary advantages.

*Financial Intermediaries*

Restrictive monetary actions may have an effect on housing by affecting adversely the flow of funds into financial intermediaries which extend most of the housing credit. Yet, a review of some measures of industry performance does not indicate that financial intermediaries are any more severely affected by a relatively slow rate of monetary expansion than is business in general. A chief intermediary is the savings and loan associations. Chart 8 shows yearly profits of all savings and loan institutions since 1951 and yearly rates of change of profits. A striking feature of the chart is that since 1951 savings and loan companies in the aggregate have had increased absolute profits each year. Also, during periods of monetary restraint profits grew at an expanding rate, except in the 1966 period when a trend toward a slower rate of increase already had begun.

From 1952 to 1966 profits of savings and loan companies rose at a 16 per cent average annual rate, and in 1966 they went up 7.3 per cent. Mutual savings banks had similar results. Their net income grew at an 11 per cent average rate between 1953 and 1966, and 10 per cent during 1966.

Profits of a mutual association may not be comparable with earnings of other firms which deduct the cost of obtaining funds as an expense. But, even if the cost of attract-

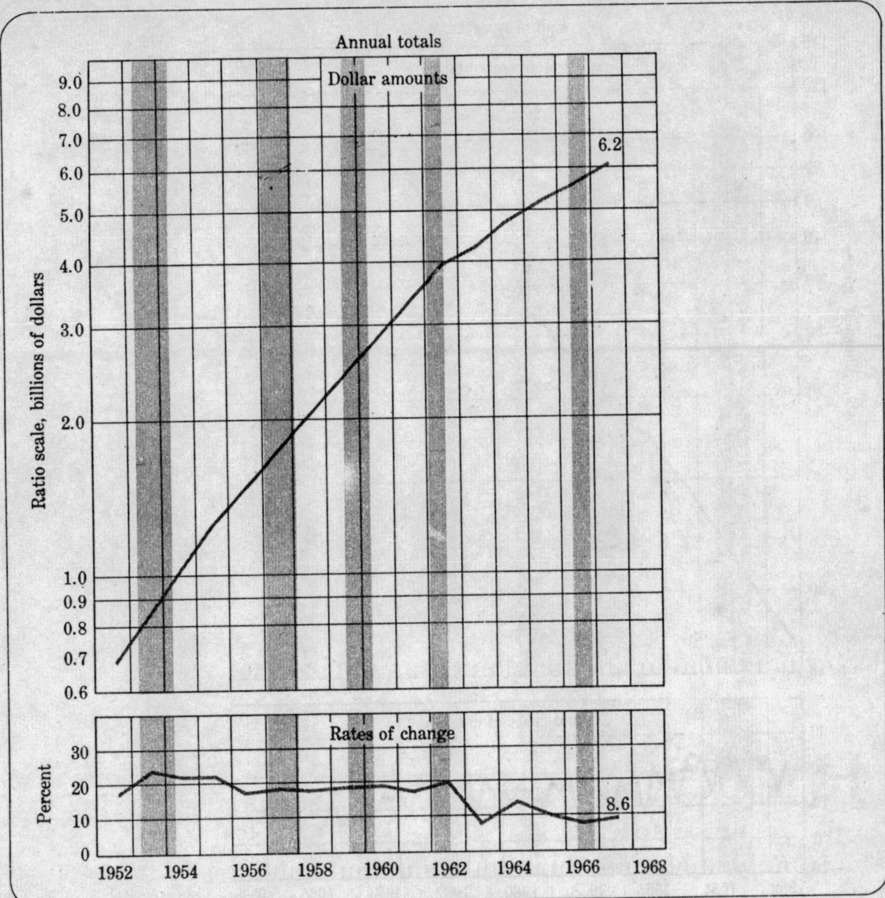


**CHART 8** Net income of all savings and loan associations. *Shaded areas are periods of slow growth or decline in money stock. Latest data plotted: 1967 preliminary.*

ing share accounts (i.e., dividends) is deducted from profits, the remaining additions to reserves have been sizeable each year since 1952. Even in the adverse year of 1966, savings and loan associations were able to add $600 million to their reserves, and the ratio of reserves to total savings balances rose from 7.90 per cent to 8.18 per cent.

Savings and loan associations have been hindered temporarily during periods of slow monetary growth in securing savings. There have been several setbacks in the rate of increase in savings capital of these institutions during periods of monetary restraint, and for one quarter (third quarter 1966) there was a moderate net decline (Chart 9). Rising interest rates make yields on savings accounts, which are regulated by FHLB "rate controls," relatively less attractive than rates paid in the free market. To a great extent the real problem has been not in the rising market interest rates, but in rate controls on the savings and loan associations. Nevertheless, despite all the market imperfections, increases in net savings funds in savings and loan associations have been at an average

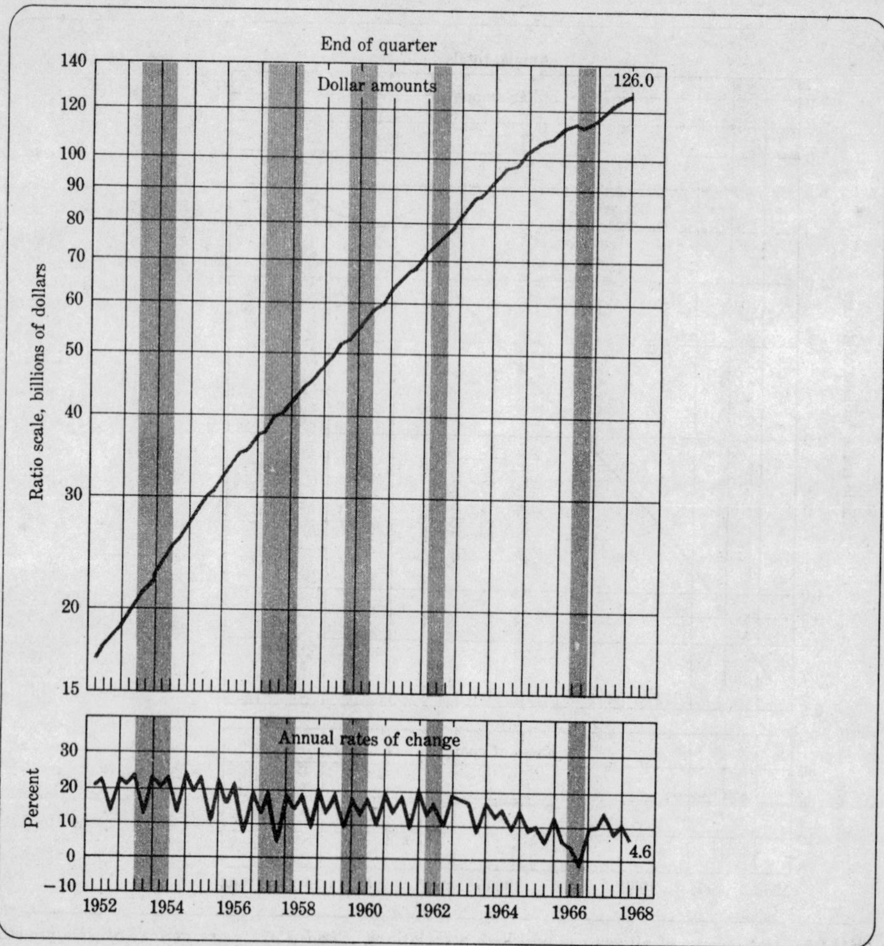


**CHART 9** Savings capital of all savings and loan associations. *Shaded areas are periods of slow growth or decline in money stock. Latest data plotted: first quarter 1968 preliminary.*

13.6 per cent annual rate since 1952; in the most adverse year—1966—they rose 4 per cent. Similarly, deposits in mutual savings banks increased at a 7 per cent average annual rate in the 1952-1966 period and 5 per cent during 1966.

Financial intermediaries perform an economic function by borrowing short-term funds and lending them for long terms. Therefore, a sharp unexpected rise in the market interest rate structure puts them at a temporary disadvantage. To compete for funds to make new loans and provide for withdrawals, they must raise interest rate payments on all their outstanding deposits,[7] but yields on their assets are fixed. As a result, expenses rise much more rapidly than earnings in the short run. Because of this situation, some feel that a rapid rise in market interest rates accompanied by higher rates

[7] There are exceptions, of course, such as paying higher rates on certificates or for funds left for a longer period.

paid by intermediaries may cause a general collapse of these financial institutions. It is partially for this reason that interest rates paid by financial intermediaries are regulated.

Although an industry that borrows short and lends long may incur losses for a period when interest rates rise sharply, most financial intermediaries have considerable ability to withstand these temporary periods when their terms of trade are adverse. In addition to their own resources, savings and loan associations and mutual savings banks may borrow from Federal Home Loan Banks.

For example, the book value of aggregate reserves and undivided profits of savings and loan institutions is nearly twice the size of their yearly dividend payments. They also have cash and Government security holdings from which payments could be made totaling over double their yearly dividend payments. These ratios prevailed even at the end of 1966, after the associations had endured their most adverse year. This means that the average association could remain solvent in an accounting sense and pay its dividends for nearly two years, even though it had no net profits. Yet, in every year since World War II, these associations have had greater profits than in the previous year.

Also, throughout the period of rising interest rates, greater returns will be flowing in from the loans made at the higher rates; in 1967, for example, repayments of regular instalments, interest, and advance repayments because of house sales amounted to about 15 per cent of average total outstanding mortgages at savings and loan associations. Even more important, periods of monetary restraint rarely have lasted even a year in length, and after a few months of slower monetary growth interest rates have had a tendency to come down.

## Conclusions

This analysis is tentative; a complete study would require an examination of the data presented in much more detail, as well as additional evidence bearing on the subject of discriminatory effects of monetary policy. Nevertheless, it appears from the information thus far developed that the requirements of the housing industry should not act as a constraint on monetary policy designed for the general welfare.

In this analysis, periods of extreme monetary restraint were studied. With the advantage of hindsight, it now appears that in most of these periods monetary actions were unduly restrictive, since all economic recessions since 1952 commenced during these periods. Housing was affected during periods of slow monetary growth, particularly in the first few months, but indications are that the housing industry was affected little more than was activity in general throughout all the periods of restraint. The widespread belief that housing has been seriously hurt by monetary restraint probably has resulted from mistakenly identifying rising market interest rates with monetary restraint. Interest rates, unadjusted for price developments and for Government borrowing, and unrelated to changing profit expectations of businesses, are usually a poor guide to either the rate of monetary expansion or its impact on economic activity.

Conversely, the evidence is strong that housing is seriously affected by excessive total demand for goods and services and inflation. Not only do the excesses drive up the costs of constructing houses, but these huge demands and the inflationary pressures push up market interest rates, which tend to bear heavily on the housing industry.

Little evidence has been found to indicate that the housing industry or the financial intermediaries are affected in such a manner which makes them gain from excessive monetary expansion. It seems that they, as most other sectors, flourish best in an economy growing at a relatively steady rate without inflation. The housing industry might be benefited, however, by a repeal or a liberalization of laws, regulations, and practices that interfere with the free flow of funds from the saver to the ultimate borrower.